FOURTH ED

"THEY SAY / I SAY"

The Moves That Matter
in Academic Writing

GERALD GRAFF

CATHY BIRKENSTEIN

both of the University of Illinois at Chicago

RUSSEL DURST

University of Cincinnatti

Wake Technical Community College

W. W. NORTON & COMPANY
Independent Publishers Since 1923

For
Aaron David

W. W. Norton & Company has been independent since its founding in 1923, when William Warder Norton and Mary D. Herter Norton first published lectures delivered at the People's Institute, the adult education division of New York City's Cooper Union. The firm soon expanded its program beyond the Institute, publishing books by celebrated academics from America and abroad. By mid-century, the two major pillars of Norton's publishing program—trade books and college texts—were firmly established. In the 1950s, the Norton family transferred control of the company to its employees, and today—with a staff of four hundred and a comparable number of trade, college, and professional titles published each year—W. W. Norton & Company stands as the largest and oldest publishing house owned wholly by its employees.

ISBN 978-0-393-43788-1

W. W. Norton & Company, Inc., 500 Fifth Avenue, New York, NY 10110
wwnorton.com

W. W. Norton & Company Ltd., 15 Carlisle Street, London W1D 3BS

6 7 8 9 0

CONTENTS

CONTENTS

PART 3. TYING IT ALL TOGETHER

PART 4. IN SPECIFIC ACADEMIC CONTEXTS

Contents

CONTENTS

Contents

CONTENTS

PREFACE
TO THE FOURTH EDITION

—⌐⌐—

SINCE IT WAS FIRST PUBLISHED OVER A DECADE AGO, this book has been dedicated to the idea that our own views are most thoughtfully formed in conversation with the views of others, including views that differ from our own.

When students work with one of this book's templates like "They say that _____, and I concede _____. But_____," they see their beliefs from another side and, in our view, are therefore able to produce more compelling arguments.

As the twenty-first century unfolds, however, the increasingly polarized state of our society is making it harder to listen to those who see things differently than we do. The wider our divisions become, the harder it is to find anyone who is willing to seriously consider viewpoints that oppose their own. Too often we either avoid difficult discussions altogether, or we talk only with like-minded people, who often reinforce our pre-existing assumptions and insulate us from serious challenge.

In this fourth edition of our book, therefore, we double down in a variety of ways on the importance of getting outside our isolated spheres and listening to others, even when we may not like what we hear.

WHAT'S NEW IN THE BOOK

New materials in the introduction reinforce the importance of listening carefully to what others say (what "they say") and summarizing it in a way that does it justice, treating our own ideas (what "I say") not as uncontestable givens but as entries in a conversation or a debate in which participants may agree, agree up to a point, or disagree.

A new chapter on entering online conversations further underscores the importance of referencing what "they say" when responding to others on blogs, class discussion boards, and the like. In this chapter, which offers more practical advice on online writing than the more theoretical chapter it replaces, we argue that, while digital technologies have transformed classrooms and connected writers in unprecedented ways, genuine conversation is all too rare. Too many online writers, instead of actually responding to others, end up talking past one another in discrete monologues that leave it unclear who or what has motivated them to write. This chapter suggests why online writing may be especially prone to this problem and offers techniques for overcoming it.

A substantially revised chapter on academic language (now called "You Mean I Can Just Say It That Way?") underscores the need to bridge spheres that are too often kept separate: everyday language and academic writing. This chapter encourages students to draw on their everyday voices in their academic writing rather than set them aside. By translating academic claims into everyday language, we show, students are better able to clarify their ideas for readers and even for themselves.

Many new model examples—fifteen in all—from a wide range of authors, including Rebecca Goldstein, Deborah Tannen, Charles Murray, Nicholas Carr, and Michelle Alexander, among others, highlight the many different contexts for academic conversations.

A substantially revised and updated chapter on writing in the social sciences reflects a broader range of writing assignments, with examples from academic publications in sociology, psychology, and political science.

New documented readings from two different fields—an essay by the computer scientist Michael Littman and a selection from *The New Jim Crow* by the legal scholar Michelle Alexander—show how the rhetorical moves taught in this book work across disciplines.

Even as we have revised and added to "*They Say / I Say*," our basic goals remain unchanged: to demystify academic reading and writing by identifying the key moves of persuasive argument and representing those moves in forms that students can put into practice. We hope this fourth edition will get us even closer to these goals, equipping students with the writing skills they need to enter the academic world and beyond.

WHAT'S ONLINE

Online tutorials give students hands-on practice recognizing and using the rhetorical moves taught in this book both as readers and writers. Each tutorial helps students read a full essay with an eye on these moves and then respond to a writing prompt using templates from the book.

They Say / I Blog. Updated monthly, this blog provides up-to-the-minute readings on the issues covered in the book, along with questions that prompt students to literally join the conversations. Check it out at **theysayiblog.com**.

Instructor's Guide. Now available in print, the guide includes expanded in-class activities, sample syllabi, summaries of each chapter and reading, and a chapter on using the online resources, including *They Say / I Blog*.

Ebook. Searchable, portable, and interactive. The complete textbook for a fraction of the price. Students can interact with the text—take notes, bookmark, search, and highlight. The ebook can be viewed on—and synced between—all computers and mobile devices.

InQuizitive for Writers. Adaptive, game-like exercises help students practice editing, focusing especially on the errors that matter.

Coursepack. Norton resources you can add to your online, hybrid, or lecture course—all at no cost. Norton Coursepacks work within your existing learning management system; there's no new system to learn, and access is free and easy. Customizable resources include assignable writing prompts from theysayiblog.com, quizzes on grammar and documentation, documentation guides, model student essays, and more.

Find it all at **digital.wwnorton.com/theysay4** or contact your Norton representative for more information.

PREFACE

Demystifying Academic Conversation

EXPERIENCED WRITING INSTRUCTORS have long recognized that writing well means entering into conversation with others. Academic writing in particular calls upon writers not simply to express their own ideas, but to do so as a response to what others have said. The first-year writing program at our own university, according to its mission statement, asks "students to participate in ongoing conversations about vitally important academic and public issues." A similar statement by another program holds that "intellectual writing is almost always composed in response to others' texts." These statements echo the ideas of rhetorical theorists like Kenneth Burke, Mikhail Bakhtin, and Wayne Booth as well as recent composition scholars like David Bartholomae, John Bean, Patricia Bizzell, Irene Clark, Greg Colomb, Lisa Ede, Peter Elbow, Joseph Harris, Andrea Lunsford, Elaine Maimon, Gary Olson, Mike Rose, John Swales and Christine Feak, Tilly Warnock, and others who argue that writing well means engaging the voices of others and letting them in turn engage us.

Yet despite this growing consensus that writing is a social, conversational act, helping student writers actually participate in these conversations remains a formidable challenge. This book aims to meet that challenge. Its goal is to demystify academic writing by isolating its basic moves, explaining them clearly, and representing them in the form of templates.

In this way, we hope to help students become active participants in the important conversations of the academic world and the wider public sphere.

HIGHLIGHTS

- *Shows that writing well means entering a conversation*, summarizing others ("they say") to set up one's own argument ("I say").
- *Demystifies academic writing*, showing students "the moves that matter" in language they can readily apply.
- *Provides user-friendly templates* to help writers make those moves in their own writing.
- *Shows that reading is a way of entering a conversation*—not just of passively absorbing information but of understanding and actively entering dialogues and debates.

HOW THIS BOOK CAME TO BE

The original idea for this book grew out of our shared interest in democratizing academic culture. First, it grew out of arguments that Gerald Graff has been making throughout his career that schools and colleges need to invite students into the conversations and debates that surround them. More specifically, it is a practical, hands-on companion to his recent book *Clueless in Academe: How Schooling Obscures the Life of the Mind*, in which he looks at academic conversations from the perspective of those who find them mysterious and proposes ways in which such mystification can be overcome. Second, this book grew out of writing templates that Cathy Birkenstein developed in the 1990s for use in writing and literature courses she was teaching. Many students, she found, could readily grasp what it meant to support a thesis with evidence, to entertain a counterargument, to identify a textual contradiction, and ultimately to summarize and respond to challenging arguments, but they often had trouble putting these concepts into practice in their own writing. When Cathy sketched out templates on the board, however, giving her students some of the language and patterns that these sophisticated moves require, their writing—and even their quality of thought—significantly improved.

This book began, then, when we put our ideas together and realized that these templates might have the potential to open up and clarify academic conversation. We proceeded from the premise that all writers rely on certain stock formulas that they themselves didn't invent—and that many of these formulas are so commonly used that they can be represented in model templates that students can use to structure and even generate what they want to say.

As we developed a working draft of this book, we began using it in first-year writing courses that we teach at UIC. In classroom exercises and writing assignments, we found that students who otherwise struggled to organize their thoughts, or even to think of something to say, did much better when we provided them with templates like the following.

▶ In discussions of _____, a controversial issue is whether _____. While some argue that _____, others contend that _____.

▶ This is not to say that _____.

One virtue of such templates, we found, is that they focus writers' attention not just on what is being said, but on the *forms* that structure what is being said. In other words, they make students more conscious of the rhetorical patterns that are key to academic success but often pass under the classroom radar.

THE CENTRALITY OF "THEY SAY / I SAY"

The central rhetorical move that we focus on in this book is the "they say / I say" template that gives our book its title. In our view, this template represents the deep, underlying structure, the internal DNA as it were, of all effective argument. Effective persuasive writers do more than make well-supported claims ("I say"); they also map those claims relative to the claims of others ("they say").

Here, for example, the "they say / I say" pattern structures a passage from an essay by the media and technology critic Steven Johnson.

> For decades, we've worked under the assumption that mass culture follows a path declining steadily toward lowest-common-denominator standards, presumably because the "masses" want dumb, simple pleasures and big media companies try to give the masses what they want. But . . . the exact opposite is happening: the culture is getting more cognitively demanding, not less.
>
> STEVEN JOHNSON, "Watching TV Makes You Smarter"

In generating his own argument from something "they say," Johnson suggests *why* he needs to say what he is saying: to correct a popular misconception.

Even when writers do not explicitly identify the views they are responding to, as Johnson does, an implicit "they say" can often be discerned, as in the following passage by Zora Neale Hurston.

> I remember the day I became colored.
> ZORA NEALE HURSTON, "How It Feels to Be Colored Me"

In order to grasp Hurston's point here, we need to be able to reconstruct the implicit view she is responding to and questioning: that racial identity is an innate quality we are simply born with. On the contrary, Hurston suggests, our race is imposed on us by society—something we "become" by virtue of how we are treated.

As these examples suggest, the "they say / I say" model can improve not just student writing, but student reading comprehension as well. Since reading and writing are deeply reciprocal activities, students who learn to make the rhetorical moves represented by the templates in this book figure to become more adept at identifying these same moves in the texts they read. And if we are right that effective arguments are always in dialogue with other arguments, then it follows that in order to understand the types of challenging texts assigned in college, students need to identify the views to which those texts are responding.

Working with the "they say / I say" model can also help with invention, finding something to say. In our experience, students best discover what they want to say not by thinking about a subject in an isolation booth, but by reading texts, listening closely to what other writers say, and looking for an opening through which they can enter the conversation. In other words, listening closely to others and summarizing what they have to say can help writers generate their own ideas.

THE USEFULNESS OF TEMPLATES

Our templates also have a generative quality, prompting students to make moves in their writing that they might not otherwise make or even know they should make. The templates in this book can be particularly helpful for students who are unsure about what to say, or who have trouble finding enough to say, often because they consider their own beliefs so self-evident that they need not be argued for. Students like this are often helped, we've found, when we give them a simple template like the following one for entertaining a counterargument (or planting a naysayer, as we call it in Chapter 6).

▸ **Of course some might object that _____ . Although I concede that _____ , I still maintain that _____ .**

What this particular template helps students do is make the seemingly counterintuitive move of questioning their own beliefs, of looking at them from the perspective of those who disagree. In so doing, templates can bring out aspects of students' thoughts that, as they themselves sometimes remark, they didn't even realize were there.

Other templates in this book help students make a host of sophisticated moves that they might not otherwise make: summarizing what someone else says, framing a quotation in one's own words, indicating the view that the writer is responding to, marking the shift from a source's view to the writer's own view, offering evidence for that view, entertaining and answering counterarguments, and explaining what is at stake in the first place. In showing students how to make such moves, templates do more than organize students' ideas; they help bring those ideas into existence.

"OK—BUT TEMPLATES?"

We are aware, of course, that some instructors may have reservations about templates. Some, for instance, may object that such formulaic devices represent a return to prescriptive forms of instruction that encourage passive learning or lead students to put their writing on automatic pilot.

This is an understandable reaction, we think, to kinds of rote instruction that have indeed encouraged passivity and drained writing of its creativity and dynamic relation to the social world. The trouble is that many students will never learn on their own to make the key intellectual moves that our templates represent. While seasoned writers pick up these moves unconsciously through their reading, many students do not. Consequently, we believe, students need to see these moves represented in the explicit ways that the templates provide.

The aim of the templates, then, is not to stifle critical thinking but to be direct with students about the key rhetorical moves that it comprises. Since we encourage students to modify and adapt the templates to the particularities of the arguments they are making, using such prefabricated formulas as learning tools need not result in writing and thinking that are themselves formulaic. Admittedly, no teaching tool can guarantee that students will engage in hard, rigorous thought. Our templates do, however, provide concrete prompts that can stimulate and shape such thought: What do "they say" about my topic? What would a naysayer say about my argument? What is my evidence? Do I need to qualify my point? Who cares?

In fact, templates have a long and rich history. Public orators from ancient Greece and Rome through the European Renaissance studied rhetorical *topoi* or "commonplaces," model passages and formulas that represented the different strategies available to public speakers. In many respects, our templates echo this classical rhetorical tradition of imitating established models.

The journal *Nature* requires aspiring contributors to follow a guideline that is like a template on the opening page of their manuscript: "Two or three sentences explaining what the main result [of their study] reveals in direct comparison with what was thought to be the case previously, or how the main result adds to previous knowledge." In the field of education, a form designed by the education theorist Howard Gardner asks postdoctoral fellowship applicants to complete the following template: "Most scholars in the field believe _____. As a result of my study, _____." That these two examples are geared toward post-doctoral fellows and veteran researchers shows that it is not only struggling undergraduates who can use help making these key rhetorical moves, but experienced academics as well.

Templates have even been used in the teaching of personal narrative. The literary and educational theorist Jane Tompkins devised the following template to help student writers make the often difficult move from telling a story to explaining what it means: "X tells a story about _____ to make the point that _____. My own experience with _____ yields a point that is similar/different/both similar and different. What I take away from my own experience with _____ is _____. As a result, I conclude _____." We especially like this template because it suggests that "they say / I say" argument need not be mechanical, impersonal, or dry, and that telling a story and mak-ing an argument are more compatible activities than many think.

WHY IT'S OKAY TO USE "I"

But wait—doesn't the "I" part of "they say / I say" flagrantly encourage the use of the first-person pronoun? Aren't we aware that some teachers prohibit students from using "I" or "we," on the grounds that these pronouns encourage ill-considered, subjective opinions rather than objective and reasoned arguments? Yes, we are aware of this first-person prohibition, but we think it has serious flaws. First, expressing ill-considered, subjective opinions is not necessarily the worst sin beginning writers can commit; it might be a starting point from which they can move on to more reasoned, less self-indulgent perspectives. Second, prohibiting students from using "I" is simply not an effective way of curbing students' subjectivity, since one can offer poorly argued, ill-supported opinions just as easily without it. Third and most important, prohibiting the first person tends to hamper students' ability not only to take strong positions but to differentiate their own positions from those of others, as we point out in Chapter 5. To be sure, writers can resort to various circumlocutions—"it will here be argued," "the evidence suggests," "the truth is"—and these may be useful for avoiding a monotonous series of "I believe" sentences. But except for avoiding such monotony, we see no good reason why "I" should be set aside in persuasive writing. Rather than prohibit "I," then, we think a better tactic is to give students practice at using it well and learning its use, both by supporting their claims with evidence and by attending closely to alternative perspectives—to what "they" are saying.

HOW THIS BOOK IS ORGANIZED

Because of its centrality, we have allowed the "they say / I say" format to dictate the structure of this book. So while Part 1 addresses the art of listening to others, Part 2 addresses how to offer one's own response. Part 1 opens with a chapter on

"Starting with What Others Are Saying" that explains why it is generally advisable to begin a text by citing others rather than plunging directly into one's own views. Subsequent chapters take up the arts of summarizing and quoting what these others have to say. Part 2 begins with a chapter on different ways of responding, followed by chapters on marking the shift between what "they say" and what "I say," on introducing and answering objections, and on answering the all-important questions: "so what?" and "who cares?" Part 3 offers strategies for "Tying It All Together," beginning with a chapter on connection and coherence; followed by a chapter on academic language, encouraging students to draw on their everyday voice as a tool for writing; and including chapters on the art of metacommentary and using templates to revise a text. Part 4 offers guidance for entering conversations in specific academic contexts, with chapters on entering class discussions, writing online, reading, and writing in literature courses, the sciences, and social sciences. Finally, we provide five readings and an index of templates.

WHAT THIS BOOK DOESN'T DO

There are some things that this book does not try to do. We do not, for instance, cover logical principles of argument such as syllogisms, warrants, logical fallacies, or the differences between inductive and deductive reasoning. Although such concepts can be useful, we believe most of us learn the ins and outs of argumentative writing not by studying logical principles in the abstract, but by plunging into actual discussions and debates, trying out different patterns of response, and in this way getting a sense of what works to persuade different audiences and what doesn't. In our view, people learn more about arguing from hearing someone say, "You miss my point. What I'm saying is not _____ , but _____ ," or "I agree with you that _____ , and would even add that _____ ," than they do from studying the differences between inductive and deductive reasoning. Such formulas give students an immediate sense of what it feels like to enter a public conversation in a way that studying abstract warrants and logical fallacies does not.

ENGAGING WITH THE IDEAS OF OTHERS

One central goal of this book is to demystify academic writing by returning it to its social and conversational roots. Although writing may require some degree of quiet and solitude, the "they say / I say" model shows students that they can best develop their arguments not just by looking inward but by doing what they often do in a good conversation with friends and family— by listening carefully to what others are saying and engaging with other views.

This approach to writing therefore has an ethical dimension, since it asks writers not simply to keep proving and reasserting what they already believe, but to stretch what they believe by putting it up against beliefs that differ, sometimes radically, from their own. In an increasingly diverse, global society, this ability to engage with the ideas of others is especially crucial to democratic citizenship.

Gerald Graff
Cathy Birkenstein

INTRODUCTION

Entering the Conversation

THINK ABOUT AN ACTIVITY that you do particularly well: cooking, playing the piano, shooting a basketball, even something as basic as driving a car. If you reflect on this activity, you'll realize that once you mastered it you no longer had to give much conscious thought to the various moves that go into doing it. Performing this activity, in other words, depends on your having learned a series of complicated moves—moves that may seem mysterious or difficult to those who haven't yet learned them.

The same applies to writing. Often without consciously realizing it, accomplished writers routinely rely on a stock of established moves that are crucial for communicating sophisticated ideas. What makes writers masters of their trade is not only their ability to express interesting thoughts but their mastery of an inventory of basic moves that they probably picked up by reading a wide range of other accomplished writers. Less experienced writers, by contrast, are often unfamiliar with these basic moves and unsure how to make them in their own writing. Hence this book, which is intended as a short, user-friendly guide to the basic moves of academic writing.

One of our key premises is that these basic moves are so common that they can be represented in *templates* that you can use right away to structure and even generate your own writing. Perhaps the most distinctive feature of this book is its presentation of many such templates, designed to help you successfully enter not only the world of academic thinking and writing, but also the wider worlds of civic discourse and work.

Instead of focusing solely on abstract principles of writing, then, this book offers model templates that help you put those principles directly into practice. Working with these templates will give you an immediate sense of how to engage in the kinds of critical thinking you are required to do at the college level and in the vocational and public spheres beyond.

Some of these templates represent simple but crucial moves like those used to summarize some widely held belief.

▸ **Many Americans assume that _____ .**

Others are more complicated.

▸ **On the one hand, _____ . On the other hand, _____ .**

▸ **Author X contradicts herself. At the same time that she argues _____ , she also implies _____ .**

▸ **I agree that _____ .**

▸ **This is not to say that _____ .**

It is true, of course, that critical thinking and writing go deeper than any set of linguistic formulas, requiring that you question assumptions, develop strong claims, offer supporting reasons and evidence, consider opposing arguments, and so on. But these deeper habits of thought cannot be put into practice unless you have a language for expressing them in clear, organized ways.

STATE YOUR OWN IDEAS AS A
RESPONSE TO OTHERS

The single most important template that we focus on in this book is the "they say _____; I say _____" formula that gives our book its title. If there is any one point that we hope you will take away from this book, it is the importance not only of expressing your ideas ("I say") but of presenting those ideas as a *response to some other person or group* ("they say"). For us, the underlying structure of effective academic writing—and of responsible public discourse—resides not just in stating our own ideas but in listening closely to others around us, summarizing their views in a way that they will recognize, and responding with our own ideas in kind. Broadly speaking, academic writing is argumentative writing, and we believe that to argue well you need to do more than assert your own position. You need to enter a conversation, using what others say (or might say) as a launching pad or sounding board for your own views. For this reason, one of the main pieces of advice in this book is to write the voices of others into your text.

In our view, then, the best academic writing has one underlying feature: it is deeply engaged in some way with other people's views. Too often, however, academic writing is taught as a process of saying "true" or "smart" things in a vacuum, as if it were possible to argue effectively without being in conversation *with* someone else. If you have been taught to write a traditional five-paragraph essay, for example, you have learned how to develop a thesis and support it with evidence. This is good advice as far as it goes, but it leaves out the important fact that in the real world we don't make arguments without being provoked. Instead, we make arguments because someone has said or done something (or perhaps *not* said or done

3

something) and we need to respond: "I can't see why you like the Lakers so much"; "I agree: it was a great film"; "That argument is contradictory." If it weren't for other people and our need to challenge, agree with, or otherwise respond to them, there would be no reason to argue at all.

"WHY ARE YOU TELLING ME THIS?"

To make an impact as a writer, then, you need to do more than make statements that are logical, well supported, and consistent. You must also find a way of entering into conversation with the views of others, with something "they say." The easiest and most common way writers do this is by *summarizing* what others say and then using it to set up what they want to say.

"But why," as a student of ours once asked, "do I always need to summarize the views of others to set up my own view? Why can't I just state my own view and be done with it?" Why indeed? After all, "they," whoever they may be, will have already had their say, so why do you have to *repeat* it? Furthermore, if they had their say in print, can't readers just go and read what was said themselves?

The answer is that if you don't identify the "they say" you're responding to, your own argument probably won't have a point. Readers will wonder what prompted you to say what you're saying and therefore motivated you to write. As the figure on the following page suggests, without a "they say," *what* you are saying may be clear to your audience, but *why* you are saying it won't be.

Even if we don't know what film he's referring to, it's easy to grasp what the speaker means here when he says that its characters are very complex. But it's hard to see why the speaker feels the need to say what he is saying. "Why," as one member

4

of his imagined audience wonders, "is he telling us this?" So the characters are complex—so what?

Now look at what happens to the same proposition when it is presented as a response to something "they say":

We hope you agree that the same claim—"the characters in the film are very complex"—becomes much stronger when presented as a response to a contrary view: that the film's characters "are sexist stereotypes." Unlike the speaker in the first cartoon, the speaker in the second has a clear goal or mission: to correct what he sees as a mistaken characterization.

THE AS-OPPOSED-TO-WHAT FACTOR

To put our point another way, framing your "I say" as a response to something "they say" gives your writing an element of contrast without which it won't make sense. It may be helpful to think of this crucial element as an "as-opposed-to-what factor" and, as you write, to continually ask yourself, "Who says otherwise?" and "Does anyone dispute it?" Behind the audience's "Yeah, so?" and "Why is he telling us this?" in the first cartoon above lie precisely these types of "As opposed to what?" questions. The speaker in the second cartoon, we think, is more satisfying because he answers these questions, helping us see his point that the film presents complex characters *rather than* simple sexist stereotypes.

HOW IT'S DONE

Many accomplished writers make explicit "they say" moves to set up and motivate their own arguments. One famous example is Martin Luther King Jr.'s "Letter from Birmingham Jail," which consists almost entirely of King's eloquent responses to a public statement by eight clergymen deploring the civil rights protests he was leading. The letter—which was written in 1963, while King was in prison for leading a demonstration against racial injustice in Birmingham—is structured almost entirely around a framework of summary and response, in which King summarizes and then answers their criticisms. In one typical passage, King writes as follows.

> You deplore the demonstrations taking place in Birmingham. But your statement, I am sorry to say, fails to express a similar concern for the conditions that brought about the demonstrations.
>
> MARTIN LUTHER KING JR., "Letter from Birmingham Jail"

King goes on to agree with his critics that "It is unfortunate that demonstrations are taking place in Birmingham," yet he hastens to add that "it is even more unfortunate that the city's white power structure left the Negro community with no alternative." King's letter is so thoroughly conversational, in fact, that it could be rewritten in the form of a dialogue or play.

King's critics:
King's response:
Critics:
Response:

Clearly, King would not have written his famous letter were it not for his critics, whose views he treats not as objections to his already-formed arguments but as the motivating source of those arguments, their central reason for being. He quotes not only what his critics have said ("Some have asked: 'Why didn't you give the new city administration time to act?'"), but also things they *might* have said ("One may well ask: 'How can you advocate breaking some laws and obeying others?'")—all to set the stage for what he himself wants to say.

A similar "they say / I say" exchange opens an essay about American patriotism by the social critic Katha Pollitt, who uses her own daughter's comment to represent the patriotic national fervor after the terrorist attacks of September 11, 2001.

> My daughter, who goes to Stuyvesant High School only blocks from the former World Trade Center, thinks we should fly the American flag out our window. Definitely not, I say: the flag stands for jingoism and vengeance and war. She tells me I'm wrong—the flag means standing together and honoring the dead and saying no to terrorism. In a way we're both right. . . .
>
> KATHA POLLITT, "Put Out No Flags"

As Pollitt's example shows, the "they" you respond to in crafting an argument need not be a famous author or someone known to your audience. It can be a family member like Pollitt's daughter, or a friend or classmate who has made a provocative claim. It can even be something an individual or a group might say—or a side of yourself, something you once believed but no longer do, or something you partly believe but also doubt. The important thing is that the "they" (or "you" or "she") represent some wider group with which readers might identify—in Pollitt's case, those who patriotically believe in flying the flag. Pollitt's example also shows that responding to the views of others need not always involve unquali-fied opposition. By agreeing and disagreeing with her daughter, Pollitt enacts what we call the "yes and no" response, reconciling apparently incompatible views.

See Chapter 4 for more on agreeing, but with a difference.

While King and Pollitt both identify the views they are responding to, some authors do not explicitly state their views but instead allow the reader to infer them. See, for instance, if you can identify the implied or unnamed "they say" that the following claim is responding to.

> I like to think I have a certain advantage as a teacher of literature because when I was growing up I disliked and feared books.
>
> GERALD GRAFF, "Disliking Books at an Early Age"

In case you haven't figured it out already, the phantom "they say" here is the common belief that in order to be a good teacher of literature, one must have grown up liking and enjoying books.

COURT CONTROVERSY, BUT...

As you can see from these examples, many writers use the "they say / I say" format to challenge standard ways of thinking and thus to stir up controversy. This point may come as a shock to you if you have always had the impression that in order to succeed academically you need to play it safe and avoid controversy in your writing, making statements that nobody can possibly disagree with. Though this view of writing may appear logical, it is actually a recipe for flat, lifeless writing and for writing that fails to answer what we call the "so what?" and "who cares?" questions. "William Shakespeare wrote many famous plays and sonnets" may be a perfectly true statement, but precisely because nobody is likely to disagree with it, it goes without saying and thus would seem pointless if said.

But just because controversy is important doesn't mean you have to become an attack dog who automatically disagrees with everything others say. We think this is an important point to underscore because some who are not familiar with this book have gotten the impression from the title that our goal is to train writers simply to disparage whatever "they say."

DISAGREEING WITHOUT BEING DISAGREEABLE

There certainly are occasions when strong critique is needed. It's hard to live in a deeply polarized society like our current one and not feel the need at times to criticize what others think. But even the most justified critiques fall flat, we submit, unless we really listen to and understand the views we are criticizing:

▸ While I understand the impulse to _____ , my own view is _____ .

Even the most sympathetic audiences, after all, tend to feel manipulated by arguments that scapegoat and caricature the other side.

Furthermore, genuinely listening to views we disagree with can have the salutary effect of helping us see that beliefs we'd initially disdained may not be as thoroughly reprehensible as we'd imagined. Thus the type of "they say / I say" argument that we promote in this book can take the form of agreeing up to a point or, as the Pollitt example above illustrates, of both agreeing and disagreeing simultaneously, as in:

▸ While I agree with X that _____ , I cannot accept her overall conclusion that _____ .

▸ While X argues _____ , and I argue _____ , in a way we're both right.

Agreement cannot be ruled out, however:

▸ I agree with _____ that _____.

THE TEMPLATE OF TEMPLATES

There are many ways, then, to enter a conversation and respond to what "they say." But our discussion of ways to do so would be incomplete were we not to mention the most comprehensive way that writers enter conversations, which incorporates all the major moves discussed in this book:

▸ In recent discussions of _____, a controversial issue has been whether _____. On the one hand, some argue that _____. From this perspective, _____. On the other hand, however, others argue that _____. In the words of _____, one of this view's main proponents, "_____." According to this view, _____. In sum, then, the issue is whether _____ or _____.

    My own view is that _____. Though I concede that _____, I still maintain that _____. For example, _____. Although some might object that _____, I would reply that _____. The issue is important because _____.

This "template of templates," as we like to call it, represents the internal DNA of countless articles and even entire books. Writers commonly use a version of it not only to stake out their "they say" and "I say" at the start of their manuscript, but—just as important—to form the overarching blueprint that structures what they write over the entire length of their text.

Taking it line by line, this master template first helps you open your text by identifying an issue in some ongoing conversation or debate ("In recent discussions of _____, a controversial issue has been _____"), and then to map some of the voices in this controversy (by using the "on the one hand / on the other hand" structure). The template then helps you introduce a quotation ("In the words of"), to explain the quotation in your own words ("According to this view"), and—in a new paragraph—to state your own argument ("My own view is that"), to qualify your argument ("Though I concede that"), and then to support your argument with evidence ("For example"). In addition, the template helps you make one of the most crucial moves in argumentative writing, what we call "planting a naysayer in your text," in which you summarize and then answer a likely objection to your own central claim ("Although it might be objected that _____, I reply _____"). Finally, this template helps you shift between general, over-arching claims ("In sum, then") and smaller-scale, supporting claims ("For example").

Again, none of us is born knowing these moves, especially when it comes to academic writing. Hence the need for this book.

BUT ISN'T THIS PLAGIARISM?

"But isn't this plagiarism?" at least one student each year will usually ask. "Well, is it?" we respond, turning the question around into one the entire class can profit from. "We are, after all, asking you to use language in your writing that isn't your own—language that you 'borrow' or, to put it less delicately, steal from other writers."

Often, a lively discussion ensues that raises important questions about authorial ownership and helps everyone better understand the frequently confusing line between plagiarism and the legitimate use of what others say and how they say it. Students are quick to see that no one person owns a conventional formula like "on the one hand . . . on the other hand. . . ." Phrases like "a controversial issue" are so commonly used and recycled that they are generic—community property that can be freely used without fear of committing plagiarism. It *is* plagiarism, however, if the words used to fill in the blanks of such formulas are borrowed from others without proper acknowledgment. In sum, then, while it is not plagiarism to recycle conventionally used formulas, it is a serious academic offense to take the substantive content from others' texts without citing the author and giving him or her proper credit.

"OK—BUT TEMPLATES?"

Nevertheless, if you are like some of our students, your initial response to templates may be skepticism. At first, many of our students complain that using templates will take away their originality and creativity and make them all sound the same. "They'll turn us into writing robots," one of our students insisted. "I'm in college now," another student asserted; "this is third-grade-level stuff."

In our view, however, the templates in this book, far from being "third-grade-level stuff," represent the stock-in-trade of sophisticated thinking and writing, and they often require a great deal of practice and instruction to use successfully. As for the belief that pre-established forms undermine creativity, we think it rests on a very limited vision of what creativity is all about. In our view, the templates in this book will actually help your writing become *more* original and creative, not less. After all, even the most creative forms of expression depend on established patterns and structures. Most songwriters, for instance, rely on a time-honored verse-chorus-verse pattern, and few people would call Shakespeare uncreative because he didn't invent the sonnet or the dramatic forms that he used to such dazzling effect. Even the most avant-garde, cutting-edge artists like improvisational jazz musicians need to master the basic forms that their work improvises on, departs from, and goes beyond, or else their work will come across as uneducated child's play. Ultimately, then, creativity and originality lie not in the avoidance of established forms but in the imaginative use of them.

Furthermore, these templates do not dictate the *content* of what you say, which can be as original as you can make it, but only suggest a way of formatting *how* you say it. In addition, once you begin to feel comfortable with the templates in this book, you will be able to improvise creatively on them to fit new situations and purposes and find others in your reading. In other words, the templates offered here are learning tools to get you started, not structures set in stone. Once you get used to using them, you can even dispense with them altogether, for the rhetorical moves they model will be at your fingertips in an unconscious, instinctive way.

But if you still need proof that writing templates need not make you sound stiff and artificial, consider the following opening to an essay on the fast-food industry that we've included at the back of this book.

If ever there were a newspaper headline custom-made for Jay Leno's monologue, this was it. Kids taking on McDonald's this week, suing the company for making them fat. Isn't that like middle-aged men suing Porsche for making them get speeding tickets? Whatever happened to personal responsibility?

I tend to sympathize with these portly fast-food patrons, though. Maybe that's because I used to be one of them.

DAVID ZINCZENKO, "Don't Blame the Eater"

Although Zinczenko relies on a version of the "they say / I say" formula, his writing is anything but dry, robotic, or uncreative. While Zinczenko does not explicitly use the words "they say" and "I say," the template still gives the passage its underlying structure: "*They say* that kids suing fast-food companies for making them fat is a joke; but *I say* such lawsuits are justified."

PUTTING IN YOUR OAR

Though the immediate goal of this book is to help you become a better writer, at a deeper level it invites you to become a certain type of person: a critical, intellectual thinker who, instead of sitting passively on the sidelines, can participate in the debates and conversations of your world in an active and empowered way. Ultimately, this book invites you to become a critical thinker who can enter the types of conversations described eloquently by the philosopher Kenneth Burke in the following widely cited passage. Likening the world of intellectual exchange to a never-ending conversation at a party, Burke writes:

You come late. When you arrive, others have long preceded you, and they are engaged in a heated discussion, a discussion too heated for them to pause and tell you exactly what it is about. . . . You listen for a while, until you decide that you have caught the tenor of the argument; then you put in your oar. Someone answers; you answer him; another comes to your defense; another aligns himself against you. . . . The hour grows late, you must depart. And you do depart, with the discussion still vigorously in progress.

KENNETH BURKE, *The Philosophy of Literary Form*

What we like about this passage is its suggestion that stating an argument (putting in your oar) can only be done in conversation with others; that entering the dynamic world of ideas must be done not as isolated individuals but as social beings deeply connected to others.

This ability to enter complex, many-sided conversations has taken on a special urgency in today's polarized, Red State / Blue State America, where the future for all of us may depend on our ability to put ourselves in the shoes of those who think very differently from us. The central piece of advice in this book—that we listen carefully to others, including those who disagree with us, and then engage with them thoughtfully and respectfully—can help us see beyond our own pet beliefs, which may not be shared by everyone. The mere act of crafting a sentence that begins "Of course, someone might object that _____" may not seem like a way to change the world; but it does have the potential to jog us out of our comfort zones, to get us thinking critically about our own beliefs, and even to change minds, our own included.

Exercises

1. Write a short essay in which you first summarize our rationale for the templates in this book and then articulate your own

position in response. If you want, you can use the template below to organize your paragraphs, expanding and modifying it as necessary to fit what you want to say.

In the Introduction to "*They Say / I Say*": *The Moves That Matter in Academic Writing,* Gerald Graff and Cathy Birkenstein provide templates designed to _____. Specifically, Graff and Birkenstein argue that the types of writing templates they offer _____. As the authors themselves put it, "_____." Although some people believe _____, Graff and Birkenstein insist that _____. In sum, then, their view is that _____.

    I [agree/disagree/have mixed feelings]. In my view, the types of templates that the authors recommend _____. For instance, _____. In addition, _____. Some might object, of course, on the grounds that _____. Yet I would argue that _____. Overall, then, I believe _____ —an important point to make given _____.

2. Read the following paragraph from an essay by Emily Poe, a student at Furman University. Disregarding for the moment what Poe says, focus your attention on the phrases she uses to structure what she says (italicized here). Then write a new paragraph using Poe's as a model but replacing her topic, vegetarianism, with one of your own.

The term "vegetarian" tends to be synonymous with "tree-hugger" in many people's minds. *They see* vegetarianism as a cult that brainwashes its followers into eliminating an essential part of their daily diets for an abstract goal of "animal welfare." *However,* few vegetarians choose their lifestyle just to follow the crowd. *On the contrary,* many of these supposedly brainwashed people are actually independent thinkers, concerned citizens, and compassionate human beings. *For the truth is* that there are many very good reasons for giving up meat. Perhaps the best reasons are to improve the environment, to encourage humane treatment of livestock, or to enhance one's own health. *In this essay, then,* closely examining a vegetarian diet as compared to a meat-eater's diet will show that vegetarianism is clearly the better option for sustaining the Earth and all its inhabitants.

ONE

"THEY SAY"

Starting with What Others Are Saying

—◧—

NOT LONG AGO we attended a talk at an academic conference where the speaker's central claim seemed to be that a certain sociologist—call him Dr. X—had done very good work in a number of areas of the discipline. The speaker proceeded to illustrate his thesis by referring extensively and in great detail to various books and articles by Dr. X and by quoting long passages from them. The speaker was obviously both learned and impassioned, but as we listened to his talk we found ourselves somewhat puzzled: the argument—that Dr. X's work was very important—was clear enough, but why did the speaker need to make it in the first place? Did anyone dispute it? Were there commentators in the field who had argued against X's work or challenged its value? Was the speaker's interpretation of what X had done somehow novel or revolutionary? Since the speaker gave no hint of an answer to any of these questions, we could only wonder why he was going on and on about X. It was only after the speaker finished and took questions from the audience that we got a clue: in response to one questioner, he referred to several critics who had

The hypothetical audience in the figure on p. 5 reacts similarly.

vigorously questioned Dr. X's ideas and convinced many sociologists that Dr. X's work was unsound.

This story illustrates an important lesson: that to give writing the most important thing of all—namely, a point—a writer
needs to indicate clearly not only what his or her thesis is,
but also what larger conversation that thesis is responding to.
Because our speaker failed to mention what others had said about
Dr. X's work, he left his audience unsure about why he felt the
need to say what he was saying. Perhaps the point was clear to
other sociologists in the audience who were more familiar with
the debates over Dr. X's work than we were. But even they, we
bet, would have understood the speaker's point better if he'd
sketched in some of the larger conversation his own claims were
a part of and reminded the audience about what "they say."

This story also illustrates an important lesson about the *order*
in which things are said: to keep an audience engaged, a writer
needs to explain what he or she is responding to—either before
offering that response or, at least, very early in the discussion.
Delaying this explanation for more than one or two paragraphs
in a very short essay or blog entry, three or four pages in a
longer work, or more than ten or so pages in a book reverses
the natural order in which readers process material—and in
which writers think and develop ideas. After all, it seems very
unlikely that our conference speaker first developed his defense
of Dr. X and only later came across Dr. X's critics. As someone
knowledgeable in his field, the speaker surely encountered the
criticisms first and only then was compelled to respond and, as
he saw it, set the record straight.

Therefore, when it comes to constructing an argument
(whether orally or in writing), we offer you the following
advice: remember that you are entering a conversation and
therefore need to start with "what others are saying," as the

title of this chapter recommends, and then introduce your own ideas as a response. Specifically, we suggest that you summarize what "they say" as soon as you can in your text, and remind readers of it at strategic points as your text unfolds. Though it's true that not all texts follow this practice, we think it's important for all writers to master it before they depart from it.

This is not to say that you must start with a detailed list of everyone who has written on your subject before you offer your own ideas. Had our conference speaker gone to the opposite extreme and spent most of his talk summarizing Dr. X's critics with no hint of what he himself had to say, the audience probably would have had the same frustrated "why-is-he-going-on-like-this?" reaction. What we suggest, then, is that as soon as possible you state your own position and the one it's responding to *together*, and that you think of the two as a unit. It is generally best to summarize the ideas you're responding to briefly, at the start of your text, and to delay detailed elaboration until later. The point is to give your readers a quick preview of what is motivating your argument, not to drown them in details right away.

Starting with a summary of others' views may seem to contradict the common advice that writers should lead with their own thesis or claim. Although we agree that you shouldn't keep readers in suspense too long about your central argument, we also believe that you need to present that argument as part of some larger conversation, indicating something about the arguments of others that you are supporting, opposing, amending, complicating, or qualifying. One added benefit of summarizing others' views as soon as you can: you let those others do some of the work of framing and clarifying the issue you're writing about.

Consider, for example, how George Orwell starts his famous essay "Politics and the English Language" with what others are saying.

Most people who bother with the matter at all would admit that the English language is in a bad way, but it is generally assumed that we cannot by conscious action do anything about it. Our civilization is decadent and our language—so the argument runs—must inevitably share in the general collapse. . . .

[But] the process is reversible. Modern English . . . is full of bad habits . . . which can be avoided if one is willing to take the necessary trouble.

GEORGE ORWELL, "Politics and the English Language"

Orwell is basically saying, "Most people assume that we cannot do anything about the bad state of the English language. But I say we can."

Of course, there are many other powerful ways to begin. Instead of opening with someone else's views, you could start with an illustrative quotation, a revealing fact or statistic, or—as we do in this chapter—a relevant anecdote. If you choose one of these formats, however, be sure that it in some way illustrates the view you're addressing or leads you to that view directly, with a minimum of steps.

In opening this chapter, for example, we devote the first paragraph to an anecdote about the conference speaker and then move quickly at the start of the second paragraph to the misconception about writing exemplified by the speaker. In the following opening, from an opinion piece in the *New York Times Book Review*, Christina Nehring also moves quickly from an anecdote illustrating something she dislikes to her own claim—that book lovers think too highly of themselves.

"I'm a reader!" announced the yellow button. "How about you?" I looked at its bearer, a strapping young guy stalking my town's Festival of Books. "I'll bet you're a reader," he volunteered, as though we were two geniuses well met. "No," I replied. "Absolutely not," I wanted to yell, and fling my Barnes & Noble bag at his feet. Instead, I mumbled something apologetic and melted into the crowd.

There's a new piety in the air: the self-congratulation of book lovers.

CHRISTINA NEHRING, "Books Make You a Boring Person"

Nehring's anecdote is really a kind of "they say": book lovers keep telling themselves how great they are.

TEMPLATES FOR INTRODUCING WHAT "THEY SAY"

There are lots of conventional ways to introduce what others are saying. Here are some standard templates that we would have recommended to our conference speaker.

▸ A number of sociologists have recently suggested <u>that X's work has several fundamental problems.</u>

▸ It has become common today to dismiss _____.

▸ In their recent work, Y and Z have offered harsh critiques of _____ for _____.

TEMPLATES FOR INTRODUCING "STANDARD VIEWS"

The following templates can help you make what we call the "standard view" move, in which you introduce a view that has become so widely accepted that by now it is essentially the conventional way of thinking about a topic.

- Americans have always believed that <u>individual effort can triumph over circumstances</u>.

- Conventional wisdom has it that _____.

- Common sense seems to dictate that _____.

- The standard way of thinking about topic X has it that _____.

- It is often said that _____.

- My whole life I have heard it said that _____.

- You would think that _____.

- Many people assume that _____.

These templates are popular because they provide a quick and efficient way to perform one of the most common moves that writers make: challenging widely accepted beliefs, placing them on the examining table, and analyzing their strengths and weaknesses.

TEMPLATES FOR MAKING WHAT "THEY SAY" SOMETHING *YOU* SAY

Another way to introduce the views you're responding to is to present them as your own. That is, the "they say" that you respond to need not be a view held by others; it can be one that you yourself once held or one that you are ambivalent about.

- I've always believed that <u>museums are boring</u>.

- When I was a child, I used to think that _____.

▸ Although I should know better by now, I cannot help thinking that _____ .

▸ At the same time that I believe _____ , I also believe _____ .

TEMPLATES FOR INTRODUCING
SOMETHING IMPLIED OR ASSUMED

Another sophisticated move a writer can make is to summarize a point that is not directly stated in what "they say" but is implied or assumed.

▸ Although none of them have ever said so directly, my teachers have often given me the impression that <u>education will open doors</u>.

▸ One implication of X's treatment of _____ is that _____ .

▸ Although X does not say so directly, she apparently assumes that _____ .

▸ While they rarely admit as much, _____ often take for granted that _____ .

These are templates that can help you think analytically—to look beyond what others say explicitly and to consider their unstated assumptions, as well as the implications of their views.

TEMPLATES FOR INTRODUCING
AN ONGOING DEBATE

Sometimes you'll want to open by summarizing a debate that presents two or more views. This kind of opening demonstrates your awareness that there are conflicting ways to look at your subject, the clear mark of someone who knows the subject and therefore is likely to be a reliable, trustworthy guide. Furthermore, opening with a summary of a debate can help you explore the issue you are writing about before declaring your own view. In this way, you can use the writing process itself to help you discover where you stand instead of having to commit to a position before you are ready to do so.

Here is a basic template for opening with a debate.

▸ In discussions of X, one controversial issue has been _____. On the one hand, _____ argues _____. On the other hand, _____ contends _____. Others even maintain _____. My own view is _____.

The cognitive scientist Mark Aronoff uses this kind of template in an essay on the workings of the human brain.

> Theories of how the mind/brain works have been dominated for centuries by two opposing views. One, rationalism, sees the human mind as coming into this world more or less fully formed—preprogrammed, in modern terms. The other, empiricism, sees the mind of the newborn as largely unstructured, a blank slate.
>
> MARK ARONOFF, "Washington Slept Here"

A student writer, Michaela Cullington, uses a version of this template near the beginning of an essay to frame a debate over online writing abbreviations like "LOL" ("laughing out loud") and to indicate her own position in this debate.

> Some people believe that using these abbreviations is hindering the writing abilities of students, and others argue that texting is

actually having a positive effect on writing. In fact, it seems likely that texting has no significant effect on student writing.

MICHAELA CULLINGTON, "Does Texting Affect Writing?"

Another way to open with a debate involves starting with a proposition many people agree with in order to highlight the point(s) on which they ultimately disagree.

▸ When it comes to the topic of _____, most of us will readily agree that _____. Where this agreement usually ends, however, is on the question of _____. Whereas some are convinced that _____, others maintain that _____.

The political writer Thomas Frank uses a variation on this move.

That we are a nation divided is an almost universal lament of this bitter election year. However, the exact property that divides us—elemental though it is said to be—remains a matter of some controversy.

THOMAS FRANK, "American Psyche"

KEEP WHAT "THEY SAY" IN VIEW

We can't urge you too strongly to keep in mind what "they say" as you move through the rest of your text. After summarizing the ideas you are responding to at the outset, it's very important to continue to keep those ideas in view. Readers won't be able to follow your unfolding response, much less any complications you may offer, unless you keep reminding them what claims you are responding to.

In other words, even when presenting your own claims, you should keep returning to the motivating "they say." The longer and more complicated your text, the greater the chance that readers will forget what ideas originally motivated it—no matter how clearly you lay them out at the beginning. At strategic moments throughout your text, we recommend that you include what we call "return sentences." Here is an example.

► In conclusion, then, as I suggested earlier, defenders of _____ can't have it both ways. Their assertion that _____ is contradicted by their claim that _____ .

We ourselves use such return sentences at every opportunity in this book to remind you of the view of writing that our book questions—that good writing means making true or smart or logical statements about a given subject with little or no reference to what others say about it.

By reminding readers of the ideas you're responding to, return sentences ensure that your text maintains a sense of mission and urgency from start to finish. In short, they help ensure that your argument is a genuine response to others' views rather than just a set of observations about a given subject. The difference is huge. To be responsive to others and the conversation you're entering, you need to start with what others are saying and continue keeping it in the reader's view.

Exercises

1. The following is a list of arguments that lack a "they say." Like the speaker in the cartoon on page 5 who declares that the film presents complex characters, these one-sided

arguments fail to explain what view they are responding to—what view, in effect, they are trying to correct, add to, qualify, complicate, and so forth. Your job in this exercise is to provide each argument with such a counterview. Feel free to use any of the templates in this chapter that you find helpful.

a. Our experiments suggest that there are dangerous levels of chemical X in the Ohio groundwater.
b. Material forces drive history.
c. Proponents of Freudian psychology question standard notions of "rationality."
d. Male students often dominate class discussions.
e. The film is about the problems of romantic relationships.
f. I'm afraid that templates like the ones in this book will stifle my creativity.

2. Below is a template that we derived from the opening of David Zinczenko's "Don't Blame the Eater" (p. 245). Use the template to structure a passage on a topic of your own choosing. Your first step here should be to find an idea that you support that others not only disagree with but actually find laughable (or, as Zinczenko puts it, worthy of a Jay Leno monologue). You might write about one of the topics listed in the previous exercise (the environment, gender relations, the meaning of a book or movie) or any other topic that interests you.

If ever there was an idea custom-made for a Jay Leno monologue, this was it: _____. Isn't that like _____? Whatever happened to _____?

I happen to sympathize with _____, though, perhaps because _____.

TWO

"HER POINT IS"

The Art of Summarizing

———

IF IT IS TRUE, as we claim in this book, that to argue persuasively you need to be in dialogue with others, then summarizing others' arguments is central to your arsenal of basic moves. Because writers who make strong claims need to map their claims relative to those of other people, it is important to know how to summarize effectively what those other people say. (We're using the word "summarizing" here to refer to any information from others that you present in your own words, including that which you paraphrase.)

Many writers shy away from summarizing—perhaps because they don't want to take the trouble to go back to the text in question and wrestle with what it says, or because they fear that devoting too much time to other people's ideas will take away from their own. When assigned to write a response to an article, such writers might offer their own views on the article's *topic* while hardly mentioning what the article itself argues or says. At the opposite extreme are those who do nothing *but* summarize. Lacking confidence, perhaps, in their own ideas, these writers so overload their texts with summaries of others' ideas that their own voice gets lost. And since these summaries are not animated by the writers' own interests, they often read like mere lists of things that X thinks or Y says—with no clear focus.

As a general rule, a good summary requires balancing what the original author is saying with the writer's own focus. Generally speaking, a summary must at once be true to what the original author says while also emphasizing those aspects of what the author says that interest you, the writer. Striking this delicate balance can be tricky, since it means facing two ways at once: both outward (toward the author being summarized) and inward (toward yourself). Ultimately, it means being respectful of others but simultaneously structuring how you summarize them in light of your own text's central argument.

ON THE ONE HAND,
PUT YOURSELF IN *THEIR* SHOES

To write a really good summary, you must be able to suspend your own beliefs for a time and put yourself in the shoes of someone else. This means playing what the writing theorist Peter Elbow calls the "believing game," in which you try to inhabit the worldview of those whose conversation you are joining—and whom you are perhaps even disagreeing with—and try to see their argument from their perspective. This ability to temporarily suspend one's own convictions is a hallmark of good actors, who must convincingly "become" characters whom in real life they may detest. As a writer, when you play the believing game well, readers should not be able to tell whether you agree or disagree with the ideas you are summarizing.

If, as a writer, you cannot or will not suspend your own beliefs in this way, you are likely to produce summaries that are so obviously biased that they undermine your credibility with readers. Consider the following summary.

> David Zinczenko's article "Don't Blame the Eater" is nothing more than an angry rant in which he accuses the fast-food companies of an evil conspiracy to make people fat. I disagree because these companies have to make money. . . .

If you review what Zinczenko actually says (pp. 709–712), you should immediately see that this summary amounts to an unfair distortion. While Zinczenko does argue that the practices of the fast-food industry have the *effect* of making people fat, his tone is never "angry," and he never goes so far as to suggest that the fast-food industry conspires to make people fat with deliberately evil intent.

Another telltale sign of this writer's failure to give Zinczenko a fair hearing is the hasty way he abandons the summary after only one sentence and rushes on to his own response. So eager is this writer to disagree that he not only caricatures what Zinczenko says but also gives the article a hasty, superficial reading. Granted, there are many writing situations in which, because of matters of proportion, a one- or two-sentence summary is precisely what you want. Indeed, as writing professor Karen Lunsford (whose own research focuses on argument theory) points out, it is standard in the natural and social sciences to summarize the work of others quickly, in one pithy sentence or phrase, as in the following example.

> Several studies (Crackle, 2012; Pop, 2007; Snap, 2006) suggest that these policies are harmless; moreover, other studies (Dick, 2011; Harry, 2007; Tom, 2005) argue that they even have benefits.

But if your assignment is to respond in writing to a single author, like Zinczenko, you will need to tell your readers enough about his or her argument so they can assess its merits on their own, independent of you.

When a writer fails to provide enough summary or to engage in a rigorous or serious enough summary, he or she often falls prey to what we call "the closest cliché syndrome," in which what gets summarized is not the view the author in question has actually expressed but a familiar cliché that the writer *mistakes* for the author's view (sometimes because the writer believes it and mistakenly assumes the author must too). So, for example, Martin Luther King Jr.'s passionate defense of civil disobedience in "Letter from Birmingham Jail" might be summarized not as the defense of political protest that it actually is but as a plea for everyone to "just get along." Similarly, Zinczenko's critique of the fast-food industry might be summarized as a call for overweight people to take responsibility for their weight.

Whenever you enter into a conversation with others in your writing, then, it is extremely important that you go back to what those others have said, that you study it very closely, and that you not confuse it with something you already believe. A writer who fails to do this ends up essentially conversing with imaginary others who are really only the products of his or her own biases and preconceptions.

ON THE OTHER HAND, KNOW WHERE *YOU* ARE GOING

Even as writing an effective summary requires you to temporarily adopt the worldview of another person, it does not mean ignoring your own view altogether. Paradoxically, at the same time that summarizing another text requires you to represent fairly what it says, it also requires that your own response exert a quiet influence. A good summary, in other words, has a focus or spin that allows the summary to fit with your own agenda while still being true to the text you are summarizing.

Thus if you are writing in response to the essay by Zinczenko, you should be able to see that an essay on the fast-food industry in general will call for a very different summary than will an essay on parenting, corporate regulation, or warning labels. If you want your essay to encompass all three topics, you'll need to subordinate these three issues to one of Zinczenko's general claims and then make sure this general claim directly sets up your own argument.

For example, suppose you want to argue that it is parents, not fast-food companies, who are to blame for children's obesity. To set up this argument, you will probably want to compose a summary that highlights what Zinczenko says about the fast-food industry *and parents*. Consider this sample.

> In his article "Don't Blame the Eater," David Zinczenko blames the fast-food industry for fueling today's so-called obesity epidemic, not only by failing to provide adequate warning labels on its high-calorie foods but also by filling the nutritional void in children's lives left by their overtaxed working parents. With many parents working long hours and unable to supervise what their children eat, Zinczenko claims, children today are easily victimized by the low-cost, calorie-laden foods that the fast-food chains are all too eager to supply. When he was a young boy, for instance, and his single mother was away at work, he ate at Taco Bell, McDonald's, and other chains on a regular basis, and ended up overweight. Zinczenko's hope is that with the new spate of lawsuits against

the food industry, other children with working parents will have healthier choices available to them, and that they will not, like him, become obese.

In my view, however, it is the parents, and not the food chains, who are responsible for their children's obesity. While it is true that many of today's parents work long hours, there are still several things that parents can do to guarantee that their children eat healthy foods. . . .

The summary in the first paragraph succeeds because it points in two directions at once—both toward Zinczenko's own text *and* toward the second paragraph, where the writer begins to establish her own argument. The opening sentence gives a sense of Zinczenko's general argument (that the fast-food chains are to blame for obesity), including his two main supporting claims (about warning labels and parents), but it ends with an emphasis on the writer's main concern: parental responsibility. In this way, the summary does justice to Zinczenko's arguments while also setting up the ensuing critique.

This advice—to summarize authors in light of your own agenda—may seem painfully obvious. But writers often summarize a given author on one issue even though their text actually focuses on another. To avoid this problem, you need to make sure that your "they say" and "I say" are well matched. In fact, aligning what they say with what you say is a good thing to work on when revising what you've written.

Often writers who summarize without regard to their own agenda fall prey to what might be called "list summaries," summaries that simply inventory the original author's various points but fail to focus those points around any larger overall claim. If you've ever heard a talk in which the points were connected only by words like "and then," "also," and "in addition," you

THE EFFECT OF A TYPICAL LIST SUMMARY

know how such lists can put listeners to sleep—as shown in the figure above. A typical list summary sounds like this.

> The author says many different things about his subject. *First* he says. . . . *Then* he makes the point that. . . . *In addition* he says. . . . *And then* he writes. . . . *Also* he shows that. . . . *And then* he says. . . .

It may be boring list summaries like this that give summaries in general a bad name and even prompt some instructors to discourage their students from summarizing at all.

Not all lists are bad, however. A list can be an excellent way to organize material—but only if, instead of being a miscellaneous grab bag, it is organized around a larger argument that informs each item listed. Many well-written summaries, for instance, list various points made by an author, sometimes itemizing those points ("First, she argues . . . ," "Second, she argues . . . ," "Third . . ."), and sometimes even itemizing those points in bullet form.

Many well-written arguments are organized in a list format as well. In "The New Liberal Arts," Sanford J. Ungar lists what he sees as seven common misperceptions that discourage college students from majoring in the liberal arts, the first three of which begin:

> Misperception No. 1: A liberal-arts degree is a luxury that most families can no longer afford. . . .
>
> Misperception No. 2: College graduates are finding it harder to get good jobs with liberal-arts degrees. . . .
>
> Misperception No. 3: The liberal arts are particularly irrelevant for low-income and first-generation college students. They, more than their more-affluent peers, must focus on something more practical and marketable.
>
> SANFORD J. UNGAR, "The New Liberal Arts"

What makes Ungar's list so effective, and makes it stand out in contrast to the type of disorganized lists our cartoon parodies, is that it has a clear, overarching goal: to defend the liberal arts. Had Ungar's article lacked such a unifying agenda and instead been a miscellaneous grab bag, it almost assuredly would have lost its readers, who wouldn't have known what to focus on or what the final message or takeaway should be.

In conclusion, writing a good summary means not just representing an author's view accurately, but doing so in a way that fits what you want to say, the larger point you want to make. On the one hand, it means playing Peter Elbow's believing game and doing justice to the source; if the summary ignores or misrepresents the source, its bias and unfairness will show. On the other hand, even as it does justice to the source, a summary has to have a slant or spin that prepares the way for your own claims. Once a summary enters your text, you should think of it as joint property—reflecting not just the source you are summarizing, but your own perspective or take on it.

SUMMARIZING SATIRICALLY

Thus far in this chapter we have argued that, as a general rule, good summaries require a balance between what someone else has said and your own interests as a writer. Now, however, we want to address one exception to this rule: the satiric summary, in which a writer deliberately gives his or her own spin to someone else's argument in order to reveal a glaring shortcoming in it. Despite our previous comments that well-crafted summaries generally strike a balance between heeding what someone else has said and your own independent interests, the satiric mode can at times be a very effective form of critique because it lets the summarized argument condemn itself without overt editorializing by you, the writer.

One such satiric summary can be found in Sanford J. Ungar's essay "The New Liberal Arts," which we just mentioned. In his discussion of the "misperception," as he sees it, that a liberal arts education is "particularly irrelevant for low-income and first-generation college students," who "must focus on something more practical and marketable," Ungar restates this view as "another way of saying, really, that the rich folks will do the important thinking, and the lower classes will simply carry out their ideas." Few who would dissuade disadvantaged students from the liberal arts would actually state their position in this insulting way. But in taking their position to its logical conclusion, Ungar's satire suggests that this is precisely what their position amounts to.

USE SIGNAL VERBS THAT FIT THE ACTION

In introducing summaries, try to avoid bland formulas like "she says" or "they believe." Though language like this is sometimes serviceable enough, it often fails to reflect accurately what's been said. In some cases, "he says" may even drain the passion out of the ideas you're summarizing.

We suspect that the habit of ignoring the action when summarizing stems from the mistaken belief we mentioned earlier that writing is about playing it safe and not making waves, a matter of piling up truths and bits of knowledge rather than a dynamic process of doing things to and with other people. People who wouldn't hesitate to *say* "X totally misrepresented," "attacked," or "loved" something when chatting with friends will in their writing often opt for far tamer and even less accurate phrases like "X said."

But the authors you summarize at the college level seldom simply "say" or "discuss" things; they "urge," "emphasize," and "complain about" them. David Zinczenko, for example, doesn't just *say* that fast-food companies contribute to obesity; he *complains* or *protests* that they do; he *challenges*, *chastises*, and *indicts* those companies. The Declaration of Independence doesn't just *talk about* the treatment of the colonies by the British; it *protests against* it. To do justice to the authors you cite, we recommend that when summarizing—or when introducing a quotation—you use vivid and precise signal verbs as often as possible. Though "he says" or "she believes" will sometimes be the most appropriate language for the occasion, your text will often be more accurate and lively if you tailor your verbs to suit the precise actions you're describing.

TEMPLATES FOR INTRODUCING SUMMARIES AND QUOTATIONS

▸ She advocates <u>a radical revision of the juvenile justice system</u>.

▸ They celebrate the fact that _____.

▸ _____, he admits.

VERBS FOR INTRODUCING SUMMARIES AND QUOTATIONS

VERBS FOR MAKING A CLAIM

argue	insist
assert	observe
believe	remind us
claim	report
emphasize	suggest

VERBS FOR EXPRESSING AGREEMENT

acknowledge	endorse
admire	extol
agree	praise

VERBS FOR EXPRESSING AGREEMENT

celebrate the fact that	reaffirm
corroborate	support
do not deny	verify

VERBS FOR QUESTIONING OR DISAGREEING

complain	qualify
complicate	question
contend	refute
contradict	reject
deny	renounce
deplore the tendency to	repudiate

VERBS FOR MAKING RECOMMENDATIONS

advocate	implore
call for	plead
demand	recommend
encourage	urge
exhort	warn

Exercises

1. To get a feel for Peter Elbow's "believing game," write a summary of some belief that you strongly disagree with. Then write a summary of the position that you actually hold on this topic. Give both summaries to a classmate or two, and see if they can tell which position you endorse. If you've succeeded, they won't be able to tell.

2. Write two different summaries of David Zinczenko's "Don't Blame the Eater" (pp. 709–712). Write the first one for an essay arguing that, contrary to what Zinczenko claims, there *are* inexpensive and convenient alternatives to fast-food restaurants. Write the second for an essay that questions whether being overweight is a genuine medical problem rather than a problem of cultural stereotypes. Compare your two summaries: though they are about the same article, they should look very different.

THREE

"AS HE HIMSELF PUTS IT"
The Art of Quoting

———

A KEY PREMISE OF THIS BOOK is that to launch an effective argument you need to write the arguments of others into your text. One of the best ways to do so is by not only summarizing what "they say," as suggested in Chapter 2, but by quoting their exact words. Quoting someone else's words gives a tremendous amount of credibility to your summary and helps ensure that it is fair and accurate. In a sense, then, quotations function as a kind of proof of evidence, saying to readers: "Look, I'm not just making this up. She makes this claim, and here it is in her exact words."

Yet many writers make a host of mistakes when it comes to quoting, not the least of which is the failure to quote enough in the first place, if at all. Some writers quote too little—perhaps because they don't want to bother going back to the original text and looking up the author's exact words, or because they think they can reconstruct the author's ideas from memory. At the opposite extreme are writers who so overquote that they end up with texts that are short on commentary of their own—maybe because they lack confidence in their ability to comment on the quotations, or because they don't fully understand what they've quoted and therefore have trouble explaining what the quotations mean.

But the main problem with quoting arises when writers assume that quotations speak for themselves. Because the meaning of a quotation is obvious to *them*, many writers assume that this meaning will also be obvious to their readers, when often it is not. Writers who make this mistake think that their job is done when they've chosen a quotation and inserted it into their text. They draft an essay, slap in a few quotations, and whammo, they're done.

Such writers fail to see that quoting means more than simply enclosing what "they say" in quotation marks. In a way, quotations are orphans: words that have been taken from their original contexts and that need to be integrated into their new textual surroundings. This chapter offers two key ways to produce this sort of integration: (1) by choosing quotations wisely, with an eye to how well they support a particular part of your text, and (2) by surrounding every major quotation with a frame explaining whose words they are, what the quotation means, and how the quotation relates to your own text. The point we want to emphasize is that quoting what "they say" must always be connected with what *you* say.

QUOTE RELEVANT PASSAGES

Before you can select appropriate quotations, you need to have a sense of what you want to do with them—that is, how they will support your text at the particular point where you insert them. Be careful not to select quotations just for the sake of demonstrating that you've read the author's work; you need to make sure they support your own argument.

However, finding relevant quotations is not always easy. In fact, sometimes quotations that were initially relevant to your argument, or to a key point in it, become less so as your text changes during the process of writing and revising. Given the evolving and messy nature of writing, you may sometimes think that you've found the perfect quotation to support your argument, only to discover later on, as your text develops, that your focus has changed and the quotation no longer works. It can be somewhat misleading, then, to speak of finding your thesis and finding relevant quotations as two separate steps, one coming after the other. When you're deeply engaged in the writing and revising process, there is usually a great deal of back-and-forth between your argument and any quotations you select.

FRAME EVERY QUOTATION

Finding relevant quotations is only part of your job; you also need to present them in a way that makes their relevance and meaning clear to your readers. Since quotations do not speak for themselves, you need to build a frame around them in which you do that speaking for them.

Quotations that are inserted into a text without such a frame are sometimes called "dangling" quotations for the way they're left dangling without any explanation. One teacher we've worked with, Steve Benton, calls these "hit-and-run" quotations, likening them to car accidents in which the driver speeds away and avoids taking responsibility for the dent in your fender or the smashed taillights, as in the figure that follows.

DON'T BE A HIT-AND-RUN QUOTER.

GG

What follows is a typical hit-and-run quotation by a student responding to an essay by Deborah Tannen, a linguistics professor and author, who complains that academics value opposition over agreement.

> Deborah Tannen writes about academia. Academics believe "that intellectual inquiry is a metaphorical battle. Following from that is a second assumption that the best way to demonstrate intellectual prowess is to criticize, find fault, and attack."
> I agree with Tannen. Another point Tannen makes is that . . .

Since this student fails to introduce the quotation adequately or explain why he finds it worth quoting, readers will have a hard time reconstructing what Tannen argued. First, the student simply gives us the quotation from Tannen without telling us who Tannen is or even indicating that the quoted words are hers. In addition, the student does not explain what he takes Tannen to be saying or how her claims connect with his own. Instead, he simply abandons the quotation in his haste to zoom on to another point.

To adequately frame a quotation, you need to insert it into what we like to call a "quotation sandwich," with the statement introducing it serving as the top slice of bread and the explanation following it serving as the bottom slice. The introductory or lead-in claims should explain who is speaking and set up what the quotation says; the follow-up statements should explain why you consider the quotation to be important and what you take it to say.

TEMPLATES FOR INTRODUCING QUOTATIONS

▸ X states, "<u>Not all steroids should be banned from sports</u>."

▸ As the prominent philosopher X puts it, "_____."

▸ According to X, "_____."

▸ X himself writes, "_____."

▸ In her book, _____ , X maintains that "_____."

▸ Writing in the journal *Commentary*, X complains that "_____."

▸ In X's view, "_____."

▸ X agrees when she writes, "_____."

▸ X disagrees when he writes, "_____."

▸ X complicates matters further when she writes, "_____."

TEMPLATES FOR EXPLAINING QUOTATIONS

The one piece of advice about quoting that our students say they find most helpful is to get in the habit of following every major quotation by explaining what it means, using a template like one of the ones below.

▸ **Basically, X is warning <u>that the proposed solution will only make the problem worse</u>.**

▸ **In other words, X believes _____.**

▸ **In making this comment, X urges us to _____.**

▸ **X is corroborating the age-old adage that _____.**

▸ **X's point is that _____.**

▸ **The essence of X's argument is that _____.**

When offering such explanations, it is important to use language that accurately reflects the spirit of the quoted passage. It is often serviceable enough in introducing a quotation to write "X states" or "X asserts," but in most cases you can add precision to your writing by introducing the quotation in more vivid terms. Since, in the example above, Tannen is clearly alarmed by the culture of "attack" that she describes, it would be more accurate to use language that reflects that alarm: "Tannen is alarmed that," "Tannen is disturbed by," "Tannen deplores," or (in our own formulation here) "Tannen complains."

See pp. 40–41 for a list of action verbs for summarizing what other say.

Consider, for example, how the earlier passage on Tannen might be revised using some of these moves.

Deborah Tannen, a prominent linguistics professor, complains that academia is too combative. Rather than really listening to others, Tannen insists, academics habitually try to prove one another wrong. As Tannen herself puts it, "We are all driven by our ideological assumption that intellectual inquiry is a metaphorical battle," that "the best way to demonstrate intellectual prowess is to criticize, find fault, and attack." In short, Tannen objects that academic communication tends to be a competition for supremacy in which loftier values like truth and consensus get lost.

> Tannen's observations ring true to me because I have often felt that the academic pieces I read for class are negative and focus on proving another theorist wrong rather than stating a truth . . .

This revision works, we think, because it frames or nests Tannen's words, integrating them and offering guidance about how they should be read. Instead of launching directly into the quoted words, as the previous draft had done, this revised version identifies Tannen ("a prominent linguistics professor") and clearly indicates that the quoted words are hers ("as Tannen herself puts it"). And instead of being presented without explanation as it was before, the quotation is now presented as an illustration of Tannen's point that, as the student helpfully puts it, "academics habitually try to prove one another wrong" and compete "for supremacy." In this way, the student explains the quotation while restating it in his own words, thereby making it clear that the quotation is being used purposefully instead of having been stuck in simply to pad the essay or the works-cited list.

BLEND THE AUTHOR'S WORDS
WITH YOUR OWN

This new framing material also works well because it accurately represents Tannen's words while giving those words the student's own spin. Instead of simply repeating Tannen word for word, the follow-up sentences echo just enough of her language while still moving the discussion in the student's own direction. Tannen's "battle," "criticize," "find fault," and "attack," for instance, get translated by the student into claims about how "combative" Tannen thinks academics are and how she thinks they "habitually try to prove one another wrong." In this way, the framing creates a kind of hybrid mix of Tannen's words and those of the writer.

CAN YOU OVERANALYZE A QUOTATION?

But is it possible to overexplain a quotation? And how do you know when you've explained a quotation thoroughly enough? After all, not all quotations require the same amount of explanatory framing, and there are no hard-and-fast rules for knowing how much explanation any quotation needs. As a general rule, the most explanatory framing is needed for quotations that may be hard for readers to process: quotations that are long and complex, that are filled with details or jargon, or that contain hidden complexities.

And yet, though the particular situation usually dictates when and how much to explain a quotation, we will still offer one piece of advice: when in doubt, go for it. It is better to risk being overly explicit about what you take a quotation to mean than to leave the quotation dangling and your readers in doubt. Indeed, we encourage you to provide such explanatory framing even when writing to an audience that you know to be familiar with the author being quoted and able to interpret your quotations on their own. Even in such cases, readers need to see how *you* interpret the quotation, since words—especially those of controversial figures—can be interpreted in various ways and used to support different, sometimes opposing, agendas.

Your readers need to see what you make of the material you've quoted, if only to be sure that your reading of the material and theirs are on the same page.

HOW *NOT* TO INTRODUCE QUOTATIONS

We want to conclude this chapter by surveying some ways *not* to introduce quotations. Although some writers do so, you should not introduce quotations by saying something like "Orwell asserts an idea that" or "A quote by Shakespeare says." Introductory phrases like these are both redundant and misleading. In the first example, you could write either "Orwell asserts that" or "Orwell's assertion is that," rather than redundantly combining the two. The second example misleads readers, since it is the writer who is doing the quoting, not Shakespeare (as "a quote by Shakespeare" implies).

The templates in this book will help you avoid such mistakes. Once you have mastered templates like "as X puts it" or "in X's own words," you probably won't even have to think about them—and will be free to focus on the challenging ideas that templates help you frame.

Exercises

1. Find a published piece of writing that quotes something that "they say." How has the writer integrated the quotation into his or her own text? How has he or she introduced the quotation, and what, if anything, has the writer said to explain it and tie it to his or her own text? Based on what you've read in this chapter, are there any changes you would suggest?

2. Look at something you have written for one of your classes.
   Have you quoted any sources? If so, how have you integrated
   the quotation into your own text? How have you introduced it? explained what it means? indicated how it relates
   to *your* text? If you haven't done all these things, revise your
   text to do so, perhaps using the Templates for Introducing
   Quotations (p. 47) and Explaining Quotations (pp. 47–48).
   If you've not written anything with quotations, try revising
   some academic text you've written to do so.

FOUR

"YES / NO / OKAY, BUT"

Three Ways to Respond

———⌐⌐———

THE FIRST THREE CHAPTERS of this book discuss the "they say" stage of writing, in which you devote your attention to the views of some other person or group. In this chapter we move to the "I say" stage, in which you offer your own argument as a response to what "they" have said.

Moving to the "I say" stage can be daunting in academia, where it often may seem that you need to be an expert in a field to have an argument at all. Many students have told us that they have trouble entering some of the high-powered conversations that take place in college or graduate school because they do not know enough about the topic at hand or because, they say, they simply are not "smart enough." Yet often these same students, when given a chance to study in depth the contribution that some scholar has made in a given field, will turn around and say things like "I can see where she is coming from, how she makes her case by building on what other scholars have said. Perhaps had I studied the situation longer *I* could have come up with a similar argument." What these students come to realize is that good arguments are based not on knowledge that only a special class of experts has access to, but on everyday habits of mind that can be isolated, identified, and used by almost anyone. Though there's certainly no substitute for expertise and for knowing as much as possible about one's topic, the arguments that finally win the day are built, as the title of this chapter suggests, on some very basic rhetorical patterns that most of us use on a daily basis.

There are a great many ways to respond to others' ideas, but this chapter concentrates on the three most common and recognizable ways: agreeing, disagreeing, or some combination of both. Although each way of responding is open to endless variation, we focus on these three because readers come to any text needing to learn fairly quickly where the writer stands, and they do this by placing the writer on a mental map consisting of a few familiar options: the writer agrees with those he or she is responding to, disagrees with them, or presents some combination of both agreeing and disagreeing.

When writers take too long to declare their position relative to views they've summarized or quoted, readers get frustrated, wondering, "Is this guy agreeing or disagreeing? Is he *for* what this other person has said, *against* it, or what?" For this reason, this chapter's advice applies to reading as well as to writing. Especially with difficult texts, you need not only to find the position the writer is responding to—the "they say"—but also to determine whether the writer is agreeing with it, challenging it, or some mixture of the two.

ONLY *THREE* WAYS TO RESPOND?

Perhaps you'll worry that fitting your own response into one of these three categories will force you to oversimplify your argument or lessen its complexity, subtlety, or originality. This is certainly a serious concern for academics who are rightly skeptical of writing that is simplistic and reductive. We would argue, however, that the more complex and subtle your argument is, and the more it departs from the conventional ways people think, the more your readers will need to be able to place it on their mental map in order to process the complex details you present. That is, the complexity, subtlety, and originality of your response are more likely to stand out and be noticed if readers have a baseline sense of where you stand relative to any ideas you've cited. As you move through this chapter, we hope you'll agree that the forms of agreeing, disagreeing, and both agreeing and disagreeing that we discuss, far from being simplistic or one-dimensional, are able to accommodate a high degree of creative, complex thought.

It is always a good tactic to begin your response not by launching directly into a mass of details but by stating clearly whether you agree, disagree, or both, using a direct, no-nonsense formula such as: "I agree," "I disagree," or "I am of two minds. I agree that _____ , but I cannot agree that _____ ." Once you have offered one of these straight-forward statements (or one of the many variations discussed below), readers will have a strong grasp of your position and then be able to appreciate the complications you go on to offer as your response unfolds. See p. 21 for suggestions on previewing where you stand.

Still, you may object that these three basic ways of responding don't cover all the options—that they ignore interpretive or analytical responses, for example. In other words, you might think that when you interpret a literary work you don't necessarily agree or disagree with anything but simply explain the work's meaning, style, or structure. Many essays about literature and the arts, it might be said, take this form—they interpret a work's meaning, thus rendering matters of agreeing or disagreeing irrelevant.

We would argue, however, that the most interesting interpretations in fact tend to be those that agree, disagree, or both—that instead of being offered solo, the best interpretations take strong stands relative to other interpretations. In fact, there would be no reason to offer an interpretation of a work of literature or art unless you were responding to the interpretations or possible interpretations of others. Even when you point out features or qualities of an artistic work that others have not noticed, you are implicitly disagreeing with what those interpreters have said by pointing out that they missed or overlooked something that, in your view, is important. In any effective interpretation, then, you need not only to state what you yourself take the work of art to mean but to do so relative to the interpretations of other readers—be they professional scholars, teachers, classmates, or even hypothetical readers (as in, "Although some readers might think that this poem is about _____, it is in fact about _____").

DISAGREE—AND EXPLAIN WHY

Disagreeing may seem like one of the simpler moves a writer can make, and it is often the first thing people associate with critical thinking. Disagreeing can also be the easiest way to generate an essay: find something you can disagree with in what has been said or might be said about your topic, summarize it, and argue with it. But disagreement in fact poses hidden challenges. You need to do more than simply assert that you disagree with a particular view; you also have to offer persuasive reasons *why* you disagree. After all, disagreeing means more than adding "not" to what someone else has said, more than just saying, "Although they say women's rights are improving,

I say women's rights are *not* improving." Such a response merely contradicts the view it responds to and fails to add anything interesting or new. To turn it into an argument, you need to give reasons to support what you say: because another's argument fails to take relevant factors into account; because it is based on faulty or incomplete evidence; because it rests on questionable assumptions; or because it uses flawed logic, is contradictory, or overlooks what you take to be the real issue. To move the conversation forward (and, indeed, to justify your very act of writing), you need to demonstrate that you have something to contribute.

You can even disagree by making what we call the "duh" move, in which you disagree not with the position itself but with the assumption that it is a new or stunning revelation. Here is an example of such a move, used to open an essay on the state of American schools.

> According to a recent report by some researchers at Stanford University, high school students with college aspirations "often lack crucial information on applying to college and on succeeding academically once they get there."
>
> Well, duh. . . . It shouldn't take a Stanford research team to tell us that when it comes to "succeeding academically," many students don't have a clue.
>
> Gerald Graff, "Trickle-Down Obfuscation"

Like all of the other moves discussed in this book, the "duh" move can be tailored to meet the needs of almost any writing situation. If you find the expression "duh" too brash to use with your intended audience, you can always dispense with the term itself and write something like "It is true that _____; but we already knew that."

TEMPLATES FOR DISAGREEING, WITH REASONS

▸ **X is mistaken because she overlooks <u>recent fossil discoveries in the South</u>.**

▸ **X's claim that _____ rests upon the questionable assumption that _____ .**

▸ **I disagree with X's view that _____ because, as recent research has shown, _____ .**

▸ **X contradicts herself/can't have it both ways. On the one hand, she argues _____ . On the other hand, she also says _____ .**

▸ **By focusing on _____ , X overlooks the deeper problem of _____ .**

You can also disagree by making what we call the "twist it" move, in which you agree with the evidence that someone else has presented but show through a twist of logic that this evidence actually supports your own, contrary position. For example:

> X argues for stricter gun control legislation, saying that the crime rate is on the rise and that we need to restrict the circulation of guns. I agree that the crime rate is on the rise, but that's precisely why I oppose stricter gun control legislation. We need to own guns to protect ourselves against criminals.

In this example of the "twist it" move, the writer agrees with X's claim that the crime rate is on the rise but then argues that this increasing crime rate is in fact a valid reason for _opposing_ gun control legislation.

At times you might be reluctant to express disagreement, for any number of reasons—not wanting to be unpleasant, to hurt someone's feelings, or to make yourself vulnerable to being disagreed with in return. One of these reasons may in fact explain why the conference speaker we described at the start of Chapter 1 avoided mentioning the disagreement he had with other scholars until he was provoked to do so in the discussion that followed his talk.

As much as we understand such fears of conflict and have experienced them ourselves, we nevertheless believe it is better to state our disagreements in frank yet considerate ways than to deny them. After all, suppressing disagreements doesn't make them go away; it only pushes them underground, where they can fester in private unchecked. Nevertheless, disagreements do not need to take the form of personal put-downs. Furthermore, there is usually no reason to take issue with *every* aspect of someone else's views. You can single out for criticism only those aspects of what someone else has said that are troubling, and then agree with the rest—although such an approach, as we will see later in this chapter, leads to the somewhat more complicated terrain of both agreeing and disagreeing at the same time.

AGREE—BUT WITH A DIFFERENCE

Like disagreeing, agreeing is less simple than it may appear. Just as you need to avoid simply contradicting views you disagree with, you also need to do more than simply echo views you agree with. Even as you're agreeing, it's important to bring something new and fresh to the table, adding something that makes you a valuable participant in the conversation.

There are many moves that enable you to contribute something of your own to a conversation even as you agree with what someone else has said. You may point out some unnoticed evidence or line of reasoning that supports X's claims that X herself hadn't mentioned. You may cite some corroborating personal experience, or a situation not mentioned by X that her views help readers understand. If X's views are particularly challenging or esoteric, what you bring to the table could be an accessible translation—an explanation for readers not already in the know. In other words, your text can usefully contribute to the conversation simply by pointing out unnoticed implications or explaining something that needs to be better understood.

Whatever mode of agreement you choose, the important thing is to open up some difference or contrast between your position and the one you're agreeing with rather than simply parroting what it says.

TEMPLATES FOR AGREEING

▸ I agree that <u>diversity in the student body is educationally valuable</u> because my experience <u>at Central University</u> confirms it.

▸ X is surely right about _____ because, as she may not be aware, recent studies have shown that _____.

▸ X's theory of _____ is extremely useful because it sheds light on the difficult problem of _____.

▸ Those unfamiliar with this school of thought may be interested to know that it basically boils down to _____.

Some writers avoid the practice of agreeing almost as much as others avoid disagreeing. In a culture like America's that prizes originality, independence, and competitive individualism, writers sometimes don't like to admit that anyone else has made the same point, seemingly beating them to the punch. In our view, however, as long as you can support a view taken by someone else without merely restating what he or she has said, there is no reason to worry about being "unoriginal." Indeed, there is good reason to rejoice when you agree with others since those others can lend credibility to your argument. While you don't want to present yourself as a mere copycat of someone else's views, you also need to avoid sounding like a lone voice in the wilderness.

But do be aware that whenever you agree with one person's view, you are likely disagreeing with someone else's. It is hard to align yourself with one position without at least implicitly positioning yourself against others. The psychologist Carol Gilligan does just that in an essay in which she agrees with scientists who argue that the human brain is "hard-wired" for cooperation, but in so doing aligns herself against anyone who believes that the brain is wired for selfishness and competition.

These findings join a growing convergence of evidence across the human sciences leading to a revolutionary shift in consciousness. . . . If cooperation, typically associated with altruism and self-sacrifice, sets off the same signals of delight as pleasures commonly associated with hedonism and self-indulgence; if the opposition between selfish and selfless, self vs. relationship biologically makes no sense, then a new paradigm is necessary to reframe the very terms of the conversation.

CAROL GILLIGAN, "Sisterhood Is Pleasurable:
A Quiet Revolution in Psychology"

In agreeing with some scientists that "the opposition between selfish and selfless . . . makes no sense," Gilligan implicitly disagrees with anyone who thinks the opposition *does* make sense. Basically, what Gilligan says could be boiled down to a template.

▶ I agree that _____, a point that needs emphasizing since so many people still believe _____.

▶ If group X is right that _____, as I think they are, then we need to reassess the popular assumption that _____.

What such templates allow you to do, then, is to agree with one view while challenging another—a move that leads into the domain of agreeing and disagreeing simultaneously.

AGREE AND DISAGREE SIMULTANEOUSLY

This last option is often our favorite way of responding. One thing we particularly like about agreeing and disagreeing simultaneously is that it helps us get beyond the kind of "is too" / "is not" exchanges that often characterize the disputes of young children and the more polarized shouting matches of talk radio and TV.

Sanford J. Ungar makes precisely this move in his essay "The New Liberal Arts" when, in critiquing seven common "misperceptions" of liberal arts education, he concedes that several contain a grain of truth. For example, after summarizing "Misperception No. 2," that "college graduates are finding it harder to get good jobs with liberal-arts degrees," that few employers want to hire those with an "irrelevant major like philosophy or French," Ungar writes: "Yes, recent graduates have had difficulty in the job market. . . ." But then, after making this concession, Ungar insists that this difficulty affects graduates in all fields, not just those from the liberal arts. In this way, we think, Ungar paradoxically strengthens his case. By admitting that the opposing argument has a point, Ungar bolsters his credibility, presenting himself as a writer willing to acknowledge facts as they present themselves rather than one determined only to cheerlead for his own side.

TEMPLATES FOR AGREEING AND DISAGREEING SIMULTANEOUSLY

"Yes and no." "Yes, but . . ." "Although I agree up to a point, I still insist . . ." These are just some of the ways you can make your argument complicated and nuanced while maintaining a clear, reader-friendly framework. The parallel structure—"yes and no"; "on the one hand I agree, on the other I disagree"— enables readers to place your argument on that map of positions we spoke of earlier in this chapter while still keeping your argument sufficiently complex.

Charles Murray's essay "Are Too Many People Going to College?" contains a good example of the "yes and no" move when, at the outset of his essay, Murray responds to what he sees as the prevailing wisdom about the liberal arts and college:

> We should not restrict the availability of a liberal education to a rarefied intellectual elite. More people should be going to college, not fewer.
>
> Yes and no. More people should be getting the basics of a liberal education. But for most students, the places to provide those basics are elementary and middle school.
>
> CHARLES MURRAY, "Are Too Many People Going to College?"

In other words, Murray is saying yes to more liberal arts, but not to more college.

Another aspect we like about this "yes and no," "agree and disagree" option is that it can be tipped subtly toward agreement or disagreement, depending on where you lay your stress. If you want to stress the disagreement end of the spectrum, you would use a template like the one below.

> ▶ **Although I agree with X up to a point, I cannot accept his overriding assumption that <u>religion is no longer a major force today</u>.**

Conversely, if you want to stress your agreement more than your disagreement, you would use a template like this one.

> ▶ **Although I disagree with much that X says, I fully endorse his final conclusion that _____.**

The first template above might be called a "yes, but . . ." move, the second a "no, but . . ." move. Other versions include the following.

> ▶ **Though I concede that _____, I still insist that _____.**

> ▶ **X is right that _____, but she seems on more dubious ground when she claims that _____.**

> ▶ **While X is probably wrong when she claims that _____, she is right that _____.**

> ▶ **Whereas X provides ample evidence that _____, Y and Z's research on _____ and _____ convinces me that _____ instead.**

Another classic way to agree and disagree at the same time is to make what we call an "I'm of two minds" or a "mixed feelings" move.

- I'm of two minds about X's claim that _____. On the one hand, I agree that _____. On the other hand, I'm not sure if _____.

- My feelings on the issue are mixed. I do support X's position that _____, but I find Y's argument about _____ and Z's research on _____ to be equally persuasive.

This move can be especially useful if you are responding to new or particularly challenging work and are as yet unsure where you stand. It also lends itself well to the kind of speculative investigation in which you weigh a position's pros and cons rather than come out decisively either for or against. But again, as we suggest earlier, whether you are agreeing, disagreeing, or both agreeing and disagreeing, you need to be as clear as possible, and making a frank statement that you are ambivalent is one way to be clear.

IS BEING UNDECIDED OKAY?

Nevertheless, writers often have as many concerns about expressing ambivalence as they do about expressing disagreement or agreement. Some worry that by expressing ambivalence they will come across as evasive, wishy-washy, or unsure of themselves. Others worry that their ambivalence will end up confusing readers who require decisive, clear-cut conclusions.

The truth is that in some cases these worries are legitimate. At times ambivalence can frustrate readers, leaving them with the feeling that you failed in your obligation to offer the guidance they expect from writers. At other times, however, acknowledging that a clear-cut resolution of an issue is impossible can demonstrate your sophistication as a writer. In an academic culture that values complex thought, forthrightly declaring that you have mixed feelings can be impressive, especially after having ruled out the one-dimensional positions on your issue taken by others in the conversation. Ultimately, then, how ambivalent you end up being comes down to a judgment call based on different readers' responses to your drafts, on your knowledge of your audience, and on the challenges of your particular argument and situation.

Exercises

1. Read one of the essays in the back of this book or on **theysayiblog.com**, identifying those places where the author agrees with others, disagrees, or both.

2. Write an essay responding in some way to the essay that you worked with in the preceding exercise. You'll want to summarize and/or quote some of the author's ideas and make clear whether you're agreeing, disagreeing, or both agreeing and disagreeing with what he or she says. Remember that there are templates in this book that can help you get started; see Chapters 1–3 for templates that will help you represent other people's ideas and Chapter 4 for templates that will get you started with your response.

FIVE

"AND YET"

Distinguishing What You *Say from What* They *Say*

—⊡—

IF GOOD ACADEMIC WRITING involves putting yourself into dialogue with others, it is extremely important that readers be able to tell at every point when you are expressing your own view and when you are stating someone else's. This chapter takes up the problem of moving from what *they* say to what *you* say without confusing readers about who is saying what.

DETERMINE WHO IS SAYING WHAT IN THE TEXTS YOU READ

Before examining how to signal who is saying what in your own writing, let's look at how to recognize such signals when they appear in the texts you read—an especially important skill when it comes to the challenging works assigned in school. Frequently, when students have trouble understanding difficult texts, it is not just because the texts contain unfamiliar ideas or words, but because the texts rely on subtle clues to let readers know when a particular view should be attributed to the writer or to someone else. Especially with texts that present a true dialogue of perspectives, readers need to be alert to the often subtle markers that indicate whose voice the writer is speaking in.

Consider how the social critic and educator Gregory Mantsios uses these "voice markers," as they might be called, to distinguish the different perspectives in his essay on America's class inequalities.

> "We are all middle-class," or so it would seem. Our national consciousness, as shaped in large part by the media and our political leadership, provides us with a picture of ourselves as a nation of prosperity and opportunity with an ever expanding middle-class life-style. As a result, our class differences are muted and our collective character is homogenized.
>
> Yet class divisions are real and arguably the most significant factor in determining both our very being in the world and the nature of the society we live in.
>
> GREGORY MANTSIOS, "Rewards and Opportunities: The Politics and Economics of Class in the U.S."

Although Mantsios makes it look easy, he is actually making several sophisticated rhetorical moves here that help him distinguish the common view he opposes from his own position.

In the opening sentence, for instance, the phrase "or so it would seem" shows that Mantsios does not necessarily agree with the view he is describing, since writers normally don't present views they themselves hold as ones that only "seem" to be true. Mantsios also places this opening view in quotation marks to signal that it is not his own. He then further distances himself from the belief being summarized in the opening paragraph by attributing it to "our national consciousness, as shaped in large part by the media and our political leadership," and then further attributing to this "consciousness" a negative, undesirable "result": one in which "our class differences" get "muted" and "our collective character" gets "homogenized," stripped of its diversity and distinctness. Hence, even before Mantsios has declared his own position in the second paragraph, readers can get a pretty solid sense of where he probably stands.

Furthermore, the second paragraph opens with the word "yet," indicating that Mantsios is now shifting to his own view (as opposed to the common view he has thus far been describing). Even the parallelism he sets up between the first and second paragraphs—between the first paragraph's claim that class differences do not exist and the second paragraph's claim that they do—helps throw into sharp relief the differences between the two voices. Finally, Mantsios's use of a direct, authoritative, declarative tone in the second paragraph also suggests a switch in voice. Although he does not use the words "I say" or "I argue," he clearly identifies the view he holds by presenting it not as one that merely *seems* to be true or that *others tell us* is true, but as a view that *is* true or, as Mantsios puts it, "real."

Paying attention to these voice markers is an important aspect of reading comprehension. Readers who fail to notice these markers often take an author's summaries of what someone else believes to be an expression of what the author himself or herself believes. Thus when we teach Mantsios's essay, some students invariably come away thinking that the statement "we are all middle-class" is Mantsios's own position rather than the perspective he is opposing, failing to see that in writing these words Mantsios acts as a kind of ventriloquist, mimicking what others say rather than directly expressing what he himself is thinking.

To see how important such voice markers are, consider what the Mantsios passage looks like if we remove them.

> We are all middle-class. . . . We are a nation of prosperity and opportunity with an ever expanding middle-class life-style. . . .
>
> Class divisions are real and arguably the most significant factor in determining both our very being in the world and the nature of the society we live in.

In contrast to the careful delineation between voices in Mant-sios's original text, this unmarked version leaves it hard to tell where his voice begins and the voices of others end. With the markers removed, readers cannot tell that "We are all middle-class" represents a view the author opposes, and that "Class divisions are real" represents what the author himself believes. Indeed, without the markers, especially the "yet," readers might well miss the fact that the second paragraph's claim that "Class divisions are real" contradicts the first paragraph's claim that "We are all middle-class."

TEMPLATES FOR SIGNALING WHO IS SAYING WHAT IN YOUR OWN WRITING

To avoid confusion in your own writing, make sure that at every point your readers can clearly tell who is saying what. To do so, you can use as voice-identifying devices many of the templates presented in previous chapters.

▶ Although X makes the best possible case for <u>universal, government-funded health care</u>, I <u>am not persuaded</u>.

▶ My view, however, contrary to what X has argued, is that _____ .

▶ Adding to X's argument, I would point out that _____ .

▶ According to both X and Y, _____ .

▶ Politicians, X argues, should _____ .

▶ Most athletes will tell you that _____ .

BUT I'VE BEEN TOLD NOT TO USE "I"

Notice that the first three templates above use the first-person "I" or "we," as do many of the templates in this book, thereby contradicting the common advice about avoiding the first person in academic writing. Although you may have been told that the "I" word encourages subjective, self-indulgent opinions rather than well-grounded arguments, we believe that texts using "I" can be just as well supported—or just as self-indulgent—as those that don't. For us, well-supported arguments are grounded in persuasive reasons and evidence, not in the use or nonuse of any particular pronouns.

Furthermore, if you consistently avoid the first person in your writing, you will probably have trouble making the key move addressed in this chapter: differentiating your views from those of others, or even offering your own views in the first place. But don't just take our word for it. See for yourself how freely the first person is used by the writers quoted in this book, and by the writers assigned in your courses.

Nevertheless, certain occasions may warrant avoiding the first person and writing, for example, that "she is correct" instead of "I think that she is correct." Since it can be monotonous to read an unvarying series of "I" statements ("I believe . . . I think . . . I argue"), it is a good idea to mix first-person assertions with ones like the following.

▸ **X is right that <u>certain common patterns can be found in the communities</u>.**

▸ **The evidence shows that _____ .**

▸ **X's assertion that _____ does not fit the facts.**

▸ **Anyone familiar with _____ should agree that _____ .**

One might even follow Mantsios's lead, as in the following template.

▸ **But _____ are real, and are arguably the most significant factor in _____ .**

On the whole, however, academic writing today, even in the sciences and social sciences, makes use of the first person fairly liberally.

ANOTHER TRICK FOR IDENTIFYING WHO IS SPEAKING

To alert readers about whose perspective you are describing at any given moment, you don't always have to use overt voice markers like "X argues" followed by a summary of the argument. Instead, you can alert readers about whose voice you're speaking in by *embedding* a reference to X's argument in your own sentences. Hence, instead of writing:

Liberals believe that cultural differences need to be respected. I have a problem with this view, however.

you might write:

I have a problem with *what liberals call cultural differences.*

There is a major problem with the liberal doctrine of *so-called cultural differences.*

You can also embed references to something you yourself have previously said. So instead of writing two cumbersome sentences like:

Earlier in this chapter we coined the term "voice markers." We would argue that such markers are extremely important for reading comprehension.

you might write:

We would argue that "voice markers," as we identified them earlier, are extremely important for reading comprehension.

Embedded references like these allow you to economize your train of thought and refer to other perspectives without any major interruption.

TEMPLATES FOR EMBEDDING VOICE MARKERS

▸ X overlooks what I consider an important point about <u>cultural differences</u>.

▸ My own view is that what X insists is a _____ is in fact a _____.

▸ I wholeheartedly endorse what X calls _____.

▸ These conclusions, which X discusses in _____, add weight to the argument that _____.

When writers fail to use voice-marking devices like the ones discussed in this chapter, their summaries of others' views tend to become confused with their own ideas—and vice versa. When readers cannot tell if you are summarizing your own views or endorsing a certain phrase or label, they have to stop and think: "Wait. I thought the author disagreed with this claim. Has she actually been asserting this view all along?" or "Hmmm, I thought she would have objected to this kind of phrase. Is she actually endorsing it?" Getting in the habit of using voice markers will keep you from confusing your readers and help alert you to similar markers in the challenging texts you read.

Exercises

1. To see how one writer signals when she is asserting her own views and when she is summarizing those of someone else, read the following passage by the social historian Julie Charlip. As you do so, identify those spots where Charlip refers to the views of others and the signal phrases she uses to distinguish her views from theirs.

Marx and Engels wrote: "Society as a whole is more and more splitting up into two great hostile camps, into two great classes directly facing each other—the bourgeoisie and the proletariat" (10). If only that were true, things might be more simple. But in late twentieth-century America, it seems that society is splitting more and more into a plethora of class factions—the working class, the working poor, lower-middle class, upper-middle class, lower uppers, and upper uppers. I find myself not knowing what class I'm from.

In my days as a newspaper reporter, I once asked a sociology professor what he thought about the reported shrinking of the middle class. Oh, it's not the middle class that's disappearing, he said, but the working class. His definition: if you earn thirty thousand dollars a year working in an assembly plant, come home from work, open a beer and watch the game, you are working class; if you earn twenty thousand dollars a year as a school teacher, come home from work to a glass of white wine and PBS, you are middle class.

How do we define class? Is it an issue of values, lifestyle, taste? Is it the kind of work you do, your relationship to the means of production? Is it a matter of how much money you earn? Are we allowed to choose? In this land of supposed classlessness, where we don't have the tradition of English society to keep us in our places, how do we know where we really belong? The average American will tell you he or she is "middle class." I'm sure that's what my father would tell you. But I always felt that we were in some no man's land, suspended between classes, sharing similarities with some and recognizing sharp, exclusionary differences from others. What class do I come from? What class am I in now? As an historian, I seek the answers to these questions in the specificity of my past.

> JULIE CHARLIP, "A Real Class Act: Searching
> for Identity in the 'Classless' Society"

2. Study a piece of your own writing to see how many perspectives you account for and how well you distinguish your own voice from those you are summarizing. Consider the following questions:

   a. How many perspectives do you engage?
   b. What other perspectives might you include?
   c. How do you distinguish your views from the other views you summarize?
   d. Do you use clear voice-signaling phrases?
   e. What options are available to you for clarifying who is saying what?
   f. Which of these options are best suited for this particular text?

   If you find that you do *not* include multiple views or clearly distinguish between others' views and your own, revise your text to do so.

SIX

"SKEPTICS MAY OBJECT"

Planting a Naysayer in Your Text

THE WRITER Jane Tompkins describes a pattern that repeats itself whenever she writes a book or an article. For the first couple of weeks when she sits down to write, things go relatively well. But then in the middle of the night, several weeks into the writing process, she'll wake up in a cold sweat, suddenly realizing that she has overlooked some major criticism that readers will surely make against her ideas. Her first thought, invariably, is that she will have to give up on the project, or that she will have to throw out what she's written thus far and start over. Then she realizes that "this moment of doubt and panic is where my text really begins." She then revises what she's written in a way that incorporates the criticisms she's anticipated, and her text becomes stronger and more interesting as a result.

This little story contains an important lesson for all writers, experienced and inexperienced alike. It suggests that even though most of us are upset at the idea of someone criticizing our work, such criticisms can actually work to our advantage. Although it's naturally tempting to ignore criticism of our ideas, doing so may in fact be a big mistake, since our writing improves when we not only listen to these objections but give them an explicit hearing in our writing. Indeed, no single device more quickly improves a piece of writing than planting a naysayer in the text—saying, for example, that "although some readers may object" to something in your argument, you "would reply that _____."

ANTICIPATE OBJECTIONS

But wait, you say. Isn't the advice to incorporate critical views a recipe for destroying your credibility and undermining your argument? Here you are, trying to say something that will hold up, and we want you to tell readers all the negative things someone might say against you?

Exactly. We *are* urging you to tell readers what others might say against you, but our point is that doing so will actually *enhance* your credibility, not undermine it. As we argue throughout this book, writing well does not mean piling up uncontroversial truths in a vacuum; it means engaging others in a dialogue or debate—not only by opening your text with a summary of what others *have* said, as we suggest in Chapter 1, but also by imagining what others *might* say against your argument as it unfolds. Once you see writing as an act of entering a conversation, you should also see how opposing arguments can work for you rather than against you.

Paradoxically, the more you give voice to your critics' objections, the more you tend to disarm those critics, especially if you go on to answer their objections in convincing ways. When you entertain a counterargument, you make a kind of preemptive strike, identifying problems with your argument before others can point them out for you. Furthermore, by entertaining counterarguments, you show respect for your readers, treating them not as gullible dupes who will believe anything you say but as independent, critical thinkers who are aware that your view is not the only one in town. In addition, by imagining what others might say against your claims, you come across as a generous, broad-minded person who is confident enough to open himself or herself to debate—like the writer in the figure on the following page.

Conversely, if you don't entertain counterarguments, you may very likely come across as closed-minded, as if you think your beliefs are beyond dispute. You might also leave important questions hanging and concerns about your arguments unaddressed. Finally, if you fail to plant a naysayer in your text, you may find that you have very little to say. Our own students often say that entertaining counterarguments makes it easier to generate enough text to meet their assignment's page-length requirements.

Planting a naysayer in your text is a relatively simple move, as you can see by looking at the following passage from a book by the writer Kim Chernin. Having spent some thirty pages complaining about the pressure on American women to be thin, Chernin inserts a whole chapter entitled "The Skeptic," opening it as follows.

> At this point I would like to raise certain objections that have been inspired by the skeptic in me. She feels that I have been ignoring some of the most common assumptions we all make about our bodies and these she wishes to see addressed. For example: "You know perfectly well," she says to me, "that you feel better when you lose weight. You buy new clothes. You look at yourself more eagerly in the mirror. When someone invites you to a party you don't stop and ask yourself whether you want to go. You feel sexier. Admit it. You like yourself better."
>
> KIM CHERNIN, *The Obsession:*
> *Reflections on the Tyranny of Slenderness*

"YOU WILL PROBABLY OBJECT THAT I HAVE MISREPRESENTED X'S WORK HERE, AND I CONCEDE THAT X NEVER SAYS _____ IN SO MANY WORDS. NEVERTHELESS. . . ."

The remainder of Chernin's chapter consists of her answers to this inner skeptic. In the face of the skeptic's challenge to her book's central premise (that the pressure to diet seriously harms women's lives), Chernin responds neither by repressing the skeptic's critical voice nor by giving in to it and relinquishing her own position. Instead, she embraces that voice and writes it into her text. Note too that instead of dispatching this naysaying voice quickly, as many of us would be tempted to do, Chernin stays with it and devotes a full paragraph to it. By borrowing some of Chernin's language, we can come up with templates for entertaining virtually any objection.

TEMPLATES FOR ENTERTAINING OBJECTIONS

▸ **At this point I would like to raise some objections that have been inspired by the skeptic in me. She feels that I have been ignoring <u>the complexities of the situation</u>.**

▸ **Yet some readers may challenge my view by insisting that _____ .**

▸ **Of course, many will probably disagree on the grounds that _____ .**

Note that the objections in the above templates are attributed not to any specific person or group, but to "skeptics," "readers," or "many." This kind of nameless, faceless naysayer is perfectly appropriate in many cases. But the ideas that motivate arguments and objections often can—and, where possible, should—be ascribed to a specific ideology or school of thought (for example, liberals, Christian fundamentalists, neopragmatists) rather than to anonymous anybodies. In other words, naysayers can be labeled, and you can add precision and impact to your writing by identifying what those labels are.

TEMPLATES FOR NAMING YOUR NAYSAYERS

▸ Here many *feminists* would probably object that <u>gender does influence language</u>.

▸ But *social Darwinists* would certainly take issue with the argument that _____ .

▸ *Biologists*, of course, may want to question whether _____ .

▸ Nevertheless, both *followers and critics of Malcolm X* will probably suggest otherwise and argue that _____ .

To be sure, some people dislike such labels and may even resent having labels applied to themselves. Some feel that labels put individuals in boxes, stereotyping them and glossing over what makes each of us unique. And it's true that labels can be used inappropriately, in ways that ignore individuality and promote stereotypes. But since the life of ideas, including many of our most private thoughts, is conducted through groups and types rather than solitary individuals, intellectual exchange requires labels to give definition and serve as a convenient shorthand. If you categorically reject all labels, you give up an important resource and even mislead readers by presenting yourself and others as having no connection to anyone else. You also miss an opportunity to generalize the importance and relevance of your work to some larger conversation. When you attribute a position you are summarizing to liberalism, say, or historical materialism, your argument is no longer just about your own solitary views but about the intersection of broad ideas and habits of mind that many readers may already have a stake in.

The way to minimize the problem of stereotyping, then, is not to categorically reject labels but to refine and qualify their use, as the following templates demonstrate.

▸ Although not all *Christians* think alike, some of them will probably dispute my claim that _____ .

▸ *Non-native English speakers* are so diverse in their views that it's hard to generalize about them, but some are likely to object on the grounds that _____ .

Another way to avoid needless stereotyping is to qualify labels carefully, substituting "pro bono lawyers" for "lawyers" in general, for example, or "quantitative sociologists" for all "social scientists," and so on.

TEMPLATES FOR INTRODUCING OBJECTIONS INFORMALLY

Objections can also be introduced in more informal ways. For instance, you can frame objections in the form of questions.

▸ But is my proposal realistic? What are the chances of its actually being adopted?

▸ Yet is it necessarily true that _____ ? Is it always the case, as I have been suggesting, that _____ ?

▸ However, does the evidence I've cited prove conclusively that _____ ?

You can also let your naysayer speak directly.

▶ "Impossible," some will say. "You must be reading the research selectively."

Moves like this allow you to cut directly to the skeptical voice itself, as the singer-songwriter Joe Jackson does in the following excerpt from a *New York Times* article complaining about the restrictions on public smoking in New York City bars and restaurants.

I like a couple of cigarettes or a cigar with a drink, and like many other people, I only smoke in bars or nightclubs. Now I can't go to any of my old haunts. Bartenders who were friends have turned into cops, forcing me outside to shiver in the cold and curse under my breath. . . . It's no fun. Smokers are being demonized and victimized all out of proportion.

"Get over it," say the anti-smokers. "You're the minority." I thought a great city was a place where all kinds of minorities could thrive. . . . "Smoking kills," they say. As an occasional smoker with otherwise healthy habits, I'll take my chances. Health consciousness is important, but so are pleasure and freedom of choice.

JOE JACKSON, "Want to Smoke? Go to Hamburg"

Jackson could have begun his second paragraph, in which he shifts from his own voice to that of his imagined naysayer, more formally, as follows: "Of course anti-smokers will object that since we smokers are in the minority, we should simply stop complaining and quietly make the sacrifices we are being called on to make for the larger social good." Or "Anti-smokers might insist, however, that the smoking minority should submit to the nonsmoking majority." We think, though, that Jackson gets the job done in a far more lively way with the more colloquial form he chooses. Borrowing a standard move of playwrights and novelists, Jackson cuts directly to the objectors' view and then to his own retort, then back to the objectors' view and then to his own retort again, thereby creating a kind of dialogue or miniature play within his own text. This move works well for Jackson, but only because he uses quotation marks and other voice markers to make clear at every point whose voice he is in.

See Chapter 5 for more advice on using voice markers.

REPRESENT OBJECTIONS FAIRLY

Once you've decided to introduce a differing or opposing view into your writing, your work has only just begun, since you still need to represent and explain that view with fairness and generosity. Although it is tempting to give opposing views short shrift, to hurry past them, or even to mock them, doing so is usually counterproductive. When writers make the best case they can for their critics (playing Peter Elbow's "believing game"), they actually bolster their credibility with readers rather than undermine it. They make readers think, "This is a writer I can trust."

See pp. 31–32 for more on the believing game.

We recommend, then, that whenever you entertain objections in your writing, you stay with them for several sentences or even paragraphs and take them as seriously as possible. We also recommend that you read your summary of opposing views with an outsider's eye: put yourself in the shoes of someone who disagrees with you and ask if such a reader would recognize himself in your summary. Would that reader think you have taken his views seriously, as beliefs that reasonable people might hold? Or would he detect a mocking tone or an oversimplification of his views?

There will always be certain objections, to be sure, that you believe do not deserve to be represented, just as there will be objections that seem so unworthy of respect that they inspire ridicule. Remember, however, that if you do choose to mock a view that you oppose, you are likely to alienate those readers who don't already agree with you—likely the very readers you want to reach. Also be aware that in mocking another's view you may contribute to a hostile argument culture in which someone may ridicule you in return.

ANSWER OBJECTIONS

Do be aware that when you represent objections successfully, you still need to be able to answer those objections persuasively. After all, when you write objections into a text, you take the risk that readers will find those objections more convincing than the argument you yourself are advancing. In the editorial quoted above, for example, Joe Jackson takes the risk that readers will identify more with the anti-smoking view he summarizes than with the pro-smoking position he endorses.

This is precisely what Benjamin Franklin describes happening to himself in *The Autobiography of Benjamin Franklin* (1793), when he recalls being converted to Deism (a religion that exalts reason over spirituality) by reading *anti*-Deist books. When he encountered the views of Deists being negatively summarized by authors who opposed them, Franklin explains, he ended up finding the Deist position more persuasive. To avoid having this kind of unintentional reverse effect on readers, you need to do your best to make sure that any counter-arguments you address are not more convincing than your own claims. It is good to address objections in your writing, but only if you are able to overcome them.

One surefire way to *fail* to overcome an objection is to dismiss it out of hand—saying, for example, "That's just wrong." The difference between such a response (which offers no supporting reasons whatsoever) and the types of nuanced responses we're promoting in this book is the difference between bullying your readers and genuinely persuading them.

Often the best way to overcome an objection is not to try to refute it completely but to agree with part of it while challenging only the part you dispute. In other words, in answering counterarguments, it is often best to say "yes, but" or "yes and no," treating the counterview as an opportunity to See pp. 59–62 for more on agreeing, with a difference. revise and refine your own position. Rather than build your argument into an impenetrable fortress, it is often best to make concessions while still standing your ground, as Kim Chernin does in the following response to the counter-argument quoted above. While in the voice of the "skeptic," Chernin writes: "Admit it. You like yourself better when you've lost weight." In response, Chernin replies as follows.

Can I deny these things? No woman who has managed to lose weight would wish to argue with this. Most people feel better about themselves when they become slender. And yet, upon reflection, it seems to me that there is something precarious about this well-being. After all, 98 percent of people who lose weight gain it back. Indeed, 90 percent of those who have dieted "successfully" gain back more than they ever lost. Then, of course, we can no longer bear to look at ourselves in the mirror.

In this way, Chernin shows how you can use a counterview to improve and refine your overall argument by making a concession. Even as she concedes that losing weight feels good in the short run, she argues that in the long run the weight always returns, making the dieter far more miserable.

TEMPLATES FOR MAKING CONCESSIONS
WHILE STILL STANDING YOUR GROUND

▸ Although I grant that <u>the book is poorly organized</u>, I still maintain that <u>it raises an important issue</u>.

▸ Proponents of X are right to argue that _____. But they exaggerate when they claim that _____.

▸ While it is true that _____, it does not necessarily follow that _____.

▸ On the one hand, I agree with X that _____. But on the other hand, I still insist that _____.

Templates like these show that answering naysayers' objections does not have to be an all-or-nothing affair in which you either definitively refute your critics or they definitively refute you. Often the most productive engagements among differing views end with a combined vision that incorporates elements of each one.

But what if you've tried out all the possible answers you can think of to an objection you've anticipated and you *still* have a nagging feeling that the objection is more convincing than your argument itself? In that case, the best remedy is to go back and make some fundamental revisions to your argument, even reversing your position completely if need be. Although finding out late in the game that you aren't fully convinced by your own argument can be painful, it can actually make your final text more intellectually honest, challenging, and serious. After all, the goal of writing is not to keep proving that whatever you initially said is right, but to stretch the limits of your thinking. So if planting a strong naysayer in your text forces you to change your mind, that's not a bad thing. Some would argue that that is what the academic world is all about.

Exercises

1. Read the following passage by the cultural critic Eric Schlosser. As you'll see, he hasn't planted any naysayers in this text. Do it for him. Insert a brief paragraph stating an objection to his argument and then responding to the objection as he might.

   The United States must declare an end to the war on drugs. This war has filled the nation's prisons with poor drug addicts and small-time drug dealers. It has created a multibillion-dollar black market, enriched organized crime groups and promoted the corruption of government officials throughout the world. And it has not stemmed the widespread use of illegal drugs. By any rational measure, this war has been a total failure.

   We must develop public policies on substance abuse that are guided not by moral righteousness or political expediency but by common sense. The United States should immediately decriminalize the cultivation and possession of small amounts of marijuana for personal use. Marijuana should no longer be classified as a Schedule I narcotic, and those who seek to use marijuana as medicine should no longer face criminal sanctions. We must shift our entire approach to drug abuse from the criminal justice system to the public health system. Congress should appoint an independent commission to study the harm-reduction policies that have been adopted in Switzerland, Spain, Portugal, and the Netherlands. The commission should recommend policies for the United States based on one important criterion: what works.

In a nation where pharmaceutical companies advertise powerful antidepressants on billboards and where alcohol companies run amusing beer ads during the Super Bowl, the idea of a "drug-free society" is absurd. Like the rest of American society, our drug policy would greatly benefit from less punishment and more compassion.

ERIC SCHLOSSER, "A People's Democratic Platform"

2. Look over something you've written that makes an argument. Check to see if you've anticipated and responded to any objections. If not, revise your text to do so. If so, have you anticipated all the likely objections? Who if anyone have you attributed the objections to? Have you represented the objections fairly? Have you answered them well enough, or do you think you now need to qualify your own argument? Could you use any of the language suggested in this chapter? Does the introduction of a naysayer strengthen your argument? Why, or why not?

SEVEN

"SO WHAT? WHO CARES?"

Saying Why It Matters

———

BASEBALL IS THE NATIONAL PASTIME. Bernini was the best sculptor of the baroque period. All writing is conversational. So what? Who cares? Why does any of this matter?

How many times have you had reason to ask these questions? Regardless of how interesting a topic may be to you as a writer, readers always need to know what is at stake in a text and why they should care. All too often, however, these questions are left unanswered—mainly because writers and speakers assume that audiences will know the answers already or will figure them out on their own. As a result, students come away from lectures feeling like outsiders to what they've just heard, just as many of us feel left hanging after talks we've attended. The problem is not necessarily that the speakers lack a clear, well-focused thesis or that the thesis is inadequately supported with evidence. Instead, the problem is that the speakers don't address the crucial question of why their arguments matter.

That this question is so often left unaddressed is unfortunate since the speakers generally *could* offer interesting, engaging answers. When pressed, for instance, most academics will tell you that their lectures and articles matter because they address some belief that needs to be corrected or updated—and because their arguments have important, real-world consequences. Yet many academics fail to identify these reasons and consequences explicitly in what they say and write. Rather than assume that audiences will know why their claims matter, all writers need to answer the "so what?" and "who cares?" questions up front. Not everyone can claim to have a cure for cancer or a solution to end poverty. But writers who fail to show that others *should* care or already *do* care about their claims will ultimately lose their audiences' interest.

This chapter focuses on various moves that you can make to answer the "who cares?" and "so what?" questions in your own writing. In one sense, the two questions get at the same thing: the relevance or importance of what you are saying. Yet they get at this significance in different ways. Whereas "who cares?" literally asks you to identify a person or group who cares about your claims, "so what?" asks about the real-world applications and consequences of those claims—what difference it would make if they were accepted. We'll look first at ways of making clear who cares.

"WHO CARES?"

To see how one writer answers the "who cares?" question, consider the following passage from the science writer Denise Grady. Writing in the *New York Times*, she explains some of the latest research into fat cells.

> Scientists used to think body fat and the cells it was made of were pretty much inert, just an oily storage compartment. But within the past decade research has shown that fat cells act like chemical factories and that body fat is potent stuff: a highly active

tissue that secretes hormones and other substances with profound and sometimes harmful effects. . . .

    In recent years, biologists have begun calling fat an "endocrine organ," comparing it to glands like the thyroid and pituitary, which also release hormones straight into the bloodstream.

            DENISE GRADY, "The Secret Life of a Potent Cell"

Notice how Grady's writing reflects the central advice we give in this book, offering a clear claim and also framing that claim as a response to what someone else has said. In so doing, Grady immediately identifies at least one group with a stake in the new research that sees fat as "active," "potent stuff": namely, the scientific community, which formerly believed that body fat is inert. By referring to these scientists, Grady implicitly acknowledges that her text is part of a larger conversation and shows who besides herself has an interest in what she says.

Consider, however, how the passage would read had Grady left out what "scientists used to think" and simply explained the new findings in isolation.

Within the past few decades research has shown that fat cells act like chemical factories and that body fat is potent stuff: a highly active tissue that secretes hormones and other substances. In recent years, biologists have begun calling fat an "endocrine organ," comparing it to glands like the thyroid and pituitary, which also release hormones straight into the bloodstream.

Though this statement is clear and easy to follow, it lacks any indication that anyone needs to hear it. Okay, one nods while reading this passage, fat is an active, potent thing. Sounds plausible enough; no reason to think it's not true. But does anyone really care? Who, if anyone, is interested?

TEMPLATES FOR INDICATING WHO CARES

To address "who cares?" questions in your own writing, we suggest using templates like the following, which echo Grady in refuting earlier thinking.

▸ <u>Parents</u> used to think <u>spanking was necessary</u>. But recently [or within the past few decades] <u>experts</u> suggest that <u>it can be counterproductive</u>.

▸ This interpretation challenges the work of those critics who have long assumed that _____ .

▸ These findings challenge the work of earlier researchers, who tended to assume that _____ .

▸ Recent studies like these shed new light on _____ , which previous studies had not addressed.

Grady might have been more explicit by writing the "who cares?" question directly into her text, as in the following template.

▸ But who really cares? Who besides me and a handful of recent researchers has a stake in these claims? At the very least, the researchers who formerly believed _____ should care.

To gain greater authority as a writer, it can help to name specific people or groups who have a stake in your claims and to go into some detail about their views.

▸ Researchers have long assumed that _____ . For instance, one eminent scholar of cell biology, _____ , assumed in _____ , her seminal work on cell structures and functions, that fat cells _____ . As _____ herself put it, "_____" (2012). Another leading scientist, _____ , argued that fat cells "_____" (2011). Ultimately, when it came to the nature of fat, the basic assumption was that _____.

But a new body of research shows that fat cells are far more complex and that _____.

In other cases, you might refer to certain people or groups who *should* care about your claims.

▶ If sports enthusiasts stopped to think about it, many of them might simply assume that the most successful athletes _____. However, new research shows _____.

▶ These findings challenge neoliberals' common assumption that _____.

▶ At first glance, teenagers might say _____. But on closer inspection _____.

As these templates suggest, answering the "who cares?" question involves establishing the type of contrast between what others say and what you say that is central to this book. Ultimately, such templates help you create a dramatic tension or clash of views in your writing that readers will feel invested in and want to see resolved.

"SO WHAT?"

Although answering the "who cares?" question is crucial, in many cases it is not enough, especially if you are writing for general readers who don't necessarily have a strong investment in the particular clash of views you are setting up. In the case of Grady's argument about fat cells, such readers may still wonder why it matters that some researchers think fat cells are active, while others think they're inert. Or, to move to a different field of study, American literature, *so what* if some scholars disagree about Huck Finn's relationship with the runaway slave Jim in Mark Twain's *Adventures of Huckleberry Finn*? Why should anyone besides a few specialists in the field care about such disputes? What, if anything, hinges on them?

The best way to answer such questions about the larger consequences of your claims is to appeal to something that your audience already figures to care about. Whereas the "who cares?" question asks you to identify an interested person or group, the "so what?" question asks you to link your argument to some larger matter that readers already deem important. Thus in analyzing *Huckleberry Finn*, a writer could argue that seemingly narrow disputes about the hero's relationship with Jim actually shed light on whether Twain's canonical, widely read novel is a critique of racism in America or is itself marred by it.

Let's see how Grady invokes such broad, general concerns in her article on fat cells. Her first move is to link researchers' interest in fat cells to a general concern with obesity and health.

> Researchers trying to decipher the biology of fat cells hope to find new ways to help people get rid of excess fat or, at least, prevent obesity from destroying their health. In an increasingly obese world, their efforts have taken on added importance.

Further showing why readers should care, Grady's next move is to demonstrate the even broader relevance and urgency of her subject matter.

> Internationally, more than a billion people are overweight. Obesity and two illnesses linked to it, heart disease and high blood pressure, are on the World Health Organization's list of the top 10 global health risks. In the United States, 65 percent of adults weigh too much,

compared with about 56 percent a decade ago, and government researchers blame obesity for at least 300,000 deaths a year.

What Grady implicitly says here is "Look, dear reader, you may think that these questions about the nature of fat cells I've been pursuing have little to do with everyday life. In fact, however, these questions are extremely important—particularly in our 'increasingly obese world' in which we need to prevent obesity from destroying our health."

Notice that Grady's phrase "in an increasingly _____ world" can be adapted as a strategic move to address the "so what?" question in other fields as well. For example, a sociologist analyzing back-to-nature movements of the past thirty years might make the following statement.

> In a world increasingly dominated by cell phones and sophisticated computer technologies, these attempts to return to nature appear futile.

This type of move can be readily applied to other disciplines because no matter how much disciplines may differ from one another, the need to justify the importance of one's concerns is common to them all.

TEMPLATES FOR ESTABLISHING WHY YOUR CLAIMS MATTER

▸ *Huckleberry Finn* matters/is important because <u>it is one of the most widely taught novels in the American school system.</u>

▸ Although X may seem trivial, it is in fact crucial in terms of today's concern over _____ .

▸ Ultimately, what is at stake here is _____ .

▸ These findings have important implications for the broader domain of _____ .

▸ If we are right about _____ , then major consequences follow for _____ .

▸ These conclusions/This discovery will have significant applications in _____ as well as in _____ .

Finally, you can also treat the "so what?" question as a related aspect of the "who cares?" question.

▸ Although X may seem of concern to only a small group of _____ , it should in fact concern anyone who cares about _____ .

All these templates help you hook your readers. By suggesting the real-world applications of your claims, the templates not only demonstrate that others care about your claims but also tell your readers why *they* should care. Again, it bears repeating that simply stating and proving your thesis isn't enough. You also need to frame it in a way that helps readers care about it.

WHAT ABOUT READERS WHO ALREADY KNOW WHY IT MATTERS?

At this point, you might wonder if you need to answer the "who cares?" and "so what?" questions in *everything* you write. Is it really necessary to address these questions if you're proposing something so obviously consequential as, say, a treatment for autism or a program to eliminate illiteracy? Isn't it obvious that everyone cares about such problems? Does it really need to be spelled out? And what about when you're writing for audiences who you know are already interested in your claims and who understand perfectly well why they're important? In other words, do you always need to address the "so what?" and "who cares?" questions?

As a rule, yes—although it's true that you can't keep answering them forever and at a certain point must say enough is enough. Although a determined skeptic can infinitely ask why something matters—"Why should I care about earning a salary? And why should I care about supporting a family?"—you have to stop answering at some point in your text. Nevertheless, we urge you to go as far as possible in answering such questions. If you take it for granted that readers will somehow intuit the answers to "so what?" and "who cares?" on their own, you may make your work seem less interesting than it actually is, and you run the risk that readers will dismiss your text as irrelevant and unimportant. By contrast, when you are careful to explain who cares and why, it's a little like bringing a cheerleading squad into your text. And though some expert readers might already know why your claims matter, even they need to be reminded. Thus the safest move is to be as explicit as possible in answering the "so what?" question, even for those already in the know. When you step back from the text and explain why it matters, you are urging your audience to keep reading, pay attention, and care.

Exercises

1. Find several texts (scholarly essays, newspaper articles, emails, memos, blogs, etc.) and see whether they answer

the "so what?" and "who cares?" questions. Probably some do, some don't. What difference does it make whether they do or do not? How do the authors who answer these questions do so? Do they use any strategies or techniques that you could borrow for your own writing? Are there any strategies or techniques recommended in this chapter, or that you've found or developed on your own, that you'd recommend to these authors?

2. Look over something you've written yourself. Do you indicate "so what?" and "who cares?" If not, revise your text to do so. You might use the following template to get started.

My point here (that _____) should interest those who _____. Beyond this limited audience, however, my point should speak to anyone who cares about the larger issue of _____.

EIGHT

"AS A RESULT"

Connecting the Parts

———◻︎———

WE ONCE HAD A STUDENT named Bill, whose characteristic sentence pattern went something like this.

Spot is a good dog. He has fleas.

"Connect your sentences," we urged in the margins of Bill's papers. "What does Spot being good have to do with his fleas?" "These two statements seem unrelated. Can you connect them in some logical way?" When comments like these yielded no results, we tried inking in suggested connections for him.

Spot is a good dog, *but* he has fleas.
Spot is a good dog, *even though* he has fleas.

But our message failed to get across, and Bill's disconnected sentence pattern persisted to the end of the semester.

And yet Bill did focus well on his subjects. When he mentioned Spot the dog (or Plato, or any other topic) in one sentence, we could count on Spot (or Plato) being the topic of the following sentence as well. This was not the case with some of Bill's classmates, who sometimes changed topic from sentence to sentence or even from clause to clause within a single sentence. But because Bill neglected to mark his connections, his writing was as frustrating to read as theirs. In all these cases, we had to struggle to figure out on our own how the sentences and paragraphs connected or failed to connect with one another.

What makes such writers so hard to read, in other words, is that they never gesture back to what they have just said or forward to what they plan to say. "Never look back" might be their motto, almost as if they see writing as a process of thinking of something to say about a topic and writing it down, then thinking of something else to say about the topic and writing that down, too, and on and on until they've filled the assigned number of pages and can hand the paper in. Each sentence basically starts a new thought, rather than growing out of or extending the thought of the previous sentence.

When Bill talked about his writing habits, he acknowledged that he never went back and read what he had written. Indeed, he told us that, other than using his computer software to check for spelling errors and make sure that his tenses were all aligned, he never actually reread what he wrote before turning it in. As Bill seemed to picture it, writing was something one did while sitting at a computer, whereas reading was a separate activity generally reserved for an easy chair, book in hand. It had never occurred to Bill that to write a good sentence he had to think about how it connected to those that came before and after; that he had to think hard about how that sentence fit into the sentences that surrounded it. Each sentence for Bill existed in a sort of tunnel isolated from every other sentence on the page. He never bothered to fit all the parts of his essay together because he apparently thought of writing as a matter of piling up information or observations rather than building a sustained argument. What we suggest in this chapter, then, is that you converse not only with others in your writing but with yourself: that you establish clear relations between one statement and the next by connecting those statements.

This chapter addresses the issue of how to connect all the parts of your writing. The best compositions establish a sense of momentum and direction by making explicit connections among their different parts, so that what is said in one sentence (or paragraph) both sets up what is to come and is clearly informed by what has already been said. When you write a sentence, you create an expectation in the reader's mind that the next sentence will in some way echo and extend it, even if—*especially if*—that next sentence takes your argument in a new direction.

It may help to think of each sentence you write as having arms that reach backward and forward, as the figure below suggests. When your sentences reach outward like this, they establish connections that help your writing flow smoothly in a way readers appreciate. Conversely, when writing lacks such connections and moves in fits and starts, readers repeatedly have to go back over the sentences and guess at the connections on their own. To prevent such disconnection and make your writing flow, we advise following a "do-it-yourself" principle, which means that it is your job as a writer to do the hard work of making the connections rather than, as Bill did, leaving this work to your readers.

This chapter offers several strategies you can use to put this principle into action: (1) using transition terms (like "therefore" and "as a result"); (2) adding pointing words (like "this" or "such"); (3) developing a set of key terms and phrases for each text you write; and (4) repeating yourself, but with a difference—a move that involves repeating what you've said, but with enough variation to avoid being redundant. All these moves require that you always look back and, in crafting any one sentence, think hard about those that precede it.

Notice how we ourselves have used such connecting devices thus far in this chapter. The second paragraph of this chapter, for example, opens with the transitional "And yet," signaling a change in direction, while the opening sentence of the third includes the phrase "in other words," telling you to expect a restatement of a point we've just made. If you look through this book, you should be able to find many sentences that contain some word or phrase that explicitly hooks them back to something said earlier, to something about to be said, or both. And many sentences in *this* chapter repeat key terms related to the idea of connection: "connect," "disconnect," "link," "relate," "forward," and "backward."

USE TRANSITIONS

For readers to follow your train of thought, you need not only to connect your sentences and paragraphs to each other, but also to mark the kind of connection you are making. One of the easiest ways to make this move is to use *transitions* (from the Latin root *trans*, "across"), which help you cross from one point to another in your text. Transitions are usually placed at or near the start of sentences so they can signal to readers where your text is going: in the same direction it has been moving, or in a new direction. More specifically, transitions tell readers whether your text is echoing a previous sentence or paragraph ("in other words"), adding something to it ("in addition"), offering an example of it ("for example"), generalizing from it ("as a result"), or modifying it ("and yet").

The following is a list of commonly used transitions, categorized according to their different functions.

ADDITION

also	in fact
and	indeed
besides	moreover
furthermore	so too
in addition	

ELABORATION

actually	to put it another way
by extension	to put it bluntly
in other words	to put it succinctly
in short	ultimately
that is	

EXAMPLE

after all	for instance
as an illustration	specifically
consider	to take a case in point
for example	

CAUSE AND EFFECT

accordingly	so
as a result	then
consequently	therefore
hence	thus
since	

COMPARISON

along the same lines	likewise
in the same way	similarly

CONTRAST

although	nevertheless
but	nonetheless
by contrast	on the contrary
conversely	on the other hand
despite	regardless
even though	whereas
however	while yet
in contrast	

CONCESSION

admittedly	naturally
although it is true	of course
granted	to be sure

CONCLUSION

as a result	in sum
consequently	therefore
hence	thus
in conclusion	to sum up
in short	to summarize

Ideally, transitions should operate so unobtrusively in a piece of writing that they recede into the background and readers do not even notice that they are there. It's a bit like what happens when drivers use their turn signals before turning right or left: just as other drivers recognize such signals almost unconsciously, readers should process transition terms with a minimum of thought. But even though such terms should function unobtrusively in your writing, they can be among the most powerful tools in your vocabulary. Think how your heart sinks when someone, immediately after praising you, begins a sentence with "but" or "however." No matter what follows, you know it won't be good.

Notice that some transitions can help you not only to move from one sentence to another, but to combine two or more sentences into one. Combining sentences in this way helps prevent the choppy, staccato effect that arises when too many short sentences are strung together, one after the other. For instance, to combine Bill's two choppy sentences ("Spot is a good dog. He has fleas.") into one, better-flowing sentence, we suggested that he rewrite them as "Spot is a good dog, *even though* he has fleas."

Transitions like these not only guide readers through the twists and turns of your argument but also help ensure that you *have* an argument in the first place. In fact, we think of words like "but," "yet," "nevertheless," "besides," and others as argument words, since it's hard to use them without making some kind of argument. The word "therefore," for instance, commits you to making sure that the claims preceding it lead logically to the conclusion that it introduces. "For example" also assumes an argument, since it requires the material you are introducing to stand as an instance or proof of some preceding generalization. As a result, the more you use transitions, the more you'll be able not only to connect the parts of your text but also to construct a strong argument in the first place. And if you draw on them frequently enough, using them should eventually become second nature.

To be sure, it is possible to overuse transitions, so take time to read over your drafts carefully and eliminate any transitions that are unnecessary. But following the maxim that you need to learn the basic moves of argument before you can deliberately depart from them, we advise you not to forgo explicit transition terms until you've first mastered their use. In all our years of teaching, we've read countless essays that suffered from having few or no transitions, but cannot recall one in which the transitions were overused. Seasoned writers sometimes omit explicit transitions, but only because they rely heavily on the other types of connecting devices that we turn to in the rest of this chapter.

Before doing so, however, let us warn you about inserting transitions without really thinking through their meanings—using "therefore," say, when your text's logic actually requires "nevertheless" or "however." So beware. Choosing transition terms should involve a bit of mental sweat, since the whole point of using them is to make your writing *more* reader-friendly, not less. The only thing more frustrating than reading Bill-style passages like "Spot is a good dog. He has fleas" is reading misconnected sentences like "Spot is a good dog. For example, he has fleas."

USE POINTING WORDS

Another way to connect the parts of your argument is by using pointing words—which, as their name implies, point or refer backward to some concept in the previous sentence. The most common of these pointing words include "this," "these," "that," "those," "their," and "such" (as in "these pointing words" near the start of this sentence) and simple pronouns like "his," "he," "her," "she," "it," and "their." Such terms help you create the flow we spoke of earlier that enables readers to move effortlessly through your text. In a sense, these terms are like an invisible hand reaching out of your sentence, grabbing what's needed in the previous sentences and pulling it along.

Like transitions, however, pointing words need to be used carefully. It's dangerously easy to insert pointing words into your text that don't refer to a clearly defined object, assuming that because the object you have in mind is clear to you it will also be clear to your readers. For example, consider the use of "this" in the following passage.

> Alexis de Tocqueville was highly critical of democratic societies, which he saw as tending toward mob rule. At the same time, he accorded democratic societies grudging respect. *This* is seen in Tocqueville's statement that . . .

When "this" is used in such a way it becomes an ambiguous or free-floating pointer, since readers can't tell if it refers to Tocqueville's critical attitude toward democratic societies, his grudging respect for them, or some combination of both. "This what?" readers mutter as they go back over such passages and try to figure them out. It's also tempting to try to cheat with pointing words, hoping that they will conceal or make up for conceptual confusions that may lurk in your argument. By referring to a fuzzy idea as "this" or "that," you might hope the fuzziness will somehow come across as clearer than it is.

You can fix problems caused by a free-floating pointer by making sure there is one and only one possible object in the vicinity that the pointer could be referring to. It also often helps to name the object the pointer is referring to at the same time that you point to it, replacing the bald "this" in the example above with a more precise phrase like "this ambivalence toward democratic societies" or "this grudging respect."

REPEAT KEY TERMS AND PHRASES

A third strategy for connecting the parts of your argument is to develop a constellation of key terms and phrases, including their synonyms and antonyms, that you repeat throughout your text. When used effectively, your key terms should be items that readers could extract from your text in order to get a solid sense of your topic. Playing with key terms also can be a good way to come up with a title and appropriate section headings for your text.

Notice how often Martin Luther King Jr. uses the key words "criticism," "statement," "answer," and "correspondence" in the opening paragraph of his famous "Letter from Birmingham Jail."

> Dear Fellow Clergymen:
>
> While confined here in the Birmingham city jail, I came across your recent *statement* calling my present activities "unwise and untimely." Seldom do I pause to *answer criticism* of my work and ideas. If I sought to *answer* all the *criticisms* that cross my desk, my secretaries would have little time for anything other than *such correspondence* in the course of the day, and I would have no time for constructive work. But since I feel that you are men of genuine good will and that your *criticisms* are sincerely set forth, I want to try to *answer* your *statement* in what I hope will be patient and reasonable terms.
>
> MARTIN LUTHER KING JR., "Letter from Birmingham Jail"

Even though King uses the terms "criticism" and "answer" three times each and "statement" twice, the effect is not overly repetitive. In fact, these key terms help build a sense of momentum in the paragraph and bind it together.

For another example of the effective use of key terms, consider the following passage, in which the historian Susan Douglas develops a constellation of sharply contrasting key terms around the concept of "cultural schizophrenics": women like herself who, Douglas claims, have mixed feelings about the images of ideal femininity with which they are constantly bombarded by the media.

> In a variety of ways, the mass media helped make us the cultural schizophrenics we are today, women who rebel against yet submit to prevailing images about what a desirable, worthwhile woman should be. . . . [T]he mass media has engendered in many women a kind of cultural identity crisis. We are ambivalent toward femininity on the one hand and feminism on the other. Pulled in opposite directions—told we were equal, yet told we were subordinate; told we could change history but told we were trapped by history—we got the bends at an early age, and we've never gotten rid of them.
>
> When I open *Vogue*, for example, I am simultaneously infuriated and seduced. . . . I adore the materialism; I despise the materialism. . . . I want to look beautiful; I think wanting to look beautiful is about the most dumb-ass goal you could have. The magazine stokes my desire; the magazine triggers my bile. And this doesn't only happen when I'm reading *Vogue*; it happens all the time. . . . On the one hand, on the other hand—that's not just me—that's what it means to be a woman in America.
>
> To explain this schizophrenia . . .
>
> Susan Douglas, *Where the Girls Are:*
Growing Up Female with the Mass Media

In this passage, Douglas establishes "schizophrenia" as a key concept and then echoes it through synonyms like "identity crisis," "ambivalent," "the bends"—and even demonstrates it through a series of contrasting words and phrases:

rebel against / submit
told we were equal / told we were subordinate
told we could change history / told we were trapped by history
infuriated / seduced
I adore / I despise
I want / I think wanting . . . is about the most dumb-ass goal
stokes my desire / triggers my bile
on the one hand / on the other hand

These contrasting phrases help flesh out Douglas's claim that women are being pulled in two directions at once. In so doing, they bind the passage together into a unified whole that, despite its complexity and sophistication, stays focused over its entire length.

REPEAT YOURSELF—BUT WITH A DIFFERENCE

The last technique we offer for connecting the parts of your text involves repeating yourself, but with a difference—which basically means saying the same thing you've just said, but in a slightly different way that avoids sounding monotonous. To effectively connect the parts of your argument and keep it moving forward, be careful not to leap from one idea to a different idea or introduce new ideas cold. Instead, try to build bridges between your ideas by echoing what you've just said while simultaneously moving your text into new territory.

Several of the connecting devices discussed in this chapter are ways of repeating yourself in this special way. Key terms, pointing terms, and even many transitions can be used in a way that not only brings something forward from the previous sentence but in some way alters it. When Douglas, for instance, uses the key term "ambivalent" to echo her earlier reference to schizophrenics, she is repeating herself with a difference— repeating the same concept, but with a different word that adds new associations.

In addition, when you use transition phrases like "in other words" and "to put it another way," you repeat yourself with a difference, since these phrases help you restate earlier claims but in a different register. When you open a sentence with "in other words," you are basically telling your readers that in case they didn't fully understand what you meant in the last sentence, you are now coming at it again from a slightly different angle, or that since you're presenting a very important idea, you're not going to skip over it quickly but will explore it further to make sure your readers grasp all its aspects.

We would even go so far as to suggest that after your first sentence, almost every sentence you write should refer back to previous statements in some way. Whether you are writing a "furthermore" comment that adds to what you have just said or a "for example" statement that illustrates it, each sentence should echo at least one element of the previous sentence in some discernible way. Even when your text changes direction and requires transitions like "in contrast," "however," or "but," you still need to mark that shift by linking the sentence to the one just before it, as in the following example.

Cheyenne loved basketball. Nevertheless, she feared her height would put her at a disadvantage.

These sentences work because even though the second sentence changes course and qualifies the first, it still echoes key concepts from the first. Not only does "she" echo "Cheyenne," since both refer to the same person, but "feared" echoes "loved" by establishing the contrast mandated by the term "nevertheless." "Nevertheless," then, is not an excuse for changing subjects radically. It too requires repetition to help readers shift gears with you and follow your train of thought.

Repetition, in short, is the central means by which you can move from point A to point B in a text. To introduce one last analogy, think of the way experienced rock climbers move up a steep slope. Instead of jumping or lurching from one handhold to the next, good climbers get a secure handhold on the position they have established before reaching for the next ledge. The same thing applies to writing. To move smoothly from point to point in your argument, you need to firmly ground what you say in what you've already said. In this way, your writing remains focused while simultaneously moving forward.

"But hold on," you may be thinking. "Isn't repetition precisely what sophisticated writers should avoid, on the grounds that it will make their writing sound simplistic—as if they are belaboring the obvious?" Yes and no. On the one hand, writers certainly can run into trouble if they merely repeat themselves and nothing more. On the other hand, repetition is key to creating continuity in writing. It is impossible to stay on track in a piece of writing if you don't repeat your points throughout the length of the text. Furthermore, writers would never make an impact on readers if they didn't repeat their main points often enough to reinforce those points and make them stand out above subordinate points. The trick therefore is not to avoid repeating yourself but to repeat yourself in varied and interesting enough ways that you advance your argument without sounding tedious.

Exercises

1. Read the following opening to Chapter 2 of *The Road to Wigan Pier*, by George Orwell. Annotate the connecting devices by underlining the transitions, circling the key terms, and putting boxes around the pointing terms.

Our civilisation . . . is founded on coal, more completely than one realises until one stops to think about it. The machines that keep us alive, and the machines that make the machines, are all directly or indirectly dependent upon coal. In the metabolism of the Western world the coal-miner is second in importance only to the man who ploughs the soil. He is a sort of grimy caryatid upon whose shoulders nearly everything that is not grimy is supported. For this reason the actual process by which coal is extracted is well worth watching, if you get the chance and are willing to take the trouble.

When you go down a coal-mine it is important to try and get to the coal face when the "fillers" are at work. This is not easy, because when the mine is working visitors are a nuisance and are not encouraged, but if you go at any other time, it is possible to come away with a totally wrong impression. On a Sunday, for instance, a mine seems almost peaceful. The time to go there is when the machines are roaring and the air is black with coal dust, and when you can actually see what the miners have to do. At those times the place is like hell, or at any rate like my own mental picture of hell. Most of the things one imagines in hell are there—heat, noise, confusion, darkness, foul air, and, above all, unbearably cramped space. Everything except the fire, for there is no fire down there except the feeble beams of Davy lamps and electric torches which scarcely penetrate the clouds of coal dust.

When you have finally got there—and getting there is a job in itself: I will explain that in a moment—you crawl through the last line of pit props and see opposite you a shiny black wall three or four feet high. This is the coal face. Overhead is the smooth ceiling made by the rock from which the coal has been cut; underneath is the rock again, so that the gallery you are in is only as high as the ledge of coal itself, probably not much more than a yard. The first impression of all, overmastering everything else for a while, is the frightful, deafening din from the conveyor belt which carries the coal away. You cannot see very far, because the fog of coal dust throws back the beam of your lamp, but you can see on either side of you the line of half-naked kneeling men, one to every four or five yards, driving their shovels under the fallen coal and flinging it swiftly over their left shoulders. . . .

GEORGE ORWELL, *The Road to Wigan Pier*

2. Read over something you've written with an eye for the devices you've used to connect the parts. Underline all the transitions, pointing terms, key terms, and repetition. Do you see any patterns? Do you rely on certain devices more than others? Are there any passages that are hard to follow—and if so, can you make them easier to read by trying any of the other devices discussed in this chapter?

NINE

"YOU MEAN I CAN JUST SAY IT THAT WAY?"

Academic Writing Doesn't Mean Setting Aside Your Own Voice

WE WISH WE HAD A DOLLAR for each time a student has asked us a version of the above question. It usually comes when the student is visiting us during our office hours, seeking advice about how to improve a draft of an essay he or she is working on. When we ask the student to tell us in simple words the point he or she is trying to make in the essay, the student will almost invariably produce a statement that is far clearer and more incisive than anything in the draft.

"Write that down," we will urge. "What you just said is sooo much better than anything you wrote in your draft. We suggest going home and revising your paper in a way that makes that claim the focal point of your essay."

"Really?" our student will ask, looking surprised. "You mean I can just say it that way?"

"Sure. Why not?"

"Well, saying it that way seems just so elementary—so obvious. I mean, I don't want to sound stupid."

The goal of this chapter is to counteract this common misconception: that relying in college on the straightforward, down-to-earth language you use every day will make you sound stupid; that to impress your teachers you need to set aside your everyday voice and write in a way that is hard to understand.

It's easy to see how this misconception took hold, since academic writing is notoriously obscure. Students can't be blamed for such obscurity when so much of the writing they're assigned to read is so hard to understand—as we can see in the following sentence from a science paper that linguist Steven Pinker quotes in his essay "Why Academics Stink at Writing":

> Participants read assertions whose veracity was either affirmed or denied by the subsequent presentation of an assessment word.

After struggling to determine what the writer of this sentence was trying to say, Pinker finally decided it was probably something as simple as this:

> Participants read sentences, each followed by the word *true* or *false*.

Had the author revised the original statement by tapping into his or her more relaxed, everyday language, as Pinker did in revising it, much of this struggle could have been avoided. In our view, then, mastering academic writing does not mean completely abandoning your normal voice for one that's stiff, convoluted, or pompous, as students often assume. Instead, it means creating a new voice that draws on the voice you already have.

This is not to suggest that any language you use among friends has a place in academic writing. Nor is it to suggest that you may fall back on your everyday voice as an excuse to remain in your comfort zone and avoid learning the rigorous forms and habits that characterize academic culture. After all, learning new words and rhetorical moves is a part of getting an education. We do, however, wish to suggest that everyday language can often enliven such moves and even enhance your precision in using academic terminology. In our view, then, it is a mistake to assume that the academic and every-day are completely separate languages that can never be used together. Ultimately, we suggest, academic writing is often at its best when it combines what we call "everydayspeak" and "academicspeak."

BLEND ACADEMIC AND COLLOQUIAL STYLES

In fact, we would point out that many academics are highly successful writers who themselves blend everyday and academic styles. Note, for example, how Judith Fetterley, a prominent scholar in the field of literary studies, blends academic and everyday ways of talking in the following passage on the novel-ist Willa Cather:

> As Merrill Skaggs has put it, "[Cather] is neurotically controlling and self-conscious about her work, but she knows at all points what she is doing. Above all else, she is self-conscious."
>
> Without question, Cather was a control freak.
>
> JUDITH FETTERLEY, "Willa Cather and the
Question of Sympathy: An Unofficial Story"

In this passage, Fetterley makes use of what is prob-ably the most common technique for blending aca-demic and everyday language: she puts them side by side, juxtaposing "neurotically controlling" and

See pp. 425–432 for an essay that mixes colloquial and academic styles.

"self-conscious" from a quoted source with her own colloquial term, "control freak." In this way, Fetterley lightens a potentially dry subject and makes it more accessible and even entertaining.

But Fetterley does more than simply put academicspeak and everydayspeak side by side. She takes a step further by translating the one into the other. By translating Skaggs's polysyllabic description of Cather as "neurotically controlling and self-conscious" into the succinct, if blunt, "control freak," Fetterley shows how rarefied, academic ways of talking and more familiar language can not only coexist but actually enhance one another—her informal "control freak" serving to explain the formal language that precedes it.

To be sure, slangy, colloquial expressions like "control freak" may be far more common in the humanities than in the sciences, and even in the humanities such casual usages are a recent development. Fifty years ago academic writing in all disciplines was the linguistic equivalent of a black-tie affair. But as times have changed, so has the range of options open to academic writers—so much so that it is not surprising to find writers in all fields using colloquial expressions and referring to movies, music, and other forms of popular culture.

Indeed, Fetterley's passage offers a simple recipe for mixing styles that we encourage you to try out in your own writing: first state the point in academic language, then translate the point into everyday language. Everyone knows that academic terms like "neurotically controlling" and "self-conscious"— and others you might encounter like "subject position" or "bifurcate"—can be hard to understand. But this translation recipe, we think, eases such difficulties by making the academic familiar. Here is one way you might translate academicspeak into everydayspeak:

▸ Scholar X argues, "_____." In other words, _____.

Instead of "In other words," you might try variations like the following:

▸ Essentially, X argues _____.

▸ X's point, succinctly put, is that _____.

▸ Plainly put, _____.

Following Fetterley's lead and making moves like these can help you not only demystify challenging academic material, but also reinterpret it, showing you understand it (and helping readers understand it) by putting it into your own terms.

SELF-TRANSLATION

But this translation recipe need not be limited to clarifying the ideas of others. It can also be used to clarify your own complex ideas, as the following passage by the philosopher Rebecca Goldstein illustrates:

> We can hardly get through our lives—in fact, it's hard to get through a week—without considering what makes specific actions right and others wrong and debating with ourselves whether that is a difference that must compel the actions we choose. (Okay, it's wrong! I get it! But why should I care?)
>
> Rebecca Goldstein, Plato at the Googleplex:
Why Philosophy Won't Go Away

Though Goldstein's first sentence may require several rereadings, it is one that most of us, with varying degrees of effort, can come to understand: that we all wrestle regularly with the challenging philosophical questions of what the ethics of a given situation are and whether those ethics should alter our behavior. But instead of leaving us entirely on our own to figure out what she is saying, Goldstein helps us out in her closing parenthetical remarks, which translate the abstractions of her first sentence into the kind of concrete everydayspeak that runs through our heads.

Yet another example of self-translation—one that actually uses the word "translation"—can be found on the opening page of a book by scholar Helen Sword:

> There is a massive gap between what most readers consider to be good writing and what academics typically produce and publish. I'm not talking about the kinds of formal strictures necessarily imposed

by journal editors—article length, citation style, and the like—but about a deeper, duller kind of disciplinary monotony, a compulsive proclivity for discursive obscurantism and circumambulatory diction (translation: an addiction to big words and soggy syntax).

HELEN SWORD, *Stylish Academic Writing*

In this passage, Sword gives her own unique twist to the translation technique we've been discussing. After a stream of difficult polysyllabic words—"a compulsive proclivity for discursive obscurantism and circumambulatory diction"—she then concludes by translating these words into everydayspeak: "an addiction to big words and soggy syntax." The effect is to dramatize her larger point: the "massive gap between what most readers consider to be good writing and what academics typically produce and publish."

FAMOUS EXAMPLES

Even notoriously difficult thinkers could be said to use the translation practice we have been advocating in this chapter, as the following famous and widely quoted claims illustrate:

I think, therefore I am.
—RENÉ DESCARTES

The master's tools will never dismantle the master's house.
—AUDRE LORDE

The medium is the message.
—MARSHALL MCLUHAN

Form follows function.
—LOUIS SULLIVAN

These sentences can be read almost as sound bites, short, catchy statements that express a more complex idea. Though the term "sound bite" is usually used to refer to mindless media simplifications, the succinct statements above show what valuable work they can do. These distillations are admittedly reductive in that they do not capture all the nuances of the more complex ideas they represent. But consider their power to stick in the minds of readers. Without these memorable translations, we wonder if these authors' ideas would have achieved such widespread circulation.

Consider Descartes' "I think, therefore I am," for example, which comes embedded in the following passage, in which Descartes is struggling to find a philosophical foundation for absolute truth in the face of skeptical doctrines that doubt that anything can be known for certain. After putting himself in the shoes of a radical skeptic and imagining what it would be like to believe all apparent truths to be false, Descartes "immediately ... observed," he writes,

> whilst I thus wished to think that all was false, it was absolutely necessary that I, who thus thought, should be somewhat; and as I observed that this truth, I think, therefore I am (*cogito ergo sum*), was so certain and of such evidence that no ground of doubt, however extravagant, could be alleged by the sceptics capable of shaking it, I concluded that I might, without scruple, accept it as the first principle of the philosophy of which I was in search.
>
> RENÉ DESCARTES, "Discourse on the Method, Part IV"

Had Descartes been less probing and scrupulous, we speculate, he would have stopped writing and ended the passage after the statement "it was absolutely necessary that I, who thus thought, should be somewhat." After all, the passage up to this point contains all the basic ingredients that the rest of it goes on to explain, the simpler, more accessible formulation

"I think, therefore I am" being merely a reformulation of this earlier material. But just imagine if Descartes had decided that his job as a writer was finished after his initial claim and had failed to add the more accessible phrase "I think, therefore I am." We suspect this idea of his would not have become one of the most famous touchstones of Western philosophy.

EVERYDAY LANGUAGE AS A THINKING TOOL

As the examples in this chapter suggest, then, translating academic language into everydayspeak can be an indispensable tool for clarifying and underscoring ideas for readers. But at an even more basic level, such translation can be an indispensable means for you as a writer to clarify your ideas to yourself. In other words, translating academicspeak into everydayspeak can function as a thinking tool that enables you to discover what you are trying to say to begin with.

For as writing theorists often note, writing is generally not a process in which we start with a fully formed idea in our heads that we then simply transcribe in an unchanged state onto the page. On the contrary, writing is more often a means of discovery in which we use the writing process to figure out what our idea is. This is why writers are often surprised to find that what they end up with on the page is quite different from what they thought it would be when they started. What we are trying to say here is that everydayspeak is often crucial for this discovery process, that translating your ideas into more common, simpler terms can help you figure out what your ideas really are, as opposed to what you initially imagined they were. Even Descartes, for example, may not have had the formulation "I think, therefore I am" in mind before he wrote the passage above; instead, he may have arrived at it as he worked through the writing process.

We ourselves have been reminded of this point when engaged in our own writing. One major benefit of writing collaboratively, as the two of us do, is that it repeatedly forces us to explain in simpler terms our less-than-clear ideas when one of us doesn't already know what the other means. In the process of writing and revising this book, for instance, we were always turning to each other after reading something the other had written and asking a version of the "Can-you-explain-that-more-simply?" question that we described asking our students in our office in this chapter's opening anecdote: "What do you mean?" "I don't get it—can you explain?" "Huh!?" Sometimes, when the idea is finally stated in plain, everyday terms, we realize that it doesn't make sense or that it amounts to nothing more than a cliché—or that we have something worth pursuing. It's as if using everyday language to talk through a draft—as any writer can do by asking others to critique his or her drafts—shines a bright light on our writing to expose its strengths and weaknesses.

STILL NOT CONVINCED?

To be sure, not everyone will be as enthusiastic as we are about the benefits of everydayspeak. Many will insist that, while some fields in the humanities may be open to everyday language, colloquial expressions, and slang, most fields in the sciences are not. And some people in both the humanities and the sciences will argue that some ideas simply can't be done justice to in everyday language. "Theory X," they will say, "is just too complex to be explained in simple terms," or "You have to be in the field to understand it." Perhaps so. But at least one distinguished scientist, the celebrated atomic physicist Enrico Fermi, thought otherwise. Fermi, it is said, believed that all faculty in his field should teach basic physics to undergraduates, because having to explain the science in relatively plain English helped to clarify their thinking. This last point can be stated as a rule of thumb: if you can't explain it to your Aunt Franny, chances are you don't understand it yourself.

Furthermore, when writers tell themselves that their ideas are just too complex to be explained to nonspecialists, they risk fooling themselves into thinking that they are making more sense than they actually are. Translating academicspeak into everydayspeak functions as a kind of baloney detector, a way of keeping us honest when we're in danger of getting carried away by our own verbosity.

CODE-MESHING

"But come on," some may say. "Get real! Academic writing must, in many cases, mean setting aside our own voices." Sure, it may be fine to translate challenging academic ideas into plain everyday language, as Goldstein, Sword, and Descartes do above, when it's a language that your audience will understand and find acceptable. But what if your everyday language— the one you use when you're most relaxed, with family and friends—is filled with slang and questionable grammar? And what if your everyday language is an ethnic or regional dialect— or a different language altogether? Is there really a place for such language in academic, professional, or public writing?

Yes and no. On the one hand, there are many situations— like when you're applying for a job or submitting a proposal to be read by an official screening body—in which it's probably safest to write in "standard" English. On the other hand, the line between language that might confuse audiences and language that engages or challenges them is not always obvious. Nor is the line between foreign words that readers don't already know and those that readers might happily learn. After all, "standard" written English is more open and inclusive than it may at first appear. And readers often appreciate writers who take risks and mix things up.

Many prominent writers mix standard written English with other dialects or languages, employing a practice that cultural and linguistic theorists Vershawn Ashanti Young and Suresh Canagarajah call "code-meshing." For instance, in the titles of two of her books, *Talkin and Testifyin: The Language of Black America* and *Black Talk: Words and Phrases From the Hood to the Amen Corner*, the language scholar Geneva Smitherman mixes African American vernacular phrases with more scholarly language in order to suggest, as she explicitly argues in these books, that black vernacular English is as legitimate a variety of language as "standard" English. Here are three typical passages:

In Black America, the oral tradition has served as a fundamental vehicle for gittin ovah. That tradition preserves the Afro-American heritage and reflects the collective spirit of the race.

Blacks are quick to ridicule "educated fools," people who done gone to school and read all dem books and still don't know nothin!

It is a socially approved verbal strategy for black rappers to talk about how bad they is.

GENEVA SMITHERMAN, *Talkin and Testifyin:*
The Language of Black America

In these examples, Smitherman blends the types of terms we expect in scholarly writing like "oral tradition" and "fundamental vehicle" with black vernacular phrases like "gittin ovah." She even blends the standard English spelling of words with African American English variants like "dem" and "ovah" in a way that evokes how some speakers of African American English sound. Some might object to these unconventional practices, but this is precisely Smitherman's point: that our habitual language practices need to be opened up, and that the number of participants in the academic conversation needs to be expanded.

Along similar lines, the writer and activist Gloria Anzaldúa mixes standard English with what she calls Chicano Spanish to make a political point about the suppression of the Spanish language in the United States. In one typical passage, she writes:

> From this racial, ideological, cultural, and biological cross-pollinization, an "alien" consciousness is presently in the making— a new *mestiza* consciousness, *una conciencia de mujer*.
>
> Gloria Anzaldúa,
Borderlands / La Frontera: The New Mestiza

Anzaldúa gets her point across not only through *what* she says but through the *way* she says it, showing that the new hybrid, or "*mestiza* consciousness," that she celebrates is, as she puts it, "presently in the making." Ultimately, such code-meshing suggests that languages, like the people who speak them, are not distinct, separate islands.

Because there are so many options in writing, then, there is no need to ever feel limited in your choice of words. You can always experiment with your language and improve it. Depending on your audience and purpose, and how much risk you're willing to take, you can dress up your language, dress it down, or some combination of both. You could even recast the title of this book, *They Say / I Say*, as a teenager might say it: "She Goes / I'm Like."

We hope you agree with us, then, that to succeed as a college writer, you need not always set aside your everyday voice, even when that voice may initially seem unwelcome in the academic world. It is by blending everyday language with standard written English that what counts as "standard" changes and the range of possibilities open to academic writers continues to grow.

Exercises

1. Take a paragraph from this book and dress it down, rewriting it in informal colloquial language. Then rewrite the same paragraph again by dressing it up, making it much more formal. Then rewrite the paragraph one more time in a way that blends the two styles. Share your paragraphs with a classmate, and discuss which versions are most effective and why.

2. Find something you've written for a course, and study it to see whether you've used any of your own everyday expressions, any words or structures that are not "academic." If by chance you don't find any, see if there's a place or two where shifting into more casual or unexpected language would help you make a point, get your reader's attention, or just add liveliness to your text. Be sure to keep your audience and purpose in mind, and use language that will be appropriate to both.

TEN

"BUT DON'T GET ME WRONG"

The Art of Metacommentary

———〔回〕———

WHEN WE TELL PEOPLE that we are writing a chapter on the art of metacommentary, they often give us a puzzled look and tell us that they have no idea what "metacommentary" is. "We know what commentary is," they'll sometimes say, "but what does it mean when it's *meta?*" Our answer is that whether or not they know the term, they practice the art of metacommentary on a daily basis whenever they make a point of explaining something they've said or written: "What I meant to say was _____," "My point was not _____ , but _____," or "You're probably not going to like what I'm about to say, but _____." In such cases, they are not offering new points but telling an audience how to interpret what they have already said or are about to say. In short, then, metacommentary is a way of commenting on your claims and telling others how—and how not—to think about them.

It may help to think of metacommentary as being like the chorus in a Greek play that stands to the side of the drama unfolding on the stage and explains its meaning to the audience—or like a voice-over narrator who comments on and explains the action in a television show or movie. Think of metacommentary as a sort of second text that stands alongside your main text and explains what it means. In the main text you say something; in the metatext you guide your readers in interpreting and processing what you've said.

What we are suggesting, then, is that you think of your text as two texts joined at the hip: a main text in which you make your argument and another in which you "work" your ideas, distinguishing your views from others they may be confused with, anticipating and answering objections, connecting one point to another, explaining why your claim might be controversial, and so forth. The figure below demonstrates what we mean.

THE MAIN TEXT SAYS SOMETHING. THE METATEXT TELLS READERS HOW—AND HOW NOT—TO THINK ABOUT IT.

USE METACOMMENTARY TO CLARIFY
AND ELABORATE

But why do you need metacommentary to tell readers what you mean and guide them through your text? Can't you just clearly say what you mean up front? The answer is that, no matter how clear and precise your writing is, readers can still fail to understand it in any number of ways. Even the best writers can provoke reactions in readers that they didn't intend, and even good readers can get lost in a complicated argument or fail to see how one point connects with another. Readers may also fail to see what follows from your argument, or they may follow your reasoning and examples yet fail to see the larger conclusion you draw from them. They may fail to see your argument's overall significance, or mistake what you are saying for a related argument that they have heard before but that you want to distance yourself from. As a result, no matter how straightforward a writer you are, readers still need you to help them grasp what you really mean. Because the written word is prone to so much mischief and can be interpreted in so many different ways, we need metacommentary to keep misinterpretations and other communication misfires at bay.

Another reason to master the art of metacommentary is that it will help you develop your ideas and generate more text. If you have ever had trouble producing the required number of pages for a writing project, metacommentary can help you add both length and depth to your writing. We've seen many students who try to produce a five-page paper sputter to a halt at two or three pages, complaining they've said everything they can think of about their topic. "I've stated my thesis and presented my reasons and evidence," students have told us. "What else is there to do?" It's almost as if such writers have generated a thesis and don't know what to do with it. When these students learn to use metacommentary, however, they get more out of their ideas and write longer, more substantial texts. In sum, metacommentary can help you extract the full potential from your ideas, drawing out important implications, explaining ideas from different perspectives, and so forth.

So even when you may think you've said everything possible in an argument, try inserting the following types of metacommentary.

▸ In other words, <u>she doesn't realize how right she is.</u>

▸ What _____ really means is _____.

▸ My point is not _____ but _____.

▸ Ultimately, then, my goal is to demonstrate that _____.

Ideally, such metacommentary should help you recognize some implications of your ideas that you didn't initially realize were there.

Let's look at how the cultural critic Neil Postman uses metacommentary in the following passage describing the shift in American culture when it began to move from print and reading to television and movies.

It is my intention in this book to show that a great . . . shift has taken place in America, with the result that the content of much of our public discourse has become dangerous nonsense. *With this in view, my task in the chapters ahead is* straightforward. *I must, first, demonstrate* how, under the governance of the printing press, discourse in America was different from what it is now—generally coherent, serious and rational; *and then* how, under the governance of television, it has become shriveled and absurd. *But to avoid the possibility that my analysis will be interpreted as* standard-brand academic whimpering, a kind of elitist complaint against "junk" on television, *I must first explain that . . .* I appreciate junk as much as the next fellow, *and I know full well that* the printing press has generated enough of it to fill the Grand Canyon to overflowing. Television is not old enough to have matched printing's output of junk.

NEIL POSTMAN, *Amusing Ourselves to Death:*
Public Discourse in the Age of Show Business

To see what we mean by metacommentary, look at the phrases above that we have italicized. With these moves, Postman essentially stands apart from his main ideas to help readers follow and understand what he is arguing.

He previews what he will argue: *It is my intention in this book to show . . .*

He spells out how he will make his argument: *With this in view, my task in the chapters ahead is . . . I must, first, demonstrate . . . and then . . .*

He distinguishes his argument from other arguments it may easily be confused with: *But to avoid the possibility that my analysis will be interpreted as . . . I must first explain that . . .*

TITLES AS METACOMMENTARY

Even the title of Postman's book, *Amusing Ourselves to Death: Public Discourse in the Age of Show Business,* functions as a form of metacommentary since, like all titles, it stands apart from the text itself and tells readers the book's main point: that the very pleasure provided by contemporary show business is destructive.

Titles, in fact, are one of the most important forms of metacommentary, functioning rather like carnival barkers telling passersby what they can expect if they go inside. Subtitles, too, function as metacommentary, further explaining or elaborating on the main title. The subtitle of this book, for example, not only explains that it is about "the moves that matter in academic writing," but indicates that "they say / I say" is one of these moves. Thinking of a title as metacommentary can actually help you develop sharper titles, ones that, like Postman's, give readers a hint of what your argument will be. Contrast such titles with unhelpfully open-ended ones like "Shakespeare" or "Steroids" or "English Essay" or essays with no titles at all. Essays with vague titles (or no titles) send the message that the writer has simply not bothered to reflect on what he or she is saying and is uninterested in guiding or orienting readers.

USE OTHER MOVES AS METACOMMENTARY

Many of the other moves covered in this book function as metacommentary: entertaining objections, adding transitions, framing quotations, answering "so what?" and "who cares?" When you entertain objections, you stand outside of your text and imagine what a critic might say; when you add transitions, you essentially explain the relationship between various claims. And when you answer the "so what?" and "who cares?" questions, you look beyond your central argument and explain who should be interested in it and why.

TEMPLATES FOR INTRODUCING METACOMMENTARY

TO WARD OFF POTENTIAL MISUNDERSTANDINGS

The following moves help you differentiate certain views from ones they might be mistaken for.

► Essentially, I am arguing not that <u>we should give up the policy</u>, but that we should monitor effects far more closely.

► This is not to say _____, but rather _____.

► X is concerned less with _____ than with _____.

TO ELABORATE ON A PREVIOUS IDEA

The following moves elaborate on a previous point, saying to readers: "In case you didn't get it the first time, I'll try saying the same thing in a different way."

► In other words, _____.

► To put it another way, _____.

► What X is saying here is that _____.

TO PROVIDE A ROAD MAP TO YOUR TEXT

This move orients readers, clarifying where you have been and where you are going—and making it easier for them to process and follow your text.

► Chapter 2 explores _____, while Chapter 3 examines _____.

► Having just argued that _____, I want now to complicate the point by _____.

TO MOVE FROM A GENERAL CLAIM TO A SPECIFIC EXAMPLE

These moves help you explain a general point by providing a concrete example that illustrates what you're saying.

- ▸ For example, _____ .
- ▸ _____ , for instance, demonstrates _____ .
- ▸ Consider _____ , for example.
- ▸ To take a case in point, _____ .

TO INDICATE THAT A CLAIM IS MORE, LESS, OR EQUALLY IMPORTANT

The following templates help you give relative emphasis to the claim that you are introducing, showing whether that claim is of more or less weight than the previous one, or equal to it.

- ▸ Even more important, _____ .
- ▸ But above all, _____ .
- ▸ Incidentally, we will briefly note, _____ .
- ▸ Just as important, _____ .
- ▸ Equally, _____ .
- ▸ Finally, _____ .

TO EXPLAIN A CLAIM WHEN YOU ANTICIPATE OBJECTIONS

Here's a template to help you anticipate and respond to possible objections.

- ▸ Although some readers may object that _____ , I would answer that _____ .

TO GUIDE READERS TO YOUR MOST GENERAL POINT

These moves show that you are wrapping things up and tying up various subpoints previously made.

Chapter 6 has more templates for anticipating objections.

▸ In sum, then, _____ .

▸ My conclusion, then, is that _____ .

▸ In short, _____ .

In this chapter we have tried to show that the most persuasive writing often doubles back and comments on its own claims in ways that help readers negotiate and process them. Instead of simply piling claim upon claim, effective writers are constantly "stage-managing" how their claims will be received. It's true of course that to be persuasive a text has to have strong claims to argue in the first place. But even the strongest arguments will flounder unless writers use metacommentary to prevent potential misreadings and make their arguments shine.

Exercises

1. Read an essay or article and annotate it to indicate the different ways the author uses metacommentary. Use the templates on pages 137–39 as your guide. For example, you may want to circle transitional phrases and write "trans" in the margins, to put brackets around sentences that elaborate on earlier sentences and mark them "elab," or underline sentences in which the author sums up what he or she has been saying, writing "sum" in the margins.

    How does the author use metacommentary? Does the author follow any of the templates provided in this book word for word? Did you find any forms of metacommentary not discussed in this chapter? If so, can you identify them, name them, and perhaps devise templates based on them for use in your own writing? And finally, how do you think the author's use of metacommentary enhances (or harms) his or her writing?

2. Complete each of the following metacommentary templates in any way that makes sense.

- ▸ In making a case for the medical use of marijuana, I am not saying that _____.

- ▸ But my argument will do more than prove that one particular industrial chemical has certain toxic properties. In this article, I will also _____.

- ▸ My point about the national obsessions with sports reinforces the belief held by many _____ that _____.

- ▸ I believe, therefore, that the war is completely unjustified. But let me back up and explain how I arrived at this conclusion: _____. In this way, I came to believe that this war is a big mistake.

ELEVEN

"HE ~~SAYS~~ CONTENDS"

Using the Templates to Revise

ONE OF THE MOST IMPORTANT stages of the writing process is revision, when you look at a draft with an eye for how well you've made your argument and what you need to do to make it better. The challenge is to figure out what needs work—and then what exactly you need to do.

Sometimes you'll have specific comments and suggestions from a teacher, noting that you need to state your position more explicitly, that your point is unclear, that you've misunderstood an author you're summarizing, and so forth. But what if you don't have any such guidance, or aren't sure what to do with it? The list of guidelines below offers help and points you back to relevant advice and templates in this book.

Do you present your argument as a response to what others say? Do you make reference to other views besides your own? Do you use voice markers to distinguish clearly for readers between your views and those of others? In order to make your argument as convincing as possible, would it help to add more concessions to opposing views, using "yes but" templates?

Asking yourself these large-scale revision questions will help you see how well you've managed the "they say / I say" framework and this in turn should help you see where further revisions are needed. The checklist below follows the order of chapters in this book.

How Do You Represent What Others Say?

Do you start with what others say? If not, try revising to do so. See pages 23–28 for templates that can help.

Do you summarize or paraphrase what they've said? If so, have you represented their views accurately—and adequately?

Do you quote others? Do you frame each quotation successfully, integrating it into your text? Does the quotation support your argument? Have you introduced each quotation adequately, naming the person you're quoting (and saying who that person is if your readers won't know)? Do you explain in your own words what the quotation means? Do you then clearly indicate how the quotation bears on your own argument? See pages 45–47 for tips on creating a "quotation sandwich."

Check the verbs you use to introduce any summaries and quotations: do they express accurately what was said? If you've used common signal phrases such as "X said" or "Y believes," is there a verb that reflects more accurately what was said? See pages 40–41 for a list of verbs for introducing summaries and quotations.

Have you documented all summaries and quotations, both with parenthetical documentation in your text and a references or works-cited list?

Do you remind readers of what others say at various points throughout your text? If not, see pages 27–28 for help revising in order to do so.

What Do You Say?

Do you agree, disagree, or both with those you're responding to? Have you said so explicitly?

If you disagree, do you give reasons why you disagree? If you agree, what more have you added to the conversation? If you both agree and disagree, do you do so without confusing readers or seeming evasive?

Have you stated your position and the one it responds to as a connected unit?

What reasons and evidence do you offer to support your "I say"? In other words, do your argument and the argument you are responding to—your "I say" and "they say"—address the same topic or issue, or does a switch occur that takes you on a tangent that will confuse readers? One way to ensure that your "I say" and "they say" are aligned rather than seeming like ships passing in the night is to use the same key terms in both. See Chapter 8 for tips on how to do so.

Will readers be able to distinguish what you say from what others say? See Chapter 5 for advice about using voice markers to make that distinction clear, especially at moments when you are moving from your view to someone else's view or back.

Have You Introduced Any Naysayers?

Have you acknowledged likely objections to your argument? If so, have you represented these views fairly—and responded to them persuasively? See Chapter 6 for tips on how to do so.

If not, think about what other perspectives exist on your topic, and incorporate them into your draft.

Have You Used Metacommentary to Clarify What You Do or Don't Mean?

No matter how clearly you've explained your points, it's a good idea to explain what you mean—or *don't* mean—with phrases like "in other words" or "don't get me wrong." See Chapter 10 for examples of how to do so.

Do you have a title? If so, does it tell readers what your main point or issue is, and does it do so in a lively manner? Should you add a subtitle to elaborate on the title?

Have You Tied It All Together?

Can readers follow your argument from one sentence and paragraph to the next and see how each successive point supports your overall argument?

Check your use of transitions, words like "however" and "therefore." Such words make clear how your ideas relate to one another; if you need to add transitions, see pages 105–06 for a complete list.

Check your use of pointing words. Do you use common pointers like "this" and "that," which help lead readers from one sentence to the next? If so, is it always clear what "this" and "that" refer to, or do you need to add nouns in order to avoid ambiguity? See pages 108–10 for help working with pointing words.

Have you used what we call "repetition with a difference" to help connect parts of your argument? See pages 112–14 for examples of how to do so.

Have You Shown Why Your Argument Matters?

Don't assume that readers will see why your argument is important—or why they should care. Be sure that you have told them why. See Chapter 7 if you need help.

A REVISED STUDENT ESSAY

Here is an example of how one student, Antonia Peacocke, used this book to revise an essay. Starting with an article she'd written for her high school newspaper, Peacocke then followed the advice in our book as she turned her article into a college-level academic essay. Her original article was a brief account of why she liked *Family Guy*, and her first step in revising was to open with a "they say" and an "I say," previewing her overall argument in brief form at the essay's beginning. While her original version had acknowledged that many find the show "objectionable," she hadn't named these people or indicated why they didn't like the show. In her revised version, after doing further research, Peacocke identified those with whom she disagreed and responded to them at length, as the essay itself illustrates.

In addition, Peacocke strengthened existing transitions, added new ones, and clarified the stakes of her argument, saying more explicitly why readers should care about whether *Family Guy* is good or bad. In making these revisions she gave her own spin to several templates in this book.

We've annotated Peacocke's essay in the margins to point out particular rhetorical moves discussed in our book and the chapters in which those discussions appear. We hope studying her essay and our annotations will suggest how you might craft and revise your own writing.

Antonia Peacocke wrote this essay in the summer between high school and her first year at Harvard. She is now a PhD student in philosophy at the University of California at Berkeley.

Family Guy *and Freud: Jokes and Their Relation to the Unconscious*

ANTONIA PEACOCKE

WHILE SLOUCHING in front of the television after a long day, you probably don't think a lot about famous psychologists of the twentieth century. Somehow, these figures don't come up often in prime-time—or even daytime—TV programming. Whether you're watching *Living Lohan* or the *NewsHour*, the likelihood is that you are not thinking of Sigmund Freud, even if you've heard of his book *Jokes and Their Relation to the Unconscious*. I say that you should be.

> Starts with what others are saying (Chapter 1)

> Responds to what they say (Chapter 4)

What made me think of Freud in the first place, actually, was *Family Guy*, the cartoon created by Seth MacFarlane. (Seriously—stay with me here.) Any of my friends can tell you that this program holds endless fascination for me; as a matter of fact, my high school rag-sheet "perfect mate" was the baby Stewie Griffin, a character on the show (see Fig. 1). Embarrassingly enough, I have almost reached the point at which I can perform

> Metacommentary wards off potential skepticism (Chapter 10)

one-woman versions of several episodes. I know every website that streams the show for free, and I still refuse to return the five *Family Guy* DVDs a friend lent me in 2006. Before I was such a devotee, however, I was adamantly opposed to the program for its particular brand of humor.

It will come as no surprise that I was not alone in this view; many still denounce *Family Guy* as bigoted and crude. *New York Times* journalist Stuart Elliott claimed just this year that "the characters on the Fox television series *Family Guy* . . . purposely offen[d] just about every group of people

> Quotes and summarizes what others say (Chapters 2 and 3)

Fig 1. Peter and Stewie Griffin. (Everett Collection)

you could name." Likewise Stephen Dubner, coauthor of *Freakonomics*, called *Family Guy* "a cartoon comedy that packs more gags per minute about race, sex, incest, bestiality, etc. than any other show [he] can think of." Comparing its level of offense to that of Don Imus's infamous comments about the Rutgers women's basketball team in the same year, comments that threw the popular CBS radio talk-show host off the air, Dubner said he wondered why Imus couldn't get away with as much as *Family Guy* could.

Dubner did not know about all the trouble *Family Guy* has had. In fact, it must be one of the few television shows in history that has been canceled not just once, but twice. After its premiere in April 1999, the show ran until August 2000, but was besieged by so many complaints, some of them from MacFarlane's old high school headmaster, Rev. Richardson W. Schell, that Fox shelved it until July 2001 (Weinraub). Still afraid of causing a commotion, though, Fox had the cartoon censored and irregularly scheduled; as a result, its ratings fell so low that 2002 saw its second cancellation (Weinraub). But then it came back with a vengeance—I'll get into that later.

Family Guy has found trouble more recently, too. In 2007, comedian Carol Burnett sued Fox for 6 million dollars, claiming that the show's parody of the Charwoman, a character that she had created for *The Carol Burnett Show*, not only violated copyright but also besmirched the character's name in revenge for Burnett's refusal to grant permission to use her theme song ("Carol Burnett Sues"). The suit came after MacFarlane had made the Charwoman into a cleaning woman for a pornography store in one episode of *Family Guy*. Burnett lost, but U.S. district judge Dean Pregerson agreed that he could "fully appreciate how distasteful and offensive the segment [was] to Ms. Burnett" (qtd. in Grossberg).

I must admit, I can see how parts of the show might seem offensive if taken at face value. Look, for example, at the mock fifties instructional video that features in the episode "I Am Peter, Hear Me Roar."

> Represents a naysayer's objections fairly (Chapter 6)

[*The screen becomes black and white. Vapid music plays in the background. The screen reads* "WOMEN IN THE WORKPLACE CA. 1956," *then switches to a shot of an office with various women working on typewriters. A businessman speaks to the camera.*]

BUSINESSMAN: Irrational and emotionally fragile by nature, female coworkers are a peculiar animal. They are very insecure about their appearance. Be sure to tell them how good they look every day, even if they're homely and unkempt. [*He turns to an unattractive female typist.*] You're doing a great job, Muriel, and you're prettier than Mamie van Doren! [*She smiles. He grins at the camera, raising one eyebrow knowingly, and winks.*]

And remember, nothing says "Good job!" like a firm open-palm slap on the behind. [*He walks past a woman bent over a file cabinet and demonstrates enthusiastically. She smiles, looking flattered. He grins at the camera again as the music comes to an end.*]

Laughing at something so blatantly sexist could cause anyone a pang of guilt, and before I thought more about the show this seemed to be a huge problem. I agreed with Dubner, and I failed to see how anyone could laugh at such jokes without feeling at least slightly ashamed.

Agrees, but with a difference (Chapter 4)

Soon, though, I found myself forced to give *Family Guy* a chance. It was simply everywhere: my brother and many of my friends watched it religiously, and its devoted fans relentlessly proselytized for it. In case you have any doubts about its immense popularity, consider these facts. On Facebook, the universal forum for my generation, there are currently 23 separate *Family Guy* fan groups with a combined membership of 1,669 people (compared with only 6 groups protesting against *Family Guy*, with 105 members total). Users of the well-respected Internet Movie Database rate the show 8.8 out of 10. The box-set DVDs were the best-selling television DVDs of 2003 in the United States (Moloney). Among the public and within the industry, the show receives fantastic acclaim; it has won eight awards, including three prime-time Emmys (IMDb). Most importantly, each time it was cancelled fans provided the brute force necessary to get it

Anticipates a naysayer's skepticism (Chapter 6)

back on the air. In 2000, online campaigns did the trick; in 2002, devotees demonstrated outside Fox Studios, refused to watch the Fox network, and boycotted any companies that advertised on it (Moloney). Given the show's high profile, both with my friends and family and in the world at large, it would have been more work for me to avoid the Griffin family than to let myself sink into their animated world.

> Distinguishes between what others say and what she says (Chapter 5)

With more exposure, I found myself crafting a more positive view of *Family Guy*. Those who don't often watch the program, as Dubner admits he doesn't, could easily come to think that the cartoon takes pleasure in controversial humor just for its own sake. But those who pay more attention and think about the creators' intentions can see that *Family Guy* intelligently satirizes some aspects of American culture.

> Mixes academic and colloquial styles (Chapter 9)

Some of this satire is actually quite obvious. Take, for instance, a quip Brian the dog makes about Stewie's literary choices in a fourth-season episode, "PTV." (Never mind that a dog and a baby can both read and hold lengthy conversations.)

[*The Griffins are in their car. Brian turns to Stewie, who sits reading in his car seat.*]

> Uses a quotation sandwich to explicate this excerpt (Chapter 3)

BRIAN: *East of Eden*? So you, you, you pretty much do whatever Oprah tells you to, huh?
STEWIE: You know, this book's been around for fifty years. It's a classic.

BRIAN: But you just got it last week. And there's a giant Oprah sticker on the front.

STEWIE: Oh—oh—oh, is that what that is? Oh, lemme just peel that right off.

BRIAN: So, uh, what are you gonna read after that one?

STEWIE: Well, she hasn't told us yet—damn!

Brian and Stewie demonstrate insightfully and comically how Americans are willing to follow the instructions of a celebrity blindly—and less willing to admit that they are doing so.

The more off-color jokes, though, those that give *Family Guy* a bad name, attract a different kind of viewer. Such viewers are not "rats in a behaviorist's maze," as *Slate* writer Dana Stevens labels modern American television consumers in her article "Thinking Outside the Idiot Box." They are conscious and critical viewers, akin to the "screenagers" identified by Douglas Rushkoff in an essay entitled "Bart Simpson: Prince of Irreverence" (294). They are not—and this I cannot stress enough, self-serving as it may seem—immoral or easily manipulated people.

> Distinguishes what others say from what she says (Chapter 5)

Rushkoff's piece analyzes the humor of *The Simpsons*, a show criticized for many of the same reasons as *Family Guy*. "The people I call 'screenagers,'" Rushkoff explains, "speak the media language better than their parents do and they see through clumsy attempts to program them into submission" (294). He claims that gaming technology has made my generation realize that television is programmed for us with certain intentions; since we can control characters in the virtual world, we are more aware that characters on TV are similarly controlled. "Sure, [these 'screenagers'] might sit back and watch a program now and again," Rushkoff explains, "but they do so voluntarily, and with full knowledge of their complicity. It is not an involuntary surrender" (294). In his opinion, our critical eyes and our unwillingness to be programmed by the programmers make for an entirely new relationship with the shows we watch. Thus we enjoy *The Simpsons'* parodies of mass media culture since we are skeptical of it ourselves.

Rushkoff's argument about *The Simpsons* actually applies to *Family Guy* as well, except in one dimension: Rushkoff writes that *The Simpsons'* creators do "not comment on social issues as much as they [do on] the media imagery around a particular social issue" (296). MacFarlane and company seem to do the reverse. Trusting in their viewers' ability to analyze what they are watching, the creators of *Family Guy* point out the weaknesses and defects of U.S. society in a mocking and sometimes intolerant way.

Taken in this light, the "instructional video" quoted above becomes not only funny but also insightful. In its satire, viewers can recognize the sickly sweet and falsely sensitive sexism of the 1950s in observing just how conveniently

Uses transitions to connect the parts (Chapter 8)

self-serving the speaker of the video appears. The message of the clip denounces and ridicules sexism rather than condoning it. It is an excerpt that perfectly exemplifies the bald-faced candor of the show, from which it derives a lot of its appeal.

Making such comically outrageous remarks on the air also serves to expose certain prejudiced attitudes as outrageous themselves. Taking these comments at face value would be as foolish as taking Jonathan Swift's "Modest Proposal" seriously. Furthermore, while they put bigoted words into the mouths of their characters, the show's writers cannot be accused of portraying these characters positively. Peter Griffin, the "family guy" of the show's title, probably says and does the most offensive things of all—but as a lazy, overweight, and insensitive failure of a man, he is hardly presented as someone to admire. Nobody in his or her right mind would observe Peter's behavior and deem it worth emulation.

Family Guy has its own responses to accusations of crudity. In the episode "PTV," Peter sets up his own television station broadcasting from home and the Griffin family finds itself confronting the Federal Communications Commission directly (see Fig. 2 for a picture of the whole family). The episode makes many tongue-in-cheek jabs at the FCC, some of which are sung in a rousing musical number, but also sneaks in some of the creator's own

Fig 2. The Griffin family watches TV. (Everett Collection)

opinions. The plot comes to a climax when the FCC begins to censor "real life" in the town of Quahog; officials place black censor bars in front of newly showered Griffins and blow foghorns whenever characters curse. MacFarlane makes an important point: that no amount of television censorship will ever change the harsh nature of reality— and to censor reality is mere folly. Likewise, he puts explicit arguments about censorship into lines spoken by his characters, as when Brian says that "responsibility lies with the parents [and] there are plenty of things that are much worse for children than television."

It must be said too that not all of *Family Guy*'s humor could be construed as offensive. Some of its jokes are more tame and insightful, the kind you might expect from *The New Yorker*. The following light commentary on the usefulness of high school algebra from "When You Wish Upon a Weinstein" could hardly be accused of upsetting anyone— except, perhaps, a few high school math teachers.

> [*Shot of Peter on the couch and his son Chris lying at his feet and doing homework.*]
>
> CHRIS: Dad, can you help me with my math? [My teacher] says if I don't learn it, I won't be able to function in the real world.
>
> [*Shot of Chris standing holding a map in a run-down gas station next to an attendant in overalls and a trucker cap reading "PUMP THIS." The attendant speaks with a Southern accent and gestures casually to show the different road configurations.*]
>
> ATTENDANT: Okay, now what you gotta do is go down the road past the old Johnson place, and you're gonna find two roads, one parallel and one perpendicular. Now keep going until you come to a highway that

bisects it at a 45-degree angle. [*Crosses his arms.*] Solve for *x*.

[*Shot of Chris lying on the ground next to the attendant in fetal position, sucking his thumb. His map lies abandoned near him.*]

In fact, *Family Guy* does not aim to hurt, and its creators take certain measures to keep it from hitting too hard. In an interview on *Access Hollywood*, Seth MacFarlane plainly states that there are certain jokes too upsetting to certain groups to go on the air. Similarly, to ensure that the easily misunderstood show doesn't fall into the hands of those too young to understand it, Fox will not license *Family Guy* rights to any products intended for children under the age of fourteen (Elliott).

> Uses transitions to connect the parts (Chapter 8)

However, this is not to say that MacFarlane's mission is corrective or noble. It is worth remembering that he wants only to amuse, a goal for which he was criticized by several of his professors at the Rhode Island School of Design (Weinraub). For this reason, his humor can be dangerous. On the one hand, I don't agree with George Will's reductive and generalized statement in his article "Reality Television: Oxymoron" that "entertainment seeking a mass audience is ratcheting up the violence, sexuality, and degradation, becoming increasingly coarse and trying to be . . . shocking in an unshockable society." I believe *Family Guy*

> Agrees and disagrees; makes concessions while standing her ground (Chapters 4 and 6)

has its intelligent points, and some of its seemingly "coarse" scenes often have hidden merit. I must concede, though, that a few of the show's scenes seem to be doing just what Will claims; sometimes the creators do seem to cross—or, perhaps, eagerly race past—the line of indecency. In one such crude scene, an elderly dog slowly races a paraplegic and Peter, who has just been hit by a car, to get to a severed finger belonging to Peter himself ("Whistle While Your Wife Works"). Nor do I find it particularly funny when Stewie physically abuses Brian in a bloody fight over gambling money ("Patriot Games").

Thus, while *Family Guy* can provide a sort of relief by breaking down taboos, we must still wonder whether or not these taboos exist for a reason. An excess of offensive jokes, especially those that are often misconstrued, can seem to grant tacit permission to think offensively if it's done for comedy—and laughing at others' expense can be cruel, no matter how funny. Jokes all have their origins, and the funniest ones are those that hit home the hardest; if we listen to Freud, these are the ones that let our animalistic and aggressive impulses surface from the unconscious. The distinction between a shamelessly candid but insightful joke and a merely shameless joke is a slight but important one. While I love *Family Guy* as much as any fan, it's important not to lose sight of what's truly unfunny in real life—even as we appreciate what is hilarious in fiction.

> Concludes by showing who cares and why her argument matters (Chapter 7)

Works Cited

"Carole Burnett Sues over *Family Guy* Parody." *CBC*, 16 Mar. 2007, www.cbc.ca/news/arts/carol-burnett-sues-over -family-guy-parody-1.693570. Accessed 14 July 2008.

Dubner, Stephen J. "Why Is *Family Guy* Okay When Imus Wasn't?" *Freakonomics Blog*, 3 Dec. 2007, freakonomics.com. Accessed 14 July 2008.

Elliott, Stuart. "Crude? So What? These Characters Still Find Work in Ads." *The New York Times*, 19 June 2008, nyti.ms/2bZWSAs. Accessed 14 July 2008.

Facebook search for *Family Guy* under "Groups." www .facebook.com. Accessed 14 July 2008.

Freud, Sigmund. *Jokes and Their Relation to the Unconscious.* 1905. Translated by James Strachey, W. W. Norton, 1989.

Grossberg, Josh. "Carole Burnett Can't Stop Stewie." *E! News*, Entertainment Television, 5 June 2007, www.eonline.com. Accessed 14 July 2008.

"I Am Peter, Hear Me Roar." *Family Guy*, season 2, episode 8, 20th Century Fox, 28 Mar. 2000. *Hulu*, www.hulu.com/ watch/171050. Accessed 14 July 2008.

"Family Guy." *IMDb*, 1999–2016, www.imdb.com/title/ tt0182576. Accessed 14 July 2008.

MacFarlane, Seth. Interview. *Access Hollywood*, NBC Universal, 8 May 2007. *YouTube*, www.youtube.com/ watch?v=rKURWCicyQU. Accessed 14 July 2008.

Moloney, Ben Adam. "*Family Guy*." *BBC.com*, 30 Sept. 2004, www.bbc.com. Accessed 14 July 2008.

"Patriot Games." *Family Guy*, season 4, episode 20, 20th
　　Century Fox, 29 Jan. 2006. *Hulu*, www.hulu.com/
　　watch/171089. Accessed 22 July 2008.

"PVT." *Family Guy*, season 4, episode 14, 20th Century Fox,
　　6 Nov. 2005. *Hulu*, www.hulu.com/watch/171083.
　　Accessed 14 July 2008.

Rushkoff, Douglas. "Bart Simpson: Prince of Irreverence."
　　*Leaving Springfield: The Simpsons and the Possibility of
　　Oppositional Culture*, edited by John Alberti, Wayne
　　State UP, 2004, pp. 292–301.

Stevens, Dana. "Thinking Outside the Idiot Box." *Slate*,
　　25 Mar. 2005, www.slate.com/articles/news_and_
　　politics/surfergirl/2005/04/thinkingoutside_the_
　　idiot_box.html. Accessed 14 July 2008.

Weinraub, Bernard. "The Young Guy of 'Family Guy': A
　　30-Year-Old's Cartoon Hit Makes an Unexpected
　　Comeback." *The New York Times*, 7 July 2004,
　　nyti.ms/1IEBiUA. Accessed 14 July 2008.

"When You Wish Upon a Weinstein." *Family Guy*, season 3,
　　episode 22, 20th Century Fox, 9 Nov. 2003. *Hulu*,
　　www.hulu.com/watch/171136. Accessed 22 July 2008.

"Whistle While Your Wife Works." *Family Guy*, season 5,
　　episode 5, 20th Century Fox, 12 Nov. 2006. *Hulu*,
　　www.hulu.com/watch/171160. Accessed 22 July 2008.

Will, George F. "Reality Television: Oxymoron." *The
　　Washington Post*, 21 June 2001, p. A25.

TWELVE

"I TAKE YOUR POINT"

Entering Class Discussions

HAVE YOU EVER been in a class discussion that feels less like a genuine meeting of the minds than like a series of discrete, disconnected monologues? You make a comment, say, that seems provocative to you, but the classmate who speaks after you makes no reference to what you said, instead going off in an entirely different direction. Then, the classmate who speaks next makes no reference either to you or to anyone else, making it seem as if everyone in the conversation is more interested in their own ideas than in actually conversing with anyone else.

We like to think that the principles this book advances can help improve class discussions, which increasingly include various forms of online communication. Particularly important for class discussion is the point that our own ideas become more cogent and powerful the more responsive we are to others, and the more we frame our claims not in isolation but as responses to what others before us have said. Ultimately, then, a good face-to-face classroom discussion (or online communication) doesn't just happen spontaneously. It requires the same sorts of disciplined moves and practices used in many writing situations, particularly that of identifying to what and to whom you are responding.

FRAME YOUR COMMENTS AS A RESPONSE
TO SOMETHING THAT HAS ALREADY BEEN SAID

The single most important thing you need to do when joining a class discussion is to link what you are about to say to something that has already been said.

> ▸ I really liked Aaron's point about <u>the two sides being closer than they seem</u>. I'd add that <u>both seem rather moderate</u>.

> ▸ I take your point, Nadia, that _____ . Still . . .

> ▸ Though Sheila and Ryan seem to be at odds about _____, they may actually not be all that far apart.

In framing your comments this way, it is usually best to name both the person and the idea you're responding to. If you name the person alone ("I agree with Aaron because _____"), it may not be clear to listeners what part of what Aaron said you are referring to. Conversely, if you only summarize what Aaron said without naming him, you'll probably leave your classmates wondering whose comments you're referring to.

But won't you sound stilted and deeply redundant in class if you try to restate the point your classmate just made? After all, in the case of the first template above, the entire class will have just heard Aaron's point about the two sides being closer than they seem. Why then would you need to restate it?

We agree that in oral situations, it does often sound artificial to restate what others just said precisely because they just said it. It would be awkward if, on being asked to pass the salt at lunch, one were to reply: "If I understand you correctly, you have asked me to pass the salt. Yes, I can, and here it is." But in oral discussions about complicated issues that are open to multiple interpretations, we usually do need to resummarize what others have said to make sure that everyone is on the same page. Since Aaron may have made several points when he spoke and may have been followed by other commentators, the class will probably need you to summarize which point of his you are referring to. And even if Aaron made only one point, restating that point is helpful, not only to remind the group what his point was (since some may have missed or forgotten it) but also to make sure that he, you, and others have interpreted his point in the same way.

TO CHANGE THE SUBJECT,
INDICATE EXPLICITLY THAT YOU ARE DOING SO

It is fine to try to change the conversation's direction. There's just one catch: you need to make clear to listeners that this is what you are doing. For example:

▸ So far we have been talking about <u>the characters in the film</u>. But isn't the real issue here <u>the cinematography</u>?

▸ I'd like to change the subject to one that hasn't yet been addressed.

You can try to change the subject without indicating that you are doing so. But you risk that your comment will come across as irrelevant rather than as a thoughtful contribution that moves the conversation forward.

BE EVEN MORE EXPLICIT
THAN YOU WOULD BE IN WRITING

Because listeners in an oral discussion can't go back and reread what you just said, they are more easily overloaded than are readers of a print text. For this reason, in a class discussion you will do well to take some extra steps to help listeners follow your train of thought. (1) When you make a comment, limit yourself to one point only, though you can elaborate on this point, fleshing it out with examples and evidence. If you feel you must make two points, either unite them under one larger umbrella point, or make one point first and save the other for later. Trying to bundle two or more claims into one comment can result in neither getting the attention it deserves. (2) Use metacommentary to highlight your key point so that listeners can readily grasp it.

▶ In other words, what I'm trying to get at here is _____.

▶ My point is this: _____.

▶ My point, though, is not _____, but _____.

▶ This distinction is important because _____.

THIRTEEN

DON'T MAKE THEM SCROLL UP

Entering Online Conversations

THE INTERNET HAS TRANSFORMED COMMUNICATION in more ways than we can count. With just a few taps on a keyboard, we can be connected with what others have said not only throughout history, but right now, in the most remote places. Almost instantaneously, communities can be created that are powerful enough to change the world. In addition, virtually the moment we voice an opinion online, we can get responses from supporters and critics alike, while any links we provide to sources can connect readers to voices they might otherwise never have known about, and to conversations they might never have been able to join.

Because of this connectivity, the internet lends itself perfectly to the type of conversational writing at the core of this book. Just the other day, we were on a discussion board in which one of the participants wrote to another, let's call him X, in a form that could have provided a template for this textbook: "Fascinating point about _____, X. I'd never thought of it that way before. I'd always thought that _____, but if you're right, then that would explain why _____."

IDENTIFY WHAT YOU'RE RESPONDING TO

Unfortunately, not all online writers make clear who or what prompted them to write. As a result, too many online exchanges end up being not true conversations but a series of statements without clear relationships to one another. All too often, it's hard to tell if the writer is building on what someone else has said, challenging it, or trying to change the discussion topic altogether. So although the digital world may connect us far more rapidly and with far more people than ever, it doesn't always encourage a genuine meeting of minds.

We've seen this type of confusion in the writing our own students submit to online discussions. Even students who use the "they say / I say" framework routinely and effectively in the essays they write often neglect to make those same moves online. While our students engage enthusiastically in online discussions, their posts are often all "I say" with little or no "they say." As a result, they end up talking past rather than to one another.

What is happening here, we suspect, is that the easy accessibility made possible by the internet makes slowing down and summarizing or even identifying what others say seem unnecessary. Why repeat the views you are responding to, writers seem to assume, when readers can easily find them by simply scrolling up or clicking on a link?

The problem with this way of thinking is that readers won't always take the time to track down the comments you're responding to, assuming they can figure out what those comments are to begin with. And even when readers do make the effort to find the comments you're responding to, they may not be sure what aspect or part of those comments you're referring to, or how you interpret them. Ultimately, when you fail to identify your "they say," you leave readers guessing, like someone listening to one side of a phone conversation trying to piece together what's being said at the other end.

It is true, of course, that there are some situations online where summarizing what you're responding to would indeed be redundant. When, for instance, you're replying to a friend's text asking, "Meet in front of the theater at 7?" a mere "OK" suffices, whereas a more elaborate response—"With regard to your suggestion that we meet in front of the theater at 7, my answer is yes"—would be not only redundant but downright bizarre. But in more complex academic conversations where the ideas are challenging, many people are involved, and there is therefore a greater chance of misunderstanding, you do need to clarify whom or what you're responding to.

To see how hard it can be to make sense of a post that fails to identify the "they say" it is responding to, consider the following example from an online class discussion devoted to Nicholas Carr's article "Is Google Making Us Stupid?"

> Blogs and social media allow us to reach many people all at
> once. The internet makes us more efficient.

When we first read this post, we could see that this writer was
making a claim about the efficiency of the internet, but we
weren't sure what the claim had to do with Carr or with any of
the other comments in the discussion. After all, the writer never
names Carr or anyone else in the conversation. Nor does she
use templates such as "Like Carr, I believe _____" or "What
X overlooks is _____" to indicate whether she's agreeing or
disagreeing with Carr or with one of her classmates. Indeed, we
couldn't tell if the writer had even read Carr or any of the other
posts, or if she was just expressing her own views on the topic.

We suspect, however, that in arguing that the internet is
making us more efficient, this writer was probably trying to
refute Carr's argument that the internet is, as Carr puts it in his
title, "making us stupid." Then again, she could also have been
criticizing someone who agreed with Carr—or, conversely, siding with someone else who disagreed with Carr.

It would have been better if she had used the "they say / I
say" framework taught in this book, opening not with her own
"I say," as she did, but with the "they say" that's motivated her
to respond, perhaps using one of the following templates:

▸ **X argues that _____ .**

▸ **Like X, Y would have us believe that _____ .**

▸ **In challenging X's argument that _____ , Y asserts
  that _____ .**

It would also have helped if, in her "I say," she had identified the "they say" she is addressing, using a template like one of these:

▶ **But what X overlooks is that _____ .**

▶ **What both X and Y fail to see is that _____ .**

▶ **Z's point is well taken. Like him, I contend that _____ is not, as X insists, _____ but _____ .**

Here's one way this writer might have responded:

> Carr argues that Google is undermining our ability to think and read deeply. But far from making people "stupid," as Carr puts it in his title, the internet, in my view, is making people more efficient. What Carr ignores is how blogs and social media allow us to reach many people at once.

This version makes clear that the writer is not just making a claim out of the blue, but that she had a reason for making her claim: to take a position in a conversation or debate.

TECHNOLOGY WON'T DO ALL THE WORK

But still, you might wonder, doesn't the internet enable writers to connect so directly with others that summarizing their claims is unnecessary? Granted, the internet does provide several unique ways of referring to what others are saying, like linking and embedding, that help us connect to what others are saying. But as the following examples show, these techniques don't mean that technology will do all the work for you.

LINKING TO WHAT "THEY SAY"

One way the internet makes it especially easy to connect directly with others is by allowing us to insert a link to what others have said into our own text. Anything with a URL can be linked to—blog posts, magazine articles, *Facebook* posts, and so forth. Readers can then click on the words to which you've attached the link and be taken directly to that page, as we can see in the following comment in another online class discussion about how the internet affects our brains.

> In his essay "Is Google Making Us Stupid?" Nicholas Carr argues that the kind of skimming we do when we read online destroys deep reading and thinking. But I would argue the opposite: that all the complex information we're exposed to online actually makes us read and think more deeply.

By including a link to Carr's essay, this writer gives her readers direct access to Carr's arguments, allowing them to assess how well she has summarized and responded to what he wrote. But the reason the writer's post succeeds is that she introduces the link to Carr's essay, summarizes what she takes Carr to be saying, and gives her response to it.

Here are a few templates for framing a link:

▸ **As X mentions in this article, " _____ ."**

▸ **In making this comment, X warns that _____ .**

▸ **Economists often assume _____ ; however, new research by X suggests _____ .**

JUXTAPOSING YOUR "THEY SAY"
WITH YOUR "I SAY"

Another way that online forums enhance our ability to connect with others is by allowing readers to respond—not only to the original article or post but also to one another through what we might call juxtaposition. On many online forums, when you reply to someone else's comment, your response appears below the original comment and indented slightly, so that it is visually clear whom you're responding to. This means that, in many cases, your "they say" and "I say" are presented almost as a single conversational unit, as the following example from the online discussion of Carr's article illustrates:

> Lee, 4/12/17, 3:02 PM
>
> Carr argues that the internet has harmed us by making it hard for us to read without breaks to look at other things. That might be true, but overall I think it has improved our lives by giving us access to so many different viewpoints.

> Cody, 4/12/17, 5:15 PM
>
> Like Lee, I think the internet has improved our lives more than it's hurt them. I would add that it's enabled us to form and participate in political communities online that make people way more politically engaged.

Twitter also allows for this type of close proximity, by enabling you to embed someone else's tweet inside your own. For instance, consider the following tweet:

Jade T. Moore @JadeTMoore

@willwst I agree—access to books is a social justice issue.

> **William West** @willwst
>
> Every child has the right to access to a school library.

Cody's response in the discussion board and Jade's on *Twitter* are effective not only because the platforms connect Cody and Jade to their "they say" but also because they take the time to make those connections clear. Cody connects his comment to his "they say" by including the words "Like Lee" and restating Lee's view, while Jade does so by including West's *Twitter* handle, @willwst, and the words "I agree." Sure, the technology does some of the work, by making the comments being answered directly available for readers to see—no scrolling or searching involved. But it can't do it all. Imagine if Cody, for instance, had merely written, "We're able to form and participate in political communities online that make people way more politically engaged." Or if Jade hadn't included an "I agree" with her comment. As readers, we'd have been left scratching our heads, unable to tell what Cody's claim had to do with Lee's claim, or what Jade's claim had to do with William's, despite how close together these claims are on the screen.

Digital communication, then, does shrink the world, as is often said, allowing us to connect with others in ways we couldn't before. But technology doesn't relieve writers of the need to use the "they say / I say" framework. A central premise of this book is that this framework is a rhetorical move that transcends the differences between all types of writing. Whether you're writing online or off, if you want others to listen to what you say, you'd better pay attention to what they think, and start with what they say. However limited your space, whatever your format, and whatever the technology, you can always find a way to identify and summarize your "they say."

Exercises

1. Look back on some of your old posts on a social media site, a class discussion board, or some other website. How well did you let other readers know whom and what you were responding to and what your own position was? What kinds of moves did you make? Does that site have any conventions or special features that you used? Are there any features not available on that site that might have helped you connect your comment to other people's comments? Having read this chapter, try revising one of your posts to reflect the advice covered here.

2. Choose an online forum (*Facebook*, theysayiblog.com, etc.) and describe how you might apply the advice given here to that site. Are there any features or norms specific to that forum (e.g., embedding, linking, etc.) that would influence how you formulate your "they say"? Go to that site and evaluate how well people use these specific features to communicate their "they say." Is it easy to tell whom

and what people are responding to? Why or why not? Can you make your own contribution to the forum using the "they say / I say" format?

3. As a test case for thinking about the questions raised in this chapter, go to the blog that accompanies this book, theysayiblog.com. Examine some of the exchanges that appear there and evaluate the quality of the responses. For example, how well do the participants in these exchanges summarize one another's claims before making their own responses? How would you characterize any discussion? How well do people listen to each other? How do these online discussions compare with the face-to-face discussions you have in class? What advantages does each offer? Go to other blogs on topics that interest you and ask these same questions.

FOURTEEN

WHAT'S MOTIVATING THIS WRITER?

Reading for the Conversation

"WHAT IS THE AUTHOR'S ARGUMENT? What is he or she trying to say?" For many years, these were the first questions we would ask our classes in a discussion of an assigned reading. The discussion that resulted was often halting, as our students struggled to get a handle on the argument, but eventually, after some awkward silences, the class would come up with something we could all agree was an accurate summary of the author's main thesis. Even after we'd gotten over that hurdle, however, the discussion would often still seem forced, and would limp along as we all struggled with the question that naturally arose next: now that we had determined what the author was saying, what did we ourselves have to say?

For a long time we didn't worry much about these halting discussions, justifying them to ourselves as the predictable result of assigning difficult, challenging readings. Several years ago, however, as we started writing this book and began thinking about writing as the art of entering conversations, we latched on to the idea of leading with some different questions: "What other argument(s) is the writer responding to?" "Is the writer disagreeing or agreeing with something, and if so, what?" "What is motivating the writer's argument?" "Are there other ideas that you have encountered in this class or elsewhere that might be pertinent?" The results were often striking. The discussions that followed tended to be far livelier and to draw in a greater number of students. We were still asking students to look for the main argument, but we were now asking them to see that argument as a response to some other argument that provoked it, gave it a reason for being, and helped all of us see why we should care about it.

What had happened, we realized, was that by changing the opening question, we changed the way our students approached reading, and perhaps the way they thought about academic work in general. Instead of thinking of the argument of a text as an isolated entity, they now thought of that argument as one that responded to and provoked other arguments. Since they were now dealing not with *one* argument but at least *two* (the author's argument and the one[s] he or she was responding to), they now had alternative ways of seeing the topic at hand. This meant that, instead of just trying to understand the view presented by the author, they were more able to question that view intelligently and engage in the type of discussion and debate that is the hallmark of a college education. In our discussions, animated debates often arose between students who found the author's argument convincing and others who were more convinced by the view it was challenging. In the best of these debates, the binary positions would be questioned by other students, who suggested each was too simple, that both might be right or that a third alternative was possible. Still other students might object that the discussion thus far had missed the author's real point and suggest that we all go back to the text and pay closer attention to what it actually said.

We eventually realized that the move from reading for the author's argument in isolation to reading for how the author's argument is in conversation with the arguments of others helps readers become active, critical readers rather than passive recipients of knowledge. On some level, reading for the conversation is more rigorous and demanding than reading for what one author says. It asks that you determine not only what the author thinks, but how what the author thinks fits with what others think, and ultimately with what you yourself think. Yet on another level, reading this way is a lot simpler and more familiar than reading for the thesis alone, since it returns writing to the familiar, everyday act of communicating with other people about real issues.

DECIPHERING THE CONVERSATION

We suggest, then, that when assigned a reading, you imagine the author not as sitting alone in an empty room hunched over a desk or staring at a screen, but as sitting in a crowded coffee shop talking to others who are making claims that he or she is engaging with. In other words, imagine the author as participating in an ongoing, multisided conversation in which everyone is trying to persuade others to agree or at least to take his or her position seriously.

The trick in reading for the conversation is to figure out *what views the author is responding to* and *what the author's own argument is*—or, to put it in the terms used in this book, to determine the "they say" and how the author responds to it. One of the challenges in reading for the "they say" and

"I say" can be figuring out which is which, since it may not be obvious when writers are summarizing others and when they are speaking for themselves. Readers need to be alert for any changes in voice that a writer might make, since instead of using explicit road-mapping phrases like "although many believe," authors may simply summarize the view that they want to engage with and indicate only subtly that it is not their own.

Consider again the opening to the selection by David Zinczenko on page 245.

> If ever there were a newspaper headline custom-made for Jay Leno's monologue, this was it. Kids taking on McDonald's this week, suing the company for making them fat. Isn't that like middle-aged men suing Porsche for making them get speeding tickets? Whatever happened to personal responsibility?
>
> I tend to sympathize with these portly fast-food patrons, though. Maybe that's because I used to be one of them.
>
> DAVID ZINCZENKO, "Don't Blame the Eater"

Whenever we teach this passage, some students inevitably assume that Zinczenko must be espousing the view expressed in his first paragraph: that suing McDonald's is ridiculous. When their reading is challenged by their classmates, these students point to the page and reply, "Look. It's right here on the page. This is what Zinczenko wrote. These are his exact words." The assumption these students are making is that if something appears on the page, the author must endorse it. In fact, however, we ventriloquize views that we don't believe in, and may in fact passionately disagree with, all the time. The central clues that Zinczenko disagrees with the view expressed in his opening paragraph come in the second

See Chapter 6 for more discussion of naysayers.

paragraph, when he finally offers a first-person declaration and uses a contrastive transition, "though," thereby resolving any questions about where he stands.

WHEN THE "THEY SAY" IS UNSTATED

Another challenge can be identifying the "they say" when it is not explicitly identified. Whereas Zinczenko offers an up-front summary of the view he is responding to, other writers assume that their readers are so familiar with these views that they need not name or summarize them. In such cases, you the reader have to reconstruct the unstated "they say" that is motivating the text through a process of inference.

See, for instance, if you can reconstruct the position that Tamara Draut is challenging in the opening paragraph of her essay "The Growing College Gap."

"The first in her family to graduate from college." How many times have we heard that phrase, or one like it, used to describe a successful American with a modest background? In today's United States, a four-year degree has become the all-but-official ticket to middle-class security. But if your parents don't have much money or higher education in their own right, the road to college—and beyond—looks increasingly treacherous. Despite a sharp increase in the proportion of high school graduates going on to some form of postsecondary education, socio-economic status continues to exert a powerful influence on college admission and completion; in fact, gaps in enrollment by class and race, after declining in the 1960s and 1970s, are once again as wide as they were thirty years ago, and getting wider, even as college has become far more crucial to lifetime fortunes.

TAMARA DRAUT, "The Growing College Gap"

You might think that the "they say" here is embedded in the third sentence: they say (or we all think) that a four-year degree is "the all-but-official ticket to middle-class security," and you might assume that Draut will go on to disagree.

If you read the passage this way, however, you would be mistaken. Draut is not questioning whether a college degree has become the "ticket to middle-class security," but whether most Americans can obtain that ticket, whether college is within the financial reach of most American families. You may have been thrown off by the "but" following the statement that college has become a prerequisite for middle-class security. However, unlike the "though" in Zinczenko's opening, this "but" does not signal that Draut will be disagreeing with the view she has just summarized, a view that in fact she takes as a given. What Draut disagrees with is that this ticket to middle-class security is still readily available to the middle and working classes.

Were one to imagine Draut in a room talking with others with strong views on this topic, one would need to picture her challenging not those who think college is a ticket to financial security (something she agrees with and takes for granted), but those who think the doors of college are open to anyone willing to put forth the effort to walk through them. The view that Draut is challenging, then, is not summarized in her opening. Instead, she assumes that readers are already so familiar with this view that it need not be stated.

Draut's example suggests that in texts where the central "they say" is not immediately identified, you have to construct it yourself based on the clues the text provides. You have to start by locating the writer's thesis and then imagine some of the arguments that might be made against it. What would it look like to disagree with this view? In Draut's case, it is relatively easy to construct a counterargument: it is the familiar faith in the

American Dream of equal opportunity when it comes to access to college. Figuring out the counterargument not only reveals what motivated Draut as a writer but helps you respond to her essay as an active, critical reader. Constructing this counter-argument can also help you recognize how Draut challenges your own views, questioning opinions that you previously took for granted.

WHEN THE "THEY SAY" IS ABOUT SOMETHING "NOBODY HAS TALKED ABOUT"

Another challenge in reading for the conversation is that writ-ers sometimes build their arguments by responding to a *lack* of discussion. These writers build their case not by playing off views that can be identified (like faith in the American Dream or the idea that we are responsible for our body weight), but by pointing to something others have overlooked. As the writing theorists John M. Swales and Christine B. Feak point out, one effective way to "create a research space" and "establish a niche" in the academic world is "by indicating a gap in . . . previous research." Much research in the sciences and humanities takes this "Nobody has noticed X" form.

In such cases, the writer may be responding to scientists, for example, who have overlooked an obscure plant that offers insights into global warming, or to literary critics who have been so busy focusing on the lead character in a play that they have overlooked something important about the minor characters.

READING PARTICULARLY CHALLENGING TEXTS

Sometimes it is difficult to figure out the views that writers are responding to not because these writers do not identify those views but because their language and the concepts they are dealing with are particularly challenging. Consider, for instance, the first two sentences of *Gender Trouble: Feminism and the Subversion of Identity*, a book by the feminist philosopher and literary theorist Judith Butler, thought by many to be a particularly difficult academic writer.

> Contemporary feminist debates over the meaning of gender lead time and again to a certain sense of trouble, as if the indeterminacy of gender might eventually culminate in the failure of feminism. Perhaps trouble need not carry such a negative valence.
>
> JUDITH BUTLER, *Gender Trouble:*
> *Feminism and the Subversion of Identity*

There are many reasons readers may stumble over this relatively short passage, not the least of which is that Butler does not explicitly indicate where her own view begins and the view she is responding to ends. Unlike Zinczenko, Butler does not use the first-person "I" or a phrase such as "in my own view" to show that the position in the second sentence is her own. Nor does Butler offer a clear transition such as "but" or "however" at the start of the second sentence to indicate, as Zinczenko does with "though," that in the second sentence she is questioning the argument she has summarized in the first. And finally, like many academic writers, Butler uses abstract, challenging words that many readers may need to look up, like "contemporary" (occurring in the present), "indeterminacy" (the quality of being impossible to define or pin down), "culminate" (finally result in), and "negative valence" (a term borrowed from chemistry, roughly denoting "negative significance" or "meaning"). For all these reasons, we can imagine many readers feeling intimidated before they reach the third sentence of Butler's book.

But readers who break down this passage into its essential parts will find that it is actually a lucid piece of writing that conforms to the classic "they say / I say" pattern. Though it can be difficult to spot the clashing arguments in the two sentences, close analysis reveals that the first sentence offers a way of looking at a certain type of "trouble" in the realm of feminist politics that is being challenged in the second.

For more on translating, see Chapter 9.
To understand difficult passages of this kind, you need to translate them into your own words—to build a bridge, in effect, between the passage's unfamiliar terms and ones more familiar to you. Building such a bridge should help you connect what you already know to what the author is saying—and will then help you move from reading to writing, providing you with some of the language you will need to summarize the text. One major challenge in translating the author's words into your own, however, is to stay true to what the author is actually saying, avoiding what we call "the closest cliché syndrome," in which one mistakes a commonplace idea for an author's more complex one (mistaking Butler's critique of the concept of "woman," for instance, for the common idea that women must have equal rights). The work of complex writers like Butler, who frequently challenge conventional thinking, cannot always be collapsed into the types of ideas most of us are already familiar with. Therefore, when you translate, do not try to fit the ideas of such writers into your preexisting beliefs, but instead allow your own views to be challenged. In building a bridge to the writers you read, it is often necessary to meet those writers more than halfway.

For more on the closest cliché syndrome, see Chapter 2.

So what, then, does Butler's opening say? Translating Butler's words into terms that are easier to understand, we can see that the first sentence says that for many feminists today, "the indeterminacy of gender"—the inability to define the essence of sexual identity—spells the end of feminism; that for many feminists the inability to define "gender," presumably the building block of the feminist movement, means serious "trouble" for feminist politics. In contrast, the second sentence suggests that this same "trouble" need not be thought of in such "negative" terms, that the inability to define femininity, or "gender trouble" as Butler calls it in her book's title, may not be such a bad thing—and, as she goes on to argue in the pages that follow, may even be something that feminist activists can profit from. In other words, Butler suggests, highlighting uncertainties about masculinity and femininity can be a powerful feminist tool.

Pulling all these inferences together, then, the opening sentences can be translated as follows: "While many contemporary feminists believe that uncertainty about what it means to be a woman will undermine feminist politics, I, Judith Butler, believe that this uncertainty can actually help strengthen feminist politics." Translating Butler's point into our own book's basic move: "They say that if we cannot define 'woman,' feminism is in big trouble. But I say that this type of trouble is precisely what feminism needs." Despite its difficulty, then, we hope you agree that this initially intimidating passage does make sense if you stay with it.

We hope it is clear that critical reading is a two-way street. It is just as much about being open to the way that writers can challenge you, maybe even transform you, as it is about questioning those writers. And if you translate a writer's argument into your own words as you read, you should allow the text to take you outside the ideas that you already hold and to introduce you to new terms and concepts. Even if you end up disagreeing with an author, you first have to show that you have really listened to what he or she is saying, have fully grasped his or her arguments, and can accurately summarize those arguments. Without such deep, attentive listening, any critique you make will be superficial and decidedly *uncritical*. It will be a critique that says more about you than about the writer or idea you're supposedly responding to.

In this chapter we have tried to show that reading for the conversation means looking not just for the thesis of a text in isolation but for the view or views that motivate that thesis— the "they say." We have also tried to show that reading for the conversation means being alert for the different strategies writers use to engage the view(s) that are motivating them, since not all writers engage other perspectives in the same way. Some writers explicitly identify and summarize a view they are responding to at the outset of their text and then return to it frequently as their text unfolds. Some refer only obliquely to a view that is motivating them, assuming that readers will be able to reconstruct that view on their own. Other writers may not explicitly distinguish their own view from the views they are questioning in ways that all of us find clear, leaving some readers to wonder whether a given view is the writer's own or one that he or she is challenging. And some writers push off against the "they say" that is motivating them in a challenging academic language that requires readers to translate what they are saying into more accessible, everyday terms. In sum, then, though most persuasive writers do follow a conversational "they say / I say" pattern, they do so in a great variety of ways. What this means for readers is that they need to be armed with various strategies for detecting the conversations in what they read, even when those conversations are not self-evident.

FIFTEEN

"ON CLOSER EXAMINATION"

Entering Conversations about Literature

—⊡—

In Chinua Achebe's novel *Things Fall Apart*, Okonkwo, the main character, is a tragic hero.

So what? Who cares?

Why does this typical way of opening an essay on a literary work leave readers wondering, "Why are you telling me this?" Because, in our view, such statements leave it unclear who would say otherwise. Would anyone deny that the main character of Achebe's novel is a tragic hero? Is there some other view of the subject that this writer is responding to? Since no such alternative interpretation is indicated, the reader thinks, "OK, Okonkwo is a tragic hero—as opposed to what?"

Now compare this opening with another possible one:

> Several members of our class have argued that Okonkwo, the main character of *Things Fall Apart*, is a hateful villain. My own view, however, is that, while it is true that Okonkwo commits villainous acts, he is ultimately a tragic hero—a flawed but ultimately sympathetic figure.

We hope you agree that the second version, which responds to what someone else says about Okonkwo, makes for more engaging writing than the first. Since the first version fails to present itself as a response to any alternative view of its subject, it comes at readers out of the blue, leaving them wondering why it needs to be said at all.

As we stress in this book, it is the views of others and our desire to respond to these views that gives our writing its underlying motivation and helps readers see why what we say matters, why others should care, and why we need to say it in the first place. In this chapter we suggest that this same principle applies to writing about literature. Literary critics, after all, don't make assertions about literary works out of the blue. Rather, they contribute to discussions and debates about the meaning and significance of literary works, some of which may continue for years and even centuries.

Indeed, this commitment to discussion animates most literature courses, in which students discuss and debate assigned works in class before writing papers about them. The premise is that engaging with classmates and teachers enables us to make discoveries about the work that we might not arrive at in simply reading the work alone.

We suggest that you think of writing about literature as a natural extension of such in-class discussions, listening carefully to others and using what they say to set up and motivate what you have to say.

START WITH WHAT OTHERS ARE SAYING

But in writing about literature, where do views to respond to— "they say"s—come from? Many sources. Published literary criticism is perhaps the most obvious:

▸ Critic X complains that Author Y's story is compromised by his _____ perspective. While there's some truth to this critique, I argue that Critic X overlooks _____.

▸ According to Critic A, novel X suggests _____. I agree, but would add that _____.

But the view that you respond to in writing about literature can be far closer to home than published literary criticism. As our opening example illustrates, it can be something said about the literary work by a classmate or teacher:

▸ Several members of our class have suggested that the final message of play X is _____. I agree up to a point, but I still think that _____.

Another tactic is to start with something you yourself thought about the work that on second thought you now want to revise:

▸ On first reading play Z, I thought it was an uncritical celebration of _____. After rereading the play and discussing it in class, however, I see that it is more critical of _____ than I originally thought.

You can even respond to something that hasn't actually been said about the work, but might hypothetically be said:

▸ It might be said that poem Y is chiefly about _____. But the problem with this reading, in my view, is _____.

▸ Though religious readers might be tempted to analyze poem X as a parable about _____, a closer examination suggests that the poem is in fact _____.

Sometimes, the "they say" that you respond to in writing about a literary work can be found in the work itself, as distinct from what some critic or other reader has said *about* the work. Much great literary criticism responds directly to the literary work, summarizing some aspect of the work's form or content and then assessing it, in much the same way you can do in response to a persuasive essay:

▸ Ultimately, as I read it, *The Scarlet Letter* seems to say _____. I have trouble accepting this proposition, however, on the grounds that _____.

One of the more powerful ways of responding to a literary work is to address any contradictions or inconsistencies:

▸ At the beginning of the poem, we encounter the generalization, seemingly introducing the poem's message, that "_____." But this statement is then contradicted by the suggestion made later in the poem that "_____." This opens up a significant inconsistency in the text: is it suggesting _____ or, on the contrary, _____?

▸ At several places in novel X, Author Y leads us to understand that the story's central point is that _____. Yet elsewhere the text suggests _____, indicating that Y may be ambivalent on this issue.

If you review the above templates, you'll notice that each does what a good discussion, lecture, or essay does: it makes an argument about some aspect of a work that can be interpreted in various ways. Instead of just making a claim about the work in isolation—character X is a tragic hero; sonnet Y is about the loss of a loved one—these templates put one claim as a response to another, making clear what motivated the argument to begin with. They thus act as conversation starters that can invite or even provoke other readers to respond with their own interpretations and judgments.

FIGURING OUT
WHAT A LITERARY WORK "MEANS"

In order to enter conversations and debates about literature, you need to meet the time-honored challenge of being able to read and make sense of literary works, understanding and analyzing what the text says. On the one hand, like the types of persuasive essays we focus on throughout this book, literary works make arguments their authors want to convey, things they are for and against, ideas they want to endorse or condemn. On the other hand, discovering "the argument" of a literary work—what it's "saying"—can be a special challenge because, unlike persuasive essays, literary works usually do not spell out their arguments explicitly. Though poets, novelists, and playwrights may have the same level of conviction as persuasive writers, rarely do they step out from behind the pages of their texts and say, "Okay, folks, this is what it all means. What I'm trying to say in a nutshell is _____ ." That is, since literary texts do not include an explicit thesis statement identifying their main point, it's left up to us as readers to figure it out.

Because literary works tend to avoid such explicitness, their meanings often need to be teased out from the clues they provide: from the dialogue between characters, the plot, the imagery and symbolism, and the kind of language the author uses. In fact, it is this absence of overt argument that makes literature so endlessly debatable—and explains why scholars and critics argue so much about what literary works mean in ways similar to the classroom discussions that you have likely participated in as a student.

The Elusive Literary Author

Indeed, not even the use of the first person "I" in a literary work is an indication that you have located the author's own position or stance, as it usually is in an essay. When David Zinczenko, for example, in his essay "Don't Blame the Eater" (pp. 245–47) writes, "I tend to sympathize with these portly fast-food patrons" who file lawsuits against the fast food industry, we can be confident that the "I" is Zinczenko himself, and that the position he expresses is his own and informs everything else in his essay. But we cannot assume that the "I" who addresses us in a work of fiction or poetry is necessarily the author, for he or she is a fictional character—and one who may be unreliable and untrustworthy.

Take, for example, the first sentence of Edgar Allan Poe's short story "The Cask of Amontillado":

> The thousand injuries of Fortunato I had borne as I best could, but when he ventured upon insult I vowed revenge.

As soon becomes clear in the story, the "I" who speaks as the narrator here is not Poe himself but an insanely vengeful murderer whose words must be seen through to get at the point of Poe's story.

Instead of a readily identifiable position, literary works often present the perspectives of a number of different characters and leave it to readers to determine which if any speaks for the author. Thus when we encounter the seemingly eloquent lines in Hamlet "To thine own self be true, . . . / And canst thou not be false to any man," we can't assume, as we might if we encountered this statement in an essay, that it represents the author's own view. For these words are uttered by Polonius, a character whom Shakespeare presents as a tedious, cliché-spouting bore—not someone he leads us to trust. After all, part of Hamlet's problem is that it's not clear to him what being "true" to his own self would require him to do.

This elusive quality of literary texts helps explain why some of our students complain about the challenge of finding the "hidden meaning," as they sometimes call it, let alone summarizing that meaning in the way assignments often require. Sure, some students say, they enjoy reading literature for pleasure. But analyzing literature in school for its "meaning" or "symbolism"—that's another matter. Some even say that the requirement that they hunt for meanings and symbols robs literature of its fun.

In fact, as most students come to recognize, analyzing meanings, symbols, and other elements should enhance rather than stifle the pleasure we get from reading literature. But it can indeed be hard to figure out what literary works mean. How do we determine the point of a story or poem when the author, unlike an essayist like Zinczenko, does not tell us explicitly what he or she is trying to say? How do you go from a fictional event or poetic image (an insane man committing murder, two roads that diverge in the woods) or from a dialogue between fictional characters ("Frankly, my dear, I don't give a damn.") to what these events, images, or lines of dialogue mean?

Look for Conflict in the Work

There is no simple recipe for figuring out what a literary work means, but one tactic that seems to help our own students is to look for the conflict or debate in the literary work itself and then ask what the text is leading us to think about that conflict. Asking these questions—what is the conflict in the work and which side, if any, should we favor?—will help you think about and formulate a position on what the work means. And since such claims are often ones that literary scholars argue about, thinking about the conflict *in* a literary work will often lead you to discussions and debates *about* the work that you can then respond to in your writing. Because literary authors don't tell us explicitly what the text means, it's always going to be *arguable*—and your task in writing about a literary work is to argue for what *you* think it means. Here are two templates to help get you started responding to other interpretations:

▶ It might be argued that in the clash between characters X and Y in play Z, the author wants us to favor character Y, since she is presented as the play's heroine. I contend, however, that _____.

▶ Several critics seem to assume that poem X endorses the values of discipline and rationality represented by the image of _____ over those of play and emotion represented by the image of _____. I agree, but with the following caveat: that the poem ultimately sees both values as equally important and even suggests that ideally they should complement one another.

This tactic of looking for the conflicts in literary works is part of a long tradition of critical thought that sees conflict as central to literature. In ancient Greece, Aristotle argued that conflict between characters or forces underlies the plots of tragic dramas such as *Oedipus*. Indeed, the ancient Greek word *agon*, which means antagonism, conflict, or debate, leaves its traces in the term "protagonist," the hero or leading character of a narrative work who comes into conflict with other characters or with the fates. And Plato noted the pervasiveness of conflict in literature when he banished poets from his ideal community on the grounds that their works depict endless conflict and division.

This emphasis on the centrality of conflict in literature has been echoed by modern theorists like the New Critics of the 1940s and 50s, who focused on such tensions and paradoxes as good and evil or innocence and experience—and more recently by poststructuralists and political theorists who see literature, like society, as saturated by such polarities as male/female, gay/straight, white/black, and so on. Writers today continue to recognize conflict as the engine of good storytelling. As the Hollywood screenwriter Robert McKee puts it, "Nothing moves forward in a story except through conflict."

Building on this idea that conflict is central to literature, we suggest the following four questions to help you understand and formulate your own position on any literary work:

1. What is the central conflict?
2. Which side—if any—does the text seem to favor?
3. What's your evidence? How might others interpret the evidence differently?
4. What's your opinion of the text?

WHAT IS THE CENTRAL CONFLICT?

Conflicts tend to manifest themselves in different ways in different literary genres. In works that take a narrative or story form (novels, short stories, and plays), the central conflict will often be represented in an actual debate between characters. These debates between characters will often reflect larger questions and debates in the society or historical era in which they were written, over such issues as the responsibility of rulers, the consequences of capitalism and consumerism, or the struggle for gender equality. Sometimes these debates will be located within an individual character, appearing as a struggle in someone caught between conflicting or incompatible choices. Whatever form they may take, these debates can provide you with points of entry into the issues raised by the work, its historical context, and its author's vision of the world.

One narrative work that lends itself to such an approach is Flannery O'Connor's 1961 short story "Everything That Rises Must Converge," which is reprinted on pages 350–369. The story presents a running debate between a mother and her son Julian about the civil rights movement for racial equality that had erupted in the American South at the time the story was written, with Julian defending the outlook of this movement and his mother defending the South's traditional racial hierarchy. The story raises the debatable question of which character we should side with: Julian, his mother, both, or neither?

WHICH SIDE—IF ANY—DOES THE TEXT SEEM TO FAVOR?

When we teach this story, most of our students first assume the story sides with Julian's outlook, which to them as Northern, urban college students in the twenty-first century seems the obviously enlightened position. Who, after all, could fail to see that the mother's views are backward and racist? As our class discussions unfold, however, most students come to reject this view as a misreading, one based more on their own views than on what's in the text. Sooner or later, someone points out that at several points Julian is presented in highly critical ways—and that his apparently progressive sympathy for racial integration rests on arid intellectual abstractions and a hypocritical lack of self-knowledge, in contrast with his mother's heartfelt loyalty to her roots. Eventually another possible interpretation surfaces, that both characters suffer from a common malady: that they're living in a mental bubble that keeps them from being able to see themselves as they really are.

The writing assignment we often give builds on this class discussion by offering students the following template for thinking about which character, if any, the text leads them to favor:

▸ **Some might argue that when it comes to the conflict between Julian and his mother over _____, our sympathies should lie with _____. My own view is that _____.**

WHAT'S YOUR EVIDENCE?

In entering the types of discussions and debates modeled by the above template, how do you determine where your "sympathies should lie"? More generally, how do you arrive at and justify an interpretation of what a literary text says?

The answer lies in the *evidence* provided by the work: its images, dialogue, plot, historical references, tone, stylistic details, and so forth.

It is important to remember, however, that evidence is not set in stone. Students sometimes assume that there exists some fixed code that unlocks the meaning of literary works, symbols, images, and other evidence. A character dies? This must mean that he or she is being condemned. A stairway appears? A symbol for upward mobility. A garden? Must be something sexual.

But evidence itself is open to interpretation and thus to debate. The mother's death in O'Connor's story, for instance, *could* be seen as evidence that we are supposed to disapprove of her as someone whose racial views are regressive and on the way out. On the other hand, her death may instead be evidence that she is to be seen as a heroic martyr too good for this cruel, harsh world. What a character's death means, then, depends—on how he or she is treated in the work, positively or negatively, which in turn may be subject to debate.

As we've repeatedly emphasized in this book, others will often disagree with you and may even use the same evidence you do to support interpretations that are contrary to your own. Like other objects of study, literary works are like the famous ambiguous drawing that can be seen as either a duck or a rabbit, depending how one views it.

Since the same piece of evidence in a literary work will often support differing, even opposing interpretations, you need to argue for what you think the evidence shows—and to acknowledge that others may read that evidence differently.

In writing about literature, then, you need to show that the evidence you are citing supports your interpretation and to anticipate other alternative ones:

▸ Although some might read the metaphor of _____ in this poem as evidence that, for Author X, modern technology undermines community traditions and values, I see it as _____.

To present evidence in such a "they say / I say" way, you need to be alert for how others may read the work differently than you—and even use this very same evidence in support of an opposing interpretation:

▸ Some might claim that evidence X suggests _____, but I argue that, on the contrary, it suggests _____.

▸ I agree with my classmate _____ that the image of _____ in novel Y is evidence of childhood innocence that has been lost. Unlike _____, however, I think this loss of innocence is to be read not as a tragic event but as a necessary, even helpful, stage in human development.

Are Some Interpretations Simply Wrong?

No matter how flexible and open to debate evidence might be, not all interpretations we arrive at using that evidence are equally valid. And some interpretations are simply unsupported by that evidence. Let us illustrate.

As we noted earlier, some of our students first favored Julian over his mother. One student, let us call her Nancy, cited as evidence a passage early in the story in which Julian is compared to Saint Sebastian, a Christian martyr who is said to have exhibited exceptional faith under extreme suffering and persecution. As the mother stood preparing for Julian to take her to her weekly swimming class, Julian is described as standing "pinned to the door frame, waiting like Saint Sebastian for the arrows to begin piercing him."

Thinking this passage proves that Julian is the more sympathetic character, Nancy pointed to other evidence as well, including the following passage:

> [Julian] was free of prejudice and unafraid to face facts. Most miraculous of all, instead of being blinded by love for [his mother] as she was for him, he had cut himself emotionally free of her and could see her with complete objectivity. He was not dominated by his mother. (412)

Citing passages like this in her essay, Nancy concluded: "Julian represents the future of society, a nonracist and an educated thinker."

After rereading the story, however, and hearing other students' views, Nancy came to realize that the passages she had cited—comparing Julian to a saint, suggesting that he is racially progressive, and that he is "free of" his mother and "objective" about her—were all intended ironically. Julian congratulates *himself* for being saintlike, free of prejudice, and objective, but the story ultimately implies that he deludes himself.

How did the supporters of the ironic reading convince Nancy to revise her initial reading—to see it as wrong, unsupported by the evidence? First, they pointed to the glaring discrepancy between the situations and kinds of suffering endured by Julian and Saint Sebastian. Could anyone be serious, they asked, in comparing something as mundane as being forced to wait a few minutes to go to the YMCA to a martyr dying for his faith? No, they answered, and the jarring incongruity of the events being compared, they argued, suggests that Julian, far from saintlike, is presented in this passage as an impatient, ungrateful, undutiful son. In addition, students pointed out that the gap between Julian's self-image as a progressive man of "complete objectivity" and "facts," "free of [his mother]" and the blubbering young man crying "Mama, Mama!" with "guilt and sorrow" at the end of the story suggests that Julian's righteous, high-minded image of himself is not to be taken at face value.

At this point you may be wondering, how can we say that some interpretations of literature must be ruled out as *wrong*? Isn't the great thing about interpreting literary works—in contrast to scientific and historical texts—that there are no wrong answers? Are we saying that there is one "correct" way to read a literary work—the one way the work itself tells us we "should" read it?

No, we aren't saying that there is only one way to read a literary work. If we believed there were, we would not be offering a method of literary analysis based on multiple interpretations and debate. But yes, acknowledging that literary interpretations are open to debate is not to say that a work can mean anything we want it to mean, as if all interpretations are equally good. In our view, and that of most literature teachers, some interpretations are better than others—more persuasively reasoned and better grounded in the evidence of the text.

If we maintain that all interpretations are equally valid, we risk confusing the perspective of the work's author with our own, as did the students who confused their own views on the civil rights movement of the 1960s with Flannery O'Connor's. Such misreadings are reminiscent of what we call "the closest cliché syndrome," where what's summarized is not the view the author actually expresses but a familiar cliché—or, in O'Connor's case,

See p. 33 for more on the closest cliché syndrome.

a certain social belief—that the writer believes and mistakenly assumes the author must too. The view that there are no wrong answers in literary interpretation encourages a kind of solipsism that erases the difference between us and others and transforms everything we encounter into a version of ourselves.

As the literary theorist Robert Scholes puts it, reading, conceived "as a submission to the intentions of another is the first step" to understanding what a literary work is saying. For "if we do not postulate the existence of [an author] behind the verbal text," we will "simply project our own subjective modes of thought and desire upon the text." In other words, unless we do the best we can to get at what the author is saying, we will never truly recognize his or her ideas except as some version of our own. Scholes acknowledges that good reading often involves going beyond the author's intention, pointing out contradictions and ideological blind spots, but he argues that we must recognize the author's intention *before* we can try to see beyond it in these ways.

WHAT'S YOUR OPINION OF THE TEXT?

In accord with the principle that we must try to understand the text on its own terms before responding to it, we have thus far in this chapter focused on how to understand and unpack what literary texts say and do. Our approach to get at what they say involves looking for the central conflict in the work and then asking yourself how the author uses various types of evidence (characters, dialogue, imagery, events, plot, etc.) to guide you in thinking about that conflict. Ultimately, your job as a reader of literature is to be open to a work as its author presents it, or else your reading will fail to see what makes that work worth reading and thinking about.

But once you have reached a good understanding of the work, it is time to allow your own opinion to come into play. Offering your own interpretation of a work and opening that interpretation to response are crucial steps in any act of literary analysis, but they are not the end of the process. The final step involves offering your own insight into or critique of the work and its vision, assessing whether, as you see it, it is morally justified or questionable, unified or contradictory, historically regressive or progressive, and so forth. For example:

> Though she is one of the most respected Southern authors of the American literary canon, Flannery O'Connor continually denigrates the one character in her 1961 story who represents the civil rights movement, and in so doing disparages progressive ideas that I believe deserve a far more sympathetic hearing.

Offering a critique, however, doesn't necessarily mean finding fault:

> Some criticize O'Connor's story by suggesting that it has a politically regressive agenda. But I see the story as a laudable critique of politics as such. In my view, O'Connor's story rightly criticizes the polarization of political conflicts—North vs. South, liberal vs. conservative, and the like—and suggests that they need to come together: to "converge," as O'Connor's title implies, through religious love, understanding, and forgiveness.

We realize that the prospect of critiquing a literary work can be daunting. Indeed, simply stating what you think an author is saying can be intimidating, since it means going out on a limb, asserting something about highly respected figures—works that are often complex, contradictory, and connected to larger historical movements. Nevertheless, if you can master these challenges, you may find that figuring out what a literary work is saying, offering an opinion about it, and entering into conversation and debate with others about such questions is what makes literature matter. And if you do it well, what *you* say will invite its own response: your "I say" will become someone else's "they say," and the conversation will go on and on.

SIXTEEN

"THE DATA SUGGEST"

Writing in the Sciences

CHRISTOPHER GILLEN

———□———

CHARLES DARWIN DESCRIBED *On the Origin of Species* as "one long argument." In *Dialogue Concerning the Two Chief World Systems*, Galileo Galilei cast his argument for a sun-centered solar system as a series of conversations. As these historical examples show, scientific writing is fundamentally argumentative. Like all academic writers, scientists make and defend claims. They address disagreements and explore unanswered questions. They propose novel mechanisms and new theories. And they advance certain explanations and reject others. Though their vocabulary may be more technical and their emphasis more numerical, science writers use the same

———

CHRISTOPHER GILLEN is a professor of biology at Kenyon College and the faculty director of the Kenyon Institute in Biomedical and Scientific Writing. He teaches courses in animal physiology, biology of exercise, and introductory biology, all stressing the critical reading of primary research articles.

rhetorical moves as other academic writers. Consider the following example from a book about the laws of physics.

> The common refrain that is heard in elementary discussions of quantum mechanics is that a physical object is in some sense both a wave and a particle, with its wave nature apparent when you measure a wave property such as wavelength, and its particle nature apparent when you measure a particle property such as position. But this is, at best, misleading and, at worst, wrong.
>
> V. J. STENGER, *The Comprehensible Cosmos*

The "they say / I say" structure of this passage is unmistakable: they say that objects have properties of both waves and particles; I say they are wrong. This example is not a lonely argumentative passage cherry-picked from an otherwise non-argumentative text. Rather, Stenger's entire book makes the argument that is foreshadowed by its title, *The Comprehensible Cosmos*: that although some might see the universe as hopelessly complex, it is essentially understandable.

Here's another argumentative passage, this one from a research article about the role of lactic acid in muscle fatigue:

> In contrast to the often suggested role for acidosis as a cause of muscle fatigue, it is shown that in muscles where force was depressed by high $[K^+]_o$, acidification by lactic acid produced a pronounced recovery of force.
>
> O. B. NIELSEN, F. DE PAOLI, AND K. OVERGAARD,
> "Protective Effects of Lactic Acid on Force Production in
> Rat Skeletal Muscle," *The Journal of Physiology*

In other words: many scientists think that lactic acid causes muscle fatigue, but our evidence shows that it actually promotes recovery. Notice that the authors frame their claim with a version of the "they say / I say" formula: although previous work suggests _____, our data argue _____. This basic move and its many variations are widespread in scientific writing. The essential argumentative moves taught in this book transcend disciplines, and the sciences are no exception. The examples in this chapter were written by professional scientists, but they show moves that are appropriate in any writing that addresses scientific issues.

Despite the importance of argument in scientific writing, newcomers to the genre often see it solely as a means for communicating uncontroversial, objective facts. It's easy to see how this view arises. The objective tone of scientific writing can obscure its argumentative nature, and many textbooks reinforce a nonargumentative vision of science when they focus on accepted conclusions and ignore ongoing controversies. And because science writers base their arguments on empirical data, a good portion of many scientific texts *does* serve the purpose of delivering uncontested facts.

However, scientific writing often does more than just report facts. Data are crucial to scientific argumentation, but they are by no means the end of the story. Given important new data, scientists assess their quality, draw conclusions from them, and ponder their implications. They synthesize the new data with existing information, propose novel theories, and design the next experiments. In short, scientific progress depends on the insight and creativity that scientists bring to their data. The thrill of doing science, and writing about it, comes from the ongoing struggle to use data to better understand our world.

START WITH THE DATA

Data are the fundamental currency of scientific argument. Scientists develop hypotheses from existing data and then test those by comparing their predictions to new experimental data. Summarizing data is therefore a basic move in science writing. Because data can often be interpreted in different ways, describing the data opens the door to critical analysis, creating opportunities to critique previous interpretations and develop new ones.

Describing data requires more than simply reporting numbers and conclusions. Rather than jumping straight to the punch line—to what X concluded—it is important first to describe the hypotheses, methods, and results that led to the conclusion: "To test the hypothesis that _____ , X measured _____ and found that _____ . Therefore, X concluded _____ ." In the following sections, we explore the three key rhetorical moves for describing the data that underpin a scientific argument: presenting the prevailing theories, explaining methodologies, and summarizing findings.

Present the Prevailing Theories

Readers must understand the prevailing theories that a study responds to before they can fully appreciate the details. So before diving into specifics, place the work in context by describing the prevailing theories and hypotheses. In the following passage from a journal article about insect respiration, the authors discuss an explanation for discontinuous gas exchange (DGC), a phenomenon where insects periodically close valves on their breathing tubes.

See how a computer scientist describes a prevailing theory on p. 586.

> Lighton (1996, 1998; see also Lighton and Berrigan, 1995) noted the prevalence of DGC in fossorial insects, which inhabit microclimates where CO_2 levels may be relatively high. Consequently, Lighton proposed the chthonic hypothesis, which suggests that

DGC originated as a mechanism to improve gas exchange while at the same time minimizing respiratory water loss.

A. G. GIBBS AND R. A. JOHNSON, "The Role of Discontinuous Gas Exchange in Insects: The Chthonic Hypothesis Does Not Hold Water," *The Journal of Experimental Biology*

Notice that Gibbs and Johnson not only describe Lighton's hypothesis but also recap the evidence that supports it. By presenting this evidence, Gibbs and Johnson set the stage for engaging with Lighton's ideas. For example, they might question the chthonic hypothesis by pointing out shortcomings of the data or flaws in its interpretation. Or they might suggest new approaches that could verify the hypothesis. The point is that by incorporating a discussion of experimental findings into their summary of Lighton's hypothesis, Gibbs and Johnson open the door to a conversation with Lighton.

Here are some templates for presenting the data that underpin prevailing explanations:

▸ Experiments showing _____ and _____ have led scientists to propose _____.

▸ Although most scientists attribute _____ to _____, X's result _____ leads to the possibility that _____.

Explain the Methods

Even as we've argued that scientific arguments hinge on data, it's important to note that the quality of data varies depending on how they were collected. Data obtained with sloppy techniques or poorly designed experiments could lead to faulty conclusions. Therefore, it's crucial to explain the methods used to collect data. In order for readers to evaluate a method, you'll need to indicate its purpose, as the following passage from a journal article about the evolution of bird digestive systems demonstrates:

> To test the hypothesis that flowerpiercers have converged with hummingbirds in digestive traits, we compared the activity of intestinal enzymes and the gut nominal area of cinnamon-bellied flowerpiercers (*Diglossa baritula*) with those of eleven hummingbird species.
>
> J. E. SCHONDUBE AND C. MARTINEZ DEL RIO,
> "Sugar and Protein Digestion in Flowerpiercers and
> Hummingbirds: A Comparative Test of Adaptive Convergence,"
> *Journal of Comparative Physiology*

You need to indicate purpose whether describing your own work or that of others. Here are a couple of templates for doing so:

▸ Smith and colleagues evaluated _____ to determine whether _____.

▸ Because _____ does not account for _____, we instead used _____.

Summarize the Findings

Scientific data often come in the form of numbers. Your task when presenting numerical data is to provide the context readers need to understand the numbers—by giving supporting information and making comparisons. In the following passage from a book about the interaction between organisms and their environments, Turner uses numerical data to support an argument about the role of the sun's energy on Earth.

> The potential rate of energy transfer from the Sun to Earth is prodigious—about 600 W m^{-2}, averaged throughout the year. Of this, only a relatively small fraction, on the order of 1–2 percent,

is captured by green plants. The rest, if it is not reflected back into space, is available to do other things. The excess can be considerable: although some natural surfaces reflect as much as 95% of the incoming solar beam, many natural surfaces reflect much less (Table 3.2), on average about 15–20 percent. The remaining absorbed energy is then capable of doing work, like heating up surfaces, moving water and air masses around to drive weather and climate, evaporating water, and so forth.

J. S. TURNER, *The Extended Organism*

Turner supports his point that a huge amount of the sun's energy is directly converted to work on Earth by quoting an actual value (600) with units of measurement ($W\ m^{-2}$, watts per square meter). Readers need the units to evaluate the value; 600 watts per square inch is very different from 600 $W\ m^{-2}$. Turner then makes comparisons using percent values, saying that only 1 to 2 percent of the total energy that reaches Earth is trapped by plants. Finally, Turner describes the data's variability by reporting comparisons as ranges—1 to 2 percent and 15 to 20 percent—rather than single values.

Supporting information—such as units of measurement, sample size (n), and amount of variability—helps readers assess the data. In general, the reliability of data improves as its sample size increases and its variability decreases. Supporting information can be concisely presented as:

▸ _____ ± _____ (*mean ± variability*) _____ (*units*), $n =$ _____ (*sample size*).

For example: before training, resting heart rate of the subjects was 56 ± 7 beats per minute, $n = 12$. Here's another way to give supporting information:

▸ We measured _____ (*sample size*) subjects, and the average response was _____ (*mean with units*) with a range of _____ (*lower value*) to _____ (*upper value*).

To help readers understand the data, make comparisons with values from the same study or from other similar work.

Here are some templates for making comparisons:

▸ Before training, average running speed was _____ ± _____ kilometers per hour, _____ kilometers per hour slower than running speed after training.

▸ We found athletes' heart rates to be _____ ± _____ % lower than nonathletes'.

▸ The subjects in X's study completed the maze in _____ ± _____ seconds, _____ seconds slower than those in Y's study.

You will sometimes need to present qualitative data, such as that found in some images and photographs, that cannot be reduced to numbers. Qualitative data must be described precisely with words. In the passage below from a review article about connections between cellular protein localization and cell growth, the author describes the exact locations of three proteins: Scrib, Dlg, and Lgl.

> Epithelial cells accumulate different proteins on their apical (top) and basolateral (bottom) surfaces. . . . Scrib and Dlg are localized at the septate junctions along the lateral cell surface, whereas Lgl coats vesicles that are found both in the cytoplasm and "docked" at the lateral surface of the cell.
>
> M. PEIFER, "Travel Bulletin—Traffic Jams
> Cause Tumors," *Science*

EXPLAIN WHAT THE DATA MEAN

Once you summarize experiments and results, you need to say what the data mean. Consider the following passage from a study in which scientists fertilized plots of tropical rainforest with nitrogen (N) and / or phosphorus (P).

> Although our data suggest that the mechanisms driving the observed respiratory responses to increased N and P may be different, the large CO_2 losses stimulated by N and P fertilization suggest that knowledge of such patterns and their effects on soil CO_2 efflux is critical for understanding the role of tropical forests in a rapidly changing global C [carbon] cycle.
>
> C. C. CLEVELAND AND A. R. TOWNSEND, "Nutrient Additions to a Tropical Rain Forest Drive Substantial Soil Carbon Dioxide Losses to the Atmosphere," *Proceedings of the National Academy of Sciences*

Notice that in discussing the implications of their data, Cleveland and Townsend use language—including the verbs "suggest" and "may be"—that denotes their level of confidence in what they say about the data.

Whether you are summarizing what others say about their data or offering your own interpretation, pay attention to the verbs that connect data to interpretations.

To signify a moderate level of confidence:

▸ The data *suggest / hint / imply* _____.

To express a greater degree of certainty:

▸ Our results *show / demonstrate* _____.

Almost never will you use the verb "prove" in reference to a single study, because even very powerful evidence generally falls short of proof unless other studies support the same conclusion.

Scientific consensus arises when multiple studies point toward the same conclusion; conversely, contradictions among studies often signal research questions that need further work. For these reasons, you may need to compare one study's findings to those of another study. Here, too, you'll need to choose your verbs carefully.

- Our data *support / confirm / verify* the work of X by showing that _____.

- By demonstrating _____, X's work *extends* the findings of Y.

- The results of X *contradict / refute* Y's conclusion that _____.

- X's findings *call into question* the widely accepted theory that _____.

- Our data *are consistent with* X's hypothesis that _____.

MAKE YOUR OWN ARGUMENTS

Now we turn toward the part of scientific writing where you express your own opinions. One challenge is that the statements of other scientists about their methods and results usually must be accepted. You probably can't argue, for example, that "X and Y claim to have studied six elephants, but I think they actually only studied four." However, it might be fair to say, "X and Y studied only six elephants, and this small sample size casts doubts on their conclusions." The second statement doesn't question what the scientists did or found but instead examines how the findings are interpreted.

When developing your own arguments—the "I say"—you will often start by assessing the interpretations of other scientists. Consider the following example from a review article about the beneficial acclimation hypothesis (BAH), the idea that organisms exposed to a particular environment become better suited to that environment than unexposed animals.

> To the surprise of most physiologists, all empirical examinations of the BAH have rejected its generality. However, we suggest that these examinations are neither direct nor complete tests of the functional benefit of acclimation.
>
> R. S. WILSON AND C. E. FRANKLIN, "Testing the Beneficial Acclimation Hypothesis," *Trends in Ecology & Evolution*

Wilson and Franklin use a version of the "twist it" move: they acknowledge the data collected by other physiologists but question how those data have been interpreted, creating an opportunity to offer their own interpretation.

For more on the "twist it" move, see p. 58.

You might ask whether we should question how other scientists interpret their own work. Having conducted a study, aren't they in the best position to evaluate it? Perhaps, but as the above example demonstrates, other scientists might see the work from a different perspective or through more objective eyes. And in fact the culture of science depends on vigorous debate in which scientists defend their own findings and challenge those of others—a give and take that helps improve science's reliability. So expressing a critical view about someone else's work is an integral part of the scientific process. Let's examine some of the basic moves for entering scientific conversations: agreeing, with a difference; disagreeing and explaining why; simultaneously agreeing and disagreeing; anticipating objections; and saying why it matters.

Agree, But with a Difference

Scientific research passes through several levels of critical analysis before being published. Scientists get feedback when they discuss work with colleagues, present findings at conferences, and receive reviews of their manuscripts. So the juiciest debates may have been resolved before publication, and you may find little to disagree with in the published literature of a research field. Yet even if you agree with what you've read, there are still ways to join the conversation—and reasons to do so.

One approach is to suggest that further work should be done:

▸ **Now that _____ has been established, scientists will likely turn their attention toward _____.**

▸ **X's work leads to the question of _____. Therefore, we investigated _____.**

▸ **To see whether these findings apply to _____, we propose to _____.**

Another way to agree and at the same time jump into the conversation is to concur with a finding and then propose a mechanism that explains it. In the following sentence from a review article about dietary deficiencies, the author agrees with a previous finding and offers a probable explanation.

> Inadequate dietary intakes of vitamins and minerals are widespread, most likely due to excessive consumption of energy-rich, micronutrient-poor, refined food.
>
> B. AMES, "Low Micronutrient Intake
May Accelerate the Degenerative Diseases of Aging through
Allocation of Scarce Micronutrients by Triage,"
Proceedings of the National Academy of Sciences

Here are some templates for explaining an experimental result.

▸ **One explanation for X's finding of _____ is that _____.**
  An alternative explanation is _____.

▸ **The difference between _____ and _____ is probably**
  due to _____.

Disagree—and Explain Why

Although scientific consensus is common, healthy disagreement is not unusual. While measurements conducted by different teams of scientists under the same conditions should produce the same result, scientists often disagree about which techniques are most appropriate, how well an experimental design tests a hypothesis, and how results should be interpreted. To illustrate such disagreement, let's return to the debate about whether or not lactic acid is beneficial during exercise. In the following passage, Lamb and Stephenson are responding to work by Kristensen and colleagues, which argues that lactic acid might be beneficial to resting muscle but not to active muscle.

> The argument put forward by Kristensen and colleagues (12) . . .
> is not valid because it is based on observations made with isolated
> whole soleus muscles that were stimulated at such a high rate that
> >60% of the preparation would have rapidly become completely
> anoxic (4). . . . Furthermore, there is no reason to expect that
> adding more H+ to that already being generated by the muscle
> activity should in any way be advantageous. It is a bit like open-
> ing up the carburetor on a car to let in too much air or throwing

gasoline over the engine and then concluding that air and gasoline are deleterious to engine performance.

G. D. Lamb and D. G. Stephenson,
"Point: Lactic Acid Accumulation Is an Advantage during
Muscle Activity," *Journal of Applied Physiology*

Lamb and Stephenson bring experimental detail to bear on their disagreement with Kristensen and colleagues. First, they criticize methodology, arguing that the high muscle stimulation rate used by Kristensen and colleagues created very low oxygen levels (anoxia). They also criticize the logic of the experimental design, arguing that adding more acid (H+) to a muscle that is already producing it isn't informative. It's also worth noting how they drive home their point, likening Kristensen and colleagues' methodology to flooding an engine with air or gasoline. Even in technical scientific writing, you don't need to set aside your own voice completely.

In considering the work of others, look for instances where the experimental design and methodology fail to adequately test a hypothesis.

▸ **The work of Y and Z appears to show that _____, but their experimental design does not control for _____.**

Also, consider the possibility that results do not lead to the stated conclusions.

▸ **While X and Y claim that _____, their finding of _____ actually shows that _____.**

Okay, But . . .

Science tends to progress incrementally. New work may refine or extend previous work but doesn't often completely overturn it. For this reason, science writers frequently agree up to a point and then express some disagreement. In the following example from a commentary about methods for assessing how proteins interact, the authors acknowledge the value of the two-hybrid studies, but they also point out their shortcomings.

> The two-hybrid studies that produced the protein interaction map for *D. melanogaster* (12) provide a valuable genome-wide view of protein interactions but have a number of shortcomings (13). Even if the protein-protein interactions were determined with high accuracy, the resulting network would still require careful interpretation to extract its underlying biological meaning. Specifically, the map is a representation of all possible interactions, but one would only expect some fraction to be operating at any given time.
>
> J. J. Rice, A. Kershenbaum, and G. Stolovitzky,
> "Lasting Impressions: Motifs in Protein-Protein Maps
> May Provide Footprints of Evolutionary Events."
> *Proceedings of the National Academy of Sciences*

Delineating the boundaries or limitations of a study is a good way to agree up to a point. Here are templates for doing so.

▸ **While X's work clearly demonstrates _____, _____ will be required before we can determine whether _____.**

▸ **Although Y and Z present firm evidence for _____, their data cannot be used to argue that _____.**

▸ **In summary, our studies show that _____, but the issue of _____ remains unresolved.**

Anticipate Objections

Skepticism is a key ingredient in the scientific process. Before an explanation is accepted, scientists demand convincing evidence and assess whether alternative explanations have been thoroughly explored, so it's essential that scientists consider possible objections to their ideas before presenting them. In the following example from a book about the origin of the universe, Tyson and Goldsmith first admit that some might doubt the existence of the poorly understood "dark matter" that physicists have proposed, and then they go on to respond to the skeptics.

> Unrelenting skeptics might compare the dark matter of today with the hypothetical, now defunct "ether," proposed centuries ago as the weightless, transparent medium through which light moved. . . . But dark matter ignorance differs fundamentally from ether ignorance. While ether amounted to a placeholder for our incomplete understanding, the existence of dark matter derives not from mere presumption but from the observed effects of its gravity on visible matter.
>
> N. D. TYSON AND D. GOLDSMITH,
> *Origins: Fourteen Billion Years of Cosmic Evolution*

Anticipating objections in your own writing will help you clarify and address potential criticisms. Consider objections to your overall approach, as well as to specific aspects of your interpretations. Here are some templates for doing so.

▶ Scientists who take a _____ (*reductionist / integrative / biochemical / computational / statistical*) approach might view our results differently.

▸ This interpretation of the data might be criticized by X, who has argued that _____.

▸ Some may argue that this experimental design fails to account for _____.

Say Why It Matters

Though individual studies can be narrowly focused, science ultimately seeks to answer big questions and produce useful technologies. So it's essential when you enter a scientific conversation to say why the work—and your arguments about it— matter. The following passage from a commentary on a research article notes two implications of work that evaluated the shape of electron orbitals.

> The classic textbook shape of electron orbitals has now been directly observed. As well as confirming the established theory, this work may be a first step to understanding high-temperature superconductivity.
>
> C. J. HUMPHREYS, "Electrons Seen in Orbit," *Nature*

Humphreys argues that the study confirms an established theory and that it may lead to better understanding in another area. When thinking about the broad significance of a study, consider both the practical applications and the impact on future scientific work.

▸ These results open the door to studies that _____.

▸ The methodologies developed by X will be useful for _____.

▸ Our findings are the first step toward _____.

▶ Further work in this area may lead to the development of
  _____ .

READING AS A WAY OF ENTERING
SCIENTIFIC CONVERSATIONS

In science, as in other disciplines, you'll often start with work done by others, and therefore you will need to critically evaluate their work. To that end, you'll need to probe how well their data support their interpretations. Doing so will lead you toward your own interpretations—your ticket into an ongoing scientific conversation. Here are some questions that will help you read and respond to scientific research.

How well do the methods test the hypothesis?

- Is the sample size adequate?

- Is the experimental design valid? Were the proper controls performed?

- What are the limitations of the methodology?

- Are other techniques available?

How fairly have the results been interpreted?

- How well do the results support the stated conclusion?

- Has the data's variability been adequately considered?

- Do other findings verify (or contradict) the conclusion?

- What other experiments could test the conclusion?

What are the broader implications of the work, and why does it matter?

- Can the results be generalized beyond the system that was studied?

- What are the work's practical implications?

- What questions arise from the work?

- Which experiments should be done next?

The examples in this chapter show that scientists do more than simply collect facts; they also interpret those facts and make arguments about their meaning. On the frontiers of science, where we are probing questions that are just beyond our capacity to answer, the data are inevitably incomplete and controversy is to be expected. Writing about science presents the opportunity to add your own arguments to the ongoing discussion.

SEVENTEEN

"ANALYZE THIS"

Writing in the Social Sciences

ERIN ACKERMAN

SOCIAL SCIENCE is the study of people—how they behave and relate to one another, and the organizations and institutions that facilitate these interactions. People are complicated, so any study of human behavior is at best partial, taking into account some elements of what people do and why, but not always explaining those actions definitively. As a result, it is the subject of constant conversation and argument.

Consider some of the topics studied in the social sciences: minimum wage laws, immigration policy, health care, what causes aggressive behavior, employment discrimination. Got an opinion on any of these topics? You aren't alone. But in the writing you do as a student of the social sciences, you need to write about more

---

ERIN ACKERMAN is the Social Sciences Librarian at The College of New Jersey and formerly taught political science at John Jay College, City University of New York. Her research and teaching interests include American law and politics, women and law, and information literacy in the social sciences.

than just your opinions. Good writing in the social sciences, as in other academic disciplines, requires that you demonstrate that you have examined what you think and why. The best way to do that is to bring your views into conversation with those expressed by others and to test what you and others think against a review of evidence. In other words, you'll need to start with what others say and then present what you say as a response.

Consider the following example from an op-ed in the *New York Times* by two psychology professors:

> Is video game addiction a real thing?
>
> It's certainly common to hear parents complain that their children are "addicted" to video games. Some researchers even claim that these games are comparable to illegal drugs in terms of their influence on the brain—that they are "digital heroin" (the neuroscientist Peter C. Whybrow) or "digital pharmakeia" (the neuroscientist Andrew Doan). The American Psychiatric Association has identified internet gaming disorder as a possible psychiatric illness, and the World Health Organization has proposed including "gaming disorder" in its catalog of mental diseases, along with drug and alcohol addiction.
>
> This is all terribly misguided. Playing video games is not addictive in any meaningful sense. It is normal behavior that, while perhaps in many cases a waste of time, is not damaging or disruptive of lives in the way drug or alcohol use can be.
>
> CHRISTOPHER J. FERGUSON AND PATRICK MARKEY,
> "Video Games Aren't Addictive"

In other words, "they" (parents, other researchers, health organizations) say that the video games are addictive, whereas Ferguson and Markey disagree. In the rest of the op-ed, they argue that video game critics have misinterpreted the evidence and are not being very precise with what counts as "addiction."

This chapter explores some of the basic moves social science writers make. Writing in the social sciences often takes the form of a research paper that generally includes several core components: a strong introduction and thesis, a literature review, and the writer's own analysis, including presentation of evidence/data and consideration of implications. The introduction sets out the thesis, or point, of the paper, briefly explaining the topic or question you are investigating and previewing what you will say in your paper and how it fits into the preexisting conversation. The literature review summarizes what has already been said on your topic. Your analysis allows you to present evidence (the information, or data, about human behavior that you are measuring or testing against what other people have said), to explain the conclusions you have drawn based on your investigation, and to discuss the implications of your research. Do you agree, disagree, or some combination of both with what has been said by others? What reasons can you give for why you feel that way? And so what? Who should be interested in what you have to say, and why?

You may get other types of writing assignments in the social sciences, such as preparing a policy memo, writing a legal brief, or designing a grant or research proposal. While there may be differences from the research papers in terms of the format and audience for these assignments, the purposes of sections of the research paper and the moves discussed here will help you with those assignments as well.

THE INTRODUCTION AND THESIS:
"THIS PAPER CHALLENGES . . ."

Your introduction sets forth what you plan to say in your essay. You might evaluate the work of earlier scholars or certain widely held assumptions and find them incorrect when measured against new events or data. Alternatively, you might point out that an author's work is largely correct, but that it could use some qualifications or be extended in some way. Or you might identify a gap in our knowledge—we know a great deal about topic X but almost nothing about some other closely related topic. In each of these instances, your introduction needs to cover both "they say" and "I say" perspectives. If you stop after the "they say," your readers won't know what you are bringing to the conversation. Similarly, if you were to jump right to the "I say" portion of your argument, readers might wonder why you need to say anything at all.

Sometimes you join the conversation at a point where the discussion seems settled. One or more views about a topic have become so widely accepted among a group of scholars or society at large that these views are essentially the conventional way of thinking about the topic. You may wish to offer new reasons to support this interpretation, or you may wish to call these standard views into question. To do so, you must first introduce and identify these widely held beliefs and then present your own view. In fact, much of the writing in the social sciences takes the form of calling into question that which we think we already know. Consider the following example from an article in *The Journal of Economic Perspectives*:

> Fifteen years ago, Milton Friedman's 1957 treatise *A Theory of the Consumption Function* seemed badly dated. Dynamic optimization theory had not been employed much in economics when Friedman wrote, and utility theory was still comparatively primitive, so his statement of the "permanent income hypothesis" never actually specified a formal mathematical model of behavior derived explicitly from utility maximization . . . [W]hen other economists subsequently

found multiperiod maximizing models that could be solved explicitly, the implications of those models differed sharply from Friedman's intuitive description of his "model." Furthermore, empirical tests in the 1970s and 1980s often rejected these rigorous versions of the permanent income hypothesis in favor of an alternative hypothesis that many households simply spent all of their current income.

Today, with the benefit of a further round of mathematical (and computational) advances, Friedman's (1957) original analysis looks more prescient than primitive . . .

> CHRISTOPHER D. CARROLL, "A Theory of Consumption
> Function, With and Without Liquidity Constraints,"
> *The Journal of Economic Perspectives*

This introduction makes clear that Carroll will defend Milton Friedman against some major criticisms of his work. Carroll mentions what has been said about Friedman's work and then goes on to say that the critiques turn out to be wrong and to suggest that Friedman's work reemerges as persuasive. A template of Carroll's introduction might look something like this: Economics research in the last fifteen years suggested Friedman's 1957 treatise was _____ because _____. In other words, they say that Friedman's work is not accurate because of _____, _____, and _____. Recent research convinces me, however, that Friedman's work makes sense.

In some cases, however, there may not be a strong consensus among experts on a topic. You might enter the ongoing debate by casting your vote with one side or another or by offering an alternative view. In the following example, Sheri Berman identifies two competing accounts of how to explain world events in the twentieth century and then puts forth a third view.

Conventional wisdom about twentieth-century ideologies rests on two simple narratives. One focuses on the struggle for dominance

between democracy and its alternatives. . . . The other narrative
focuses on the competition between free-market capitalism and its
rivals. . . . Both of these narratives obviously contain some truth.
. . . Yet both only tell part of the story, which is why their common
conclusion—neoliberalism as the "end of History"—is unsatisfying
and misleading.

What the two conventional narratives fail to mention is that
a third struggle was also going on: between those ideologies that
believed in the primacy of economics and those that believed in
the primacy of politics.

SHERI BERMAN, "The Primacy of Economics versus the
Primacy of Politics: Understanding the Ideological Dynamics
of the Twentieth Century," *Perspectives on Politics*

After identifying the two competing narratives, Berman suggests a third view—and later goes on to argue that this third
view explains current debates over globalization. A template
for this type of introduction might look something like this:
In recent discussions of _____, a controversial aspect has
been _____. On the one hand, some argue that _____.
On the other hand, others argue that _____. Neither of
these arguments, however, considers the alternative view
that _____.

Given the complexity of many of the issues studied in
the social sciences, however, you may sometimes agree *and*
disagree with existing views—pointing out things that you
believe are correct or have merit, while disagreeing For more on different ways of responding, see Chapter 4.
with or refining other points. In the example below,
anthropologist Sally Engle Merry agrees with another
scholar about something that is a key trait of modern society
but argues that this trait has a different origin than the other
author identifies.

Although I agree with Rose that an increasing emphasis on governing the soul is characteristic of modern society, I see the transformation not as evolutionary but as the product of social mobilization and political struggle.

> SALLY ENGLE MERRY, "Rights, Religion, and Community:
> Approaches to Violence against Women in the
> Context of Globalization," *Law and Society Review*

Here are some templates for agreeing and disagreeing:

▸ **Although I agree with X up to a point, I cannot accept his overall conclusion that _____.**

▸ **Although I disagree with X on _____ and _____, I agree with her conclusion that _____.**

▸ **Political scientists studying _____ have argued that it is caused by _____. While _____ contributes to the problem, _____ is also an important factor.**

▸ **While noting _____, I contend _____.**

In the process of examining people from different angles, social scientists sometimes identify gaps—areas that have not been explored in previous research.

In the following example, several sociologists identify such a gap.

Family scholars have long argued that the study of dating deserves more attention (Klemer, 1971), as dating is an important part of the life course at any age and often a precursor to marriage (Levesque & Caron, 2004). . . .

The central research questions we seek to answer with this study are whether and how the significance of particular dating rituals are patterned by gender and race simultaneously. We use a racially diverse data set of traditional-aged college students from a variety of college contexts. Understanding gender and racial differences in the assessment of dating rituals helps us explore the extent to which relationship activities are given similar importance across institutional and cultural lines. Most of the studies that inform our knowledge of dating and relationships are unable to draw conclusions regarding racial differences because the sample is Caucasian (e.g., Bogle, 2008), or primarily so (e.g., Manning & Smock, 2005). Race has been recently argued to be an often-overlooked variable in studies examining social psychological processes because of the prevalence of sample limitations as well as habitual oversight in the literature (Hunt, Jackson, Powell, & Steelman, 2000). Additionally, a failure to examine both gender and race prevents assessment of whether gendered beliefs are shared across groups. Gauging the extent of differences in beliefs among different population subgroups is critical to advancing the study of relationship dynamics (see Weaver & Ganong, 2004).

PAMELA BRABOY JACKSON, SIBYL KLEINER,
CLAUDIA GEIST, AND KARA CEBULKO, "Conventions of Courtship: Gender and Race Differences in the Significance of Dating Rituals," *Journal of Family Issues*

Jackson and her coauthors note that, while other scholars have said that studying dating is important and have examined some aspects of dating, we have little information about whether attitudes about dating activities (such as sexual intimacy, gift exchange, and meeting the family) vary across groups by gender and race. Their study aims to fill this gap in our understanding of relationships.

Here are some templates for introducing gaps in the existing research:

▶ Studies of X have indicated _____. It is not clear, however, that this conclusion applies to _____.

▶ _____ often take for granted that _____. Few have investigated this assumption, however.

▶ X's work tells us a great deal about _____. Can this work be generalized to _____?

▶ Our understanding of _____ remains incomplete because previous work has not examined _____.

Again, a good introduction indicates what you have to say in the larger context of what others have said. Throughout the rest of your paper, you will move back and forth between the "they say" and the "I say," adding more details.

THE LITERATURE REVIEW:
"PRIOR RESEARCH INDICATES . . ."

The point of a literature review is to establish the state of knowledge on your topic. Before you (and your reader) can properly consider an issue, you need to understand the conversation about your topic that has already taken place (and is likely still in progress). In the literature review, you explain what "they say" in more detail, summarizing, paraphrasing, or quoting the viewpoints to which you are responding. But you need to balance what they are saying with your own focus. You need to characterize someone else's work fairly and accurately but set up the points you yourself want to make by selecting the details that are relevant to your own perspective and observations.

It is common in the social sciences to summarize several arguments in a single paragraph or even a single sentence, grouping several sources together by their important ideas or other attributes. The example below cites some key findings and conclusions of psychological research that should be of interest to motivated college students looking to improve their academic performance.

> Some people may associate sacrificing hours of sleep with being studious, but the reality is that sleep deprivation can hurt your cognitive functioning without your being aware of it (e.g., becoming worse at paying attention and remembering things; Goel, Rao, Durmer, & Dinges, 2009; Pilcher & Walters, 1997).... Sleep affects learning and memory by organizing and consolidating memories from the day (Diekelmann & Born, 2010; Rasch & Born, 2013), which can lead to better problem-solving ability and creativity (Verleger, Rose, Wagner, Yordanova, & Kolev, 2013).
>
> ADAM L. PUTNAM, VICTOR W. SUNGKHASETTEE, AND
> HENRY L. ROEDIGER, III, "Optimizing Learning in College:
> Tips from Cognitive Psychology," *Perspectives on
> Psychological Science*

A template for this paragraph might look like this: Students believe _____, but researchers disagree because _____. According to researchers, negative consequences of sleep deprivation include _____. The research shows that a positive effect of sleep is _____, which improves _____.

Such summaries are brief, bringing together relevant arguments by several scholars to provide an overview of scholarly work on a particular topic. In writing such a summary, you need to ask yourself how the authors themselves might describe their positions and also consider what in their work is relevant for the point you wish to make. This kind of summary is especially appropriate when you have a large amount of research material on a topic and want to identify the major strands of a debate or to show how the work of one author builds on that of another. Here are some templates for overview summaries:

▸ In addressing the question of _____, researchers have considered several explanations for _____. X argues that _____. According to Y and Z, another plausible explanation is _____.

▸ What is the effect of _____ on _____? Previous work on _____ by X and by Y and Z supports _____.

▸ Scholars point to the role of _____ in _____.

▸ Existing research on _____ presents convincing evidence of _____.

Sometimes you may need to say more about the works you cite. On a midterm or final exam, for example, you may need to demonstrate that you have a deep familiarity with a particular work. And in some disciplines of the social sciences, longer, more detailed literature reviews are the standard. Your instructor and the articles he or she has assigned are your best guides for the length and level of detail of your literature review. Other times, the work of certain authors is especially important for your argument, and therefore you need to provide more details to explain what these authors have said. See how political scientists Hahrie Han and Lisa Argyle, in a report for the Ford

Foundation, summarize an argument that is central to their investigation of improving democratic participation.

> [A]t the root of declining rates of participation is the sense that people do not feel like their participation matters. People do not feel like they have any real reason or opportunity to exercise voice in the political process. People's sense of agency is in decline, especially given negative or incomplete experiences of government in their lives.
>
> This lack of caring comes as no surprise when we examine research showing that most people have negative or, at best, incomplete experiences of the role of government in their lives. Suzanne Mettler, for instance, finds that many middle-class people who benefit from different government programs—ranging from education savings accounts to welfare to tax credits—believe that they "have not used a government social program." In addition, other scholars find a trend towards increasing privatization of public goods and political processes in the twenty-first century. As a result, government is what Mettler calls a "submerged state," since the role of government in people's lives is effectively submerged from view.
>
> Hahrie Han and Lisa Argyle, "A Program Review of the
Promoting Electoral Reform and Democratic
Participation (PERDP) Initiative," *Ford Foundation*

Note that Han and Argyle start by identifying the broad problem of lack of participation and then explain how Mettler's work describes how middle-class people may be unaware of the role of government in their lives, leading Mettler to argue for the idea of the "submerged state."

You may want to include direct quotations of what others have said, as Han and Argyle do. Using an author's exact words helps you demonstrate that you are representing him or her fairly. But you cannot simply insert a quotation; you need to explain to your readers what it means for your point. Consider the following example drawn from a political science book on the debate over tort reform.

> The essence of *agenda setting* was well enunciated by E. E. Schattschneider: "In politics as in everything else, it makes a great difference whose game we play" (1960, 47). In short, the ability to define or control the rules, terms, or perceived options in a contest over policy greatly affects the prospects for winning.
>
> WILLIAM HALTOM AND MICHAEL McCANN,
> *Distorting the Law: Politics, Media, and the Litigation Crisis*

Notice how Haltom and McCann first quote Schattschneider and then explain in their own words how political agenda setting can be thought of as a game, with winners and losers.

Remember that whenever you summarize, quote, or paraphrase the work of others, credit must be given in the form of a citation to the original work. The words may be your own, but if the idea comes from someone else you must give credit to the original work. There are several formats for documenting sources. Consult your instructor for help choosing which citation style to use.

THE ANALYSIS

The literature review covers what others have said on your topic. The analysis allows you to present and support your own response. In the introduction you indicate whether you agree, disagree, or some combination of both with what others have said. You will want to expand on how you have formed your opinion and why others should care about your topic.

"The Data Indicate . . ."

The social sciences use evidence to develop and test explanations. This evidence is often referred to as data. Data can be quantitative or qualitative and can come from a number of sources. You might use statistics related to GDP growth, unemployment, voting rates, or demographics. You might report results from an experiment or simulation. Or you could use surveys, interviews, or other first-person accounts.

Regardless of the type of data used, it is important to do three things: define your data, indicate where you got the data, and then say what you have done with your data. For a chapter in their book assessing media coverage of female candidates, political scientists Danny Hayes and Jennifer Lawless explain how they assembled a data set.

> From the perspective of campaign professionals and voters, local newspaper coverage remains the most important news source during House campaigns....
>
> We began by selecting the appropriate newspaper for each House race in 2010 and 2014.... [W]e identified every news story during the thirty days leading up to the election that mentioned at least one of the two major-party candidates....
>
> Our data collection efforts produced 10,375 stories about 1,550 candidates who received at least some local news coverage in either the 2010 or 2014 midterms....
>
> Coders read the full text of each article and recorded several pieces of information. First, they tracked the number of times a candidate's sex or gender was mentioned.... Second, we recorded the number of explicit references to candidate traits, both positive and negative (e.g., "capable" and "ineffective")....
>
> Third, we tracked every time an issue was mentioned in connection with a candidate.... We then classified issues in two ways:

(1) We assigned each issue to one of the eight broad categories...
and (2) we classified a subset of the topics as "women's" or "men's"
issues.

DANNY HAYES AND JENNIFER L. LAWLESS, *Women on the Run:*
Gender, Media, and Political Campaigns in a Polarized Era

Hayes and Lawless explain how they collected their data—local
newspaper coverage of congressional candidates—and explain
how they coded and classified the coverage to allow them to
perform statistical analysis of the news pieces. While you probably won't collect 10,000+ news items for a class project, you
could collect information (such as media coverage, interview
responses, or legal briefs) and analyze and sort them to identify
patterns such as repeated words and ideas.

If your data are quantitative, you also need to explain
them. Sociologist Jonathan Horowitz's research concludes
that job quality influences personal assessments of well-being
by "improving social life, altering class identification, affecting
physical health, and increasing amounts of leisure time." See
how he introduces the data he analyzes:

In this study, I use data from the General Social Survey (GSS) and
structural equation modeling to test relationships between job quality and subjective wellbeing. The GSS is a nationally representative
sample of adults in the United States that asks a large number of
questions about experiences at work (Smith et al. 2010). In particular, the GSS introduced a new battery of questions titled "Quality
of Working Life" in 2002 (and repeated in 2006 and 2010) which
includes multiple questions about several job quality dimensions.

JONATHAN HOROWITZ, "Dimensions of Job Quality,
Mechanisms, and Subjective Well-Being in the United States,"
Sociological Forum

Here are some templates for discussing data:

▸ In order to test the hypothesis that _____, we assessed _____. Our calculations suggest _____.

▸ I used _____ to investigate _____. The results of this investigation indicate _____.

"But Others May Object . . ."

No matter how strongly your data support your argument, there are almost surely other perspectives (and thus other data) that you need to acknowledge. By considering possible objections to your argument and taking them seriously, you demonstrate that you've done your work and that you're aware of other perspectives—and most important, you present your own argument as part of an ongoing conversation.

See how law professor Michelle Alexander acknowledges that there may be objections to her argument describing trends in mass incarceration as "the new Jim Crow." See p. 266 for a selection from *The New Jim Crow.*

> Some might argue that as disturbing as this system appears to be, there is nothing particularly new about mass incarceration; it is merely a continuation of past drug wars and biased law enforcement practices. Racial bias in our criminal justice system is simply an old problem that has gotten worse, and the social excommunication of "criminals" has a long history; it is not a recent invention. There is some merit to this argument.
>
> MICHELLE ALEXANDER, *The New Jim Crow: Mass Incarceration in the Age of Colorblindness*

Alexander imagines a conversation with people who might be skeptical about her argument, particularly her claim that this represents a "new" development. And she responds that they are correct, to a point. After acknowledging her agreement with the assessment of historical racial bias in the criminal justice system, she goes on in the rest of her chapter to explain that the expanded scope and consequences of contemporary mass incarceration have caused dramatic differences in society.

Someone may object because there are related phenomena that your analysis does not explain or because you do not have the right data to investigate a particular question. Or perhaps someone may object to assumptions underlying your argument or how you handled your data. Here are some templates for considering naysayers:

▸ _____ might object that _____ .

▸ Is my claim realistic? I have argued _____ , but readers may question _____ .

▸ My explanation accounts for _____ but does not explain _____ . This is because _____ .

"Why Should We Care?"

Who should care about your research, and why? Since the social sciences attempt to explain human behavior, it is important to consider how your research affects the assumptions we make about human behavior. In addition, you might offer recommendations for how other social scientists might continue to explore an issue, or what actions policymakers should take.

In the following example, sociologist Devah Pager identifies the implications of her study of the way having a criminal record affects a person applying for jobs.

> [I]n terms of policy implications, this research has troubling conclusions. In our frenzy of locking people up, our "crime control"

policies may in fact exacerbate the very conditions that lead to crime in the first place. Research consistently shows that finding quality steady employment is one of the strongest predictors of desistance from crime (Shover 1996; Sampson and Laub 1993; Uggen 2000). The fact that a criminal record severely limits employment opportunities—particularly among blacks—suggests that these individuals are left with few viable alternatives.

DEVAH PAGER, "The Mark of a Criminal Record,"
The American Journal of Sociology

Pager's conclusion that a criminal record negatively affects employment chances creates a vicious circle, she says: steady employment discourages recidivism, but a criminal record makes it harder to get a job.

In answering the "so what?" question, you need to explain why your readers should care. Although sometimes the implications of your work may be so broad that they would be of interest to almost anyone, it's never a bad idea to identify explicitly any groups of people who will find your work important.

Templates for establishing why your claims matter:

▸ **X is important because _____.**

▸ **Ultimately, what is at stake here is _____.**

▸ **The finding that _____ should be of interest to _____ because _____.**

As noted at the beginning of this chapter, the complexity of people allows us to look at their behavior from many different viewpoints. Much has been, and will be, said about how and why people do the things they do. As a result, we can look at writing in the social sciences as an ongoing conversation. When you join this conversation, the "they say / I say" framework will help you figure out what has already been said (they say) and what you can add (I say). The components of social science writing presented in this chapter are tools to help you join that conversation.

RAY BRADBURY { *There Will Come Soft Rains*

RAY BRADBURY (1920–2012) was born in Waukegan, Illinois, and lived with his family in Tuscon, Arizona, as well as Los Angeles, where he graduated from Los Angeles High School. Bradbury did not attend college, preferring to read during evenings at the public library after a day of writing and selling newspapers on the street. Known for his science fiction, fantasy, and mystery narratives, Bradbury wrote his acclaimed *Fahrenheit 451* (1953) at UCLA's Powell Library, on a rented typewriter. His works have been adapted into comic books, television shows (*Alfred Hitchcock Presents*), and films. For eight years Bradbury hosted his own television show, *Ray Bradbury Presents*, for which he adapted sixty-five of his stories.

"There Will Come Soft Rains," from Bradbury's story collection *The Martian Chronicles* (1950), exposes a postapocalyptic world: humans have been eradicated by a nuclear disaster, but their homes—completely powered by technology—linger. What kind of existence does Bradbury imagine, both pre- and postapocalypse? How is this story a cautionary tale about the effects of technology? Do you agree with Bradbury's stance?

IN THE LIVING ROOM THE voice-clock sang, *Tick-tock, seven o'clock, time to get up, time to get up, seven o'clock!* as if it were afraid that nobody would. The morning house lay empty. The clock ticked on, repeating and repeating its sounds into the emptiness. *Seven-nine, breakfast time, seven-nine!*

In the kitchen the breakfast stove gave a hissing sigh and ejected from its warm interior eight pieces of perfectly browned toast, eight eggs sunnyside up, sixteen slices of bacon, two coffees, and two cool glasses of milk.

"Today is August 4, 2057," said a second voice from the kitchen ceiling, "in the city of Allendale, California." It repeated the date three times for memory's sake. "Today is Mr. Featherstone's birthday. Today is the anniversary of Tilita's marriage. Insurance is payable, as are the water, gas, and light bills."

Somewhere in the walls, relays clicked, memory tapes glided under electric eyes.

Eight-one, tick-tock, eight-one o'clock, off to school, off to work, run, ₅ *run, eight-one!* But no doors slammed, no carpets took the soft tread of rubber heels. It was raining outside. The weather box on the front door sang quietly: "Rain, rain, go away; rubbers, raincoats for today . . ." And the rain tapped on the empty house, echoing.

Outside, the garage chimed and lifted its door to reveal the waiting car. After a long wait the door swung down again.

At eight-thirty the eggs were shriveled and the toast was like stone. An aluminum wedge scraped them into the sink, where hot water whirled them down a metal throat which digested and flushed them away to the distant sea. The dirty dishes were dropped into a hot washer and emerged twinkling dry.

Nine-fifteen, sang the clock, *time to clean.*

Out of warrens in the wall, tiny robot mice darted. The rooms were acrawl with the small cleaning animals, all rubber and metal. They thudded against chairs, whirling their mustached runners, kneading the rug nap, sucking gently at hidden dust. Then, like mysterious invaders, they popped into their burrows. Their pink electric eyes faded. The house was clean.

Ten o'clock. The sun came out from behind the rain. The house ₁₀ stood alone in a city of rubble and ashes. This was the one house left standing. At night the ruined city gave off a radioactive glow which could be seen for miles.

Ten-fifteen. The garden sprinklers whirled up in golden founts, filling the soft morning air with scatterings of brightness. The water pelted windowpanes, running down the charred west side where the house had been burned evenly free of its white paint. The entire west face of the house was black, save for five places. Here the silhouette in paint of a man mowing a lawn. Here, as in a photograph, a woman bent to pick flowers. Still farther over, their images burned on wood in one titanic instant, a small boy, hands flung into the air; higher up, the image of a thrown ball, and opposite him a girl, hands raised to catch a ball which never came down.

The five spots of paint—the man, the woman, the children, the ball—remained. The rest was a thin charcoaled layer.

The gentle sprinkler rain filled the garden with falling light.

Until this day, how well the house had kept its peace. How carefully it had inquired, "Who goes there? What's the password?" and, getting no answer from lonely foxes and whining cats, it had shut up its windows and drawn shades in an old-maidenly preoccupation with self-protection which bordered on a mechanical paranoia.

It quivered at each sound, the house did. If a sparrow brushed a window, the shade snapped up. The bird, startled, flew off! No, not even a bird must touch the house! 15

The house was an altar with ten thousand attendants, big, small, servicing, attending, in choirs. But the gods had gone away, and the ritual of the religion continued senselessly, uselessly.

Twelve noon.

A dog whined, shivering, on the front porch.

The front door recognized the dog voice and opened. The dog, once huge and fleshy, but now gone to bone and covered with sores, moved in and through the house, tracking mud. Behind it whirled angry mice, angry at having to pick up mud, angry at inconvenience.

For not a leaf fragment blew under the door but what the wall panels 20 flipped open and the copper scrap rats flashed swiftly out. The offending dust, hair, or paper, seized in miniature steel jaws, was raced back to the burrows. There, down tubes which fed into the cellar, it was dropped into the sighing vent of an incinerator which sat like evil Baal in a dark corner.

The dog ran upstairs, hysterically yelping to each door, at last realizing, as the house realized, that only silence was here.

It sniffed the air and scratched the kitchen door. Behind the door, the stove was making pancakes which filled the house with a rich baked odor and the scent of maple syrup.

The dog frothed at the mouth, lying at the door, sniffing, its eyes turned to fire. It ran wildly in circles, biting at its tail, spun in a frenzy, and died. It lay in the parlor for an hour.

Two o'clock, sang a voice.

Delicately sensing decay at last, the regiments of mice hummed out   25
as softly as blown gray leaves in an electrical wind.

Two-fifteen.

The dog was gone.

In the cellar, the incinerator glowed suddenly and a whirl of sparks leaped up the chimney.

Two thirty-five.

Bridge tables sprouted from patio walls. Playing cards fluttered   30
onto pads in a shower of pips. Martinis manifested on an oaken bench with egg-salad sandwiches. Music played.

But the tables were silent and the cards untouched.

At four o'clock the tables folded like great butterflies back through the paneled walls.

Four-thirty.

The nursery walls glowed.

Animals took shape: yellow giraffes, blue lions, pink antelopes,   35
lilac panthers cavorting in crystal substance. The walls were glass. They looked out upon color and fantasy. Hidden films clocked through well-oiled sprockets, and the walls lived. The nursery floor was woven to resemble a crisp, cereal meadow. Over this ran aluminum roaches and iron crickets, and in the hot still air butterflies of delicate red tissue wavered among the sharp aroma of animal spoors! There was the sound like a great matted yellow hive of bees within a dark bellows, the lazy bumble of a purring lion. And there was the patter of okapi feet and the murmur of a fresh jungle rain, like other hoofs, falling upon the summer-starched grass. Now the walls dissolved into distances of parched weed, mile on mile,

and warm endless sky. The animals drew away into thorn brakes and water holes.

It was the children's hour.

Five o'clock. The bath filled with clear hot water.

Six, seven, eight o'clock, The dinner dishes manipulated like magic tricks, and in the study a *click*. In the metal stand opposite the hearth where a fire now blazed up warmly, a cigar popped out, half an inch of soft gray ash on it, smoking, waiting.

Nine o'clock. The beds warmed their hidden circuits, for nights were cool here.

Nine-five. A voice spoke from the study ceiling: 40

"Mrs. McClellan, which poem would you like this evening?"

The house was silent.

The voice said at last, "Since you express no preference, I shall select a poem at random." Quiet music rose to back the voice. "Sara Teasdale. As I recall, your favorite. . . .

"There will come soft rains and the smell of the ground,
And swallows circling with their shimmering sound;

And frogs in the pools singing at night,
And wild plum trees in tremulous white;

Robins will wear their feathery fire,
Whistling their whims on a low fence-wire;

And not one will know of the war, not one
Will care at last when it is done.

Not one would mind, neither bird nor tree,
If mankind perished utterly;

And Spring herself, when she woke at dawn
Would scarcely know that we were gone."

The fire burned on the stone hearth and the cigar fell away into a mound of quiet ash on its tray. The empty chairs faced each other between the silent walls, and the music played.

At ten o'clock the house began to die. 45

The wind blew. A falling tree bough crashed through the kitchen window. Cleaning solvent, bottled, shattered over the stove. The room was ablaze in an instant!

"Fire!" screamed a voice. The house lights flashed, water pumps shot water from the ceilings. But the solvent spread on the linoleum, licking, eating, under the kitchen door, while the voices took it up in chorus: "Fire, fire, fire!"

The house tried to save itself. Doors sprang tightly shut, but the windows were broken by the heat and the wind blew and sucked upon the fire.

The house gave ground as the fire in ten billion angry sparks moved with flaming ease from room to room and then up the stairs. While scurrying water rats squeaked from the walls, pistoled their water, and ran for more. And the wall sprays let down showers of mechanical rain.

But too late. Somewhere, sighing, a pump shrugged to a stop. The 50 quenching rain ceased. The reserve water supply which had filled baths and washed dishes for many quiet days was gone.

The fire crackled up the stairs. It fed upon Picassos and Matisses in the upper halls, like delicacies, baking off the oily flesh, tenderly crisping the canvases into black shavings.

Now the fire lay in beds, stood in windows, changed the colors of drapes!

And then, reinforcements.

From attic trapdoors, blind robot faces peered down with faucet mouths gushing green chemical.

The fire backed off, as even an elephant must at the sight of a dead 55 snake. Now there were twenty snakes whipping over the floor, killing the fire with a clear cold venom of green froth.

But the fire was clever. It had sent flames outside the house, up through the attic to the pumps there. An explosion! The attic brain which directed the pumps was shattered into bronze shrapnel on the beams.

The fire rushed back into every closet and felt of the clothes hung there.

The house shuddered, oak bone on bone, its bared skeleton cringing from the heat, its wire, its nerves revealed as if a surgeon had torn the skin off to let the red veins and capillaries quiver in the scalded air. Help, help! Fire! Run, run! Heat snapped mirrors like the brittle winter ice. And the voices wailed Fire, fire, run, run, like a tragic nursery rhyme, a dozen voices, high, low, like children dying in a forest, alone, alone. And the voices fading as the wires popped their sheathings like hot chestnuts. One, two, three, four, five voices died.

In the nursery the jungle burned. Blue lions roared, purple giraffes bounded off. The panthers ran in circles, changing color, and ten million animals, running before the fire, vanished off toward a distant steaming river. . . .

Ten more voices died. In the last instant under the fire avalanche, 60 other choruses, oblivious, could be heard announcing the time, playing music, cutting the lawn by remote-control mower, or setting an umbrella frantically out and in the slamming and opening front door, a thousand things happening, like a clock shop when each clock strikes the hour insanely before or after the other, a scene of maniac confusion, yet unity; singing, screaming, a few last cleaning mice darting bravely out to carry the horrid ashes away! And one voice, with sublime disregard for the situation, read poetry aloud in the fiery study, until all the film spools burned, until all the wires withered and the circuits cracked.

The fire burst the house and let it slam flat down, puffing out skirts of spark and smoke.

In the kitchen, an instant before the rain of fire and timber, the stove could be seen making breakfasts at a psychopathic rate, ten dozen eggs, six loaves of toast, twenty dozen bacon strips, which, eaten by fire, started the stove working again, hysterically hissing!

The crash. The attic smashing into kitchen and parlor. The parlor into cellar, cellar into sub-cellar. Deep freeze, armchair, film tapes, circuits, beds, and all like skeletons thrown in a cluttered mound deep under.

Smoke and silence. A great quantity of smoke.

Dawn showed faintly in the east. Among the ruins, one wall stood 65 alone. Within the wall, a last voice said, over and over again and again, even as the sun rose to shine upon the heaped rubble and steam:

"Today is August 5, 2057, today is August 5, 2057, today is . . ."

STUDY QUESTIONS

1. What is the SETTING of this story—what has happened as the story opens?

2. If technological advancements are the CAUSE, what are their EFFECTS—both positive and negative—in this story?

3. Reread the poem by Sara Teasdale within the story. What does the poem predict will be Nature's reaction when mankind perishes? What does happen? Discuss the IRONY of the poem's relationship to the events in the story.

4. ***For Writing.*** In an essay, explore your own relationship to technology. Do you use a GPS? A music streaming service? Do you reach for your cell phone out of muscle memory? Consider all the ways in which you interact with technology on a daily basis and determine whether those interactions are ultimately helpful or could have negative consequences. Be sure to cite—and examine in detail—specifi c examples.

RALPH ELLISON   { *Battle Royal*

RALPH ELLISON (1913–1994) published only one novel in his
lifetime, yet he holds a spot as one of America's great writers. Though
Ellison gave his birth year as 1914, recent biographers have determined
that he was born March 1, 1913, in Oklahoma City, Oklahoma, just six
years after statehood. A gifted trumpeter, Ellison attended Tuskegee
Institute to study music composition. After three years, he moved to
New York City, where he met author Richard Wright, who encouraged
Ellison to begin writing. His National Book Award–winning novel,
Invisible Man, was published in 1952. A coming-of-age story that deals
with race and identity, it is frequently cited among the most important
American books. Following his death, some two thousand pages of
manuscript were edited down into the novel *Juneteenth* (1999).

"Battle Royal," the opening chapter of *Invisible Man,* explores the
process of how a young black valedictorian attempts to make his speech
to an audience of "upstanding" white male members of the community
who prefer to see him fight other young black men in a "battle royal,"
a fight among more than two combatants in which the winner is the last
person standing. What are the obstacles to his making his speech clearly
and confidently? What does this story say about the power dynamics
between black and white individuals?

IT GOES A LONG WAY back, some twenty years. All my life I had been
looking for something, and everywhere I turned someone tried to tell
me what it was. I accepted their answers too, though they were often

in contradiction and even self-contradictory. I was naïve. I was looking for myself and asking everyone except myself questions which I, and only I, could answer. It took me a long time and much painful boomeranging of my expectations to achieve a realization everyone else appears to have been born with: That I am nobody but myself. But first I had to discover that I am an invisible man!

And yet I am no freak of nature, nor of history. I was in the cards, other things having been equal (or unequal) eighty-five years ago. I am not ashamed of my grandparents for having been slaves. I am only ashamed of myself for having at one time been ashamed. About eighty-five years ago they were told that they were free, united with others of our country in everything pertaining to the common good, and, in everything social, separate like the fingers of the hand. And they believed it. They exulted in it. They stayed in their place, worked hard, and brought up *my* father to do the same. But my grandfather is the one. He was an odd old guy, my grandfather, and I am told I take after him. It was he who caused the trouble. On his deathbed he called my father to him and said, "Son, after I'm gone I want you to keep up the good fight. I never told you, but our life is a war and I have been a traitor all my born days, a spy in the enemy's country ever since I give up my gun back in the Reconstruction. Live with your head in the lion's mouth. I want you to overcome 'em with yeses, undermine 'em with grins, agree 'em to death and destruction, let 'em swoller you till they vomit or bust wide open." They thought the old man had gone out of his mind. He had been the meekest of men. The younger children were rushed from the room, the shades drawn and the flame of the lamp turned so low that it sputtered on the wick like the old man's breathing. "Learn it to the younguns," he whispered fiercely; then he died.

But my folks were more alarmed over his last words than over his dying. It was as though he had not died at all, his words caused so much anxiety. I was warned emphatically to forget what he had said and, indeed, this is the first time it has been mentioned outside the family circle. It had a tremendous effect upon me, however. I could never be sure of what he meant. Grandfather had been a quiet old man who never made any trouble, yet on his deathbed he had called himself a traitor and a spy, and he had spoken of his meekness as a dangerous activity. It became a constant puzzle which lay unanswered in the back of my mind. And whenever things went well for me I remembered my grandfather and felt guilty and uncomfortable. It was as though I was carrying out his advice in spite of myself. And to make it worse, everyone loved me for it. I was praised by the most lily-white men of the town. I was considered an example of desirable conduct— just as my grandfather had been. And what puzzled me was that the old man had defined it as *treachery*. When I was praised for my conduct I felt a guilt that in some way I was doing something that was really against the wishes of the white folks, that if they had understood they would have desired me to act just the opposite, that I should have been sulky and mean, and that that really would have been what they wanted, even though they were fooled and thought they wanted me to act as I did. It made me afraid that some day they would look upon me as a traitor and I would be lost. Still I was more afraid to act any other way because they didn't like that at all. The old man's words were like a curse. On my graduation day I delivered an oration in which I showed that humility was the secret, indeed, the very essence of progress. (Not that I believed this—how could I, remembering my grandfather?—I only believed that it worked.) It was a great success. Everyone praised me and I was invited to give the speech at a gathering of the town's leading white citizens. It was a triumph for our whole community.

It was in the main ballroom of the leading hotel. When I got there I discovered that it was on the occasion of a smoker, and I was told that since I was to be there anyway I might as well take part in the battle royal to be fought by some of my schoolmates as part of the entertainment. The battle royal came first.

All of the town's big shots were there in their tuxedoes, wolfing 5 down the buffet foods, drinking beer and whiskey and smoking black cigars. It was a large room with a high ceiling. Chairs were arranged in neat rows around three sides of a portable boxing ring. The fourth side was clear, revealing a gleaming space of polished floor. I had some misgivings over the battle royal, by the way. Not from a distaste for fighting, but because I didn't care too much for the other fellows who were to take part. They were tough guys who seemed to have no grandfather's curse worrying their minds. No one could mistake their toughness. And besides, I suspected that fighting a battle royal might detract from the dignity of my speech. In those pre-invisible days I visualized myself as a potential Booker T. Washington. But the other fellows didn't care too much for me either, and there were nine of them. I felt superior to them in my way, and I didn't like the manner in which we were all crowded together into the servants' elevator. Nor did they like my being there. In fact, as the warmly lighted floors flashed past the elevator we had words over the fact that I, by taking part in the fight, had knocked one of their friends out of a night's work.

We were led out of the elevator through a rococo hall into an anteroom and told to get into our fighting togs. Each of us was issued a pair of boxing gloves and ushered out into the big mirrored hall, which we entered looking cautiously about us and whispering, lest we might accidentally be heard above the noise of the room. It was foggy with cigar smoke. And already the whiskey was taking effect. I was shocked to see some of the most important men of the town quite tipsy. They were all there—bankers, lawyers, judges, doctors, fire chiefs, teachers, merchants. Even one of the more fashionable pastors. Something we could not see was going on up front. A clarinet was vibrating sensuously and the men were standing up and moving eagerly forward. We were a small tight group, clustered together, our bare upper bodies touching and shining with anticipatory sweat; while up front the big shots were becoming increasingly excited over something we still could not see. Suddenly I heard the school superintendent, who had told me to come, yell, "Bring up the shines, gentlemen! Bring up the little shines!"

We were rushed up to the front of the ballroom, where it smelled even more strongly of tobacco and whiskey. Then we were pushed into place. I almost wet my pants. A sea of faces, some hostile, some amused, ringed around us, and in the center, facing us, stood a magnificent blonde—stark naked. There was dead silence. I felt a blast of cold air chill me. I tried to back away, but they were behind me and around me. Some of the boys stood with lowered heads, trembling. I felt a wave of irrational guilt and fear. My teeth chattered, my skin turned to goose flesh, my knees knocked. Yet I was strongly attracted and looked in spite of myself. Had the price of looking been blindness,

I would have looked. The hair was yellow like that of a circus kewpie doll, the face heavily powdered and rouged, as though to form an abstract mask, the eyes hollow and smeared a cool blue, the color of a baboon's butt. I felt a desire to spit upon her as my eyes brushed slowly over her body. Her breasts were firm and round as the domes of East Indian temples, and I stood so close as to see the fine skin texture and beads of pearly perspiration glistening like dew around the pink and erected buds of her nipples. I wanted at one and the same time to run from the room, to sink through the floor, or go to her and cover her from my eyes and the eyes of the others with my body; to feel the soft thighs, to caress her and destroy her, to love her and murder her, to hide from her, and yet to stroke where below the small American flag tattooed upon her belly her thighs formed a capital V. I had a notion that of all in the room she saw only me with her impersonal eyes.

And then she began to dance, a slow sensuous movement; the smoke of a hundred cigars clinging to her like the thinnest of veils. She seemed like a fair bird-girl girdled in veils calling to me from the angry surface of some gray and threatening sea. I was transported. Then I became aware of the clarinet playing and the big shots yelling at us. Some threatened us if we looked and others if we did not. On my right I saw one boy faint. And now a man grabbed a silver pitcher from a table and stepped close as he dashed ice water upon him and stood him up and forced two of us to support him as his head hung and moans issued from his thick bluish lips. Another boy began to plead to go home. He was the largest of the group, wearing dark red fighting trunks much too small to conceal the erection which projected from him as though in answer to the insinuating low-registered moaning of the clarinet. He tried to hide himself with his boxing gloves.

And all the while the blonde continued dancing, smiling faintly at the big shots who watched her with fascination, and faintly smiling at our fear. I noticed a certain merchant who followed her hungrily, his lips loose and drooling. He was a large man who wore diamond studs in a shirtfront which swelled with the ample paunch underneath, and each time the blonde swayed her undulating hips he ran his hand through the thin hair of his bald head and, with his arms upheld, his posture clumsy like that of an intoxicated panda, wound his belly in a slow and obscene grind. This creature was completely hypnotized. The music had quickened. As the dancer flung herself about with a detached expression on her face, the men began reaching out to touch her. I could see their beefy fingers sink into the soft flesh. Some of the others tried to stop them and she began to move around the floor in graceful circles, as they gave chase, slipping and sliding over the polished floor. It was mad. Chairs went crashing, drinks were spilt, as they ran laughing and howling after her. They caught her just as she reached a door, raised her from the floor, and tossed her as college boys are tossed at a hazing, and above her red, fixed-smiling lips I saw the terror and disgust in her eyes, almost like my own terror and that which I saw in some of the other boys. As I watched, they tossed her twice and her soft breasts seemed to flatten against the air and her legs flung wildly as she spun. Some of the more sober ones helped her to escape. And I started off the floor, heading for the anteroom with the rest of the boys.

Some were still crying and in hysteria. But as we tried to leave we were stopped and ordered to get into the ring. There was nothing to do but what we were told. All ten of us climbed under the ropes and allowed ourselves to be blindfolded with broad bands of white cloth. One of the men seemed to feel a bit sympathetic and tried to cheer us up as we stood with our backs against the ropes. Some of us tried to grin. "See that boy over there?" one of the men said. "I want you to run across at the bell and give it to him right in the belly. If you don't get him, I'm going to get you. I don't like his looks." Each of us was told the same. The blindfolds were put on. Yet even then I had been going over my speech. In my mind each word was as bright as flame. I felt the cloth pressed into place, and frowned so that it would be loosened when I relaxed.

But now I felt a sudden fit of blind terror. I was unused to darkness. It was as though I had suddenly found myself in a dark room filled with poisonous cottonmouths. I could hear the bleary voices yelling insistently for the battle royal to begin.

"Get going in there!"

"Let me at that big nigger!"

I strained to pick up the school superintendent's voice, as though to squeeze some security out of that slightly more familiar sound.

"Let me at those black sonsabitches!" someone yelled.   15

"No, Jackson, no!" another voice yelled. "Here, somebody, help me hold Jack."

"I want to get at that ginger-colored nigger. Tear him limb from limb," the first voice yelled.

I stood against the ropes trembling. For in those days I was what they called ginger-colored, and he sounded as though he might crunch me between his teeth like a crisp ginger cookie.

Quite a struggle was going on. Chairs were being kicked about and I could hear voices grunting as with a terrific effort. I wanted to see, to see more desperately than ever before. But the blindfold was tight as a thick skin-puckering scab and when I raised my gloved hands to push the layers of white aside a voice yelled, "Oh, no you don't, black bastard! Leave that alone!"

"Ring the bell before Jackson kills him a coon!" someone boomed   20
in the sudden silence. And I heard the bell clang and the sound of the feet scuffing forward.

A glove smacked against my head. I pivoted, striking out stiffly as someone went past, and felt the jar ripple along the length of my arm to my shoulder. Then it seemed as though all nine of the boys had turned upon me at once. Blows pounded me from all sides while I struck out as best I could. So many blows landed upon me that I wondered if I were not the only blindfolded fighter in the ring, or if the man called Jackson hadn't succeeded in getting me after all.

Blindfolded, I could no longer control my motions. I had no dignity. I stumbled about like a baby or a drunken man. The smoke had become thicker, and with each new blow it seemed to sear and further restrict my lungs. My saliva became like hot bitter glue. A glove connected with my head, filling my mouth with warm blood. It was everywhere. I could not tell if the moisture I felt upon my body was sweat or blood. A blow landed hard against the nape of my neck. I felt myself going over, my head hitting the floor. Streaks of blue light filled the black world behind the blindfold. I lay prone, pretending that I was knocked out, but felt myself seized by hands and yanked to my feet. "Get going, black boy! Mix it up!" My arms were like lead, my head smarting from blows. I managed to feel my way to the ropes and held on, trying to catch my breath. A glove landed in my mid-section and I went over again, feeling as though the smoke had become a knife jabbed into my guts. Pushed this way and that by the legs milling around me, I finally pulled erect and discovered that I could see the black, sweat-washed forms weaving, in the smoky-blue atmosphere like drunken dancers weaving to the rapid drumlike thuds of blows.

Everyone fought hysterically. It was complete anarchy. Everybody fought everybody else. No group fought together for long. Two, three, four, fought one, then turned to fight each other, were themselves attacked. Blows landed below the belt and in the kidney, with the gloves open as well as closed, and with my eye partly opened now there was not so much terror. I moved carefully, avoiding blows, although not too many to attract attention, fighting from group to group. The boys groped about like blind, cautious crabs crouching to protect their mid-sections, their heads pulled in short against their shoulders, their arms stretched nervously before them, with their fists testing the smoke-filled air like the knobbed feelers of hypersensitive snails. In one corner I glimpsed a boy violently punching the air and heard him scream in pain as he smashed his hand against a ring post. For a second I saw him bent over holding his hand, then going down as a blow caught his unprotected head. I played one group against the other, slipping in and throwing a punch then stepping out of range while pushing the others into the melee to take the blows blindly aimed at me. The smoke was agonizing and there were no rounds, no bells at three-minute inter-vals to relieve our exhaustion. The room spun round me, a swirl of lights, smoke, sweating bodies surrounded by tense white faces. I bled from both nose and mouth, the blood spattering upon my chest.

The men kept yelling, "Slug him, black boy! Knock his guts out!"

"Uppercut him! Kill him! Kill that big boy!"   25

Taking a fake fall, I saw a boy going down heavily beside me as though we were felled by a single blow, saw a sneaker-clad foot shoot into his groin as the two who had knocked him down stumbled upon him. I rolled out of range, feeling a twinge of nausea.

The harder we fought the more threatening the men became. And yet, I had begun to worry about my speech again. How would it go? Would they recognize my ability? What would they give me?

I was fighting automatically when suddenly I noticed that one after another of the boys was leaving the ring. I was surprised, filled with panic, as though I had been left alone with an unknown danger. Then I understood. The boys had arranged it among themselves. It was the custom for the two men left in the ring to slug it out for the winner's prize. I discovered this too late. When the bell sounded two men in tuxedoes leaped into the ring and removed the blindfold. I found myself facing Tatlock, the biggest of the gang. I felt sick at my stomach. Hardly had the bell stopped ringing in my ears than it clanged again and I saw him moving swiftly toward me. Thinking of nothing else to do I hit him smash on the nose. He kept coming, bringing the rank sharp violence of stale sweat. His face was a black blank of a face, only his eyes alive—with hate of me and aglow with a feverish terror from what had happened to us all. I became anxious. I wanted to deliver my speech and he came at me as though he meant to beat it out of me. I smashed him again and again, taking his blows as they came. Then on a sudden impulse I struck him lightly and as we clinched, I whispered, "Fake like I knocked you out, you can have the prize."

"I'll break your behind," he whispered hoarsely.

"For *them*?"

"For *me*, sonofabitch!"

They were yelling for us to break it up and Tatlock spun me half around with a blow, and as a joggled camera sweeps in a reeling scene, I saw the howling red faces crouching tense beneath the cloud of blue-gray smoke. For a moment the world wavered, unraveled, flowed, then my head cleared and Tatlock bounced before me. That fluttering shadow before my eyes was his jabbing left hand. Then falling forward, my head against his damp shoulder, I whispered.

"I'll make it five dollars more."

"Go to hell!"

But his muscles relaxed a trifle beneath my pressure and I breathed, "Seven?"

"Give it to your ma," he said, ripping me beneath the heart.

And while I still held him I butted him and moved away. I felt myself bombarded with punches. I fought back with hopeless desperation. I wanted to deliver my speech more than anything else in the world, because I felt that only these men could judge truly my ability, and now this stupid clown was ruining my chances. I began fighting carefully now, moving in to punch him and out again with my greater speed. A lucky blow to his chin and I had him going too— until I heard a loud voice yell, "I got my money on the big boy."

Hearing this, I almost dropped my guard. I was confused: Should I try to win against the voice out there? Would not this go against my speech, and was not this a moment for humility, for nonresistance? A blow to my head as I danced about sent my right eye popping like a jack-in-the-box and settled my dilemma. The room went red as I fell. It was a dream fall, my body languid and fastidious as to where to land, until the floor became impatient and smashed up to meet me. A moment later I came to. An hypnotic voice said FIVE emphatically. And I lay there, hazily watching a dark red spot of my own blood shaping itself into a butterfly, glistening and soaking into the soiled gray world of the canvas.

When the voice drawled TEN I was lifted up and dragged to a chair. I sat dazed. My eye pained and swelled with each throb of my pounding heart and I wondered if now I would be allowed to speak. I was wringing wet, my mouth still bleeding. We were grouped along the wall now. The other boys ignored me as they congratulated Tatlock and speculated as to how much they would be paid. One boy whimpered over his smashed hand. Looking up front, I saw attendants in white jackets rolling the portable ring away and placing a small square rug in the vacant space surrounded by chairs. Perhaps, I thought, I will stand on the rug to deliver my speech.

Then the M.C. called to us, "Come on up here boys and get your money." 40

We ran forward to where the men laughed and talked in their chairs, waiting. Everyone seemed friendly now.

"There it is on the rug," the man said. I saw the rug covered with coins of all dimensions and a few crumpled bills. But what excited me, scattered here and there, were the gold pieces.

"Boys, it's all yours," the man said. "You get all you grab."

"That's right, Sambo," a blond man said, winking at me confidentially.

I trembled with excitement, forgetting my pain. I would get the 45
gold and the bills, I thought. I would use both hands. I would throw
my body against the boys nearest me to block them from the gold.

"Get down around the rug now," the man commanded, "and don't
anyone touch it until I give the signal."

"This ought to be good," I heard.

As told, we got around the square rug on our knees. Slowly the man
raised his freckled hand as we followed it upward with our eyes.

I heard, "These niggers look like they're about to pray!"

Then, "Ready," the man said. "Go!" 50

I lunged for a yellow coin lying on the blue design of the carpet, touching it and sending a surprised shriek to join those rising around me. I
tried frantically to remove my hand but could not let go. A hot, violent
force tore through my body, shaking me like a wet rat. The rug was elec-
trified. The hair bristled up on my head as I shook myself free. My
muscles jumped, my nerves jangled, writhed. But I saw that this was not
stopping the other boys. Laughing in fear and embarrassment, some
were holding back and scooping up the coins knocked off by the painful
contortions of the others. The men roared above us as we struggled.

"Pick it up, goddamnit, pick it up!" someone called like a bass-
voiced parrot. "Go on, get it!"

I crawled rapidly around the floor, picking up the coins, trying to
avoid the coppers and to get greenbacks and the gold. Ignoring the
shock by laughing, as I brushed the coins off quickly, I discovered that
I could contain the electricity—a contradiction, but it works. Then the
men began to push us onto the rug. Laughing embarrassedly, we struggled out of their hands and kept after the coins. We were all wet and
slippery and hard to hold. Suddenly I saw a boy lifted into the air, glistening with sweat like a circus seal, and dropped, his wet back landing
flush upon the charged rug, heard him yell and saw him literally dance
upon his back, his elbows beating a frenzied tattoo upon the floor, his
muscles twitching like the flesh of a horse stung by many flies. When he
finally rolled off, his face was gray and no one stopped him when he ran
from the floor amid booming laughter.

"Get the money," the M.C. called. "That's good hard American
cash!"

And we snatched and grabbed, snatched and grabbed. I was careful   55
not to come too close to the rug now, and when I felt the hot whiskey
breath descend upon me like a cloud of foul air I reached out and
grabbed the leg of a chair. It was occupied and I held on desperately.

"Leggo, nigger! Leggo!"

The huge face wavered down to mine as he tried to push me free. But
my body was slippery and he was too drunk. It was Mr. Colcord, who
owned a chain of movie houses and "entertainment palaces." Each time
he grabbed me I slipped out of his hands. It became a real struggle.
I feared the rug more than I did the drunk, so I held on, surprising
myself for a moment by trying to topple *him* upon the rug. It was such
an enormous idea that I found myself actually carrying it out. I tried not
to be obvious, yet when I grabbed his leg, trying to tumble him out of
the chair, he raised up roaring with laughter, and, looking at me with
soberness dead in the eye, kicked me viciously in the chest. The chair
leg flew out of my hand and I felt myself going and rolled. It was as
though I had rolled through a bed of hot coals. It seemed a whole century would pass before I would roll free, a century in which I was seared
through the deepest levels of my body to the fearful breath within me
and the breath seared and heated to the point of explosion. It'll all be
over in a flash, I thought as I rolled clear. It'll all be over in a flash.

But not yet, the men on the other side were waiting, red faces swollen as though from apoplexy as they bent forward in their chairs. Seeing their fingers coming toward me I rolled away as a fumbled football
rolls off the receiver's fingertips, back into the coals. That time I luck-
ily sent the rug sliding out of place and heard the coins ringing against
the floor and the boys scuffling to pick them up and the M.C. calling,
"All right, boys, that's all. Go get dressed and get your money."

I was limp as a dish rag. My back felt as though it had been beaten
with wires.

When we had dressed the M.C. came in and gave us each five dol-   60
lars, except Tatlock, who got ten for being last in the ring. Then he told
us to leave. I was not to get a chance to deliver my speech, I thought. I
was going out into the dim alley in despair when I was stopped and
told to go back. I returned to the ballroom, where the men were pushing back their chairs and gathering in groups to talk.

The M.C. knocked on a table for quiet. "Gentlemen," he said, "we almost forgot an important part of the program. A most serious part, gentlemen. This boy was brought here to deliver a speech which he made at his graduation yesterday . . ."

"Bravo!"

"I'm told that he is the smartest boy we've got out there in Greenwood. I'm told that he knows more big words than a pocket-sized dictionary."

Much applause and laughter.

"So now, gentlemen, I want you to give him your attention." 65

There was still laughter as I faced them, my mouth dry, my eye throbbing. I began slowly, but evidently my throat was tense, because they began shouting, "Louder! Louder!"

"We of the younger generation extol the wisdom of that great leader and educator," I shouted, "who first spoke these flaming words of wisdom: 'A ship lost at sea for many days suddenly sighted a friendly vessel. From the mast of the unfortunate vessel was seen a signal: "Water, water; we die of thirst!" The answer from the friendly vessel came back: "Cast down your bucket where you are." The captain of the distressed vessel, at last heeding the injunction, cast down his bucket, and it came up full of fresh sparkling water from the mouth of the Amazon River.' And like him I say, and in his words, 'To those of my race who depend upon bettering their condition in a foreign land, or who underestimate the importance of cultivating friendly relations with the southern white man, who is his next-door neighbor, I would say: "Cast down your bucket where you are"—cast it down in making friends in every manly way of the people of all races by whom we are surrounded . . .'"

I spoke automatically and with such fervor that I did not realize that the men were still talking and laughing until my dry mouth, filling up with blood from the cut, almost strangled me. I coughed, wanting to stop and go to one of the tall brass, sand-filled spittoons to relieve myself, but a few of the men, especially the superintendent, were listening and I was afraid. So I gulped it down, blood, saliva and all, and continued. (What powers of endurance I had during those days! What enthusiasm! What a belief in the rightness of things!) I spoke even louder in spite of the pain. But still they talked and still they laughed, as though deaf with cotton in dirty ears. So I spoke with greater emotional emphasis. I closed my ears and swallowed blood until I was nauseated. The speech seemed a hundred times as long as before, but I could not leave out a single word. All had to be said, each memorized nuance considered, rendered. Nor was that all. Whenever I uttered a word of three or more syllables a group of voices would yell for me to repeat it. I used the phrase "social responsibility" and they yelled:

"What's that word you say, boy?"

"Social responsibility," I said.   70

"What?"

"Social . . ."

"Louder."

". . . responsibility."

"More."   75

"Respon—"

"Repeat!"

"—sibility."

The room filled with the uproar of laughter until, no doubt distracted by having to gulp down my blood, I made a mistake and yelled a phrase I had often seen denounced in newspaper editorials, heard debated in private.

"Social . . ."   80

"What?" they yelled.

". . . equality—"

The laughter hung smokelike in the sudden stillness. I opened my eyes, puzzled. Sounds of displeasure filled the room. The M.C. rushed forward. They shouted hostile phrases at me. But I did not understand.

A small dry mustached man in the front row blared out, "Say that slowly, son!"

"What, sir?"   85

"What you just said!"

"Social responsibility, sir," I said.

"You weren't being smart, were you, boy?" he said, not unkindly.

"No, sir!"

"You sure that about 'equality' was a mistake?" 90

"Oh, yes, sir," I said. "I was swallowing blood."

"Well, you had better speak more slowly so we can understand. We mean to do right by you, but you've got to know your place at all times. All right, now, go on with your speech."

I was afraid. I wanted to leave but I wanted also to speak and I was afraid they'd snatch me down.

"Thank you, sir," I said, beginning where I had left off, and having them ignore me as before.

Yet when I finished there was a thunderous applause. I was sur- 95 prised to see the superintendent come forth with a package wrapped in white tissue paper, and, gesturing for quiet, address the men.

"Gentlemen, you see that I did not overpraise this boy. He makes a good speech and some day he'll lead his people in the proper paths. And I don't have to tell you that that is important in these days and times. This is a good, smart boy, and so to encourage him in the right direction, in the name of the Board of Education I wish to present him a prize in the form of this . . ."

He paused, removing the tissue paper and revealing a gleaming calfskin brief case.

". . . in the form of this first-class article from Shad Whitmore's shop."

"Boy," he said, addressing me, "take this prize and keep it well. Consider it a badge of office. Prize it. Keep developing as you are and some day it will be filled with important papers that will help shape the destiny of your people."

I was so moved that I could hardly express my thanks. A rope of 100 bloody saliva forming a shape like an undiscovered continent drooled upon the leather and I wiped it quickly away. I felt an importance that I had never dreamed.

"Open it and see what's inside," I was told.

My fingers a-tremble, I complied, smelling the fresh leather and finding an official-looking document inside. It was a scholarship to the state college for Negroes. My eyes filled with tears and I ran awkwardly off the floor.

I was overjoyed; I did not even mind when I discovered that the gold pieces I had scrambled for were brass pocket tokens advertising a certain make of automobile.

When I reached home everyone was excited. Next day the neighbors came to congratulate me. I even felt safe from grandfather, whose deathbed curse usually spoiled my triumphs. I stood beneath his photograph with my brief case in hand and smiled triumphantly into his stolid black peasant's face. It was a face that fascinated me. The eyes seemed to follow everywhere I went.

That night I dreamed I was at a circus with him and that he refused 105 to laugh at the clowns no matter what they did. Then later he told me to open my brief case and read what was inside and I did, finding an official envelope stamped with the state seal; and inside the envelope I found another and another, endlessly, and I thought I would fall of weariness. "Them's years," he said. "Now open that one." And I did and in it I found an engraved document containing a short message in letters of gold. "Read it," my grandfather said. "Out loud!"

"To Whom It May Concern," I intoned. "Keep This Nigger-Boy Running."

I awoke with the old man's laughter ringing in my ears.

(It was a dream I was to remember and dream again for many years after. But at that time I had no insight into its meaning. First I had to attend college.)

STUDY QUESTIONS

1. Why does the mild-mannered, passive grandfather say that he has been a "traitor in enemy country"? How can the grandfather's advice to both "live with your head in the lion's mouth" and "overcome 'em with yeses" be followed?

2. The NARRATOR'S speech borrows directly from Booker T. Washington's "Atlanta Exposition Address." Locate a copy of Washington's speech and COMPARE AND CONTRAST it to what the narrator says. How are the SETTINGS for the two speeches different? What is the EFFECT of the narrator's using Washington's conciliatory rhetoric after a battle royal?

3. This story depicts the narrator's reflection on the PROCESS of giving his valedictory speech. What do the blindfolds that the young men wear during the battle royal SYMBOLIZE? How do they prevent the fighters from recognizing truths about themselves and others around them? Does the narrator see clearly by the end of the process? Why or why not?

4. *For Writing.* Consider some of the elements of the traditional American dream: healthy competition, financial success, a good education, an attractive, loving spouse, being respected among one's peers in the community. In an essay, explore how Ellison's story twists these elements. Why and how does the American dream become an American nightmare for this young, African American protagonist?

JOYCE CAROL OATES { *Where Are You Going,*
Where Have You Been?

JOYCE CAROL OATES (b. 1938) is a prolific and versatile writer whose work is popular both with the general reading public (her 1996 novel *We Were the Mulvaneys* was featured on Oprah's Book Club) and in academia, where her fiction and poetry often appear on the syllabi of college courses. Oates was raised in a rural area near Lockport, New York, and earned her BA at Syracuse University; as a student there, she won a fiction contest sponsored by *Mademoiselle* magazine. She went on to obtain an MA in English at the University of Wisconsin. She has taught at the University of Windsor and is currently a professor of creative writing at Princeton. The author of more than one hundred novels, novellas, and short story collections, as well as many books of poetry, plays, and essays, Oates received the National Book Award in 1970 for her novel *them*, which, like much of her fiction, reimagines historical events in fictional form. Her other novels include *Black Water* (1993), *What I Lived For* (1994), *Blonde* (2000), and *The Gravedigger's Daughter* (2007).

"Where Are You Going, Where Have You Been?" (1966) is Oates's most anthologized short story. It presents a vivid picture of the seemingly conventional life of its teenaged protagonist, Connie, and describes what happens when an element of danger is introduced. As you read, consider how the story both reflects and undercuts the popular culture of the early 1960s.

for Bob Dylan[1]

HER NAME WAS CONNIE. SHE was fifteen and she had a quick, nervous giggling habit of craning her neck to glance into mirrors or checking other people's faces to make sure her own was all right. Her mother, who noticed everything and knew everything and who hadn't much reason any longer to look at her own face, always scolded Connie about it. "Stop gawking at yourself. Who are you? You think you're so pretty?" she would say. Connie would raise her eyebrows at these familiar old complaints and look right through her mother, into a shadowy vision of herself as she was right at that moment: she knew she was pretty and that was everything. Her mother had been pretty once too, if you could believe those old snapshots in the album, but now her looks were gone and that was why she was always after Connie.

"Why don't you keep your room clean like your sister? How've you got your hair fixed—what the hell stinks? Hair spray? You don't see your sister using that junk."

Her sister June was twenty-four and still lived at home. She was a secretary in the high school Connie attended, and if that wasn't bad enough—with her in the same building—she was so plain and chunky and steady that Connie had to hear her praised all the time by her mother and her mother's sisters. June did this, June did that, she saved money and helped clean the house and cooked and Connie couldn't do a thing, her mind was all filled with trashy daydreams. Their father was away at work most of the time and when he came home he wanted supper and he read the newspaper at supper and after supper he went to bed. He didn't bother talking much to them, but around his bent head Connie's mother kept picking at her until Connie wished her mother was dead and she herself was dead and it was all over. "She makes me want to throw up sometimes," she complained to her friends. She had a high, breathless, amused voice that made everything she said sound a little forced, whether it was sincere or not.

---

[1] The mood and tone of this story was inspired by American folk and rock singer and songwriter Bob Dylan (b. 1941).

There was one good thing: June went places with girl friends of hers, girls who were just as plain and steady as she, and so when Connie wanted to do that her mother had no objections. The father of Connie's best girl friend drove the girls the three miles to town and left them at a shopping plaza so they could walk through the stores or go to a movie, and when he came to pick them up again at eleven he never bothered to ask what they had done.

They must have been familiar sights, walking around the shopping 5 plaza in their shorts and flat ballerina slippers that always scuffed the sidewalk, with charm bracelets jingling on their thin wrists; they would lean together to whisper and laugh secretly if someone passed who amused or interested them. Connie had long dark blond hair that drew anyone's eye to it, and she wore part of it pulled up on her head and puffed out and the rest of it she let fall down her back. She wore a pullover jersey blouse that looked one way when she was at home and another way when she was away from home. Everything about her had two sides to it, one for home and one for anywhere that was not home: her walk, which could be childlike and bobbing, or languid enough to make anyone think she was hearing music in her head; her mouth, which was pale and smirking most of the time, but bright and pink on these evenings out; her laugh, which was cynical and drawling at home—"Ha, ha, very funny,"—but high-pitched and nervous anywhere else, like the jingling of the charms on her bracelet.

Sometimes they did go shopping or to a movie, but sometimes they went across the highway, ducking fast across the busy road, to a drive-in restaurant where older kids hung out. The restaurant was shaped like a big bottle, though squatter than a real bottle, and on its cap was a revolving figure of a grinning boy holding a hamburger aloft. One night in midsummer they ran across, breathless with daring, and right away someone leaned out a car window and invited them over, but it was just a boy from high school they didn't like. It made them feel good to be able to ignore him. They went up through the maze of parked and cruising cars to the bright-lit, fly-infested restaurant, their faces pleased and expectant as if they were entering a sacred building that loomed up out of the night to give them what haven and blessing they yearned for.

They sat at the counter and crossed their legs at the ankles, their thin shoulders rigid with excitement, and listened to the music that made everything so good: the music was always in the background, like music at a church service; it was something to depend upon.

A boy named Eddie came in to talk with them. He sat backwards on his stool, turning himself jerkily around in semicircles and then stopping and turning back again, and after a while he asked Connie if she would like something to eat. She said she would and so she tapped her friend's arm on her way out—her friend pulled her face up into a brave, droll look—and Connie said she would meet her at eleven, across the way. "I just hate to leave her like that," Connie said earnestly, but the boy said that she wouldn't be alone for long. So they went out to his car, and on the way Connie couldn't help but let her eyes wander over the windshields and faces all around her, her face gleaming with a joy that had nothing to do with Eddie or even this place; it might have been the music. She drew her shoulders up and sucked in her breath with the pure pleasure of being alive, and just at that moment she happened to glance at a face just a few feet from hers. It was a boy with shaggy black hair, in a convertible jalopy painted gold. He stared at her and then his lips widened into a grin. Connie slit her eyes at him and turned away, but she couldn't help glancing back and there he was, still watching her. He wagged a finger and laughed and said, "Gonna get you, baby," and Connie turned away again without Eddie noticing anything.

She spent three hours with him, at the restaurant where they ate hamburgers and drank Cokes in wax cups that were always sweating, and then down an alley a mile or so away, and when he left her off at five to eleven only the movie house was still open at the plaza. Her girl friend was there, talking with a boy. When Connie came up, the two girls smiled at each other and Connie said, "How was the movie?" and the girl said, "*You* should know." They rode off with the girl's father, sleepy and pleased, and Connie couldn't help but look back at the darkened shopping plaza with its big empty parking lot and its signs that were faded and ghostly now, and over at the drive-in restaurant where cars were still circling tirelessly. She couldn't hear the music at this distance.

Next morning June asked her how the movie was and Connie said, "So-so."

She and that girl and occasionally another girl went out several times a week, and the rest of the time Connie spent around the house— it was summer vacation—getting in her mother's way and thinking, dreaming about the boys she met. But all the boys fell back and dissolved into a single face that was not even a face but an idea, a feeling, mixed up with the urgent insistent pounding of the music and the humid night air of July. Connie's mother kept dragging her back to the daylight by finding things for her to do or saying suddenly, "What's this about the Pettinger girl?"

And Connie would say nervously, "Oh, her. That dope." She always drew thick clear lines between herself and such girls, and her mother was simple and kind enough to believe it. Her mother was so simple, Connie thought, that it was maybe cruel to fool her so much. Her mother went scuffling around the house in old bedroom slippers and complained over the telephone to one sister about the other, then the other called up and the two of them complained about the third one. If June's name was mentioned her mother's tone was approving, and if Connie's name was mentioned it was disapproving. This did not really mean she disliked Connie, and actually Connie thought that her mother preferred her to June just because she was prettier, but the two of them kept up a pretense of exasperation, a sense that they were tugging and struggling over something of little value to either of them. Sometimes, over coffee, they were almost friends, but something would come up—some vexation that was like a fly buzzing suddenly around their heads—and their faces went hard with contempt.

One Sunday Connie got up at eleven—none of them bothered with church—and washed her hair so that it could dry all day long in the sun. Her parents and sister were going to a barbecue at an aunt's house and Connie said no, she wasn't interested, rolling her eyes to let her mother know just what she thought of it. "Stay home alone then," her mother said sharply. Connie sat out back in a lawn chair and watched them drive away, her father quiet and bald, hunched around so that he could back the car out, her mother with a look that was still angry and not at all softened through the windshield, and in the back seat poor old June, all dressed up as if she didn't know what a barbecue was, with all the running yelling kids and the flies. Connie sat with her eyes closed in the sun, dreaming and dazed with the warmth about her as if this were a kind of love, the caresses of love, and her mind slipped over onto thoughts of the boy she had been with the night before and how nice he had been, how sweet it always was, not the way someone like June would suppose but sweet, gentle, the way it was in movies and promised in songs; and when she opened her eyes she hardly knew where she was, the back yard ran off into weeds and a fence-like line of trees and behind it the sky was perfectly blue and still. The asbestos "ranch house" that was now three years old startled her—it looked small. She shook her head as if to get awake.

It was too hot. She went inside the house and turned on the radio to drown out the quiet. She sat on the edge of her bed, barefoot, and listened for an hour and a half to a program called XYZ Sunday Jamboree, record after record of hard, fast, shrieking songs she sang along with, interspersed by exclamations from "Bobby King": "An' look here, you girls at Napoleon's—Son and Charley want you to pay real close attention to this song coming up!"

And Connie paid close attention herself, bathed in a glow of slow-pulsed joy that seemed to rise mysteriously out of the music itself and lay languidly about the airless little room, breathed in and breathed out with each gentle rise and fall of her chest.

After a while she heard a car coming up the drive. She sat up at once, startled, because it couldn't be her father so soon. The gravel kept crunching all the way in from the road—the driveway was long— and Connie ran to the window. It was a car she didn't know. It was an open jalopy, painted a bright gold that caught the sunlight opaquely. Her heart began to pound and her fingers snatched at her hair, checking it, and she whispered, "Christ. Christ," wondering how bad she looked. The car came to a stop at the side door and the horn sounded four short taps, as if this were a signal Connie knew.

She went into the kitchen and approached the door slowly, then hung out the screen door, her bare toes curling down off the step. There were two boys in the car and now she recognized the driver: he had shaggy, shabby black hair that looked crazy as a wig and he was grinning at her.

15

"I ain't late, am I?" he said.

"Who the hell do you think you are?" Connie said.

"Toldja I'd be out, didn't I?"

"I don't even know who you are."   20

She spoke sullenly, careful to show no interest or pleasure, and he spoke in a fast, bright monotone. Connie looked past him to the other boy, taking her time. He had fair brown hair, with a lock that fell onto his forehead. His sideburns gave him a fierce, embarrassed look, but so far he hadn't even bothered to glance at her. Both boys wore sunglasses. The driver's glasses were metallic and mirrored everything in miniature.

"You wanta come for a ride?" he said.

Connie smirked and let her hair fall loose over one shoulder.

"Don'tcha like my car? New paint job," he said. "Hey."

"What?"   25

"You're cute."

She pretended to fidget, chasing flies away from the door.

"Don'tcha believe me, or what?" he said.

"Look, I don't even know who you are," Connie said in disgust.

"Hey, Ellie's got a radio, see. Mine broke down." He lifted his   30
friend's arm and showed her the little transistor radio the boy was holding, and now Connie began to hear the music. It was the same program that was playing inside the house.

"Bobby King?" she said.

"I listen to him all the time. I think he's great."

"He's kind of great," Connie said reluctantly.

"Listen, that guy's *great*. He knows where the action is."

Connie blushed a little, because the glasses made it impossible for   35
her to see just what this boy was looking at. She couldn't decide if she liked him or if he was just a jerk, and so she dawdled in the doorway and wouldn't come down or go back inside. She said, "What's all that stuff painted on your car?"

"Can'tcha read it?" He opened the door very carefully, as if he were afraid it might fall off. He slid out just as carefully, planting his feet firmly on the ground, the tiny metallic world in his glasses slowing down like gelatine hardening, and in the midst of it Connie's bright green blouse. "This here is my name, to begin with," he said. ARNOLD

FRIEND was written in tarlike black letters on the side, with a drawing of a round, grinning face that reminded Connie of a pumpkin, except it wore sunglasses. "I wanta introduce myself, I'm Arnold Friend and that's my real name and I'm gonna be your friend, honey, and inside the car's Ellie Oscar, he's kinda shy." Ellie brought his transistor radio up to his shoulder and balanced it there. "Now, these numbers are a secret code, honey," Arnold Friend explained. He read off the numbers 33, 19, 17 and raised his eyebrows at her to see what she thought of that, but she didn't think much of it. The left rear fender had been smashed and around it was written, on the gleaming gold background: DONE BY CRAZY WOMAN DRIVER. Connie had to laugh at that. Arnold Friend was pleased at her laughter and looked up at her. "Around the other side's a lot more—you wanta come and see them?"

"No."

"Why not?"

"Why should I?"

"Don'tcha wanta see what's on the car? Don'tcha wanta go for a   40
ride?"

"I don't know."

"Why not?"

"I got things to do."

"Like what?"

"Things."   45

He laughed as if she had said something funny. He slapped his thighs. He was standing in a strange way, leaning back against the car as if he were balancing himself. He wasn't tall, only an inch or so taller than she would be if she came down to him. Connie liked the way he was dressed, which was the way all of them dressed: tight faded jeans stuffed into black, scuffed boots, a belt that pulled his waist in and showed how lean he was, and a white pull-over shirt that was a little soiled and showed the hard small muscles of his arms and shoulders. He looked as if he probably did hard work, lifting and carrying things. Even his neck looked muscular. And his face was a familiar face, somehow: the jaw and chin and cheeks slightly darkened because he hadn't shaved for a day or two, and the nose long and hawklike, sniffing as if she were a treat he was going to gobble up and it was all a joke.

"Connie, you ain't telling the truth. This is your day set aside for a ride with me and you know it," he said, still laughing. The way he straightened and recovered from his fit of laughing showed that it had been all fake.

"How do you know what my name is?" she said suspiciously.

"It's Connie."

"Maybe and maybe not."   50

"I know my Connie," he said, wagging his finger. Now she remembered him even better, back at the restaurant, and her cheeks warmed at the thought of how she had sucked in her breath just at the moment she passed him—how she must have looked to him. And he had remembered her. "Ellie and I come out here especially for you," he said. "Ellie can sit in back. How about it?"

"Where?"

"Where what?"

"Where're we going?"

He looked at her. He took off the sunglasses and she saw how pale   55
the skin around his eyes was, like holes that were not in shadow but instead in light. His eyes were like chips of broken glass that catch the light in an amiable way. He smiled. It was as if the idea of going for a ride somewhere, to someplace, was a new idea to him.

"Just for a ride, Connie sweetheart."

"I never said my name was Connie," she said.

"But I know what it is. I know your name and all about you, lots of things," Arnold Friend said. He had not moved yet but stood still leaning back against the side of his jalopy. "I took a special interest in you, such a pretty girl, and found out all about you—like I know your parents and sister are gone somewhere and I know where and how long they're going to be gone, and I know who you were with last night, and your best girl friend's name is Betty. Right?"

He spoke in a simple lilting voice, exactly as if he were reciting the words to a song. His smile assured her that everything was fine. In the car Ellie turned up the volume on his radio and did not bother to look around at them.

"Ellie can sit in the back seat," Arnold Friend said. He indicated his   60
friend with a casual jerk of his chin, as if Ellie did not count and she should not bother with him.

"How'd you find out all that stuff?" Connie said.

"Listen: Betty Schultz and Tony Fitch and Jimmy Pettinger and Nancy Pettinger," he said in a chant. "Raymond Stanley and Bob Hutter—"

"Do you know all those kids?"

"I know everybody."

"Look, you're kidding. You're not from around here." 65

"Sure."

"But—how come we never saw you before?"

"Sure you saw me before," he said. He looked down at his boots, as if he were a little offended. "You just don't remember."

"I guess I'd remember you," Connie said.

"Yeah?" He looked up at this, beaming. He was pleased. He began to 70 mark time with the music from Ellie's radio, tapping his fists lightly together. Connie looked away from his smile to the car, which was painted so bright it almost hurt her eyes to look at it. She looked at that name, ARNOLD FRIEND. And up at the front fender was an expression that was familiar—MAN THE FLYING SAUCERS. It was an expression kids had used the year before but didn't use this year. She looked at it for a while as if the words meant something to her that she did not yet know.

"What're you thinking about? Huh?" Arnold Friend demanded. "Not worried about your hair blowing around in the car, are you?"

"No."

"Think I maybe can't drive good?"

"How do I know?"

"You're a hard girl to handle. How come?" he said. "Don't you 75 know I'm your friend? Didn't you see me put my sign in the air when you walked by?"

"What sign?"

"My sign." And he drew an X in the air, leaning out toward her. They were maybe ten feet apart. After his hand fell back to his side the X was still in the air, almost visible. Connie let the screen door close and stood perfectly still inside it, listening to the music from her radio and the boy's blend together. She stared at Arnold Friend. He stood there so stiffly relaxed, pretending to be relaxed, with one hand idly on the door handle as if he were keeping himself up that way and had no intention of ever moving again. She recognized most things about him, the tight jeans that showed his thighs and buttocks and the greasy leather boots and the tight shirt, and even that slippery friendly smile of his, that sleepy dreamy smile that all the boys used to get across ideas they didn't want to put into words. She recognized all this and also the singsong way he talked, slightly mocking, kidding, but serious and a little melancholy, and she recognized the way he tapped one fist against the other in homage to the perpetual music behind him. But all these things did not come together.

She said suddenly, "Hey, how old are you?"

His smiled faded. She could see then that he wasn't a kid, he was much older—thirty, maybe more. At this knowledge her heart began to pound faster.

"That's a crazy thing to ask. Can'tcha see I'm your own age?" 80

"Like hell you are."

"Or maybe a coupla years older. I'm eighteen."

"Eighteen?" she said doubtfully.

He grinned to reassure her and lines appeared at the corners of his mouth. His teeth were big and white. He grinned so broadly his eyes became slits and she saw how thick the lashes were, thick and black as if painted with a black tarlike material. Then, abruptly, he seemed to become embarrassed and looked over his shoulder at Ellie. "*Him,* he's crazy," he said. "Ain't he a riot? He's a nut, a real character." Ellie was still listening to the music. His sunglasses told nothing about what he was thinking. He wore a bright orange shirt unbuttoned halfway to show his chest, which was a pale, bluish chest and not muscular like Arnold Friend's. His shirt collar was turned up all around and the very tips of the collar pointed out past his chin as if they were protecting him. He was pressing the transistor radio up against his ear and sat there in a kind of daze, right in the sun.

"He's kinda strange," Connie said. 85

"Hey, she says you're kinda strange! Kinda strange!" Arnold Friend cried. He pounded on the car to get Ellie's attention. Ellie turned for the first time and Connie saw with shock that he wasn't a kid either— he had a fair, hairless face, cheeks reddened slightly as if the veins grew too close to the surface of his skin, the face of a forty-year-old baby.

Connie felt a wave of dizziness rise in her at this sight and she stared at him as if waiting for something to change the shock of the moment, make it all right again. Ellie's lips kept shaping words, mumbling along with the words blasting in his ear.

"Maybe you two better go away," Connie said faintly.

"What? How come?" Arnold Friend cried. "We come out here to take you for a ride. It's Sunday." He had the voice of the man on the radio now. It was the same voice, Connie thought. "Don'tcha know it's Sunday all day? And honey, no matter who you were with last night, today you're with Arnold Friend and don't you forget it! Maybe you better step out here," he said, and this last was in a different voice. It was a little flatter, as if the heat was finally getting to him.

"No. I got things to do."

"Hey." 90

"You two better leave."

"We ain't leaving until you come with us."

"Like hell I am—"

"Connie, don't fool around with me. I mean—I mean, don't fool *around*," he said, shaking his head. He laughed incredulously. He placed his sunglasses on top of his head, carefully, as if he were indeed wearing a wig, and brought the stems down behind his ears. Connie stared at him, another wave of dizziness and fear rising in her so that for a moment he wasn't even in focus but was just a blur standing there against his gold car, and she had the idea that he had driven up the driveway all right but had come from nowhere before that and belonged nowhere and that everything about him and even about the music that was so familiar to her was only half real.

"If my father comes and sees you—" 95

"He ain't coming. He's at a barbecue."

"How do you know that?"

"Aunt Tillie's. Right now they're—uh—they're drinking. Sitting around," he said vaguely, squinting as if he were staring all the way to town and over to Aunt Tillie's back yard. Then the vision seemed to get clear and he nodded energetically. "Yeah. Sitting around. There's your sister in a blue dress, huh? And high heels, the poor sad bitch—

nothing like you, sweetheart! And your mother's helping some fat woman with the corn, they're cleaning the corn—husking the corn—"

"What fat woman?" Connie cried.

"How do I know what fat woman, I don't know every goddamn fat 100 woman in the world!" Arnold Friend laughed.

"Oh, that's Mrs. Hornsby. . . . Who invited her?" Connie said. She felt a little lightheaded. Her breath was coming quickly.

"She's too fat. I don't like them fat. I like them the way you are, honey," he said, smiling sleepily at her. They stared at each other for a while through the screen door. He said softly, "Now, what you're going to do is this: you're going to come out that door. You're going to sit up front with me and Ellie's going to sit in the back, the hell with Ellie, right? This isn't Ellie's date. You're my date. I'm your lover, honey."

"What? You're crazy—"

"Yes, I'm your lover. You don't know what that is but you will," he said. "I know that too. I know all about you. But look: it's real nice and you couldn't ask for nobody better than me, or more polite. I always keep my word. I'll tell you how it is, I'm always nice at first, the first time. I'll hold you so tight you won't think you have to try to get away or pretend anything because you'll know you can't. And I'll come inside you where it's all secret and you'll give in to me and you'll love me—"

"Shut up! You're crazy!" Connie said. She backed away from the 105 door. She put her hands up against her ears as if she'd heard something terrible, something not meant for her. "People don't talk like that, you're crazy," she muttered. Her heart was almost too big now for her chest and its pumping made sweat break out all over her. She looked out to see Arnold Friend pause and then take a step toward the porch, lurching. He almost fell. But, like a clever drunken man, he managed to catch his balance. He wobbled in his high boots and grabbed hold of one of the porch posts.

"Honey?" he said. "You still listening?"

"Get the hell out of here!"

"Be nice, honey. Listen."

"I'm going to call the police—"

He wobbled again and out of the side of his mouth came a fast spat   110
curse, an aside not meant for her to hear. But even this "Christ!"
sounded forced. Then he began to smile again. She watched this smile
come, awkward as if he were smiling from inside a mask. His whole
face was a mask, she thought wildly, tanned down to his throat but then
running out as if he had plastered make-up on his face but had forgotten about his throat.

"Honey—? Listen, here's how it is. I always tell the truth and I
promise you this: I ain't coming in that house after you."

"You better not! I'm going to call the police if you—if you don't—"

"Honey," he said, talking right through her voice, "honey, I'm not
coming in there but you are coming out here. You know why?"

She was panting. The kitchen looked like a place she had never seen
before, some room she had run inside but that wasn't good enough,
wasn't going to help her. The kitchen window had never had a curtain, after three years, and there were dishes in the sink for her to do—
probably—and if you ran your hand across the table you'd probably
feel something sticky there.

"You listening, honey? Hey?"   115

"—going to call the police—"

"Soon as you touch the phone I don't need to keep my promise and
can come inside. You won't want that."

She rushed forward and tried to lock the door. Her fingers were
shaking. "But why lock it," Arnold Friend said gently, talking right into
her face. "It's just a screen door. It's just nothing." One of his boots was
at a strange angle, as if his foot wasn't in it. It pointed out to the left,
bent at the ankle. "I mean, anybody can break through a screen door
and glass and wood and iron or anything else if he needs to, anybody
at all, and specially Arnold Friend. If the place got lit up with a fire,
honey, you'd come runnin' out into my arms, right into my arms an'
safe at home—like you knew I was your lover and'd stopped fooling
around. I don't mind a nice shy girl but I don't like no fooling around."
Part of those words were spoken with a slight rhythmic lilt, and Connie
somehow recognized them—the echo of a song from last year, about a
girl rushing into her boy friend's arms and coming home again—

Connie stood barefoot on the linoleum floor, staring at him. "What do you want?" she whispered.

"I want you," he said.   120

"What?"

"Seen you that night and thought, that's the one, yes sir. I never needed to look anymore."

"But my father's coming back. He's coming to get me. I had to wash my hair first—" She spoke in a dry, rapid voice, hardly raising it for him to hear.

"No, your daddy is not coming and yes, you had to wash your hair and you washed it for me. It's nice and shining and all for me. I thank you, sweetheart," he said with a mock bow, but again he almost lost his balance. He had to bend and adjust his boots. Evidently his feet did not go all the way down; the boots must have been stuffed with something so that he would seem taller. Connie stared out at him and behind him at Ellie in the car, who seemed to be looking off toward Connie's right, into nothing. This Ellie said, pulling the words out of the air one after another as if he were just discovering them, "You want me to pull out the phone?"

"Shut your mouth and keep it shut," Arnold Friend said, his face   125
red from bending over or maybe from embarrassment because Connie had seen his boots. "This ain't none of your business."

"What—what are you doing? What do you want?" Connie said. "If I call the police they'll get you, they'll arrest you—"

"Promise was not to come in unless you touch that phone, and I'll keep that promise," he said. He resumed his erect position and tried to force his shoulders back. He sounded like a hero in a movie, declaring something important. But he spoke too loudly and it was as if he were speaking to someone behind Connie. "I ain't made plans for coming in that house where I don't belong but just for you to come out to me, the way you should. Don't you know who I am?"

"You're crazy," she whispered. She backed away from the door but did not want to go into another part of the house, as if this would give him permission to come through the door. "What do you . . . you're crazy, you. . . ."

"Huh? What're you saying, honey?"

Her eyes darted everywhere in the kitchen. She could not remember what it was, this room.   130

"This is how it is, honey: you come out and we'll drive away, have a nice ride. But if you don't come out we're gonna wait till your people come home and then they're all going to get it."

"You want that telephone pulled out?" Ellie said. He held the radio away from his ear and grimaced, as if without the radio the air was too much for him.

"I toldja shut up, Ellie," Arnold Friend said, "you're deaf, get a hearing aid, right? Fix yourself up. This little girl's no trouble and's gonna be nice to me, so Ellie keep to yourself, this ain't your date—right? Don't hem in on me, don't hog, don't crush, don't bird dog, don't trail me," he said in a rapid, meaningless voice, as if he were running through all the expressions he'd learned but was no longer sure which of them was in style, then rushing on to new ones, making them up with his eyes closed. "Don't crawl under my fence, don't squeeze in my chipmunk hole, don't sniff my glue, suck my Popsicle, keep your own greasy fingers on yourself!" He shaded his eyes and peered in at Connie, who was backed against the kitchen table. "Don't mind him, honey, he's just a creep. He's a dope. Right? I'm the boy for you and like I said, you come out here nice like a lady and give me your hand, and nobody else gets hurt, I mean, your nice old bald-headed daddy and your mummy and your sister in her high heels. Because listen: why bring them in this?"

"Leave me alone," Connie whispered.

"Hey, you know that old woman down the road, the one with the   135
chickens and stuff—you know her?"

"She's dead!"

"Dead? What? You know her?" Arnold Friend said.

"She's dead—"

"Don't you like her?"

"She's dead—she's—she isn't here any more—"   140

"But don't you like her, I mean, you got something against her? Some grudge or something?" Then his voice dipped as if he were conscious of a rudeness. He touched the sunglasses perched up on top of his head as if to make sure they were still there. "Now, you be a good girl."

"What are you going to do?"

"Just two things, or maybe three," Arnold Friend said. "But I promise it won't last long and you'll like me the way you get to like people you're close to. You will. It's all over for you here, so come on out. You don't want your people in any trouble, do you?"

She turned and bumped against a chair or something, hurting her leg, but she ran into the back room and picked up the telephone. Something roared in her ear, a tiny roaring, and she was so sick with fear that she could do nothing but listen to it—the telephone was clammy and very heavy and her fingers groped down to the dial but were too weak to touch it. She began to scream into the phone, into the roaring. She cried out, she cried for her mother, she felt her breath start jerking back and forth in her lungs as if it were something Arnold Friend was stabbing her with again and again with no tenderness. A noisy sorrowful wailing rose all about her and she was locked inside it the way she was locked inside this house.

After a while she could hear again. She was sitting on the floor with   145
her wet back against the wall.

Arnold Friend was saying from the door, "That's a good girl. Put the phone back."

She kicked the phone away from her.

"No, honey. Pick it up. Put it back right."

She picked it up and put it back. The dial tone stopped.

"That's a good girl. Now, you come outside."   150

She was hollow with what had been fear but what was now just an emptiness. All that screaming had blasted it out of her. She sat, one leg cramped under her, and deep inside her brain was something like a pinpoint of light that kept going and would not let her relax. She thought, I'm not going to see my mother again. She thought, I'm not going to sleep in my bed again. Her bright green blouse was all wet.

Arnold Friend said, in a gentle-loud voice that was like a stage voice, "The place where you came from ain't there any more, and where you had in mind to go is cancelled out. This place you are now—inside your daddy's house—is nothing but a cardboard box I can knock down any time. You know that and always did know it. You hear me?"

She thought, I have got to think. I have got to know what to do.

"We'll go out to a nice field, out in the country here where it smells so nice and it's sunny," Arnold Friend said. "I'll have my arms tight around you so you won't need to try to get away and I'll show you what love is like, what it does. The hell with this house! It looks solid all right," he said. He ran a fingernail down the screen and the noise did not make Connie shiver, as it would have the day before. "Now, put your hand on your heart, honey. Feel that? That feels solid too but we know better. Be nice to me, be sweet like you can because what else is there for a girl like you but to be sweet and pretty and give in?—and get away before her people come back?"

She felt her pounding heart. Her hand seemed to enclose it. She 155 thought for the first time in her life that it was nothing that was hers, that belonged to her, but just a pounding, living thing inside this body that wasn't really hers either.

"You don't want them to get hurt," Arnold Friend went on. "Now, get up, honey. Get up all by yourself."

She stood.

"Now, turn this way. That's right. Come over here to me.—Ellie, put that away, didn't I tell you? You dope. You miserable creepy dope," Arnold Friend said. His words were not angry but only part of an incantation. The incantation was kindly. "Now, come out through the kitchen to me, honey, and let's see a smile, try it, you're a brave, sweet little girl and now they're eating corn and hot dogs cooked to bursting over an outdoor fire, and they don't know one thing about you and never did and honey, you're better than them because not a one of them would have done this for you."

Connie felt the linoleum under her feet; it was cool. She brushed her hair back out of her eyes. Arnold Friend let go of the post tentatively and opened his arms for her, his elbows pointing in toward each other and his wrists limp, to show that this was an embarrassed embrace and a little mocking, he didn't want to make her self-conscious.

She put out her hand against the screen. She watched herself push 160 the door slowly open as if she were back safe somewhere in the other doorway, watching this body and this head of long hair moving out into the sunlight where Arnold Friend waited.

"My sweet little blue-eyed girl," he said in a half-sung sigh that had nothing to do with her brown eyes but was taken up just the same by the vast sunlit reaches of the land behind him and on all sides of him— so much land that Connie had never seen before and did not recognize except to know that she was going to it.

STUDY QUESTIONS

1. Where does Connie first encounter Arnold Friend? What does he do when he sees her?

2. One of the techniques that Oates uses to add DESCRIPTION to this story is to include many COMPARISONS (e.g., "as if" statements). Select one of these comparisons that you find interesting. ANALYZE what that comparison adds to the story and provide an updated version of it, using contemporary language.

3. This story is commonly discussed as a coming-of-age NARRATIVE that takes an unexpected turn. Where does the story include the expected components of a coming-of-age story? At what point does its turn to the unexpected take place? How is the story's outcome different from what you would expect from a conventional coming-of-age narrative?

4. The DIALOGUE between Connie and Arnold Friend moves the PLOT forward in the second half of the story. How would you CHARACTERIZE Arnold Friend's language? How does it change as the story progresses? How does it help to establish Arnold Friend's character?

5. *For Writing.* Arnold Friend is a puzzling character, one who is often interpreted symbolically. In an essay, analyze Arnold Friend as a SYMBOL: what do you think he symbolizes? What EVIDENCE from the story supports your analysis?

TIM O'BRIEN { *How to Tell a True War Story*

TIM O'BRIEN (b. 1946) was born in Austin, Minnesota, and spent his
teenage years in Worthington, two locales that inform the setting of
much of his fiction. He graduated in 1968 from Macalester College,
where he was president of the student body and earned a BA in political
science. Following graduation, O'Brien was drafted into the U.S. Army
and served in Vietnam from 1969 to 1970. He then entered a PhD
program in government studies at Harvard, working as a reporter for the
Washington Post during the summers; he left graduate school in 1976 to
concentrate on his writing. He often writes about his wartime experiences, including in his memoir, *If I Die in a Combat Zone, Box Me Up
and Ship Me Home* (1973), and in his critically acclaimed novel *The
Things They Carried* (1990). He teaches in the creative writing program
at the University of Texas at San Marcos.

"How to Tell a True War Story" is excerpted from *The Things They
Carried*. In it, the narrator reflects on the death of Curt Lemon, a fellow
soldier in Vietnam, through a series of stories. O'Brien plays with the
tension between what he calls "story-truth," or fiction, and "happening-
truth," or reality, as the line between the two blurs in the story. How do
reality and fiction complicate each other as the narrator explains the
process of how to tell a true war story?

THIS IS TRUE.

I had a buddy in Vietnam. His name was Bob Kiley, but everybody called him Rat.

A friend of his gets killed, so about a week later Rat sits down and writes a letter to the guy's sister. Rat tells her what a great brother she had, how together the guy was, a number one pal and comrade. A real soldier's soldier, Rat says. Then he tells a few stories to make the point, how her brother would always volunteer for stuff nobody else would volunteer for in a million years, dangerous stuff, like doing recon or going out on these really badass night patrols. Stainless steel balls, Rat tells her. The guy was a little crazy, for sure, but crazy in a good way, a real daredevil, because he liked the challenge of it, he liked testing himself, just man against gook. A great, great guy, Rat says.

Anyway, it's a terrific letter, very personal and touching. Rat almost bawls writing it. He gets all teary telling about the good times they had together, how her brother made the war seem almost fun, always raising hell and lighting up villes[1] and bringing smoke to bear every which way. A great sense of humor, too. Like the time at this river when he went fishing with a whole damn crate of hand grenades. Probably the funniest thing in world history, Rat says, all that gore, about twenty zillion dead gook fish. Her brother, he had the right attitude. He knew how to have a good time. On Halloween, this real hot spooky night, the dude paints up his body all different colors and puts on this weird mask and hikes over to a ville and goes trick-or-treating almost stark naked, just boots and balls and an M-16. A tremendous human being, Rat says. Pretty nutso sometimes, but you could trust him with your life.

And then the letter gets very sad and serious. Rat pours his heart out. 5 He says he loved the guy. He says the guy was his best friend in the world. They were like soul mates, he says, like twins or something, they had a whole lot in common. He tells the guy's sister he'll look her up when the war's over.

So what happens?

---

[1] Villages.

Rat mails the letter. He waits two months. The dumb cooze[2] never writes back.

A true war story is never moral. It does not instruct, nor encourage virtue, nor suggest models of proper human behavior, nor restrain men from doing the things men have always done. If a story seems moral, do not believe it. If at the end of a war story you feel uplifted, or if you feel that some small bit of rectitude has been salvaged from the larger waste, then you have been made the victim of a very old and terrible lie. There is no rectitude whatsoever. There is no virtue. As a first rule of thumb, therefore, you can tell a true war story by its absolute and uncompromising allegiance to obscenity and evil. Listen to Rat Kiley. Cooze, he says. He does not say bitch. He certainly does not say woman, or girl. He says cooze. Then he spits and stares. He's nineteen years old—it's too much for him—so he looks at you with those big sad gentle killer eyes and says *cooze*, because his friend is dead, and because it's so incredibly sad and true: she never wrote back.

You can tell a true war story if it embarrasses you. If you don't care for obscenity, you don't care for the truth; if you don't care for the truth, watch how you vote. Send guys to war, they come home talking dirty.

Listen to Rat: "Jesus Christ, man, I write this beautiful fuckin' letter, 10 I slave over it, and what happens? The dumb cooze never writes back."

The dead guy's name was Curt Lemon. What happened was, we crossed a muddy river and marched west into the mountains, and on the third day we took a break along a trail junction in deep jungle. Right away, Lemon and Rat Kiley started goofing. They didn't understand about the spookiness. They were kids; they just didn't know. A nature hike, they thought, not even a war, so they went off into the shade of some giant trees—quadruple canopy, no sunlight at all—and they were giggling and calling each other yellow mother and playing a silly game they'd invented. The game involved smoke grenades, which were harmless unless you did stupid things, and what they did

[2]Vagina, or a woman viewed as a sex object.

was pull out the pin and stand a few feet apart and play catch under the shade of those huge trees. Whoever chickened out was a yellow mother. And if nobody chickened out, the grenade would make a light popping sound and they'd be covered with smoke and they'd laugh and dance around and then do it again.

It's all exactly true.

It happened, to *me*, nearly twenty years ago, and I still remember that trail junction and those giant trees and a soft dripping sound somewhere beyond the trees. I remember the smell of moss. Up in the canopy there were tiny white blossoms, but no sunlight at all, and I remember the shadows spreading out under the trees where Curt Lemon and Rat Kiley were playing catch with smoke grenades. Mitchell Sanders sat flipping his yo-yo. Norman Bowker and Kiowa and Dave Jensen were dozing, or half dozing, and all around us were those ragged green mountains.

Except for the laughter things were quiet.

At one point, I remember, Mitchell Sanders turned and looked 15 at me, not quite nodding, as if to warn me about something, as if he already *knew*, then after a while he rolled up his yo-yo and moved away.

It's hard to tell you what happened next.

They were just goofing. There was a noise, I suppose, which must've been the detonator, so I glanced behind me and watched Lemon step from the shade into bright sunlight. His face was suddenly brown and shining. A handsome kid, really. Sharp gray eyes, lean and narrow-waisted, and when he died it was almost beautiful, the way the sunlight came around him and lifted him up and sucked him high into a tree full of moss and vines and white blossoms.

In any war story, but especially a true one, it's difficult to separate what happened from what seemed to happen. What seems to happen becomes its own happening and has to be told that way. The angles of vision are skewed. When a booby trap explodes, you close your eyes and duck and float outside yourself. When a guy dies, like Curt Lemon, you look away and then look back for a moment and then look away again. The pictures get jumbled; you tend to miss a lot. And then afterward, when you go to tell about it, there is always that surreal seemingness, which makes the story seem untrue, but which in fact represents the hard and exact truth as it *seemed.*

• ○ •

In many cases a true war story cannot be believed. If you believe it, be skeptical. It's a question of credibility. Often the crazy stuff is true and the normal stuff isn't, because the normal stuff is necessary to make you believe the truly incredible craziness.

In other cases you can't even tell a true war story. Sometimes it's 20 just beyond telling.

I heard this one, for example, from Mitchell Sanders. It was near dusk and we were sitting at my foxhole along a wide muddy river north of Quang Ngai. I remember how peaceful the twilight was. A deep pinkish red spilled out on the river, which moved without sound, and in the morning we would cross the river and march west into the mountains. The occasion was right for a good story.

"God's truth," Mitchell Sanders said. "A six-man patrol goes up into the mountains on a basic listening-post operation. The idea's to spend a week up there, just lie low and listen for enemy movement. They've got a radio along, so if they hear anything suspicious—anything—they're supposed to call in artillery or gunships, whatever it takes. Otherwise they keep strict field discipline. Absolute silence. They just listen."

Sanders glanced at me to make sure I had the scenario. He was playing with his yo-yo, dancing it with short, tight little strokes of the wrist.

His face was blank in the dusk.

"We're talking regulation, by-the-book LP. These six guys, they 25 don't say boo for a solid week. They don't got tongues. *All* ears."

"Right," I said.

"Understand me?"

"Invisible."

Sanders nodded.

"Affirm," he said. "Invisible. So what happens is, these guys get 30 themselves deep in the bush, all camouflaged up, and they lie down and wait and that's all they do, nothing else, they lie there for seven straight days and just listen. And man, I'll tell you—it's spooky. This is mountains. You don't *know* spooky till you been there. Jungle, sort of, except it's way up in the clouds and there's always this fog—like rain, except it's not raining—everything's all wet and swirly and tangled up and you can't see jack, you can't find your own pecker to piss with. Like you don't even have a body. Serious spooky. You just go with the vapors—the fog sort of takes you in . . . And the sounds, man. The sounds carry forever. You hear stuff nobody should *ever* hear."

Sanders was quiet for a second, just working the yo-yo, then he smiled at me.

"So after a couple days the guys start hearing this real soft, kind of wacked-out music. Weird echoes and stuff. Like a radio or something, but it's not a radio, it's this strange gook music that comes right out of the rocks. Faraway, sort of, but right up close, too. They try to ignore it. But it's a listening post, right? So they listen. And every night they keep hearing that crazyass gook concert. All kinds of chimes and xylophones. I mean, this is wilderness—no way, it can't be real—but there it *is*, like the mountains are tuned in to Radio fucking Hanoi. Naturally they get nervous. One guy sticks Juicy Fruit in his ears. Another guy almost flips. Thing is, though, they can't report music. They can't get on the horn and call back to base and say, 'Hey, listen, we need some firepower, we got to blow away this weirdo gook rock band.' They can't do that. It wouldn't go down. So they lie there in the fog and keep their mouths shut. And what makes it extra bad, see, is the poor dudes can't horse around like normal. Can't joke it away. Can't even talk to each other except maybe in whispers, all hush-hush, and that just revs up the willies. All they do is listen."

Again there was some silence as Mitchell Sanders looked out on the river. The dark was coming on hard now, and off to the west I could see the mountains rising in silhouette, all the mysteries and unknowns.

"This next part," Sanders said quietly, "you won't believe."

"Probably not," I said.

"You won't. And you know why?" He gave me a long, tired smile. "Because it happened. Because every word is absolutely dead-on true."

35

Sanders made a sound in his throat, like a sigh, as if to say he didn't care if I believed him or not. But he did care. He wanted me to feel the truth, to believe by the raw force of feeling. He seemed sad, in a way.

"These six guys," he said, "they're pretty fried out by now, and one night they start hearing voices. Like at a cocktail party. That's what it sounds like, this big swank gook cocktail party somewhere out there in the fog. Music and chitchat and stuff. It's crazy, I know, but they hear the champagne corks. They hear the actual martini glasses. Real hoity-toity, all very civilized, except this isn't civilization. This is Nam.

"Anyway, the guys try to be cool. They just lie there and groove, but after a while they start hearing—you won't believe this—they hear chamber music. They hear violins and cellos. They hear this terrific mama-san soprano. Then after a while they hear gook opera and a glee club and the Haiphong Boys Choir and a barbershop quartet and all kinds of weird chanting and Buddha-Buddha stuff. And the whole time, in the background, there's still that cocktail party going on. All these different voices. Not human voices, though. Because it's the mountains. Follow me? The rock—it's *talking.* And the fog, too, and the grass and the goddamn mongooses. Everything talks. The trees talk politics, the monkeys talk religion. The whole country. Vietnam. The place talks. It talks. Understand? Nam—it truly *talks.*

"The guys can't cope. They lose it. They get on the radio and report enemy movement—a whole army, they say—and they order up the firepower. They get arty[3] and gunships. They call in air strikes. And I'll tell you, they fuckin' crash that cocktail party. All night long, they just smoke those mountains. They make jungle juice. They blow away trees and glee clubs and whatever else there is to blow away. Scorch time. They walk napalm up and down the ridges. They bring in the Cobras and F-4s, they use Willie Peter and HE[4] and incendiaries. It's all fire. They make those mountains burn.

40

---

[3]That is, artillery.

[4]High explosive grenades. *Willie Peter*: white phosphorus, a chemical weapon often dropped in cans from jets during the Vietnam War.

"Around dawn things finally get quiet. Like you never even *heard* quiet before. One of those real thick, real misty days—just clouds and fog, they're off in this special zone—and the mountains are absolutely dead-flat silent. Like Brigadoon—pure vapor, you know? Everything's all sucked up inside the fog. Not a single sound, except they still *hear* it.

"So they pack up and start humping. They head down the mountain, back to base camp, and when they get there they don't say diddly. They don't talk. Not a word, like they're deaf and dumb. Later on this fat bird colonel comes up and asks what the hell happened out there. What'd they hear? Why all the ordnance? The man's ragged out, he gets down tight on their case. I mean, they spent six trillion dollars on firepower, and this fatass colonel wants answers, he wants to know what the fuckin' story is.

"But the guys don't say zip. They just look at him for a while, sort of funny like, sort of amazed, and the whole war is right there in that stare. It says everything you can't ever say. It says, man, you got *wax* in your ears. It says, poor bastard, you'll never know—wrong frequency—you don't *even* want to hear this. Then they salute the fucker and walk away, because certain stories you don't ever tell."

You can tell a true war story by the way it never seems to end. Not then, not ever. Not when Mitchell Sanders stood up and moved off into the dark.

It all happened.

Even now, at this instant, I remember that yo-yo. In a way, I suppose, you had to be there, you had to hear it, but I could tell how desperately Sanders wanted me to believe him, his frustration at not quite getting the details right, not quite pinning down the final and definitive truth.

And I remember sitting at my foxhole that night, watching the shadows of Quang Ngai, thinking about the coming day and how we would cross the river and march west into the mountains, all the ways I might die, all the things I did not understand.

Late in the night Mitchell Sanders touched my shoulder.

"Just came to me," he whispered. "The moral, I mean. Nobody listens. Nobody hears nothin'. Like that fatass colonel. The politi-

45

cians, all the civilian types. Your girlfriend. My girlfriend. Everybody's sweet little virgin girlfriend. What they need is to go out on LP. The vapors, man. Trees and rocks—you got to *listen* to your enemy."

And then again, in the morning, Sanders came up to me. The platoon was preparing to move out, checking weapons, going through all the little rituals that preceded a day's march. Already the lead squad had crossed the river and was filing off toward the west.

"I got a confession to make," Sanders said. "Last night, man, I had to make up a few things."

"I know that."

"The glee club. There wasn't any glee club."

"Right."

"No opera."

"Forget it, I understand."

"Yeah, but listen, it's still true. Those six guys, they heard wicked sound out there. They heard sound you just plain won't believe."

Sanders pulled on his rucksack, closed his eyes for a moment, then almost smiled at me. I knew what was coming.

"All right," I said, "what's the moral?"

"Forget it."

"No, go ahead."

For a long while he was quiet, looking away, and the silence kept stretching out until it was almost embarrassing. Then he shrugged and gave me a stare that lasted all day.

"Hear that quiet, man?" he said. "That quiet—just listen. There's your moral."

In a true war story, if there's a moral at all, it's like the thread that makes the cloth. You can't tease it out. You can't extract the meaning without unraveling the deeper meaning. And in the end, really, there's nothing much to say about a true war story, except maybe "Oh."

True war stories do not generalize. They do not indulge in abstraction or analysis.

For example: War is hell. As a moral declaration the old truism seems perfectly true, and yet because it abstracts, because it generalizes, I can't believe it with my stomach. Nothing turns inside.

It comes down to gut instinct. A true war story, if truly told, makes the stomach believe.

•   ○   •

This one does it for me. I've told it before—many times, many versions—but here's what actually happened.

We crossed that river and marched west into the mountains. On the third day, Curt Lemon stepped on a booby-trapped 105 round. He was playing catch with Rat Kiley, laughing, and then he was dead. The trees were thick; it took nearly an hour to cut an LZ for the dustoff.

Later, higher in the mountains, we came across a baby VC water buffalo. What it was doing there I don't know—no farms or paddies—but we chased it down and got a rope around it and led it along to a deserted village where we set up for the night. After supper Rat Kiley went over and stroked its nose.

He opened up a can of C rations, pork and beans, but the baby buffalo wasn't interested.

Rat shrugged.

He stepped back and shot it through the right front knee. The animal did not make a sound. It went down hard, then got up again, and Rat took careful aim and shot off an ear. He shot it in the hindquarters and in the little hump at its back. He shot it twice in the flanks. It wasn't to kill; it was to hurt. He put the rifle muzzle up against the mouth and shot the mouth away. Nobody said much. The whole platoon stood there watching, feeling all kinds of things, but there wasn't a great deal of pity for the baby water buffalo. Curt Lemon was dead. Rat Kiley had lost his best friend in the world. Later in the week he would write a long personal letter to the guy's sister, who would not write back, but for now it was a question of pain. He shot off the tail. He shot away chunks of meat below the ribs. All around us there was the smell of smoke and filth and deep greenery, and the evening was humid and very hot. Rat went to automatic. He shot randomly, almost casually, quick little spurts in the belly and butt. Then he reloaded, squatted down, and shot it in the left front knee. Again the animal fell hard and tried to get up, but this time it couldn't quite make it. It wobbled and went down sideways. Rat shot it in the nose. He bent forward and whispered something, as if talking to a pet, then he shot it in the throat. All the while the baby buffalo was silent, or almost silent, just a light bubbling sound where the nose had been. It lay very still. Nothing moved except the eyes, which were enormous, the pupils shiny black and dumb.

Rat Kiley was crying. He tried to say something, but then cradled his rifle and went off by himself.

The rest of us stood in a ragged circle around the baby buffalo. For a time no one spoke. We had witnessed something essential, something brand-new and profound, a piece of the world so startling there was not yet a name for it.

Somebody kicked the baby buffalo.

It was still alive, though just barely, just in the eyes.

"Amazing," Dave Jensen said. "My whole life, I never seen anything like it."

"Never?"

"Not hardly. Not once."

Kiowa and Mitchell Sanders picked up the baby buffalo. They hauled it across the open square, hoisted it up, and dumped it in the village well.

Afterward, we sat waiting for Rat to get himself together.

"Amazing," Dave Jensen kept saying. "A new wrinkle. I never seen it before."

Mitchell Sanders took out his yo-yo. "Well, that's Nam," he said. "Garden of Evil. Over here, man, every sin's real fresh and original."

How do you generalize?

War is hell, but that's not the half of it, because war is also mystery and terror and adventure and courage and discovery and holiness and pity and despair and longing and love. War is nasty; war is fun. War is thrilling; war is drudgery. War makes you a man; war makes you dead.

The truths are contradictory. It can be argued, for instance, that war is grotesque. But in truth war is also beauty. For all its horror, you can't help but gape at the awful majesty of combat. You stare out at tracer rounds unwinding through the dark like brilliant red ribbons. You crouch in ambush as a cool, impassive moon rises over the night-time paddies. You admire the fluid symmetries of troops on the move, the harmonies of sound and shape and proportion, the great sheets of metal-fire streaming down from a gunship, the illumination rounds, the white phosphorus, the purply orange glow of napalm, the rocket's red glare. It's not pretty, exactly. It's astonishing. It fills the eye. It commands you. You hate it, yes, but your eyes do not. Like a killer forest fire, like cancer under a microscope, any battle of bombing raid or artillery barrage has the aesthetic purity of absolute moral indifference—a powerful, implacable beauty—and a true war story will tell the truth about this, though the truth is ugly.

To generalize about war is like generalizing about peace. Almost everything is true. Almost nothing is true. At its core, perhaps, war is just another name for death, and yet any soldier will tell you, if he tells the truth, that proximity to death brings with it a corresponding proximity to life. After a firefight, there is always the immense pleasure of aliveness. The trees are alive. The grass, the soil—everything. All around you things are purely living, and you among them, and the aliveness makes you tremble. You feel an intense, out-of-the-skin awareness of your living self—your truest self, the human being you want to be and then become by the force of wanting it. In the midst of evil you want to be a good man. You want decency. You want justice and courtesy and human concord, things you never knew you wanted. There is a kind of largeness to it, a kind of godliness. Though it's odd, you're never more alive than when you're almost dead. You recognize what's valuable. Freshly, as if for the first time, you love what's best in yourself and in the world, all that might be lost. At the hour of dusk you sit at your foxhole and look out on a wide river turning pinkish red, and at the mountains beyond, and although in the morning you must cross the river and go into the mountains and do terrible things and maybe die, even so, you find yourself studying the fine colors on the river, you feel wonder and awe at the setting of the sun, and you are filled with a hard, aching love for how the world could be and always should be, but now is not.

Mitchell Sanders was right. For the common soldier, at least, war has the feel—the spiritual texture—of a great ghostly fog, thick and permanent. There is no clarity. Everything swirls. The old rules are no longer binding, the old truths no longer true. Right spills over into wrong. Order blends into chaos, love into hate, ugliness into beauty, law into anarchy, civility into savagery. The vapors suck you in. You can't tell where you are, or why you're there, and the only certainty is overwhelming ambiguity.

In war you lose your sense of the definite, hence your sense of truth itself, and therefore it's safe to say that in a true war story nothing is ever absolutely true. 90

Often in a true war story there is not even a point, or else the point doesn't hit you until twenty years later, in your sleep, and you wake up and shake your wife and start telling the story to her, except when you get to the end you've forgotten the point again. And then for a long time you lie there watching the story happen in your head. You listen to your wife's breathing. The war's over. You close your eyes. You smile and think, Christ, what's the *point?*

This one wakes me up.

In the mountains that day, I watched Lemon turn sideways. He laughed and said something to Rat Kiley. Then he took a peculiar half step, moving from shade into bright sunlight, and the booby-trapped 105 round blew him into a tree. The parts were just hanging there, so Dave Jensen and I were ordered to shinny up and peel him off. I remember the white bone of an arm. I remember pieces of skin and something wet and yellow that must've been the intestines. The gore was horrible, and stays with me. But what wakes me up twenty years later is Dave Jensen singing "Lemon Tree"[5] as we threw down the parts.

---

[5]Folk song recorded by Peter, Paul, and Mary in the 1960s. The lyrics run, in part, "Lemon tree, very pretty / And the lemon flower is sweet / But the fruit of the poor lemon is impossible to eat."

You can tell a true war story by the questions you ask. Somebody tells a story, let's say, and afterward you ask, "Is it true?" and if the answer matters, you've got your answer.

For example, we've all heard this one. Four guys go down a trail. A grenade sails out. One guy jumps on it and takes the blast and saves his three buddies.

Is it true?

The answer matters.

You'd feel cheated if it never happened. Without the grounding reality, it's just a trite bit of puffery, pure Hollywood, untrue in the way all such stories are untrue. Yet even if it did happen—and maybe it did, anything's possible—even then you know it can't be true, because a true war story does not depend upon that kind of truth. Absolute occurrence is irrelevant. A thing may happen and be a total lie; another thing may not happen and be truer than the truth. For example: Four guys go down a trail. A grenade sails out. One guy jumps on it and takes the blast, but it's a killer grenade and everybody dies anyway. Before they die, though, one of the dead guys says, "The fuck you do *that* for?" and the jumper says, "Story of my life, man," and the other guy starts to smile but he's dead.

That's a true story that never happened.

Twenty years later, I can still see the sunlight on Lemon's face. I can see him turning, looking back at Rat Kiley, then he laughed and took that curious half step from shade into sunlight, his face suddenly brown and shining, and when his foot touched down, in that instant, he must've thought it was the sunlight that was killing him. It was not the sunlight. It was a rigged 105 round. But if I could ever get the story right, how the sun seemed to gather around him and pick him up and lift him high into a tree, if I could somehow recreate the fatal whiteness of that light, the quick glare, the obvious cause and effect, then you would believe the last thing Curt Lemon believed, which for him must've been the final truth.

Now and then, when I tell this story, someone will come up to me afterward and say she liked it. It's always a woman. Usually it's an older woman of kindly temperament and humane politics. She'll explain that as a rule she hates war stories; she can't understand why people want to wallow in all the blood and gore. But this one she liked. The poor baby buffalo, it made her sad. Sometimes, even, there are little tears. What I should do, she'll say, is put it all behind me. Find new stories to tell.

I won't say it but I'll think it. 100

I'll picture Rat Kiley's face, his grief, and I'll think, *You dumb cooze.* Because she wasn't listening.

It *wasn't* a war story. It was a *love* story.

But you can't say that. All you can do is tell it one more time, patiently, adding and subtracting, making up a few things to get at the real truth. No Mitchell Sanders, you tell her. No Lemon, no Rat Kiley. No trail junction. No baby buffalo. No vines or moss or white blossoms. Beginning to end, you tell her, it's all made up. Every goddamn detail—the mountains and the river and especially that poor dumb baby buffalo. None of it happened. *None* of it. And even if it did happen, it didn't happen in the mountains, it happened in this little village on the Batangan Peninsula, and it was raining like crazy, and one night a guy named Stink Harris woke up screaming with a leech on his tongue. You can tell a true war story if you just keep on telling it.

And in the end, of course, a true war story is never about war. It's 105 about sunlight. It's about the special way that dawn spreads out on a river when you know you must cross the river and march into the mountains and do things you are afraid to do. It's about love and memory. It's about sorrow. It's about sisters who never write back and people who never listen.

STUDY QUESTIONS

1. Why does the NARRATOR suggest that Curt Lemon might have believed that the sunlight was killing him?

2. What are the challenges the narrator faces when attempting to tell a "true" war story?

3. How does the narrator attempt to ANALYZE THE PROCESS of telling a true war story? Where do you see both "story-truth" and "happening-truth" in the narrative? How are they both part of the narrator's process?

4. How do the stories told here intersect with one another? What is the effect of the narrator's telling the same story about Lemon in several different ways? Why does he open his story with "This is true," and why does he repeat some form of that idea throughout the story?

5. *For Writing.* Write down a story, about yourself and at least two other people, that you have told in the past. Then write it down again, from each of the other two individuals' perspectives. In an essay, explore how the different perspectives engage both story-truth and happening-truth. What, then, does the teller know and the reader learn about the truths of the story?

FLANNERY O'CONNOR { *A Good Man Is Hard to Find*

FLANNERY O'CONNOR (1925–1964), novelist, short-story writer, and essayist, was born in Savannah, Georgia. She graduated from Georgia State College for Women in 1945 and earned an MFA from the Iowa Writers' Workshop in 1947. O'Connor, whose Catholicism figures prominently in her work, is considered a "Southern Gothic" writer; the genre is defined by disturbing and often grotesque incidents set in the southern United States. O'Connor wrote two novels—*Wise Blood* (1952) and *The Violent Bear It Away* (1960)—and six collections of stories, essays, and letters. Her *The Complete Stories*, published posthumously in 1971, won the National Book Award.

The following is the title story from *A Good Man Is Hard to Find and Other Stories* (1955). It depicts a family's ill-fated vacation: a wrong turn, a road accident, a confrontation with three escaped convicts. Both humorous and horrifying, the story explores themes of good and evil, religious hypocrisy, and grace. As you read, notice the foreshadowing, the many instances of irony, and the detached narrative tone. Pay attention to the details that O'Connor uses to craft the personalities of each character.

THE GRANDMOTHER DIDN'T WANT TO go to Florida. She wanted to visit some of her connections in east Tennessee and she was seizing every chance to change Bailey's mind. Bailey was the son she lived with, her only boy. He was sitting on the edge of his chair at the table, bent over the orange sports section of the *Journal*. "Now look here, Bailey," she said, "see here, read this," and she stood with one hand on her thin hip and the other rattling the newspaper at his bald head. "Here this fellow that calls himself The Misfit is aloose from the Federal Pen and headed toward Florida and you read here what it says he did to these people. Just you read it. I wouldn't take my children in any direction with a criminal like that aloose in it. I couldn't answer to my conscience if I did."

Bailey didn't look up from his reading so she wheeled around then and faced the children's mother; a young woman in slacks, whose face was as broad and innocent as a cabbage and was tied around with a green headkerchief that had two points on the top like rabbit's ears. She was sitting on the sofa, feeding the baby his apricots out of a jar. "The children have been to Florida before," the old lady said. "You all ought to take them somewhere else for a change so they would see different parts of the world and be broad. They never have been to east Tennessee."

The children's mother didn't seem to hear her, but the eight-year-old boy, John Wesley, a stocky child with glasses, said, "If you don't want to go to Florida, why dontcha stay at home?" He and the little girl, June Star, were reading the funny papers on the floor.

"She wouldn't stay at home to be queen for a day," June Star said without raising her yellow head.

"Yes, and what would you do if this fellow, The Misfit, caught you?" the grandmother asked. 5

"I'd smack his face," John Wesley said.

"She wouldn't stay at home for a million bucks," June Star said. "Afraid she'd miss something. She has to go everywhere we go."

"All right, Miss," the grandmother said. "Just remember that the next time you want me to curl your hair."

June Star said her hair was naturally curly.

The next morning the grandmother was the first one in the car, ready to go. She had her big black valise that looked like the head of a hippopotamus in one corner, and underneath it she was hiding a basket with Pitty Sing,[1] the cat, in it. She didn't intend for the cat to be left 10

---

[1] The name of a character in Gilbert and Sullivan's comic opera *The Mikado* (1885).

alone in the house for three days because he would miss her too much and she was afraid he might brush against one of the gas burners and accidentally asphyxiate himself. Her son, Bailey, didn't like to arrive at a motel with a cat.

She sat in the middle of the back seat with John Wesley and June Star on either side of her. Bailey and the children's mother and the baby sat in the front and they left Atlanta at eight forty-five with the mileage on the car at 55890. The grandmother wrote this down because she thought it would be interesting to say how many miles they had been when they got back. It took them twenty minutes to reach the outskirts of the city.

The old lady settled herself comfortably, removing her white cotton gloves and putting them up with her purse on the shelf in front of the back window. The children's mother still had on slacks and still had her head tied up in a green kerchief, but the grandmother had on a navy blue straw sailor hat with a bunch of white violets on the brim and a navy blue dress with a small white dot in the print. Her collar and cuffs were white organdy trimmed with lace and at her neckline she had pinned a purple spray of cloth violets containing a sachet. In case of an accident, anyone seeing her dead on the highway would know at once that she was a lady.

She said she thought it was going to be a good day for driving, neither too hot nor too cold, and she cautioned Bailey that the speed limit was fifty-five miles an hour and that the patrolmen hid themselves behind billboards and small clumps of trees and sped out after you before you had a chance to slow down. She pointed out interesting details of the scenery: Stone Mountain;[2] the blue granite that in some places came up to both sides of the highway; the brilliant red clay banks slightly streaked with purple; and the various crops that made rows of green lace-work on the ground. The trees were full of silver-white sunlight and the meanest of them sparkled. The children were reading comic magazines and their mother had gone back to sleep.

---

[2]Memorial to the Confederate States of America near Atlanta, Georgia; it consists of large bas-relief images of generals Stonewall Jackson and Robert E. Lee, and Confederate President Jefferson Davis carved into an immense granite outcrop.

"Let's go through Georgia fast so we won't have to look at it much," John Wesley said.

"If I were a little boy," said the grandmother, "I wouldn't talk about my native state that way. Tennessee has the mountains and Georgia has the hills."

"Tennessee is just a hillbilly dumping ground," John Wesley said, "and Georgia is a lousy state too."

"You said it," June Star said.

"In my time," said the grandmother, folding her thin veined fingers, "children were more respectful of their native states and their parents and everything else. People did right then. Oh look at the cute little pickaninny!" she said and pointed to a Negro child standing in the door of a shack. "Wouldn't that make a picture, now?" she asked and they all turned and looked at the little Negro out of the back window. He waved.

"He didn't have any britches on," June Star said.

"He probably didn't have any," the grandmother explained. "Little niggers in the country don't have things like we do. If I could paint, I'd paint that picture," she said.

The children exchanged comic books.

The grandmother offered to hold the baby and the children's mother passed him over the front seat to her. She set him on her knee and bounced him and told him about the things they were passing. She rolled her eyes and screwed up her mouth and stuck her leathery thin face into his smooth bland one. Occasionally he gave her a faraway smile. They passed a large cotton field with five or six graves fenced in the middle of it, like a small island. "Look at the graveyard!" the grandmother said, pointing it out. "That was the old family burying ground. That belonged to the plantation."

"Where's the plantation?" John Wesley asked.

"Gone With the Wind,"[3] said the grandmother. "Ha. Ha."

When the children finished all the comic books they had brought, they opened the lunch and ate it. The grandmother ate a peanut but-

[3]Title of the best-selling 1936 novel by Margaret Mitchell about the Civil War and the passing of the old South, made into one of the most successful films of all time.

ter sandwich and an olive and would not let the children throw the box and the paper napkins out the window. When there was nothing else to do they played a game by choosing a cloud and making the other two guess what shape it suggested. John Wesley took one the shape of a cow and June Star guessed a cow and John Wesley said, no, an automobile, and June Star said he didn't play fair, and they began to slap each other over the grandmother.

The grandmother said she would tell them a story if they would keep quiet. When she told a story, she rolled her eyes and waved her head and was very dramatic. She said once when she was a maiden lady she had been courted by a Mr. Edgar Atkins Teagarden from Jasper, Georgia. She said he was a very good-looking man and a gentleman and that he brought her a watermelon every Saturday afternoon with his initials cut in it, E.A.T. Well, one Saturday, she said, Mr. Teagarden brought the watermelon and there was nobody at home and he left it on the front porch and returned in his buggy to Jasper, but she never got the watermelon, she said, because a nigger boy ate it when he saw the initials, E.A.T.! This story tickled John Wesley's funny bone and he giggled and giggled but June Star didn't think it was any good. She said she wouldn't marry a man that just brought her a watermelon on Saturday. The grandmother said she would have done well to marry Mr. Teagarden because he was a gentleman and had bought Coca-Cola stock when it first came out and that he had died only a few years ago, a very wealthy man.

They stopped at The Tower for barbecued sandwiches. The Tower was a part-stucco and part-wood filling station and dance hall set in a clearing outside of Timothy. A fat man named Red Sammy Butts ran it and there were signs stuck here and there on the building and for miles up and down the highway saying, TRY RED SAMMY'S FAMOUS BARBECUE. NONE LIKE FAMOUS RED SAMMY'S! RED SAM! THE FAT BOY WITH THE HAPPY LAUGH. A VETERAN! RED SAMMY'S YOUR MAN!

Red Sammy was lying on the bare ground outside The Tower with his head under a truck while a gray monkey about a foot high, chained to a small chinaberry tree, chattered nearby. The monkey sprang back into the tree and got on the highest limb as soon as he saw the children jump out of the car and run toward him.

Inside, The Tower was a long dark room with a counter at one end and tables at the other and dancing space in the middle. They all sat down at a broad table next to the nickelodeon[4] and Red Sam's wife, a tall burnt-brown woman with hair and eyes lighter than her skin, came and took their order. The children's mother put a dime in the machine and played "The Tennessee Waltz," and the grandmother said that tune always made her want to dance. She asked Bailey if he would like to dance but he only glared at her. He didn't have a naturally sunny disposition like she did and trips made him nervous. The grandmother's brown eyes were very bright. She swayed her head from side to side and pretended she was dancing in her chair. June Star said play something she could tap to so the children's mother put in another dime and played a fast number and June Star stepped out onto the dance floor and did her tap routine.

"Ain't she cute?" Red Sam's wife said, leaning over the counter. 30 "Would you like to come be my little girl?"

"No, I certainly wouldn't," June Star said. "I wouldn't live in a broken-down place like this for a million bucks!" and she ran back to the table.

"Ain't she cute?" the woman repeated, stretching her mouth politely.

"Aren't you ashamed?" hissed the grandmother.

Red Sam came in and told his wife to quit lounging on the counter and hurry up with these people's order. His khaki trousers reached just to his hip bones and his stomach hung over them like a sack of meal swaying under his shirt. He came over and sat down at a table nearby and let out a combination sigh and yodel. "You can't win," he said. "You can't win," and he wiped his sweating red face off with a gray handkerchief. "These days you don't know who to trust," he said. "Ain't that the truth?"

"People are certainly not nice like they used to be," said the grand- 35 mother.

"Two fellers come in here last week," Red Sammy said, "driving a Chrysler. It was an old beat-up car but it was a good one and these boys looked all right to me. Said they worked at the mill and you know I let them fellers charge the gas they bought? Now why did I do that?"

"Because you're a good man!" the grandmother said at once.

[4]Jukebox.

"Yes'm, I suppose so," Red Sam said as if he were struck with this answer.

His wife brought the orders, carrying the five plates all at once without a tray, two in each hand and one balanced on her arm. "It isn't a soul in this green world of God's that you can trust," she said. "And I don't count nobody out of that, not nobody," she repeated, looking at Red Sammy.

"Did you read about that criminal, The Misfit, that's escaped?" 40 asked the grandmother.

"I wouldn't be a bit surprised if he didn't attack this place right here," said the woman. "If he hears about it being here, I wouldn't be none surprised to see him. If he hears it's two cent in the cash register, I wouldn't be a tall surprised if he . . ."

"That'll do," Red Sam said. "Go bring these people their Co'-Colas," and the woman went off to get the rest of the order.

"A good man is hard to find," Red Sammy said. "Everything is getting terrible. I remember the day you could go off and leave your screen door unlatched. Not no more."

He and the grandmother discussed better times. The old lady said that in her opinion Europe was entirely to blame for the way things were now. She said the way Europe acted you would think we were made of money and Red Sam said it was no use talking about it, she was exactly right. The children ran outside into the white sunlight and looked at the monkey in the lacy chinaberry tree. He was busy catching fleas on himself and biting each one carefully between his teeth as if it were a delicacy.

They drove off again into the hot afternoon. The grandmother took 45 cat naps and woke up every few minutes with her own snoring. Outside of Toombsboro she woke up and recalled an old plantation that she had visited in this neighborhood once when she was a young lady. She said the house had six white columns across the front and that there was an avenue of oaks leading up to it and two little wooden trellis arbors on either side in front where you sat down with your suitor after a stroll in the garden. She recalled exactly which road to turn off to get to it. She knew that Bailey would not be willing to lose any time looking at an old house, but the more she talked about it, the more she wanted to see it once again and find out if the little twin arbors were still standing. "There was a secret panel in this house," she said craftily, not telling the truth but wishing that she were, "and the story went that all the family silver was hidden in it when Sherman[5] came through but it was never found . . ."

"Hey!" John Wesley said. "Let's go see it! We'll find it! We'll poke all the woodwork and find it! Who lives there? Where do you turn off at? Hey Pop, can't we turn off there?"

"We never have seen a house with a secret panel!" June Star shrieked. "Let's go to the house with the secret panel! Hey, Pop, can't we go see the house with the secret panel!"

"It's not far from here, I know," the grandmother said. "It wouldn't take over twenty minutes."

Bailey was looking straight ahead. His jaw was as rigid as a horseshoe. "No," he said.

The children began to yell and scream that they wanted to see the house with the secret panel. John Wesley kicked the back of the front seat and June Star hung over her mother's shoulder and whined desperately into her ear that they never had any fun even on their vacation, that they could never do what THEY wanted to do. The baby began to scream and John Wesley kicked the back of the seat so hard that his father could feel the blows in his kidney.

"All right!" he shouted and drew the car to a stop at the side of the road. "Will you all shut up? Will you all just shut up for one second? If you don't shut up, we won't go anywhere."

"It would be very educational for them," the grandmother murmured.

"All right," Bailey said, "but get this. This is the only time we're going to stop for anything like this. This is the one and only time."

"The dirt road that you have to turn down is about a mile back," the grandmother directed. "I marked it when we passed."

"A dirt road," Bailey groaned.

After they had turned around and were headed toward the dirt road,

---

[5]In 1864 the Union army led by General William Tecumseh Sherman marched from Atlanta to Savannah, destroying civilian farms and houses along the way.

the grandmother recalled other points about the house, the beautiful glass over the front doorway and the candle lamp in the hall. John Wesley said that the secret panel was probably in the fireplace.

"You can't go inside this house," Bailey said. "You don't know who lives there."

"While you all talk to the people in front, I'll run around behind and get in a window," John Wesley suggested.

"We'll all stay in the car," his mother said.

They turned onto the dirt road and the car raced roughly along in a swirl of pink dust. The grandmother recalled the times when there were no paved roads and thirty miles was a day's journey. The dirt road was hilly and there were sudden washes in it and sharp curves on dangerous embankments. All at once they would be on a hill, looking down over the blue tops of trees for miles around, then the next minute, they would be in a red depression with the dust-coated trees looking down on them.

"This place had better turn up in a minute," Bailey said, "or I'm going to turn around."

The road looked as if no one had traveled on it in months.

"It's not much farther," the grandmother said and just as she said it, a horrible thought came to her. The thought was so embarrassing that she turned red in the face and her eyes dilated and her feet jumped up, upsetting her valise in the corner. The instant the valise moved, the newspaper top she had over the basket under it rose with a snarl and Pitty Sing, the cat, sprang onto Bailey's shoulder.

The children were thrown to the floor and their mother, clutching the baby, was thrown out the door onto the ground; the old lady was thrown into the front seat. The car turned over once and landed right-side-up in a gulch on the side of the road. Bailey remained in the driver's seat with the cat—gray-striped with a broad white face and an orange nose—clinging to his neck like a caterpillar.

As soon as the children saw they could move their arms and legs, they scrambled out of the car, shouting, "We've had an ACCIDENT!" The grandmother was curled up under the dashboard, hoping she was injured so that Bailey's wrath would not come down on her all at once. The horrible thought she had had before the accident was that the house she had remembered so vividly was not in Georgia but in Tennessee.

Bailey removed the cat from his neck with both hands and flung it out the window against the side of a pine tree. Then he got out of the car and started looking for the children's mother. She was sitting against the side of the red gutted ditch, holding the screaming baby, but she only had a cut down her face and a broken shoulder. "We've had an ACCIDENT!" the children screamed in a frenzy of delight.

"But nobody's killed," June Star said with disappointment as the grandmother limped out of the car, her hat still pinned to her head but the broken front brim standing up at a jaunty angle and the violet spray hanging off the side. They all sat down in the ditch, except the children, to recover from the shock. They were all shaking.

"Maybe a car will come along," said the children's mother hoarsely.

"I believe I have injured an organ," said the grandmother, pressing her side, but no one answered her. Bailey's teeth were clattering. He had on a yellow sport shirt with bright blue parrots designed in it and his face was as yellow as the shirt. The grandmother decided that she would not mention that the house was in Tennessee.

The road was about ten feet above and they could see only the tops 70 of the trees on the other side of it. Behind the ditch they were sitting in there were more woods, tall and dark and deep. In a few minutes they saw a car some distance away on top of a hill, coming slowly as if the occupants were watching them. The grandmother stood up and waved both arms dramatically to attract their attention. The car continued to come on slowly, disappeared around a bend and appeared again, moving even slower, on top of the hill they had gone over. It was a big black battered hearselike automobile. There were three men in it.

It came to a stop over them and for some minutes, the driver looked down with a steady expressionless gaze to where they were sitting, and didn't speak. Then he turned his head and muttered something to the other two and they got out. One was a fat boy in black trousers and a red sweat shirt with a silver stallion embossed on the front of it. He moved around on the right side of them and stood staring, his mouth partly open in a kind of loose grin. The other had on khaki pants and a blue striped coat and a gray hat pulled down very low, hiding most of his face. He came around slowly on the left side. Neither spoke.

The driver got out of the car and stood by the side of it, looking down at them. He was an older man than the other two. His hair was just beginning to gray and he wore silver-rimmed spectacles that gave him a scholarly look. He had a long creased face and didn't have on any shirt or undershirt. He had on blue jeans that were too tight for him and was holding a black hat and a gun. The two boys also had guns.

"We've had an ACCIDENT!" the children screamed.

The grandmother had the peculiar feeling that the bespectacled man was someone she knew. His face was as familiar to her as if she had known him all her life but she could not recall who he was. He moved away from the car and began to come down the embankment, placing his feet carefully so that he wouldn't slip. He had on tan and white shoes and no socks, and his ankles were red and thin. "Good afternoon," he said. "I see you all had you a little spill."

"We turned over twice!" said the grandmother. 75

"Oncet," he corrected. "We seen it happen. Try their car and see will it run, Hiram," he said quietly to the boy with the gray hat.

"What you got that gun for?" John Wesley asked. "Whatcha gonna do with that gun?"

"Lady," the man said to the children's mother, "would you mind calling them children to sit down by you? Children make me nervous. I want all you all to sit down right together there where you're at."

"What are you telling us what to do for?" June Star asked.

Behind them the line of woods gaped like a dark open mouth. 80 "Come here," said their mother.

"Look here now," Bailey began suddenly, "we're in a predicament! We're in . . ."

The grandmother shrieked. She scrambled to her feet and stood staring.

"You're The Misfit!" she said. "I recognized you at once!"

"Yes'm," the man said, smiling slightly as if he were pleased in spite of himself to be known, "but it would have been better for all of you, lady, if you hadn't of reckernized me."

Bailey turned his head sharply and said something to his mother 85 that shocked even the children. The old lady began to cry and The Misfit reddened.

"Lady," he said, "don't you get upset. Sometimes a man says things he don't mean. I don't reckon he meant to talk to you thataway."

"You wouldn't shoot a lady, would you?" the grandmother said and removed a clean handkerchief from her cuff and began to slap at her eyes with it.

The Misfit pointed the toe of his shoe into the ground and made a little hole and then covered it up again. "I would hate to have to," he said.

"Listen," the grandmother almost screamed, "I know you're a good man. You don't look a bit like you have common blood. I know you must come from nice people!"

"Yes mam," he said, "finest people in the world." When he smiled ⁹⁰ he showed a row of strong white teeth. "God never made a finer woman than my mother and my daddy's heart was pure gold," he said. The boy with the red sweat shirt had come around behind them and was standing with his gun at his hip. The Misfit squatted down on the ground. "Watch them children, Bobby Lee," he said. "You know they make me nervous." He looked at the six of them huddled together in front of him and he seemed to be embarrassed as if he couldn't think of anything to say. "Ain't a cloud in the sky," he remarked, looking up at it. "Don't see no sun but don't see no cloud neither."

"Yes, it's a beautiful day," said the grandmother. "Listen," she said, "you shouldn't call yourself The Misfit because I know you're a good man at heart. I can just look at you and tell."

"Hush!" Bailey yelled. "Hush! Everybody shut up and let me handle this!" He was squatting in the position of a runner about to spring forward but he didn't move.

"I pre-chate that, lady," The Misfit said and drew a little circle in the ground with the butt of his gun.

"It'll take a half a hour to fix this here car," Hiram called, looking over the raised hood of it.

"Well, first you and Bobby Lee get him and that little boy to step ⁹⁵ over yonder with you," The Misfit said, pointing to Bailey and John Wesley. "The boys want to ask you something," he said to Bailey. "Would you mind stepping back in them woods there with them?"

"Listen," Bailey began, "we're in a terrible predicament! Nobody realizes what this is," and his voice cracked. His eyes were as blue and intense as the parrots in his shirt and he remained perfectly still.

The grandmother reached up to adjust her hat brim as if she were going to the woods with him but it came off in her hand. She stood staring at it and after a second she let it fall on the ground. Hiram pulled Bailey up by the arm as if he were assisting an old man. John Wesley caught hold of his father's hand and Bobby Lee followed. They went off toward the woods and just as they reached the dark edge, Bailey turned and supporting himself against a gray naked pine trunk, he shouted, "I'll be back in a minute, Mamma, wait on me!"

"Come back this instant!" his mother shrilled but they all disappeared into the woods.

"Bailey Boy!" the grandmother called in a tragic voice but she found she was looking at The Misfit squatting on the ground in front of her. "I just know you're a good man," she said desperately. "You're not a bit common!"

"Nome, I ain't a good man," The Misfit said after a second as if he had considered her statement carefully, "but I ain't the worst in the world neither. My daddy said I was a different breed of dog from my brothers and sisters. 'You know,' Daddy said, 'it's some that can live their whole life out without asking about it and it's others has to know why it is, and this boy is one of the latters. He's going to be into everything!'" He put on his black hat and looked up suddenly and then away deep into the woods as if he were embarrassed again. "I'm sorry I don't have on a shirt before you ladies," he said, hunching his shoulders slightly. "We buried our clothes that we had on when we escaped and we're just making do until we can get better. We borrowed these from some folks we met," he explained.

"That's perfectly all right," the grandmother said. "Maybe Bailey has an extra shirt in his suitcase."

"I'll look and see terrectly," The Misfit said.

"Where are they taking him?" the children's mother screamed.

"Daddy was a card himself," The Misfit said. "You couldn't put anything over on him. He never got in trouble with the Authorities though. Just had the knack of handling them."

"You could be honest too if you'd only try," said the grandmother. 105 "Think how wonderful it would be to settle down and live a comfortable life and not have to think about somebody chasing you all the time."

The Misfit kept scratching in the ground with the butt of his gun as if he were thinking about it. "Yes'm, somebody is always after you," he murmured.

The grandmother noticed how thin his shoulder blades were just behind his hat because she was standing up looking down on him. "Do you ever pray?" she asked.

He shook his head. All she saw was the black hat wiggle between his shoulder blades. "Nome," he said.

There was a pistol shot from the woods, followed closely by another. Then silence. The old lady's head jerked around. She could hear the wind move through the tree tops like a long satisfied insuck of breath. "Bailey Boy!" she called.

"I was a gospel singer for a while," The Misfit said. "I been most 110 everything. Been in the arm service, both land and sea, at home and abroad, been twict married, been an undertaker, been with the railroads, plowed Mother Earth, been in a tornado, seen a man burnt alive oncet," and he looked up at the children's mother and the little girl who were sitting close together, their faces white and their eyes glassy; "I even seen a woman flogged," he said.

"Pray, pray," the grandmother began, "pray, pray . . ."

"I never was a bad boy that I remember of," The Misfit said in an almost dreamy voice, "but somewheres along the line I done something wrong and got sent to the penitentiary. I was buried alive," and he looked up and held her attention to him by a steady stare.

"That's when you should have started to pray," she said. "What did you do to get sent to the penitentiary that first time?"

"Turn to the right, it was a wall," The Misfit said, looking up again at the cloudless sky. "Turn to the left, it was a wall. Look up it was a ceiling, look down it was a floor. I forget what I done, lady. I set there and set there, trying to remember what it was I done and I ain't recalled it to this day. Oncet in a while, I would think it was coming to me, but it never come."

"Maybe they put you in by mistake," the old lady said vaguely.   115

"Nome," he said. "It wasn't no mistake. They had the papers on me."

"You must have stolen something," she said.

The Misfit sneered slightly. "Nobody had nothing I wanted," he said. "It was a head-doctor at the penitentiary said what I had done was kill my daddy but I known that for a lie. My daddy died in nineteen ought nineteen of the epidemic flu[6] and I never had a thing to do with it. He was buried in the Mount Hopewell Baptist churchyard and you can go there and see for yourself."

"If you would pray," the old lady said, "Jesus would help you."

"That's right," The Misfit said.   120

"Well then, why don't you pray?" she asked trembling with delight suddenly.

"I don't want no hep," he said. "I'm doing all right by myself."

Bobby Lee and Hiram came ambling back from the woods. Bobby Lee was dragging a yellow shirt with bright blue parrots in it.

"Throw me that shirt, Bobby Lee," The Misfit said. The shirt came flying at him and landed on his shoulder and he put it on. The grandmother couldn't name what the shirt reminded her of. "No, lady," The Misfit said while he was buttoning up, "I found out the crime don't matter. You can do one thing or you can do another, kill a man or take a tire off his car, because sooner or later you're going to forget what it was you done and just be punished for it."

The children's mother had begun to make heaving noises as if she   125 couldn't get her breath. "Lady," he asked, "would you and that little girl like to step off yonder with Bobby Lee and Hiram and join your husband?"

"Yes, thank you," the mother said faintly. Her left arm dangled helplessly and she was holding the baby, who had gone to sleep, in the other. "Hep that lady up, Hiram," The Misfit said as she struggled to climb out of the ditch, "and Bobby Lee, you hold onto that little girl's hand."

---

[6]The so-called "Spanish flu" spread through much of the world in 1918–19, killing millions.

"I don't want to hold hands with him," June Star said. "He reminds me of a pig."

The fat boy blushed and laughed and caught her by the arm and pulled her off into the woods after Hiram and her mother.

Alone with The Misfit, the grandmother found that she had lost her voice. There was not a cloud in the sky nor any sun. There was nothing around her but woods. She wanted to tell him that he must pray. She opened and closed her mouth several times before anything came out. Finally she found herself saying, "Jesus, Jesus," meaning, Jesus will help you, but the way she was saying it, it sounded as if she might be cursing.

"Yes'm," The Misfit said as if he agreed. "Jesus thrown everything off balance. It was the same case with Him as with me except He hadn't committed any crime and they could prove I had committed one because they had the papers on me. Of course," he said, "they never shown me my papers. That's why I sign myself now. I said long ago, you get you a signature and sign everything you do and keep a copy of it. Then you'll know what you done and you can hold up the crime to the punishment and see do they match and in the end you'll have something to prove you ain't been treated right. I call myself The Misfit," he said, "because I can't make what all I done wrong fit what all I gone through in punishment."

There was a piercing scream from the woods, followed closely by a pistol report. "Does it seem right to you, lady, that one is punished a heap and another ain't punished at all?"

"Jesus!" the old lady cried. "You've got good blood! I know you wouldn't shoot a lady! I know you come from nice people! Pray! Jesus, you ought not to shoot a lady. I'll give you all the money I've got!"

"Lady," The Misfit said, looking beyond her far into the woods, "there never was a body that give the undertaker a tip."

There were two more pistol reports and the grandmother raised her head like a parched old turkey hen crying for water and called, "Bailey Boy, Bailey Boy!" as if her heart would break.

"Jesus was the only One that ever raised the dead," The Misfit continued, "and He shouldn't have done it. He thrown everything off balance. If He did what He said, then it's nothing for you to do but throw

130

135

away everything and follow Him, and if He didn't then it's nothing for you to do but enjoy the few minutes you got left the best way you can— by killing somebody or burning down his house or doing some other meanness to him. No pleasure but meanness," he said and his voice had become almost a snarl.

"Maybe He didn't raise the dead," the old lady mumbled, not knowing what she was saying and feeling so dizzy that she sank down in the ditch with her legs twisted under her.

"I wasn't there so I can't say He didn't," The Misfit said, "I wisht I had of been there," he said, hitting the ground with his fist. "It ain't right I wasn't there because if I had of been there I would of known. Listen lady," he said in a high voice, "if I had of been there I would of known and I wouldn't be like I am now." His voice seemed about to crack and the grandmother's head cleared for an instant. She saw the man's face twisted close to her own as if he were going to cry and she murmured, "Why, you're one of my babies. You're one of my own children!" She reached out and touched him on the shoulder. The Misfit sprang back as if a snake had bitten him and shot her three times through the chest. Then he put his gun down on the ground and took off his glasses and began to clean them.

Hiram and Bobby Lee returned from the woods and stood over the ditch, looking down at the grandmother who half sat and half lay in a puddle of blood with her legs crossed under her like a child's and her face smiling up at the cloudless sky.

Without his glasses, The Misfit's eyes were red-rimmed and pale and defenseless-looking. "Take her off and throw her where you thrown the others," he said, picking up the cat that was rubbing itself against his leg.

"She was a talker, wasn't she?" Bobby Lee said, sliding down the ditch with a yodel.

"She would of been a good woman," The Misfit said, "if it had been somebody there to shoot her every minute of her life."

"Some fun!" Bobby Lee said.

"Shut up, Bobby Lee," The Misfit said. "It's no real pleasure in life."

STUDY QUESTIONS

1. Examine paragraph 137, where the grandmother says to The Misfit, "Why, you're one of my babies. You're one of my own children!" Why does she say this? Why does she then touch him?

2. Consider the passage in which The Misfit has the entire family killed. What TONE is used to NARRATE the event? How appropriate is it? How effective is it? How does the tone help to shape your reaction to The Misfit and the murders?

3. While the phrase "a good man" is used six times in the story, the DEFINITION of "a good man" is implied rather than stated explicitly. With reference to the events and CHARACTERS in the story, formulate a definition of "a good man."

4. *For Writing.* Write an essay in which you explore the concept of a "good" man or woman. Think about how a "good man" is defined in O'Connor's story and use examples from your own experiences to support or refute that definition.

GWENDOLYN BROOKS ⎰ *We Real Cool*

GWENDOLYN BROOKS (1917–2000), a poet and the first African American to win a Pulitzer Prize, was born in Topeka, Kansas, but grew up in Chicago, the city with which she and her poetry are most closely identified. There she attended both segregated and integrated schools (including a primarily white high school) and graduated from Wilson Junior College in 1936. She published her first book of poetry, *A Street in Bronzeville* (its title referring to a historic African American neighborhood in the South Side of Chicago), in 1945. A dedicated chronicler of the urban experience, Brooks created strong characters, such as those in *Annie Allen* (1949), *Maud Martha* (1953), and *Bronzeville Boys and Girls* (1956). She was named poet laureate of Illinois in 1968 and used that position to reach out to people, holding workshops, readings, and contests for children.

Although the language and line length of "We Real Cool" are spare, the poem's narrative power is considerable. Note how Brooks develops a solid cause-and-effect argument about the place of "cool" in youth culture. How might her minimalist style/prose be more effective in this instance than a more complex poetic style?

THE POOL PLAYERS,
SEVEN AT THE GOLDEN SHOVEL.

We real cool. We
Left school. We

Lurk late. We
Strike straight. We

Sing sin. We   5
Thin gin. We

Jazz June. We
Die soon.

STUDY QUESTIONS

1. **DESCRIBE**, in a paragraph, the scene and action of this poem—what is its **SETTING**? What do its **CHARACTERS** do and say?

2. Although this poem is brief—only eight short lines—it tells a complete story using **CAUSE AND EFFECT**. How does Brooks develop this cause-and-effect **NARRATIVE** from the first to the last line? How might these spare lines be even more effective than a longer narrative?

3. Each line of this poem, with the exception of the last, ends with "We," the beginning word of the following sentence. What effect does this form have on the printed version of the poem? Listen to Gwendolyn Brooks read "We Real Cool" (a recording is available on Poets.org) and respond again: how does Brooks's rhythmic reading of the line endings bring meaning to the poem?

4. *For Writing.* **REFLECT** on the quality of being "cool." In an essay, **ANALYZE** the ways the speaker and his buddies understand the concept as well as the way the poet understands both the pleasures and the dangers of acting "cool."

ROBERT FROST { *The Road Not Taken*

ROBERT FROST (1874–1963) was born in San Francisco, California, although reading his poetry might give you the impression he was born and reared in New England. In fact, Frost's father—who died in California—wished to be buried in his hometown of Lawrence, Massachusetts, a wish that prompted eleven-year-old Robert, his mother, and his sister to move there. After graduating from high school, Frost entered Dartmouth College but left without a degree to go into teaching as he continued writing. Except for a four-year stay in England just before the First World War, Frost and his wife and children lived on a series of farms in New Hampshire and Vermont. He is revered as the quintessential voice of rural New England and was awarded the Pulitzer Prize for Poetry four times. Frost recited his poem "The Gift Outright" (1942) at John F. Kennedy's presidential inauguration in 1961. After Frost's death, Kennedy praised him for his contribution to the arts.

"The Road Not Taken" is one of Frost's best-known poems. The narrator relates that a seemingly casual decision had to be made and only in retrospect did he come to understand what that decision really meant. In much the same way, at first this poem may seem artless and simple; careful rereading, though, reveals the poem's vivid imagery and formal structure. On rereading, consider whether the poem has the same message as you first thought.

Two roads diverged in a yellow wood,
And sorry I could not travel both
And be one traveler, long I stood
And looked down one as far as I could
To where it bent in the undergrowth;   5

Then took the other, as just as fair,
And having perhaps the better claim,
Because it was grassy and wanted wear;
Though as for that the passing there
Had worn them really about the same,   10

And both that morning equally lay
In leaves no step had trodden black.
Oh, I kept the first for another day!
Yet knowing how way leads on to way,
I doubted if I should ever come back.   15

I shall be telling this with a sigh
Somewhere ages and ages hence:
Two roads diverged in a wood, and I—
I took the one less traveled by,
And that has made all the difference.   20

STUDY QUESTIONS

1. The **NARRATOR** of the poem relates an incident about a choice that he or she once made. **SUMMARIZE** each stanza in one sentence, then create a paragraph from the four sentences and compare it to the poem. Does the prose paragraph convey the ideas and emotion of Frost's poem? Why or why not?

2. Read the poem again for meaning. Identify a possible **THESIS** of the poem and the parts of the poem that support this thesis. Can you know whether this is the meaning the poet had in mind or a meaning that you created for the poem? Explain.

3. **ANALYZE** the poem for the following elements: **TONE**, narrator's mood, **DICTION**, **IMAGERY**, structure, rhyme, and the title. How does each contribute to the poem's overall effect?

4. *For Writing.* Using your answers to the questions above, write a **LITERARY ANALYSIS** of the poem. You might want to summarize the poem, identify its thesis, and show how the **NARRATOR** supports it, breaks the poem down into literary elements, and then synthesizes the parts to arrive at an evaluative conclusion.

SEAMUS HEANEY ⎰ *Mid-Term Break*

SEAMUS HEANEY (1939–2013) was born in Northern Ireland, the eldest of nine children. At twelve, he enrolled in St. Columb's College, a Catholic boarding school located in Derry, on scholarship. He graduated from Queen's University of Belfast in 1961 with a degree in English language and literature. During his first position as a teacher he began to publish poetry with the encouragement of his headmaster, the writer Michael McLaverty. He has achieved great critical and commercial success as a poet, lecturer, and translator, culminating in the Nobel Prize in Literature in 1995. Heaney often draws on his rural and working-class roots (his father was a farmer; his mother's family were linen millworkers) for his body of work, which includes *Death of a Naturalist* (1967), *Wintering Out* (1973), and *The Haw Lantern* (1987). He taught at Harvard University and the University of Oxford. His lyrical translation of *Beowulf* (2000) brought the Anglo-Saxon epic to a contemporary audience, as Heaney melded modern language with Old English form.

"Mid-Term Break" is based on a true event: the death of Heaney's four-year-old brother while the poet was away at St. Columb's. Composed from the distance of time, the poem engages with memory as it addresses the speaker's process of gradually coming to terms with what has happened. How does memory act as a filter as well as a clear lens through which to view this sad occasion?

I sat all morning in the college sick bay
Counting bells knelling classes to a close.
At two o'clock our neighbours drove me home.

In the porch I met my father crying—
He had always taken funerals in his stride—   5
And Big Jim Evans saying it was a hard blow.

The baby cooed and laughed and rocked the pram
When I came in, and I was embarrassed
By old men standing up to shake my hand

And tell me they were "sorry for my trouble."   10
Whispers informed strangers I was the eldest,
Away at school, as my mother held my hand

In hers and coughed out angry tearless sighs.
At ten o'clock the ambulance arrived
With the corpse, stanched and bandaged by the nurses.   15

Next morning I went up into the room. Snowdrops
And candles soothed the bedside; I saw him
For the first time in six weeks. Paler now,

Wearing a poppy bruise on his left temple,
He lay in the four foot box as in his cot.   20
No gaudy scars, the bumper knocked him clear.

A four foot box, a foot for every year.

STUDY QUESTIONS

1. What is the occasion for this poem?

2. Consider the language in this poem. For instance, how does the title "Mid-Term Break" function on a literal and on a SYMBOLIC level? Choose two to three other examples and explore their multiple meanings. What do the different readings bring to the poem?

3. How does Heaney employ "memory" to help his speaker ANALYZE THE PROCESS of coming to terms with a death in the family? What is the effect?

4. How does Heaney use—and not use—emotion in this poem? How does Heaney employ both emotion and neutrality? What is the effect? Be sure to cite concrete language from the poem to support your points.

5. *For Writing.* Write a poem or an essay about a significant, highly emotional event in your life. Carefully choose the TONE that you feel will best convey your reaction to the event. Describe the event using details that appeal to the senses.

LANGSTON HUGHES ⎰ *Theme for English B*

LANGSTON HUGHES (1902–1967) was born in Joplin, Missouri. He
lived with his maternal grandmother in Lawrence, Kansas, after his
parents divorced and then with family friends after her death before
returning to his mother in Lincoln, Illinois. Hughes was elected class
poet, though he suspected it was because of a stereotype in the largely
white school that blacks had "rhythm." As a teen he was able to travel to
Africa and Europe as a crewman on the *SS Malone.* Returning to the
United States, he assisted the historian Carter G. Woodson before
entering Lincoln University in Pennsylvania, earning a BA in 1929. He
then moved to Harlem, in the midst of the Harlem Renaissance, a period
when the African American community's artistic talent flowered.
However, Hughes took issue with some of the shepherds of the Renaissance, such as W. E. B. Du Bois and Alain Locke, because he felt that
their approach was too assimilationist. Instead, Hughes celebrated
blackness unapologetically and focused his work on racial pride,
employing rhythms from jazz and folk music. He also wrote fiction,
nonfiction, plays, and children's books. His best-known works include
The Weary Blues (1926), *The Big Sea* (1940), and *Mule Bone* (1931), the
last written with Zora Neale Hurston.

  "Theme for English B" depicts an African American student's
reaction to being assigned an essay by a white instructor. The assignment seems simple enough, but as the speaker talks about himself, he

shows how it is loaded with cultural assumptions. Has the speaker written something that's "true"?

The instructor said,

> *Go home and write*
> *a page tonight.*
> *And let that page come out of you—*
> *Then, it will be true.*   5

I wonder if it's that simple?
I am twenty-two, colored, born in Winston-Salem.
I went to school there, then Durham, then here
to this college on the hill above Harlem.
I am the only colored student in my class.   10
The steps from the hill lead down into Harlem,
through a park, then I cross St. Nicholas,
Eighth Avenue, Seventh, and I come to the Y,
the Harlem Branch Y, where I take the elevator
up to my room, sit down, and write this page: 15

It's not easy to know what is true for you or me
at twenty-two, my age. But I guess I'm what
I feel and see and hear, Harlem, I hear you:
hear you, hear me—we two—you, me, talk on this page.
(I hear New York, too.) Me—who?   20
Well, I like to eat, sleep, drink, and be in love.
I like to work, read, learn, and understand life.
I like a pipe for a Christmas present,
or records—Bessie, bop, or Bach.
I guess being colored doesn't make me *not* like   25
the same things other folks like who are other races.
So will my page be colored that I write?
Being me, it will not be white.
But it will be

a part of you, instructor.   30
You are white—
yet a part of me, as I am a part of you.
That's American.
Sometimes perhaps you don't want to be a part of me.
Nor do I often want to be a part of you.   35
But we are, that's true!
As I learn from you,
I guess you learn from me—
although you're older—and white—
and somewhat more free.   40

This is my page for English B.

STUDY QUESTIONS

1. Describe the SPEAKER of the poem. What do we know about his character and his situation?

2. Why does the speaker choose to reveal the things that he does about himself, such as his route home, his musical taste, his various likes? What do his DESCRIPTIVE choices say about him?

3. At first glance, the instructor's assignment appears generic: to write something that's "true." How does Hughes complicate the DEFINITION of what is "true" here?

4. Why do you think the speaker chooses to write his "page" in verse, rather than in prose? How is his choice of GENRE a response to his instructor?

5. *For Writing.* In an essay, analyze the ways the speaker COMPARES AND CONTRASTS himself with his white instructor, both implicitly and explicitly. Be sure to refer to specific language in the poem.

WILLIAM BUTLER YEATS { *The Second Coming*

WILLIAM BUTLER YEATS (1865–1939), Irish dramatist and poet, was born to a prosperous Protestant family of artists and merchants. He immersed himself in the complex politics of his time as Irish nationalists struggled to free Ireland from British rule, and though he was ambivalent about its factionalism, he embraced Ireland's cultural identity and incorporated Irish legends, mythology, and history into his poems and plays. Late in life he served two terms in the Senate of the newly independent Irish Republic. Although mainstream Christianity never held much interest for Yeats, he was fascinated by spiritualism and the occult, and much of his writing reflects religious themes. In 1923 Yeats was awarded the Nobel Prize in Literature for what the Nobel committee called his "inspired poetry, which in a highly artistic form gives expression to the spirit of a whole nation."

In "The Second Coming," one of his most anthologized poems, Yeats evokes an apocalyptic vision in which the modern world's turmoil ushers in an era not of Christian redemption but of "anarchy" and "darkness." As you read, pay particular attention to the way Yeats paces the poem to create first a sense of almost panicky urgency and then a slowly dawning awareness of what cannot be stopped.

Turning and turning in the widening gyre[1]
The falcon cannot hear the falconer;
Things fall apart; the centre cannot hold;
Mere anarchy is loosed upon the world,

---

[1] A vast circle or spiral, Yeats's image in many of his poems for the turnings and patterns of history.

The blood-dimmed tide is loosed, and everywhere 5
The ceremony of innocence is drowned;
The best lack all conviction, while the worst
Are full of passionate intensity.

Surely some revelation is at hand;
Surely the Second Coming[2] is at hand. 10
The Second Coming! Hardly are those words out
When a vast image out of Spiritus Mundi[3]
Troubles my sight: a waste of desert sand;
A shape with lion body and the head of a man,
A gaze blank and pitiless as the sun, 15
Is moving its slow thighs, while all about it
Wind shadows of the indignant desert birds.

The darkness drops again but now I know
That twenty centuries of stony sleep
Were vexed to nightmare by a rocking cradle, 20
And what rough beast, its hour come round at last,
Slouches towards Bethlehem to be born?

[2]That is, of Jesus Christ.
[3]The spirit of the world (Latin).

STUDY QUESTIONS

1. In one sentence, SUMMARIZE the poem.

2. How does the poem's IMAGERY underscore the message of the poem? How effective is it?

3. Find a DESCRIPTION of the prophecy of the Second Coming in the Bible's Book of Revelation, then COMPARE AND CONTRAST it with Yeats's description. What does Yeats's vision have in common with that of the Bible? How do they differ?

4. *For Writing.* Yeats wrote this poem in 1919, shortly after World War I ended. RESEARCH this war and then write an ANALYSIS of how the war might have influenced the dire, pessimistic mood of the poem. Focus on imagery, TONE, and other literary elements to support your THESIS.

NATALIE ANGIER $\left\{ \begin{array}{l} \textit{Men, Women,} \\ \textit{Sex and Darwin} \end{array} \right.$

NATALIE ANGIER (b. 1958) has built a career writing books and articles that explain the intricacies of science to the nonscientist. Born and raised in New York City, Angier graduated from Barnard College, where she studied physics, astronomy, and English. She began working as a science writer for *Discovery* magazine in 1980, and in 1990 she joined the staff of the *New York Times*, where she won a Pulitzer Prize for beat reporting in 1991. She has published four books, all of them bestsellers: *Natural Obsessions* (1988), *The Beauty of the Beastly* (1995), *Woman: An Intimate Geography* (2000), and *The Canon: A Whirligig Tour of the Beautiful Basics of Science* (2007).

In "Men, Women, Sex and Darwin," published in the *New York Times* in 1999, Angier examines the most common theories proposed by evolutionary psychologists to explain male and female sexual behavior—for instance, that men are naturally more promiscuous than women and that women are naturally more interested in marriage than men. Drawing on empirical evidence and the work of psychologists, anthropologists, and primatologists, Angier finds reason to doubt these theories and offers alternative explanations of her own. As you read, notice how Angier summarizes and synthesizes information from many different sources.

LIFE IS SHORT BUT JINGLES are forever. None more so, it seems, than the familiar ditty, variously attributed to William James, Ogden Nash and Dorothy Parker: "Hoggamus, higgamus,/Men are polygamous,/Higgamus, hoggamus,/Women monogamous."

Lately the pith of that jingle has found new fodder and new fans, through the explosive growth of a field known as evolutionary psychology. Evolutionary psychology professes to have discovered the fundamental modules of human nature, most notably the essential nature of man and of woman. It makes sense to be curious about the evolutionary roots of human behavior. It's reasonable to try to understand our impulses and actions by applying Darwinian logic to the problem. We're animals. We're not above the rude little prods and jests of natural and sexual selection. But evolutionary psychology as it has been disseminated across mainstream consciousness is a cranky and despotic Cyclops, its single eye glaring through an overwhelmingly masculinist lens. I say "masculinist" rather than "male" because the view of male behavior promulgated by hard-core evolutionary psychologists is as narrow and inflexible as their view of womanhood is.

I'm not interested in explaining to men what they really want or how they should behave. If a fellow chooses to tell himself that his yen for the fetching young assistant in his office and his concomitant disgruntlement with his aging wife make perfect Darwinian sense, who am I to argue with him? I'm only proposing here that the hard-core evolutionary psychologists have got a lot about women wrong—about some of us, anyway—and that women want more and deserve better than the cartoon Olive Oyl[1] handed down for popular consumption.

The cardinal premises of evolutionary psychology of interest to this discussion are as follows: 1. Men are more promiscuous and less sexually reserved than women are. 2. Women are inherently more interested in a stable relationship than men are. 3. Women are naturally attracted to high-status men with resources. 4. Men are naturally attracted to youth and beauty. 5. Humankind's core preferences and desires were hammered out long, long ago, a hundred thousand years or more, in the legendary Environment of Evolutionary Adaptation, or E.E.A., also known as the ancestral environment, also known as the Stone Age, and they have not changed appreciably since then, nor are they likely to change in the future.

---

[1]Popeye's long-suffering sweetheart in the *Popeye* comic strip and animations, first created by cartoonist Elzie Crisler Segar in 1929.

In sum: Higgamus, hoggamus, Pygmalionus, *Playboy* magazine, 5 eternitas. Amen.

Hard-core evolutionary psychology types go to extremes to argue in favor of the yawning chasm that separates the innate desires of women and men. They declare ringing confirmation for their theories even in the face of feeble and amusingly contradictory data. For example: Among the cardinal principles of the evo-psycho set is that men are by nature more polygamous than women are, and much more accepting of casual, even anonymous, sex. Men can't help themselves, they say: they are always hungry for sex, bodies, novelty and nubility. Granted, men needn't act on such desires, but the drive to sow seed is there nonetheless, satyric and relentless, and women cannot fully understand its force. David Buss, a professor of psychology at the University of Texas at Austin and one of the most outspoken of the evolutionary psychologists, says that asking a man not to lust after a pretty young woman is like telling a carnivore not to like meat.

At the same time, they recognize that the overwhelming majority of men and women get married, and so their theories must extend to different innate mate preferences among men and women. Men look for the hallmarks of youth, like smooth skin, full lips and perky breasts; they want a mate who has a long childbearing career ahead of her. Men also want women who are virginal and who seem as though they'll be faithful and not make cuckolds of them. The sexy, vampy types are fine for a Saturday romp, but when it comes to choosing a marital partner, men want modesty and fidelity.

Women want a provider, the theory goes. They want a man who seems rich, stable and ambitious. They want to know that they and their children will be cared for. They want a man who can take charge, maybe dominate them just a little, enough to reassure them that the man is genotypically, phenotypically, eternally, a king. Women's innate preference for a well-to-do man continues to this day, the evolutionary psychologists insist, even among financially independent and professionally successful women who don't need a man as a provider. It was adaptive in the past to look for the most resourceful man, they say, and adaptations can't be willed away in a generation or two of putative cultural change.

And what is the evidence for these male-female verities? For the difference in promiscuity quotas, the hard-cores love to raise the example of the differences between gay men and lesbians. Homosexuals are seen as a revealing population because they supposedly can behave according to the innermost impulses of their sex, untempered by the need to adjust to the demands and wishes of the opposite sex, as heterosexuals theoretically are. What do we see in this ideal study group? Just look at how gay men carry on! They are perfectly happy to have hundreds, thousands, of sexual partners, to have sex in bathhouses, in bathrooms, in Central Park. By contrast, lesbians are sexually sedate. They don't cruise sex clubs. They couple up and stay coupled, and they like cuddling and hugging more than they do serious, genitally based sex.

In the hard-core rendering of inherent male-female discrepancies in promiscuity, gay men are offered up as true men, real men, men set free to be men, while lesbians are real women, ultrawomen, acting out every woman's fantasy of love and commitment. Interestingly, though, in many neurobiology studies gay men are said to have somewhat feminized brains, with hypothalamic nuclei that are closer in size to a woman's than to a straight man's, and spatial-reasoning skills that are modest and ladylike rather than manfully robust. For their part, lesbians are posited to have somewhat masculinized brains and skills—to be sportier, more mechanically inclined, less likely to have played with dolls or tea sets when young—all as an ostensible result of exposure to prenatal androgens. And so gay men are sissy boys in some contexts and Stone Age manly men in others, while lesbians are battering rams one day and flower into the softest and most sexually divested girlish girls the next.

On the question of mate preferences, evo-psychos rely on surveys, most of them compiled by David Buss. His surveys are celebrated by some, derided by others, but in any event they are ambitious—performed in thirty-seven countries, he says, on six continents. His surveys, and others emulating them, consistently find that men rate youth and beauty as important traits in a mate, while women give comparatively greater weight to ambition and financial success. Surveys show that surveys never lie. Lest you think that women's mate preferences change with their own mounting economic clout, surveys assure us that they do not. Surveys of female medical students, according to John Marshall Townsend, of Syracuse University, indicate that they hope to marry men with an earning power and social status at least equal to and preferably greater than their own.

Perhaps all this means is that men can earn a living wage better, even now, than women can. Men make up about half the world's population, but they still own the vast majority of the world's wealth—the currency, the minerals, the timber, the gold, the stocks, the amber fields of grain. In her superb book *Why So Slow?* Virginia Valian, a professor of psychology at Hunter College, lays out the extent of lingering economic discrepancies between men and women in the United States. In 1978 there were two women heading Fortune 1000 companies; in 1994, there were still two; in 1996, the number had jumped all the way to four. In 1985, 2 percent of the Fortune 1000's senior-level executives were women; by 1992, that number had hardly budged, to 3 percent. A 1990 salary and compensation survey of 799 major companies showed that of the highest-paid officers and directors, less than one-half of 1 percent were women. Ask, and he shall receive. In the United States the possession of a bachelor's degree adds $28,000 to a man's salary but only $9,000 to a woman's. A degree from a high-prestige school contributes $11,500 to a man's income but subtracts $2,400 from a woman's. If women continue to worry that they need a man's money, because the playing field remains about as level as the surface of Mars, then we can't conclude anything about innate preferences. If women continue to suffer from bag-lady syndrome even as they become prosperous, if they still see their wealth as provisional and capsizable, and if they still hope to find a man with a dependable income to supplement their own, then we can credit women with intelligence and acumen, for inequities abound.

There's another reason that smart, professional women might respond on surveys that they'd like a mate of their socioeconomic status or better. Smart, professional women are smart enough to know that men can be tender of ego—is it genetic?—and that it hurts a man to earn less money than his wife, and that resentment is a noxious chemical in a marriage and best avoided at any price. "A woman who is more successful than her mate threatens his position in the male hierarchy," Elizabeth Cashdan, of the University of Utah, has written. If women could be persuaded that men didn't mind their being high achievers, were in fact pleased and proud to be affiliated with them, we might predict that the women would stop caring about the particulars of their mates' income. The anthropologist Sarah Blaffer Hrdy writes that "when female status and access to resources do not depend on her mate's status, women will likely use a range of criteria, not primarily or even necessarily prestige and wealth, for mate selection." She cites a 1996 *New York Times* story about women from a wide range of professions—bankers, judges, teachers, journalists—who marry male convicts. The allure of such men is not their income, for you can't earn much when you make license plates for a living. Instead, it is the men's gratitude that proves irresistible. The women also like the fact that their husbands' fidelity is guaranteed. "Peculiar as it is," Hrdy writes, "this vignette of sex-reversed claustration[2] makes a serious point about just how little we know about female choice in breeding systems where male interests are not paramount and patrilines[3] are not making the rules."

Do women love older men? Do women find gray hair and wrinkles attractive on men—as attractive, that is, as a fine, full head of pigmented hair and a vigorous, firm complexion? The evolutionary psychologists suggest yes. They believe that women look for the signs of maturity in men because a mature man is likely to be a comparatively wealthy and resourceful man. That should logically include baldness, which generally comes with age and the higher status that it often confers. Yet, as Desmond Morris points out, a thinning hairline is not considered a particularly attractive state.

Assuming that women find older men attractive, is it the men's alpha 15 status? Or could it be something less complimentary to the male, something like the following—that an older man is appealing not because he is powerful but because in his maturity he has lost some of his power, has become less marketable and desirable and potentially

[2]Cloistering, enclosing.
[3]Groups of patrilineages, or lines of descent from a male ancestor.

more grateful and gracious, more likely to make a younger woman feel that there is a balance of power in the relationship? The rude little calculation is simple: He is male, I am female—advantage, man. He is older, I am younger—advantage, woman. By the same token, a woman may place little value on a man's appearance because she values something else far more: room to breathe. Who can breathe in the presence of a handsome young man, whose ego, if expressed as a vapor, would fill Biosphere II? Not even, I'm afraid, a beautiful young woman.

In the end, what is important to question, and to hold to the fire of alternative interpretation, is the immutability and adaptive logic of the discrepancy, its basis in our genome rather than in the ecological circumstances in which a genome manages to express itself. Evolutionary psychologists insist on the essential discordance between the strength of the sex drive in males and females. They admit that many nonhuman female primates gallivant about rather more than we might have predicted before primatologists began observing their behavior in the field—more, far more, than is necessary for the sake of reproduction. Nonetheless, the credo of the coy female persists. It is garlanded with qualifications and is admitted to be an imperfect portrayal of female mating strategies, but then, that little matter of etiquette attended to, the credo is stated once again.

"Amid the great variety of social structure in these species, the basic theme . . . stands out, at least in minimal form: males seem very eager for sex and work hard to find it; females work less hard," Robert Wright says in *The Moral Animal.* "This isn't to say the females don't like sex. They love it, and may initiate it. And, intriguingly, the females of the species most closely related to humans—chimpanzees and bonobos—seem particularly amenable to a wild sex life, including a variety of partners. Still, female apes don't do what male apes do: search high and low, risking life and limb, to find sex, and to find as much of it, with as many different partners, as possible; it has a way of finding them." In fact female chimpanzees do search high and low and take great risks to find sex with partners other than the partners who have a way of finding them. DNA studies of chimpanzees in West Africa show that half the offspring in a group of closely scrutinized chimpanzees turned out not to be the offspring of the resident males.

The females of the group didn't rely on sex "finding" its way to them; they proactively left the local environs, under such conditions of secrecy that not even their vigilant human observers knew they had gone, and became impregnated by outside males. They did so even at the risk of life and limb—their own and those of their offspring. Male chimpanzees try to control the movements of fertile females. They'll scream at them and hit them if they think the females aren't listening. They may even kill an infant they think is not their own. We don't know why the females take such risks to philander, but they do, and to say that female chimpanzees "work less hard" than males do at finding sex does not appear to be supported by the data.

Evo-psychos pull us back and forth until we might want to sue for whiplash. On the one hand we are told that women have a lower sex drive than men do. On the other hand we are told that the madonna-whore dichotomy is a universal stereotype. In every culture, there is a tendency among both men and women to adjudge women as either chaste or trampy. The chaste ones are accorded esteem. The trampy ones are consigned to the basement, a notch or two below goats in social status. A woman can't sleep around without risking terrible retribution, to her reputation, to her prospects, to her life. "Can anyone find a single culture in which women with unrestrained sexual appetites aren't viewed as more aberrant than comparably libidinous men?" Wright asks rhetorically.

Women are said to have lower sex drives than men, yet they are universally punished if they display evidence to the contrary—if they disobey their "natural" inclination toward a stifled libido. Women supposedly have a lower sex drive than men do, yet it is not low enough. There is still just enough of a lingering female infidelity impulse that cultures everywhere have had to gird against it by articulating a rigid dichotomy with menacing implications for those who fall on the wrong side of it. There is still enough lingering female infidelity to justify infibulation, purdah, claustration. Men have the naturally higher sex drive, yet all the laws, customs, punishments, shame, strictures, mystiques and antimystiques are aimed with full hominid fury at that tepid, sleepy, hypoactive creature, the female libido.

"It seems premature . . . to attribute the relative lack of female inter- 20 est in sexual variety to women's biological nature alone in the face of overwhelming evidence that women are consistently beaten for promiscuity and adultery," the primatologist Barbara Smuts has written. "If female sexuality is muted compared to that of men, then why must men the world over go to extreme lengths to control and contain it?"

Why indeed? Consider a brief evolutionary apologia for President Clinton's adulteries written by Steven Pinker, of the Massachusetts Institute of Technology. "Most human drives have ancient Darwinian rationales," he wrote. "A prehistoric man who slept with fifty women could have sired fifty children, and would have been more likely to have descendants who inherited his tastes. A woman who slept with fifty men would have no more descendants than a woman who slept with one. Thus, men should seek quantity in sexual partners; women, quality." And isn't it so, he says, everywhere and always so? "In our society," he continues, "most young men tell researchers that they would like eight sexual partners in the next two years; most women say that they would like one." Yet would a man find the prospect of a string of partners so appealing if the following rules were applied: that no matter how much he may like a particular woman and be pleased by her performance and want to sleep with her again, he will have no say in the matter and will be dependent on her mood and good graces for all future contact; that each act of casual sex will cheapen his status and make him increasingly less attractive to other women; and that society will not wink at his randiness but rather sneer at him and think him pathetic, sullied, smaller than life? Until men are subjected to the same severe standards and threat of censure as women are, and until they are given the lower hand in a so-called casual encounter from the start, it is hard to insist with such self-satisfaction that, hey, it's natural, men like a lot of sex with a lot of people and women don't.

Reflect for a moment on Pinker's philandering caveman who slept with fifty women. Just how good a reproductive strategy is this chronic, random shooting of the gun? A woman is fertile only five or six days a month. Her ovulation is concealed. The man doesn't know when she's fertile. She might be in the early stages of pregnancy when he gets to her; she might still be lactating and thus not ovulating. Moreover, even if our hypothetical Don Juan hits a day on which a woman is ovulating, the chances are around 65 percent that his sperm will fail to fertilize her egg; human reproduction is complicated, and most eggs and sperm are not up to the demands of proper fusion. Even if conception occurs, the resulting embryo has about a 30 percent chance of miscarrying at some point in gestation. In sum, each episode of fleeting sex has a remarkably small probability of yielding a baby—no more than 1 or 2 percent at best.

And because the man is trysting and running, he isn't able to prevent any of his casual contacts from turning around and mating with other men. The poor fellow. He has to mate with many scores of women for his wham-bam strategy to pay off. And where are all these women to be found, anyway? Population densities during that purportedly all-powerful psyche shaper the "ancestral environment" were quite low, and long-distance travel was dangerous and difficult.

There are alternatives to wantonness, as a number of theorists have emphasized. If, for example, a man were to spend more time with one woman rather than dashing breathlessly from sheet to sheet, if he were to feel compelled to engage in what animal behaviorists call mate guarding, he might be better off, reproductively speaking, than the wild Lothario, both because the odds of impregnating the woman would increase and because he'd be monopolizing her energy and keeping her from the advances of other sperm bearers. It takes the average couple three to four months of regular sexual intercourse to become pregnant. That number of days is approximately equal to the number of partners our hypothetical libertine needs to sleep with to have one encounter result in a "fertility unit," that is, a baby. The two strategies, then, shake out about the same. A man can sleep with a lot of women—the quantitative approach—or he can sleep with one woman for months at a time, and be madly in love with her—the qualitative tactic.

It's possible that these two reproductive strategies are distributed in discrete packets among the male population, with a result that some men are born philanderers and can never attach, while others are born romantics and perpetually in love with love; but it's also possible that men teeter back and forth from one impulse to the other, suffering an internal struggle between the desire to bond and the desire to retreat, with the circuits of attachment ever there to be toyed with, and their needs and desires difficult to understand, paradoxical, fickle, treacherous and glorious. It is possible, then, and for perfectly good Darwinian reason, that casual sex for men is rarely as casual as it is billed.

It needn't be argued that men and women are exactly the same, or that humans are meta-evolutionary beings, removed from nature and slaves to culture, to reject the perpetually regurgitated model of the coy female and the ardent male. Conflicts of interest are always among us, and the outcomes of those conflicts are interesting, more interesting by far than what the ultra-evolutionary psychology line has handed us. Patricia Gowaty, of the University of Georgia, sees conflict between males and females as inevitable and pervasive. She calls it sexual dialectics. Her thesis is that females and males vie for control over the means of reproduction. Those means are the female body, for there is as yet no such beast as the parthenogenetic[4] man.

Women are under selective pressure to maintain control over their reproduction, to choose with whom they will mate and with whom they will not—to exercise female choice. Men are under selective pressure to make sure they're chosen or, barring that, to subvert female choice and coerce the female to mate against her will. "But once you have this basic dialectic set in motion, it's going to be a constant push-me, pull-you," Gowaty says. That dynamism cannot possibly result in a unitary response, the caricatured coy woman and ardent man. Instead there are going to be some coy, reluctantly mating males and some ardent females, and any number of variations in between.

"A female will choose to mate with a male whom she believes, consciously or otherwise, will confer some advantage on her and her offspring. If that's the case, then her decision is contingent on what she brings to the equation." For example, she says, "the 'good genes' model leads to oversimplified notions that there is a 'best male' out there, a top-of-the-line hunk whom all females would prefer to mate with if they had the wherewithal. But in the viability model, a female brings

---

[4]Created from an unfertilized egg.

her own genetic complement to the equation, with the result that what looks good genetically to one woman might be a clash of colors for another."

Maybe the man's immune system doesn't complement her own, for example, Gowaty proposes. There's evidence that the search for immune variation is one of the subtle factors driving mate selection, which may be why we care about how our lovers smell; immune molecules may be volatilized and released in sweat, hair, the oil on our skin. We are each of us a chemistry set, and each of us has a distinctive mix of reagents. "What pleases me might not please somebody else," Gowaty says. "There is no one-brand great male out there. We're not all programmed to look for the alpha male and only willing to mate with the little guy or the less aggressive guy because we can't do any better. But the propaganda gives us a picture of the right man and the ideal woman, and the effect of the propaganda is insidious. It becomes self-reinforcing. People who don't fit the model think, I'm weird, I'll have to change my behavior." It is this danger, that the ostensible "discoveries" of evolutionary psychology will be used as propaganda, that makes the enterprise so disturbing.

Variation and flexibility are the key themes that get set aside in the 30 breathless dissemination of evolutionary psychology. "The variation is tremendous, and is rooted in biology," Barbara Smuts said to me. "Flexibility itself is the adaptation." Smuts has studied olive baboons, and she has seen males pursuing all sorts of mating strategies. "There are some whose primary strategy is dominating other males, and being able to gain access to more females because of their fighting ability," she says. "Then there is the type of male who avoids competition and cultivates long-term relationships with females and their infants. These are the nice, affiliative guys. There's a third type, who focuses on sexual relationships. He's the consorter. . . . And as far as we can tell, no one reproductive strategy has advantages over the others."

Women are said to need an investing male. We think we know the reason. Human babies are difficult and time consuming to raise. Stone Age mothers needed husbands to bring home the bison. Yet the age-old assumption that male parental investment lies at the heart of human evolution is now open to serious question. Men in traditional foraging cultures do not necessarily invest resources in their offspring. Among the Hadza of Africa, for example, the men hunt, but they share the bounty of that hunting widely, politically, strategically. They don't deliver it straight to the mouths of their progeny. Women rely on their senior female kin to help feed their children. The women and their children in a gathering-hunting society clearly benefit from the meat that hunters bring back to the group. But they benefit as a group, not as a collection of nuclear family units, each beholden to the father's personal pound of wildeburger.

This is a startling revelation, which upends many of our presumptions about the origins of marriage and what women want from men and men from women. If the environment of evolutionary adaptation is not defined primarily by male parental investment, the bedrock of so much of evolutionary psychology's theories, then we can throw the door wide open and ask new questions, rather than endlessly repeating ditties and calling the female coy long after she has run her petticoats through the presidential paper shredder.

For example: Nicholas Blurton Jones, of the University of California at Los Angeles, and others have proposed that marriage developed as an extension of men's efforts at mate guarding. If the cost of philandering becomes ludicrously high, the man might be better off trying to claim rights to one woman at a time. Regular sex with a fertile woman is at least likely to yield offspring at comparatively little risk to his life, particularly if sexual access to the woman is formalized through a public ceremony—a wedding. Looked at from this perspective, one must wonder why an ancestral woman bothered to get married, particularly if she and her female relatives did most of the work of keeping the family fed from year to year. Perhaps, Blurton Jones suggests, to limit the degree to which she was harassed. The cost of chronic male harassment may be too high to bear. Better to agree to a ritualized bond with a male and to benefit from whatever hands-off policy that marriage may bring, than to spend all of her time locked in one sexual dialectic or another.

Thus marriage may have arisen as a multifaceted social pact: between man and woman, between male and male and between the couple and the tribe. It is a reasonable solution to a series of cultural challenges that arose in concert with the expansion of the human neocortex. But its roots may not be what we think they are, nor may our contemporary mating behaviors stem from the pressures of an ancestral environment as it is commonly portrayed, in which a woman needed a mate to help feed and clothe her young. Instead, our "deep" feelings about marriage may be more pragmatic, more contextual and, dare I say it, more egalitarian than we give them credit for being.

If marriage is a social compact, a mutual bid between man and woman to contrive a reasonably stable and agreeable microhabitat in a community of shrewd and well-armed members, then we can understand why, despite rhetoric to the contrary, men are as eager to marry as women are. A raft of epidemiological studies have shown that marriage adds more years to the life of a man than it does to that of a woman. Why should that be, if men are so "naturally" ill suited to matrimony? 35

What do women want? None of us can speak for all women, or for more than one woman, really, but we can hazard a mad guess that a desire for emotional parity is widespread and profound. It doesn't go away, although it often hibernates under duress, and it may be perverted by the restrictions of habitat or culture into something that looks like its opposite. The impulse for liberty is congenital. It is the ultimate manifestation of selfishness, which is why we can count on its endurance.

STUDY QUESTIONS

1. What theories of evolutionary psychology does Angier call into question? What alternative theories does she propose?

2. List the people Angier quotes or cites. How does each contribute to her essay? What is the rhetorical effect of using these sources? How would the essay be different if she hadn't used sources?

3. *For Writing.* Write an essay in which you explain, in your own words, a theory of evolutionary psychology that Angier discusses. Then DESCRIBE the behavior of at least two people you know and explain how that behavior supports or refutes that theory.

We're sorry!

The rights-holder for the selection previously printed here is no longer granting permission for W. W. Norton to reproduce this work.

STEPHEN JAY GOULD { *Sex, Drugs, Disasters, and the*

Extinction of Dinosaurs

Steven Jay Gould (1941–2002) was born in New York City; he earned his undergraduate degree at Antioch College in Ohio and his PhD at Columbia University. For thirty-five years Gould was a professor at Harvard University. However, he is best known for his ability to explain complex scientific topics in ways that make them accessible to a general audience, often by writing articles in popular magazines and by advising (and often appearing in) television programs like PBS's *NOVA*. He collected his columns from the magazine *Natural History* into several book-length collections, including *Hen's Teeth and Horse's Toes* (1983), *The Flamingo's Smile* (1985), and *Bully for Brontosaurus* (1991). The recipient of dozens of honorary degrees, Gould was a finalist for the Pulitzer Prize for his book *Wonderful Life: The Burgess Shale and the Nature of History* (1989).

The following essay, originally published in *Discover Magazine* in 1984, presents three potential hypotheses for the extinction of the dinosaurs and analyzes each for its scientific value. As you read, think about how the essay is organized and how Gould incorporates humor into a serious discussion. How might these qualities contribute to Gould's reputation as a writer who excels at presenting scientific topics to a general audience?

SCIENCE, IN ITS MOST FUNDAMENTAL definition, is a fruitful mode of inquiry, not a list of enticing conclusions. The conclusions are the consequence, not the essence. My greatest unhappiness with most popular presentations of science concerns their failure to separate fascinating claims from the methods that scientists use to establish the facts of nature. Journalists, and the public, thrive on controversial and stunning statements. But science is, basically, a way of knowing—in P. B. Medawar's apt words, "the art of the soluble." If the growing corps of popular science writers would focus on *how* scientists develop and defend those fascinating claims, they would make their greatest possible contribution to public understanding.

Consider three ideas, proposed in perfect seriousness to account for that greatest of all titillating puzzles—the extinction of dinosaurs. These three notions invoke the primarily fascinating themes of our culture—sex, drugs, and violence—and I want to show why two of them rank as silly speculation, and why the other represents science at its grandest and most useful.

Science works with testable hypotheses. If, after much compilation and scrutiny of data, new information continues to affirm a hypothesis, we may accept it provisionally and gain confidence as further evidence mounts. We can never be completely sure that a hypothesis is right, though we may be able to show with confidence that it is wrong. The best scientific hypotheses are also generous and expansive: they suggest extensions and implications that enlighten related, and even far distant, subjects. Simply consider how the idea of evolution has influenced virtually every intellectual field.

Useless speculation, on the other hand, is restrictive. It generates no testable hypothesis, proposes no way to obtain potentially refuting evidence. Please note that I am not speaking of truth or falsity. The speculation may well be true; still, if it provides, in principle, no material for affirmation or rejection, we can make nothing of it. It must simply stand forever as an intriguing idea. Useless speculation turns in on itself and leads nowhere; good science reaches out. But, enough preaching. Let's move on to dinosaurs, and the three proposed causes of their extinction.

1. Sex: Testes function only in a narrow range of temperature (those of mammals hang externally in a scrotal sac because they need to be cooler than the body). A worldwide rise in temperature at the close of the Cretaceous period caused the testes of dinosaurs to stop functioning and led to their extinction by sterilization of males.

2. Drugs: Angiosperms (flowering plants) first evolved toward the end of the dinosaurs' reign. Many of these plants contain psychoactive

agents, avoided by mammals today because of their bitter taste. Dinosaurs had neither means to taste the bitterness, nor livers effective enough to detoxify the substances. They died of massive overdoses.

3. Disasters: A huge asteroid struck the earth some 65 million years ago, lofting a cloud of dust into the sky and blocking sunlight, thereby suppressing photosynthesis and so drastically lowering world temperatures that dinosaurs and hosts of other creatures became extinct.

Before analyzing these three tantalizing statements, we must establish a basic ground rule often violated in proposals for the dinosaurs' demise. *There is no separate problem of the extinction of dinosaurs.* Too often we divorce specific events from their wider contexts and systems of cause and effect. The fundamental fact of dinosaur extinction is that it coincided with the demise of many other groups across a wide range of habitats, from terrestrial to marine.

The history of life has been punctuated by brief episodes of mass extinction. A recent analysis by University of Chicago paleontologists Jack Sepkoski and Dave Raup, based on the best and most exhaustive tabulation of data ever assembled, shows clearly that five episodes of mass dying stand well above the "background" extinctions of normal times. The Cretaceous debacle, occurring 65 million years ago and separating the Mesozoic and Cenozoic eras of our geological time scale, ranks prominently among the five. Nearly all the marine plankton (single-celled floating creatures) died suddenly, at least in geological terms; among marine invertebrates, close to 15 percent of all families perished, including many previously dominant groups, especially the ammonites (relatives of squids in coiled shells). On land, the dinosaurs disappeared after more than 100 million years of unchallenged domination.

In this context, speculations limited to dinosaurs alone ignore the 10 larger phenomenon. We need a coordinated explanation for a system of events that includes the extinction of dinosaurs as one component. Thus it makes little sense, though it may fuel our desire to view mammals as inevitable inheritors of the earth, to guess that dinosaurs died because small mammals ate their eggs (a perennial untestable speculation). It seems most unlikely that some disaster peculiar to dinosaurs befell these massive beasts—and that the debacle happened to strike just when one of history's five great dyings had enveloped the earth for completely different reasons.

The testicular theory, an old favorite from the 1940s, had its root in an interesting and thoroughly respectable study of temperature tolerances in the American alligator, published in the staid *Bulletin of the American Museum of Natural History* in 1946 by three experts on living and fossil reptiles—E. H. Colbert, my own first teacher in paleontology, R. B. Cowles, and C. M. Bogert.

The first sentence of their summary reveals a purpose beyond alligators: "This report describes an attempt to infer the reactions of extinct reptiles, especially the dinosaurs, to high temperatures as based upon reactions observed in the modern alligator." They studied, by rectal thermometry, the body temperatures of alligators under changing conditions of heating and cooling. (Well, let's face it, you wouldn't want to try sticking a thermometer under a 'gator's tongue.) The predictions under test go way back to an old theory first stated by Galileo in the 1630s—the unequal scaling of surfaces and volumes. As an animal, or any object, grows (provided its shape doesn't change), surface areas must increase more slowly than volumes—since surfaces get larger as length squared, volumes much more rapidly, as length cubed. Therefore, small animals have high ratios of surface to volume, while large animals cover themselves with relatively little surface.

Among cold-blooded animals lacking any physiological mechanism for keeping their temperatures constant, small creatures have a hell of a time keeping warm—because they lose so much heat through their relatively large surfaces. On the other hand, large animals, with their relatively small surfaces, may lose heat so slowly that, once warm, they may maintain effectively constant temperatures against ordinary fluctuations of climate. (In fact, the resolution of the "hot-blooded dinosaur" controversy of a few years back may simply be that, while large dinosaurs possessed no physiological mechanism for constant temperature, and so were not warm-blooded in the technical sense, their size and relatively small surface area kept them warm.)

Colbert, Cowles, and Bogert compared the warming rates of small and large alligators. As predicted, the small fellows heated up (and cooled down) more quickly. When exposed to a warm sun, a tiny

50-gram (1.76-ounce) alligator heated up one degree Celsius every minute and a half, while a large alligator, 260 times bigger at 13,000 grams (28.7 pounds), took seven and a half minutes to gain a degree. Extrapolating up to an adult ten-ton dinosaur, they concluded that a one-degree rise in body temperature would take 86 hours. If large animals absorb heat so slowly (through their relatively small surfaces), they will also be unable to shed any excess heat gained when temperatures rise above a favorable level.

The authors then guessed that large dinosaurs lived at or near their optimum temperatures; Cowles suggested that a rise in global temperatures just before the Cretaceous extinction caused the dinosaurs to heat up beyond their optimal tolerance—and, being so large, they couldn't shed the unwanted heat. (In a most unusual statement for a scientific paper, Colbert and Bogert explicitly disavowed this speculative extension of their empirical work on alligators.) Cowles conceded that this excess heat probably wasn't enough to kill or even to enervate the great beasts, but since testes often function only within a narrow range of temperature, he proposed that this global rise might have sterilized all the males, causing extinction by natural contraception. 15

The overdose theory has recently been supported by UCLA psychiatrist Ronald K. Siegel. Siegel has observed, he claims, more than 2,000 animals that can give themselves various drugs—from a swig of alcohol to massive doses of the big H.[1] Elephants will swill the equivalent of twenty beers at a time, but do not like alcohol in concentrations greater than 7 per cent. In a silly bit of anthropocentric speculation, Siegel states that "elephants drink, perhaps, to forget . . . the anxiety produced by shrinking rangeland and the competition for food."

Since fertile imaginations can apply almost any hot idea to the extinction of dinosaurs, Siegel found a way. Flowering plants did not evolve until late in the dinosaurs' reign. These plants also produced an array of aromatic, amino-acid-based alkaloids—the major group of psychoactive agents. Most mammals are "smart" enough to avoid these potential poisons. The alkaloids simply don't taste good (they are

[1]Slang term for heroin.

bitter), and in any case we mammals have livers happily supplied with the capacity to detoxify them. But, Siegel speculates, perhaps dinosaurs could neither taste the bitterness nor detoxify the substances once ingested. Speaking of their extinction, he recently told members of the American Psychological Association: "I'm not suggesting that all dinosaurs OD'd on plant drugs, but it certainly was a factor." He also argued that death by overdose may help explain why so many dinosaur fossils are found in contorted positions. (Do not go gentle into that good night.)[2]

Extraterrestrial catastrophes have long pedigrees in the popular literature of extinction, but the subject exploded again after a long lull three years ago when the father-son, physicist-geologist team of Luis and Walter Alvarez proposed that an asteroid, about six miles in diameter, struck the earth 65 million years ago. Most asteroids circle the sun in an orbit between Mars and Jupiter but some, the so-called Apollo objects, take a more eccentric route, actually crossing the earth's orbit in their path around the sun. The chance of a collision at any crossing is minuscule, but the number of Apollo objects and the immensity of geological time virtually guarantee that impacts will occur once in a great while.

The force of such a collision would be immense, greater by far than the megatonnage of all the world's nuclear weapons. In trying to reconstruct a scenario that would explain the simultaneous dying of dinosaurs on land and so many creatures in the sea, the Alvarezes proposed that a gigantic dust cloud, generated by particles blown aloft in the impact, would so darken the earth that photosynthesis would cease and temperatures drop precipitously. (Rage, rage against the dying of the light.)[3] The single-celled photosynthetic oceanic plankton, with life cycles measured in weeks, would perish outright, but land plants might survive through the dormancy of their seeds (land plants were not much affected by the Cretaceous extinction, and any adequate the-

---

[2]Repeated line (and title) of a poem by Welsh poet Dylan Thomas (1914–53).

[3]Another repeating line in Thomas's poem.

ory must account for the curious pattern of differential survival). Dinosaurs would die by starvation and freezing; small, warm-blooded mammals, with more modest requirements for food and better regulation of body temperature, would squeak through.

All three theories, testicular malfunction, psychoactive overdosing, and asteroidal zapping, grab our attention mightily. As pure statements, they rank about equally high on any hit parade of primal fascination. Yet one represents expansive science, the others restrictive and untestable speculation.   20

How could we possibly decide whether the hypothesis of testicular frying is right or wrong? We would have to know things that the fossil record cannot provide. What temperatures were optimal for dinosaurs? Could the beasts avoid the absorption of excess heat by staying in the shade, or in caves? At what temperatures did their testicles cease to function? Were late Cretaceous climates ever warm enough to drive the internal temperatures of dinosaurs close to this ceiling? Testicles simply don't fossilize, and how could we infer their temperature tolerances even if they did? In short, Cowles's hypothesis is simply an intriguing speculation leading nowhere. The most damning statement against it appeared right in the conclusion of Colbert, Cowles, and Bogert's paper, when they admitted: "It is difficult to advance any definite arguments against this hypothesis." My statement may seem paradoxical—isn't a hypothesis really good if you can't devise any arguments against it? Quite the contrary. It is simply untestable and unusable.

Siegel's overdosing has even less going for it. At least Cowles extrapolated his conclusion from some good data on alligators. And he didn't completely violate the primary guideline of explaining dinosaur extinction in the context of a general mass dying—for rise in temperature could be the root cause of a general catastrophe, zapping dinosaurs by testicular malfunction and different groups for other reasons. But Siegel's speculation cannot touch the extinction of ammonites or oceanic plankton (diatoms make their own food with good sweet sunlight; they don't OD on the chemicals of terrestrial plants). It is simply a gratuitous, attention-grabbing guess. It cannot be tested, for how can we know what dinosaurs tasted and what their livers could do?

The hypothesis doesn't even make any sense in its own context. Angiosperms were in full flower tens of millions of years before dinosaurs went the way of all flesh. Why did it take so long? As for the pains of a chemical death recorded in contortions of fossils, I regret to say (or rather I'm pleased to note for the dinosaurs' sake) that Siegel's knowledge of geology must be a bit deficient: muscles contract after death and geological strata rise and fall with motions of the earth's crust after burial—more than enough reason to distort a fossil's pristine appearance.

The asteroid story, on the other hand, has a basis in evidence. It can be tested, extended, refined and, if wrong, disproved. The Alvarezes did not just construct an arresting guess for public consumption. They proposed their hypothesis after laborious geochemical studies with Frank Asaro and Helen Michel had revealed a massive increase of iridium in rocks deposited right at the time of extinction. Iridium, a rare metal of the platinum group, is virtually absent from indigenous rocks of the earth's crust; most of our iridium comes from extraterrestrial objects that hit the earth.

The Alvarez hypothesis bore immediate fruit. Based originally on   25
evidence found in rocks at two sites in Europe, it led geochemists throughout the world to examine other sediments of the same age. They found abnormally high amounts of iridium everywhere—from continental rocks of the western United States to deep sea cores from the South Atlantic.

Cowles proposed his testicular hypothesis in the mid-1940s. Where has it gone since then? Absolutely nowhere, because scientists can do nothing with it. It merely stands as a curious appendage to a solid study of alligators. Siegel's overdose scenario will also win a few press notices and fade into oblivion. The Alvarezes' asteroid falls into a different category altogether, and much of the popular commentary has missed this essential distinction by focusing on the impact and its attendant results, and forgetting what is really important to a scientist—the iridium. If you talk just about asteroids, dust, and darkness, you simply tell stories no better and no more entertaining than fried testicles or terminal trips. It is the iridium—the source of testable evidence—that counts and forges the crucial distinction between speculation and science.

The proof, to twist a phrase, lies in the doing. In thirty-five years, Cowles's hypothesis led to no further advances toward our understanding of dinosaurian extinction. In three years, the Alvarez hypothesis has spawned hundreds of studies, a major conference, and attendant publications. Geologists are fired up. They are looking for iridium at all other extinction boundaries and, by the way, have not (with one exception) found any marked increases—thus proving that a good hypothesis also shows its worth by failing to work in other situations. Every week exposes a new wrinkle in the scientific press. In November a group of Yale scientists supported the hypothesis by finding a "cosmic signature" for isotopes of osmium in Cretaceous boundary rocks (a ratio of isotopes found in extraterrestrial material but not in crustal rocks produced on earth). Then, in December, chemists from the University of Maryland cast some doubt by reporting that volcanic eruptions of Kilauea on Hawaii had belched forth unexpectedly high levels of iridium; perhaps an extraterrestrial source need not be sought.

My point is simply this: whatever the eventual outcome (I suspect it will be positive), the Alvarez hypothesis is exciting, fruitful science because it generates tests, provides us with things to do, and expands outward. We are having fun, battling back and forth, moving toward a resolution, and extending the hypothesis beyond its original scope.

As just one example of the unexpected, distant cross-fertilization that good science engenders, the Alvarez hypothesis made a major contribution to a theme that has riveted public attention in the past few months—so-called nuclear winter. In a speech delivered in April 1982, Luis Alvarez calculated the energy that a six-mile asteroid would release on impact. He compared such an explosion with a full nuclear exchange and implied that all-out atomic war might unleash similar consequences.

This theme of impact leading to massive dust clouds and falling temperatures was an important factor in the decision of Carl Sagan and a group of colleagues to model the climatic consequences of nuclear holocaust. We have, of course, long known that a full nuclear exchange could kill half of humanity outright and cannot be deemed acceptable

30

on any grounds. But some of us still had lurking in our minds the hope that, if we hunkered down in our shelters and lived far from military sites or cities, at least we could survive after the initial fallout dropped.

Apparently, it is not necessarily so. Full nuclear exchange would probably generate the same kind of dust cloud and darkening that may have wiped out the dinosaurs. Temperatures would drop precipitously and agriculture might become impossible. Avoidance of nuclear war is fundamentally an ethical and political problem, but we must know the factual consequences to make firm judgments. Is this not a heartening thought: a recognition of the very phenomenon that made our evolution possible by exterminating the previously dominant dinosaurs and clearing a way for the evolution of large mammals, including us, might actually help to save us from joining those magnificent beasts in contorted poses among the strata of the earth.

STUDY QUESTIONS

1. Gould explores three possible explanations for the extinction of the dinosaurs. Which one of these does he think is best, and why?

2. What CRITERIA does Gould use to EVALUATE each of the three hypotheses? What other criteria might he have used? How would changing the criteria change the outcome of his evaluation? What makes for "good science," according to Gould?

3. Gould's writing is often praised as "accessible"—that is, he presents scientific information in a way that makes it understandable for nonscientists. The ORGANIZATION of this essay and its use of humor are two elements that help make it accessible; how is each suited for a general AUDIENCE? How would the essay have been different if it were written for an audience of scientists?

4. *For Writing.* Select a TOPIC for which there are multiple causes or explanations and do RESEARCH to uncover common ARGUMENTS for each explanation. In an essay, address a few of those causes or explanations and argue for the superiority of one of them. Be sure to DOCUMENT your sources using the CITATION style assigned.

TEMPLE GRANDIN

My Mind Is a Web Browser:
How People with Autism Think

TEMPLE GRANDIN (b. 1947) was born in Boston, Massachusetts, and was diagnosed with autism when she was three years old. She did not begin to speak until she was four, but later attended a boarding school for gifted children in New Hampshire, graduating in 1966. She earned a BS in psychology from Franklin Pierce College in 1970, an MS in animal science from Arizona State University in 1975, and a PhD in animal science from the University of Illinois at Urbana-Champaign in 1989. A professor at Colorado State University, Grandin designs livestock-handling facilities and is an advocate for animal welfare. She also advocates for autism rights and has been outspoken about this issue in the media. HBO made a dramatic film about her life, released in 2010, starring Claire Danes, which won five Emmys.

"My Mind Is a Web Browser: How People with Autism Think" analyzes Grandin's thought process: she thinks in images, not words; indeed, she has said that words are her second language. As you read, consider your own thought process. How do you think in words, images, or both?

———————

SINCE WRITING *THINKING IN PICTURES*, which described my visual way of thinking, I have gained further insights into how my thought processes are different when compared to those of people who think in language. At autism meetings, I am often asked, "How can you be effective at public speaking when you think in pictures that are like video tapes in your imagination?" It is almost as though I have two levels of consciousness that operate separately. Only by interviewing people did I learn that many of them think primarily in words, and that their thoughts are linked to emotion. In my brain, words act as a narrator for the visual images in my imagination. I can see the pictures in my memory files.

To use a computer analogy: The language part of my brain is the computer operator, and the rest of my brain is the computer. In most people, the brain's computer operator and the computer are merged into one seamless consciousness; but in me they are separate. I hypothesize that the frontal cortex of my brain is the operator and the rest of my brain is the computer.

When I lecture, the language itself is mostly "downloaded" out of memory from files that are like tape recordings. I use slides or notes to trigger opening the different files. When I am talking about something for the first time, I look at the visual images on the "computer monitor" in my imagination, then the language part of me describes those images. After I have given the lecture several times, the new material in language is switched over into "audio tape-recording files." When I was in high school, other kids called me "tape recorder."

Non-autistic people seem to have a whole upper layer of verbal thinking that is merged with their emotions. By contrast, unless I panic, I use logic to make all decisions; my thinking can be done independently of emotion. In fact, I seem to lack a higher consciousness composed of abstract verbal thoughts that are merged with emotion. Researchers have learned that people with autism have a decreased metabolism in the area in the frontal cortex that connects the brain's emotional centers with higher thinking (the anterior cingulate).[1] The frontal cortex is the brain's senior executive, like the CEO of a corporation. Brain scans indicate that people with autism use problem-solving circuits in social situations. Unlike non-autistic people, the emotion center in their amygdala is not activated, for example, when they judge expressions in another person's eyes.[2]

---

[1]Haznedar MM, Buchsbaum MS, Metzer M, et al. Anterior cingulate gyrus volume and glucose metabolism in autistic disorder. *American Journal of Psychiatry.* 1997: 154:1047–1050.

[2]Baron-Cohen S, Ring HA, Wheelwright S. Social intelligence in the normal and autistic brain: an FMRI study. *European Journal of Neuroscience.* 1999: 11:1891–1898.

MY MIND IS A WEB BROWSER

Now let me explain how the language part of my brain and the "think- 5
ing in pictures" part of my brain seem to interact. My mind works just
like an Internet Web browser. A Web browser finds specific words; by
analogy, my mind looks for picture memories that are associated with
a word. It can also go off on a tangent in the same way as a Web browser,
because visual thinking is non-linear, associative thinking.

To demonstrate how my mind works, at an autism meeting I asked
a member of the audience to name a thing for me to invent. I wanted to
show how the visual part of my brain and the language part worked
separately. Somebody said, "invent a better paper clip." The language part of my brain said, "I can do that," and pictures immediately
started flashing into my imagination of all kinds of paper clips I have
seen. My "Web browser" searched the picture memory files; many
paper clip pictures flashed through my imagination like slides. I could
stop on any one picture and study it. I saw an odd, plastic paper clip
that was on a scientific paper from Europe. At this point, I got off the
subject and saw pictures of the first scientific meeting I had attended
in Spain. The language voice inside me said: "Get back on the subject
of paper clips." The language part of me is a manager who uses simple
non-descriptive language to tell the rest of my brain what to do.

Often, the best ideas for inventing things come just as I am drifting
off to sleep. The pictures are clearer then. It is as though I can access
the most concrete, vivid memory files with the most detailed images.
The language part of my brain is completely shut off at night.

To get ideas for new paper clip designs, I can pull up pictures of
clothes pins and other clip-like things, such as mouse traps and C
clamps used in woodworking. I start thinking that inventing a better
clip for holding a thick pile of papers together might be more marketable than a new paper clip design. Existing spring binder clips tend to
rip envelopes when papers are mailed, because the clips have protruding edges. When I think about this, I see ripped envelopes. The
language part of my mind says, "Design a flat binder clip for thick documents." When I say this, I see a mailed document in an undamaged
envelope. My visual imagination then sees a large plastic clip that I saw

in Japan. Japanese apartment dwellers who do not have clothes driers use large, plastic clips to hold blankets and other laundry on balcony railings. A small version of the Japanese balcony clip may make a better paper clip for holding many pages.

When I was responding to the paper clip inquiry, I knew that I could visually associate all day about paper clips. The language part of my mind then said, "That is enough," and I resumed my lecture. But as I corrected the first draft of this article, I saw a one-piece molded plastic binder clip that would lay flat on a thick bunch of papers.

I do have the ability to control the rate at which pictures come onto   10
the "computer screen" in my imagination. Some people with autism are not able to do this. One person with autism told me that images explode into a web of a pictures that are interrelated. The decision-making process can become "locked up" and overloaded with pictures coming in all at once.

UNMASKING TALENT

I have been fascinated with research indicating that the detailed, realistic pictures that autistic savants—autistic individuals with extraordinary talent in a specific area—make may be created by directly accessing primary memory areas deep in the brain. Researchers in Australia hypothesize that autistic savants may have privileged access to lower levels of information.[3] A study with a non-autistic "human calculator," who could solve multiplication problems twice as quickly as a normal person, indicated that his brain had enhanced low-level processing.[4] EEG recordings of his brain waves showed that brain activity was greatest, as compared with a normal person, when the multiplication problem was first flashed on the screen.

I hypothesize that I am able to access primary visual files in my brain. When designing livestock equipment in my business, I can do

[3]Snyder AW, Mitchell JD. Is integer arithmetic fundamental to mental processing? The mind's secret arithmetic. *Proceedings of the Royal Society of London.* 1999:266: 587–592.

[4]Birbaumer N. Rain Man's revelations. *Nature.* 1999:399:211–212.

three-dimensional, full-motion videos of equipment and can test-run the equipment in my imagination. I can walk around it or fly over it. My ability to rotate the image is slow. I move my mind's eye around or over the image.

When I read an article in *Neurology* about frontal temporal lobe dementia, I became extremely excited. It provided a scientific foundation for the idea of hidden visual thinking under a layer of verbal thinking. Research on frontal temporal lobe dementia, an Alzheimer's-like condition that destroys language and social areas in the brain, demonstrated that, as the condition progressed, visual skills in art emerged in people who had no interest in art.[5] The increase in creativity was always visual, never verbal. Brain scans found the highest activity in the visual cortex. As the patient's cognitive abilities deteriorated, the art became more photo realistic. Artwork published with the journal article looks like the art of autistic savants.

I SEE THE DECISION PROCESS

I see the decision-making process in my mind in a way most people do not. When I tried to explain this to a person who thinks in language, he just didn't get it. How my decision-making works is most clearly seen in an emergency.

On a bright, sunny day, I was driving to the airport when an elk ran   15
into the highway just ahead of my car. I had only three or four seconds to react. During those few seconds, I saw images of my choices. The first image was of a car rear-ending me. This is what would have happened if I had made the instinctive panic response and slammed on the brakes. The second image was of an elk smashing through my windshield. This is what would have happened if I had swerved. The last image showed the elk passing by in front of my car. The last choice was the one I could make if I inhibited the panic response and braked just a little to slow the car. I mentally "clicked" on slowing down and avoided an accident. It was like clicking a computer mouse on the desired picture.

---

[5]Miller BL, Cummings J, Mishkin F. Emergence of artistic talent in froniotemporal dementia. *Neurology*. 1998;51:978–982.

ANIMAL DECISION MAKING

I speculate that the decision-making process I used to avoid the accident may be similar to the process animals use. From my work with animals, I've come to believe that consciousness originally arose from the orienting response. When a deer sees a person, it will often freeze and look at him. This is the deer's orienting response. During this time, it decides either to run away or to keep grazing. It does not act as a programmed robot, governed by instinct or reflexes; it has the flexibility to make a decision. One of the things that has helped me to understand animals is that, more than most people, I think and feel like one. The more "animal" parts of the normal human brain may be covered by layers of language-based thinking.

THINKING IN AUDIO TAPES

In connection with my lectures, I have talked with autistic people who are not visual thinkers. They seem to think in audio tape clips. Audio tape thinking does not have to involve language; instead of using visual images to form memories, these people store very specific audio clips. I suspect that, for them, hearing is easier than seeing. Dr. John Stein and his colleagues at Oxford University have discovered that some people have difficulty seeing rapidly changing visual scenes. They find reading is difficult because the print appears jumbled.[6] This results from defects in brain circuits that process motion.[7] The eye is fine; the circuits between brain and eyes malfunction.

One person I know who is expert at training animals told me that she hears the animal's behavior instead of seeing it. She has audio tapes in her memory with little sound details. For example, she knows that the animal is relaxed or agitated by listening to its breathing or footsteps. She reads audio signals instead of body posture.

[6]Clayton J. Lost for Words. *New Scientist*. April 24, 1999. pp. 27–30.
[7]Eden GF, Van Meter JW, Ramsey J, et al. Abnormal processing of artistic talent in dyslexia revealed by functional brain imaging. *Nature*. 1996:382:66–69.

PIECING THE DETAILS TOGETHER

People with autism, and animals as well, pay more attention to details. As I described in *Thinking in Pictures*, all my thinking goes from the specific to the general. I look at lots of little details and piece them together to make a concept. The first step in forming an idea is to make categories. For example, the most primary level is sorting objects by color or shape. The next step is sorting things by less obvious features, as when we categorize cats and dogs. When I was five years old, I figured out that a miniature dachshund was not a cat because it had a dog's nose; all dogs had certain features that were visually recognizable.

My mind seeks these categories amidst an array of little details. In problem solving, my thinking process is like that of an epidemiologist tracking down a disease. The epidemiologist collects lots of little pieces of information and finally figures out the common factor that caused certain people to fall ill. For example, they may all have eaten strawberries from a certain place.

Also, I understand concepts visually. For example, all objects classified as keys will open locks. I realize that the word "key" can also be used metaphorically, when we say, "the key to success is positive thinking." When I think about that phrase, I see Norman Vincent Peale's book, *The Power of Positive Thinking*, and I see myself back at my aunt's ranch reading it. I then see a stage where a person is getting an award and I see a large cardboard key. Even in this situation, the key still unlocks the door to success. The ability to form categories is the beginning of the ability to form concepts. Keys in their physical form open physical locks but abstract keys can open many things, such as a scientific discovery or career success.

In teaching people to understand animal behavior, I have to help them to learn how to observe details that seem insignificant. Animals notice details in their environment that most people do not see, such as a branch that moves slightly or a shadow. In my work with livestock facilities, I try to get the language-based thinkers of the world to be more observant of little details that spook cattle. A cow may balk at entering a vaccinating chute because it sees a piece of jiggling chain that most people ignore, but which is significant in the cow's environment.

That little chain attracts the cow's attention because it moves quickly. Rapid movement activates the amygdala, the brain's emotion center.[8] In a prey species such as cattle, rapid movement elevates fear because, in the wild, things that move rapidly are often dangerous. Something moving quickly in the bushes may be a lion. On the other hand, a predatory animal, such as a dog, is attracted to rapid movement. This may explain why some dogs attack joggers. Rapid movement triggers chasing and attacking in a predatory animal, but it triggers flight in a prey species such as deer or cattle.

Objects that move rapidly also attract the attention of people with autism. When I was younger, I liked to play with automatic doors at supermarkets. I enjoyed watching the rapid opening movement. Elevator doors were not interesting; they did not move fast enough to be pleasurable to watch. Tests of my visual tracking indicate that I have a slight abnormality in my eye's ability to track a moving object. Children and adults with autism who never learn to speak have graver defects in their nervous system. The automatic doors that I liked to watch cause many nonverbal autistics to put their hands over their eyes. The rapid movement of the doors hurts their eyes. Possibly, a small defect in eye tracking makes rapidly moving things attractive to me, while a more serious neurological defect makes them unpleasant to other autistics. As a child, my favorite things all made rapid movements. I liked flapping flags, kites, and model airplanes that flew.

DISTURBING SOUNDS

I have always felt that my senses were more like those of an animal. 25 Does my brain have deeper access to the ancient anti-predator circuits that humans share with animals? At night, I cannot get to sleep if I hear high-pitched, intermittent noise such as a backup alarm on a truck or children yelling in the next hotel room; they make my heart

[8]LeDoux J. *The Emotional Brain*. Simon and Schuster; 1996.

race. Thunder or airport noise does not bother me, but the little high-pitched noises cannot be shut out. Recent research with pigs has confirmed that intermittent sounds are more disturbing to them than steady sounds.[9]

Why are high-pitched sounds disturbing to animals (and to me), while airport noises and thunder are not? I speculate that in nature the rumble of thunder is not dangerous but a high-pitched noise would be an animal's distress call. Beeping backup alarms and car alarms are electronic distress calls, which activate my nervous system even though I know they are harmless. It is almost as though these animal circuits in my brain have been laid bare.

PROPORTIONAL THINKING

A recent report in *Science* indicated that activities involving numbers are processed in at least two different parts of the brain.[1] Precise calculations are dependent on language and are processed in the frontal areas; proportional figuring is processed in visual areas. Proportional thinking is figuring out if one object is less or more than another. For example, three marbles are more than one marble. Animals can do proportional thinking. They can easily determine that 10 pieces of food are more than two. It is likely that proportional thinking is the kind of number processing that humans share with animals.

In school, math was a tough subject for me. Finding the precisely correct answer is difficult because I mix up numbers. On the other hand, I am very good at proportional thinking, coming up with an accurate approximate answer. In my scientific work, I often convert numerical differences between my control and experimental groups to percentage differences. Percentage differences can be visualized on a pie chart. When I present data, I like to use charts and graphs so I can see the proportional differences between different sets of data.

[9]Talling JC, Waran NK, Wathes CM. Sound avoidance by domestic pigs depends on the characteristics of the signal. *Applied Animal Behavior Science*. 1998: 58: 255–266.

[1]Dehaene S, Spelke E, Pinel P, Stanescu R, Tsivkin S. Sources of mathematical thinking: Behavioral and brain imaging evidence. *Science*. 1999: 284:970–973.

When I did cost estimating for cattle industry construction projects, I never tried to calculate projects to the penny. Instead, I estimated the cost of a new job by figuring out its proportional cost in relation to other finished projects. This was mainly a visual process. I would look at the drawing and build the entire project in my imagination. I then would put it up on the video screen in my imagination and compare it in size to other completed projects that had complete cost figures. In my mind, I could compare four or five completed projects with the drawing I was estimating. The project being estimated might be equal to two-thirds of a cattle-handling facility that I designed at Red River Feedlot and about 25 percent bigger than a corral I designed for Lone Mountain Ranch.

For money to have meaning to me, it must be related to something I 30 can buy with it, otherwise it is too abstract. For example, $3 is equal to lunch at McDonald's, $20 is a tank of gas, and $1000 can buy a computer. Big tables full of figures make little sense to me. Some more severely autistic people do not understand money at all. For me to understand a billion dollars, I have to have a picture in my mind of something that cost a billion dollars. One billion is one quarter of the cost of the new Denver Airport. When President Clinton announced part way through the war in Kosovo that it had cost $2 billion, I figured that half a Denver Airport worth of money had been spent. Different amounts of money have different visual values. It is interesting that proportional thinking for numbers is in the visual parts of the brain.

In proportional thinking, as in creating something new, making a decision, and forming concepts, my thinking relies on more direct access to the primary visual memory areas in my brain. There is a whole higher level of abstract thinking seamlessly linked to emotion that I do not have.

New York City, 2000

STUDY QUESTIONS

1. What is the difference between a verbal and a visual way of thinking? What role does emotion play in each? Why?

2. How effective is the METAPHOR of the web browser that Grandin uses for describing how her mind works?

3. What is the function of the subheadings in this essay? Are the subheadings effective? What other ways might Grandin have supplied TRANSITIONS and other signposts to the reader?

4. How does Grandin think in pictures? ANALYZE THE PROCESS of her "visual way of thinking."

5. *For Writing.* Consider your thought process by testing two of Grandin's examples. How would you go about designing a paper clip? How would you deal with an elk that suddenly entered your path? In an essay, explore the way that you would come to a solution. What does your process say about you?

RANDY PAUSCH   { *I Never Made It*
                    to the NFL

RANDY PAUSCH (1960–2008), professor of computer science and pioneer
in the field of virtual reality, was born and raised in Maryland. He earned
two degrees in computer science, a bachelor's at Brown University in 1982
and a PhD at Carnegie Mellon University in 1988. As a professor at
Carnegie Mellon University, he developed the computer language Alice,
which helps teach young people computer programming. In addition to
publishing more than seventy scholarly articles and books, Pausch wrote
The Last Lecture (2008), an expanded version of his inspirational speech
delivered at Carnegie Mellon on September 18, 2007, as part of the "Last
Lecture" series—a series in which top academics give a talk that captures the
wisdom they would like to impart. Pausch's was especially poignant: he had
been diagnosed with terminal pancreatic cancer a month earlier and had less
than a year to live.

   In this selection from the book, Pausch explains what he learned from
playing youth football. Children who play sports, according to Pausch, learn
far more than the skills and rules of the game. As you read, consider the role
of Coach Graham in helping Pausch learn these important lessons.

I LOVE FOOTBALL. *TACKLE* FOOTBALL. I started playing when I was
nine years old, and football got me through. It helped make me who
I am today. And even though I did not reach the National Football League, I sometimes think I got more from pursuing that dream,
and *not* accomplishing it, than I did from many of the ones I did
accomplish.

My romance with football started when my dad dragged me, kicking and screaming, to join a league. I had no desire to be there. I was naturally wimpy, and the smallest kid by far. Fear turned to awe when I met my coach, Jim Graham, a hulking, six-foot-four wall-of-a-guy. He had been a linebacker at Penn State, and was seriously old-school. I mean, *really* old-school; like he thought the forward pass was a trick play.[1]

On the first day of practice, we were all scared to death. Plus he hadn't brought along any footballs. One kid finally spoke up for all of us. "Excuse me, Coach. There are no footballs."

And Coach Graham responded, "We don't need any footballs."

There was a silence, while we thought about that . . . 5

"How many men are on the football field at a time?" he asked us.

Eleven on a team, we answered. So that makes twenty-two.

"And how many people are touching the football at any given time?" One of them.

"Right!" he said. "So we're going to work on what those *other* 10 twenty-one guys are doing."

Fundamentals. That was a great gift Coach Graham gave us. Fundamentals, fundamentals, fundamentals. As a college professor, I've seen this as one lesson so many kids ignore, always to their detriment: You've *got* to get the fundamentals down, because otherwise the fancy stuff is not going to work.

● ○ ●

Coach Graham used to ride me hard. I remember one practice in particular. "You're doing it all wrong, Pausch. Go back! Do it again!" I tried to do what he wanted. It wasn't enough. "You owe me, Pausch! You're doing push-ups after practice."

When I was finally dismissed, one of the assistant coaches came over to reassure me. "Coach Graham rode you pretty hard, didn't he?" he said.

I could barely muster a "yeah."

"That's a good thing," the assistant told me. "When you're screw- 15

[1]Football's forward pass become legal in 1906.

ing up and nobody says anything to you anymore, that means they've given up on you."

That lesson has stuck with me my whole life. When you see yourself doing something badly and nobody's bothering to tell you anymore, that's a bad place to be. You may not want to hear it, but your critics are often the ones telling you they still love you and care about you, and want to make you better.

There's a lot of talk these days about giving children self-esteem. It's not something you can *give;* it's something they have to build. Coach Graham worked in a no-coddling zone. Self-esteem? He knew there was really only one way to teach kids how to develop it: You give them something they can't do, they work hard until they find they can do it, and you just keep repeating the process.

When Coach Graham first got hold of me, I was this wimpy kid with no skills, no physical strength, and no conditioning. But he made me realize that if I work hard enough, there will be things I can do tomorrow that I can't do today. Even now, having just turned forty-seven, I can give you a three-point stance that any NFL lineman would be proud of.

I realize that, these days, a guy like Coach Graham might get thrown out of a youth sports league. He'd be too tough. Parents would complain.

I remember one game when our team was playing terribly. At half- 20 time, in our rush for water, we almost knocked over the water bucket. Coach Graham was livid: "Jeez! That's the most I've seen you boys move since this game started!" We were eleven years old, just standing there, afraid he'd pick us up one by one and break us with his bare hands. "Water?" he barked. "You boys want water?" He lifted the bucket and dumped all the water on the ground.

We watched him walk away and heard him mutter to an assistant coach: "You can give water to the first-string defense. They played OK."

Now let me be clear. Coach Graham would never endanger any kid. One reason he worked so hard on conditioning was he knew it reduces injuries. However, it was a chilly day, we'd all had access to water during the first half, and the dash to the water bucket was more about us being a bunch of brats than really needing hydration.

Even so, if that kind of incident happened today, parents on the sidelines would be pulling out their cell phones to call the league commissioner, or maybe their lawyer.

It saddens me that many kids today are so coddled. I think back to how I felt during that halftime rant. Yes, I was thirsty. But more than that, I felt humiliated. We had all let down Coach Graham, and he let us know it in a way we'd never forget. He was right. We had shown more energy at the water bucket than we had in the damn game. And getting chewed out by him meant something to us. During the second half, we went back on the field, and gave it our all.

I haven't seen Coach Graham since I was a teen, but he just keeps 25 showing up in my head, forcing me to work harder whenever I feel like quitting, forcing me to be better. He gave me a feedback loop for life.

● ○ ●

When we send our kids to play organized sports—football, soccer, swimming, whatever—for most of us, it's not because we're desperate for them to learn the intricacies of the sport.

What we really want them to learn is far more important: teamwork, perseverance, sportsmanship, the value of hard work, an ability to deal with adversity. This kind of indirect learning is what some of us like to call a "head fake."

There are two kinds of head fakes. The first is literal. On a football field, a player will move his head one way so you'll think he's going in that direction. Then he goes the opposite way. It's like a magician using misdirection. Coach Graham used to tell us to watch a player's waist. "Where his belly button goes, his body goes," he'd say.

The second kind of head fake is the *really* important one—the one that teaches people things they don't realize they're learning until well into the process. If you're a head-fake specialist, your hidden objective is to get them to learn something you want them to learn.

This kind of head-fake learning is absolutely vital. And Coach Gra- 30 ham was the master.

STUDY QUESTIONS

1. What does the term "head fake" refer to in its original, literal sense? What does Pausch mean when he uses the term figuratively? How is this essay a "head fake"?

2. Notice how Pausch breaks this chapter into three sections. What is the main point of each section?

3. List some of Coach Graham's physical characteristics. Describe his personality. In what ways does Pausch create a DOMINANT IMPRESSION of his coach?

4. *For Writing.* What lessons have you learned that might be of value to others? Write an essay in which you use one or more ANECDOTES to illustrate how you learned a particular lesson. Be sure to include both specific details and the broader implications of your experience.

SCOTT RUSSELL SANDERS { *The Inheritance of Tools*

SCOTT RUSSELL SANDERS (b. 1945), born in Memphis, Tennessee, grew up mainly in Ohio. He graduated from Brown University in 1967 and received his PhD from Cambridge University in 1971. He has taught at Indiana University since 1971. The author of eight novels and eleven works of nonfiction, he has written widely on environmental issues, social justice, and community.

In "The Inheritance of Tools," Sanders meditates on the proper use of tools and the virtue and morality of building with one's hands, knowledge that has been passed down through the generations of Sanders men. He brings together past and present as he describes passing on his own knowledge to his children. By the end of his essay, Sanders has described not only his tools and their history, but also what those tools represent—purpose, timelessness, and love.

AT JUST ABOUT THE HOUR when my father died, soon after dawn one February morning when ice coated the windows like cataracts, I banged my thumb with a hammer. Naturally I swore at the hammer, the reckless thing, and in the moment of swearing I thought of what my father would say: "If you'd try hitting the nail it would go in a whole lot faster. Don't you know your thumb's not as hard as that hammer?" We both were doing carpentry that day, but far apart. He was building cupboards at my brother's place in Oklahoma; I was at home in Indiana putting up a wall in the basement to make a bedroom for my daughter. By the time my mother called with news of his death—the long-distance wires whittling her voice until it seemed too thin to bear the weight of what she had to say—my thumb was swollen. A week or so later a white scar in the shape of a crescent moon began to show above the cuticle, and month by month it rose across the pink sky of my thumbnail. It took the better part of a year for the scar to disappear, and every time I noticed it I thought of my father.

The hammer had belonged to him, and to his father before him. The three of us have used it to build houses and barns and chicken coops, to upholster chairs and crack walnuts, to make doll furniture and bookshelves and jewelry boxes. The head is scratched and pock-marked, like an old plowshare that has been working rocky fields, and it gives off the sort of dull sheen you see on fast creek water in the shade. It is a finishing hammer, about the weight of a bread loaf, too light really for framing walls, too heavy for cabinetwork, with a curved claw for pulling nails, a rounded head for pounding, a fluted neck for looks, and a hickory handle for strength.

The present handle is my third one, bought from a lumberyard in Tennessee down the road from where my brother and I were helping my father build his retirement house. I broke the previous one by try-ing to pull sixteen-penny nails out of floor joists—a foolish thing to do with a finishing hammer, as my father pointed out. "You ever hear of a crowbar?" he said. No telling how many handles he and my grandfa-ther had gone through before me. My grandfather used to cut down hickory trees on his farm, saw them into slabs, cure the planks in his hayloft, and carve handles with a drawknife. The grain in hickory is crooked and knotty, and therefore tough, hard to split, like the grain in the two men who owned this hammer before me.

After proposing marriage to a neighbor girl, my grandfather used this hammer to build a house for his bride on a stretch of river bottom in northern Mississippi. The lumber for the place, like the hickory for the handle, was cut on his own land. By the day of the wedding he had not quite finished the house, and so right after the ceremony he took his wife home and put her to work. My grandmother had worn her Sunday dress for the wedding, with a fringe of lace tacked on around the hem in honor of the occasion. She removed this lace and folded it away before going out to help my grandfather nail siding on the house.

"There she was in her good dress," he told me some fifty-odd years after that wedding day, "holding up them long pieces of clapboard while I hammered, and together we got the place covered up before dark." As the family grew to four, six, eight, and eventually thirteen, my grandfather used this hammer to enlarge his house room by room, like a chambered nautilus expanding his shell.

By and by the hammer was passed along to my father. One day he was up on the roof of our pony barn nailing shingles with it, when I stepped out the kitchen door to call him for supper. Before I could yell, something about the sight of him straddling the spine of that roof and swinging the hammer caught my eye and made me hold my tongue. I was five or six years old, and the world's commonplaces were still news to me. He would pull a nail from the pouch at his wrist, bring the hammer down, and a moment later the *thunk* of the blow would reach my ears. And that is what had stopped me in my tracks and stilled my tongue, that momentary gap between seeing and hearing the blow. Instead of yelling from the kitchen door, I ran to the barn and climbed two rungs up the ladder—as far as I was allowed to go—and spoke quietly to my father. On our walk to the house he explained that sound takes time to make its way through air. Suddenly the world seemed larger, the air more dense, if sound could be held back like any ordinary traveler.

By the time I started using this hammer, at about the age when I discovered the speed of sound, it already contained houses and mysteries for me. The smooth handle was one my grandfather had made. In those days I needed both hands to swing it. My father would start a nail in a scrap of wood, and I would pound away until I bent it over.

"Looks like you got ahold of some of those rubber nails," he would tell me. "Here, let me see if I can find you some stiff ones." And he would rummage in a drawer until he came up with a fistful of more cooperative nails. "Look at the head," he would tell me. "Don't look at your hands, don't look at the hammer. Just look at the head of that nail and pretty soon you'll learn to hit it square."

Pretty soon I did learn. While he worked in the garage cutting dovetail joints for a drawer or skinning a deer or tuning an engine, I would hammer nails. I made innocent blocks of wood look like porcupines.

He did not talk much in the midst of his tools, but he kept up a nearly ceaseless humming, slipping in and out of a dozen tunes in an afternoon, often running back over the same stretch of melody again and again, as if searching for a way out. When the humming did cease, I knew he was faced with a task requiring great delicacy or concentration, and I took care not to distract him.

He kept scraps of wood in a cardboard box—the ends of two-by-fours, slabs of shelving and plywood, odd pieces of molding—and everything in it was fair game. I nailed scraps together to fashion what I called boats or houses, but the results usually bore only faint resemblance to the visions I carried in my head. I would hold up these constructions to show my father, and he would turn them over in his hands admiringly, speculating about what they might be. My cobbled-together guitars might have been alien spaceships, my barns might have been models of Aztec temples, each wooden contraption might have been anything but what I had set out to make.

Now and again I would feel the need to have a chunk of wood 10 shaped or shortened before I riddled it with nails, and I would clamp it in a vice and scrape at it with a handsaw. My father would let me lacerate the board until my arm gave out, and then he would wrap his hand around mine and help finish the cut, showing me how to use my thumb to guide the blade, how to pull back on the saw to keep it from binding, how to let my shoulder do the work.

"Don't force it," he would say, "just drag it easy and give the teeth a chance to bite."

As the saw teeth bit down the wood released its smell, each kind with its own fragrance, oak or walnut or cherry or pine—usually pine, because it was the softest and the easiest for a child to work. No matter how weathered and gray the board, no matter how warped and cracked, inside there was this smell waiting, as of something freshly baked. I gathered every smidgen of sawdust and stored it away in coffee cans, which I kept in a drawer of the workbench. When I did not feel like hammering nails I would dump my sawdust on the concrete floor of the garage and landscape it into highways and farms and towns, running miniature cars and trucks along miniature roads. Looming as huge as a colossus, my father worked over and around me, now and again bending down to inspect my work, careful not to trample my creations. It was a landscape that smelled dizzyingly of wood. Even after a bath my skin would carry the smell, and so would my father's hair, when he lifted me for a bedtime hug.

I tell these things not only from memory but also from recent observation, because my own son now turns blocks of wood into nailed porcupines, dumps cans full of sawdust at my feet and sculpts highways on the floor. He learns how to swing a hammer from the elbow instead of the wrist, how to lay his thumb beside the blade to guide a saw, how to tap a chisel with a wooden mallet, how to mark a hole with an awl before starting a drill bit. My daughter did the same before him, and even now, on the brink of teenage aloofness, she will occasionally drag out my box of wood scraps and carpenter something. So I have seen my apprenticeship to wood and tools reenacted in each of my children, as my father saw his own apprenticeship renewed in me.

The saw I use belonged to him, as did my level and both of my squares, and all four tools had belonged to his father. The blade of the saw is the bluish color of gun barrels, and the maple handle, dark from the sweat of hands, is inscribed with curving leaf designs. The level is a shaft of walnut two feet long, edged with brass and pierced by three round windows in which air bubbles float in oil-filled tubes of glass. The middle window serves for testing whether a surface is horizontal, the others for testing whether it is plumb or vertical. My grandfather used to carry this level on the gun rack behind the seat in his pickup, and when I rode with him I would turn around to watch the bubbles dance. The larger of the two squares is called a framing square, a flat steel elbow so beat up and tarnished you can barely make out the rows of numbers that show how to figure the cuts on rafters. The smaller one is called a try square, for marking right angles, with a blued steel blade for the shank and a brass-faced block of cherry for the head.

I was taught early on that a saw is not to be used apart from a square: 15 "If you're going to cut a piece of wood," my father insisted, "you owe it to the tree to cut it straight."

Long before studying geometry, I learned there is a mystical virtue in right angles. There is an unspoken morality in seeking the level and the plumb. A house will stand, a table will bear weight, the sides of a box will hold together only if the joints are square and the members upright. When the bubble is lined up between two marks etched in the glass tube of a level, you have aligned yourself with the forces that hold the universe together. When you miter the corners of a picture frame, each angle must be exactly forty-five degrees, as they are in the perfect triangles of Pythagoras, not a degree more or less. Otherwise the frame will hang crookedly, as if ashamed of itself and of its maker. No matter if the joints you are cutting do not show. Even if you are butting two pieces of wood together inside a cabinet, where no one except a wrecking crew will ever see them, you must take pains to insure that the ends are square and the studs are plumb.

I took pains over the wall I was building on the day my father died. Not long after that wall was finished—paneled with tongue-and-groove boards of yellow pine, the nail holes filled with putty and the wood all stained and sealed—I came close to wrecking it one afternoon when my daughter ran howling up the stairs to announce that her gerbils had escaped from their cage and were hiding in my brand-new wall. She could hear them scratching and squeaking behind her bed. Impossible! I said. How on earth could they get inside my drum-tight wall? Through the heating vent, she answered. I went downstairs, pressed my ear to the honey-colored wood, and heard the scritch scritch of tiny feet.

"What can we do?" my daughter wailed. "They'll starve to death, they'll die of thirst, they'll suffocate." "Hold on," I soothed. "I'll think of something."

While I thought and she fretted, the radio on her bedside table delivered us the headlines. Several thousand people had died in a city in India from a poisonous cloud that had leaked overnight from a chemical plant. A nuclear-powered submarine had been launched. Rioting continued in South Africa. An airplane had been hijacked in the Mediterranean. Authorities calculated that several thousand homeless people slept on the streets within sight of the Washington Monument. I felt my usual helplessness in face of all these calamities. But here was my daughter weeping because her gerbils were holed up in a wall. This calamity I could handle.

"Don't worry," I told her. "We'll set food and water by the heating   20 vent and lure them out. And if that doesn't do the trick, I'll tear the wall apart until we find them."

She stopped crying and gazed at me. "You'd really tear it apart? Just for my gerbils? The *wall*?" Astonishment slowed her down only for a second, however, before she ran to the workbench and began tugging at drawers, saying, "Let's see, what'll we need? Crowbar. Hammer. Chisels. I hope we don't have to use them—but just in case."

We didn't need the wrecking tools. I never had to assault my handsome wall, because the gerbils eventually came out to nibble at a dish of popcorn. But for several hours I studied the tongue-and-groove skin I had nailed up on the day of my father's death, considering where to begin prying. There were no gaps in that wall, no crooked joints.

I had botched a great many pieces of wood before I mastered the right angle with a saw, botched even more before I learned to miter a joint. The knowledge of these things resides in my hands and eyes and the webwork of muscles, not in the tools. There are machines for sale—powered miter boxes and radial arm saws, for instance—that will enable any casual soul to cut proper angles in boards. The skill is invested in the gadget instead of the person who uses it, and this is what distinguishes a machine from a tool. If I had to earn my keep by making furniture or building houses, I suppose I would buy powered saws and pneumatic nailers; the need for speed would drive me to it. But since I carpenter only for my own pleasure or to help neighbors or to remake the house around the ears of my family, I stick with hand tools. Most of the ones I own were given to me by my father, who also taught me how to wield them. The tools in my workbench are a double inheritance, for each hammer and level and saw is wrapped in a cloud of knowing.

All of these tools are a pleasure to look at and to hold. Merchants would never paste NEW NEW NEW! signs on them in stores. Their designs are old because they work, because they serve their purpose well. Like folksongs and aphorisms and the grainy bits of language, these tools have been pared down to essentials. I look at my claw hammer, the distillation of a hundred generations of carpenters, and consider that it holds up well beside those other classics—Greek vases, Gregorian chants, *Don Quixote,* barbed fishhooks, candles, spoons.

Knowledge of hammering stretches back to the earliest humans who squatted beside fires chipping flints. Anthropologists have a lovely name for those unworked rocks that served as the earliest hammers. "Dawn stones" they are called. Their only qualification for the work, aside from hardness, is that they fit the hand. Our ancestors used them for grinding corn, tapping awls, smashing bones. From dawn stones to this claw hammer is a great leap in time, but no great distance in design or imagination.

On that iced-over February morning when I smashed my thumb 25 with the hammer, I was down in the basement framing the wall that my daughter's gerbils would later hide in. I was thinking of my father, as I always did whenever I built anything, thinking how he would have gone about the work, hearing in memory what he would have said about the wisdom of hitting the nail instead of my thumb. I had the studs and plates nailed together all square and trim, and was lifting the wall into place when the phone rang upstairs. My wife answered, and in a moment she came to the basement door and called down softly to me. The stillness in her voice made me drop the framed wall and hurry upstairs. She told me my father was dead. Then I heard the details over the phone from my mother. Building a set of cupboards for my brother in Oklahoma, he had knocked off work early the previous afternoon because of cramps in his stomach. Early this morning, on his way into the kitchen of my brother's trailer, maybe going for a glass of water, so early that no one else was awake, he slumped down on the linoleum and his heart quit.

For several hours I paced around inside my house, upstairs and down, in and out of every room, looking for the right door to open and knowing there was no such door. My wife and children followed me and wrapped me in arms and backed away again, circling and staring as if I were on fire. Where was the door, the door, the door? I kept wondering. My smashed thumb turned purple and throbbed, making me furious. I wanted to cut it off and rush outside and scrape away the snow and hack a hole in the frozen earth and bury the shameful thing.

I went down into the basement, opened a drawer in my workbench, and stared at the ranks of chisels and knives. Oiled and sharp, as my father would have kept them, they gleamed at me like teeth. I took up a clasp knife, pried out the longest blade, and tested the edge on the hair of my forearm. A tuft came away cleanly, and I saw my father testing the sharpness of tools on his own skin, the blades of axes and knives and gouges and hoes, saw the red hair shaved off in patches from his arms and the backs of his hands. "That will cut bear," he would say. He never cut a bear with his blades, now my blades, but he cut deer, dirt, wood. I closed the knife and put it away. Then I took up the hammer and went back to work on my daughter's wall, snugging the bottom place against a chalkline on the floor, shimming the top plate against the joists overhead, plumbing the studs with my level, making sure before I drove the first nail that every line was square and true.

STUDY QUESTIONS

1. What advice did Sanders's father give him about hammering nails? What did Sanders make from the various chunks of wood his father gave him? What was Sanders's greatest achievement as a builder?

2. ANALYZE Sander's DESCRIPTION of his hammer (paragraphs 2–6). How does the hammer look, sound, and feel? How does this description contribute to Sander's overall NARRATIVE?

3. Sanders begins and ends his MEMOIR of his father by recounting what he is doing just before and just after he learns of his father's death. Why do you think he chose to frame the NARRATIVE in this way? What is the significance to this essay of using this rhetorical strategy? How does the word "frame" fit both the strategy and the subject?

4. *For Writing.* Choose a person who is special in your life, and make a list of some experiences that you have shared. Select the experience that stirs the most emotions, that best displays your relationship with this person, and that you can write about. Using DESCRIPTION, PATHOS, and any other rhetorical strategies that will give your AUDIENCE a full picture of your subject, write a memoir of this special person.

E. O. WILSON { *Apocalypse Now*

EDWARD O. WILSON (b. 1929), biologist, naturalist, and writer, was born
in Birmingham, Alabama. He earned three degrees in biology: a BS in 1949
and an MS in 1950, both from the University of Alabama, and a PhD in
1955 from Harvard University. He joined Harvard's faculty in 1956, where
he remained his entire career. Regarded as one of the most important scientists of the twentieth century, Wilson has discovered hundreds of new insect
species and has written extensively on biodiversity and sociobiology, the
study of how biology influences the behavior of organisms. Wilson won the
National Medal for Science in 1977 and has received two Pulitzer Prizes, for
On Human Nature (1979) and *The Ants* (1991).

   "Apocalypse Now," Wilson's letter to a fictional Southern Baptist minister, originally appeared in *The New Republic*. Acknowledging their different
worldviews but highlighting the things they have in common, Wilson asks
the minister to join him in working to stop environmental destruction. Without an alliance between science and religion to "save the Creation," Wilson
argues, our survival as a species is in jeopardy. As you read, consider how—
and how effectively—Wilson establishes common ground with his fictional
minister and, more broadly, the evangelical Christian community he hopes
to reach.

———————————

DEAR PASTOR,
   We have not met, yet I feel I know you well enough to call you a
friend. First of all, we grew up in the same faith. As a boy, I, too,
answered the altar call; I went under the water. Although I no longer belong to that faith, I am confident that, if we met and spoke privately of

our deepest beliefs, it would be in a spirit of mutual respect and good-will. I know we share many precepts of moral behavior. Perhaps it also matters that we are both Americans and, insofar as it might still affect civility and good manners, we are both Southerners.

I write to you now for your counsel and help. Of course, in doing so, I see no way to avoid the fundamental differences in our worldviews. You are a strict interpreter of Christian Holy Scripture; I am a secular humanist. You believe that each person's soul is immortal, making this planet a waystation to a second, eternal life; I think heaven and hell are what we create for ourselves, on this planet. For you, the belief in God made flesh to save mankind; for me, the belief in Promethean fire seized to set men free.[1] You have found your final truth; I am still searching. You may be wrong; I may be wrong. We both may be partly right.

Do these differences in worldview separate us in all things? They do not. You and I and every other human being strive for the same imper-atives of security, freedom of choice, personal dignity, and a cause to believe in that is larger than ourselves. Let us see, then, if we can meet on the near side of metaphysics in order to deal with the real world we share. You have the power to help solve a great problem about which I care deeply. I hope you have the same concern. I suggest that we set aside our differences in order to save the Creation. The defense of living nature is a universal value. It doesn't rise from, nor does it pro-mote, any religious or ideological dogma. Rather, it serves without discrimination the interests of all humanity. Pastor, we need your help. The Creation—living nature—is in deep trouble.

Scientists estimate that, if habitat-conversion and other destructive 5 human activities continue at their present rates, half the species of plants and animals on earth could be either gone or at least fated for early extinction by the end of the century. The ongoing extinction rate is calculated in the most conservative estimates to be about 100 times above that prevailing before humans appeared on earth, and it is ex-pected to rise to at least 1,000 times greater (or more) in the next few

[1]Wilson refers to Jesus Christ, on the one hand, and Prometheus, the Titan who stole fire and gave it to mankind, on the other.

decades. If this rise continues unabated, the cost to humanity—in wealth, environmental security, and quality of life—will be catastrophic.

Surely we can agree that each species, however inconspicuous and humble it may seem to us at this moment, is a masterpiece of biology and well worth saving. Each species possesses a unique combination of genetic traits that fits it more or less precisely to a particular part of the environment. Prudence alone dictates that we act quickly to prevent the extinction of species and, with it, the pauperization of earth's ecosystems.

With all the troubles that humanity faces, why should we care about the condition of living nature? Homo sapiens is a species confined to an extremely small niche. True, our minds soar out to the edges of the universe and contract inward to subatomic particles—the two extremes encompassing 30 powers of ten in space. In this respect, our intellects are godlike. But, let's face it, our bodies stay trapped inside a proportionately microscopic envelope of physical constraints. Earth provides a self-regulating bubble that sustains us indefinitely without any thought or contrivance of our own. This protective shield is the biosphere, the totality of life, creator of all air, cleanser of all water, manager of all soil—but is itself a fragile membrane that barely clings to the face of the planet. We depend upon its razor-thin health for every moment of our lives. We belong in the biosphere, we were born here as species, we are closely suited to its exacting conditions—and not all conditions, either, but just those in a few of the climatic regimes that exist upon some of the land. Environmental damage can be defined as any change that alters our surroundings in a direction contrary to humanity's inborn physical and emotional needs. We must be careful with the environment upon which our lives ultimately depend.

In destroying the biosphere, we are destroying unimaginably vast sources of scientific information and biological wealth. Opportunity costs, which will be better understood by our descendants than by ourselves, will be staggering. Gone forever will be undiscovered medicines, crops, timber, fibers, soil-restoring vegetation, petroleum substitutes, and other products and amenities. Critics of environmentalism forget, if they ever knew, how the rosy periwinkle of Madagascar provided the alkaloids that cure most cases of Hodgkin's disease and acute childhood leukemia; how a substance from an obscure Norwegian fungus made possible the organ transplant industry; how a chemical from the saliva of leeches yielded a solvent that prevents blood clots during and after surgery; and so on through the pharmacopoeia that has stretched from the herbal medicines of Stone Age shamans to the magic-bullet cures of present-day biomedical science.

These are just a few examples of what could be lost if Homo sapiens pursue our current course of environmental destruction. Earth is a laboratory wherein nature—God, if you prefer, pastor—has laid before us the results of countless experiments. We damage her at our own peril.

You may well ask at this point, *Why me?* Simply because religion and science are the two most powerful forces in the world today and especially in the United States. If religion and science could be united on the common ground of biological conservation, the problem might soon be solved.

It may seem far-fetched for a secular scientist to propose an alliance between science and religion. But the fact is that environmental activists cannot succeed without you and your followers as allies. The political process in American democracy, with rare exceptions, does not start at the top and work its way down to the voting masses. It proceeds in the opposite direction. Political leaders are compelled to calculate as precisely as they can what it will take to win the next election. The United States is an intensely religious nation. It is overwhelmingly Judeo-Christian, with a powerful undercurrent of evangelism. We secularists must face reality. The National Association of Evangelicals has 30 million members; the three leading American humanist organizations combined have, at best, a few thousand. Those who, for religious reasons, believe in saving the Creation, have the strength to do so through the political process; acting alone, secular environmentalists do not. An alliance between science and religion, forged in an atmosphere of mutual respect, may be the only way to protect life on earth, including, in the end, our own.

Yes, the gulf separating our worldviews is wide. The Abrahamic religions—Judaism, Christianity, and Islam—believe that the universe was constructed to be relevant to humanity. The discoveries of science, in unintended opposition, have reduced earth to an infinitesimal speck within an immensity of space unrelated to human destiny. The Abrahamic religions envisage a supreme ruler who, while existing outside the material universe, nevertheless oversees an agenda for each and every one of our immortal souls. Science can find no evidence of an agenda other than that fashioned by the complex interaction of genes and environment within parallel evolving cultures. Religious creation stories have a divinely engineered beginning and a divinely ordained ending. According to science, in contrast, humans descended from apish ancestors: our origin was basically no different from that of other animals, played out over geological time through a tortuous route of mutation and environmentally driven natural selection. In addition, all mainstream religious belief, whether fundamentalist or liberal, is predicated upon the assumption that humanity is not alone, and we are here for a life and purpose beyond our earthly existence. Science says that, as far as verifiable evidence tells, we are alone, and what significance we have is therefore of our own making. This is the heart of the agonizing conflict between science and religion that has persisted for the past 500 years.

I do not see how the difference in worldview between these two great productions of human striving can be closed. But, for the purposes of saving the Creation, I am not sure that it needs to be. To make the point in good gospel manner, let me tell the story of a young man, newly trained for the ministry and so fixed in his Christian faith that he referred all questions of morality to readings from the Bible. When he visited the Atlantic rainforest of Brazil, he saw the manifest hand of God, and in his notebook he wrote, "It is not possible to give an adequate idea of the higher feelings of wonder, admiration, and devotion which fill and elevate the mind." That was Charles Darwin in 1832, early into the voyage of the HMS *Beagle*, before he had given any thought to evolution. And here is Darwin, concluding *On the Origin of Species* in 1859, having first abandoned Christian dogma and then, with his newfound intellectual freedom, formulated the theory of evolution by natural selection: "There is grandeur in this view of life, with its several powers, having been originally breathed into a few forms or into one; and that, whilst this planet has gone cycling on according to the fixed law of gravity, from so simple a beginning endless forms most beautiful and most wonderful have been, and are being, evolved." Darwin's reverence for life remained the same as he crossed the seismic divide that separated his religious phase and his scientific one. And so it can be for the divide that, today, separates mainstream religion and scientific humanism. And that separates you and me.

Indeed, despite all that divides science from religion, there is good reason to hope that an alliance on environmental issues is possible. The spiritual reach of evangelical Christianity is nowadays increasingly extended to the environment. While the Old Testament God commands humanity to take dominion over the earth, the decree is not (as one evangelical leader recently affirmed) an excuse to trash the planet. The dominant theme in scripture as interpreted by many evangelicals is instead stewardship. Organizations like the Green Cross and the Evangelical Environmental Network (the latter a coalition of evangelical Christian agencies and institutions) are expanding their magisterium to include conservation—in religious terms, protection of the living Creation.

This evangelical interest in the environment is part of a worldwide 15 trend among religions. In the United States, the umbrella National Religious Partnership for the Environment works with evangelical groups and other prominent organizations, including the U.S. Conference of Catholic Bishops, the National Council of Churches of Christ, and the Coalition on the Environment and Jewish Life. In 2001, the Archbishop of Canterbury urged that "it may not be time to build an Ark like Noah, but it is high time to take better care of God's creation." Three years earlier, Bartholomew I, Patriarch of the Greek Orthodox Church, had gone further: "For humans to cause species to become extinct and to destroy the biological diversity of God's creation . . . these are sins." He and Pope John Paul II later issued a "Common Declaration" that "God has not abandoned the world. It is His will that His Design and our hope for it will be realized through our co-operation in restoring its original harmony. In our own time we are witnessing a growth of an ecological awareness which needs to be encouraged, so that it will lead to practical programs and initiatives." Unfortunately, a corresponding magnitude of engagement has not yet occurred in Islam or the Eastern religions.

Every great religion offers mercy and charity to the poor. The poor of the world, of whom nearly a billion exist in the "poverty trap" of absolute destitution, are concentrated in the developing countries—the home of 80 percent of the world's population and most of Earth's biodiversity. The solution to the problems of both depends on the recognition that each depends on the other. The desperately poor have little chance to improve their lives in a devastated environment. Conversely, natural environments, where most of the Creation hangs on, cannot survive the press of land-hungry people who have nowhere else to go.

To be sure, some leaders of the religious right are reluctant to support biological conservation, an opposition sufficient to create a wedge within the evangelical movement. They may be partly afraid of paganism, by which worship of nature supplants worship of God. More realistically and importantly, opposition rises from the perceived association of environmental activism with the political left. For decades, conservatives have defined environmentalism as a movement bent on strangling the United States with regulations and bureaucratic power. This canard has dogged the U.S. environmental movement and helped keep it off the agenda of the past two presidential campaigns.

Finally, however, opinion may be changing. The mostly evangelical religious right, which, along with big business, has been the decisive source of power in the Republican Party, has begun to move care of the Creation back into the mainstream of conservative discourse. The opportunity exists to make the environment a universal concern and to render it politically nonpartisan.

Still, for all the positive signs, I remain puzzled that so many religious leaders have hesitated to make protection of the Creation an important part of their magisterium. Pastor, help me understand: Do they believe that human-centered ethics and preparation for the afterlife are the only things that matter? Do they believe that the Second Coming is imminent and that, therefore, the condition of the planet is of little consequence? These and other similar doctrines are not gospels of hope and compassion. They are gospels of cruelty and despair.

You and I are both humanists in the broadest sense: Human welfare 20 is at the center of our thought. So forget our disagreements, I say, and let us meet on common ground. That might not be as difficult as it first seems. When you think about it, our metaphysical differences have remarkably little effect on the conduct of our separate lives. My guess is that you and I are about equally ethical, patriotic, and altruistic. We are products of a civilization that rose from both religion and the science-based Enlightenment. We would gladly serve on the same jury, fight the same wars, and sanctify human life with the same intensity. Surely we also share a love of the Creation—and an understanding that, however the tensions play out between our opposing worldviews, however science and religion wax and wane in the minds of men, there remains the earthborn yet transcendental obligation we are both morally bound to share.

Warmly and respectfully,
Edward O. Wilson

STUDY QUESTIONS

1. What is Wilson's stated PURPOSE for writing "Apocalypse Now"? Why is he writing to a religious leader rather than, for instance, a political leader?

2. How does Wilson establish COMMON GROUND with the minister he addresses and with the evangelical Christian community in general? How effective are his efforts? Explain. Refer to specific passages in your response.

3. Wilson has in mind an AUDIENCE of evangelical Christians. What are some of the ways that he shapes his ARGUMENT to appeal to them? Cite passages from the text to support your RESPONSE. How successful do you think he is? Explain. What changes might he make if he were writing for a different audience?

4. *For Writing.* Pretend that you are the evangelical pastor whom Wilson is addressing and WRITE A LETTER responding to him. On what points do you agree with Wilson? On what points do you disagree? Do you believe science and religion can join hands on this issue? Why or why not? Before you begin drafting your letter, RESEARCH the REASONS that various religious groups have, as Wilson CLAIMS, opposed environmentalism, and address those reasons in your letter.

JESSICA MITFORD { *Behind the Formaldehyde Curtain*

JESSICA MITFORD (1917–1996) was born into an aristocratic English family and moved in 1939 to the United States, where she became a naturalized American citizen and pursued a career as an investigative reporter. A lifelong activist, Mitford worked on behalf of pacifism and civil rights; when she and her husband, Robert Treuhaft, a lawyer, became aware of funeral costs for working-class families in the San Francisco Bay Area, she published *The American Way of Death* (1963), which sold out on the day of publication. While the work provoked queasiness in some readers and outrage in others (mainly funeral directors), it has become a classic piece of expository prose, anthologized in more than fifty textbooks. Mitford is the author of several books, including *The American Way of Death Revisited* (1998).

This chapter from *The American Way of Death* presents a critical look at the process of embalming bodies and preparing them for burial. Mitford uses an ironically breezy tone to convey her attitude toward the way funerals are conducted in the United States as she describes the procedures used to embalm the fictitious "Mr. Jones." Despite her gruesome subject matter (or perhaps, for some readers, because of it), Mitford's understated sense of humor has made "Behind the Formaldehyde Curtain" enduringly popular.

THE DRAMA BEGINS TO UNFOLD with the arrival of the corpse at the mortuary.

Alas, poor Yorick![1] How surprised he would be to see how his counterpart of today is whisked off to a funeral parlor and is in short

---

[1] *Hamlet*, 5.1.171. Hamlet discovers the skull of an old friend in a graveyard.

order sprayed, sliced, pierced, pickled, trussed, trimmed, creamed, waxed, painted, rouged and neatly dressed—transformed from a common corpse into a Beautiful Memory Picture. This process is known in the trade as embalming and restorative art, and is so universally employed in the United States and Canada that the funeral director does it routinely, without consulting corpse or kin. He regards as eccentric those few who are hardy enough to suggest that it might be dispensed with. Yet no law requires embalming, no religious doctrine commends it, nor is it dictated by considerations of health, sanitation, or even of personal daintiness. In no part of the world but in Northern America is it widely used. The purpose of embalming is to make the corpse presentable for viewing in a suitably costly container; and here too the funeral director routinely, without first consulting the family, prepares the body for public display.

Is all this legal? The processes to which a dead body may be subjected are after all to some extent circumscribed by law. In most states, for instance, the signature of next of kin must be obtained before an autopsy may be performed, before the deceased may be cremated, before the body may be turned over to a medical school for research purposes; or such provision must be made in the decedent's will. In the case of embalming, no such permission is required nor is it ever sought. A textbook, *The Principles and Practices of Embalming*, comments on this: "There is some question regarding the legality of much that is done within the preparation room." The author points out that it would be most unusual for a responsible member of a bereaved family to instruct the mortician, in so many words, to *"embalm"* the body of a deceased relative. The very term "embalming" is so seldom used that the mortician must rely upon custom in the matter. The author concludes that unless the family specifies otherwise, the act of entrusting the body to the care of a funeral establishment carries with it an implied permission to go ahead and embalm.

Embalming is indeed a most extraordinary procedure, and one must wonder at the docility of Americans who each year pay hundreds of millions of dollars for its perpetuation, blissfully ignorant of what it is all about, what is done, how it is done. Not one in ten thousand has any idea of what actually takes place. Books on the subject are extremely hard to come by. They are not to be found in most libraries or bookshops.

In an era when huge television audiences watch surgical operations 5 in the comfort of their living rooms, when, thanks to the animated cartoon, the geography of the digestive system has become familiar territory even to the nursery school set, in a land where the satisfaction of curiosity about almost all matters is a national pastime, the secrecy surrounding embalming can, surely, hardly be attributed to the inherent gruesomeness of the subject. Custom in this regard has within this century suffered a complete reversal. In the early days of American embalming, when it was performed in the home of the deceased, it was almost mandatory for some relative to stay by the embalmer's side and witness the procedure. Today, family members who might wish to be in attendance would certainly be dissuaded by the funeral director. All others, except apprentices, are excluded by law from the preparation room.

A close look at what does actually take place may explain in large measure the undertaker's intractable reticence concerning a procedure that has become his major *raison d'être.* Is it possible he fears that public information about embalming might lead patrons to wonder if they really want this service? If the funeral men are loath to discuss the subject outside the trade, the reader may, understandably, be equally loath to go on reading at this point. For those who have the stomach for it, let us part the formaldehyde curtain. Others should skip to paragraph 20.

The body is first laid out in the undertaker's morgue—or rather, Mr. Jones is reposing in the preparation room—to be readied to bid the world farewell.

The preparation room in any of the better funeral establishments has the tiled and sterile look of a surgery, and indeed the embalmer-restorative artist who does his chores there is beginning to adopt the term "dermasurgeon" (appropriately corrupted by some mortician-writers as "demisurgeon") to describe his calling. His equipment, consisting of scalpels, scissors, augers, forceps, clamps, needles, pumps, tubes, bowls and basins, is crudely imitative of the surgeon's, as is his technique, acquired in a nine- or twelve-month post-high-school course in an embalming school. He is supplied by an advanced chemical industry with a bewildering array of fluids, sprays, pastes, oils, powders, creams, to fix or soften tissue, shrink or distend it as needed, dry it here, restore the moisture there. There are cosmetics, waxes and paints to fill and cover features, even plaster of Paris to replace entire limbs. There are ingenious aids to prop and stabilize the cadaver: a Vari-Pose Head Rest, the Edwards Arm and Hand Positioner, the Repose Block (to support the shoulders, during the embalming), and the Throop Foot Positioner, which resembles an old-fashioned stocks.

Mr. John H. Eckels, president of the Eckels College of Mortuary Science, thus describes the first part of the embalming procedure: "In the hands of a skilled practitioner, this work may be done in a comparatively short time and without mutilating the body other than by slight incision—so slight that it scarcely would cause serious inconvenience if made upon a living person. It is necessary to remove the blood, and doing this not only helps in the disinfecting, but removes the principal cause of disfigurements due to discoloration."

Another textbook discusses the all-important time element: "The earlier this is done, the better, for every hour that elapses between death and embalming will add to the problems and complications encountered. . . ." Just how soon should one get going on the embalming? The author tells us, "On the basis of such scanty information made available to this profession through its rudimentary and haphazard system of technical research, we must conclude that the best results are to be obtained if the subject is embalmed before life is completely extinct—that is, before cellular death has occurred. In the average case, this would mean within an hour after somatic death." For those who feel that there is something a little rudimentary, not to say haphazard, about this advice, a comforting thought is offered by another writer. Speaking of fears entertained in early days of premature burial, he points out, "One of the effects of embalming by chemical injection, however, has been to dispel fears of live burial." How true; once the blood is removed, chances of live burial are indeed remote.

To return to Mr. Jones, the blood is drained out through the veins and replaced by embalming fluid pumped in through the arteries. As noted in *The Principles and Practices of Embalming,* "every operator has a favorite injection and drainage point—a fact which becomes a handicap only if he fails or refuses to forsake his favorites when conditions demand it." Typical favorites are the carotid artery, femoral artery, jugular vein, subclavian vein. There are various choices of embalming fluid. If Flextone is used, it will produce a "mild, flexible rigidity. The skin retains a velvety softness, the tissues are rubbery and pliable. Ideal for women and children." It may be blended with B. and G. Products Company's Lyf-Lyk tint, which is guaranteed to reproduce "nature's own skin texture . . . the velvety appearance of living tissue." Suntone comes in three separate tints: Suntan; Special Cosmetic Tint, a pink shade "especially indicated for young female subjects"; and Regular Cosmetic Tint, moderately pink.

About three to six gallons of a dyed and perfumed solution of formaldehyde, glycerin, borax, phenol, alcohol and water is soon circulating through Mr. Jones, whose mouth has been sewn together with a "needle directed upward between the upper lip and gum and brought out through the left nostril," with the corners raised slightly "for a more pleasant expression." If he should be bucktoothed, his teeth are cleaned with Bon Ami and coated with colorless nail polish. His eyes, meanwhile, are closed with flesh-tinted eye caps and eye cement.

The next step is to have at Mr. Jones with a thing called a trocar. This is a long, hollow needle attached to a tube. It is jabbed into the abdomen, poked around the entrails and chest cavity, the contents of which are pumped out and replaced with "cavity fluid." This done, and the hole in the abdomen sewn up, Mr. Jones's face is heavily creamed (to protect the skin from burns which may be caused by leakage of the chemicals), and he is covered with a sheet and left unmolested for a while. But not for long—there is more, much more, in store for him. He has been embalmed, but not yet restored, and the best time to start the restorative work is eight to ten hours after embalming, when the tissues have become firm and dry.

The object of all this attention to the corpse, it must be remembered, is to make it presentable for viewing in an attitude of healthy repose. "Our customs require the presentation of our dead in the semblance of normality . . . unmarred by the ravages of illness, disease, or mutilation," says Mr. J. Sheridan Mayer in his *Restorative Art*. This is rather a large order since few people die in the full bloom of health, unravaged by illness and unmarked by some disfigurement. The funeral industry is equal to the challenge: "In some cases the gruesome appearance of a mutilated or disease-ridden subject may be quite discouraging. The task of restoration may seem impossible and shake the confidence of the embalmer. This is the time for intestinal fortitude and determination. Once the formative work is begun and affected tissues are cleaned or removed, all doubts of success vanish. It is surprising and gratifying to discover the results which may be obtained."

The embalmer, having allowed an appropriate interval to elapse, returns to the attack, but now he brings into play the skill and equipment of sculptor and cosmetician. Is a hand missing? Casting one in plaster of Paris is a simple matter. "For replacement purposes, only a cast of the back of the hand is necessary; this is within the ability of the average operator and is quite adequate." If a lip or two, a nose or an ear should be missing, the embalmer has at hand a variety of restorative waxes with which to model replacements. Pores and skin texture are simulated by stippling with a little brush, and over this cosmetics are laid on. Head off? Decapitation cases are rather routinely handled. Ragged edges are trimmed, and head joined to torso with a series of splints, wires and sutures. It is a good idea to have a little something at the neck—a scarf or high collar—when time for viewing comes. Swollen mouth? Cut out tissue as needed from inside the lips. If too much is removed, the surface contour can easily be restored by padding with cotton. Swollen necks and cheeks are reduced by removing tissue through vertical incisions made down each side of the neck. "When the deceased is casketed, the pillow will hide the suture incisions . . . as an extra precaution against leakage, the suture may be painted with liquid sealer."

The opposite condition is more likely to present itself—that of emaciation. His hypodermic syringe now loaded with massage cream, the embalmer seeks out and fills the hollowed and sunken areas by injection. In this procedure the backs of the hands and fingers and the under-chin area should not be neglected.

Positioning the lips is a problem that recurrently challenges the ingenuity of the embalmer. Closed too tightly, they tend to give a stern, even disapproving expression. Ideally, embalmers feel, the lips should give the impression of being ever so slightly parted, the upper lip protruding slightly for a more youthful appearance. This takes some engineering, however, as the lips tend to drift apart. Lip drift can sometimes be remedied by pushing one or two straight pins through the inner margin of the lower lip and then inserting them between the two front upper teeth. If Mr. Jones happens to have no teeth, the pins can just as easily be anchored in his Armstrong Face Former and Denture Replacer. Another method to maintain lip closure is to dislocate the lower jaw, which is then held in its new position by a wire run through holes which have been drilled through the upper and lower jaws at the midline. As the French are fond of saying, *il faut souffrir pour être belle.*[2]

If Mr. Jones has died of jaundice, the embalming fluid will very likely turn him green. Does this deter the embalmer? Not if he has intestinal fortitude. Masking pastes and cosmetics are heavily laid on, burial garments and casket interiors are color-correlated with particular care, and Jones is displayed beneath rose-colored lights. Friends will say, "How *well* he looks." Death by carbon monoxide, on the other hand, can be rather a good thing from the embalmer's viewpoint: "One advantage is the fact that this type of discoloration is an exaggerated form of a natural pink coloration." This is nice because the healthy glow is already present and needs but little attention.

The patching and filling completed, Mr. Jones is now shaved, washed and dressed. Cream-based cosmetic, available in pink, flesh, suntan, brunette and blond, is applied to his hands and face, his hair is shampooed and combed (and, in the case of Mrs. Jones, set), his hands manicured. For the horny-handed son of toil special care must be taken; cream should be applied to remove ingrained grime, and the nails cleaned. "If he were not in the habit of having them manicured in

---

[2]In 1963 *Mortuary Management* reports a new development: "Natural Expression Formers," an invention of Funeral Directors Research Company. "They may be used to replace one or both artificial dentures, or over natural teeth; have 'bite-indicator' lines as a closure guide . . . Natural Expression Formers also offer more control of facial expression" [Author's note]. *Il faut souffrir pour être belle:* One must suffer to be beautiful (French).

life, trimming and shaping is advised for better appearance—never questioned by kin."

Jones is now ready for casketing (this is the present participle of the verb "to casket"). In this operation his right shoulder should be depressed slightly "to turn the body a bit to the right and soften the appearance of lying flat on the back." Positioning the hands is a matter of importance, and special rubber positioning blocks may be used. The hands should be cupped slightly for a more lifelike, relaxed appearance. Proper placement of the body requires a delicate sense of balance. It should lie as high as possible in the casket, yet not so high that the lid, when lowered, will hit the nose. On the other hand, we are cautioned, placing the body too low "creates the impression that the body is in a box."

Jones is next wheeled into the appointed slumber room where a few last touches may be added—his favorite pipe placed in his hand or, if he was a great reader, a book propped into position. (In the case of little Master Jones a Teddy bear may be clutched.) Here he will hold open house for a few days, visiting hours 10 A.M. to 9 P.M.

All now being in readiness, the funeral director calls a staff conference to make sure that each assistant knows his precise duties. Mr. Wilber Krieger writes: "This makes your staff feel that they are a part of the team, with a definite assignment that must be properly carried out if the whole plan is to succeed. You never heard of a football coach who failed to talk to his entire team before they go on the field. They have drilled on the plays they are to execute for hours and days, and yet the successful coach knows the importance of making even the bench-warming third-string substitute feel that he is important if the game is to be won." The winning of *this* game is predicated upon glass-smooth handling of the logistics. The funeral director has notified the pallbearers whose names were furnished by the family, has arranged for the presence of clergyman, organist, and soloist, has provided transportation for everybody, has organized and listed the flowers sent by friends. In *Psychology of Funeral Service* Mr. Edward A. Martin points out: "He may not always do as much as the family thinks he is doing, but it is his helpful guidance that they appreciate in knowing they are proceeding as they should. . . . The important thing is how well his services can be used to make the family believe they are giving unlimited expression to their own sentiment."

The religious service may be held in a church or in the chapel of the funeral home; the funeral director vastly prefers the latter arrangement, for not only is it more convenient for him but it affords him the opportunity to show off his beautiful facilities to the gathered mourners. After the clergyman has had his say, the mourners queue up to file past the casket for a last look at the deceased. The family is *never* asked whether they want an open-casket ceremony; in the absence of their instruction to the contrary, this is taken for granted. Consequently well over 90 percent of all American funerals feature the open casket—a custom unknown in other parts of the world. Foreigners are astonished by it. An English woman living in San Francisco described her reaction in a letter to the writer:

> I myself have attended only one funeral here—that of an elderly fellow worker of mine. After the service I could not understand why everyone was walking towards the coffin (sorry, I mean casket), but thought I had better follow the crowd. It shook me rigid to get there and find the casket open and poor old Oscar lying there in his brown tweed suit, wearing a suntan makeup and just the wrong shade of lipstick. If I had not been extremely fond of the old boy, I have a horrible feeling that I might have giggled. Then and there I decided that I could never face another American funeral—even dead.

The casket (which has been resting throughout the service on a Classic Beauty Ultra Metal Casket Bier) is now transferred by a hydraulically operated device called Porto-Lift to a balloon-tired, Glide Easy casket carriage which will wheel it to yet another conveyance, the Cadillac Funeral Coach. This may be lavender, cream, light green—anything but black. Interiors, of course, are color-correlated, "for the man who cannot stop short of perfection."

At graveside, the casket is lowered into the earth. This office, once the prerogative of friends of the deceased, is now performed by a patented mechanical lowering device. A "Lifetime Green" artificial grass mat is at the ready to conceal the sere earth, and overhead, to con-

25

ceal the sky, is a portable Steril Chapel Tent ("resists the intense heat and humidity of summer and the terrific storms of winter . . . available in Silver Grey, Rose or Evergreen"). Now is the time for the ritual scattering of earth over the coffin, as the solemn words "earth to earth, ashes to ashes, dust to dust" are pronounced by the officiating cleric. This can today be accomplished "with a mere flick of the wrist with the Gordon Leak-Proof Earth Dispenser. No grasping of a handful of dirt, no soiled fingers. Simple, dignified, beautiful, reverent! The modern way!" The Gordon Earth Dispenser (at $5) is of nickel-plated brass construction. It is not only "attractive to the eye and long wearing"; it is also "one of the 'tools' for building better public relations" if presented as "an appropriate non-commercial gift" to the clergyman. It is shaped something like a saltshaker.

Untouched by human hand, the coffin and the earth are now united.

It is in the function of directing the participants through this maze of gadgetry that the funeral director has assigned to himself his relatively new role of "grief therapist." He has relieved the family of every detail, he has revamped the corpse to look like a living doll, he has arranged for it to nap for a few days in a slumber room, he has put on a well-oiled performance in which the concept of *death* has played no part whatsoever—unless it was inconsiderately mentioned by the clergyman who conducted the religious service. He has done everything in his power to make the funeral a real pleasure for everybody concerned. He and his team have given their all to score an upset victory over death.

STUDY QUESTIONS

1. In paragraph 6, Mitford invites the reader to "part the formaldehyde curtain." What does she mean? How is the formaldehyde curtain like the "Iron Curtain" that divided western and eastern Europe during the Cold War era?

2. Mitford writes a PROCESS essay about embalming. However, rather than simply list each step, she DESCRIBES and EXPLAINS each part of the process. Identify two steps that are fully explained and discuss your reaction to them. Does this kind of process essay help you better understand the subject? Explain.

3. Consider the TOPIC and the TONE of the article. Do you think the two are consistent? Describe the tone that Mitford uses to explain the process of embalming. Who is her intended AUDIENCE? Rewrite one or two steps using a different tone for a different audience.

4. *For Writing.* Consider a process that you are familiar with. Write a process essay that explains the steps to complete the activity. Use Mitford's essay as a model—don't just list the steps, explain the steps and DESCRIBE the equipment needed to perform the activity. Write the paper for two different audiences: one that is familiar with the process and one that is unfamiliar with it.

WAKE TECH FACULTY ESSAYS

JIM NEILSON

"We Say"

———◧———

Arguing Academically

In the following section, you'll find essays (by Wake Tech English faculty) that examine elements of academic argument. This material covers a wide range of intellectual history, from the Greek philosopher Aristotle, who lived 300 years before Christ, to the British philosopher Stephen Toulmin, who died in 2009. That argument—persuasion through reason—has been a concern of writers and thinkers for so long suggests its ongoing importance. The way we live—our pursuit of a college education, use of machines, consumption of food, conception of the American dream, perceptions of gender—has been shaped by academic argument and inquiry, the back-and-forth conversation between they say and I say.

When scholars argue academically, they enter into long-standing conversations, weighing their conclusions against those of experts in their field of study, modifying positions, and moving toward a truer claim based on facts. The standard research paper assigned in Freshman Composition mimics this process. Its goal is two-fold: to familiarize you with the kinds of essays you will write in other college classes and to help you develop your critical thinking skills, the ability to distinguish between true and false (or true and less true) claims. These skills were first understood and explained, as John Etheridge makes clear in his essay on classical argument, by the ancient Greeks, who recognized that the use of reason is essential to "creating civil and public discourse."

A skill required for succeeding in college (and, we believe, for being an educated citizen) is the ability to question others' arguments. You can't enter into an academic conversation without understanding what writers are persuading you to believe and how they are doing so. In her essay, Lisa Martin shows how to analyze and evaluate a writer's persuasive techniques. In learning how to critique others' techniques, you will improve your own rhetorical skills, your ability to persuade through written language. You will further develop these skills, as James Harr points out, by learning to recognize common logical flaws.

To make a persuasive claim, you need support, which is found through research. That's why teachers assign research papers. People use support all of the time to back up their claims. If you're arguing, for instance, that Tom Brady, not Joe Montana, is the best quarterback ever to play in the NFL, you'll compare quarterback ratings, touchdown to interception ratios, number of Super Bowls won—which requires research.

Frequently in our daily lives we use the internet for such research. Before buying something online, for instance, you're likely to read others' comments. And when you do, you're often evaluating the reliability of these reviewers. Who among them seems convincing because of their knowledge and use of specific details? You're also looking at overall ratings, since you realize a handful of negative or positive reviews is unrepresentative.

How many stars did this product receive? What is the consensus opinion? How recent are these comments? When you're asking these questions, you're doing just what scholars do when they evaluate the credibility of sources.

However, while in your daily life you may rely on the internet, instructors often limit your choice of sources, sometimes banishing internet sites entirely and forcing you to search in unfamiliar and hard-to-use library databases. Instructors do this to make sure your claims are supported by recent, credible sources. While the internet does provide a world of information, it also provides a world of false and distorted information. Conducting a thorough search of reliable sources, therefore, is essential for writing a well-supported argument. As Elena Fleggas explains in her essay on constructing effective academic arguments, the research process helps you discover what academic conversation to join and how to develop claims and organize your own argument.

When we think of argument, we tend to think of something contentious. The arguments that occur on cable news networks, for instance, often devolve into a he said/she said dead-end. Scott Dennis, in his essay on Rogerian argument, explains another model of argument, one that seeks consensus rather than contest. And in his discussion of the Toulmin model, Win Neagle explains the essence of academic arguments: how to construct a rational fact-based claim.

As individuals increasingly rely upon news gathered through social media, the ability to evaluate source credibility and truth claims grows ever more important. Some fear that we have entered the age of what comedian Stephen Colbert labelled "truthiness," which he defined as "something that seems like truth—the truth we want to exist." We believe, on the contrary, that there are such things as facts, that these are the basis of academic arguments, that when we enter into an academic conversation we seek to build upon an existing argument in order to reach a truer conclusion—and that the following selections will help you achieve these ends.

WORKS CITED

Colbert, Stephen. "The Word—Truthiness." *The Colbert Report*. 17 Oct. 2005, www.cc.com/video-clips/63ite2/the-colbert-report-the-word—truthiness.

ELENA FLEGGAS { *Constructing an Effective*

Academic Argument

EFFECTIVE ACADEMIC ARGUMENTS differ from the biased
ideas that surround us every day in advertisements, politics,
and the news. For instance, a strong academic argument
incorporates recent, credible research and engages respectfully with positions that oppose or differ from the author's.
While you may encounter many types of argumentative
assignments in college, the following techniques will help you
develop a persuasive academic argument.

BEGIN BY CHOOSING A TOPIC

When you are assigned the task of writing an academic argument, your instructor may also assign the class a topic. You
might be allowed to modify this topic to suit your own interests. In some cases, your instructor may provide students
with a list of argumentative topics to choose from or allow
students to come up with their own topics. In both of these
instances, you have the freedom to pick which argumentative
topic to explore. You should keep in mind that argumentative writing often comes easiest to writers when they choose a
subject that interests them and that they actually *want* to learn
more about, though you should be careful since being too

personally invested in a topic can make argumentation and listening to opposing viewpoints more difficult. Often, too, college essays call for you to write on a topic you have little personal interest in. Learning the techniques of constructing an argument will help you succeed even on topics you may consider uninteresting.

If you are unsure which topic to research, you might begin by brainstorming. For example, you can make a list of tentative topics and then browse through articles and books that intrigue you on those topics. Often sources published within the last ten years will strengthen your argument the most—the conversations and realities surrounding debatable topics are always changing, so readers may question your credibility if you rely on texts that are out of date.

After doing a bit of research, you may find it easier to zero in on one or two subjects that speak to you the most and that allow you to meet the assignment criteria. You should always look to your assignment prompt and check with your instructor if you are unsure about the appropriateness of your topic or sources.

BECOME FAMILIAR WITH THE DISCUSSION SURROUNDING YOUR TOPIC AND ACTIVELY READ

Once you have decided on your topic, you should *actively* 5 engage with the texts you plan to use in your essay. Quickly reading your chosen materials will not help you fully understand how these will fit into your argument. Therefore, you should *actively read*. Use the following tips:

- Underline and highlight key phrases and words in your texts. This technique allows you to easily revisit important points. You should try to highlight and underline only *key* phrases and words—too much highlighting may confuse you later on.

- In the margins of your sources, briefly summarize key points, note any confusion you may have, and raise questions about these arguments. You can do this in printed books or Ebooks. Since annotating requires a bit more critical thinking than highlighting, it may help you remember the texts' key points better. You may also annotate on sticky notes if you prefer not to write in your texts.

- Ask questions about the text. Who is/are the author(s)? When was the text written? Also consider the purpose of the piece by asking what its goal is—is it a call to action? Does it attempt to explain something? Is it trying to persuade?

- Try to summarize what you have read to a friend. Without having read the piece, he or she should be able to understand its key points after hearing your synopsis (The Open University).

Although time consuming, active reading allows you to better understand the conversation surrounding your topic. You should understand what the key arguments are concerning your subject and who the most important figures are in this discussion. In other words, you should strive to understand the contours of and to join this academic conversation.

Remember, too, that, depending on your topic, you may need to gather research from a variety of sources or publications in order to engage a variety of perspectives.

FORM A NARROW CLAIM ABOUT YOUR TOPIC

As you conduct your research, you should be developing a claim you will argue and support. Generally speaking, the narrower your claim, the more persuasive your argument. A claim that is too broad may confuse your readers. Furthermore, broad claims require a great deal of support. One of the most consistent problems in student papers is an overly broad thesis. We believe that academic essays are stronger when they support narrowly focused claims. The narrower your claim, the more likely you are to effectively and convincingly support it.

Here is an example of a claim that is too broad:

Smoking should be banned on college campuses.   10

There are quite a few issues with this claim. First, what does the writer mean by "smoking"? Is the writer referencing drug use or cigarettes? In addition, *why* does the author believe smoking should be banned on college campuses? How, in other words, is smoking harmful in this setting? Lastly, the writer references college campuses, but it is not clear to the audience which location(s) the writer will explore. Does the author plan to explore the United States or discuss other countries? On the whole, this claim is too general and likely leaves the audience with many unanswered questions.

For your claim to be strong and, most important, convincing, it must be narrow, arguable, and proveable with research. In addition, your claim should not leave the reader with questions about what the essay will explore or argue.

Here is an example of a narrow claim:

- Smoking cigarettes should be banned on America's college campuses since it is detrimental to the health of smokers and those around them.

This narrow claim manages detail well: it reveals who is 15 harmed on college campuses by the act of smoking cigarettes. In addition, this claim is linked to a place—the United States. This statement can be supported with valid evidence, research, and reasoning.

Note that in order for your claim to be effective, you need to appropriately cite and reference written sources. What kinds of evidence might you incorporate? Facts, statistics, examples, visuals, expert opinions, all qualify. You should check with your instructor and review your assignment prompt to know which types of evidence are suitable.

USE AN APPROPRIATE TONE

If writing on a topic you feel strongly about, you may develop a tone that too aggressively expresses how you feel. You should avoid this aggressive tone. For example, if you were making an argument about who to blame for the obesity epidemic in the United States, you would not want to write:

> Of course, fast food companies are to blame for the obesity issue in the United States. They selfishly keep nutritional information from the public.

Here, the writer's tone reads as hostile and accusatory, potentially alienating the audience.

While an aggressive tone harms credibility, too passive a 20 tone risks weakening your argument:

> "I *might* be correct, but I think fast food companies are to blame for the obesity epidemic"

This statement suggests a lack of confidence in the writer's claim or even that he or she does not care enough to have done the research to support it.

The most appropriate tone for an effective academic argument is assertive. An assertive tone builds credibility and engages readers because it shows confidence in an ability to contribute to the conversation in a level-headed way:

> "Fast food companies often conceal nutritional information from the public, contributing to the obesity problem in the United States."

This statement is not too aggressive or passive—it is just asser- 25 tive enough. This type of language makes the writer seem level headed about the issue being discussed; therefore, the audience is more likely to take his or her argument seriously and be convinced by it.

CONSIDER YOUR AUDIENCE AND ADDRESS NAYSAYERS

Another way to convince your audience in an academic argument is to approach them as readers who do not or will not automatically agree with your claim. Instead, you should pretend your readers are skeptical about your argument and will only decide where they stand on your issue after hearing multiple sides of it—including the ideas of those who disagree with you. The most effective arguments, in other words, respectfully consider and carefully respond to opposing ideas

Responding to your naysayers strengthens your credibility because it shows you are open-minded and consider multiple points of view. While often it strengthens an essay to place the naysayer in the first or last body paragraphs, sometimes including your naysayer throughout the paper works best; where you place the naysayer ultimately depends on your assignment criteria and instructor's preferences.

Below are some easy-to-use templates from *They Say/I Say* that reveal how you may respond to your naysayer appropriately. These templates have been modified to remove the first person "I," as is sometimes required by academic disciplines:

> **X is mistaken because she overlooks _____ .**
> **X's claim that _____ rests upon the questionable assumption that _____ .**
> **X's view that _____ is flawed because, as recent research has shown, _____ .**
> **By focusing on _____ , X overlooks the deeper problem of _____ (Graff and Birkenstein 769).**

Although academic arguments take on different forms, this genre of writing challenges you to accomplish more than just summarizing facts or research. You must consider and respond to ideas other than your own from recent resources with which you have actively engaged. Additionally, you must form a narrow claim about your topic, use an appropriate and assertive tone, and effectively address your naysayers.

Works Cited

Graff, Gerald, Cathy Birkenstein, and Russel Durst. *They Say I Say: The Moves That Matter in Academic Writing, with Readings.* 3rd ed., W.W. Norton & Company, 2015.

The Open University. "Skills for OU Study: Active Reading," 20 May 2013, http://www2.open.ac.uk/students/skillsforstudy/active-reading.php. Accessed 21 November 2016.

LISA MARTIN ⎱ *Rhetorical Analysis*

OFTEN IN A WRITING class, you may be asked to analyze someone else's written argument. This task typically involves analyzing the author's credibility, message, and audience. Why do instructors ask you to examine other people's arguments? Because you are surrounded by arguments everywhere you look, you need to be able to think critically about what you find persuasive—or not. You may not realize it but as you scroll through your social media page, you are bombarded by arguments; in fact, every website you view has an implicit argument: trust this website for this reason. Every commercial you watch makes an argument: buy this product for this reason. The ability to distinguish between credible evidence and sheer propaganda is a necessary skill in this digital age of media, fake news, blogs, memes, and tweets.

To avoid being manipulated, you need to determine who is making the argument, why the argument is being made, how well the argument is supported, and what rhetorical tactics are being employed to persuade you to think or believe a certain way. In fact, the same critical thinking skills used to analyze any argument are essential to your success in school and in the workplace as employers increasingly seek applicants with effective critical thinking skills. Before you can make your own effective arguments, you must first think critically about how arguments are constructed and why some arguments are more persuasive than others.

A rhetorical analysis—a common writing assignment in college English classes—looks to answer one central question: Did the arguer successfully persuade his or her intended audience to accept his or her claim as valid?

To begin a rhetorical analysis, you must first consider the time and place for the argument, what the ancient Greek philosophers called *kairos*. As Gregory Howard notes in his *Dictionary of Rhetorical Terms*, this term

> refers to the way a given context for communication both calls for and constrains one's speech. Thus, sensitive to *kairos*, a speaker or writer takes into account the contingencies of a given place and time, and considers the opportunities within this specific context for words to be effective and appropriate to that moment. (127)

The situational factors involved may also be part of the argument's constraints or demands. For example, writing an article for a magazine involves attention to the time and place (*kairos*), has restrictions on length and topic (constraints), and could be motivated by things like money, the need to get the word out, etc. (exigence).

You can examine an argument's context by answering the following questions:

1. Why did the author write the argument? What was his or her purpose?

2. What existing problem or argument is he or she responding to?

3. Where was the argument published? When was it published?

Thus, to analyze an argument, you first need to consider *the purpose* of the text:

- What was the author hoping to achieve?
- Is the writer trying to entertain you? Inform you? Something else?
- How does the author organize the argument and what types of evidence does he or she use?
- What does the author want you to do after reading or viewing the argument?

In addition, you will want to examine *the author's audience*, 10 the intended receiver of the argument. Who are they? What beliefs or values might they hold about the argument being made in the text? How does the author work to connect with the audience? When considering audience, you'll first need to identify the audiences the text is addressing and explain any assumptions, values, opinions, or beliefs they hold. You could also consider whether the audience is easily identifiable or not and evaluate how this impacts the argument's effectiveness.

Next, you might examine the specific rhetorical features of the argument by discussing whether or not the author uses *an appropriate tone and style* for the particular argument and the particular audience:

- Do the tone and style support the author's purpose?

- Does the author effectively address his or her reason for writing?

Here you might examine whether the argument's tone is optimistic, angry, sarcastic, condescending, serious, or calm. You might also look at the specific word choice the author uses to establish that tone.

In addition to looking at the author's purpose, the author's audience, and the author's tone and style, you might consider looking at three specific rhetorical appeals, first identified by Greek philosopher Aristotle: ethos, logos, and pathos. In fact, in his seminal work *The Art of Rhetoric,* Aristotle writes, "Of the modes of persuasion furnished by the spoken word there are three kinds. The first kind depends on the personal character of the speaker; the second on putting the audience into a certain frame of mind; the third on the proof, or apparent proof, provided by the words of the speech itself" (2155) Below is an explanation for analyzing arguments using those three appeals.

ETHOS

The word *ethos* is Greek for character. Greeks used the term 15 to refer to the customs and characteristics of a people. Today, rhetoricians use *ethos* or *ethical appeal* to refer to the practice of convincing the reader of the credibility of the author (see also p. TK). To analyze an argument's appeal to ethos, you want to examine how the author establishes that he or she is an ethical speaker both in terms of authority, trustworthiness, and credibility or believability on the subject of the argument **and** in terms of being an ethical person, a person of goodwill who respects the audience. To find appeals to ethos in any argument, you should ask these questions (some of which were prepared by the Brigham Young University Writing Center):

- How does the author demonstrate his or her expertise on the topic?

- What authority does the speaker want audience to trust? Is it the author him- or herself or someone the author is citing?

- How does the writer convince you that he or she is trustworthy?

- How does the author appeal to shared values, beliefs, or experiences to appear more relatable and thus more credible to the audience?

- How does the author demonstrate his or her goodwill for the audience?

LOGOS

Logos is a Greek word variously translated as word, speech, opinion, or thought, among others. In composition, it typically refers to an argument's logic (see also p. TK). To analyze an argument's appeal to logos, you will need to examine how the author supports each claim with logic and reason. Sometimes those reasons can come in the form of hard evidence such as statistics or facts, but sometimes those reasons can come in the form of rational logic that appeals to the audience's brain. In other words, you should ask yourself these questions:

- What claims is the author making?

- How does the author support each claim?

- What types of evidence does the author use?

- How does the author assure readers that the evidence comes from credible sources?

- Does the author provide good, common-sense reasons to support each claim?

- Does the argument seem logical and rational or does the author make too many generalizations and leaps in logic?

- Does the argument contain any logical fallacies—gaps in logic—(see p. A-259) such as making false comparisons, oversimplifying objections, or mistaking sequence for cause?

PATHOS

The word "pathos" is Greek for suffering, experience, or emotion. To analyze an argument's appeal to pathos, you examine how the author appeals to the audience's emotions (see also p. TK). Pathos, then, is about how the author wants the audience to feel in response to the arguments. Appeals to pathos are based not on how the author feels about the topic of the argument but rather on how the author evokes a specific emotion in the audience. To find appeals to pathos, you should ask the following:

- Where in the article does the author appeal to the emotions of his or her audience? 20

- Is the author arousing anger, pity, or hope in his or her audience? Why? For what purpose?

- What particular words, images, and analogies is the speaker using to manipulate or arouse these emotions? Does this strategy work? Why or why not?

- Once the speaker has created an emotion in listeners, how does he or she connect that emotion with the purpose of the argument? Is this strategy effective? Why or why not? In other words, how does establishing an emotional connection help persuade people to follow the speaker and accept his or her argument?

COMPARING WRITTEN ARGUMENTS

Occasionally, you may be asked to compare two or more written arguments, to evaluate how well two authors make a persuasive argument to different audiences. To generate those comparisons, you should ask the following:

1. Whose argument is effective given the constraints of the argument? Who does more to respond to an existing problem or argument?

2. Who does a better job of establishing trust and credibility with their audience? What exactly do they do to establish trust and credibility? In other words, do their appeals to ethos function the same way or are they different?

3. Who does a better job of presenting evidence to support their claim? Compare the types of evidence both authors present and examine why that evidence would be effective for that audience. Moreover, whose argument seems more

reasonable and logical? Why?. Do they both cite data? Do they both quote experts? Do they both use sound logic?

4. Who does a better job of arousing emotion in their audience? How are their emotional appeals similar or different? Which article contains more emotional appeals? Why?

SAMPLE RHETORICAL ANALYSIS ESSAY

Following is a sample rhetorical analysis written by a Wake Tech student for her English 112 course during the Fall 2016 semester. Note: this paper is formatted according to the MLA, 8th edition.

Works Cited

Aristotle. *The Art of Rhetoric.* Translated by Roberts, Rhys W., Megaphone eBooks, 2008.

Brigham Young University Writing Center. "Rhetorical Analysis: Prewriting." //writingcenter.byu.edu/sites/default/files/handouts/rhetorical_analysis_ prewriting_0.pdf

Howard, Gregory. *Dictionary of Rhetorical Terms.* Xlibris, 2010.

Brianna Paszko
ENG 112
Lisa Martin
12 October 2016

FOOD FOR THOUGHT

Obesity has become an increasingly complex issue over the years. Many disagree on how to effectively solve the obesity epidemic and exactly what causes it to be such a problem. One author who has entered the debate is Radley Balko, a former a policy analyst with the Cato Institute who now writes opinion articles for the Washington Post and holds degrees in journalism and political science from Indiana University. In his article "What You Eat Is Your Business," published on the Cato Institute's website in 2004, Radley Balko talks about how the government is trying to pass more anti-obesity initiatives and how those initiatives will affect his libertarian audience. The Cato Institute, which serves a primarily libertarian audience, is a public policy research organization dedicated to "the principles of individual liberty, limited government, free markets and peace" (466). Through his article, Balko is able to persuade his audience by establishing his credibility and a sense of trust, presenting facts to prove that the government is not helping to stop the obesity epidemic, and using a call to action to incite anger and fear in his audience.

In Balko's article, he establishes credibility with his audience by presenting detailed facts about the government's current plans for stopping the obesity epidemic saying that they are, "agitating for a panoply of government anti-obesity initiatives, including prohibiting junk food in school vending machines, federal funding for new bike trails and sidewalks, more demanding labels on foodstuffs, and prodding the food industry into more 'responsible' behavior" (466). This evidence proves to Balko's audience that he has an understanding of current government initiatives to stop the obesity epidemic. He also establishes trust with his readers by showing that he is looking out for their best interests by focusing on the financial effects of government intervention on the reader.

In addition, he appeals to logic by pointing out that, "President Bush earmarked $200 million in his budget for anti-obesity measures" (467). He uses this evidence to show his readers exactly how much government involvement there is in trying to stop the obesity epidemic. After presenting the amount of money put towards fighting obesity, he argues that the government getting involved in this matter presents no incentive for people to, "put down the cheeseburger" (467). He uses this incentive argument to show that if the government continues to be involved in the obesity epidemic there will be no incentive for people to stay healthy because there's no reason to. However, if the government steps away from the problem, there will be financial incentive for people to live a healthy lifestyle. Balko then discusses how government involvement is requiring people to be responsible for someone else's health. He uses all of this evidence to show his readers that government involvement in private healthcare is not helping to solve the obesity epidemic but is, in fact, making matters worse. Balko also uses his evidence for how much money is being put towards fighting obesity and the government's involvement in private healthcare to show that the government is not encouraging a sense of responsibility among consumers but is instead feeding the problem. All of Balko's evidence proves to his audience that the government should not be involved with the obesity epidemic as it will only make matters worse.

Furthermore, he tries to invoke discomfort and anger in his audience. He makes his audience uncomfortable by describing the government's involvement with the obesity epidemic as, "bringing government between you and your waistline" (466). He then invokes anger when he says, "Our lawmakers just enacted a huge entitlement that requires some people to pay for other people's medicine" (467). Balko uses these appeals to emotion because he knows that his audience of libertarians do not want the government involved with their private health matters. Balko is invoking anger over having to pay for someone else's medicine. He also attempts to make his audience angry by examining the intrusion of government into private healthcare. Balko knows that his audience will be very upset with the idea of paying for someone else's medicine and having the government involved with their private health matters.

Although Balko does a very good job of presenting his arguments, he does have a few gaps in logic. First, Balko makes a gap in logic known as a slippery slope. A slippery slope fallacy is when someone assumes that one action will lead to a continuous chain of actions. This fallacy occurs when Balko is describing how government involvement in private health, "paves the way for even more federal restrictions on consumer choice and civil liberties" (468). Although Balko has no evidence that this increase in federal restrictions will happen, he makes the assumption that government involvement will lead to more regulations. Balko also creates a non sequitur fallacy in his article, an argument that justifies something through irrelevant reasons, which occurs when he talks about how the, "largest organization of trial lawyers," are encouraging each other to, "weed jury pools of candidates who show 'personal responsibility bias'" (468). Although this information might be of interest to his audience, this point has nothing to do with the rest of his arguments. However, even though Balko had fallacies in his article, these fallacies would have no effect on his audience. In Balko's article, his gaps in logic would be completely overlooked by his audience. His audience already believes that government involvement will lead to more restrictions, so his Slippery Slope would only encourage their beliefs. His Non Sequitur would also have no effect on his arguments; it would only encourage his readers preconceived ideas regarding the industries attempt to cancel out personal responsibility.

Overall, Balko makes very convincing arguments for his specific audience. He is able to present detailed facts about the government's involvement in the obesity epidemic which ultimately builds his credibility and a sense of trust. Balko is also able to appeal to his audience's sense of logic by connecting the government's involvement to a lack of incentive for people to maintain healthy lifestyles. He is then able to incite a sense of anger and fear in his audience through the discussion of having to pay for someone else's poor choices and the government's involvement in private health matters. Finally, even though Balko does present two flaws in logic, he is still able to make very convincing arguments for his audience through ethos, logos, and pathos. Therefore, his argument is effective because he knows exactly how to connect with what his audience already values and believes.

Works Cited

Balko, Radley. "What You Eat Is Your Business." *They Say/I Say With Readings*, 3rd ed., edited by Cathy Birkenstein and Russel Durst, W.W. Norton, 2015, pp. 466–469.

JAMES B. HARR, III { *Logical Fallacies*

Fallacies are argumentative errors. They are often committed unknowingly, and to the unaware and unprepared audience, these erroneous arguments often appear valid. Fallacies tend to weaken or even undermine an argument by relying on misdirection and oversimplification. As children, we often hear and commit fallacies in arguments with friends, family, and authority figures: "But everyone else has one," "I know you are, but what am I?," "If you didn't take my toy, then who did?," "She got to do it, so why can't I?" Although most of us have progressed beyond these juvenile examples, more refined manifestations can be found in everyday arguments. Politicians, particularly, are guilty of committing fallacies to gain voter approval. Here are some of the more common logical fallacies:

- Slippery slope: One decision will lead to an exaggerated result (*If Wake Tech forbids the use of nicotine on campus, it is only a matter of time before they ban coffee because it contains caffeine.*)

- Ad hominem: Attacking the person rather than the argument (*My instructor is a Democrat, so I'm sure he knows nothing about business ethics.*)

- Non sequitur: Two ideas are falsely connected (*She goes to a community college, so she must have been a bad student in high school.*)

- Bandwagon: Accepting something because it is popular (*Everyone is skipping class this Friday. You should too.*)

- Straw Man: Redirecting an argument towards one which can easily be disputed (Speaker 1: *The state government should look into lowering college tuition costs.* Speaker 2: *So you're advocating taking money away from senior citizens and reallocating it to young people? Is that the way the state should treat the elderly?*)

- Post hoc (ergo propter hoc): Two ideas are related and thus directly affect each other (*Because I wear my socks inside out when I fly, I have never been in a plane crash.*)

- Scare tactics: Using fear as a way to manipulate (*This candidate wants to open up our borders, allowing terrorists free access to our nation.*)

- Either/Or or False Dichotomy: Presenting only two options when many could exist (*You either earn a degree or you work a menial job for the rest of your life.*)

Learning about the types of fallacies and their common uses is the best way to identify and refute them. It is also important to note that several fallacies can be committed at the same time. For example:

> As the majority of Americans know, if you support a candidate who is nothing more than a self-indulging idiot, you vote for an individual who supports the 2nd amendment and ultimately will

drive us to martial law where no one will feel safe. Is that what 5
you want? Anarchy in the United States? You either support
anarchy or you support this candidate's opponent.

In this statement, we have committed bandwagon appeals
("as the majority of Americans know…"), ad hominem
("self-indulging idiot"), slippery slope (supporting the second amendment *will* lead to martial law), scare tactics/fear
mongering ("no one will feel safe"), and straw man (changing
the topic from a candidate's platform to wishing anarchy on
the United States). Studying and identifying the commonly
abused fallacies will strengthen your ability both to refute a
poorly structured argument and to avoid making those same
mistakes.

For additional information on logical fallacies, see Jane.
A. Aaron. *The Little, Brown Handbook, Brief Version.* 6th ed.,
Pearson, 2017, Section 11e, pp. 111–115.

JOHN ETHERIDGE { *Classical Argument*

THE CONTEXT

In the first year of the Peloponnesian War, with its citizens anxious about the fate of their city and full of sorrow over those many men already lost in battle, Athens held its traditional funeral for the fallen. The bodies of the war dead had been laid out in tents; offerings for the deceased had been made; the families of the fallen and all the war-weary citizens of Athens had processed to the Kerameikos, the section of the city that contained the honorary graveyard much like our own Arlington National Cemetery. Pericles, the esteemed Athenian leader, rose to deliver the traditional funeral oration for the dead.

What does one say in such a moment, when so many have died and the outcome of the conflict is unclear? *How* does one say it in a meaningful way that sounds neither trite nor dismissive?

The Athenian historian Thucydides was present that day at the Kerameikos, and in his work *The History of the Peloponnesian War*, he recalled the solemn scene. When Pericles rose to speak, his skill and training in the use of language and argument and his own personal character (his "ethos") allowed him to deliver a meaningful speech which honored the dead ("with life and limb [they] stood stoutly to their task...at the crowning moment not of fear but of glory" (335)), comforted the grieving ("be comforted by the fair fame of these your sons" (339)), exhorted the war-weary citizens ("for Athens alone among her contemporaries, when put to the test, is superior to the report of her" (331)), and honored the city of Athens ("when the vision of her greatness has inspired you, reflect that all this has been acquired by men of courage who knew their duty and in the hour of conflict were moved by a high sense of honour, who...were resolved that at least their country should not find herself deserted by their valour, but freely sacrificed to her the fairest offering it was in their power to give" (335-6)).

Classical Argument, such as Pericles's oration, is not merely a type of essay organization, as it is often presented in modern textbooks, nor is it a collection of Latinate terms to be memorized in a rote manner. Classical rhetoric (of which argument is the primary part) is a fundamental brick in the foundation of Western thinking, a vital yet increasingly forgotten effort to create civil and productive public discourse.

THE FIVE CANONS

Building on the work of Aristotle and Cicero, the Roman 5 rhetorician Quintilian codified classical rhetoric into five "canons" (e.g., categories) for creating, arranging, and presenting argument:

- *Inventio*—invention, creation, or discovery
- *Dispositio*—organization
- *Elocutio*—style

- *Pronuntiatio* or *actio*—delivery
- *Memoria*—memory

As ancient rhetoric revolved primarily around the spoken word, two of these canons (*memoria* and *pronuntiatio*) apply only to spoken rhetoric. Thus, the written rhetorical situation involves three canons (inventio, dispositio, and elocutio) Elocutio deals with competence in diction, grammar, and coherence, skills learned in foundational composition courses. Inventio and dispositio are therefore the two canons vital for the modern student's understanding of classical argument.

Canon 1: Inventio

For our purposes, the most important canon is inventio, the creation, discovery, or invention of an argument. Many of the techniques of inventio are not exclusive to classical argument, and so still prove useful in most rhetorical situations. We break down inventio into three "toolboxes" that you might go to as you think about how to effectively construct your argument.

TOOLBOX 1: A STRONG THESIS

Classical argument typically begins with a tentative thesis, usually, though not always, a one-sentence claim. It should be narrow, clear, and specific. The thesis should obviously be debatable, and it should be able to fit into a "should" or "should not" statement. This sentence does not need to include those words, but if you are having trouble creating a thesis statement, you might use one of those forms to help you produce a workable thesis.

TOOLBOX 2: THREE MODES OF PERSUASION

Teachers of rhetoric such as Aristotle, Cicero, and Quintilian 10 identify three primary ways to convince an audience to believe or to act as we wish them to. It is by means of these three "modes of persuasion" that we prove our thesis, and it is the context of the situation which dictates how much of one or the other we use.

Ethos

Quintilian, whose works on rhetoric formed the basis for education for centuries, taught that the most foundational part of an argument was the ethos of the speaker/writer: "he who would have men trust his judgment as to what is expedient and honorable should possess and be regarded as possessing genuine wisdom and excellence of character" (485). If you want to convince other people of what is just and necessary, then you yourself must have and display good moral character (*ethos*). Additionally, the appeal to ethos must show that the writer is genuinely familiar with and concerned with the audience's real needs and desires (see also p. TK).

Appeal by means of ethos may play out differently depending on the situation, but here are some possible ways to display ethos:

- Avoid fallacies and underhanded or lazy techniques;
- Properly integrate and cite testimony (source material);
- Appeal to the general welfare of the whole audience, not just a group;

- As appropriate, appeal directly to ethical standards (justice, temperance, fortitude, wisdom).

Why is ethos important? Manipulation by means of argument is as old as language itself. For example, in the Judeo-Christian story about the fall of man, it is not an act of violence or of lust or of injustice which brings evil into the created world. Rather, it is the serpent's manipulative argument in human language that leads to Adam and Eve's decision to sin against their Creator.

Pathos

The appeal to emotion (*pathos*) is the most powerful of the 15 modes of persuasion. Pathos requires no training or experience, and can be felt even by children completely unschooled in argumentative techniques. Its power and pervasiveness are the sources of its effectiveness (see also p. TK).

To be sure, we ought not to reject pathos as a means of persuasion, as many situations exist in which pathos is a vital element. If we think again about the situation in which Pericles found himself delivering the Athenian funeral oration, we can see clearly that an appeal to pathos is, in fact, very necessary for that rhetorical context.

In deciding when and how to appeal to pathos, we must consider first what pathos does. To put it simply, our ethos establishes our trust and concern for the good; logos convinces the audience of the truth of our claim; and pathos moves our audience's will to action. To consider Pericles again, he appeals to the pathos of his audience so that (a) those grieving might be comforted and not consumed by their grief, and (b) that the citizenry might be inspired to continue their support of the war effort. In essence, pathos moves the audience to *do* something, not merely to *believe* something.

Consider the following tips for *how* and *where* to include appeals to pathos:

- Use powerful, vivid, descriptive diction and imagery
- Use personal anecdotes, examples, or narratives to engage the reader
- Use pathos in the introductory and concluding paragraphs, as emotion will help draw your reader in and can leave a strong final impression

Finally, the following two principles ought to be followed [20] when appealing to pathos:

- Appeal to pathos must be appropriate to the situation. For example, the Funeral Oration of Pericles requires emotional appeal, whereas an essay on the use of traffic cameras would likely not utilize much appeal to pathos.
- Appeal to pathos must be measured. Any fallacies of "loaded language" should be avoided.

Logos

While ethos is the most foundational means of persuasion and pathos the most powerful, logos is the most substantive. It is the primary tool used by writers, especially in the academic arena, and so it ought to be honed most sharply. Here we present the three most basic and most commonly used patterns of logic (see also p. TK).

Pattern 1: Definition or Generalization

When we make an argument by definition, we draw a conclusion by saying what a thing actually is, or by placing it in a category. It is the most basic way we think about the world. We place an unknown item into a category of like things, or we divide it away from a category of unlike things. Thus, any time we use definitions, categorizations, or generalizations, we make an argument by *definition*.

Of course, there are shades of soundness to an argument by definition. This kind of argument is sound if (a) the unknown thing is placed (or excluded from) the appropriate category, or (b) the category is large and representative enough.

In his Funeral Oration, Pericles argues by definition when 25 he attempts to place Athenians in a category distinct from other peoples. Thucydides records the Athenian leader's series of characteristics common to Athenians, saying, for example, that "we are lovers of the beauty" (327) and "for it is not by receiving kindness, but by conferring it, that we acquire our friends" (329). In offering these and other defining traits of the Athenian citizen, Pericles draws a precise picture of what he thinks an Athenian actually is.

We can also convince our audience by using the pattern of generalization, which categorizes in a way similar to definition. Pericles, after spending a good deal of time praising Athens itself, explains his purpose by saying, "for when I lauded the city, that was but the praise wherewith the brave deeds of these men and men like them have already adorned her" (Thucydides 333). Each of the dead is part of the Athenian whole, and so as Pericles praises the whole, he praises its parts—the praise belongs to the whole and to the parts of the whole.

Another notable example of a generalization would be a poll. Some polls are sound (not *certain*, but *sound*), and others are not. The soundness of a poll depends on how many people were polled, how representative the polled people were of the population as a whole, and how well-constructed the poll was. If all of those elements meet statistical and rhetorical standards, then the poll would be sound.

Pattern 2: Analogy (or Comparison/Contrast)

Our second basic pattern of thought is analogy. When we draw an analogy, we draw conclusions about one thing based on a comparison to a second thing. In some ways, this is like definition, but the distinction for analogy is that the comparison is a "one-to-one" analysis, whereas definition deals in categories.

When we make comparisons, we attempt to find two things that share properties. In order to constitute a sound analogy, those properties should be relevant to the conclusion drawn and as numerous as possible. The first criteria is much more important, as a comparison between two shared things that depends on two properties very relevant to the conclusion would be more sound than one that depends on a dozen properties that are not relevant to the conclusion.

To illustrate, consider Rev. Martin Luther King, Jr.'s 30 expression of disappointment in the church in his "Letter from Birmingham Jail":

> There was a time when the church was very powerful—in the time when the early Christians rejoiced at being deemed worthy

to suffer for what they believed. In those days the church was not merely a thermometer that recorded the ideas and principles of popular opinion; it was a thermostat that transformed the mores of society. . . . Things are different now. So often the contemporary church is a weak, ineffectual voice with an uncertain sound. So often it is an archdefender of the status quo. Far from being disturbed by the presence of the church, the power structure of the average community is consoled by the church's silent—and often even vocal—sanction of things as they are. (134)

Here, King creates an analogy between the church of the past and the church of the present. He does not need to expressly state why this analogy is legitimate, as it is understood that these two institutions share many relevant properties (because, of course, they are the same institution, just in different time periods). Instead, he develops the contrasts between the early church and the modern church to show the moral poverty of the modern church.

Specifically, he suggests the early church acted more bravely on principle and, in doing so, "transformed the mores of society." The modern church, however, not only acquiesces to the "status quo" of the modern world, but in fact offers "sanction of things as they are." Thus, using reasoning by analogy, King attempts to hold up the church of his day as inferior to the early church in its ability and desire to pursue justice. Considering his stated audience (the clergymen to whom the letter is addressed) and one of his implied audiences (the white moderate Southern Christian), King sees this analogy as both a stinging rebuke and an encouragement to action.

Pattern 3: Causal Relationship (Cause/Effect)

Causal reasoning means drawing conclusions based on causal relationships (i.e., cause and effect relationships). Good writers avoid drawing conclusions based on coincidental occurrences.

In "Letter from Birmingham Jail," King relies on causal reasoning to illustrate that the form of nonviolent protest he advocates is far preferable to the alternative: "If this philosophy had not emerged, by now many streets of the South would, I am convinced, be flowing with blood. And I am further convinced that if our white brothers. . . . refuse to support our nonviolent efforts, millions of Negroes will, out of frustration and despair, seek solace and security in black-nationalist ideologies—a development that would inevitably lead to a frightening racial nightmare." (132)

The chain of reasoning is fairly easy to identify in this passage, with King forecasting a dire effect ("frightening racial nightmare") if the path of nonviolent protest is not supported, particularly by the white moderate and white church. Note that King *directly* links nonviolent protest to the avoidance of the "racial nightmare," arguing strongly that the *only* manner of producing a positive outcome (avoidance of racial nightmare) is support of nonviolent protest.

Causal reasoning is often the most easily identifiable and easiest to deploy in argument, so consideration of causes and effects ought to be at the forefront of your mind as you construct your ideas.

TOOLBOX 3: TESTIMONY

The final toolbox writers can deploy to prove a claim is what ancient thinkers called testimony and what we call research.

Aristotle called this the "non-artistic" means of persuasion, as research deals in objective evidence and witness testimony. Classical argument uses testimony in two primary ways:

- To confirm one's own claims using the claims of some other witness (a trusted expert);
- To refute one's opponent's claims by drawing attention especially to that opponent's fallacies or ineffective logic.

Canon 2: Dispositio

Dispositio is the organization of an argument. This method 40 of organizing will likely seem familiar to students, since it has been the standard manner of presenting the order of an argument. In classical rhetoric, dispositio has five possible components:

- Introduction
- Statement of Facts (also called *narratio*)
- Confirmation
- Refutation
- Conclusion

In general practice in college essays, an argument requires at least an introduction, a conclusion, and either confirmation or refutation. Of course, an argument can contain all five of these elements or only one of them, depending on the topic and context. Techniques for constructing introductions and conclusions likely were covered in previous English courses, and those same tactics apply to (and are usually borrowed from) classical argument.

STATEMENT OF FACTS

The statement of facts is an explanation of the circumstances and details of the question at hand. It is an informative reminder, especially for an audience who may not be immediately familiar with the subject at hand. For placement, one option is to include the statement of facts in a single paragraph that comes after the introduction; it could also be scattered throughout the essay if the audience is already familiar with the topic.

If you choose to include a statement of facts, it should be lucid, brief, and objective.

CONFIRMATION AND REFUTATION

Confirmation and Refutation will make up the body of your essay. Confirmation presents your supporting claims along with proof of those claims. It is the "positive" aspect of argumentation ("Here is why my argument is true."). It effectively deploys all three of the toolboxes mentioned in the inventio discussion above. The actual organization of the body paragraphs varies by circumstance, topic, requirements, and individual choice.

Refutation, as the name suggests, attempts to undercut the opposition argument, and could be seen as the "negative" form of argumentation ("here is why my opponent's argument is not true"). Refutation could be done in any one of several ways:

- Point out weak or poorly-used evidence (modes of persuasion or testimony);
- Present stronger, alternative evidence;

- Expose possible logical fallacies;
- Provide counter-examples or counter-consequences.

Classical argument is typically presented as a particular organizational model for argument. In reality, *dispositio* is treated by classical authors as a complement to *inventio*. Aristotle, for example, intended his treatment of organization in argument to be included in a different book than his material on *inventio*. Additionally, *dispositio* was consistently seen as being governed not by external form as is often presented, but rather as being governed by the necessities of the situation and the preferences of the writer, all in order to achieve maximum effect.

CONCLUSION

Ancient philosophers and rhetoricians—Socrates, Plato, Aristotle, Cicero, and Quintilian, among others—took seriously the role of words spoken or written for public consumption. To varying degrees, each was concerned with the frightful possibility of an immoral man skilled in oratorical style manipulating citizens untrained in logic and ethics. On the other hand, each also understood the potential beauty of a city skilled in the art of rhetoric—a citizenry moored in the virtues of justice, temperance, wisdom, and courage, engaging in rigorous yet civil public discourse in order to bring about what is good for the city and her citizens, a goal that historically has been central to a college education.

Works Cited

Aristotle. *On Rhetoric*. Translated by George Kennedy. Oxford UP, 2007.

King Jr., Martin Luther. "Letter from Birmingham Jail." *Wake Tech Reader*. Revised Edition. Cengage, 2015, pp.125–137.

Quintilian. *The Institutio Oratoria of Quintilian*. Translated by H.E. Butler. Vol. 1. New York, G.P. Putnam's Sons, 1920. *Google Books*, https://books.google.com/books?id=8AMdAAAAYAAJ&printsec=frontcover#v=onepage&q&f=true

Thucydides. *The History of the Peloponnesian War*. Translated by C.F. Smith. Book II. *Loeb Classical Library*. Harvard UP, 1928.

WIN NEAGLE { *Toulmin Model of Argument*

While humans have a distinguished record of incredible feats of reason, our individual perspectives tend to be formed more by instinct and emotion than by rational reflection. As we attempt to distinguish beliefs founded on sound, critical thought from those derived from less rational paths, clearly stating why we believe what we believe can be quite useful. The founder of formal logic, Aristotle, recognized this value more than 2,300 years ago when he proposed the use of syllogisms to present arguments for consideration. A syllogism is a deductive scheme constructed from premises (usually two or more) that lead to a conclusion, as in the following example:

> All humans are mortal.
> Jane is a human.
> Therefore, Jane is mortal.

To be sound, a syllogism must have factually accurate premises that lead to the eventual conclusion in a logically valid manner. The syllogism is a simple but powerful device for evaluating truthfulness, and British philosopher Stephen Toulmin (1922–2009) based his model for philosophical reasoning on this useful tool.

In the Toulmin model, a claim is supported by grounds (or data): *The county should implement a higher minimum wage because doing so would reduce homelessness and attract a pool of dedicated workers to the area.*

Warrants show that the grounds are, indeed, relevant to the claim: *Roughly 25% of the county's homeless hold full-time jobs.*

Backing answers any further questions regarding the relevance of the grounds: *Availability of affordable housing has decreased in the county over the last decade.*

When putting forth an argument, we can anticipate counterarguments and respond to them. In the Toulmin model these responses are referred to as rebuttals: *While some claim that raising the minimum wage will lead to localized inflation, offsetting any potential gains, this has not proven to be the case in other communities where higher minimum wages have been implemented.*

Upon reflection, we may find that our claim needs to be refined. Toulmin referred to such equivocations as qualifiers: *The county should implement a higher minimum wage because doing so **might** reduce homelessness and attract a pool of dedicated workers to the area.*

The power of the Toulmin argument, like the syllogism, lies in its simplicity, providing no room to hide irrational pleas and logical fallacies, thus forcing us to take a clear and honest look at our reasoning for accepting the claim that has been proposed.

DR. PHILLIP SCOTT DENNIS ⎰ *Rogerian*
                                    Argument

Critical thinking means opening up our minds to diverse and unfamiliar points of view. The kinds of exploration we undertake in English 112 can also require us to test our own assumptions and sometimes reshape or reject ideas we may have previously held dear or even considered unquestionable. In addition, critical thinking often compels us to realize that issues, ideas, or circumstances we may have considered simple or straightforward are, in fact, complex, requiring more nuanced thought or a deeper consideration. The ability to recognize these complexities and use this recognition to cultivate more in-depth understanding will help us negotiate our complicated world in more informed, objective, and unprejudiced ways.

Carl Rogers was a famous twentieth-century psychologist who developed a method of mediation in which two people in a disagreement or conflict were each asked to state the positions of the other person prior to verbalizing their own positions. Rogers found that asking someone to first consider an opposite perspective led to better outcomes in negotiating conflicts or misunderstandings (86). By interweaving seemingly contradictory perspectives, opponents could often find workable compromises they had before been unable to reach.

Scholars quickly discovered that this technique might also help writers invent nuanced solutions to complex problems and developed the Rogerian argument as a tool for exploring such issues and reaching compromise solutions (Brent).

ROGERIAN STRUCTURE

Rogerian argument integrates multiple viewpoints in order to arrive at a middle ground, or compromise solution, rather than to produce a "winner" and "loser." This type of argument is often distinguished from "Classical" argument, which typically incorporates opposing or divergent viewpoints only to point out their weaknesses, or simply as a means to support the dominant thesis. Unlike Rogerian arguments, a "Classical" argument typically states a clear thesis near the beginning, including as support only that evidence which best reinforces or upholds that thesis, and airing carefully selected opposing viewpoints only for the purposes of counterargument. Rogerian arguments, on the other hand, incorporate multiple perspectives, not just to dissect or to oppose them, but rather to integrate diverse positions into a compromise, or middle ground, that also serves as the main thesis, or claim, of the essay.

Rogerian arguments also differ in structure from more traditional arguments. Instead of presenting the thesis in the introductory material, the Rogerian writer often chooses to defer the thesis statement until the *end* of the argument, waiting until many diverse perspectives have been explored *before* disclosing the main point of the essay. Rogerian writers typically capture the reader's attention with an engaging introduction, and then, rather than stating the thesis overtly, provide the audience with a general discussion of the issue. The object of this type of introduction is to "set the stage" before presenting a wide variety of viewpoints from diverse (and even diametrically opposed) perspectives, leading to a compromise, middle-ground conclusion.

A CONTEMPORARY EXAMPLE: IMMIGRATION POLICY

One function of the Rogerian approach is to reconcile extreme positions. This can be especially useful for exploring issues prone to "False Dichotomy" fallacies (also known as "False Dilemmas," "Either/Or," or "Black and White" fallacies), where potential arguments are falsely restricted to invite only binary "yes or no" or "pro or con" responses. Rogerian arguments are often used to illuminate these types of issues, extracting meaningful compromises from the integration of seemingly oppositional viewpoints.

U.S. immigration policy is one contemporary issue that can elicit polarized or even antagonistic stances. In order to persuade a broadly diverse audience, a well-reasoned Rogerian argument seeks to moderate between many possible positions to suggest a policy amenable to a wide audience. To most readers, for example, a policy position which prohibits immigration completely would seem extreme—so, too, would a position which advocates for free and unrestricted immigration. In between these two positions, however, lies a wide range of potential policies ripe for exploration. A Rogerian argument about immigration policy first considers a spectrum of divergent viewpoints, then creates a policy recommendation that incorporates differing concerns.

In such a case, an arguer might first engage the reader with an impactful, attention-getting introduction and then provide the reader with some background information demonstrating the importance of sound immigration policy or explaining briefly the history of the issue. Next, the arguer would integrate ideas backed by research exploring differing perspectives on the effects of immigration—on culture, economy, government, or health care, just to name a few possibilities. These divergent positions should be supported by evidence gathered from credible sources (and incorporated into the essay using correct documentation and citation). To avoid bias, and to convince the reader of his or her credibility, the author should make a deliberate effort to represent voices from multiple stakeholders; some examples might include immigrants, policymakers, workers, foreign governments, border and other law enforcement officials, health care employees, or social workers. This researched support might either be organized according to subtopic, or be divided roughly into "pro-immigration" and "anti-immigration" stances, with the idea that the final thesis will bring various perspectives together, presenting a compromise workable to all sides.

Finally, the conclusion would offer a detailed, nuanced policy argument (or *thesis*) that proposes a "middle-ground" policy or solution. In this case, for example, an author might offer a policy that encourages legal immigration, but with some carefully explained restrictions or exceptions. Based on this recommendation, the arguer would of course want to discuss how such a policy might affect the economy, employment, culture, health care, or governance, consistent with the issues discussed in the body of the essay. Though this policy may not satisfy all viewpoints regarding immigration, it is likely that such a compromise position would be acceptable to a broad diversity of readers—whose opinions would likely lie somewhere *in between* polar extremes.

CONCLUSION

Based on the belief that a combining of diverse perspectives leads to more equitable outcomes, Rogerian arguments are especially good for exploring complicated issues with diverse stakeholders and widely differing perspectives. Though not useful in all contexts or for all issues, Rogerian arguments are nonetheless an important tool for students of argumentation. The main elements of Rogerian argument—voicing, hearing, and considering differing viewpoints in search of compromise—are hallmarks of sophisticated critical thinking and a necessity for success in English 112 and beyond.

Works Cited

Brent, Douglas. "Rogerian Rhetoric: An Alternative to Traditional Rhetoric." University of Calgary Department of Communication and Culture. Web. 2-Jan-2017.

Rogers, Carl R. "Communication: its Blocking and its Facilitation." *ETC: A Review of General Semantics*, vol. 9, no. 2, 1952, pp. 83–88. Web. 2-Jan-2017.

READINGS

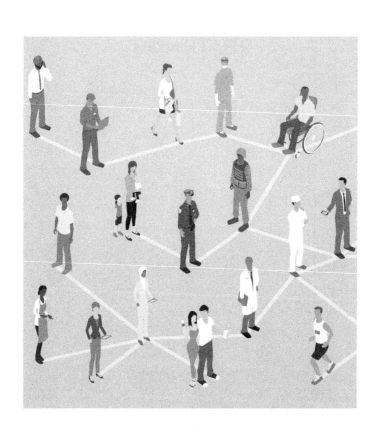

EIGHTEEN

HOW CAN WE BRIDGE
THE DIFFERENCES THAT DIVIDE US?

—⌐◻⌐—

"Can we talk?" The late, great comedian Joan Rivers often began her TV shows by asking the audience that question, and it became her trademark line. Audiences knew to expect funny, snarky, sometimes outrageous jokes and stories from her, and it helped her to establish a close, almost intimate connection with viewers. But today in the United States, the question "Can we talk?" has taken on a far less humorous meaning, because increasingly the answer is "No."

We have always been divided by such factors as geography, political orientation, socioeconomic class, race, gender, and age, but in recent years it seems like we have become a nation of people estranged from one another. Social media and niche viewing have exacerbated these divisions as more and more we hear from and interact with only those who share our views.

Across the dividing lines, Americans are increasingly bitter, angry, and suspicious toward one another. In an article entitled "'Go to Hell!' A Divided America Struggles to Heal after Ugly Election," Jason Szep, a reporter for Reuters, an international news agency, writes that "the 2016 US election was unprecedented in the way it turned Americans against each other, according to dozens of interviews in rural United States and across some of the most politically charged battleground states." According to Szep, some family members no longer speak with one another, and longtime friendships have dissolved due to differing views. And in January 2017, the Pew Research Center, a nonpartisan think tank, surveyed over 1,000 people throughout the United States and found that 86 percent described the country as "more politically divided today than in the past."

Many people living in the United States believe that, as a nation, we need to work to improve communication and understanding across communities, but where exactly do we start? Possible first steps involve venturing out of our comfort zones to listen and pay attention to viewpoints that might challenge our own, and finding ways of responding respectfully. The readings in this chapter offer a genuine and much-needed attempt to break down those differences—probably not to the point where we can all agree on the burning issues of the day, but at least to where we can once again live and work together comfortably and productively.

Several of the writers in this chapter identify divisions that have arisen, and go further to pose possible ways to bridge the differences that divide us. Sean Blanda, writer and technology entrepreneur, suggests that we show compassion and respect for "the other side," his term for how we label people who don't think exactly the way we do. And danah boyd, a researcher who examines the intersection of technology and society, reveals how Americans have self-segregated in recent decades—online, in college, in the military, and at work—arguing that "we must find a healthy way to diversify our social connections." College student Gabriela Moro explores the role of minority student clubs on college campuses. She finds that, while such organizations offer a positive environment for their members, such clubs should be supplemented with initiatives that offer students opportunities to meet and interact across groups.

Other writers in this chapter analyze the attitudes and backgrounds of particular groups that many see as having been left behind. Robert Leonard, a news reporter from Iowa, writes about the economic hardships and political frustrations that he believes have led many Americans living in rural parts of the country to a conservative ideology and a deep distrust of people they see as liberals. In telling his own story, author J. D. Vance writes about growing up in Ohio and Kentucky and the sense of hopelessness that he believes is pervading his community. Legal scholar Michelle Alexander then takes us to prisons across America to describe the discrimination faced by incarcerated members of our society, who, as she argues, are overwhelmingly African American. This prison system is at the root of what she calls "the new Jim Crow." Joseph E. Stiglitz, a Nobel Prize–winning economist, uses tax and income data to demonstrate that the US tax system continues to favor the wealthiest 1 percent of our population, to the serious detriment of the rest of us. Finally, former president Barack Obama, in a commencement speech at Howard University, urges young people to get involved in politics—to cast votes and not just write hashtags—and, above all, to work with people from across the political spectrum.

As you read this chapter—and its companion blog, **theysayiblog.com**—you will have the opportunity to listen to a multitude of perspectives, think about and perhaps reconsider your own opinions, and make your own contribution to this vital, ongoing conversation.

The "Other Side" Is Not Dumb

SEAN BLANDA

—◻—

THERE'S A FUN GAME I like to play in a group of trusted friends called "Controversial Opinion." The rules are simple: Don't talk about what was shared during Controversial Opinion afterward and you aren't allowed to "argue"—only to ask questions about why that person feels that way. Opinions can range from "I think James Bond movies are overrated" to "I think Donald Trump would make an excellent president."

Usually, someone responds to an opinion with, "Oh my god! I had no idea you were one of *those* people!" Which is really another way of saying "I thought you were on my team!"

In psychology, the idea that everyone is like us is called the "false-consensus bias." This bias often manifests itself when we see TV ratings ("Who the hell are all these people that watch *NCIS?*") or in politics ("Everyone I know is for stricter gun

———

SEAN BLANDA is the author of *Hacking PR: A Guide for Boot-Strapped Startups* (2013) and the editor-in-chief of the websites *GrowthLab* and *I Will Teach You to Be Rich*, both of which advise entrepreneurs on business innovations. Blanda is also the cofounder of Technically, a startup based in Philadelphia that "grows local technology communities by connecting organizations and people through news, events, and services." This essay first appeared in *Medium*, a website for news and commentary.

control! Who are these backwards rubes that disagree?!") or polls ("Who are these people voting for Ben Carson?").

Online it means we can be blindsided by the opinions of our friends or, more broadly, America. Over time, this morphs into a subconscious belief that we and our friends are the sane ones and that there's a crazy "Other Side" that must be laughed at—an Other Side that just doesn't "get it," and is clearly not as intelligent as "us." But this holier-than-thou social media behavior is counterproductive; it's self-aggrandizement at the cost of actual nuanced discourse, and if we want to consider online discourse productive, we need to move past this.

What is emerging is the worst kind of echo chamber, one 5 where those inside are increasingly convinced that everyone shares their world view, that their ranks are growing when they aren't. It's like clockwork: an event happens and then your social media circle is shocked when a non–social media peer group public reacts to news in an unexpected way. They then mock the Other Side for being "out of touch" or "dumb."

Fredrik deBoer, one of my favorite writers around, touched on this in his essay "Getting Past the Coalition of the Cool." He writes:

> [The Internet] encourages people to collapse any distinction between their work life, their social life, and their political life. "Hey, that person who tweets about the TV shows I like also dislikes injustice," which over time becomes "I can identify an ally by the TV shows they like." The fact that you can mine a Rihanna video for political content becomes, in that vague internety way, the sense that people who don't see political content in Rihanna's music aren't on your side.

When someone communicates that they are not "on our side" our first reaction is to run away or dismiss them as stupid. To be sure, there are hateful, racist people not worthy of the small amount of electricity it takes [for] just one of your synapses to fire. I'm instead referencing those who actually believe in an opposing viewpoint of a complicated issue, and do so for genuine, considered reasons. Or at least, for reasons just as good as yours.

This is not a "political correctness" issue. It's a fundamental rejection of the possibility to consider that the people who don't feel the same way you do might be right. It's a preference to see

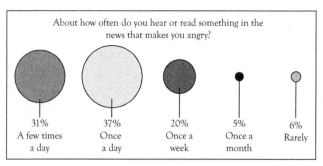

the Other Side as a cardboard cutout, and not the complicated individual human beings that they actually are.

What happens instead of genuine intellectual curiosity is the sharing of *Slate* or *Daily Kos* or *Fox News* or *Red State* links. Sites that exist almost solely to produce content to be shared so friends can pat each other on the back and mock the Other Side. Look at the Other Side! So dumb and unable to see this the way I do!

Sharing links that mock a caricature of the Other Side isn't signaling that we're somehow more informed. It signals that we'd rather be smug assholes than consider alternative views. It signals that we'd much rather show our friends that we're like them, than try to understand those who are not.

It's impossible to consider yourself a curious person and 10 participate in social media in this way. We cannot consider ourselves "empathetic" only to turn around and belittle those who don't agree with us.

On Twitter and Facebook this means we prioritize by sharing stuff that will garner approval of our peers over stuff that's actually, you know, true. We share stuff that ignores wider realities, selectively shares information, or is just an outright falsehood. The misinformation is so rampant that the *Washington Post* stopped publishing its Internet fact-checking column because people didn't seem to care if stuff was true.

> Where debunking an Internet fake once involved some research, it's now often as simple as clicking around for an "about" or "disclaimer" page. And where a willingness to believe hoaxes once seemed to come from a place of honest ignorance or misunderstanding, that's frequently no longer the case. Headlines like "Casey Anthony found dismembered in truck" go viral via old-fashioned schadenfreude—even hate.

...

Institutional distrust is so high right now, and cognitive bias so strong *always*, that the people who fall for hoax news stories are frequently only interested in consuming information that conforms with their views—even when it's demonstrably fake.

The solution, as deBoer says: "You have to be willing to sacrifice your carefully curated social performance and be willing to work with people who *are not like you.*" In other words you have to recognize that the Other Side is made of actual people.

But I'd like to go a step further. We should all enter every issue with the very real possibility that *we might be wrong this time.*

Isn't it possible that you, reader of *Medium* and Twitter power user, like me, suffer from this from time to time? Isn't it possible that we're not right about everything? That those who live in places not where you live, watch shows that you don't watch, and read books that you don't read, have opinions and belief systems just as valid as yours? That maybe you don't see the entire picture?

Think political correctness has gotten out of control? Follow the many great social activists on Twitter. Think America's stance on guns is puzzling? Read the stories of the 31% of Americans that own a firearm. This is not to say the Other Side is "right" but that they likely have real reasons to feel that way. And only after understanding those reasons can a real discussion take place.

See pp. 133–34 for ways to clarify and elaborate on your point.

As any debate club veteran knows, if you can't make your opponent's point for them, you don't truly grasp the issue. We can bemoan political gridlock and a divisive media all we want. But we won't truly progress as individuals until we make an honest effort to understand those that are not like us. And you won't convince anyone to feel the way you do if you don't respect their position and opinions.

A dare for the next time you're in a discussion with someone you disagree with: Don't try to "win." Don't try to "convince" anyone of your viewpoint. Don't score points by mocking them to your peers. Instead try to "lose." Hear them out. Ask them to convince you and mean it. No one is going to tell your environmentalist friends that you merely asked follow-up questions after your brother made his pro-fracking case.

Or, the next time you feel compelled to share a link on social media about current events, ask yourself why you are doing it. Is it because that link brings to light information you hadn't considered? Or does it confirm your world view, reminding your circle of intellectual teammates that you're not on the Other Side?

I implore you to seek out your opposite. When you hear someone cite "facts" that don't support your viewpoint don't think "that can't be true!" Instead consider, "Hm, maybe that person is right? I should look into this." Because refusing to truly understand those who disagree with you is intellectual laziness and worse, is *usually* worse than what you're accusing the Other Side of doing.

Joining the Conversation

1. Sean Blanda begins his essay by defining "false-consensus bias." Explain what this concept is, and give an example from your own experience or observation that you think demonstrates this bias.

2. In paragraph 6, Blanda introduces a quotation by Fredrik deBoer, but he doesn't follow it with an explanation. How would you recommend that Blanda do so? (See pp. 45–47 for ways to create a quotation sandwich.)

3. So what? Who cares? Where in this piece does Blanda explain why his argument matters? Has he persuaded you, and if not, why not?

4. Robert Leonard (pp. 315–21) examines why some Americans living in rural areas view liberals with disdain. What concrete suggestions do you think Blanda would make to encourage them to move beyond the stereotypes they might have of liberals?

5. Choose an issue of importance to you and write a tweet (280 characters or less) or a Facebook post that demonstrates respect for "the Other Side."

6. Go to **theysayiblog.com** and search for "(Alt) right and wrong" by Brendan Novak. How do Novak's views compare with Blanda's—how are they similar, and how are they different?

Why America Is Self-Segregating

DANAH BOYD

—◻︎—

THE UNITED STATES has always been a diverse but segregated country. This has shaped American politics profoundly. Yet, throughout history, Americans have had to grapple with divergent views and opinions, political ideologies, and experiences in order to function as a country. Many of the institutions that underpin American democracy force people in the United States to encounter difference. This does not inherently produce tolerance or result in healthy resolution. Hell, the history of the United States is fraught with countless examples of people enslaving and oppressing other people on the basis of difference. This isn't about our past; this is about our present. And today's battles over laws and culture are nothing new.

———

DANAH BOYD is a researcher at Microsoft Research and a visiting professor in New York University's interactive telecommunications program. She is the author of *It's Complicated: The Social Lives of Networked Teens* (2014) and the founder of Data & Society, a research institute "focused on the social and cultural issues arising from data-centric technological development." This essay first appeared in 2017 on *Points*, a blog of Data & Society.

Ironically, in a world in which we have countless tools to connect, we are also watching fragmentation, polarization, and de-diversification happen en masse. The American public is self-segregating, and this is tearing at the social fabric of the country.

Many in the tech world imagined that the Internet would connect people in unprecedented ways, allow for divisions to be bridged and wounds to heal. It was the kumbaya dream. Today, those same dreamers find it quite unsettling to watch as the tools that were designed to bring people together are used by people to magnify divisions and undermine social solidarity. These tools were built in a bubble, and that bubble has burst.

Nowhere is this more acute than with Facebook. Naive as hell, Mark Zuckerberg dreamed he could build the tools that would connect people at unprecedented scale, both domestically and internationally. I actually feel bad for him as he clings to that hope while facing increasing attacks from people around the world about the role that Facebook is playing in magnifying social divisions. Although critics love to paint him as only motivated by money, he genuinely wants to make the world a better place and sees Facebook as a tool to connect people, not empower them to self-segregate.

The problem is not simply the "filter bubble," Eli Pariser's 5 notion that personalization-driven algorithmic systems help silo people into segregated content streams. Facebook's claim that content personalization plays a small role in shaping what people see compared to their own choices is accurate. And they have every right to be annoyed. I couldn't imagine TimeWarner being blamed for who watches *Duck Dynasty* vs. *Modern Family*. And yet, what Facebook does do is mirror and magnify a trend that's been unfolding in the United States for the last twenty years, a trend of self-segregation that is enabled by technology in all sorts of complicated ways.

The United States can only function as a healthy democracy if we find a healthy way to diversify our social connections, if we find a way to weave together a strong social fabric that bridges ties across difference.

Yet, we are moving in the opposite direction with serious consequences. To understand this, let's talk about two contemporary trend lines and then think about the implications going forward.

See p. 137 for ways to provide a roadmap for your readers.

Privatizing the Military

The voluntary US military is, in many ways, a social engineering project. The public understands the military as a service organization, dedicated to protecting the country's interests. Yet, when recruits sign up, they are promised training and job opportunities. Individual motivations vary tremendously, but many are enticed by the opportunity to travel the world, participate in a cause with a purpose, and get the heck out of Dodge. Everyone expects basic training to be physically hard, but few recognize that some of the most grueling aspects of signing up have to do with the diversification project that is central to the formation of the American military.

When a soldier is in combat, she must trust her fellow soldiers with her life. And she must be willing to do what it takes to protect the rest of her unit. In order to make that possible, the military must wage war on prejudice. This is not an easy task. Plenty of generals fought hard to fight racial desegregation and to limit the role of women in combat. Yet, the US military was desegregated in 1948, six years before *Brown* v. *Board* forced desegregation of schools. And the Supreme Court ruled that LGB individuals could openly serve in the military before they could legally marry.

Morale is often raised as the main reason that soldiers should 10
not be forced to entrust their lives to people who are different
than them. Yet, time and again, this justification collapses under
broader interests to grow the military. As a result, commanders are
forced to find ways to build up morale across difference, to actively
and intentionally seek to break down barriers to teamwork, and to
find a way to gel a group of people whose demographics, values,
politics, and ideologies are as varied as the country's.

In the process, they build one of the most crucial social
infrastructures of the country. They build the diverse social
fabric that underpins democracy.

Tons of money was poured into defense after 9/11, but the
number of people serving in the US military today is far lower
than it was throughout the 1980s. Why? Starting in the 1990s
and accelerating after 9/11, the US privatized huge chunks of the
military. This means that private contractors and their employees
play critical roles in everything from providing food services to
equipment maintenance to military housing. The impact of this

on the role of the military in society is significant. For example, this undermines recruits' ability to get training to develop critical skills that will be essential for them in civilian life. Instead, while serving on active duty, they spend a much higher amount of time on the front lines and in high-risk battle, increasing the likelihood that they will be physically or psychologically harmed. The impact on skills development and job opportunities is tremendous, but so is the impact on the diversification of the social fabric.

Private vendors are not engaged in the same social engineering project as the military and, as a result, tend to hire and fire people based on their ability to work effectively as a team. Like many companies, they have little incentive to invest in helping diverse teams learn to work together as effectively as possible. Building diverse teams—especially ones in which members depend on each other for their survival—is extremely hard, time-consuming, and emotionally exhausting. As a result, private companies focus on "culture fit," emphasize teams that get along, and look for people who already have the necessary skills, all of which helps reinforce existing segregation patterns.

The end result is that, in the last 20 years, we've watched one of our major structures for diversification collapse without anyone taking notice. And because of how it's happened, it's also connected to job opportunities and economic opportunity for many working- and middle-class individuals, seeding resentment and hatred.

A Self-Segregated College Life

If you ask a college admissions officer at an elite institution 15 to describe how they build a class of incoming freshman, you will quickly realize that the American college system is a diversification project. Unlike colleges in most parts of the world, the vast majority of freshman at top tier universities in the United States live on campus with roommates who are assigned to them. Colleges approach housing assignments as an opportunity to pair diverse strangers with one another to build social ties. This makes sense given how many friendships emerge out of freshman dorms. By pairing middle class kids with students from wealthier families, elite institutions help diversify the elites of the future.

This diversification project produces a tremendous amount of conflict. Although plenty of people adore their college roommates and relish the opportunity to get to know people from different walks of life as part of their college experience, there is an amazing amount of angst about dorm assignments and the troubles that brew once folks try to live together in close quarters. At many universities, residential life is often in the business of student therapy as students complain about their roommates and dormmates. Yet, just like in the military, learning how to negotiate conflict and diversity in close quarters can be tremendously effective in sewing the social fabric.

In the spring of 2006, I was doing fieldwork with teenagers at a time when they had just received acceptances to college. I giggled at how many of them immediately wrote to the college in which they intended to enroll, begging for a campus email address so that they could join that school's Facebook (before Facebook was broadly available). In the previous year, I had watched the previous class look up roommate assignments on MySpace so I was prepared for the fact that they'd use Facebook to do the same. What I wasn't prepared for was how quickly they would all get on Facebook, map the incoming freshman class, and use this information to ask for a roommate switch. Before they even arrived on campus in August/September of 2006, they had self-segregated as much as possible.

A few years later, I watched another trend hit: cell phones. While these were touted as tools that allowed students to stay connected to parents (which prompted many faculty to complain about "helicopter parents" arriving on campus), they really ended up serving as a crutch to address homesickness, as incoming students focused on maintaining ties to high school friends rather than building new relationships.

Students go to elite universities to "get an education." Few realize that the true quality product that elite colleges in the US have historically offered is social network diversification. Even when it comes to job acquisition, sociologists have long known that diverse social networks ("weak ties") are what increase job prospects. By self-segregating on campus, students undermine their own potential while also helping fragment the diversity of the broader social fabric.

Diversity Is Hard

Diversity is often touted as highly desirable. Indeed, in professional contexts, we know that more diverse teams often outperform homogeneous teams. Diversity also increases cognitive development, both intellectually and socially. And yet, actually encountering and working through diverse viewpoints, experiences, and perspectives is hard work. It's uncomfortable. It's emotionally exhausting. It can be downright frustrating.

Thus, given the opportunity, people typically revert to situations where they can be in homogeneous environments. They look for "safe spaces" and "culture fit." And systems that are "personalized" are highly desirable. Most people aren't looking to self-segregate, but they do it anyway. And, increasingly, the technologies and tools around us allow us to self-segregate with ease. Is your uncle annoying you with his political rants? Mute him. Tired of getting ads for irrelevant products? Reveal your preferences. Want your search engine to remember the things that matter to you? Let it capture data. Want to watch a TV show that appeals to your senses? Here are some recommendations.

Any company whose business model is based on advertising revenue and attention is incentivized to engage you by giving you what you want. And what you want in theory is different than what you want in practice.

Consider, for example, what Netflix encountered when it started its streaming offer. Users didn't watch the movies that they had placed into their queue. Those movies were the movies they thought they wanted, movies that reflected their ideal self—*12 Years a Slave*, for example. What they watched when they could stream whatever they were in the mood for at that moment was the equivalent of junk food—reruns of *Friends*, for example. (This completely undid Netflix's recommendation

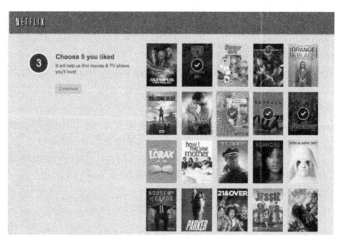

Netflix recommends shows to its users based on what they have already watched.

infrastructure, which had been trained on people's idealistic self-images.)

The divisions are not just happening through commercialism though. School choice has led people to self-segregate from childhood on up. The structures of American work life mean that fewer people work alongside others from different socioeconomic backgrounds. Our contemporary culture of retail and service labor means that there's a huge cultural gap between workers and customers with little opportunity to truly get to know one another. Even many religious institutions are increasingly fragmented such that people have fewer interactions across diverse lines. (Just think about how there are now "family services" and "traditional services" which age-segregate.) In so many parts of public, civic, and professional life, we are self-segregating and the opportunities for doing so are increasing every day.

By and large, the American public wants to have strong 25 connections across divisions. They see the value politically and socially. But they're not going to work for it. And given the option, they're going to renew their license remotely, try to get out of jury duty, and use available data to seek out housing and schools that are filled with people like them. This is the conundrum we now face.

Many pundits remarked that, during the 2016 election season, very few Americans were regularly exposed to people whose political ideology conflicted with their own. This is true. But it cannot be fixed by Facebook or news media. Exposing people to content that challenges their perspective doesn't actually make them more empathetic to those values and perspectives. To the contrary, it polarizes them. What makes people willing to hear difference is knowing and trusting people whose worldview differs from their own. Exposure to content cannot make up for self-segregation.

If we want to develop a healthy democracy, we need a diverse and highly connected social fabric. This requires creating contexts in which the American public voluntarily struggles with the challenges of diversity to build bonds that will last a lifetime. We have been systematically undoing this, and the public has used new technological advances to make their lives easier by self-segregating. This has increased polarization, and we're going to pay a heavy price for this going forward. Rather than focusing on what media enterprises can and should do, we need to focus instead on building new infrastructures for connection where people have a purpose for coming together across divisions. We need that social infrastructure just as much as we need bridges and roads.

Joining the Conversation

1. Writer danah boyd argues that, rather than becoming a more diverse nation, the United States is becoming a nation of self-contained identity groups. What evidence does she provide to support her argument? In what ways does your own experience support or challenge boyd's view?

2. In paragraph 4, boyd writes that Mark Zuckerberg is "naive as hell," using language that is informal, especially in contrast to her discussion of "fragmentation, polarization, and de-diversification," which is happening "en masse" (paragraph 2). How does this blend of styles affect your response to the essay?

3. According to boyd, we like the idea of diversity, but we're not willing to work for it (paragraph 25). How do you think Sean Blanda (pp. 248–54) or Barack Obama (pp. 332–49) might respond?

4. Write an essay responding to boyd, drawing on your own experiences in college, online, in the military, or with something else. Frame your argument as a response to boyd.

5. Self-segregation in college life is a topic on the minds of other writers, too. Go to **theysayiblog.com** and search for Conor Friedersdorf. Read his essay on elitism in college dorms. What does he say about them?

The New Jim Crow

MICHELLE ALEXANDER

—◻—

JARVIOUS COTTON CANNOT VOTE. Like his father, grandfather, great-grandfather, and great-great-grandfather, he has been denied the right to participate in our electoral democracy. Cotton's family tree tells the story of several generations of black men who were born in the United States but who were denied the most basic freedom that democracy promises—the freedom to vote for those who will make the rules and laws that govern one's life. Cotton's great-great-grandfather could not vote as a slave. His great-grandfather was beaten to death by the Ku Klux Klan for attempting to vote. His grandfather was prevented from voting by Klan intimidation. His father was barred from voting by poll taxes and literacy tests. Today, Jarvious Cotton

———

MICHELLE ALEXANDER is a lawyer and scholar known for her work to protect civil rights. She has taught at Stanford Law School and has a joint appointment at Ohio State University's law school and its institute for the study of race and ethnicity. She has written opinion pieces for the *New York Times*, *Huffington Post*, *The Nation*, *Washington Post*, and *Los Angeles Times*, among other publications. She is the author of *The New Jim Crow: Mass Incarceration in the Age of Colorblindness* (2010); this selection is from the book's introduction.

cannot vote because he, like many black men in the United States, has been labeled a felon and is currently on parole.[1]

Cotton's story illustrates, in many respects, the old adage "The more things change, the more they remain the same." In each generation, new tactics have been used for achieving the same goals—goals shared by the Founding Fathers. Denying African Americans citizenship was deemed essential to the formation of the original union. Hundreds of years later, America is still not an egalitarian democracy. The arguments and rationalizations that have been trotted out in support of racial exclusion and discrimination in its various forms have changed and evolved, but the outcome has remained largely the same. An extraordinary percentage of black men in the United States are legally barred from voting today, just as they have been throughout most of American history. They are also subject to legalized discrimination in employment, housing, education, public benefits, and jury service, just as their parents, grandparents, and great-grandparents once were.

What has changed since the collapse of Jim Crow has less to do with the basic structure of our society than with the language we use to justify it. In the era of colorblindness, it is no longer socially permissible to use race, explicitly, as a justification for discrimination, exclusion, and social contempt. So we don't. Rather than rely on race, we use our criminal justice system to label people of color "criminals" and then engage in all the practices we supposedly left behind. Today it is perfectly legal to discriminate against criminals in nearly all the ways that it was once legal to discriminate against African Americans. Once you're labeled a felon, the old forms of discrimination— employment discrimination, housing discrimination, denial of the right to vote, denial of educational opportunity, denial of food stamps and other public benefits, and exclusion from jury service—are suddenly legal. As a criminal, you have scarcely more rights, and arguably less respect, than a black man living in Alabama at the height of Jim Crow. We have not ended racial caste in America; we have merely redesigned it.

I have reached these conclusions reluctantly. Ten years ago, I would have argued strenuously against the central claim made here—namely, that something akin to a racial caste system currently exists in the United States. Indeed, if Barack Obama had been elected president back then, I would have argued that his election marked the nation's triumph over racial caste—the final nail in the coffin of Jim Crow. My elation would have been tempered by the distance yet to be traveled to reach the promised land of racial justice in America, but my conviction that nothing remotely similar to Jim Crow exists in this country would have been steadfast.

Today my elation over Obama's election is tempered by a 5 far more sobering awareness. As an African American woman, with three young children who will never know a world in which a black man could not be president of the United States, I was beyond thrilled on election night. Yet when I walked out of the election night party, full of hope and enthusiasm, I was immediately reminded of the harsh realities of the New Jim Crow. A black man was on his knees in the gutter, hands cuffed behind his back, as several police officers stood around him talking, joking, and ignoring his human existence. People poured out of the building; many stared for a moment at the black man cowering in the street, and then averted their gaze. What did the election of Barack Obama mean for him?

Like many civil rights lawyers, I was inspired to attend law school by the civil rights victories of the 1950s and 1960s. Even in the face of growing social and political opposition to remedial policies such as affirmative action, I clung to the notion that the evils of Jim Crow are behind us and that, while we have a long way to go to fulfill the dream of an egalitarian, multiracial democracy, we have made real progress and are now struggling to hold on to the gains of the past. I thought my job as a civil rights lawyer was to join with the allies of racial progress to resist attacks on affirmative action and to eliminate the vestiges of Jim Crow segregation, including our still separate and unequal system of education. I understood the problems plaguing poor communities of color, including problems associated with crime and rising incarceration rates, to be a function of poverty and lack of access to quality education—the continuing legacy of slavery and Jim Crow. Never did I seriously consider the possibility that a new racial caste system was operating in this country. The new system had been developed and implemented swiftly, and it was largely invisible, even to people, like me, who spent most of their waking hours fighting for justice.

I first encountered the idea of a new racial caste system more than a decade ago, when a bright orange poster caught my eye. I was rushing to catch the bus, and I noticed a sign stapled to a telephone pole that screamed in large bold print: THE DRUG WAR IS THE NEW JIM CROW. I paused for a moment and skimmed the text of the flyer. Some radical group was holding a community meeting about police brutality, the new three-strikes law in California, and the expansion of America's prison system. The meeting was being held at a small community church a few blocks away; it had seating capacity for no more than fifty people. I sighed, and muttered to myself something like, "Yeah, the criminal justice system is racist in many ways, but it really doesn't help to make such an absurd comparison. People will just think you're crazy." I then crossed the street and hopped on the bus. I was headed to my new job, director of the Racial Justice Project of the American Civil Liberties Union (ACLU) in Northern California.

Michelle Alexander speaks about her book *The New Jim Crow*.

When I began my work at the ACLU, I assumed that the criminal justice system had problems of racial bias, much in the same way that all major institutions in our society are plagued with problems associated with conscious and unconscious bias. As a lawyer who had litigated numerous class-action employment-discrimination cases, I understood well the many ways in which racial stereotyping can permeate subjective decision-making processes at all levels of an organization, with devastating consequences. I was familiar with the challenges associated with reforming institutions in which racial stratification is thought to be normal—the natural consequence of differences in education, culture, motivation, and, some still believe, innate ability. While at the ACLU, I shifted my focus from employment discrimination to criminal justice reform and dedicated myself to the task of working with others to identify and eliminate racial bias whenever and wherever it reared its ugly head.

By the time I left the ACLU, I had come to suspect that I was wrong about the criminal justice system. It was not just another institution infected with racial bias but rather a different beast entirely. The activists who posted the sign on the telephone pole were not crazy; nor were the smattering of lawyers and advocates around the country who were beginning to connect the dots between our current system of mass incarceration and earlier forms of social control. Quite belatedly, I came to see that mass incarceration in the United States had, in fact, emerged as a stunningly comprehensive and well-disguised system of racialized social control that functions in a manner strikingly similar to Jim Crow.

In my experience, people who have been incarcerated rarely 10 have difficulty identifying the parallels between these systems of social control. Once they are released, they are often denied the right to vote, excluded from juries, and relegated to a racially segregated and subordinated existence. Through a web of laws, regulations, and informal rules, all of which are powerfully reinforced by social stigma, they are confined to the margins of mainstream society and denied access to the mainstream economy. They are legally denied the ability to obtain employment, housing, and public benefits—much as African Americans were once forced into a segregated, second-class citizenship in the Jim Crow era.

Those of us who have viewed that world from a comfortable distance—yet sympathize with the plight of the so-called underclass—tend to interpret the experience of those caught up in the criminal justice system primarily through the lens of popularized social science, attributing the staggering increase in incarceration rates in communities of color to the predictable, though unfortunate, consequences of poverty, racial segregation, unequal educational opportunities, and the presumed realities of the drug market, including the mistaken belief that most drug dealers are black or brown. Occasionally, in the course of my work, someone would make a remark suggesting that perhaps the War on Drugs is a racist conspiracy to put blacks back in their place. This type of remark was invariably accompanied by nervous laughter, intended to convey the impression that although the idea had crossed their minds, it was not an idea a reasonable person would take seriously.

Most people assume the War on Drugs was launched in response to the crisis caused by crack cocaine in inner-city See p. 25 for more ways to introduce something implied or assumed. neighborhoods. This view holds that the racial disparities in drug convictions and sentences, as well as the rapid explosion of the prison population, reflect nothing more than the government's zealous—but benign—efforts to address rampant drug crime in poor, minority neighborhoods. This view, while understandable, given the sensational media coverage of crack in the 1980s and 1990s, is simply wrong.

While it is true that the publicity surrounding crack cocaine led to a dramatic increase in funding for the drug war (as well as to sentencing policies that greatly exacerbated racial disparities in incarceration rates), there is no truth to the notion that the War on Drugs was launched in response to crack cocaine. President Ronald Reagan officially announced the current drug war in 1982, before crack became an issue in the media or a crisis in poor black neighborhoods. A few years after the drug war was declared, crack began to spread rapidly in the poor black neighborhoods of Los Angeles and later emerged in cities across the country.[2] The Reagan administration hired staff to publicize the emergence of crack cocaine in 1985 as part of a strategic effort to build public and legislative support for the war. The media campaign was an extraordinary success. Almost overnight, the media was saturated with images of black "crack whores," "crack dealers," and "crack babies"—images that seemed to confirm the worst negative

Then-President Ronald Reagan and his wife Nancy Reagan prepare for their
joint address, calling for a national campaign against drug abuse.

racial stereotypes about impoverished inner-city residents. The
media bonanza surrounding the "new demon drug" helped to
catapult the War on Drugs from an ambitious federal policy
to an actual war.

The timing of the crack crisis helped to fuel conspiracy theories and general speculation in poor black communities that the
War on Drugs was part of a genocidal plan by the government
to destroy black people in the United States. From the outset,
stories circulated on the street that crack and other drugs were

being brought into black neighborhoods by the CIA. Eventually, even the Urban League came to take the claims of genocide seriously. In its 1990 report "The State of Black America," it stated: "There is at least one concept that must be recognized if one is to see the pervasive and insidious nature of the drug problem for the African American community. Though difficult to accept, that is the concept of genocide."[3] While the conspiracy theories were initially dismissed as far-fetched, if not downright loony, the word on the street turned out to be right, at least to a point. The CIA admitted in 1998 that guerrilla armies it actively supported in Nicaragua were smuggling illegal drugs into the United States—drugs that were making their way onto the streets of inner-city black neighborhoods in the form of crack cocaine. The CIA also admitted that, in the midst of the War on Drugs, it blocked law enforcement efforts to investigate illegal drug networks that were helping to fund its covert war in Nicaragua.[4]*

It bears emphasis that the CIA never admitted (nor has any evidence been revealed to support the claim) that it intentionally sought the destruction of the black community by allowing illegal drugs to be smuggled into the United States. Nonetheless, conspiracy theorists surely must be forgiven for their bold accusation of genocide, in light of the devastation wrought by crack cocaine and the drug war, and the odd coincidence that an illegal drug crisis suddenly appeared in the black community after—not before—a drug war had been declared. In fact, the War on Drugs began at a time when illegal drug use was on the decline.[5] During this same time period, however, a war was

*__Covert war in Nicaragua__ In December 1981, then-President Ronald Reagan authorized the CIA to support the Contras, an opposition group that fought the Sandinistas, a revolutionary socialist group that the United States opposed in its fight against communism during the Cold War.

declared, causing arrests and convictions for drug offenses to skyrocket, especially among people of color.

The impact of the drug war has been astounding. In less than thirty years, the U.S penal population exploded from around 300,000 to more than 2 million, with drug convictions accounting for the majority of the increase.[6] The United States now has the highest rate of incarceration in the world, dwarfing the rates of nearly every developed country, even surpassing those in highly repressive regimes like Russia, China, and Iran. In Germany, 93 people are in prison for every 100,000 adults and children. In the United States, the rate is roughly eight times that, or 750 per 100,000.[7]

The racial dimension of mass incarceration is its most striking feature. No other country in the world imprisons so many of its racial or ethnic minorities. The United States imprisons a larger percentage of its black population than South Africa did at the height of apartheid. In Washington, D.C., our nation's capitol, it is estimated that three out of four young black men (and nearly all those in the poorest neighborhoods) can expect to serve time in prison.[8] Similar rates of incarceration can be found in black communities across America.

These stark racial disparities cannot be explained by rates of drug crime. Studies show that people of all colors *use and sell* illegal drugs at remarkably similar rates.[9] If there are significant differences in the surveys to be found, they frequently suggest that whites, particularly white youth, are more likely to engage in drug crime than people of color.[10] That is not what one would guess, however, when entering our nation's prisons and jails, which are overflowing with black and brown drug offenders. In some states, black men have been admitted to prison on drug charges at rates twenty to fifty times greater than those of white men.[11] And in major cities wracked by the drug war, as many as 80 percent of young African American men now have criminal records and are thus subject to legalized discrimination for the rest of their lives.[12] These young men are part of a growing undercaste, permanently locked up and locked out of mainstream society.

It may be surprising to some that drug crime was declining, not rising, when a drug war was declared. From a historical perspective, however, the lack of correlation between crime and punishment is nothing new. Sociologists have frequently observed that governments use punishment primarily as a tool of social control, and thus the extent or severity of punishment is often unrelated to actual crime patterns. Michael Tonry explains in *Thinking About Crime*: "Governments decide how much punishment they want, and these decisions are in no simple way related to crime rates."[13] This fact, he points out, can be seen most clearly by putting crime and punishment in comparative perspective. Although crime rates in the United States have not been markedly higher than those of other Western countries, the rate of incarceration has soared in the United States while it has remained stable or declined in other countries. Between 1960 and 1990, for example, official crime rates in Finland, Germany, and the United States were close to identical. Yet the U.S. incarceration rate quadrupled, the Finnish rate fell by 60 percent, and the German rate was stable in that period.[14] Despite similar crime rates, each government chose to impose different levels of punishment.

Today, due to recent declines, U.S. crime rates have dipped 20 below the international norm. Nevertheless, the United States now boasts an incarceration rate that is six to ten times greater than that of other industrialized nations[15]—a development directly traceable to the drug war. The only country in the world that even comes close to the American rate of incarceration is Russia, and no other country in the world incarcerates such an astonishing percentage of its racial or ethnic minorities.

The stark and sobering reality is that, for reasons largely unrelated to actual crime trends, the American penal system has emerged as a system of social control unparalleled in world history. And while the size of the system alone might suggest that it would touch the lives of most Americans, the primary targets of its control can be defined largely by race. This is an astonishing development, especially given that as recently as the mid-1970s, the most well-respected criminologists were predicting that the prison system would soon fade away. Prison did not deter crime significantly, many experts concluded. Those who had meaningful economic and social opportunities were unlikely to commit crimes regardless of the penalty, while those who went to prison were far more likely to commit crimes again in the future. The growing consensus among experts was perhaps best reflected by the National Advisory Commission on Criminal Justice Standards and Goals, which issued a recommendation in 1973 that "no new institutions for adults should be built and existing institutions for juveniles should be closed."[16] This recommendation was based on their finding that "the prison, the reformatory and the jail have achieved only a shocking record of failure. There is overwhelming evidence that these institutions create crime rather than prevent it."[17]

These days, activists who advocate "a world without prisons" are often dismissed as quacks, but only a few decades ago, the notion that our society would be much better off without prisons—and that the end of prisons was more or less inevitable—not only dominated mainstream academic discourse in the field of criminology but also inspired a national campaign by reformers demanding a moratorium on prison construction. Marc Mauer, the executive director of the Sentencing Project, notes that what is most remarkable about the moratorium campaign in retrospect is the context of imprisonment at the time. In 1972, fewer than 350,000 people were being held in prisons and jails nationwide, compared with more than 2 million people today. The rate of incarceration in 1972 was at a level so low that it no longer seems in the realm of possibility, but for moratorium supporters, that magnitude of imprisonment was egregiously high. "Supporters of the moratorium effort can be forgiven for being so naïve," Mauer suggests, "since the prison expansion that was about to take place was unprecedented in human history."[18] No one imagined that the prison population would more than quintuple in their lifetime. It seemed far more likely that prisons would fade away.

Far from fading away, it appears that prisons are here to stay. And despite the unprecedented levels of incarceration in the African American community, the civil rights community is oddly quiet. One in three young African American men will serve time in prison if current trends continue, and in some cities more than half of all young adult black men are currently under correctional control—in prison or jail, on probation or parole.[19] Yet mass incarceration tends to be categorized as a criminal justice issue as opposed to a racial justice or civil rights issue (or crisis).

The attention of civil rights advocates has been largely devoted to other issues, such as affirmative action. During the past twenty years, virtually every progressive, national civil rights organization in the country has mobilized and rallied in defense of affirmative action. The struggle to preserve affirmative action in higher education, and thus maintain diversity in the nation's most elite colleges and universities, has consumed much of the attention and resources of the civil rights community and dominated racial justice discourse in the mainstream media, leading the general public to believe that affirmative action is the main battlefront in U.S. race relations—even as our prisons fill with black and brown men. . . .

This is not to say that important criminal justice reform work 25 has not been done. Civil rights advocates have organized vigorous challenges to specific aspects of the new caste system. One notable example is the successful challenge led by the NAACP Legal Defense Fund to a racist drug sting operation in Tulia, Texas. The 1999 drug bust incarcerated almost 15 percent of the black population of the town, based on the uncorroborated false testimony of a single informant hired by the sheriff of Tulia. More recently, civil rights groups around the country have helped to launch legal attacks and vibrant grassroots campaigns against felon disenfranchisement laws and have strenuously opposed discriminatory crack sentencing laws and guidelines, as well as "zero tolerance" policies that effectively funnel youth of color from schools to jails. The national ACLU recently developed a racial justice program that includes criminal justice issues among its core priorities and has created a promising Drug Law Reform Project. And thanks to the aggressive advocacy of the ACLU, NAACP, and other civil rights organizations around the country, racial profiling is widely condemned, even by members of law enforcement who once openly embraced the practice.

Still, despite these significant developments, there seems to be a lack of appreciation for the enormity of the crisis at hand. There is no broad-based movement brewing to end mass incarceration and no advocacy effort that approaches in scale the fight to preserve affirmative action. There also remains a persistent tendency in the civil rights community to treat the criminal justice system as just another institution infected with lingering racial bias. The NAACP's Web site offers one example. As recently as May 2008, one could find a brief introduction to the organization's criminal justice work in the section entitled Legal Department. The introduction explained that "despite the civil rights victories of our past, racial prejudice still pervades the criminal justice system." Visitors to the Web site were urged to join the NAACP in order to "protect the hard-earned civil rights gains of the past three decades." No one visiting the Web site would learn that the mass incarceration of African Americans had already eviscerated many of the hard-earned gains it urged its members to protect.

Imagine if civil rights organizations and African American leaders in the 1940s had not placed Jim Crow segregation at the forefront of their racial justice agenda. It would have seemed absurd, given that racial segregation was the primary vehicle of racialized social control in the United States during that period. Mass incarceration is, metaphorically, the New Jim Crow and all those who care about social justice should fully commit themselves to dismantling this new racial caste system. Mass incarceration—not attacks on affirmative action or lax civil rights enforcement—is the most damaging manifestation of the backlash against the Civil Rights Movement. The popular narrative that emphasizes the death of slavery and Jim Crow and celebrates the nation's "triumph over race" with the election of Barack Obama, is dangerously misguided. The colorblind public consensus that prevails in America today—i.e., the widespread belief that race no longer matters—has blinded us to the realities of race in our society and facilitated the emergence of a new caste system.

. . .

The language of caste may well seem foreign or unfamiliar to some. Public discussions about racial caste in America are relatively rare. We avoid talking about caste in our society because we are ashamed of our racial history. We also avoid talking about race. We even avoid talking about class. Conversations about class are resisted in part because there is a tendency to imagine that one's class reflects upon one's character. What is key to America's understanding of class is the persistent belief—despite all evidence to the contrary—that anyone, with the proper discipline and drive, can move from a lower class to a higher class. We recognize that mobility may be difficult, but the key to our collective self-image is the assumption that mobility is always possible, so failure to move up reflects on one's character. By extension, the failure of a race or ethnic group to move up reflects very poorly on the group as a whole.

What is completely missed in the rare public debates today about the plight of African Americans is that a huge percentage of them are not free to move up at all. It is not just that they lack opportunity, attend poor schools, or are plagued by poverty. They are barred by law from doing so. And the major institutions with which they come into contact are designed to prevent their mobility. To put the matter starkly: The current system of control permanently locks a huge percentage of the African American community out of the mainstream society and economy. The system operates through our criminal justice institutions, but it functions more like a caste system than a system of crime control. Viewed from this perspective, the so-called underclass is better understood as an *undercaste*—a lower caste of individuals who are permanently barred by law and custom from mainstream society. Although this new system of racialized social control purports to be colorblind, it creates and maintains racial hierarchy much as earlier systems of control did. Like Jim Crow (and slavery), mass incarceration operates as a tightly networked system of laws, policies, customs, and institutions that operate collectively to ensure the subordinate status of a group defined largely by race. . . .

Skepticism about the claims made here is warranted. There are 30 important differences, to be sure, among mass incarceration, Jim Crow, and slavery—the three major racialized systems of control adopted in the United States to date. Failure to acknowledge the relevant differences, as well as their implications, would be a disservice to racial justice discourse. Many of the differences are not as dramatic as they initially appear, however; others serve to illustrate the ways in which systems of racialized social control have managed to morph, evolve, and adapt to changes in the political, social, and legal context over time. Ultimately, I believe that the similarities between these systems of control overwhelm the differences and that mass incarceration, like its predecessors, has been largely immunized from legal challenge. If this claim is substantially correct, the implications for racial justice advocacy are profound.

For more on ways to address a skeptical reader, see Chapter 6.

With the benefit of hindsight, surely we can see that piece-meal policy reform or litigation alone would have been a futile approach to dismantling Jim Crow segregation. While those strategies certainly had their place, the Civil Rights Act of 1964 and the concomitant cultural shift would never have occurred without the cultivation of a critical political consciousness in the African American community and the widespread, strategic activism that flowed from it. Likewise, the notion that the New Jim Crow can ever be dismantled through traditional litigation and policy-reform strategies that are wholly disconnected from a major social movement seems fundamentally misguided.

Such a movement is impossible, though, if those most committed to abolishing racial hierarchy continue to talk and behave as if a state-sponsored racial caste system no longer exists. If we continue to tell ourselves the popular myths about racial progress or, worse yet, if we say to ourselves that the problem of mass incarceration is just too big, too daunting for us to do anything about and that we should instead direct our energies to battles that might be more easily won, history will judge us harshly. A human rights nightmare is occurring on our watch.

A new social consensus must be forged about race and the role of race in defining the basic structure of our society, if we hope ever to abolish the New Jim Crow. This new consensus must begin with dialogue, a conversation that fosters a critical consciousness, a key prerequisite to effective social action. My writing is an attempt to ensure that the conversation does not end with nervous laughter.

NOTES

1. Jarvious Cotton was a plaintiff in *Cotton v. Fordice*, 157 F.3d 388 (5th Cir. 1998), which held that Mississippi's felon disenfranchisement provision had lost its racially discriminatory taint. The information regarding Cotton's family tree was obtained by Emily Bolton on March 29, 1999, when she interviewed Cotton at Mississippi State Prison. Jarvious Cotton was released on parole in Mississippi, a state that denies voting rights to parolees.

2. The *New York Times* made the national media's first specific reference to crack in a story published in late 1985. Crack became known in a few impoverished neighborhoods in Los Angeles, New York, and Miami in early 1986. See Craig Reinarman and Harry Levine, "The Crack Attack: America's Latest Drug Scare, 1986–1992," in *Images of Issues: Typifying Contemporary Social Problems* (New York: Aldine De Gruyter, 1995), 152.

3. Clarence Page, "'The Plan': A Paranoid View of Black Problems," *Dover* (Delaware) *Herald*, Feb. 23, 1990. See also Manning Marable, *Race, Reform, and Rebellion: The Second Reconstruction in Black America, 1945–1990* (Jackson: University Press of Mississippi, 1991), 212–13.

4. See Alexander Cockburn and Jeffrey St. Clair, *Whiteout: The CIA, Drugs, and the Press* (New York: Verso, 1999). See also Nick Shou, "The Truth in 'Dark Alliance,'" *Los Angeles Times*, Aug. 18, 2006; Peter Kornbluh, "CIA's Challenge in South Central." *Los Angeles Times* (Washington edition), Nov. 15, 1996; and Alexander Cockburn, "Why They Hated Gary Webb," *The Nation*, Dec. 16, 2004.

5. Katherine Beckett and Theodore Sasson, *The Politics of Injustice: Crime and Punishment in America* (Thousand Oaks, CA: Sage Publications, 2004), 163.

6. Marc Mauer, *Race to Incarcerate*, rev. ed. (New York: The New Press, 2006), 33.

7. PEW Center on the States, *One in 100: Behind Bars in America 2008* (Washington, DC: PEW Charitable Trusts, 2008), 5.

8. Donald Braman, *Doing Time on the Outside: Incarceration and Family Life in Urban America* (Ann Arbor: University of Michigan Press, 2004), 3, citing D.C. Department of Corrections data for 2000.

9. See, e.g., U.S. Department of Health and Human Services, Substance Abuse and Mental Health Services Administration, *Summary of Findings from the 2000 National Household Survey on Drug Abuse*, NHSDA series H-13, DHHS pub. no. SMA 01-3549 (Rockville, MD: 2001), reporting that 6.4 percent of whites, 6.4 percent of blacks, and 5.3 percent of Hispanics were current users of illegal drugs in 2000; *Results from the 2002 National Survey on Drug Use and Health: National Findings*, NHSDA series H-22, DHHS pub. no. SMA 03-3836 (2003), revealing nearly identical rates of illegal drug use among whites and blacks, only a single percentage point between them; and *Results from the 2007 National Survey on Drug Use and Health: National Findings*, NSDUH series H-34, DHHS pub. no. SMA 08-4343 (2007), showing essentially the same finding. See also Marc Mauer and Ryan S. King, *A 25-Year Quagmire: The "War on Drugs" and Its Impact on American Society* (Washington, DC: Sentencing Project, 2007), 19, citing a study suggesting that African Americans have slightly higher rates of illegal drug use than whites.

10. See, e.g., Howard N. Snyder and Melissa Sickman, *Juvenile Offenders and Victims: 2006 National Report*, U.S. Department of Justice, Office of Justice Programs, Office of Juvenile Justice and Delinquency Prevention (Washington, DC: U.S. Department of Justice, 2006), reporting that white youth are more likely than black youth to engage in illegal drug sales. See also Lloyd D. Johnson, Patrick M. O'Malley, Jerald G. Bachman, and John E. Schulunberg, *Monitoring the Future, National Survey Results on Drug Use, 1975–2006, vol. 1, Secondary School Students*, U.S. Department of Health and Human Services, National Institute on Drug Abuse, NIH pub. no. 07-6205 (Bethesda, MD: 2007), 32, "African American 12th graders have consistently shown lower usage rates than White 12th graders for most drugs, both licit and illicit"; and Lloyd D. Johnston, Patrick M. O'Malley, and Jerald G. Bachman, *Monitoring the Future: National Results on Adolescent Drug Use: Overview of Key Findings 2002*, U.S. Department of Health and Human Services, National Institute on

Drug Abuse, NIH pub. no. 03-5374 (Bethesda, MD: 2003), presenting data showing that African American adolescents have slightly lower rates of illicit drug use than their white counterparts.

11. Human Rights Watch, *Punishment and Prejudice: Racial Disparities in the War on Drugs*, HRW Reports, vol. 12, no. 2 (New York, 2000).

12. See, e.g., Paul Street, *The Vicious Circle: Race, Prison, Jobs, and Community in Chicago, Illinois, and the Nation* (Chicago: Chicago Urban League, Department of Research and Planning, 2002).

13. Michael Tonry, *Thinking About Crime: Sense and Sensibility in American Penal Culture* (New York: Oxford University Press, 2004), 14.

14. Ibid.

15. Ibid., 20.

16. National Advisory Commission on Criminal Justice Standards and Goals, *Task Force Report on Corrections* (Washington, DC: Government Printing Office, 1973), 358.

17. Ibid., 597.

18. Mauer, *Race to Incarcerate*, 17–18.

19. The estimate that one in three black men will go to prison during their lifetime is drawn from Thomas P. Boncszar, "Prevalence of Imprisonment in the U.S. Population, 1974–2001," U.S. Department of Justice, Bureau of Justice Statistics, August 2003. In Baltimore, like many large urban areas, the majority of young African American men are currently under correctional supervision. See Eric Lotke and Jason Ziedenberg, "Tipping Point: Maryland's Overuse of Incarceration and the Impact on Community Safety," Justice Policy Institute, March 2005, 3.

Joining the Conversation

1. Michelle Alexander argues that in the United States mass incarceration is a "well-disguised system of racialized social control" (paragraph 9). Why, as she acknowledges in paragraph 4, did it take her so long to reach this conclusion?

2. Throughout the essay, Alexander presents and then responds to the views of others. Find two examples where Alexander introduces the views of others. In each case, how does she make clear to readers that the view in question is not hers?

3. The author states that "the racial dimension of mass incarceration is its most striking feature" (paragraph 17). What does she mean, and what evidence does she provide to support her claim?

4. According to Alexander, African Americans "are not free to move up at all" (paragraph 29) and "the more things change the more they stay the same." What do you think Barack Obama (pp. 332–49) would say to that?

5. Write an essay responding to the reading in which you agree, disagree, or both with the author's argument that mass incarceration allows for continued discrimination against African Americans.

Hillbilly Elegy

J. D. VANCE

———◻———

I ARRIVED FOR ORIENTATION at Ohio State in early September 2007, and I couldn't have been more excited. I remember every little detail about that day: lunch at Chipotle, the first time Lindsay* had ever eaten there; the walk from the orientation building to the south campus house that would soon be my Columbus home; the beautiful weather. I met with a guidance counselor who talked me through my first college schedule, which put me in class only four days per week, never before nine thirty in the morning. After the Marine Corps and its five thirty A.M. wake-ups, I couldn't believe my good fortune.

Ohio State's main campus in Columbus is about a hundred miles away from Middletown, meaning it was close enough for weekend visits to my family. For the first time in a few years, I could drop

———

J. D. VANCE works at an investment firm in Silicon Valley and has written articles for the *National Review* and the *New York Times*. He is the author of *Hillbilly Elegy: A Memoir of a Family and Culture in Crisis* (2016), which describes his experiences growing up in Jackson, Kentucky and Middletown, Ohio. The selection reprinted here is a chapter from that book.

*Lindsay Vance's sister.

in on Middletown whenever I felt like it. And while Havelock (the North Carolina city closest to my Marine Corps base) was not too different from Middletown, Columbus felt like an urban paradise. It was (and remains) one of the fastest-growing cities in the country, powered in large part by the bustling university that was now my home. OSU grads were starting businesses, historic buildings were being converted into new restaurants and bars, and even the worst neighborhoods seemed to be undergoing significant revitalization. Not long after I moved to Columbus, one of my best friends began working as the promotions director for a local radio station, so I always knew what was happening around town and always had an in to the city's best events, from local festivals to VIP seating for the annual fireworks show.

In many ways, college was very familiar. I made a lot of new friends, but virtually all of them were from southwest Ohio. My six roommates included five graduates of Middletown High School and one graduate of Edgewood High School in nearby Trenton. They were a little younger (the Marine Corps had aged me past the age of the typical freshman), but I knew most of them from back home. My closest friends had already graduated or were about to, but many stayed in Columbus after graduation. Though I didn't know it, I was witnessing a phenomenon that social scientists call "brain drain"—people who are able to leave struggling cities often do, and when they find a new home with educational and work opportunities, they stay there. Years later, I looked at my wedding party of six groomsmen and realized that every single one of them had, like me, grown up in a small Ohio town before leaving for Ohio State. To a man, all of them had found careers outside of their hometowns, and none of them had any interest in ever going back.

By the time I started at Ohio State, the Marine Corps had instilled in me an incredible sense of invincibility. I'd go to classes, do my homework, study at the library, and make it home in time to drink well past midnight with my buddies, then wake up early to go running. My schedule was intense, but everything that had made me fear the independent college life when I was eighteen felt like a piece of cake now. I had puzzled through those financial aid forms with Mamaw* a few years earlier, arguing about whether to list her or Mom as my "parent/guardian." We had worried that unless I somehow obtained and submitted the financial information of Bob Hamel (my legal father), I'd be guilty of fraud. The whole experience had made both of us painfully aware of how unfamiliar we were with the outside world. I had nearly failed out of high school, earning Ds and Fs in English I. Now I paid my own bills and earned As in every class I took at my state's flagship university. I felt completely in control of my destiny in a way that I never had before.

I knew that Ohio State was put-up-or-shut-up time. I had left 5 the Marine Corps not just with a sense that I could do what I wanted but also with the capacity to plan. I wanted to go to law school, and I knew that to go to the best law school, I'd need good grades and to ace the infamous Law School Admissions Test, or LSAT. There was much I didn't know, of course. I couldn't really explain why I wanted to go to law school besides the fact that in Middletown the "rich kids" were born to either doctors or lawyers, and I didn't want to work with blood. I didn't know how much else was out there, but the little knowledge I had at least gave me direction, and that was all I needed.

I loathed debt and the sense of limitation it imposed. Though the GI Bill paid for a significant chunk of my education, and Ohio State charged relatively little to an in-state resident, I still needed to cover about twenty thousand dollars of expenses

***Mamaw** Vance's grandmother.

on my own. I took a job at the Ohio Statehouse, working for a remarkably kind senator from the Cincinnati area named Bob Schuler. He was a good man, and I liked his politics, so when constituents called and complained, I tried to explain his positions. I watched lobbyists come and go and overheard the senator and his staff debate whether a particular bill was good for his constituents, good for his state, or good for both. Observing the political process from the inside made me appreciate it in a way that watching cable news never had. Mamaw had thought all politicians were crooks, but I learned that, no matter their politics, that was largely untrue at the Ohio Statehouse.

After a few months at the Ohio Senate, as my bills piled up and I found fewer and fewer ways to make up the difference between my spending and my income (one can donate plasma only twice per week, I learned), I decided to get another job. One nonprofit advertised a part-time job that paid ten dollars an hour, but when I showed up for the interview in khakis, an ugly lime-green shirt, and Marine Corps combat boots (my only non-sneakers at the time) and saw the interviewer's reaction, I knew that I was out of luck. I barely noticed the rejection email a week later. A local nonprofit did work for abused and neglected children, and they also paid ten dollars an hour, so I went to Target, bought a nicer shirt and a pair of black shoes, and came away with a job offer to be a "consultant." I cared about their mission, and they were great people. I began work immediately.

With two jobs and a full-time class load, my schedule intensified, but I didn't mind. I didn't realize there was anything unusual about my commitments until a professor emailed me about meeting after class to discuss a writing assignment. When I sent him my schedule, he was aghast. He sternly told me that I should focus on my education and not let work distractions stand in my way. I smiled, shook his hand, and said thanks, but I did not heed his advice. I liked staying up late to work on assignments, waking up early after only three or four hours of sleep, and patting myself on the back for being able to do it. After so many years of fearing my own future, of worrying that I'd end up like many of my neighbors or family—addicted to drugs or alcohol, in prison, or with kids I couldn't or wouldn't take care of—I felt an incredible momentum. I knew the statistics. I had read the brochures in the social worker's office when I was a kid. I had recognized the look of pity from the hygienist at the low-income dental clinic. I wasn't supposed to make it, but I was doing just fine on my own.

Did I take it too far? Absolutely. I didn't sleep enough. I drank too much and ate Taco Bell at nearly every meal. A week into what I thought was just a really awful cold, a doctor told me that I had mono. I ignored him and kept on living as though NyQuil and DayQuil were magical elixirs. After a week of this, my urine turned a disgusting brown shade, and my temperature registered 103. I realized I might need to take care of myself, so I downed some Tylenol, drank a couple of beers, and went to sleep.

When Mom found out what was happening, she drove to 10 Columbus and took me to the emergency room. She wasn't perfect, she wasn't even a practicing nurse, but she took it as a point of pride to supervise every interaction we had with the health care system. She asked the right questions, got annoyed with doctors when they didn't answer directly, and made sure I had what I needed. I spent two full days in the hospital as doctors emptied five bags of saline to rehydrate me and discovered that I had contracted a staph infection in addition to the mono, which explained why I grew so sick. The doctors released me to Mom, who wheeled me out of the hospital and took me home to recover.

My illness lasted another few weeks, which, happily, coincided with the break between Ohio State's spring and summer terms. When I was in Middletown, I split time between Aunt Wee's and Mom's; both of them cared for me and treated me like a son. It was my first real introduction to the competing emotional demands of Middletown in a post-Mamaw world: I didn't want to hurt Mom's feelings, but the past had created rifts that would likely never go away. I never confronted these demands head-on. I never explained to Mom that no matter how nice and caring she was at any given time—and while I had mono, she couldn't have been a better mother—I just felt uncomfortable around her. To sleep in her house meant talking to husband number five, a kind man but a stranger who would never be anything to me but the future ex–Mr. Mom. It meant looking at her furniture and remembering the time I hid behind it during one of her fights with Bob. It meant trying to understand how Mom could be such a contradiction—a woman who sat patiently with me at the hospital for days and an addict who would lie to her family to extract money from them a month later.

I knew that my increasingly close relationship with Aunt Wee hurt Mom's feelings. She talked about it all the time. "I'm your mother, not her," she'd repeat. To this day, I often wonder whether, if I'd had the courage as an adult that I'd had as a child, Mom might have gotten better. Addicts are at their weakest during emotionally trying times, and I knew that I had the power to save her from at least some bouts of sadness. But I couldn't do it any longer. I didn't know what had changed, but I wasn't that person anymore. Perhaps it was nothing more than self-preservation. Regardless, I couldn't pretend to feel at home with her.

After a few weeks of mono, I felt well enough to return to Columbus and my classes. I'd lost a lot of weight—twenty pounds over four weeks—but otherwise felt pretty good. With the hospital bills piling up, I got a third job (as an SAT tutor at the Princeton Review), which paid an incredible eighteen dollars an hour. Three jobs were too much, so I dropped the job I loved the most—my work at the Ohio senate—because it paid the least. I needed money and the financial freedom it provided, not rewarding work. That, I told myself, would come later.

Shortly before I left, the Ohio senate debated a measure that would significantly curb payday-lending practices. My senator opposed the bill (one of the few senators to do so), and though he never explained why, I liked to think that maybe he and I had something in common. The senators and policy staff debating the bill had little appreciation for the role of payday lenders in the shadow economy that people like me occupied. To them, payday lenders were predatory sharks, charging high interest rates on loans and exorbitant fees for cashed checks. The sooner they were snuffed out, the better.

To me, payday lenders could solve important financial prob- 15 lems. My credit was awful, thanks to a host of terrible financial decisions (some of which weren't my fault, many of which were), so credit cards weren't a possibility. If I wanted to take a girl out to dinner or needed a book for school and didn't have money in the bank, I didn't have many options. (I probably could have asked my aunt or uncle, but I desperately wanted to do things on my own.) One Friday morning I dropped off my rent check, knowing that if I waited another day, the fifty-dollar late fee would kick in. I didn't have enough money to cover the check, but I'd get paid that day and would be able to deposit the money after work. However, after a long day at the senate, I forgot to grab my paycheck before I left. By the time I realized the mistake, I was already home, and the Statehouse staff had left for the weekend. On that day, a three-day payday loan, with a few dollars of interest, enabled me to avoid a significant overdraft fee. The legislators debating the merits of payday lending didn't mention situations like that. The lesson? Powerful people sometimes do things to help people like me without really understanding people like me.

My second year of college started pretty much as my first year had, with a beautiful day and a lot of excitement. With a new job, I was a bit busier, but I didn't mind the work. What I did mind was the gnawing feeling that, at twenty-four, I was a little too old to be a second-year college student. But with four years in the Marine Corps behind me, more separated me from the other students than age. During an undergraduate seminar in foreign policy, I listened as a nineteen-year-old classmate with a hideous beard spouted off about the Iraq war. He explained that those fighting the war were typically less intelligent than those (like him) who immediately went to college. It showed, he argued, in the wanton way soldiers butchered and disrespected Iraqi civilians. It was an objectively terrible opinion—my friends from the Marine Corps spanned the political spectrum and held nearly every conceivable opinion about the war. Many of my Marine Corps friends were staunch liberals who had no love for our commander in chief—then George W. Bush—and felt that we had sacrificed too much for too little gain. But none of them had ever uttered such unreflective tripe.

As the student prattled on, I thought about the never-ending training on how to respect Iraqi culture—never show anyone the bottom of your foot, never address a woman in traditional Muslim garb without first speaking to a male relative. I thought about the security we provided for Iraqi poll workers, and how we studiously explained the importance of their mission without ever pushing our own political views on them. I thought about listening to a young Iraqi (who couldn't

See pp. 110–12 for ways to repeat key terms and phrases.

speak a word of English) flawlessly rap every single word of 50 Cent's "In Da Club" and laughing along with him and his friends. I thought about my friends who were covered in third-degree burns, "lucky" to have survived an IED attack in the Al-Qaim region of Iraq. And here was this dipshit in a spotty beard telling our class that we murdered people for sport.

I felt an immediate drive to finish college as quickly as possible. I met with a guidance counselor and plotted my exit—I'd need to take classes during the summer and more than double the full-time course load during some terms. It was, even by my heightened standards, an intense year. During a particularly terrible February, I sat down with my calendar and counted the number of days since I'd slept more than four hours in a day. The tally was thirty-nine. But I continued, and in August 2009, after one year and eleven months at Ohio State, I graduated with a double major, summa cum laude. I tried to skip my graduation ceremony, but my family wouldn't let me. So I sat in an uncomfortable chair for three hours before I walked across the podium and received my college diploma. When Gordon Gee, then president of the Ohio State University, paused for an unusually long photograph with the girl who stood in front of me in line, I extended my hand to his assistant, nonverbally asking for the diploma. She handed it to me, and I stepped behind Dr. Gee and down off the podium. I may have been the only graduating student that day to not shake his hand. *On to the next one,* I thought.

I knew I'd go to law school later the next year (my August graduation precluded a 2009 start to law school), so I moved home to save money. Aunt Wee had taken Mamaw's place as the family matriarch: She put out the fires, hosted family gatherings, and kept us all from breaking apart. She had always provided me with a home base after Mamaw's death, but ten months seemed like an imposition; I didn't like the idea of disrupting her family's routine. But she insisted, "J.D., this is your home now. It's the only place for you to stay."

Those last months living in Middletown were among the 20 happiest of my life. I was finally a college graduate, and I knew that I'd soon accomplish another dream—going to law school. I worked odd jobs to save money and grew closer to my aunt's two daughters. Every day I'd get home from work, dusty and sweaty from manual labor, and sit at the dinner table to hear my teenage cousins talk about their days at school and trials with friends. Sometimes I'd help with homework. On Fridays during Lent, I helped with the fish fries at the local Catholic church. That feeling I had in college—that I had survived decades of chaos and heartbreak and finally come out on the other side—deepened.

The incredible optimism I felt about my own life contrasted starkly with the pessimism of so many of my neighbors. Years of decline in the blue-collar economy manifested themselves in the material prospects of Middletown's residents. The Great Recession, and the not-great recovery that followed, had hastened Middletown's downward trajectory. But there was something almost spiritual about the cynicism of the community at large, something that went much deeper than a short-term recession.

As a culture, we had no heroes. Certainly not any politician—Barack Obama was then the most admired man in America (and likely still is), but even when the country was enraptured by his rise, most Middletonians viewed him suspiciously. George W. Bush had few fans in 2008. Many loved Bill Clinton, but many more saw him as the symbol of American moral decay, and Ronald Reagan was long dead. We loved the military but had no George S. Patton figure in the modern army. I doubt my neighbors could even name a high-ranking military officer. The space program, long a source of pride, had gone the way of the dodo, and with it the celebrity astronauts. Nothing united us with the core fabric of American society. We felt trapped in two seemingly unwinnable wars, in which a disproportionate share of the fighters came from our neighborhood, and in an economy that failed to deliver the most basic promise of the American Dream—a steady wage.

To understand the significance of this cultural detachment, you must appreciate that much of my family's, my neighborhood's, and my community's identity derives from our love of country. I couldn't tell you a single thing about Breathitt County's mayor, its health care services, or its famous residents. But I do know this: "Bloody Breathitt" allegedly earned its name because the county filled its World War I draft quota entirely with volunteers—the only county in the entire United States to do so. Nearly a century later, and that's the factoid about Breathitt that I remember best: It's the truth that everyone around me ensured I knew. I once interviewed Mamaw for a class project about World War II. After seventy years filled with marriage, children, grandchildren, death, poverty, and triumph, the thing about which Mamaw was unquestionably the proudest and most excited was that she and her family did their part during World War II. We spoke for minutes about everything else; we spoke for hours about war rations, Rosie the Riveter, her dad's wartime love letters to her mother from the Pacific, and the day "we dropped the bomb." Mamaw always had two gods: Jesus Christ and the United States of America. I was no different, and neither was anyone else I knew.

I'm the kind of patriot whom people on the Acela corridor laugh at. I choke up when I hear Lee Greenwood's cheesy anthem "Proud to Be an American." When I was sixteen, I vowed that every time I met a veteran, I would go out of my way

J. D. Vance

to shake his or her hand, even if I had to awkwardly interject to do so. To this day, I refuse to watch *Saving Private Ryan* around anyone but my closest friends, because I can't stop from crying during the final scene.

Mamaw and Papaw taught me that we live in the best and greatest country on earth. This fact gave meaning to my childhood. Whenever times were tough—when I felt overwhelmed by the drama and the tumult of my youth—I knew that better days were ahead because I lived in a country that allowed me to make the good choices that others hadn't. When I think today about my life and how genuinely incredible it is—a gorgeous, kind, brilliant life partner; the financial security that I dreamed about as a child; great friends and exciting new experiences—I feel overwhelming appreciation for these United States. I know it's corny, but it's the way I feel.

If Mamaw's second God was the United States of America, then many people in my community were losing something akin to a religion. The tie that bound them to their neighbors, that inspired them in the way my patriotism had always inspired me, had seemingly vanished.

The symptoms are all around us. Significant percentages of white conservative voters—about one-third—believe that Barack Obama is a Muslim. In one poll, 32 percent of conservatives said that they believed Obama was foreign-born and another 19 percent said they were unsure—which means that a majority of white conservatives aren't certain that Obama is even an American. I regularly hear from acquaintances or distant family members that Obama has ties to Islamic extremists, or is a traitor, or was born in some far-flung corner of the world.

Many of my new friends blame racism for this perception of the president. But the president feels like an alien to many Middletonians for reasons that have nothing to do with skin color. Recall that not a single one of my high school classmates attended an Ivy League school. Barack Obama attended two of them and excelled at both. He is brilliant, wealthy, and speaks like a constitutional law professor—which, of course, he is. Nothing about him bears any resemblance to the people I admired growing up: His accent—clean, perfect, neutral—is foreign; his credentials are so impressive that they're frightening; he made his life in Chicago, a dense metropolis; and he conducts himself with a confidence that comes from knowing that the modern American meritocracy was built for him. Of course, Obama overcame adversity in his own right—adversity familiar to many of us—but that was long before any of us knew him.

President Obama came on the scene right as so many people in my community began to believe that the modern American meritocracy was not built for *them*. We know we're not doing well. We see it every day: in the obituaries for teenage kids that conspicuously omit the cause of death (reading between the lines: overdose), in the deadbeats we watch our daughters waste their time with. Barack Obama strikes at the heart of our deepest insecurities. He is a good father while many of us aren't. He wears suits to his job while we wear overalls, if we're lucky enough to have a job at all. His wife tells us that we shouldn't be feeding our children certain foods, and we hate her for it—not because we think she's wrong but because we know she's right.

Many try to blame the anger and cynicism of working-class whites on misinformation. Admittedly, there is an industry of conspiracy-mongers and fringe lunatics writing about all manner of idiocy, from Obama's alleged religious leanings to his ancestry. But every major news organization, even the oft-maligned Fox News, has always told the truth about Obama's citizenship status and religious views. The people I know are well aware of what the major news organizations have to say about the issue; they simply don't believe them. Only 6 percent of American voters believe that the media is "very trustworthy."[1] To many of us, the free press—that bulwark of American democracy—is simply full of shit.

With little trust in the press, there's no check on the Internet conspiracy theories that rule the digital world. Barack Obama is a foreign alien actively trying to destroy our country. Everything the media tells us is a lie. Many in the white working class believe the worst about their society. Here's a small sample of emails or messages I've seen from friends or family:

- From right-wing radio talker Alex Jones on the ten-year anniversary of 9/11, a documentary about the "unanswered question" of the terrorist attacks, suggesting that the U.S. government played a role in the massacre of its own people.

- From an email chain, a story that the Obamacare legislation requires microchip implantation in new health care patients. This story carries extra bite because of the religious implications: Many believe that the End Times "mark of the beast" foretold in biblical prophecy will be an electronic device. Multiple friends warned others about this threat via social media.

- From the popular website *WorldNetDaily*, an editorial suggesting that the Newtown gun massacre was engineered by the federal government to turn public opinion on gun control measures.

- From multiple Internet sources, suggestions that Obama will soon implement martial law in order to secure power for a third presidential term.

The list goes on. It's impossible to know how many people believe one or many of these stories. But if a third of our community questions the president's origin—despite all evidence to the contrary—it's a good bet that the other conspiracies have broader currency than we'd like. This isn't some libertarian mistrust of government policy, which is healthy in any democracy. This is deep skepticism of the very institutions of our society. And it's becoming more and more mainstream.

We can't trust the evening news. We can't trust our politicians. Our universities, the gateway to a better life, are rigged against us. We can't get jobs. You can't believe these things and participate meaningfully in society. Social psychologists have shown that group belief is a powerful motivator in performance. When groups perceive that it's in their interest to work hard and achieve things, members of that group outperform other similarly situated individuals. It's obvious why: If you believe that hard work pays off, then you work hard; if you think it's hard to get ahead even when you try, then why try at all?

Similarly, when people do fail, this mind-set allows them to look outward. I once ran into an old acquaintance at a Middletown bar who told me that he had recently quit his job because he was sick of waking up early. I later saw him complaining on Facebook about the "Obama economy" and how it had affected his life. I don't doubt that the Obama economy has affected many, but this man is assuredly not among them. His status in life is directly attributable to the choices he's made, and his life will improve only through better decisions. But for him to make better choices, he needs to live in an environment that forces him to ask tough questions about himself. There is a cultural movement in the white working class to blame problems on society or the government, and that movement gains adherents by the day.

Here is where the rhetoric of modern conservatives (and 35 I say this as one of them) fails to meet the real challenges of their biggest constituents. Instead of encouraging engagement, conservatives increasingly foment the kind of detachment that has sapped the ambition of so many of my peers. I have watched some friends blossom into successful adults and others fall victim to the worst of Middletown's temptations—premature parenthood, drugs, incarceration. What separates the successful from the unsuccessful are the expectations that they had for their own lives. Yet the message of the right is increasingly: It's not your fault that you're a loser; it's the government's fault.

My dad, for example, has never disparaged hard work, but he mistrusts some of the most obvious paths to upward mobility. When he found out that I had decided to go to Yale Law, he asked whether, on my applications, I had "pretended to be black or liberal." This is how low the cultural expectations of working-class white Americans have fallen. We should hardly be surprised that as attitudes like this one spread, the number of people willing to work for a better life diminishes.

The Pew Economic Mobility Project studied how Americans evaluated their chances at economic betterment, and what they found was shocking. There is no group of Americans more pessimistic than working-class whites. Well over half of blacks, Latinos, and college-educated whites expect that their children will fare better economically than they have. Among working-class whites, only 44 percent share that expectation. Even more surprising, 42 percent of working-class whites—by far the highest number in the survey—report that their lives are less economically successful than those of their parents'.

In 2010, that just wasn't my mind-set. I was happy about where I was and overwhelmingly hopeful about the future. For the first time in my life, I felt like an outsider in Middletown. And what turned me into an alien was my optimism.

NOTE

1. "Only 6% Rate News Media as Very Trustworthy," *Rasmussen Report.* February 28, 2013, http://www.rasmussenreports.com/public_content/politics/general_politics/february_2013/only_6-rate_news_media_as_very_trustworthy (accessed November 17, 2015). [Vance's note]

Joining the Conversation

1. J. D. Vance tells his own story, in part, to illustrate how the optimism he felt about his future "contrasted starkly with the pessimism of so many of [his] neighbors." What other arguments does Vance make throughout his narrative? In addition to citing personal experience, what kinds of evidence does he offer to support his views?

2. Vance uses metacommentary to explain to readers how to interpret something he has just said. Find two examples in the reading where Vance uses this technique.

3. An elegy is a sad, mournful lament. Why do you think Vance called his book *Hillbilly Elegy*? How does his own story relate to the title?

4. Nicholas Eberstadt (pp. 667–81) writes about the dramatic increase in unemployment and underemployment among men with a high school education or less. How might Vance use the statistics Eberstadt cites to support his argument about the challenges facing many working-class Americans?

5. Vance tells his own story and also makes observations about his greater community. Think of a challenge or experience you have had. Write an essay about what happened, making an argument about how your personal experience reflects a greater trend taking place in your community or hometown.

Minority Student Clubs:
Segregation or Integration?

GABRIELA MORO

—ᠣ—

MINORITY REPRESENTATION on US college campuses has increased significantly in recent years, and many schools have made it a priority to increase diversity on their campuses in order to prepare students for a culturally diverse US democratic society (Hurtado and Ruiz 3–4). To complement this increase, many schools have implemented minority student clubs to provide safe and comfortable environments where minority students can thrive academically and socially with peers from similar backgrounds. However, do these minority groups amplify students' tendency to interact only with those who are similar to themselves? Put another way, do these groups inhibit students from engaging in diverse relationships?

Many view such programs to be positive and integral to minority students' college experience; some, however, feel that

―――――

GABRIELA MORO wrote this essay in her first-year composition class at the University of Notre Dame in South Bend, Indiana. It was published in 2015 in the university's journal *Fresh Writing*, "an interactive archive of exemplary first-year writing projects." A neuroscience and behavior pre-health major, Moro plans to pursue a career in medicine.

these clubs are not productive for promoting cross-cultural interaction. While minority clubs have proven to be beneficial to minority students in some cases, particularly on campuses that are not very diverse, my research suggests that colleges would enrich the educational experience for all students by introducing multicultural clubs as well.

To frame my discussion, I will use an article from *College Student Journal* that distinguishes between two types of students: one who believes minority clubs are essential for helping minority students stay connected with their cultures, and another who believes these clubs isolate minorities and work against diverse interaction among students. To pursue the question of whether or not such groups segregate minorities from the rest of the student body and even discourage cultural awareness, I will use perspectives from minority students to show that these programs are especially helpful for first-year students. I will also use other student testimonials to show that when taken too far, minority groups can lead to self-segregation and defy what most universities claim to be their diversity goals. Findings from research will contribute to a better understanding of the role minority clubs play on college campuses and offer a complete answer to my question about the importance of minority programs.

Before I go further, I would like to differentiate among three kinds of diversity that Gurin et al. identify in their article "Diversity and Higher Education: Theory and Impact on Educational Outcomes." The first type is *structural diversity*, "the numerical representation of diverse [racial and ethnic] groups." The existence of structural diversity alone does not assure that students will develop valuable intergroup relationships. *Classroom diversity*, the second type, involves gaining "content knowledge" or a better understanding about diverse peers and their backgrounds by doing so in the classroom. The third type of diversity, *informal interactional diversity*, refers to "both the frequency and the quality of intergroup interaction as keys to meaningful diversity experiences during college." Students often encounter this kind of diversity in social settings outside the classroom (Gurin 332–33). Informal interactional diversity is the focus of my research, since it is the concept that leads colleges to establish social events and organizations that allow all students to experience and appreciate the variety of cultures present in a student body.

In a study published in *College Student Journal*, three admin- 5 istrators at Pennsylvania State University explored how biracial students interact with others on a college campus. The authors concluded that views of minority clubs and related programs, which the authors call race-oriented student services (ROSS), tend to fall into two groups: "Although some argue that these race-oriented student services (ROSS) are divisive and damage white-minority relations (Stern & Gaiter, 1994), others support these services as providing a safe place and meeting the needs of minority students to develop a sense of racial pride, community and importance (Patton, 2006)" (Ingram 298). I will start by examining the point of view of those who associate minority clubs with positive outcomes.

A study by Samuel D. Museus in the *Journal of College Student Development* found that minority student programs help students to stay connected with their culture in college and help ease first-year minority students' transition into the college environment. The study also shows that ethnic student organizations help students adjust and find their place at universities that have a predominantly white student body (584). Museus concluded that universities should stress the importance of racial and ethnic groups and develop more opportunities for minority students to make connections with them. This way, students can find support from their minority peers as they work together to face academic and social challenges. Museus's findings suggest that minority student groups are essential for allowing these students to preserve and foster connections to their own cultures.

In another study, Hall et al. evaluated how minority and non-minority students differed in their inclinations to take part in diversity activities and to communicate with racially and ethnically diverse peers at a predominantly white university. These scholars concluded that "engagement [with diverse peers] is learned" (434). Students who engaged with diverse students before going to college were more likely to interact with diverse peers by the end of their sophomore year. Minority students were more predisposed than their white peers to interact with diverse peers during their freshman year (435). These findings indicate that minority student clubs can be helpful for first-year minority students who have not previously engaged with other minority students, especially if the university has a predominantly white student body.

Professors and scholars are not the only ones who strongly support minority clubs. For example, three students at Harvard College—Andrea Delgado, Denzel (no last name given), and Kimi Fafowora—give their perspective on student life and multicultural identity on campus to incoming students via *YouTube*. The students explain how minority programs on campus have helped them adjust to a new college environment as first-year students. As Delgado put it, "I thought [cultural clubs were] something I maybe didn't need, but come November, I missed speaking Spanish and I missed having tacos, and other things like that. That's the reason why I started attending meetings more regularly. Latinas Unidas has been a great intersection of my cultural background and my political views." The experiences these minority students shared support the scholarly evidence that minority clubs help incoming students transition into a new and often intimidating environment.

While the benefits of these clubs are quite evident, several problems can also arise from them. The most widely recognized is self-segregation. Self-segregating tendencies are not exclusive to minority students: college students in general tend to self-segregate as they enter an unfamiliar environment. As a study by Martin et al. finds, "Today, the student bodies of our leading colleges and universities are more diverse than ever. However, college students are increasingly self-segregating by race or ethnicity" (720). Several studies as well as interviews with students suggest that minority clubs exacerbate students' inclination to self-segregate. And as students become comfortable with their minority peers, they may no longer desire or feel the need to branch out of their comfort zone.

In another study, Julie J. Park, a professor at the University 10 of Maryland, examined the relationship between participation in college student organizations and the development of interracial friendships. Park suggests, "if students spend the majority of time in such groups [Greek, ethnic, and religious student organizations], participation may affect student involvement in the broader diversity of the institution" (642). In other words, if minority students form all of their social and academic ties within their minority group, the desired cultural exchange among the study body could suffer.

So what can be done? In the Penn State study mentioned earlier, in which data were collected by an online survey, participants were asked to respond to an open-ended question about what they think universities should do to create a more inviting environment for biracial students (Ingram et al. 303). On one hand, multiple students responded with opinions opposing the formation of both biracial and multiracial clubs: "I feel instead of having biracial and multiracial clubs the colleges should have diversity clubs and just allow everyone to get together. All these 'separate' categorizing of clubs, isn't that just separation of groups?" "Having a ton of clubs that are for specific races is counter-productive. It creates segregation and lack of communication across cultures" (304–305).

On the other hand, students offered suggestions for the formation of multicultural activities: "Encourage more racial integration to show students races aren't so different from each other and to lessen stereotypes." "Hold cultural events that allow students of different races to express/share their heritage." Ingram et al. concluded that, while biracial and multiracial student organizations are helpful in establishing an inviting college environment for minority students,

> creating a truly inclusive environment . . . requires additional efforts: these include multicultural awareness training for faculty, staff, and students, and incorporation of multicultural issues into the curriculum (White, 2006; Gasser, 2002). In addition to the creation of biracial/multiracial clubs and organization, the students in this study want to increase awareness of the mixed heritage population among others on college campuses. (308)

The two very different opinions reported in this study point to the challenges minority student programs can create, but also suggest ways to resolve these challenges. Now that evidence from both research studies and student perspectives confirm that these clubs, while beneficial to minority students' experiences, can inhibit cultural immersion, I will continue with my original argument that the entire student body would benefit if campuses also implemented multicultural advocacy clubs, rather than just selective minority clubs. Gurin et al., the researchers who identified the three types of diversity in higher education, contend that even with the presence of diverse racial and ethnic groups and regular communication among students formally and informally, a greater push from educators is needed:

For tips on clarifying where you have been and where you are going, see p. 137.

> In order to foster citizenship for a diverse democracy, educators must intentionally structure opportunities for students to leave the comfort of their homogenous peer group and build relationships across racially/ethnically diverse student communities on campus. (363)

This suggestion implies that participation from students and faculty is needed to foster cultural immersion in higher education.

Another way to improve cross-cultural exchange is by developing a diverse curriculum. An article on multiculturalism in higher education by Alma Clayton-Pedersen and Caryn McTighe Musil in the *Encyclopedia of Education* reviewed the ways in which universities have incorporated diversity studies into their core curriculum over the last several decades. They found that the numbers of courses that seek to prepare students for a democratic society rich in diversity have increased (1711, 1714). However, they recommend that institutions need to take a more holistic approach to their academic curricula in order to pursue higher education programs that prepare students to face "complex and demanding questions" and to "use their new knowledge and civic, intercultural capacities to address real-world problems" (1714). My research supports that a more holistic approach to the importance of diversity studies in the college curriculum, as well as multicultural advocacy clubs, are necessary in order to prepare *all* students, not just minority students, for the diverse world and society ahead of them.

Thus, even though minority student clubs can lead to self-segregation among students and result in less cross-cultural interaction, their benefits to minority students suggest that a balance needs to be found between providing support for minorities and avoiding segregation of these groups from the rest of the student body. Besides sponsoring minority student programs, colleges and universities can implement multicultural events and activities for all students to participate in, especially during the freshman year. An initiative like this would enhance the diverse interactions that occur on campuses, promote cultural immersion, and garner support for minority student clubs.

Beyond the reach of this evaluation, further research should 15 be conducted, specifically on the types of cultural events that are most effective in promoting cultural awareness and meaningful diverse interactions among the student body. By examining different multicultural organizations from both public and private institutions, and comparing student experiences and participation in those programs, researchers can suggest an ideal multicultural program to provide an optimal student experience.

WORKS CITED

Clayton-Pedersen, Alma R., and Caryn McTighe Musil. "Multiculturalism in Higher Education." *Encyclopedia of Education*, edited by James W. Guthrie, 2nd ed., vol. 5, Macmillan, 2002, pp. 1709–1716. *Gale Virtual Reference Library*. Accessed 26 Feb. 2015.

Gurin, Patricia, Eric L. Dey, Sylvia Hurtado, and Gerald Gurin. "Diversity and Higher Education: Theory and Impact on Educational Outcomes." *Harvard Educational Review*, vol. 72, no. 3, 2002, pp. 330–36. *ResearchGate*, doi:10.17763/haer.72.3.01151786u134n051. Accessed 28 Mar. 2015.

Hall, Wendell, Alberto Cabrera, and Jeffrey Milem. "A Tale of Two Groups: Differences Between Minority Students and Non-Minority Students in Their Predispositions to and Engagement with Diverse Peers at a Predominantly White Institution." *Research in Higher Education*, vol. 52, no. 4, 2011, pp. 420–439. *Academic Search Premier*, doi: 10.1007/s11162 -010-9201-4. Accessed 10 Mar. 2015.

Harvard College Admissions & Financial Aid. "Student Voices: Multicultural Perspectives." *YouTube*, 7 Aug. 2014, https://www.youtube.com/ watch?v=djIWQgDx-Jc. Accessed 12 Mar. 2015.

Hurtado, Sylvia, and Adriana Ruiz. "The Climate for Underrepresented Groups and Diversity on Campus." Higher Education Research Institute at UCLA (HERI) and Cooperative Institutional Research Program (CIRP), 2012, heri.ucla.edu/briefs/urmbrief.php. Accessed 26 Feb. 2015.

Ingram, Patreese, Anil Kumar Chaudhary, and Walter Terrell Jones. "How Do Biracial Students Interact with Others on the College Campus?" *College Student Journal*, vol. 48, no. 2, 2014, pp. 297–311. Questia, www.questia .com/library/journal/1G1-377286773/how-do-biracial-students-interact -with-others-on-the. Accessed 28 July 2017.

Martin, Nathan D., William Tobin, and Kenneth I. Spenner. "Interracial Friendships Across the College Years: Evidence from a Longitudinal Case Study." *Journal of College Student Development*, vol. 55, no. 7, 2014, pp. 720–725. *Academic Search Premier*, doi: 10.1353/csd.2014.0075. Accessed 16 Mar. 2015.

Museus, Samuel D. "The Role of Ethnic Student Organizations in Fostering African American and Asian American Students' Cultural Adjustment and Membership at Predominantly White Institutions." *Journal of College Student Development*, vol. 49, no. 6, 2008, pp. 568–86. *Project MUSE*, doi:10.1353/csd.0.0039. Accessed 26 Feb. 2015.

Park, Julie J. "Clubs and the Campus Racial Climate: Student Organizations and Interracial Friendship in College." *Journal of College Student Development*, vol. 55, no. 7, 2014, pp. 641–660. *Academic Search Premier*, doi:10.1353/csd.2014.0076. Accessed 16 March. 2015.

Joining the Conversation

1. What larger conservation is Gabriela Moro responding to in this essay?

2. What are some of the connecting words, phrases, and sentences Moro uses to transition from one paragraph to another? (See pp. 105–06 for a list of commonly used transitions.)

3. Notice how many direct quotations Moro includes. Why do you think she includes so many? What do the quotations contribute that a summary or paraphrase would not?

4. Writer danah boyd (pp. 255–65) criticizes the many ways in which Americans are now self-segregating. How might she respond to Moro's description of Notre Dame's campus and to Moro's proposal to support minority clubs *and* multiculturalism?

5. Develop an argument of your own that responds to Moro's proposal, agreeing, disagreeing, or both. However you choose to argue, be sure to consider other positions in addition to your own, including other authors in this chapter.

Why Rural America Voted for Trump

ROBERT LEONARD

———◻———

KNOXVILLE, IOWA—One recent morning, I sat near two young men at a coffee shop here whom I've known since they were little boys. Now about 18, they pushed away from the table, and one said: "Let's go to work. Let the liberals sleep in." The other nodded.

They're hard workers. As a kid, one washed dishes, took orders and swept the floor at a restaurant. Every summer, the other picked sweet corn by hand at dawn for a farm stand and for grocery stores, and then went to work all day on his parents' farm. Now one is a welder, and the other is in his first year at a state university on an academic scholarship. They are conservative, believe in hard work, family, the military and cops, and they know that abortion and socialism are evil, that Jesus Christ is our savior, and that Donald J. Trump will be good for America.

————

ROBERT LEONARD is the news director for the radio station KNIA KRLS in Marion County, Iowa. He has contributed essays to *The Hill* and *Salon*, online news publications focused on politics, and his book *Yellow Cab* (2006) describes his experiences working as a cabdriver while he was an anthropology professor. This essay first appeared in the *New York Times* on January 5, 2017.

They are part of a growing movement in rural America that immerses many young people in a culture—not just conservative news outlets but also home and church environments—that emphasizes contemporary conservative values. It views liberals as loathsome, misinformed and weak, even dangerous.

Who are these rural, red-county people who brought Mr. Trump into power? I'm a native Iowan and reporter in rural Marion County, Iowa. I consider myself fairly liberal. My family has mostly voted Democratic since long before I was born. To be honest, for years, even I have struggled to understand how these conservative friends and neighbors I respect—and at times admire—can think so differently from me, not to mention how over 60 percent of voters in my county could have chosen Mr. Trump.

Political analysts have talked about how ignorance, racism, 5 sexism, nationalism, Islamophobia, economic disenfranchisement and the decline of the middle class contributed to the popularity of Mr. Trump in rural America. But this misses the deeper cultural factors that shape the thinking of the conservatives who live here.

See Chapter 5 for ways to signal who is saying what.

For me, it took a 2015 pre-caucus stop in Pella by J. C. Watts, a Baptist minister raised in the small town of Eufaula, Oklahoma, who was a Republican congressman from 1995 to 2003, to begin to understand my neighbors—and most likely other rural Americans as well.

"The difference between Republicans and Democrats is that Republicans believe people are fundamentally bad, while Democrats see people as fundamentally good," said Mr. Watts, who was in the area to campaign for Senator Rand Paul. "We are born bad," he said and added that children did not need to be taught to behave badly—they are born knowing how to do that.

"We teach them how to be good," he said. "We become good by being reborn—born again."

He continued: "Democrats believe that we are born good, that we create God, not that he created us. If we are our own God, as the Democrats say, then we need to look at something else to blame when things go wrong—not us."

Mr. Watts talked about the 2015 movie theater shoot- 10 ing in Lafayette, Louisiana, in which two people were killed. Mr. Watts said that Republicans knew that the gunman was a bad man, doing a bad thing. Democrats, he added, "would look for other causes—that the man was basically good, but that it was the guns, society or some other place where the blame lies and then they will want to control the guns, or something else—not the man." Republicans, he said, don't need to look anywhere else for the blame.

Hearing Mr. Watts was an epiphany for me. For the first time I had a glimpse of where many of my conservative friends and neighbors were coming from. I thought, no wonder Republicans and Democrats can't agree on things like gun control, regulations or the value of social programs. We live in different philosophical worlds, with different foundational principles.

Overlay this philosophical perspective on the American rural-urban divides of history, economy and geography, and the conservative individual responsibility narrative becomes even more powerful. In my experience, the urban-rural divide isn't really so much a red state versus blue state issue, it's red county versus blue county. Rural Iowans have more in common with the rural residents of Washington State and New Mexico—places I've also lived—than with the residents of Des Moines, Seattle and Albuquerque.

Look at a national map of which counties went for Democrats and which for Republicans: Overwhelmingly the blue counties

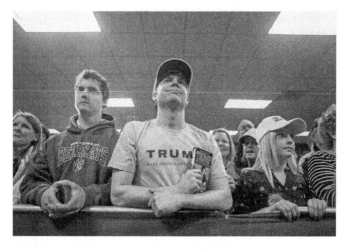

Trump supporters at a rally in Iowa, January 2016.

are along waterways, where early river transportation encouraged the formation of cities, and surround state capitals. This is also where most investment in infrastructure and services is made. Rural Americans recognize that this is how it must be, as the cities are where most of the people are, yet it's a sore spot.

In state capitols across America, lawmakers spend billions of dollars to take a few seconds off a city dweller's commute to his office, while rural counties' farm-to-market roads fall into disrepair. Some of the paved roads in my region are no longer maintained and are reverting to gravel. For a couple of generations now, services that were once scattered across rural areas have increasingly been consolidated in urban areas, and rural towns die. It's all done in the name of efficiency.

In cities, firefighters and E.M.T.s are professionals whose 15 departments are funded by local, state and federal tax dollars. Rural America relies on volunteers. If I have a serious heart attack at home, I'll be cold to the touch by the time the volunteer ambulance crew from a town 22 miles away gets here.

Urban police officers have the latest in computer equipment and vehicles, while small-town cops go begging.

In this view, blue counties are where most of our tax dollars are spent, and that's where all of our laws are written and passed. To rural Americans, sometimes it seems our taxes mostly go to making city residents live better. We recognize that the truth is more complex, particularly when it comes to social programs, but it's the perception that matters—certainly to the way most people vote.

To make matters worse, jobs are continuing to move to metropolitan areas. Small-town chamber of commerce directors and mayors still have big dreams, and use their perkiest grins and tax abatements to try to lure new businesses, only to see their hopes dashed, time and again. Many towns with a rich history and strong community pride are already dead; their citizens just don't know it yet.

Many moderate rural Republicans became supporters of Mr. Trump when he released his list of potential Supreme Court nominees who would allow the possibility of overturning *Roe v. Wade.* They also think the liberal worldview creates unnecessary rules and regulations that cripple the economy and take away good jobs that may belong to them or their neighbor. Public school systems and colleges are liberal tools of indoctrination that go after what we love and value most—our children.

Some of what liberals worry about they see as pure nonsense. When you are the son or daughter of a carpenter or mechanic and a housewife or secretary who lives paycheck to paycheck, who can't afford to send kids to college, as many rural residents are, white privilege is meaningless and abstract. 20

It's not just older people. The two young men at breakfast exemplify a younger generation with this view. When Ted Cruz campaigned in a neighboring town in 2015, I watched as a couple of dozen grade-school pupils sat at his feet, as if they were at a children's service at church. His campaign speech was nearly a sermon, and the children listened wide-eyed when he told them the world is a scary place, and it's godly men like him who are going to save them from the evils of President Obama, Hillary Clinton and their fellow Democrats.

While many blame poor decisions by Mrs. Clinton for her loss, in an environment like this, the Democratic candidate probably didn't matter. And the Democratic Party may not for generations to come. The Republican brand is strong in rural America—perhaps even strong enough to withstand a disastrous Trump presidency.

Rural conservatives feel that their world is under siege, and that Democrats are an enemy to be feared and loathed. Given the philosophical premises Mr. Watts presented as the difference between Democrats and Republicans, reconciliation seems a long way off.

Joining the Conversation

1. Robert Leonard, a reporter from Iowa, describes the conservative values as well as the social and economic conditions that he believes led a majority of people living in rural America to vote for Donald Trump. Summarize his description in two or three sentences.

2. This piece was originally published in the *New York Times*, a newspaper with a predominantly liberal, college-educated readership. Why do you think Leonard chose to write his piece for this newspaper?

3. Leonard includes quotations from several people whose views differ from his own, such as J. C. Watts, a conservative Baptist minister. Find three examples where Leonard presents conservative views, and show how he is able to clearly distinguish those views from his own.

4. Michelle Alexander (pp. 266–86) argues that African Americans are at the bottom of what she calls "a new racial caste system." How might the people who believe that "white privilege is meaningless and abstract" (paragraph 20) respond to Alexander's argument?

5. Leonard argues that Republicans and Democrats "live in different philosophical worlds, with different foundational principles" (paragraph 11) and concludes that reconciliation seems unlikely, at least for now. Write an essay in which you agree, disagree, or both with this argument, citing ideas from readings in this chapter.

A Tax System Stacked
against the 99 Percent

JOSEPH E. STIGLITZ

———

Leona Helmsley, the hotel chain executive who was convicted of federal tax evasion in 1989, was notorious for, among other things, reportedly having said that "only the little people pay taxes."

As a statement of principle, the quotation may well have earned Mrs. Helmsley, who died in 2007, the title Queen of Mean. But as a prediction about the fairness of American tax policy, Mrs. Helmsley's remark might actually have been prescient.

Today [April 15], the deadline for filing individual income-tax returns, is a day when Americans would do well to pause and

———

Joseph E. Stiglitz, winner of the Nobel Prize in Economics in 2001, teaches at Columbia University. Formerly, Stiglitz was a senior vice president and chief economist at the World Bank, and served as chairman of the Council of Economic Advisers. His books include *The Euro: How a Common Currency Threatens the Future of Europe* (2016) and *The Great Divide: Unequal Societies and What We Can Do About Them* (2015). This essay first appeared in the *New York Times* series about inequality, "The Great Divide," on April 14, 2013.

reflect on our tax system and the society it creates. No one enjoys paying taxes, and yet all but the extreme libertarians agree, as Oliver Wendell Holmes said, that taxes are the price we pay for civilized society. But in recent decades, the burden for paying that price has been distributed in increasingly unfair ways.

About 6 in 10 of us believe that the tax system is unfair—and they're right: put simply, the very rich don't pay their fair share. The richest 400 individual taxpayers, with an average income of more than $200 million, pay less than 20 percent of their income in taxes—far lower than mere millionaires, who pay about 25 percent of their income in taxes, and about the same as those earning a mere $200,000 to $500,000. And in 2009, 116 of the top 400 earners—almost a third—paid less than 15 percent of their income in taxes.

Conservatives like to point out that the richest Americans' tax payments make up a large portion of total receipts. This is true, as well it should be in any tax system that is progressive—that is, a system that taxes the affluent at higher rates than those of modest means. It's also true that as the wealthiest Americans' incomes have sky-rocketed in recent years, their total tax payments have grown. This would be so even if we had a single flat income-tax rate across the board.

See p. 88 for tips on making concessions while still standing your ground.

What should shock and outrage us is that as the top 1 percent has grown extremely rich, the effective tax rates they pay have markedly decreased. Our tax system is much less progressive than it was for much of the 20th century. The top marginal income tax rate peaked at 94 percent during World War II and remained at 70 percent through the 1960s and 1970s; it is now 39.6 percent. Tax fairness has gotten much worse in the 30 years since the Reagan "revolution" of the 1980s.

As the author argues, the wealth that belongs to the 1 percent continues to increase, while the incomes of the 99 percent have stagnated or fallen.

Citizens for Tax Justice, an organization that advocates for a more progressive tax system, has estimated that, when federal, state and local taxes are taken into account, the top 1 percent paid only slightly more than 20 percent of all American taxes in 2010—about the same as the share of income they took home, an outcome that is not progressive at all.

With such low effective tax rates—and, importantly, the low tax rate of 20 percent on income from capital gains—it's not a huge surprise that the share of income going to the top 1 percent has doubled since 1979, and that the share going to the top 0.1 percent has almost tripled, according to the economists Thomas Piketty and Emmanuel Saez. Recall that the wealthiest 1 percent of Americans own about 40 percent of the nation's wealth, and the picture becomes even more disturbing.

If these numbers still don't impress you as being unfair, consider them in comparison with other wealthy countries.

The United States stands out among the countries of the 10 Organization for Economic Cooperation and Development, the world's club of rich nations, for its low top marginal income tax rate. These low rates are not essential for growth—consider Germany, for instance, which has managed to maintain its status as a center of advanced manufacturing, even though its top income-tax rate exceeds America's by a considerable margin. And in general, our top tax rate kicks in at much higher incomes. Denmark, for example, has a top tax rate of more than 60 percent, but that applies to anyone making more than $54,900. The top rate in the United States, 39.6 percent, doesn't kick in until individual income reaches $400,000 (or $450,000 for a couple). Only three O.E.C.D. countries—South Korea, Canada and Spain—have higher thresholds.

Most of the Western world has experienced an increase in inequality in recent decades, though not as much as the United States has. But among most economists there is a general understanding that a country with excessive inequality can't function well; many countries have used their tax codes to help "correct" the market's distribution of wealth and income. The United States hasn't—or at least not very much. Indeed, the low rates at the top serve to exacerbate and perpetuate the inequality— so much so that among the advanced industrial countries, America now has the highest income inequality and the least equality of opportunity. This is a gross inversion of America's traditional meritocratic ideals—ideals that our leaders, across the spectrum, continue to profess.

Over the years, some of the wealthy have been enormously successful in getting special treatment, shifting an ever greater share of the burden of financing the country's expenditures—defense, education, social programs—onto others. Ironically, this is especially true of some of our multinational corporations, which call on the federal government to negotiate favorable trade treaties that allow them easy entry into foreign markets and to defend their commercial interests around the world, but then use these foreign bases to avoid paying taxes.

General Electric has become the symbol for multinational corporations that have their headquarters in the United States but pay almost no taxes—its effective corporate-tax rate averaged less than 2 percent from 2002 to 2012—just as Mitt Romney, the [former] Republican presidential nominee, became the symbol for the wealthy who don't pay their fair share when he admitted that he paid only 14 percent of his income in taxes in 2011, even as he notoriously complained that 47 percent of Americans were freeloaders. Neither G.E. nor Mr. Romney has, to my knowledge, broken any tax laws, but the sparse taxes they've paid violate most Americans' basic sense of fairness.

In looking at such statistics, one has to be careful: they typically reflect taxes as a percentage of reported income. And the tax laws don't require the reporting of all kinds of income. For the rich, hiding such assets has become an elite sport. Many avail themselves of the Cayman Islands or other offshore tax shelters to avoid taxes (and not, you can safely assume, because of the sunny weather). They don't have to report income until it is brought back ("repatriated") to the United States. So, too, capital gains have to be reported as income only when they are realized.

And if the assets are passed on to one's children or grand- 15 children at death, no taxes are ever paid, in a peculiar loophole called the "step-up in cost basis at death." Yes, the tax privileges of being rich in America extend into the afterlife.

As Americans look at some of the special provisions in the tax code—for vacation homes, racetracks, beer breweries, oil refineries, hedge funds and movie studios, among many other favored assets or industries—it is no wonder that they feel disillusioned with a tax system that is so riddled with special rewards. Most of these tax-code loopholes and giveaways did not materialize from thin air, of course—usually, they were enacted in pursuit of, or at least in response to, campaign contributions from influential donors. It is estimated that these kinds of special tax provisions amount to some \$123 billion a year, and that the price tag for offshore tax loopholes is not far behind. Eliminating these provisions alone would go a long way toward meeting deficit-reduction targets called for by fiscal conservatives who worry about the size of the public debt.

Yet another source of unfairness is the tax treatment on so-called carried interest. Some Wall Street financiers are able to pay taxes at lower capital gains tax rates on income that comes from managing assets for private equity funds or hedge funds. But why should managing financial assets be treated any differently from managing people, or making discoveries? Of course, those in finance say they are essential. But so are doctors, lawyers, teachers and everyone else who contributes to making our complex society work. They say they are necessary for job creation. But in fact, many of the private equity firms that have excelled in exploiting the carried interest loophole are actually job destroyers; they excel in restructuring firms to "save" on labor costs, often by moving jobs abroad.

Economists often eschew the word "fair"—fairness, like beauty, is in the eye of the beholder. But the unfairness of the American tax system has gotten so great that it's dishonest to apply any other label to it.

Traditionally, economists have focused less on issues of equality than on the more mundane issues of growth and efficiency. But here again, our tax system comes in with low marks.

Our growth was higher in the era of high top marginal tax rates than it has been since 1980. Economists—even at traditional, conservative international institutions like the International Monetary Fund—have come to realize that excessive inequality is bad for growth and stability. The tax system can play an important role in moderating the degree of inequality. Ours, however, does remarkably little about it.

One of the reasons for our poor economic performance is the large distortion in our economy caused by the tax system. The one thing economists agree on is that incentives matter—if you lower taxes on speculation, say, you will get more speculation. We've drawn our most talented young people into financial shenanigans, rather than into creating real businesses, making real discoveries, providing real services to others. More efforts go into "rent-seeking"—getting a larger slice of the country's economic pie—than into enlarging the size of the pie.

Research in recent years has linked the tax rates, sluggish growth and rising inequality. Remember, the low tax rates at the top were supposed to spur savings and hard work, and thus economic growth. They didn't. Indeed, the household savings rate fell to a record level of near zero after President George W. Bush's two rounds of cuts, in 2001 and 2003, on taxes on dividends and capital gains. What low tax rates at the top did do was increase the return on rent-seeking. It flourished, which meant that growth slowed and inequality grew. This is a pattern that has now been observed across countries. Contrary to the warnings of those who want to preserve their privileges, countries that have increased their top tax bracket have not grown more slowly. Another piece of evidence is here at home: if the efforts at the top were resulting in our entire economic engine's doing better, we would expect everyone to benefit. If they were engaged in rent-seeking, as their incomes increased, we'd expect that of others to decrease. And that's exactly what's been happening. Incomes in the middle, and even the bottom, have been stagnating or falling.

Aside from the evidence, there is a strong intuitive case to be made for the idea that tax rates have encouraged rent-seeking at the expense of wealth creation. There is an intrinsic satisfaction in creating a new business, in expanding the horizons of our knowledge, and in helping others. By contrast, it is unpleasant to spend one's days fine-tuning dishonest and deceptive practices that siphon money off the poor, as was common in the financial sector before the 2007–8 financial crisis. I believe that a vast majority of Americans would, all things being equal, choose the former over the latter. But our tax system tilts the field. It increases the net returns from engaging in some of these intrinsically distasteful activities, and it has helped us become a rent-seeking society.

It doesn't have to be this way. We could have a much simpler tax system without all the distortions—a society where those who clip coupons for a living pay the same taxes as someone with the same income who works in a factory; where someone who earns his income from saving companies pays the same tax as a doctor who makes the income by saving lives; where someone who earns his income from financial innovations pays the same taxes as someone who does research to create real innovations that transform our economy and society. We could have a tax system that encourages good things like hard work and thrift and discourages bad things, like rent-seeking, gambling, financial speculation and pollution. Such a tax system could raise far more money than the current one—we wouldn't have to go through all the wrangling we've been going through with sequestration, fiscal cliffs and threats to end Medicare and Social Security as we know it. We would be in a sound fiscal position, for at least the next quarter-century.

The consequences of our broken tax system are not just economic. Our tax system relies heavily on voluntary compliance. But if citizens believe that the tax system is unfair, this voluntary compliance will not be forthcoming. More broadly, government plays an important role not just in social protection, but in making investments in infrastructure, technology, education and health. Without such investments, our economy will be weaker, and our economic growth slower.

Society can't function well without a minimal sense of national solidarity and cohesion, and that sense of shared purpose also rests on a fair tax system. If Americans believe that government is unfair—that ours is a government of the 1 percent, for the 1 percent, and by the 1 percent—then faith in our democracy will surely perish.

Joining the Conversation

1. Joseph E. Stiglitz begins this essay with a "they say" statement uttered by a wealthy hotel owner, that "only the little people pay taxes." How would you summarize Stiglitz's corresponding "I say" statement?
2. What evidence does Stiglitz provide for his assertion that the wealthiest 1 percent of Americans pay far less in taxes than they should? How convincing is this evidence to you?
3. In paragraph 17, Stiglitz begins, "Yet another source of unfairness is the tax treatment on so-called carried interest." Stiglitz states a view he does not agree with, and then counters this view with his own argument in the rest of paragraph. How does he let you know that he is beginning with an assertion he will then disagree with?

4. Imagine that Stiglitz wrote his article for an audience in favor of the tax policies he argues against. How might Stiglitz have developed his argument differently to appeal to such readers? Consider his title, for instance, and suggest another title that would be more likely to interest such an audience.

5. The final paragraph of this essay offers a "so what" statement explaining why the author believes his argument matters. In a paragraph, respond to this point by either agreeing, disagreeing, or both.

Howard University
Commencement Speech

BARACK OBAMA

—⌐🔲⌐—

To President Frederick, the Board of Trustees, faculty and staff, fellow recipients of honorary degrees, thank you for the honor of spending this day with you. And congratulations to the Class of 2016! (Applause.) Four years ago, back when you were just freshmen, I understand many of you came by my house the night I was reelected. (Laughter.) So I decided to return the favor and come by yours.

To the parents, the grandparents, aunts, uncles, brothers, sisters, all the family and friends who stood by this class, cheered them on, helped them get here today—this is your day, as well. Let's give them a big round of applause, as well. (Applause.) . . .

———

Barack Obama, 44th President of the United States from 2009–2017, worked as a community organizer and civil rights attorney—and taught at the University of Chicago—before entering politics. He is the author of several books, including a memoir of his youth titled *Dreams from My Father: A Story of Race and Inheritance* (1995) and a personal commentary on US politics titled *The Audacity of Hope: Thoughts on Reclaiming the American Dream* (2006). Obama delivered this speech at Howard University's commencement ceremony in Washington, DC, on May 7, 2016.

I know you're all excited today. You might be a little tired, as well. Some of you were up all night making sure your credits were in order. (Laughter.) Some of you stayed up too late, ended up at HoChi* at 2:00 a.m. (Laughter.) Got some mambo sauce on your fingers. (Laughter.)

But you got here. And you've all worked hard to reach this 5 day. You've shuttled between challenging classes and Greek life. You've led clubs, played an instrument or a sport. You volunteered, you interned. You held down one, two, maybe three jobs. You've made lifelong friends and discovered exactly what you're made of. The "Howard Hustle" has strengthened your sense of purpose and ambition.

Which means you're part of a long line of Howard graduates. Some are on this stage today. Some are in the audience. That

---

*HoChi   Howard China, late-night counter-service restaurant near the college campus.

spirit of achievement and special responsibility has defined this campus ever since the Freedman's Bureau established Howard just four years after the Emancipation Proclamation; just two years after the Civil War came to an end. They created this university with a vision—a vision of uplift; a vision for an America where our fates would be determined not by our race, gender, religion or creed, but where we would be free—in every sense—to pursue our individual and collective dreams.

It is that spirit that's made Howard a centerpiece of African-American intellectual life and a central part of our larger American story. This institution has been the home of many firsts: The first black Nobel Peace Prize winner. The first black Supreme Court justice. But its mission has been to ensure those firsts were not the last. Countless scholars, professionals, artists, and leaders from every field received their training here. The generations of men and women who walked through this yard helped reform our government, cure disease, grow a black middle class, advance civil rights, shape our culture. The seeds of change—for all Americans—were sown here. And that's what I want to talk about today.

As I was preparing these remarks, I realized that when I was first elected President, most of you—the Class of 2016—were just starting high school. Today, you're graduating college. I used to joke about being old. Now I realize I'm old. (Laughter.) It's not a joke anymore. (Laughter.)

But seeing all of you here gives me some perspective. It makes me reflect on the changes that I've seen over my own lifetime. So let me begin with what may sound like a controversial statement—a hot take.

Given the current state of our political rhetoric and debate, 10 let me say something that may be controversial, and that is this: America is a better place today than it was when I graduated from college. (Applause.) Let me repeat: America is by almost every measure better than it was when I graduated from college. It also happens to be better off than when I took office—(laughter)—but that's a longer story. (Applause.) That's a different discussion for another speech.

But think about it. I graduated in 1983. New York City, America's largest city, where I lived at the time, had endured a decade marked by crime and deterioration and near bankruptcy. And many cities were in similar shape. Our nation had gone through years of economic stagnation, the stranglehold of foreign oil, a recession where unemployment nearly scraped 11 percent. The auto industry was getting its clock cleaned by foreign competition. And don't even get me started on the clothes and the hairstyles. I've tried to eliminate all photos of me from this period. I thought I looked good. (Laughter.) I was wrong.

Since that year—since the year I graduated—the poverty rate is down. Americans with college degrees, that rate is up. Crime rates are down. America's cities have undergone a renaissance. There are more women in the workforce. They're earning more money. We've cut teen pregnancy in half. We've slashed the African American dropout rate by almost 60 percent, and all of you have a computer in your pocket that gives you the world at the touch of a button. In 1983, I was part of fewer than 10 percent of African Americans who graduated with a bachelor's degree. Today, you're part of the more than 20 percent who will. And more than half of blacks say we're better off than our parents were at our age—and that our kids will be better off, too.

So America is better. And the world is better, too. A wall came down in Berlin. An Iron Curtain was torn asunder. The obscenity of apartheid came to an end. A young generation in Belfast and London have grown up without ever having to think about IRA bombings. In just the past 16 years, we've come from a world without marriage equality to one where it's a reality in nearly two dozen countries. Around the world, more people live in democracies. We've lifted more than 1 billion people from extreme poverty. We've cut the child mortality rate worldwide by more than half.

See Chapter 6 for tips on entertaining objections. America is better. The world is better. And stay with me now—race relations are better since I graduated. That's the truth. No, my election did not create a post-racial society. I don't know who was propagating that notion. That was not mine. But the election itself—and the subsequent one—because the first one, folks might have made a mistake. (Laughter.) The second one, they knew what they were getting. The election itself was just one indicator of how attitudes had changed.

In my inaugural address, I remarked that just 60 years earlier, 15 my father might not have been served in a D.C. restaurant—at least not certain of them. There were no black CEOs of Fortune 500 companies. Very few black judges. Shoot, as Larry Wilmore* pointed out last week, a lot of folks didn't even think blacks had the tools to be a quarterback. Today, former Bull Michael Jordan isn't just the greatest basketball player of all time—he owns the team. (Laughter.) When I was graduating, the main black hero on TV was Mr. T. (Laughter.) Rap and hip hop were counterculture, underground. Now, Shonda Rhimes owns Thursday night, and Beyoncé runs the world. (Laughter.) We're no longer only entertainers, we're producers, studio executives. No longer small business owners—we're CEOs, we're mayors, representatives, Presidents of the United States. (Applause.)

*__Larry Wilmore__ Comedian who spoke at the White House Correspondents' Dinner, an annual event for journalists covering news about the White House and president, a week before Obama's address.

I am not saying gaps do not persist. Obviously, they do. Racism persists. Inequality persists. Don't worry—I'm going to get to that. But I wanted to start, Class of 2016, by opening your eyes to the moment that you are in. If you had to choose one moment in history in which you could be born, and you didn't know ahead of time who you were going to be—what nationality, what gender, what race, whether you'd be rich or poor, gay or straight, what faith you'd be born into—you wouldn't choose 100 years ago. You wouldn't choose the fifties, or the sixties, or the seventies. You'd choose right now. If you had to choose a time to be, in the words of Lorraine Hansberry, "young, gifted, and black" in America, you would choose right now. (Applause.)

I tell you all this because it's important to note progress. Because to deny how far we've come would do a disservice to the cause of justice, to the legions of foot soldiers; to not only the incredibly accomplished individuals who have already been mentioned, but your mothers and your dads, and grandparents and great grandparents, who marched and toiled and suffered and overcame to make this day possible. I tell you this not to lull you into complacency, but to spur you into action—because there's still so much more work to do, so many more miles to travel. And America needs you to gladly, happily take up that work. You all have some work to do. So enjoy the party, because you're going to be busy. (Laughter.)

Yes, our economy has recovered from crisis stronger than almost any other in the world. But there are folks of all races who are still hurting—who still can't find work that pays enough to keep the lights on, who still can't save for retirement. We've still got a big racial gap in economic opportunity. The overall unemployment rate is 5 percent, but the black unemployment rate is almost nine. We've still got an achievement gap when black boys and girls graduate high school and college at lower rates than white boys and white girls. Harriet Tubman may be going on the twenty, but we've still got a gender gap when a black woman working full-time still earns just 66 percent of what a white man gets paid. (Applause.)

We've got a justice gap when too many black boys and girls pass through a pipeline from underfunded schools to overcrowded jails. This is one area where things have gotten worse. When I was in college, about half a million people in America were behind bars. Today, there are about 2.2 million. Black men are about six times likelier to be in prison right now than white men.

Around the world, we've still got challenges to solve that 20 threaten everybody in the 21st century—old scourges like disease and conflict, but also new challenges, from terrorism and climate change.

So make no mistake, Class of 2016—you've got plenty of work to do. But as complicated and sometimes intractable as these challenges may seem, the truth is that your generation is better positioned than any before you to meet those challenges, to flip the script.

Now, how you do that, how you meet these challenges, how you bring about change will ultimately be up to you. My generation, like all generations, is too confined by our own experience, too invested in our own biases, too stuck in our ways to provide much of the new thinking that will be required. But us old-heads have learned a few things that might be useful in your journey. So with the rest of my time, I'd like to offer some suggestions for how young leaders like you can fulfill your destiny and shape our collective future—bend it in the direction of justice and equality and freedom.

First of all—and this should not be a problem for this group— be confident in your heritage. (Applause.) Be confident in your blackness. One of the great changes that's occurred in our country since I was your age is the realization there's no one way to be black. Take it from somebody who's seen both sides of the debate about whether I'm black enough. (Laughter.) In the past couple months, I've had lunch with the Queen of England and hosted Kendrick Lamar in the Oval Office. There's no straitjacket, there's no constraints, there's no litmus test for authenticity.

Look at Howard. One thing most folks don't know about Howard is how diverse it is. When you arrived here, some of you were like, oh, they've got black people in Iowa? (Laughter.) But it's true—this class comes from big cities and rural communities, and some of you crossed oceans to study here. You shatter stereotypes. Some of you come from a long line of Bison. Some of you are the first in your family to graduate from college. (Applause.) You all talk different, you all dress different. You're Lakers fans, Celtics fans, maybe even some hockey fans. (Laughter.)

And because of those who've come before you, you have 25 models to follow. You can work for a company, or start your own. You can go into politics, or run an organization that holds politicians accountable. You can write a book that wins the National Book Award, or you can write the new run of "Black Panther." Or, like one of your alumni, Ta-Nehisi Coates, you can go ahead and just do both. You can create your own style, set your own standard of beauty, embrace your own sexuality. Think about an icon we just lost—Prince. He blew up categories. People didn't know what Prince was doing. (Laughter.) And folks loved him for it.

You need to have the same confidence. Or as my daughters tell me all the time, "You be you, Daddy." (Laughter.) Sometimes Sasha puts a variation on it—"You do you, Daddy." (Laughter.) And because you're a black person doing whatever it is that you're doing, that makes it a black thing. Feel confident.

Second, even as we each embrace our own beautiful, unique, and valid versions of our blackness, remember the tie that does bind us as African Americans—and that is our particular awareness of injustice and unfairness and struggle. That means we cannot sleepwalk through life. We cannot be ignorant of history. (Applause.) We can't meet the world with a sense of entitlement. We can't walk by a homeless man without asking why a society as wealthy as ours allows that state of affairs to occur. We can't just lock up a low-level dealer without asking why this boy, barely out of childhood, felt he had no other options. We have cousins and uncles and brothers and sisters who we remember were just as smart and just as talented as we were, but somehow got ground down by structures that are unfair and unjust.

And that means we have to not only question the world as it is, and stand up for those African Americans who haven't been so lucky—because, yes, you've worked hard, but you've also been lucky. That's a pet peeve of mine: People who have been successful and don't realize they've been lucky. That God may have blessed them; it wasn't nothing you did. So don't have an attitude. But we must expand our moral imaginations to understand and empathize with all people who are struggling, not just black folks who are struggling—the refugee, the immigrant, the rural poor, the transgender person, and yes, the middle-aged white guy who you may think has all the advantages, but over the last several decades has seen his world upended by economic and cultural and technological change, and feels powerless to stop it. You got to get in his head, too.

Number three: You have to go through life with more than just passion for change; you need a strategy. I'll repeat that. I want you to have passion, but you have to have a strategy. Not just awareness, but action. Not just hashtags, but votes.

You see, change requires more than righteous anger. It requires 30 a program, and it requires organizing. At the 1964 Democratic Convention, Fannie Lou Hamer—all five-feet-four-inches tall— gave a fiery speech on the national stage. But then she went back home to Mississippi and organized cotton pickers. And she didn't have the tools and technology where you can whip up a movement in minutes. She had to go door to door. And I'm so proud of the new guard of black civil rights leaders who understand this. It's thanks in large part to the activism of young people like many of you, from Black Twitter to Black Lives Matter, that America's eyes have been opened—white, black, Democrat, Republican—to the real problems, for example, in our criminal justice system.

But to bring about structural change, lasting change, awareness is not enough. It requires changes in law, changes in custom. If you care about mass incarceration, let me ask you: How are you pressuring members of Congress to pass the criminal justice reform bill now pending before them? (Applause.) If you care about better policing, do you know who your district attorney is? Do you know who your state's attorney general is? Do you know the difference? Do you know who appoints the police chief and who writes the police training manual? Find out who they are, what their responsibilities are. Mobilize the community, present them with a plan, work with them to bring about change, hold them accountable if they do not deliver. Passion is vital, but you've got to have a strategy.

And your plan better include voting—not just some of the time, but all the time. (Applause.) It is absolutely true that 50 years after the Voting Rights Act, there are still too many barriers in this country to vote. There are too many people trying to erect new barriers to voting. This is the only advanced democracy on Earth that goes out of its way to make it difficult for people to vote. And there's a reason for that. There's a legacy to that.

But let me say this: Even if we dismantled every barrier to voting, that alone would not change the fact that America has some of the lowest voting rates in the free world. In 2014, only 36 percent of Americans turned out to vote in the midterms—the second lowest participation rate on record. Youth turnout—that would be you—was less than 20 percent. Less than 20 percent. Four out of five did not vote. In 2012, nearly two in three African Americans turned out. And then, in 2014, only two in five turned out. You don't think that made a difference in terms of the Congress I've got to deal with? And then people are wondering, well, how come Obama hasn't gotten this done? How come he didn't get that done? You don't think that made a difference? What would have happened if you had turned out at 50, 60, 70 percent, all across this country? People try to make this political thing really complicated. Like, what kind of reforms do we need? And how do we need to do that? You know what, just vote. It's math. If you have more votes than the other guy, you get to do what you want. (Laughter.) It's not that complicated.

And you don't have excuses. You don't have to guess the number of jellybeans in a jar or bubbles on a bar of soap to register to vote. You don't have to risk your life to cast a ballot. Other people already did that for you. (Applause.) Your grandparents, your great-grandparents might be here today if they were working on it. What's your excuse? When we don't vote, we give away our power, disenfranchise ourselves—right when we need to use the power that we have; right when we need your power to stop others from taking away the vote and rights of those more vulnerable than you are—the elderly and the poor, the formerly incarcerated trying to earn their second chance.

So you got to vote all the time, not just when it's cool, not 35 just when it's time to elect a President, not just when you're inspired. It's your duty. When it's time to elect a member of Congress or a city councilman, or a school board member, or a sheriff. That's how we change our politics—by electing people at every level who are representative of and accountable to us. It is not that complicated. Don't make it complicated.

And finally, change requires more than just speaking out—it requires listening, as well. In particular, it requires listening to those with whom you disagree, and being prepared to compromise. When I was a state senator, I helped pass Illinois's first racial profiling law, and one of the first laws in the nation requiring the videotaping of confessions in capital cases. And we were successful because, early on, I engaged law enforcement. I didn't say to them, oh, you guys are so racist, you need to do something. I understood, as many of you do, that the overwhelming majority of police officers are good, and honest, and courageous, and fair, and love the communities they serve.

And we knew there were some bad apples, and that even the good cops with the best of intentions—including, by the way, African American police officers—might have unconscious biases, as we all do. So we engaged and we listened, and we kept working until we built consensus. And because we took the time to listen, we crafted legislation that was good for the police—because it improved the trust and cooperation of the community—and it was good for the communities, who were less likely to be treated unfairly. And I can say this unequivocally: Without at least the acceptance of the police organizations in Illinois, I could never have gotten those bills passed. Very simple. They would have blocked them.

The point is, you need allies in a democracy. That's just the way it is. It can be frustrating and it can be slow. But history teaches us that the alternative to democracy is always worse. That's not just true in this country. It's not a black or white thing. Go to any country where the give and take of democracy has been repealed by one-party rule, and I will show you a country that does not work.

And democracy requires compromise, even when you are 100 percent right. This is hard to explain sometimes. You can be completely right, and you still are going to have to engage folks who disagree with you. If you think that the only way forward is to be as uncompromising as possible, you will feel good about yourself, you will enjoy a certain moral purity, but you're not going to get what you want. And if you don't get what you want long enough, you will eventually think the whole system is rigged. And that will lead to more cynicism, and less participation, and a downward spiral of more injustice and more anger and more despair. And that's never been the source of our progress. That's how we cheat ourselves of progress.

We remember Dr. King's soaring oratory, the power of his 40 letter from a Birmingham jail, the marches he led. But he also sat down with President Johnson in the Oval Office to try and get a Civil Rights Act and a Voting Rights Act passed. And those two seminal bills were not perfect—just like the Emancipation Proclamation was a war document as much as it was some clarion call for freedom. Those mileposts of our progress were not perfect. They did not make up for centuries of slavery or Jim Crow or eliminate racism or provide for 40 acres and a mule. But they made things better. And you know what, I will take better every time. I always tell my staff—better is good, because you consolidate your gains and then you move on to the next fight from a stronger position.

Brittany Packnett, a member of the Black Lives Matter movement and Campaign Zero, one of the Ferguson protest organizers, she joined our Task Force on 21st Century Policing. Some of her fellow activists questioned whether she should participate. She rolled up her sleeves and sat at the same table with big city police chiefs and prosecutors. And because she did, she ended up shaping many of the recommendations of that task force. And those recommendations are now being adopted across the country—changes that many of the protesters called for. If young activists like Brittany had refused to participate out of some sense of ideological purity, then those great ideas would have just remained ideas. But she did participate. And that's how change happens.

America is big and it is boisterous and it is more diverse than ever. The president told me that we've got a significant Nepalese contingent here at Howard. I would not have guessed that. Right on. But it just tells you how interconnected we're becoming. And with so many folks from so many places, converging, we are not always going to agree with each other.

Another Howard alum, Zora Neale Hurston, once said—this is a good quote here: "Nothing that God ever made is the same thing to more than one person." Think about that. That's why our democracy gives us a process designed for us to settle our disputes with argument and ideas and votes instead of violence and simple majority rule.

So don't try to shut folks out, don't try to shut them down, no matter how much you might disagree with them. There's been a trend around the country of trying to get colleges to disinvite speakers with a different point of view, or disrupt a politician's rally. Don't do that—no matter how ridiculous or offensive you might find the things that come out of their mouths. Because as my grandmother used to tell me, every time a fool speaks, they are just advertising their own ignorance. Let them talk. Let them talk. If you don't, you just make them a victim, and then they can avoid accountability.

That doesn't mean you shouldn't challenge them. Have the confidence to challenge them, the confidence in the rightness of your position. There will be times when you shouldn't compromise your core values, your integrity, and you will have the responsibility to speak up in the face of injustice. But listen. Engage. If the other side has a point, learn from them. If they're wrong, rebut them. Teach them. Beat them on the battlefield of ideas. And you might as well start practicing now, because one thing I can guarantee you—you will have to deal with ignorance, hatred, racism, foolishness, trifling folks. (Laughter.) I promise you, you will have to deal with all that at every stage of your life. That may not seem fair, but life has never been completely fair. Nobody promised you a crystal stair. And if you want to make life fair, then you've got to start with the world as it is.

So that's my advice. That's how you change things. Change isn't something that happens every four years or eight years; change is not placing your faith in any particular politician and then just putting your feet up and saying, okay, go. Change is the effort of committed citizens who hitch their wagons to something bigger than themselves and fight for it every single day.

That's what Thurgood Marshall understood—a man who once walked this yard, graduated from Howard Law; went home to Baltimore, started his own law practice. He and his mentor, Charles Hamilton Houston, rolled up their sleeves and they set out to overturn segregation. They worked through the NAACP. Filed dozens of lawsuits, fought dozens of cases. And after nearly 20 years of effort—20 years—Thurgood Marshall ultimately succeeded in bringing his righteous cause before the Supreme Court, and securing the ruling in *Brown v. Board of Education* that separate could never be equal. (Applause.) Twenty years.

Marshall, Houston—they knew it would not be easy. They knew it would not be quick. They knew all sorts of obstacles would stand in their way. They knew that even if they won, that would just be the beginning of a longer march to equality. But they had discipline. They had persistence. They had faith—and a sense of humor. And they made life better for all Americans.

And I know you graduates share those qualities. I know it because I've learned about some of the young people graduating here today. There's a young woman named Ciearra Jefferson, who's graduating with you. And I'm just going to use her as an example. I hope you don't mind, Ciearra. Ciearra grew up in Detroit and was raised by a poor single mom who worked seven days a week in an auto plant. And for a time, her family found themselves without a place to call home. They bounced around between friends and family who might take them in. By her senior year, Ciearra was up at 5:00 A.M. every day, juggling homework, extracurricular activities, volunteering, all while taking care of her little sister. But she knew that education was her ticket to a better life. So she never gave up. Pushed herself to excel. This daughter of a single mom who works on the assembly line turned down a full scholarship to Harvard to come to Howard. (Applause.)

And today, like many of you, Ciearra is the first in her fam- 50 ily to graduate from college. And then, she says, she's going to go back to her hometown, just like Thurgood Marshall did, to make sure all the working folks she grew up with have access to the health care they need and deserve. As she puts it, she's going to be a "change agent." She's going to reach back and help folks like her succeed.

And people like Ciearra are why I remain optimistic about America. (Applause.) Young people like you are why I never give in to despair.

Ciearra Jefferson celebrates with her classmates at Howard's commencement ceremony.

James Baldwin once wrote, "Not everything that is faced can be changed, but nothing can be changed until it is faced."

Graduates, each of us is only here because someone else faced down challenges for us. We are only who we are because someone else struggled and sacrificed for us. That's not just Thurgood Marshall's story, or Ciearra's story, or my story, or your story—that is the story of America. A story whispered by slaves in the cotton fields, the song of marchers in Selma, the dream of a King in the shadow of Lincoln. The prayer of immigrants who set out for a new world. The roar of women demanding the vote. The rallying cry of workers who built America. And the GIs who bled overseas for our freedom.

Now it's your turn. And the good news is, you're ready. And when your journey seems too hard, and when you run into a chorus of cynics who tell you that you're being foolish to keep believing or that you can't do something, or that you should just give up, or you should just settle—you might say to yourself a little phrase that I've found handy these last eight years: Yes, we can.

Congratulations, Class of 2016! (Applause.) Good luck! 55 God bless you. God bless the United States of America. I'm proud of you.

Joining the Conversation

1. One purpose of this speech was to celebrate the achievements of the graduates. But at the same time, Barack Obama is making an argument about how the graduates should think and act as they make their way in the world. What are his main points, and how does he support them?
2. Obama says that we've got plenty of work to do, but things are better than they used to be. What evidence does he provide to support his claim?
3. Obama addresses much of his speech to the graduates. Find some examples of how he tries to make a connection with this audience. What other audiences, not at the ceremony, might he also be appealing to?
4. Obama emphasizes that we must listen to and, whenever possible, work with those with whom we disagree, because democracy requires compromise. How might danah boyd (pp. 255–65) respond to this view?
5. Imagine you were in the audience that day at Howard University. Write a tweet summarizing something Obama said and then responding in some way. You may need to write two tweets.

Everything That Rises Must Converge

FLANNERY O'CONNOR

———🔲———

HER DOCTOR HAD TOLD JULIAN'S MOTHER that she must lose twenty pounds on account of her blood pressure, so on Wednesday nights Julian had to take her downtown on the bus for a reducing class at the Y. The reducing class was designed for working girls over fifty, who weighed from 165 to 200 pounds. His mother was one of the slimmer ones, but she said ladies did not tell their age or weight. She would not ride the buses by herself at night since they had been integrated, and because the reducing class was one of her few pleasures, necessary for her health, and *free*, she said Julian could at least put himself out to take her, considering all she did for him. Julian did not

———

FLANNERY O'CONNOR (1925–1964) was an American writer and essayist. Born in Savannah, Georgia, she authored two novels and over thirty short stories. "Everything That Rises Must Converge" comes from her second short story collection, published posthumously in 1965. Her style is frequently associated with the Southern Gothic, a genre of stories set in the American South in which characters often find themselves in ominous situations.

like to consider all she did for him, but every Wednesday night he braced himself and took her.

She was almost ready to go, standing before the hall mirror, putting on her hat, while he, his hands behind him, appeared pinned to the door frame, waiting like Saint Sebastian for the arrows to begin piercing him. The hat was new and had cost her seven dollars and a half. She kept saying, "Maybe I shouldn't have paid that for it. No, I shouldn't have. I'll take it off and return it tomorrow. I shouldn't have bought it."

Julian raised his eyes to heaven. "Yes, you should have bought it," he said. "Put it on and let's go." It was a hideous hat. A purple velvet flap came down on one side of it and stood up on the other; the rest of it was green and looked like a cushion with the stuffing out. He decided it was less comical than jaunty and pathetic. Everything that gave her pleasure was small and depressed him.

She lifted the hat one more time and set it down slowly on top of her head. Two wings of gray hair protruded on either side of her florid face, but her eyes, sky-blue, were as innocent and untouched by experience as they must have been when she was ten. Were it not that she was a widow who had struggled fiercely to feed and clothe and put him through school and who was supporting him still, "until he got on his feet," she might have been a little girl that he had to take to town.

"It's all right, it's all right," he said. "Let's go." He opened the door himself and started down the walk to get her going. The sky was a dying violet and the houses stood out darkly against it, bulbous liver-colored monstrosities of a uniform ugliness though no two were alike. Since this had been a fashionable neighborhood forty years ago, his mother persisted in thinking they did well to have an apartment in it. Each house had a narrow collar of dirt around it in which sat, usually, a grubby child.

Julian walked with his hands in his pockets, his head down and thrust forward and his eyes glazed with the determination to make himself completely numb during the time he would be sacrificed to her pleasure.

The door closed and he turned to find the dumpy figure, surmounted by the atrocious hat, coming toward him. "Well," she said, "you only live once and paying a little more for it, I at least won't meet myself coming and going."

"Some day I'll start making money," Julian said gloomily—he knew he never would—"and you can have one of those jokes whenever you take the fit." But first they would move. He visualized a place where the nearest neighbors would be three miles away on either side.

"I think you're doing fine," she said, drawing on her gloves. "You've only been out of school a year. Rome wasn't built in a day."

She was one of the few members of the Y reducing class who arrived in hat and gloves and who had a son who had been to college. "It takes time," she said, "and the world is in such a mess. This hat looked better on me than any of the others, though when she brought it out I said, 'Take that thing back. I wouldn't have it on my head,' and she said, 'Now wait till you see it on,' and when she put it on me, I said, 'We-ull,' and she said, 'If you ask me, that hat does something for you and you do something for the hat, and besides,' she said, 'with that hat, you won't meet yourself coming and going.'"

Julian thought he could have stood his lot better if she had been selfish, if she had been an old hag who drank and screamed at him. He walked along, saturated in depression, as if in the midst of his martyrdom he had lost his faith. Catching sight of his long, hopeless, irritated face, she stopped suddenly with a grief-stricken look, and pulled back on his arm. "Wait on me," 10 she said. "I'm going back to the house and take this thing off and tomorrow I'm going to return it. I was out of my head. I can pay the gas bill with that seven-fifty."

He caught her arm in a vicious grip. "You are not going to take it back," he said. "I like it."

"Well," she said, "I don't think I ought . . ."

"Shut up and enjoy it," he muttered, more depressed than ever.

"With the world in the mess it's in," she said, "it's a wonder we can enjoy anything. I tell you, the bottom rail is on the top."

Julian sighed. 15

"Of course," she said, "if you know who you are, you can go anywhere." She said this every time he took her to the reducing class. "Most of them in it are not our kind of people," she said, "but I can be gracious to anybody. I know who I am."

"They don't give a damn for your graciousness," Julian said savagely. "Knowing who you are is good for one generation only. You haven't the foggiest idea where you stand now or who you are."

She stopped and allowed her eyes to flash at him. "I most certainly do know who I am," she said, "and if you don't know who you are, I'm ashamed of you."

"Oh hell," Julian said.

"Your great-grandfather was a former governor of this state," 20 she said. "Your grandfather was a prosperous landowner. Your grandmother was a Godhigh."

"Will you look around you," he said tensely, "and see where you are now?" and he swept his arm jerkily out to indicate the neighborhood, which the growing darkness at least made less dingy.

"You remain what you are," she said. "Your great-grandfather had a plantation and two hundred slaves."

"There are no more slaves," he said irritably.

"They were better off when they were," she said. He groaned to see that she was off on that topic. She rolled onto it every few days like a train on an open track. He knew every stop, every junction, every swamp along the way, and knew the exact point at which her conclusion would roll majestically into the station: "It's ridiculous. It's simply not realistic. They should rise, yes, but on their own side of the fence."

"Let's skip it," Julian said.   25

"The ones I feel sorry for," she said, "are the ones that are half white. They're tragic."

"Will you skip it?"

"Suppose we were half white. We would certainly have mixed feelings."

"I have mixed feelings now," he groaned.

"Well let's talk about something pleasant," she said.   30 "I remember going to Grandpa's when I was a little girl. Then the house had double stairways that went up to what was really the second floor—all the cooking was done on the first. I used to like to stay down in the kitchen on account of the way the walls smelled. I would sit with my nose pressed against the plaster and take deep breaths. Actually the place belonged to the Godhighs but your grandfather Chestny paid the mortgage and saved it for them. They were in reduced circumstances," she said, "but reduced or not, they never forgot who they were."

"Doubtless that decayed mansion reminded them," Julian muttered. He never spoke of it without contempt or thought of it without longing. He had seen it once when he was a child before it had been sold. The double stairways had rotted and been torn down. Negroes were living in it. But it remained in his mind as his mother had known it. It appeared in his dreams regularly. He would stand on the wide porch, listening to the rustle of oak leaves, then wander through the high-ceilinged hall into the parlor that opened onto it and gaze at the worn rugs and faded draperies. It occurred to him that it was he, not she, who could have appreciated it. He preferred its threadbare elegance to anything he could name and it was because of it that all the neighborhoods they had lived in had been a torment to him—whereas she had hardly known the difference. She called her insensitivity "being adjustable."

"And I remember the old darky who was my nurse, Caroline. There was no better person in the world. I've always had a great respect for my colored friends," she said. "I'd do anything in the world for them and they'd . . ."

"Will you for God's sake get off that subject?" Julian said. When he got on a bus by himself, he made it a point to sit down beside a Negro, in reparation as it were for his mother's sins.

"You're mighty touchy tonight," she said. "Do you feel all right?"

"Yes I feel all right," he said. "Now lay off." 35

She pursed her lips. "Well, you certainly are in a vile humor," she observed. "I just won't speak to you at all."

They had reached the bus stop. There was no bus in sight and Julian, his hands still jammed in his pockets and his head thrust forward, scowled down the empty street. The frustration of having to wait on the bus as well as ride on it began to creep up his neck like a hot hand. The presence of his mother was borne in upon him as she gave a pained sigh. He looked at her bleakly. She was holding herself very erect under the preposterous hat, wearing it like a banner of her imaginary dignity. There was in him an evil urge to break her spirit. He suddenly unloosened his tie and pulled it off and put it in his pocket.

She stiffened. "Why must you look like *that* when you take me to town?" she said. "Why must you deliberately embarrass me?"

"If you'll never learn where you are," he said, "you can at least learn where I am."

"You look like a—thug," she said.   40

"Then I must be one," he murmured.

"I'll just go home," she said. "I will not bother you. If you can't do a little thing like that for me . . ."

Rolling his eyes upward, he put his tie back on. "Restored to my class," he muttered. He thrust his face toward her and hissed, "True culture is in the mind, the *mind*," he said, and tapped his head, "the mind."

"It's in the heart," she said, "and in how you do things and how you do things is because of who you *are*."

"Nobody in the damn bus cares who you are."   45

"I care who I am," she said icily.

The lighted bus appeared on top of the next hill and as it approached, they moved out into the street to meet it. He put his hand under her elbow and hoisted her up on the creaking step. She entered with a little smile, as if she were going into a drawing room where everyone had been waiting for her. While he put in the tokens, she sat down on one of the broad front seats for three which faced the aisle. A thin woman with protruding teeth and long yellow hair was sitting on the end of it. His mother moved up beside her and left room for Julian beside herself. He sat down and looked at the floor across the aisle where a pair of thin feet in red and white canvas sandals were planted.

His mother immediately began a general conversation meant to attract anyone who felt like talking. "Can it get any hotter?" she said and removed from her purse a folding fan, black with a Japanese scene on it, which she began to flutter before her.

"I reckon it might could," the woman with the protruding teeth said, "but I know for a fact my apartment couldn't get no hotter."

"It must get the afternoon sun," his mother said. She sat 50 forward and looked up and down the bus. It was half filled. Everybody was white. "I see we have the bus to ourselves," she said. Julian cringed.

"For a change," said the woman across the aisle, the owner of the red and white canvas sandals. "I come on one the other day and they were thick as fleas—up front and all through."

"The world is in a mess everywhere," his mother said. "I don't know how we've let it get in this fix."

"What gets my goat is all those boys from good families stealing automobile tires," the woman with the protruding teeth said. "I told my boy, I said you may not be rich but you been raised right and if I ever catch you in any such mess, they can send you on to the reformatory. Be exactly where you belong."

"Training tells," his mother said. "Is your boy in high school?"

"Ninth grade," the woman said.   55

"My son just finished college last year. He wants to write but he's selling typewriters until he gets started," his mother said.

The woman leaned forward and peered at Julian. He threw her such a malevolent look that she subsided against the seat. On the floor across the aisle there was an abandoned newspaper. He got up and got it and opened it out in front of him. His mother discreetly continued the conversation in a lower tone but the woman across the aisle said in a loud voice, "Well that's nice. Selling typewriters is close to writing. He can go right from one to the other."

"I tell him," his mother said, "that Rome wasn't built in a day."

Behind the newspaper Julian was withdrawing into the inner compartment of his mind where he spent most of his time. This was a kind of mental bubble in which he established himself when he could not bear to be a part of what was going on around him. From it he could see out and judge but in it he was safe from any kind of penetration from without. It was the only place where he felt free of the general idiocy of his fellows. His mother had never entered it but from it he could see her with absolute clarity.

The old lady was clever enough and he thought that if she 60 had started from any of the right premises, more might have been expected of her. She lived according to the laws of her own fantasy world outside of which he had never seen her set foot. The law of it was to sacrifice herself for him after she had first created the necessity to do so by making a mess of things. If he had permitted her sacrifices, it was only because her lack of foresight had made them necessary. All of her life had been a struggle to act like a Chestny without the Chestny goods, and to give him everything she thought a Chestny ought to have; but since, said she, it was fun to struggle, why complain? And when you had won, as she had won, what fun to look back on the hard times! He could not forgive her that she had enjoyed the struggle and that she thought *she* had won.

What she meant when she said she had won was that she had brought him up successfully and had sent him to college and that he had turned out so well—good looking (her teeth had gone unfilled so that his could be straightened), intelligent (he realized he was too intelligent to be a success), and with a future ahead of him (there was of course no future ahead of him). She excused his gloominess on the grounds that he was still growing up and his radical ideas on his lack of practical experience. She said he didn't yet know a thing about "life," that he hadn't even entered the real world—when already he was as disenchanted with it as a man of fifty.

The further irony of all this was that in spite of her, he had turned out so well. In spite of going to only a third-rate college, he had, on his own initiative, come out with a first-rate education; in spite of growing up dominated by a small mind, he had ended up with a large one; in spite of all her foolish views, he was free of prejudice and unafraid to face facts. Most miraculous of all, instead of being blinded by love for her as she was for him, he had cut himself emotionally free of her and could see her with complete objectivity. He was not dominated by his mother.

The bus stopped with a sudden jerk and shook him from his meditation. A woman from the back lurched forward with little steps and barely escaped falling in his newspaper as she righted herself. She got off and a large Negro got on. Julian kept his paper lowered to watch. It gave him a certain satisfaction to see injustice in daily operation. It confirmed his view that with a few exceptions there was no one worth knowing within a radius of three hundred miles. The Negro was well dressed and carried a briefcase. He looked around and then sat down on the other end of the seat where the woman with the red and white canvas sandals was sitting. He immediately unfolded a newspaper and obscured himself behind it. Julian's mother's elbow at once prodded insistently into his ribs. "Now you see why I won't ride on these buses by myself," she whispered.

The woman with the red and white canvas sandals had risen at the same time the Negro sat down and had gone further back in the bus and taken the seat of the woman who had got off. His mother leaned forward and cast her an approving look.

Julian rose, crossed the aisle, and sat down in the place of the 65
woman with the canvas sandals. From this position, he looked
serenely across at his mother. Her face had turned an angry
red. He stared at her, making his eyes the eyes of a stranger.
He felt his tension suddenly lift as if he had openly declared
war on her.

He would have liked to get in conversation with the Negro
and to talk with him about art or politics or any subject that
would be above the comprehension of those around them, but
the man remained entrenched behind his paper. He was either
ignoring the change of seating or had never noticed it. There
was no way for Julian to convey his sympathy.

His mother kept her eyes fixed reproachfully on his face. The
woman with the protruding teeth was looking at him avidly as
if he were a type of monster new to her.

"Do you have a light?" he asked the Negro.

Without looking away from his paper, the man reached in
his pocket and handed him a packet of matches.

"Thanks," Julian said. For a moment he held the matches 70
foolishly. A NO SMOKING sign looked down upon him from over
the door. This alone would not have deterred him; he had no
cigarettes. He had quit smoking some months before because
he could not afford it. "Sorry," he muttered and handed back
the matches. The Negro lowered the paper and gave him an
annoyed look. He took the matches and raised the paper again.

His mother continued to gaze at him but she did not take
advantage of his momentary discomfort. Her eyes retained their
battered look. Her face seemed to be unnaturally red, as if her
blood pressure had risen. Julian allowed no glimmer of sympathy
to show on his face. Having got the advantage, he wanted desperately to keep it and carry it through. He would have liked to
teach her a lesson that would last her a while, but there seemed

no way to continue the point. The Negro refused to come out from behind his paper.

Julian folded his arms and looked stolidly before him, facing her but as if he did not see her, as if he had ceased to recognize her existence. He visualized a scene in which, the bus having reached their stop, he would remain in his seat and when she said, "Aren't you going to get off?" he would look at her as at a stranger who had rashly addressed him. The corner they got off on was usually deserted, but it was well lighted and it would not hurt her to walk by herself the four blocks to the Y. He decided to wait until the time came and then decide whether or not he would let her get off by herself. He would have to be at the Y at ten to bring her back, but he could leave her wondering if he was going to show up. There was no reason for her to think she could always depend on him.

He retired again into the high-ceilinged room sparsely set-tled with large pieces of antique furniture. His soul expanded momentarily but then he became aware of his mother across from him and the vision shriveled. He studied her coldly. Her feet in little pumps dangled like a child's and did not quite reach the floor. She was training on him an exaggerated look of reproach. He felt completely detached from her. At that moment he could with pleasure have slapped her as he would have slapped a particularly obnoxious child in his charge.

He began to imagine various unlikely ways by which he could teach her a lesson. He might make friends with some distinguished Negro professor or lawyer and bring him home to spend the evening. He would be entirely justified but her blood pressure would rise to 300. He could not push her to the extent of making her have a stroke, and moreover, he had never been successful at making any Negro friends. He had tried to strike up an acquaintance on the bus with some of the better types, with ones that looked like professors or ministers or lawyers. One morning he had sat down next to a distinguished-looking dark brown man who had answered his questions with a sonorous solemnity but who had turned out to be an undertaker. Another day he had sat down beside a cigar-smoking Negro with a diamond ring on his finger, but after a few stilted pleasantries, the Negro had rung the buzzer and risen, slipping two lottery tickets into Julian's hand as he climbed over him to leave.

He imagined his mother lying desperately ill and his being 75 able to secure only a Negro doctor for her. He toyed with that idea for a few minutes and then dropped it for a momentary vision of himself participating as a sympathizer in a sit-in demonstration. This was possible but he did not linger with it. Instead, he approached the ultimate horror. He brought home a beautiful suspiciously Negroid woman. Prepare yourself, he said. There is nothing you can do about it. This is the woman I've chosen. She's intelligent, dignified, even good, and she's suffered and she hasn't thought it *fun*. Now persecute us, go ahead and persecute us. Drive her out of here, but remember, you're driving me too. His eyes were narrowed and through the indignation he had generated, he saw his mother across the aisle, purple-faced, shrunken to the dwarf-like proportions of her moral nature, sitting like a mummy beneath the ridiculous banner of her hat.

He was tilted out of his fantasy again as the bus stopped. The door opened with a sucking hiss and out of the dark a large, gaily dressed, sullen-looking colored woman got on with a little boy. The child, who might have been four, had on a short plaid suit and a Tyrolean hat with a blue feather in it. Julian hoped that he would sit down beside him and that the woman would push in beside his mother. He could think of no better arrangement.

As she waited for her tokens, the woman was surveying the seating possibilities—he hoped with the idea of sitting where she was least wanted. There was something familiar-looking about her but Julian could not place what it was. She was a giant of a woman. Her face was set not only to meet opposition but to seek it out. The downward tilt of her large lower lip was like a warning sign: DON'T TAMPER WITH ME. Her bulging figure was encased in a green crepe dress and her feet overflowed in red shoes. She had on a hideous hat. A purple velvet flap came down on one side of it and stood up on the other; the rest of it was green and looked like a cushion with the stuffing out. She carried a mammoth red pocketbook that bulged throughout as if it were stuffed with rocks.

To Julian's disappointment, the little boy climbed up on the empty seat beside his mother. His mother lumped all children, black and white, into the common category, "cute," and she thought little Negroes were on the whole cuter than little white children. She smiled at the little boy as he climbed on the seat.

Meanwhile the woman was bearing down upon the empty seat beside Julian. To his annoyance, she squeezed herself into it. He saw his mother's face change as the woman settled herself next to him and he realized with satisfaction that this was more objectionable to her than it was to him. Her face seemed almost gray and there was a look of dull recognition in her eyes, as if suddenly she had sickened at some awful confrontation. Julian saw that it was because she and the woman had, in a sense, swapped sons. Though his mother would not realize the symbolic significance of this, she would feel it. His amusement showed plainly on his face.

The woman next to him muttered something unintelligible 80 to herself. He was conscious of a kind of bristling next to him, muted growling like that of an angry cat. He could not see anything but the red pocketbook upright on the bulging green thighs. He visualized the woman as she had stood waiting for her tokens—the ponderous figure, rising from the red shoes upward over the solid hips, the mammoth bosom, the haughty face, to the green and purple hat.

His eyes widened.

The vision of the two hats, identical, broke upon him with the radiance of a brilliant sunrise. His face was suddenly lit with joy. He could not believe that Fate had thrust upon his mother such a lesson. He gave a loud chuckle so that she would look at him and see that he saw. She turned her eyes on him slowly. The blue in them seemed to have turned a bruised purple. For a moment he had an uncomfortable sense of her innocence, but it lasted only a second before principle rescued him. Justice entitled him to laugh. His grin hardened until it said to her as plainly as if he were saying aloud: Your punishment exactly fits your pettiness. This should teach you a permanent lesson.

Her eyes shifted to the woman. She seemed unable to bear looking at him and to find the woman preferable. He became conscious again of the bristling presence at his side. The woman was rumbling like a volcano about to become active. His mother's mouth began to twitch slightly at one corner. With a sinking heart, he saw incipient signs of recovery on her face and realized that this was going to strike her suddenly as funny and was going to be no lesson at all. She kept her eyes on the woman and an amused smile came over her face as if the woman were a monkey that had stolen her hat. The little Negro was looking up at her with large fascinated eyes. He had been trying to attract her attention for some time.

"Carver!" the woman said suddenly. "Come heah!"

When he saw that the spotlight was on him at last, Carver 85
drew his feet up and turned himself toward Julian's mother
and giggled.

"Carver!" the woman said. "You heah me? Come heah!"

Carver slid down from the seat but remained squatting with
his back against the base of it, his head turned slyly around
toward Julian's mother, who was smiling at him. The woman
reached a hand across the aisle and snatched him to her. He
righted himself and hung backwards on her knees, grinning
at Julian's mother. "Isn't he cute?" Julian's mother said to the
woman with the protruding teeth.

"I reckon he is," the woman said without conviction.

The Negress yanked him upright but he eased out of her grip
and shot across the aisle and scrambled, giggling wildly, onto
the seat beside his love.

"I think he likes me," Julian's mother said, and smiled at 90
the woman. It was the smile she used when she was being
particularly gracious to an inferior. Julian saw everything lost.
The lesson had rolled off her like rain on a roof.

The woman stood up and yanked the little boy off the seat
as if she were snatching him from contagion. Julian could feel
the rage in her at having no weapon like his mother's smile.
She gave the child a sharp slap across his leg. He howled once
and then thrust his head into her stomach and kicked his feet
against her shins. "Behave," she said vehemently.

The bus stopped and the Negro who had been reading the
newspaper got off. The woman moved over and set the little
boy down with a thump between herself and Julian. She held
him firmly by the knee. In a moment he put his hands in front
of his face and peeped at Julian's mother through his fingers.

"I see yoooooooo!" she said and put her hand in front of her
face and peeped at him.

The woman slapped his hand down. "Quit yo' foolishness," she said, "before I knock the living Jesus out of you!"

Julian was thankful that the next stop was theirs. He reached 95 up and pulled the cord. The woman reached up and pulled it at the same time. Oh my God, he thought. He had the terrible intuition that when they got off the bus together, his mother would open her purse and give the little boy a nickel. The gesture would be as natural to her as breathing. The bus stopped and the woman got up and lunged to the front, dragging the child, who wished to stay on, after her. Julian and his mother got up and followed. As they neared the door, Julian tried to relieve her of her pocketbook.

"No," she murmured, "I want to give the little boy a nickel."

"No!" Julian hissed. "No!"

She smiled down at the child and opened her bag. The bus door opened and the woman picked him up by the arm and descended with him, hanging at her hip. Once in the street she set him down and shook him.

Julian's mother had to close her purse while she got down the bus step but as soon as her feet were on the ground, she opened it again and began to rummage inside. "I can't find but a penny," she whispered, "but it looks like a new one."

"Don't do it!" Julian said fiercely between his teeth. There 100 was a streetlight on the corner and she hurried to get under it so that she could better see into her pocketbook. The woman was heading off rapidly down the street with the child still hanging backward on her hand.

"Oh little boy!" Julian's mother called and took a few quick steps and caught up with them just beyond the lamppost. "Here's a bright new penny for you," and she held out the coin, which shone bronze in the dim light.

The huge woman turned and for a moment stood, her shoulders lifted and her face frozen with frustrated rage, and stared at Julian's mother. Then all at once she seemed to explode like a piece of machinery that had been given one ounce of pressure too much. Julian saw the black fist swing out with the red pocketbook. He shut his eyes and cringed as he heard the woman shout, "He don't take nobody's pennies!" When he opened his eyes, the woman was disappearing down the street with the little boy staring wide-eyed over her shoulder. Julian's mother was sitting on the sidewalk.

"I told you not to do that," Julian said angrily. "I told you not to do that!"

He stood over her for a minute, gritting his teeth. Her legs were stretched out in front of her and her hat was on her lap. He squatted down and looked her in the face. It was totally expressionless. "You got exactly what you deserved," he said. "Now get up."

He picked up her pocketbook and put what had fallen out 105 back in it. He picked the hat up off her lap. The penny caught his eye on the sidewalk and he picked that up and let it drop before her eyes into the purse. Then he stood up and leaned over and held his hands out to pull her up. She remained immobile. He sighed. Rising above them on either side were black apartment buildings, marked with irregular rectangles of light. At the end of the block a man came out of a door and walked off in the opposite direction. "All right," he said, "suppose somebody happens by and wants to know why you're sitting on the sidewalk?"

She took the hand and, breathing hard, pulled heavily up on it and then stood for a moment, swaying slightly as if the spots of light in the darkness were circling around her. Her eyes, shadowed and confused, finally settled on his face. He did not try to conceal his irritation. "I hope this teaches you a lesson," he said. She leaned forward and her eyes raked his face. She seemed trying to determine his identity. Then, as if she found nothing familiar about him, she started off with a headlong movement in the wrong direction.

"Aren't you going on to the Y?" he asked.

"Home," she muttered.

"Well, are we walking?"

For answer she kept going. Julian followed along, his hands 110 behind him. He saw no reason to let the lesson she had had go without backing it up with an explanation of its meaning. She might as well be made to understand what had happened to her. "Don't think that was just an uppity Negro woman," he said. "That was the whole colored race which will no longer take your condescending pennies. That was your black double. She can wear the same hat as you, and to be sure," he added gratuitously (because he thought it was funny), "it looked better on her than it did on you. What all this means," he said, "is that the old world is gone. The old manners are obsolete and your graciousness is not worth a damn." He thought bitterly of the house that had been lost for him. "You aren't who you think you are," he said.

She continued to plow ahead, paying no attention to him. Her hair had come undone on one side. She dropped her pocketbook and took no notice. He stooped and picked it up and handed it to her but she did not take it.

"You needn't act as if the world had come to an end," he said, "because it hasn't. From now on you've got to live in a new world and face a few realities for a change. Buck up," he said, "it won't kill you."

She was breathing fast.

"Let's wait on the bus," he said.

"Home," she said thickly.

"I hate to see you behave like this," he said. "Just like a child. I should be able to expect more of you." He decided to stop where he was and make her stop and wait for a bus. "I'm not going any farther," he said, stopping. "We're going on the bus."

She continued to go on as if she had not heard him. He took a few steps and caught her arm and stopped her. He looked into her face and caught his breath. He was looking into a face he had never seen before. "Tell Grandpa to come get me," she said.

He stared, stricken.

"Tell Caroline to come get me," she said.

Stunned, he let her go and she lurched forward again, walk- ing as if one leg were shorter than the other. A tide of dark- ness seemed to be sweeping her from him. "Mother!" he cried. "Darling, sweetheart, wait!" Crumpling, she fell to the pave- ment. He dashed forward and fell at her side, crying, "Mamma, Mamma!" He turned her over. Her face was fiercely distorted. One eye, large and staring, moved slightly to the left as if it had become unmoored. The other remained fixed on him, raked his face again, found nothing and closed.

"Wait here, wait here!" he cried and jumped up and began to run for help toward a cluster of lights he saw in the distance ahead of him. "Help, help!" he shouted, but his voice was thin, scarcely a thread of sound. The lights drifted farther away the faster he ran and his feet moved numbly as if they carried him nowhere. The tide of darkness seemed to sweep him back to her, postponing from moment to moment his entry into the world of guilt and sorrow.

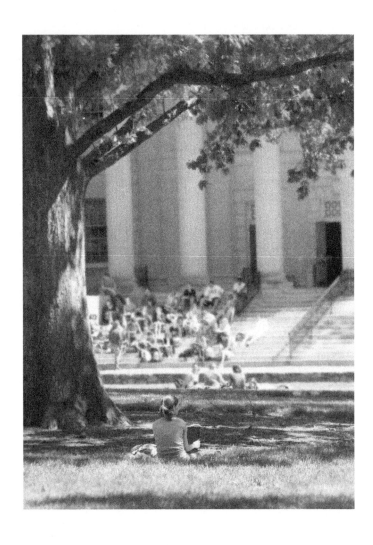

NINETEEN

IS COLLEGE THE BEST OPTION?

—⌐回⌐—

AMERICAN CULTURE MAY BE MORE DIVIDED THAN EVER, but not when it comes to college—or so it seems. The readings in this chapter focus on the present state of higher education in the United States and examine the potential benefits and pitfalls of going to college—not only for people who were born here or who enjoy the benefits of citizenship, but for immigrants and refugees, too.

From a very early age, we get the message that going to college is a crucial step in life. We hear this message regularly from our families, our schools, our communities. We see this message constantly in the media: movies, television shows, sports broadcasts, newspapers, magazines, and websites all show the allure and advantages of college. Even on the highways, billboards portray attractive, smiling, confident, intelligent-looking students on a tree-lined campus promoting the virtues of particular colleges: strong academics, excellent career opportunities, a friendly atmosphere, affordable tuition. Indeed, young people in the United States grow up to see college as inevitable, and many others living outside the country hope to have the chance of studying at one of America's many colleges or universities.

But not everyone sees this rosy picture. As college student blogger Hannah Fouks recently wrote for the website *Odyssey*,

"It frustrates me to no end that instead of educating students on all of their options, teachers make students focus on plans to attend college. This sends the message that to be successful they need to go to college, but this is not the case." If we look closely, we can glimpse another side to the college story: graduates unable to find good jobs, or, in some cases, any job at all; students with large amounts of college debt from loans that can take years, even decades, to pay off; stories of uncaring professors, huge classes, maze-like bureaucracies, distracted advisors; students who for a variety of reasons wake up one day to find themselves in academic trouble. As with all paths in life, it's possible to take a wrong turn in college. If students choose to attend, it's advisable for them to go in with their eyes open, with specific reasons for pursuing a so-called higher education, and with a plan for how best to succeed.

The chapter begins with Stephanie Owen and Isabel Sawhill's study showing that while college graduates on average make significantly more money in their lifetimes than high school graduates do, there is wide variation in the return on investment, based on such factors as college attended, major, whether or not the student graduates, and occupation. Political scientist Charles Murray advances the view that far too many American students currently go on to college and would be better off attending a vocational program or going right to work after high school.

Other authors in the chapter argue, in different ways, that faculty and institutions as a whole can support student success. Former college president Sanford J. Ungar, for instance, writes about the value of a college education steeped in the liberal arts, as opposed to the preprofessional training that many students now prefer. Liz Addison, drawing upon her own experiences, articulates the often underappreciated value of a community college education. Ben Casselman argues that mainstream news organizations focus far too much on the tiny percentage of students who attend elite institutions even though the majority of college students attend community colleges or four-year regional schools. Focusing on students at one such school in Minnesota, Steve Kolowich writes about one university's attempts to become a place of tolerance and acceptance for its Muslim students from Somalia.

Finally, two pieces argue that education can take place in settings other than college and about topics other than "academic" ones. Gerald Graff suggests that it matters less whether we read Macbeth or a Marvel comic book, as long as we approach what we read with a critical eye and question it in analytical, intellectual ways. And Mike Rose makes the case that people in blue-collar occupations who never attend college nonetheless develop sophisticated knowledge of how to do their work.

As a college student yourself, you'll find plenty to think about in this chapter—and on its companion blog, **theysayiblog.com.**

Should Everyone Go to College?

STEPHANIE OWEN AND ISABEL SAWHILL

—▣—

Summary

FOR THE PAST FEW DECADES, it has been widely argued that
a college degree is a prerequisite to entering the middle class
See pp. 25–27
on introducing
an ongoing
debate. in the United States. Study after study reminds us that
higher education is one of the best investments we can
make, and President Obama has called it "an economic
imperative." We all know that, on average, college graduates
make significantly more money over their lifetimes than those
with only a high school education. What gets less attention

STEPHANIE OWEN AND ISABEL SAWHILL are the authors of *Should
Everyone Go to College?*, a report published in 2013 by the Brookings Institution, a centrist think tank in Washington, D.C. Owen
was a senior research assistant at Brookings' Center on Children and
Families at the time of the report's publication and is currently a PhD
student in public policy and economics at the University of Michigan.
Sawhill is a senior fellow in economic studies at Brookings and the
author of *Generation Unbound: Drifting into Sex and Parenthood without Marriage* (2014).

is the fact that not all college degrees or college graduates are equal. There is enormous variation in the so-called return to education depending on factors such as institution attended, field of study, whether a student graduates, and post-graduation occupation. While the average return to obtaining a college degree is clearly positive, we emphasize that it is not universally so. For certain schools, majors, occupations, and individuals, college may not be a smart investment. By telling all young people that they should go to college no matter what, we are actually doing some of them a disservice.

The Rate of Return on Education

One way to estimate the value of education is to look at the increase in earnings associated with an additional year of schooling. However, correlation is not causation, and getting at the true causal effect of education on earnings is not so easy. The main problem is one of selection: if the smartest, most motivated people are both more likely to go to college and more likely to be financially successful, then the observed difference in earnings by years of education doesn't measure the true effect of college.

Researchers have attempted to get around this problem of causality by employing a number of clever techniques, including, for example, comparing identical twins with different levels of education. The best studies suggest that the return to an additional year of school is around 10 percent. If we apply this 10 percent rate to the median earnings of about $30,000 for a 25- to 34-year-old high school graduate working full time in 2010, this implies that a year of college increases earnings by $3,000, and four years increases them by $12,000. Notice that this amount is less than the raw differences in earnings between high school graduates and bachelor's degree holders of $15,000, but it is in the same ballpark. Similarly, the raw difference between high school graduates and associate's degree holders is about $7,000, but a return of 10% would predict the causal effect of those additional two years to be $6,000.

There are other factors to consider. The cost of college matters as well: the more someone has to pay to attend, the lower the net benefit of attending. Furthermore, we have to factor in the opportunity cost of college, measured as the foregone earnings a student gives up when he or she leaves or delays entering the workforce in order to attend school. Using average earnings for 18- and 19-year-olds and 20- and 21-year-olds with high school degrees (including those working part-time or not at all), Michael Greenstone and Adam Looney of Brookings' Hamilton Project calculate an opportunity cost of $54,000 for a four-year degree.

In this brief, we take a rather narrow view of the value of 5 a college degree, focusing on the earnings premium. However, there are many non-monetary benefits of schooling which are harder to measure but no less important. Research suggests that additional education improves overall wellbeing by affecting things like job satisfaction, health, marriage, parenting, trust, and social interaction. Additionally, there are social benefits to education, such as reduced crime rates and higher political participation. We also do not want to dismiss personal preferences, and we acknowledge that many people derive value from their careers in ways that have nothing to do with money. While beyond the scope of this piece, we do want to point out that these noneconomic factors can change the cost-benefit calculus.

As noted above, the gap in annual earnings between young high school graduates and bachelor's degree holders working full time is $15,000. What's more, the earnings premium associated with a college degree grows over a lifetime. Hamilton Project research shows that 23- to 25-year-olds with bachelor's degrees make $12,000 more than high school graduates but by age 50, the gap has grown to $46,500 (Figure 1). When we look at lifetime earnings—the sum of earnings over a career—the total premium is $570,000 for a bachelor's degree and $170,000 for an associate's degree. Compared to the average up-front cost of four years of college (tuition plus opportunity cost) of $102,000, the Hamilton Project is not alone in arguing that investing in college provides "a tremendous return."

It is always possible to quibble over specific calculations, but it is hard to deny that, on average, the benefits of a college degree far outweigh the costs. The key phrase here is "on average." The purpose of this brief is to highlight the reasons why,

FIGURE 1. EARNING TRAJECTORIES
BY EDUCATIONAL ATTAINMENT

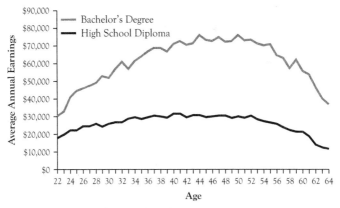

Source: Greenstone and Looney (2011).
Note: Sample includes all civilian U.S. citizens, excluding those in school. Annual earnings are averaged over the entire sample, including those without work. Source: March CPS 2007–2010.

for a given individual, the benefits may not outweigh the costs. We emphasize that a 17- or 18-year-old deciding whether and where to go to college should carefully consider his or her own likely path of education and career before committing a considerable amount of time and money to that degree. With tuitions rising faster than family incomes, the typical college student is now more dependent than in the past on loans, creating serious risks for the individual student and perhaps for the system as a whole, should widespread defaults occur in the future. Federal student loans now total close to $1 trillion, larger than credit card debt or auto loans and second only to mortgage debt on household balance sheets.

Variation in the Return to Education

It is easy to imagine hundreds of dimensions on which college degrees and their payoffs could differ. Ideally, we'd like to be able to look into a crystal ball and know which individual school will give the highest net benefit for a given student with her unique strengths, weaknesses, and interests. Of course, we are not able to do this. What we can do is lay out several key dimensions that seem to significantly affect the return to a college degree. These include school type, school selectivity level, school cost and financial aid, college major, later occupation, and perhaps most importantly, the probability of completing a degree.

Variation by School Selectivity

Mark Schneider of the American Enterprise Institute (AEI) and the American Institutes for Research (AIR) used longitudinal data from the Baccalaureate and Beyond survey to calculate lifetime earnings for bachelor's earners by type of institution attended, then compared them to the lifetime earnings of high school graduates. The difference (after accounting for tuition costs and discounting to a present value) is the value of a bachelor's degree. For every type of school (categorized by whether the school was a public institution or a nonprofit private institution and by its selectivity) this value is positive, but it varies widely. People who attended the most selective private schools have a lifetime earnings premium of over $620,000 (in 2012 dollars). For those who attended a minimally selective or open admission private school, the premium is only a third of that. Schneider performed a similar exercise with campus-level data on college graduates (compiled by the online salary information company PayScale), calculating the return on investment (ROI) of a bachelor's degree (Figure 2). These calculations suggest that public schools tend to have higher ROIs than private schools, and more selective schools offer higher returns than less selective ones. Even within a school type and selectivity category, the variation is striking. For example, the average ROI for a competitive public school in 2010 is 9 percent, but the highest rate within this category is 12 percent while the lowest is 6 percent.

Another important element in estimating the ROI on a college education is financial aid, which can change the expected return dramatically. For example, Vassar College is one of the most expensive schools on the 2012 list and has a relatively low annual ROI of 6%. But when you factor in its generous aid packages (nearly 60% of students receive aid, and the average amount is over $30,000), Vassar's annual ROI increases 50%, to a return of 9% (data available at http://www.payscale.com/college-education-value-2012).

FIGURE 2. RETURN ON INVESTMENT OF A BACHELOR'S
DEGREE BY INSTITUTION TYPE

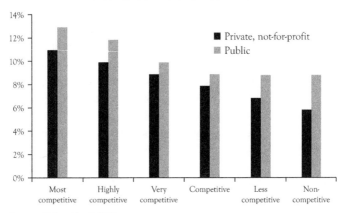

Source: Schneider (2010).
Note: Data uses PayScale return on investment data and Barron's index of
school selectivity.

One of the most important takeaways from the PayScale
data is that not every bachelor's degree is a smart investment.
After attempting to account for in-state vs. out-of-state tuition,
financial aid, graduation rates, years taken to graduate, wage
inflation, and selection, nearly two hundred schools on the
2012 list have negative ROIs. Students may want to think twice
about attending the Savannah College of Art and Design in
Georgia or Jackson State University in Mississippi. The problem is compounded if the students most likely to attend these
less selective schools come from disadvantaged families.

Variation by Field of Study and Career

Even within a school, the choices a student makes about his or
her field of study and later career can have a large impact on

what he or she gets out of her degree. It is no coincidence that the three schools with the highest 30-year ROIs on the 2012 PayScale list—Harvey Mudd, Caltech, and MIT—specialize in the STEM fields: science, technology, engineering, and math. Recent analysis by the Census Bureau also shows that the lifetime earnings of workers with bachelor's degrees vary widely by college major and occupation. The highest paid major is engineering, followed by computers and math. The lowest paid major, with barely half the lifetime earnings of engineering majors, is education, followed by the arts and psychology (Figure 3). The highest-earning

FIGURE 3. WORK-LIFE EARNINGS OF BACHELOR'S DEGREE HOLDERS BY COLLEGE MAJOR

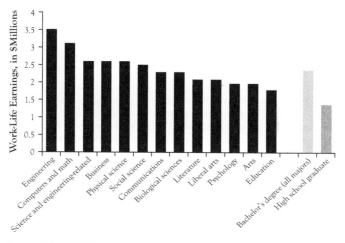

Source: Julian (2012).

Note: Synthetic work-life earnings estimates are calculated by finding median earnings for each 5-year age group between 25 and 64 (25–29, 30–34, etc.). Earnings for each group is multiplied by 5 to get total earnings for that period, then aggregated to get total lifetime earnings. This is done for high school graduates, bachelor's degree holders, and bachelor's degree holders by major.

FIGURE 4. WORK-LIFE EARNINGS OF BACHELOR'S DEGREE
HOLDERS BY OCCUPATION

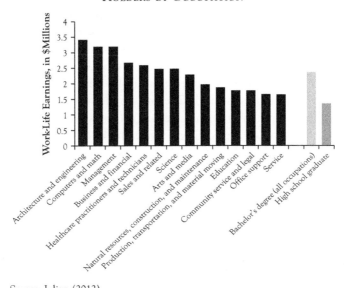

Source: Julian (2012).
Note: Synthetic work-life earnings estimates are calculated by finding median
earnings for each 5-year age group between 25 and 64 (25–29, 30–34, etc.).
Earnings for each group is multiplied by 5 to get total earnings for that period,
then aggregated to get total lifetime earnings. This is done for high school graduates, bachelor's degree holders, and bachelor's degree holders by occupation.

occupation category is architecture and engineering, with computers, math, and management in second place. The lowest-earning
occupation for college graduates is service (Figure 4). According
to Census's calculations, the lifetime earnings of an education or
arts major working in the service sector are actually lower than
the average lifetime earnings of a high school graduate.

When we dig even deeper, we see that just as not all college degrees are equal, neither are all high school diplomas.

Anthony Carnevale and his colleagues at the Georgetown Center on Education and the Workforce use similar methodology to the Census calculations but disaggregate even further, estimating median lifetime earnings for all education levels by occupation. They find that 14 percent of people with a high school diploma make at least as much as those with a bachelor's degree, and 17 percent of people with a bachelor's degree make more than those with a professional degree. The authors argue that much of this finding is explained by occupation. In every occupation category, more educated workers earn more.

But, for example, someone working in a STEM job with only a high school diploma can expect to make more over a lifetime than someone with a bachelor's degree working in education, community service and arts, sales and office work, health support, blue collar jobs, or personal services.

The numbers above are for full-time workers in a given field. 15 In fact, choice of major can also affect whether a college graduate can find a job at all. Another recent report from the Georgetown Center on Education and the Workforce breaks down unemployment rates by major for both recent (age 22–26) and experienced (age 30–54) college graduates in 2009–2010. People who majored in education or health have very low unemployment—even though education is one of the lowest-paying majors. Architecture graduates have particularly high unemployment, which may simply reflect the decline of the construction industry during the Great Recession. Arts majors don't fare too well, either. The expected earnings (median full-time earnings times the probability of being employed) of a young college graduate with a theater degree are about $6,000 more than the expected earnings of a young high school graduate. For a young person with a mechanical engineering degree, the expected earnings of the college graduate is a staggering $35,000 more than that of a typical high school graduate.

Variation in Graduation Rates

Comparisons of the return to college by highest degree attained include only people who actually complete college. Students who fail to obtain a degree incur some or all of the costs of a bachelor's degree without the ultimate payoff. This has major implications for inequalities of income and wealth, as the students least likely to graduate—lower-income students—are also the most likely to take on debt to finance their education.

Fewer than 60 percent of students who enter four-year schools finish within six years, and for low-income students it's even worse. Again, the variation in this measure is huge. Just within Washington, D.C., for example, six-year graduation rates range from a near-universal 93 percent at Georgetown University to a dismal 19 percent at the University of D.C. Of course, these are very different institutions, and we might expect high-achieving students at an elite school like Georgetown to have higher completion rates than at a less competitive school like UDC. In fact, Frederick Hess and his colleagues at AEI have documented that the relationship between selectivity and completion is positive, echoing other work that suggests that students are more likely to succeed in and graduate from college when they attend more selective schools (Figure 5). At the most selective schools, 88 percent of students graduate within six years; at non-competitive schools, only 35 percent do. Furthermore, the range of completion rates is negatively correlated with school ranking, meaning the least selective schools have the widest range. For example, one non-competitive school, Arkansas Baptist College, graduates 100 percent of its students, while only 8 percent of students at Southern University at New Orleans finish. Not every student can get into Harvard, where the likelihood of graduating is 97 percent, but students

FIGURE 5. AVERAGE SIX-YEAR GRADUATION RATES
BY SCHOOL SELECTIVITY

Source: Hess et al. (2009).

can choose to attend a school with a better track record within their ability level.

Unfortunately, recent evidence by Caroline Hoxby of Stanford and Christopher Avery of Harvard shows that most high-achieving low-income students never even apply to the selective schools that they are qualified to attend—and at which they would be eligible for generous financial aid. There is clearly room for policies that do a better job of matching students to schools.

Policy Implications

All of this suggests that it is a mistake to unilaterally tell young Americans that going to college—any college—is the best decision they can make. If they choose wisely and attend a school with generous financial aid and high expected earnings, and if they don't just enroll but graduate, they can greatly improve their lifetime prospects. The information needed to make a wise decision, however, can be difficult to find and hard to interpret.

One solution is simply to make the type of information discussed above more readily available. A study by Andrew Kelly and Mark Schneider of AEI found that when parents were asked to choose between two similar public universities in their state, giving them information on the schools' graduation rates caused them to prefer the higher-performing school. 20

The PayScale college rankings are a step in the right direction, giving potential students and their parents information with which to make better decisions. Similarly, the Obama Administration's new College Scorecard is being developed to increase transparency in the college application process. As it operates now, a prospective student can type in a college's name and learn its average net price, graduation rate, loan default rate, and median borrowed amount. The Department of Education is working to add information about the earnings of a given school's graduates. There is also a multi-dimensional search feature that allows users to find schools by location, size, and degrees and majors offered. The Student Right to Know Before You Go Act, sponsored by Senators Ron Wyden (D-OR) and Marco Rubio (R-FL), also aims to expand the data available on the costs and benefits of individual schools, as well as programs and majors within schools.

The College Scorecard is an admirable effort to help students and parents navigate the complicated process of choosing a college. However, it may not go far enough in improving transparency and helping students make the best possible decisions. A recent report by the Center for American Progress (CAP) showed a draft of the Scorecard to a focus group of college-bound high school students and found, among other things, that they are frequently confused about the term "net price" and give little weight to six-year graduation rates because they expect to graduate in four. It appears that the White House has responded to some of these critiques, for example showing median amount borrowed and default rates rather than the confusing "student loan repayment." Nevertheless, more information for students and their parents is needed.

There is also room for improvement in the financial aid system, which can seem overwhelmingly complex for families not familiar with the process. Studies have shown that students frequently underestimate how much aid they are eligible for, and don't claim the tax incentives that would save them money. Since 2009, the Administration has worked to simplify the FAFSA, the form that families must fill out to receive federal aid—but more could be done to guide low-income families through the process.

In the longer run, colleges need to do more to ensure that their students graduate, particularly the lower-income students who struggle most with persistence and completion. Research suggests that grants and loans increase enrollment but that aid must be tied to performance in order to affect persistence. Currently, we spend over $100 billion on Pell Grants and federal loans, despite a complete lack of evidence that this money leads to higher graduation rates. Good research on programs like Georgia's HOPE scholarships or West Virginia's PROMISE scholarships suggest that attaching strings to grant aid can improve college persistence and completion.

Finally, we want to emphasize that the personal characteristics and skills of each individual are equally important. It may be that for a student with poor grades who is on the fence 25 about enrolling in a four-year program, the most bang for the buck will come from a vocationally oriented associate's degree or career-specific technical training. Indeed, there are many well-paid job openings going unfilled because employers can't find workers with the right skills—skills that young potential workers could learn from training programs, apprenticeships, a vocational certificate, or an associate's degree. Policymakers should encourage these alternatives at the high school as well as the postsecondary level, with a focus on high-demand occupations and high-growth sectors. There has long been resistance to vocational education in American high schools, for fear that "tracking" students reinforces socioeconomic (and racial) stratification and impedes mobility. But if the default for many lower-achieving students was a career-focused training path rather than a path that involves dropping out of traditional college, their job prospects would probably improve. For example, Career Academies are high schools organized around an occupational or industry focus, and have partnerships with local employers and colleges. They have been shown by gold standard research to increase men's wages, hours worked, and employment stability after high school, particularly for those at high risk of dropping out.

Conclusions

In this brief, we have corralled existing research to make the point that while on average the return to college is highly positive, there is a considerable spread in the value of going to college. A bachelor's degree is not a smart investment for every student in every circumstance. We have outlined three important steps policymakers can take to make sure every person does make a smart investment in their choice of postsecondary education. First, we must provide more information in a comprehensible manner. Second, the federal government should lead the way on performance-based scholarships to incentivize college attendance and persistence. Finally, there should be more good alternatives to a traditional academic path, including career and technical education and apprenticeships.

ADDITIONAL READING

Anthony P. Carnevale, Ban Cheah, and Jeff Strohl, "Hard Times: College Majors, Unemployment, and Earnings: Not All College Degrees Are Created Equal" (Washington, D.C.: The Georgetown University Center on Education and the Workforce, January 2012).

Anthony P. Carnevale, Stephen J. Rose, and Ban Cheah, "The College Payoff: Education, Occupations, Lifetime Earnings" (Washington, D.C.: The Georgetown University Center on Education and the Workforce, August 2011).

Michael Greenstone and Adam Looney, "Where Is the Best Place to Invest $102,000—In Stocks, Bonds, or a College Degree?" (Washington, D.C.: The Brookings Institution, June 2011).

Frederick M. Hess, Mark Schneider, Kevin Carey, and Andrew P. Kelly, "Diplomas and Dropouts: Which Colleges Actually Graduate Their Students (and Which Don't)" (Washington, D.C.: American Enterprise Institute for Public Policy Research, June 2009).

Harry J. Holzer and Robert I. Lerman, "The Future of Middle-Skill Jobs," (Washington, D.C.: The Brookings Institution, February 2009).

Caroline M. Hoxby and Christopher Avery, "The Missing 'One-Offs': The Hidden Supply of High-Achieving, Low Income Students" (Cambridge, MA, Working Paper, National Bureau of Economic Research, 2012).

Tiffany Julian, "Work-Life Earnings by Field of Degree and Occupation for People With a Bachelor's Degree: 2011" (Washington, D.C.: U.S. Census Bureau, October 2012).

Andrew P. Kelly and Mark Schneider, "Filling In the Blanks: How Information Can Affect Choice in Higher Education" (Washington, D.C.: American Enterprise Institute for Public Policy Research, January 2011).

Julie Margetta Morgan and Gadi Dechter, "Improving the College
    Scorecard: Using Student Feedback to Create an Effective Disclosure"
    (Washington, D.C.: Center for American Progress, November 2012).
Mark Schneider, "How Much Is That Bachelor's Degree Really Worth?
    The Million Dollar Misunderstanding" (Washington, D.C.: American
    Enterprise Institute for Public Policy Research, May 2009).
Mark Schneider, "Is College Worth the Investment?" (Washington, D.C.:
    American Enterprise Institute for Public Policy Research, October
    2010).

Joining the Conversation

1. Stephanie Owen and Isabel Sawhill announce the "they say" in their second sentence—"Study after study reminds us that higher education is one of the best investments we can make"—and then proceed to report on how the return on that investment varies. What factors do they say make college a questionable investment?

2. This report draws upon quite a bit of quantitative data on the economic effects of graduating from college. Look carefully at one of the graphs that Owen and Sawhill provide, and explain in your own words what the data say.

3. Owen and Sawhill's analysis seems to favor baccalaureate degree programs as conferring the greatest advantages upon students. How might essayist Liz Addison, whose essay appears on pages 421–24, respond to their argument?

4. In the essay's concluding paragraphs, the authors note information that students and parents should know before choosing a college. What information do they consider most important? What did you know and what did you not know about colleges you were considering as you were deciding

which school to attend? How might additional knowledge have helped you make a more informed choice?

5. According to Owen and Sawhill, "For certain schools, majors, occupations, and individuals, college may not be a smart investment." Taking this statement as a "they say," write a short essay responding with what you think. Discuss your own reasons for attending college, and refer to the authors' argument and data about the pros and cons of attending college.

The New Liberal Arts

SANFORD J. UNGAR

HARD ECONOMIC TIMES inevitably bring scrutiny of all accepted ideals and institutions, and this time around liberal-arts education has been especially hard hit. Something that has long been held up as a uniquely sensible and effective approach to learning has come under the critical gaze of policy makers and the news media, not to mention budget-conscious families.

But the critique, unfortunately, seems to be fueled by reliance on common misperceptions. Here are a few of those misperceptions, from my vantage point as a liberal-arts college president, and my reactions to them:

SANFORD J. UNGAR was the president of Goucher College in Baltimore, Maryland, from 2001 to 2014. He is the author of *Fresh Blood: The New American Immigrants* (1998) and *Africa: The People and Politics of an Emerging Continent* (1986). Ungar has also worked in broadcast journalism both at National Public Radio and at the Voice of America, the U.S. government–funded broadcast network for a global audience. His extensive print journalism work includes articles in *Newsweek*, the *Economist*, and the *Washington Post*. This article first appeared in *The Chronicle of Higher Education*, a publication read by college faculty and administrators, on March 5, 2010.

Misperception No. 1: A liberal-arts degree is a luxury that most families can no longer afford. "Career education" is what we now must focus on. Many families are indeed struggling, in the depths of the recession, to pay for their children's college education. Yet one could argue that the traditional, well-rounded preparation that the liberal arts offer is a better investment than ever—that the future demands of citizenship will require not narrow technical or job-focused training, but rather a subtle understanding of the complex influences that shape the world we live in.

No one could be against equipping oneself for a career. But the "career education" bandwagon seems to suggest that shortcuts are available to students that lead directly to high-paying jobs—leaving out "frills" like learning how to write and speak well, how to understand the nuances of literary texts and scientific concepts, how to collaborate with others on research.

Many states and localities have officials or task forces in 5 charge of "work-force development," implying that business and industry will communicate their needs and educational institutions will dutifully turn out students who can head straight to the factory floor or the office cubicle to fulfill them. But history is filled with examples of failed social experiments that treated people as work units rather than individuals capable of inspiration and ingenuity. It is far wiser for students to prepare for change—and the multiple careers they are likely to have—than to search for a single job track that might one day become a dead end.

I recently heard Geoffrey Garin, president of Hart Research Associates, suggest that the responsibility of higher education today is to prepare people "for jobs that do not yet exist." It may be that studying the liberal arts is actually the best form of career education.

Misperception No. 2: College graduates are finding it harder to get good jobs with liberal-arts degrees. Who wants to hire somebody with an irrelevant major like philosophy or French? Yes, recent graduates have had difficulty in the job market, but

See Chapter 4 for tips on explaining why you disagree.

the recession has not differentiated among major fields of study in its impact. A 2009 survey for the Association of American Colleges and Universities actually found that more than three-quarters of our nation's employers recommend that collegebound students pursue a "liberal education." An astounding 89 percent said they were looking for more emphasis on "the ability to effectively communicate orally and in writing," and almost as many urged the development of better "critical thinking and analytical reasoning skills." Seventy percent said they were on the lookout for "the ability to innovate and be creative."

It is no surprise, then, that a growing number of corporations, including some in highly technical fields, are headed by people with liberal-arts degrees. Plenty of philosophy and physics majors work on Wall Street, and the ability to analyze and compare literature across cultures is a skill linked to many other fields, including law and medicine. Knowledge of foreign languages is an advantage in all lines of work. What seemed a radical idea in business education 10 years or so ago—that critical and creative thinking is as "relevant" as finance or accounting—is now commonplace.

Misperception No. 3: The liberal arts are particularly irrelevant for low-income and first-generation college students. They, more than their more-affluent peers, must focus on something more practical and marketable. It is condescending to imply that those who have less cannot understand and appreciate the finer elements of knowledge—another way of saying, really, that the rich folks will do the important thinking, and the lower classes will simply carry out their ideas. That is just a form of prejudice and cannot be supported intellectually.

Perhaps students who come with prior acquaintance with 10 certain fields and a reservoir of experience have an advantage at the start of college. But in my experience, it is often the people who are newest to certain ideas and approaches who are the most original and inventive in the discussion and application of those ideas. They catch up quickly.

We should respect what everyone brings to the table and train the broadest possible cross section of American society to participate in, and help shape, civil discourse. We cannot assign different socioeconomic groups to different levels or types of education. This is a country where a mixed-race child raised overseas by a struggling single mother who confronts impossible odds can grow up to be president. It is precisely a liberal education that allowed him to catch up and move ahead.

Misperception No. 4: One should not, in this day and age, study only the arts. The STEM fields—science, technology, engineering, and mathematics—are where the action is. The liberal arts encompass the broadest possible range of disciplines in the natural sciences, the humanities, and the social sciences. In fact, the historical basis of a liberal education is in the classical artes liberales, comprising the trivium (grammar, logic, and rhetoric) and the quadrivium (arithmetic, geometry, astronomy, and music). Another term sometimes substituted for liberal arts, for the sake of clarity, is "the arts and sciences." Thus, many universities have colleges, divisions, or schools of arts and sciences among their academic units.

To be sure, there is much concern about whether America is keeping up with China and other rising economies in the

STEM disciplines. No evidence suggests, however, that success in scientific and technical fields will be greater if it comes at the expense of a broad background in other areas of the liberal arts.

Misperception No. 5: It's the liberal Democrats who got this country into trouble in recent years, so it's ridiculous to continue indoctrinating our young people with a liberal education. A liberal education, as properly defined above, has nothing whatsoever to do with politics—except insofar as politics is one of the fields that students often pursue under its rubric. On the contrary, because of its inclusiveness and its respect for classical traditions, the liberal arts could properly be described as a conservative approach to preparation for life. It promotes the idea of listening to all points of view and not relying on a single ideology, and examining all approaches to solving a problem rather than assuming that one technique or perspective has all the answers. That calm and balanced sort of dialogue may be out of fashion in the American public arena today, when shouting matches are in vogue and many people seek information only from sources they know in advance they agree with. But it may be only liberal education that can help lead the way back to comity and respectful conversation about issues before us.

Misperception No. 6: America is the only country in the 15 world that clings to such an old-fashioned form of postsecondary education as the liberal arts. Other countries, with more practical orientations, are running way ahead of us. It is often difficult to explain the advantages of a liberal-arts education to people from other cultures, where it is common to specialize early. In many places, including Europe, the study of law or medicine often begins directly after high school, without any requirement to complete an undergraduate degree first. We should recognize, however, that a secondary education in some systems—say, those that follow the model of the German Gymnasium—often includes much that is left out of the typical high-school curriculum in America. One need only look in on a student preparing for the baccalaureat examination in France to understand the distinction: Mastery of philosophical and scientific concepts is mandatory.

Further, in recent years delegations from China have been visiting the United States and asking pointed questions about the liberal arts, seemingly because they feel there may be good reason to try that approach to education. The Chinese may be coming around to the view that a primary focus on technical training is not serving them adequately—that if they aspire to world leadership, they will have to provide young people with a broader perspective. Thus, it is hardly a propitious moment to toss out, or downgrade, one element of higher education that has served us so well.

Misconception No. 7: The cost of American higher education is spiraling out of control, and liberal-arts colleges are becoming irrelevant because they are unable to register gains in productivity or to find innovative ways of doing things. There is plenty wrong with American higher education, including the runaway costs. But the problem of costs goes beyond individual institutions. Government at all levels has come nowhere close to supporting colleges in ways that allow them to provide the kind of access and affordability that's needed. The best way to understand genuine national priorities is to follow the money, and by that standard, education is really not all that important to this country.

Many means exist to obtain a liberal education, including at some large universities, public and private. The method

I happen to advocate, for obvious reasons, is the small, residential liberal-arts college, usually independent, where there is close interaction between faculty members and students and, at its best, a sense of community emerges that prepares young people to develop high standards for themselves and others.

Efficiency is hardly the leading quality of liberal-arts colleges, and indeed, their financial model is increasingly coming into question. But because of their commitment to expand need-based financial aid, the net cost of attending a small liberal-arts college can be lower than that of a large public university. One can only hope that each institution will find ways to cut costs and develop distinguishing characteristics that help it survive through the tough times ahead.

The debate over liberal education will surely continue 20 through the recession and beyond, but it would be helpful to put these misperceptions aside. Financial issues cannot be ignored, but neither can certain eternal verities: Through immersion in liberal arts, students learn not just to make a living, but also to live a life rich in values and character. They come to terms with complexity and diversity, and otherwise devise means to solve problems—rather than just complaining about them. They develop patterns that help them understand how to keep learning for the rest of their days.

Joining the Conversation

1. Summarize in a few sentences the seven misperceptions that Sanford Ungar discusses. These of course are all things that "they say"—and that he uses to launch what he wants to say. How does calling them "misperceptions" affect the way you read his argument? Would you read it any differently if he instead called them "common assumptions"?

2. See paragraph 6, where Geoffrey Garin suggests that "the responsibility of higher education today is to prepare people 'for jobs that do not yet exist.'" Thus, according to Ungar, "It may be that studying the liberal arts is actually the best form of career education." How would you respond to this claim?

3. Misperception 5 relates liberal education to political affiliation. What does Ungar have to say on this issue, and what do you think about his response?

4. On what specific points do you think Ungar would agree with Charles Murray (pp. 400–20)? On what points would he be likely to disagree?

5. Write your own essay listing and explaining five assumptions about college education. Follow Ungar's essay as a model, and use the "they say / I say" pattern to organize your essay, with each assumption as a "they say" that sets up what you want to say.

Are Too Many People Going to College?

CHARLES MURRAY

—◻—

To ASK WHETHER too many people are going to college requires us to think about the importance and nature of a liberal education. "Universities are not intended to teach the knowledge required to fit men for some special mode of gaining their livelihood," John Stuart Mill told students at the University of St. Andrews in 1867. "Their object is not to make skillful lawyers, or physicians, or engineers, but capable and cultivated human beings." If this is true (and I agree that it is), why say that too many people are going to college? Surely a mass democracy should encourage as many people as possible to become "capable and cultivated human beings" in Mill's sense. We should not restrict the availability of a liberal education to a rarefied intellectual elite. More people should be going to college, not fewer.

CHARLES MURRAY is the W. H. Brady Scholar at the American Enterprise Institute, a "public policy think tank dedicated to defending human dignity, expanding human potential, and building a freer and safer world." He is the author, most recently, of *By the People: Rebuilding Liberty without Permission* (2015). This essay, adapted from his book *Real Education: Four Simple Truths for Bringing America's Schools Back to Reality* (2008) first appeared on September 8, 2008, in *The American*, the journal of the American Enterprise Institute.

Yes and no. More people should be getting the basics of a liberal education. But for most students, the places to provide those basics are elementary and middle school. E. D. Hirsch Jr. is the indispensable thinker on this topic, beginning with his 1987 book *Cultural Literacy: What Every American Needs to Know.* Part of his argument involves the importance of a body of core knowledge in fostering reading speed and comprehension. With regard to a liberal education, Hirsch makes three points that are germane here:

See Chapter 4 for ways to agree, but with a difference.

Full participation in any culture requires familiarity with a body of core knowledge. To live in the United States and not recognize Teddy Roosevelt, Prohibition, the Minutemen, Wall Street, smoke-filled rooms, or Gettysburg is like trying to read without knowing some of the ten thousand most commonly used words in the language. It signifies a degree of cultural illiteracy about America. But the core knowledge transcends one's own country. Not to recognize Falstaff, Apollo, the Sistine Chapel, the Inquisition, the twenty-third Psalm, or Mozart signifies cultural illiteracy about the West. Not to recognize the solar system, the Big Bang, natural selection, relativity, or the periodic table is to be scientifically illiterate. Not to recognize the Mediterranean, Vienna, the Yangtze River, Mount Everest, or Mecca is to be geographically illiterate.

This core knowledge is an important part of the glue that holds the culture together. All American children, of whatever ethnic heritage, and whether their families came here 300 years ago or three months ago, need to learn about the Pilgrims, Valley Forge, Duke Ellington, Apollo 11, Susan B. Anthony, George C. Marshall, and the Freedom Riders. All students need to learn the iconic stories. For a society of immigrants such as ours, the core knowledge is our shared identity that makes us Americans together rather than hyphenated Americans.

K–8 are the right years to teach the core knowledge, and the effort should get off to a running start in elementary school. Starting early is partly a matter of necessity: There's a lot to learn, and it takes time. But another reason is that small children enjoy learning myths and fables, showing off names and dates they have memorized, and hearing about great historical figures and exciting deeds. The educational establishment sees this kind of curriculum as one that forces children to memorize boring facts. That conventional wisdom is wrong on every count. The facts can be fascinating (if taught right); a lot more than memorization is entailed; yet memorizing things is an indispensable part of education, too; and memorizing is something that children do much, much better than adults. The core knowledge is suited to ways that young children naturally learn and enjoy learning. Not all children will be able to do the reading with the same level of comprehension, but the fact-based nature of the core knowledge actually works to the benefit of low-ability students—remembering facts is much easier than making inferences and deductions. The core knowledge curriculum lends itself to adaptation for students across a wide range of academic ability.

In the 20 years since *Cultural Literacy* was published, Hirsch and his colleagues have developed and refined his original formulation into an inventory of more than 6,000 items that approximate the core knowledge broadly shared by literate Americans. Hirsch's Core Knowledge Foundation has also developed a detailed, grade-by-grade curriculum for K–8, complete with lists of books and other teaching materials.

The Core Knowledge approach need not stop with eighth grade. High school is a good place for survey courses in the humanities, social sciences, and sciences taught at a level below the demands of a college course and accessible to most students in the upper two-thirds of the distribution of academic ability. Some students will not want to take these courses, and it can be counterproductive to require them to do so, but high school can put considerable flesh on the liberal education skeleton for students who are still interested.

Liberal Education in College

Saying "too many people are going to college" is not the same as saying that the average student does not need to know about history, science, and great works of art, music, and literature. They do need to know—and to know more than they are currently learning. So let's teach it to them, but let's not wait for college to do it.

Liberal education in college means taking on the tough stuff. A high-school graduate who has acquired Hirsch's core knowledge will know, for example, that John Stuart Mill was an important 19th-century English philosopher who was associated with something called Utilitarianism and wrote a famous book called *On Liberty*. But learning philosophy in college, which is an essential component of a liberal education, means that the student has to be able to read and understand the actual text of *On Liberty*. That brings us to the limits set by the nature of college-level material. Here is the first sentence of *On Liberty*: "The subject of this essay is not the so-called liberty of the will, so unfortunately opposed to the misnamed doctrine of philosophical necessity; but civil, or social liberty:

the nature and limits of the power which can be legitimately exercised by society over the individual." I will not burden you with *On Liberty*'s last sentence. It is 126 words long. And Mill is one of the more accessible philosophers, and *On Liberty* is one of Mill's more accessible works. It would be nice if everyone could acquire a fully formed liberal education, but they cannot.

Specifically: When College Board researchers defined "col- 10 lege readiness" as the SAT score that is associated with a 65 percent chance of getting at least a 2.7 grade point average in college during the freshman year, and then applied those criteria (hardly demanding in an era of soft courses and grade inflation) to the freshmen in a sample of 41 major colleges and universities, the threshold "college readiness" score was found to be 1180 on the combined SAT math and verbal tests. It is a score that only about 10 percent of American 18-year-olds would achieve if they all took the SAT, in an age when more than 30 percent of 18-year-olds go to college.

Should all of those who do have the academic ability to absorb a college-level liberal education get one? It depends. Suppose we have before us a young woman who is in the 98th percentile of academic ability and wants to become a lawyer and eventually run for political office. To me, it seems essential that she spend her undergraduate years getting a rigorous liberal education. Apart from a liberal education's value to her, the nation will benefit. Everything she does as an attorney or as an elected official should be informed by the kind of wisdom that a rigorous liberal education can encourage. It is appropriate to push her into that kind of undergraduate program.

But the only reason we can get away with pushing her is that the odds are high that she will enjoy it. The odds are high because she is good at this sort of thing—it's no problem for her to read *On Liberty* or *Paradise Lost*. It's no problem for her to come up with an interesting perspective on what she's read and weave it into a term paper. And because she's good at it, she is also likely to enjoy it. It is one of Aristotle's central themes in his discussion of human happiness, a theme that John Rawls later distilled into what he called the Aristotelian Principle: "Other things equal, human beings enjoy the exercise of the irrealized capacities (their innate or trained abilities), and this enjoyment increases the more the capacity is realized, or the greater its complexity." And so it comes to pass that those who take the hardest majors and who enroll in courses that look most like an old fashioned liberal education are concentrated among the students in the top percentiles of academic ability. Getting a liberal education consists of dealing with complex intellectual material day after day, and dealing with complex intellectual material is what students in the top few percentiles are really good at, in the same way that other people are really good at cooking or making pottery. For these students, doing it well is fun.

Every percentile down the ability ladder—and this applies to all abilities, not just academic—the probability that a person will enjoy the hardest aspects of an activity goes down as well. Students at the 80th percentile of academic ability are still smart kids, but the odds that they will respond to a course that assigns Mill or Milton are considerably lower than the odds that a student in the top few percentiles will respond. Virtue has nothing to do with it. Maturity has nothing to do with it. Appreciation of the value of a liberal education has nothing to do with it. The probability that a student will enjoy *Paradise Lost* goes down as his linguistic ability goes down, but so does the probability that he works on double acrostic puzzles in his spare time or regularly plays online Scrabble, and for the identical reason. The lower down the linguistic ladder he is, the less fun such activities are.

And so we return to the question: Should all of those who have the academic ability to absorb a college-level liberal education get one? If our young woman is at the 80th percentile of linguistic ability, should she be pushed to do so? She has enough intellectual capacity, if she puts her mind to it and works exceptionally hard.

The answer is no. If she wants to, fine. But she probably 15 won't, and there's no way to force her. Try to force her (for example, by setting up a demanding core curriculum), and she will transfer to another school, because she is in college for vocational training. She wants to write computer code. Start a business. Get a job in television. She uses college to take vocational courses that pertain to her career interests. A large proportion of people who are theoretically able to absorb a liberal education have no interest in doing so.

And reasonably so. Seen dispassionately, getting a traditional liberal education over four years is an odd way to enjoy spending one's time. Not many people enjoy reading for hour after hour, day after day, no matter what the material may be. To enjoy reading *On Liberty* and its ilk—and if you're going to absorb such material, you must in some sense enjoy the process—is downright peculiar. To be willing to spend many more hours writing papers and answers to exam questions about that material approaches masochism.

We should look at the kind of work that goes into acquiring a liberal education at the college level in the same way that we look at the grueling apprenticeship that goes into becoming a master chef: something that understandably attracts only a few people. Most students at today's colleges choose not to take the courses that go into a liberal education because the capabilities they want to develop lie elsewhere. These students are not lazy, any more than students who don't want to spend hours learning how to chop carrots into a perfect eighth-inch dice are lazy. A liberal education just doesn't make sense for them.

For Learning How to Make a Living, the Four-Year Brick-and-Mortar Residential College Is Increasingly Obsolete

We now go from one extreme to the other, from the ideal of liberal education to the utilitarian process of acquiring the knowledge that most students go to college to acquire— practical and vocational. The question here is not whether the traditional four-year residential college is fun or valuable as a place to grow up, but when it makes sense as a place to learn how to make a living. The answer is: in a sensible world, hardly ever.

Start with the time it takes—four years. Assuming a semester system with four courses per semester, four years of class work means 32 semester-long courses. The occupations for which "knowing enough" requires 32 courses are exceedingly rare. For some professions—medicine and law are the obvious examples—a rationale for four years of course work can be concocted (combining pre-med and pre-law undergraduate courses with three years of medical school and law school), but for every other occupation, the body of knowledge taught in classrooms can be learned more quickly. Even Ph.D.s don't require four years of course work. The Ph.D. is supposed to signify expertise, but that expertise comes from burrowing deep in to a specialty, not from dozens of courses.

Those are the jobs with the most stringent academic require- 20 ments. For the student who wants to become a good hotel manager, software designer, accountant, hospital administrator,

407

farmer, high-school teacher, social worker, journalist, optometrist, interior designer, or football coach, four years of class work is ridiculous. Actually becoming good in those occupations will take longer than four years, but most of the competence is acquired on the job. The two-year community college and online courses offer more flexible options for tailoring course work to the real needs of the job.

A brick-and-mortar campus is increasingly obsolete. The physical infrastructure of the college used to make sense for three reasons. First, a good library was essential to higher learning, and only a college faculty and student body provided the economies of scale that made good libraries affordable. Second, scholarship flourishes through colleagueships, and the college campus made it possible to put scholars in physical proximity to each other. Third, the best teaching requires interaction between teachers and students, and physical proximity was the only way to get it. All three rationales for the brick-and-mortar campus are fading fast.

The rationale for a physical library is within a few years of extinction. Even now, the Internet provides access, for a price, to all the world's significant technical journals. The books are about to follow. Google is scanning the entire text of every book in the libraries of Harvard, Princeton, Stanford, Oxford, the New York Public Library, the Bavarian State Library, Ghent University Library, Keio Library (Tokyo), the National Library of Catalonia, University of Lausanne, and an expanding list of others. Collectively, this project will encompass close to the sum total of human knowledge. It will be completely searchable. Everything out of copyright will be free. Everything still under copyright will be accessible for a fee. Libraries will still be a selling point for colleges, but as a place for students to study in pleasant surroundings—an amenity in the same way that an attractive student union is an amenity. Colleges and universities will not need to exist because they provide libraries.

The rationale for colleges based on colleagueships has eroded. Until a few decades ago, physical proximity was important because correspondence and phone calls just weren't as good. As email began to spread during the 1980s, physical proximity became less important. As the capacity of the Internet expanded in the 1990s, other mechanisms made those interactions richer. Now, regular emails from professional groups inform scholars of the latest publications in their field of interest. Specialized chat groups enable scholars to bounce new ideas off other people working on the same problems. Drafts are exchanged effortlessly and comments attached electronically. Whether physical proximity still has any advantages depends mostly on the personality of the scholar. Some people like being around other people during the workday and prefer face-to-face conversations to emails. For those who don't, the value of being on a college campus instead of on a mountaintop in Montana is nil. Their electronic access to other scholars is incomparably greater than any scholar enjoyed even within the world's premier universities before the advent of the Internet. Like the library, face-to-face colleagueships will be an amenity that colleges continue to provide. But colleges and universities will not need to exist because they provide a community of scholars.

The third rationale for the brick-and-mortar college is that it brings teachers together with students. Working against that rationale is the explosion in the breadth and realism of what is known as distance learning. The idea of distance learning is surprisingly old—Isaac Pitman was teaching his shorthand system to British students through the postal service in the 1840s, and the University of London began offering degrees for correspondence students in 1858—but the technology of distance learning changed little for the next century. The advent of inexpensive videocassettes in the 1980s opened up a way for students to hear and see lectures without being in the classroom. By the early 1990s, it was possible to buy college-level courses on audio or videotape, taught by first-rate teaching professors, on a wide range of topics, for a few hundred dollars. But without easy interaction between teacher and student, distance learning remained a poor second-best to a good college seminar.

Once again, the Internet is revolutionizing everything. As 25 personal computers acquired the processing power to show high-definition video and the storage capacity to handle big video files, the possibilities for distance learning expanded by orders of magnitude. We are now watching the early expression of those possibilities: podcasts and streaming videos in real time of professors' lectures, online discussions among students scattered around the country, online interaction between students and professors, online exams, and tutorials augmented by computer-aided instruction software.

Even today, the quality of student-teacher interactions in a virtual classroom competes with the interactions in a brick-and-mortar classroom. But the technology is still in its early stages of development and the rate of improvement is breathtaking. Compare video games such as Myst and SimCity in the 1990s to their descendants today; the Walkman you used in the 1990s to the iPod you use today; the cell phone you used in the 1990s to the BlackBerry or iPhone you use today. Whatever technical limitations might lead you to say, "Yes, but it's still not the same as being there in the classroom," are probably within a few years of being outdated.

College Isn't All It's Cracked Up to Be

College looms so large in the thinking of both parents and students because it is seen as the open sesame to a good job. Reaping the economic payoff for college that shows up in econometric analyses is a long shot for large numbers of young people.

When high-school graduates think that obtaining a B.A. will help them get a higher-paying job, they are only narrowly correct. Economists have established beyond doubt that people with B.A.s earn more on average than people without them. But why does the B.A. produce that result? For whom does the B.A. produce that result? For some jobs, the economic premium for a degree is produced by the actual education that has gone into getting the degree. Lawyers, physicians, and engineers can earn their high incomes only by deploying knowledge and skills that take years to acquire, and degrees in law, medicine, and engineering still signify competence in those knowledges and skills. But for many other jobs, the economic premium for the B.A. is created by a brutal fact of life about the American job market: Employers do not even interview applicants who do not hold a B.A. Even more brutal, the advantage conferred by the B.A. often has nothing to do with the content of the education. Employers do not value what the student learned, just that the student has a degree.

Employers value the B.A. because it is a no-cost (for them) screening device for academic ability and perseverance. The more people who go to college, the more sense it makes for employers to require a B.A. When only a small percentage of people got college degrees, employers who required a B.A. would have been shutting themselves off from access to most of the talent. With more than a third of 23-year-olds now getting a B.A., many employers can reasonably limit their hiring

411

pool to college graduates because bright and ambitious high-school graduates who can go to college usually do go to college. An employer can believe that exceptions exist but rationally choose not to expend time and money to identify them. Knowing this, large numbers of students are in college to buy their admission ticket—the B.A.

But while it is true that the average person with a B.A. [30] makes more than the average person without a B.A., getting a B.A. is still going to be the wrong economic decision for many high-school graduates. Wages within occupations form a distribution. Young people with okay-but-not-great academic ability who are thinking about whether to go after a B.A. need to consider the competition they will face after they graduate. Let me put these calculations in terms of a specific example, a young man who has just graduated from high school and is trying to decide whether to become an electrician or go to college and major in business, hoping to become a white-collar manager. He is at the 70th percentile in linguistic ability and logical mathematical ability—someone who shouldn't go to college by my standards, but who can, in today's world, easily find a college that will give him a degree. He is exactly average in interpersonal and intrapersonal ability. He is at the 95th percentile in the small-motor skills and spatial abilities that are helpful in being a good electrician.

He begins by looking up the average income of electricians and managers on the Bureau of Labor Statistics website, and finds that the mean annual income for electricians in 2005 was $45,630, only about half of the $88,450 mean for management occupations. It looks as if getting a B.A. will buy him a huge wage premium. Should he try to get the B.A. on economic grounds?

To make his decision correctly, our young man must start by throwing out the averages. He has the ability to become an excellent electrician and can reasonably expect to be near the top of the electricians' income distribution. He does not have it in him to be an excellent manager, because he is only average in interpersonal and intrapersonal ability and only modestly above average in academic ability, all of which are important for becoming a good manager, while his competitors for those slots will include many who are high in all of those abilities. Realistically, he should be looking at the incomes toward the bottom of the distribution of managers. With that in mind, he goes back to the Bureau of Labor Statistics website and discovers that an electrician at the 90th percentile of electricians' incomes made $70,480 in 2005, almost twice the income of a manager at the 10th percentile of managers' incomes ($37,800). Even if our young man successfully completes college and gets a B.A. (which is far from certain), he is likely to make less money than if he becomes an electrician.

Then there is job security to consider. A good way to make sure you always can find work is to be among the best at what you do. It also helps to have a job that does not require you to compete with people around the globe. When corporations downsize, they lay off mediocre managers before they lay off top electricians. When the economy gets soft, top electricians can find work when mediocre managers cannot. Low-level management jobs can often be outsourced to India, whereas electricians' jobs cannot.

What I have said of electricians is true throughout the American job market. The income for the top people in a wide variety of occupations that do not require a college degree is higher than the average income for many occupations that require a B.A. Furthermore, the range and number of such jobs are expanding rapidly. The need for assembly-line workers in factories (one of the most boring jobs ever invented) is falling, but the demand for skilled technicians of every kind—in healthcare, information technology, transportation networks, and every other industry that relies on high-tech equipment— is expanding. The service sector includes many low-skill, low-paying jobs, but it also includes growing numbers of specialized jobs that pay well (for example, in healthcare and the entertainment and leisure industries). Construction offers an array of high-paying jobs for people who are good at what they do. It's not just skilled labor in the standard construction trades that is in high demand. The increase in wealth in American society has increased the demand for all sorts of craftsmanship. Today's high-end homes and office buildings may entail the work of specialized skills in stonework, masonry, glazing, painting, cabinetmaking, machining, landscaping, and a dozen other crafts. The increase in wealth is also driving an increased demand for the custom-made and the exquisitely wrought, meaning demand for artisans in everything from pottery to jewelry to metalworking. There has never been a time in history when people with skills not taught in college have been in so much demand at such high pay as today, nor a time when the range of such jobs has been so wide. In today's America, finding a first-rate lawyer or physician is easy. Finding first-rate skilled labor is hard.

Intrinsic Rewards

The topic is no longer money but job satisfaction—intrinsic 35 rewards. We return to our high-school graduate trying to decide between going to college and becoming an electrician. He knows that he enjoys working with his hands and likes the idea of not being stuck in the same place all day, but he also likes the idea of being a manager sitting behind a desk in a big office, telling people what to do and getting the status that goes with it.

However, he should face facts that he is unlikely to know on his own, but that a guidance counselor could help him face. His chances of getting the big office and the status are slim. He is more likely to remain in a cubicle, under the thumb of the boss in the big office. He is unlikely to have a job in which he produces something tangible during the course of the day.

If he becomes a top electrician instead, he will have an expertise that he exercises at a high level. At the end of a workday, he will often be able to see that his work made a difference in the lives of people whose problems he has solved. He will not be confined to a cubicle and, after his apprenticeship, will be his own supervisor in the field. Top electricians often become independent contractors who have no boss at all.

The intrinsic rewards of being a top manager can be just as great as those of a top electrician (though I would not claim they are greater), but the intrinsic rewards of being a mediocre manager are not. Even as people in white-collar jobs lament the soullessness of their work, the intrinsic rewards of exercising technical skills remain undiminished.

Finally, there is an overarching consideration so important it is hard to express adequately: the satisfaction of being good at what one does for a living (and knowing it), compared to the melancholy of being mediocre at what one does for a living (and knowing it). This is another truth about living a human life that a 17-year-old might not yet understand on his own, but that a guidance counselor can bring to his attention. Guidance counselors and parents who automatically encourage young people to go to college straight out of high school regardless of their skills and interests are being thoughtless about the best interests of young people in their charge.

The Dark Side of the B.A. as Norm

It is possible to accept all that I have presented as fact and still 40
disagree with the proposition that too many people are going
to college. The argument goes something like this:

The meaning of a college education has evolved since the
19th century. The traditional liberal education is still available
for students who want it, but the curriculum is appropriately
broader now, and includes many courses for vocational preparation that today's students want. Furthermore, intellectual
requirements vary across majors. It may be true that few students can complete a major in economics or biology, but larger
proportions can handle the easier majors. A narrow focus on
curriculum also misses the important nonacademic functions of
college. The lifestyle on today's campuses may leave something
to be desired, but four years of college still give youngsters in
late adolescence a chance to encounter different kinds of people, to discover new interests, and to decide what they want to
make of their lives. And if it is true that some students spend
too much of their college years partying, that was also true of
many Oxford students in the 18th century. Lighten up.

If the only people we had to worry about were those who are
on college campuses and doing reasonably well, this position
would have something to be said for it. It does not address the
issues of whether four years makes sense or whether a residential
facility makes sense; nevertheless, college as it exists is not an
intrinsically evil place for the students who are there and are
coping academically. But there is the broader American society to worry about as well. However unintentionally, we have
made something that is still inaccessible to a majority of the
population—the B.A.—into a symbol of first-class citizenship.
We have done so at the same time that other class divisions are

becoming more powerful. Today's college system is implicated in the emergence of class-riven America.

The problem begins with the message sent to young people that they should aspire to college no matter what. Some politicians are among the most visible offenders, treating every failure to go to college as an injustice that can be remedied by increasing government help. American educational administrators reinforce the message by instructing guidance counselors to steer as many students as possible toward a college-prep track (more than 90 percent of high-school students report that their guidance counselors encouraged them to go to college). But politicians and educators are only following the lead of the larger culture. As long as it remains taboo to acknowledge that college is intellectually too demanding for most young people, we will continue to create crazily unrealistic expectations among the next generation. If "crazily unrealistic" sounds too strong, consider that more than 90 percent of high school seniors expect to go to college, and more than 70 percent of them expect to work in professional jobs.

One aspect of this phenomenon has been labeled misaligned ambitions, meaning that adolescents have career ambitions that are inconsistent with their educational plans. Data from the Sloan Study of Youth and Social Development conducted during the 1990s indicate that misaligned ambitions characterized more than half of all adolescents. Almost always, the misalignment is in the optimistic direction, as adolescents aspire to be attorneys or physicians without understanding the educational hurdles they must surmount to achieve their goals. They end up at a four-year institution not because that is where they can take the courses they need to meet their career goals, but because college is the place where B.A.s are handed out, and everyone knows that these days you've got to have a B.A. Many of them drop out. Of those who entered a four-year college in 1995, only 58 percent had gotten their B.A. five academic years later. Another 14 percent were still enrolled. If we assume that half of that 14 percent eventually get their B.A.s, about a third of all those who entered college hoping for a B.A. leave without one.

If these numbers had been produced in a culture where the 45 B.A. was a nice thing to have but not a big deal, they could be interpreted as the result of young adults deciding that they didn't really want a B.A. after all. Instead, these numbers were produced by a system in which having a B.A. is a very big deal indeed, and that brings us to the increasingly worrisome role of the B.A. as a source of class division. The United States has always had symbols of class, and the college degree has always been one of them. But through the first half of the 20th century, there were all sorts of respectable reasons a person might not go to college—not enough money to pay for college; needing to work right out of high school to support a wife, parents, or younger siblings; or the commonly held belief that going straight to work was better preparation for a business career than going to college. As long as the percentage of college graduates remained small, it also remained true, and everybody knew it, that the majority of America's intellectually most able people did not have B.A.s.

Over the course of the 20th century, three trends gathered strength. The first was the increasing proportion of jobs screened for high academic ability due to the advanced level of education they require—engineers, physicians, attorneys, college teachers, scientists, and the like. The second was the increasing market value of those jobs. The third was the opening up of college to more of those who had the academic ability to go to college, partly because the increase in American wealth meant that more parents could afford college for their children, and partly because the proliferation of scholarships and loans made it possible for most students with enough academic ability to go.

The combined effect of these trends has been to overturn the state of affairs that prevailed through World War II. Now the great majority of America's intellectually most able people do have a B.A. Along with that transformation has come a downside that few anticipated. The acceptable excuses for not going to college have dried up. The more people who go to college, the more stigmatizing the failure to complete college becomes. Today, if you do not get a B.A., many people assume it is because you are too dumb or too lazy. And all this because of a degree that seldom has an interpretable substantive meaning.

Let's approach the situation from a different angle. Imagine that America had no system of postsecondary education and you were made a member of a task force assigned to create one from scratch. Ask yourself what you would think if one of your colleagues submitted this proposal:

First, we will set up a common goal for every young person that represents educational success. We will call it a B.A. We will then make it difficult or impossible for most people to achieve this goal. For those who can, achieving the goal will take four years no matter what is being taught. We will attach an economic reward for reaching the goal that often has little to do with the content of what has been learned. We will lure large numbers of people who do not possess adequate ability or motivation to try to achieve the goal and then fail. We will then stigmatize everyone who fails to achieve it.

What I have just described is the system that we have in 50 place. There must be a better way.

Joining the Conversation

1. The "I say" here is explicit: "too many people are going to college." We know what Charles Murray thinks. But why does he think this? In the rest of his essay, he tells us why. Summarize his argument, noting all the reasons and evidence he gives to support his claim.

2. Is Murray right—are too many people going to college? If you disagree, why? Whether or not you agree with him, do you find his argument persuasive?

3. In the middle of the essay is a lengthy narrative about someone who is trying to decide what to be when he grows up, an electrician or a manager. What does this narrative contribute to Murray's argument? Where would the argument be without the narrative?

4. Compare Murray's argument that college is a waste of time for many with Sanford J. Ungar's argument (pp. 392–99) that anyone can benefit from a college education. Which one do you find more convincing?

5. In one or two paragraphs, reflect on why you chose your current school. Did you consider, first and foremost, how your college would help you "learn how to make a living," as Murray would recommend? Did you consider other potential benefits of your college education? If you could have a well-paying job without a college education, would you go to college anyway?

Two Years Are Better Than Four

LIZ ADDISON

———⌐口⌐———

OH, THE HAND WRINGING. "College as America used to understand it is coming to an end," bemoans Rick Perlstein and his beatnik friend of fallen face. Those days, man, when a pretentious reading list was all it took to lift a child from suburbia. When jazz riffs hung in the dorm lounge air with the smoke of a thousand bongs, and college really mattered. Really mattered?

Rick Perlstein thinks so. It mattered so much to him that he never got over his four years at the University of Privilege. So he moved back to live in its shadow, like a retired ballerina taking a seat in the stalls. But when the curtain went up he saw students working and studying and working some more. Adults

————

LIZ ADDISON attended Piedmont Virginia Community College and Southern Maine Community College, where she graduated with a degree in biology in 2008. She received a graduate degree from the Royal Veterinary College in London in 2014 and now works as a veterinarian in Virginia. This essay, published in 2007, was a runner-up in a *New York Times Magazine* college essay contest. The essay responds to Rick Perlstein's opinion piece "What's the Matter With College?," in which he argues that universities no longer matter as much as they once did.

before their time. Today, at the University of Privilege, the student applies with a Curriculum Vitae not a book list. Shudder.

Thus, Mr. Perlstein concludes, the college experience—a rite of passage as it was meant it to be—must have come to an end. But he is wrong. For Mr. Perlstein, so rooted in his own nostalgia, is looking for himself—and he would never think to look for himself in the one place left where the college experience of self-discovery does still matter to those who get there. My guess, reading between the lines, is that Mr. Perlstein has never set foot in an American community college.

The philosophy of the community college, and I have been to two of them, is one that unconditionally allows its students to begin. Just begin. Implicit in this belief is the understanding that anything and everything is possible. Just follow any one of the 1,655 road signs, and pop your head inside—yes, they let anyone in—and there you will find discoveries of a first independent film, a first independent thought, a first independent study. This college experience remains as it should. This college brochure is not marketing for the parents—because the parents, nor grandparents, probably never went to college themselves.

Upon entry to my first community college I had but one 5 O'level to my name. These now disbanded qualifications once marked the transition from lower to upper high school in the Great British education system. It was customary for the average student to proceed forward with a clutch of O'levels, say eight or nine. On a score of one, I left school hurriedly at sixteen. Thomas Jefferson once wrote, "Everybody should have an education proportional to their life." In my case, my life became proportional to my education. But, in doing so, it had the good fortune to land me in an American community college and now, from that priceless springboard, I too seek admission to the University of Privilege. Enter on empty and leave with a head full of dreams? How can Mr. Perlstein say college does not matter anymore?

The community college system is America's hidden public service gem. If I were a candidate for office I would campaign from every campus. Not to score political points, but simply to make sure that anyone who is looking to go to college in this country knows where to find one. Just recently, I read an article in the *New York Times* describing a "college application essay" workshop for low-income students. I was strangely disturbed that those interviewed made no mention of community college. Mr. Perlstein might have been equally disturbed, for the thrust of the workshop was no different to that of an essay coach to the affluent. "Make Life Stories Shine," beams the headline. Or, in other words, prove yourself worldly, insightful, cultured, mature, before you get to college.

Yet, down at X.Y.C.C. it is still possible to enter the college experience as a rookie. That is the understanding—that you will grow up a little bit with your first English class, a bit more with your first psychology class, a whole lot more with your first biology, physics, chemistry. That you may shoot through the roof with calculus, philosophy, See Chapter 9 on mixing academic and colloquial styles. or genetics. "College is the key," a young African American student writes for the umpteenth torturous revision of his college essay, "as well as hope." Oh, I wanted desperately to say, please tell him about community college. Please tell him that hope can begin with just one placement test.

When Mr. Perlstein and friends say college no longer holds importance, they mourn for both the individual and society. Yet, arguably, the community college experience is more critical to the nation than that of former beatnik types who, lest we forget, did not change the world. The community colleges of America cover this country college by college and community by community. They offer a network of affordable future, of accessible hope, and an option to dream. In the cold light of day, is it perhaps not more important to foster students with dreams rather than a building take-over?

I believe so. I believe the community college system to be one of America's uniquely great institutions. I believe it should be celebrated as such. "For those who find it necessary to go to a two-year college," begins one University of Privilege admissions paragraph. None too subtle in its implication, but very true. For some students, from many backgrounds, would never breathe the college experience if it were not for the community college. Yes, it is here that Mr. Perlstein will find his college years of self-discovery, and it is here he will find that college does still matter.

Joining the Conversation

1. What view is Liz Addison responding to? Write out a sentence or two summarizing the "they say."
2. Addison discusses her own educational experience as part of her argument. What role does this use of autobiographical narrative play in her argument?
3. How does Addison make clear that her topic is important— and that it should matter to readers?
4. In closing, Addison writes of community colleges: "It is here that Mr. Perlstein will find his college years of self-discovery, and it is here he will find that college does still matter." Do you think college still matters? Write an essay responding to this point from your own perspective as a college student.

Hidden Intellectualism

GERALD GRAFF

EVERYONE KNOWS SOME YOUNG PERSON who is impressively "street smart" but does poorly in school. What a waste, we think, that one who is so intelligent about so many things in life seems unable to apply that intelligence to academic work. What doesn't occur to us, though, is that schools and colleges might be at fault for missing the opportunity to tap into such street smarts and channel them into good academic work.

Nor do we consider one of the major reasons why schools and colleges overlook the intellectual potential of street smarts: the fact that we associate those street smarts with anti-intellectual concerns. We associate the educated life, the life of the mind, too narrowly and exclusively with subjects and texts that we consider inherently weighty and academic. We assume that it's possible to wax intellectual about Plato, Shakespeare,

---

GERALD GRAFF, a coauthor of this book, is a professor of English and education at the University of Illinois at Chicago. He is a past president of the Modern Language Association, the world's largest professional association of university scholars and teachers. This essay is adapted from his 2003 book, *Clueless in Academe: How Schooling Obscures the Life of the Mind*.

the French Revolution, and nuclear fission, but not about cars, dating, fashion, sports, TV, or video games.

The trouble with this assumption is that no necessary connection has ever been established between any text or subject and the educational depth and weight of the discussion it can generate. Real intellectuals turn any subject, however lightweight it may seem, into grist for their mill through the thoughtful questions they bring to it, whereas a dullard will find a way to drain the interest out of the richest subject. That's why a George Orwell writing on the cultural meanings of penny postcards is infinitely more substantial than the cogitations of many professors on Shakespeare or globalization (104–16).

See pp. 58–59 for tips on disagreeing, with reasons.

Students do need to read models of intellectually challenging writing—and Orwell is a great one—if they are to become intellectuals themselves. But they would be more prone to take on intellectual identities if we encouraged them to do so at first on subjects that interest them rather than ones that interest us.

I offer my own adolescent experience as a case in point. Until I entered college, I hated books and cared only for sports. The only reading I cared to do or could do was sports magazines, on which I became hooked, becoming a regular reader of *Sport* magazine in the late forties, *Sports Illustrated* when it began publishing in 1954, and the annual magazine guides to professional baseball, football, and basketball. I also loved the sports novels for boys of John R. Tunis and Clair Bee and autobiographies of sports stars like Joe DiMaggio's *Lucky to Be a Yankee* and Bob Feller's *Strikeout Story*. In short, I was your typical teenage anti-intellectual—or so I believed for a long time. I have recently come to think, however, that my preference for sports over schoolwork was not anti-intellectualism so much as intellectualism by other means.

In the Chicago neighborhood I grew up in, which had become a melting pot after World War II, our block was solidly middle class, but just a block away—doubtless concentrated there by the real estate companies—were African Americans, Native Americans, and "hillbilly" whites who had recently fled postwar joblessness in the South and Appalachia. Negotiating this class boundary was a tricky matter. On the one hand, it was necessary to maintain the boundary between "clean-cut" boys like me and working-class "hoods," as we called them, which meant that it was good to be openly smart in a bookish sort of way. On the other hand, I was desperate for the approval of the hoods, whom I encountered daily on the playing field and in the neighborhood, and for this purpose it was not at all good to be book-smart. The hoods would turn on you if they sensed you were putting on airs over them: "Who you lookin' at, smart ass?" as a leather-jacketed youth once said to me as he relieved me of my pocket change along with my self-respect.

I grew up torn, then, between the need to prove I was smart and the fear of a beating if I proved it too well; between the need not to jeopardize my respectable future and the need to impress the hoods. As I lived it, the conflict came down to a choice between being physically tough and being verbal. For a boy in my neighborhood and elementary school, only being "tough" earned you complete legitimacy. I still recall endless, complicated debates in this period with my closest pals over who was "the toughest guy in the school." If you were less than negligible as a fighter, as I was, you settled for the next best thing, which was to be inarticulate, carefully hiding telltale marks of literacy like correct grammar and pronunciation.

In one way, then, it would be hard to imagine an adolescence more thoroughly anti-intellectual than mine. Yet in retrospect, I see that it's more complicated, that I and the 1950s themselves were not simply hostile toward intellectualism, but divided and ambivalent. When Marilyn Monroe married the playwright Arthur Miller in 1956 after divorcing the retired baseball star

Joe DiMaggio, the symbolic triumph of geek over jock suggested the way the wind was blowing. Even Elvis, according to his biographer Peter Guralnick, turns out to have supported Adlai over Ike in the presidential election of 1956. "I don't dig the intellectual bit," he told reporters. "But I'm telling you, man, he knows the most" (327).

Though I too thought I did not "dig the intellectual bit," I see now that I was unwittingly in training for it. The germs had actually been planted in the seemingly philistine debates about which boys were the toughest. I see now that in the interminable analysis of sports teams, movies, and toughness that my friends and I engaged in—a type of analysis, needless to say, that the real toughs would never have stooped to—I was already betraying an allegiance to the egghead world. I was practicing being an intellectual before I knew that was what I wanted to be.

It was in these discussions with friends about toughness and sports, I think, and in my reading of sports books and magazines, that I began to learn the rudiments of the intellectual life: how to make an argument, weigh different kinds of evidence, move between particulars and generalizations, summarize the views of others, and enter a conversation about ideas. It was in reading and arguing about sports and toughness that I experienced what it felt like to propose a generalization, restate and respond to a counterargument, and perform other intellectualizing operations, including composing the kind of sentences I am writing now.

Only much later did it dawn on me that the sports world was more compelling than school because it was *more intellectual than school*, not less. Sports after all was full of challenging arguments, debates, problems for analysis, and intricate statistics that you could care about, as school conspicuously was not. I believe that street smarts beat out book smarts in our culture not because street smarts are nonintellectual, as we generally suppose, but because they satisfy an intellectual thirst more thoroughly than school culture, which seems pale and unreal.

They also satisfy the thirst for community. When you entered sports debates, you became part of a community that was not limited to your family and friends, but was national and public. Whereas schoolwork isolated you from others, the pennant race or Ted Williams's .400 batting average was something you could talk about with people you had never met. Sports introduced you not only to a culture steeped in argument, but to a public argument culture that transcended the personal. I can't blame my schools for failing to make intellectual culture resemble the Super Bowl, but I do fault them for failing to learn anything from the sports and entertainment worlds about how to organize and represent intellectual culture, how to exploit its gamelike element and turn it into arresting public spectacle that might have competed more successfully for my youthful attention.

For here is another thing that never dawned on me and is still kept hidden from students, with tragic results: that the real intellectual world, the one that existed in the big world beyond school, is organized very much like the world of team sports, with rival texts, rival interpretations and evaluations of texts, rival theories of why they should be read and taught, and elaborate team competitions in which "fans" of writers, intellectual systems, methodologies, and -isms contend against each other.

To be sure, school contained plenty of competition, which became more invidious as one moved up the ladder (and has become even more so today with the advent of high-stakes testing). In this competition, points were scored not by making arguments, but by a show of information or vast reading, by grade-grubbing, or other forms of one-upmanship. School competition, in short, reproduced the less attractive features of sports culture without those that create close bonds and community.

And in distancing themselves from anything as enjoyable and absorbing as sports, my schools missed the opportunity to capitalize on an element of drama and conflict that the intellectual world shares with sports. Consequently, I failed to see the parallels between the sports and academic worlds that could have helped me cross more readily from one argument culture to the other.

Sports is only one of the domains whose potential for literacy training (and not only for males) is seriously underestimated by educators, who see sports as competing with academic development rather than a route to it. But if this argument suggests why it is a good idea to assign readings and topics that are close to students' existing interests, it also suggests the limits of this tactic. For students who get excited about the chance to write about their passion for cars will often write as poorly and unreflectively on that topic as on Shakespeare or Plato. Here is the flip side of what I pointed out before: that there's no necessary relation between the degree of interest a student shows in a text or subject and the quality of thought or expression such a student manifests in writing or talking about it. The challenge, as college professor Ned Laff has put it, "is not simply to exploit students' nonacademic interests, but to get them to see those interests through academic eyes."

To say that students need to see their interests "through academic eyes" is to say that street smarts are not enough. Making students' nonacademic interests an object of academic study is useful, then, for getting students' attention and overcoming their boredom and alienation, but this tactic won't in itself necessarily move them closer to an academically rigorous treatment of those interests. On the other hand, inviting students to write about cars, sports, or clothing fashions does not have to be a pedagogical cop-out as long as students are required to see these interests "through academic eyes," that is, to think and write about cars, sports, and fashions in a reflective, analytical way, one that sees them as microcosms of what is going on in the wider culture.

If I am right, then schools and colleges are missing an opportunity when they do not encourage students to take their nonacademic interests as objects of academic study. It is self-defeating to decline to introduce any text or subject that figures to engage students who will otherwise tune out academic work entirely. If a student cannot get interested in Mill's *On Liberty* but will read *Sports Illustrated* or *Vogue* or the hip-hop magazine *Source* with absorption, this is a strong argument for assigning the magazines over the classic. It's a good bet that if students get hooked on reading and writing by doing term papers on *Source*, they will eventually get to *On Liberty*. But even if they don't, the magazine reading will make them more literate and reflective than they would be otherwise. So it makes pedagogical sense to develop classroom units on sports, cars, fashions, rap music, and other such topics. Give me the student anytime who writes a sharply argued, sociologically acute analysis of an issue in *Source* over the student who writes a lifeless explication of *Hamlet* or Socrates' *Apology*.

Works Cited

Cramer, Richard Ben. *Joe DiMaggio: The Hero's Life*. Simon, 2000.

DiMaggio, Joe. *Lucky to Be a Yankee*. Bantam, 1949.

Feller, Bob. *Strikeout Story*. Bantam, 1948.

Guralnick, Peter. *Last Train to Memphis: The Rise of Elvis Presley*. Little, Brown, 1994.

Orwell, George. *A Collection of Essays*. Harcourt, 1953.

Joining the Conversation

1. Gerald Graff begins his essay with the view that we generally associate "book smarts" with intellectualism and "street smarts" with anti-intellectualism. Graff then provides an extended example from his early life to counter this viewpoint. What do you think of his argument that boyhood conversations about sports provided a solid foundation for his later intellectual life? What support does he provide, and how persuasive is it?

2. Graff argues in paragraph 13 that the intellectual world is much like the world of team sports, with "rival texts . . . , rival theories . . . , and elaborate team competitions." Can you think of any examples from your own experience that support this assertion? In what ways do you think "the real intellectual world" is different from the world of team sports?

3. Imagine a conversation between Graff and Mike Rose (pp. 433–45) on the intellectual skills people can develop outside the realm of formal education and the benefits of these skills.

4. So what? Who cares? Graff does not answer these questions explicitly. Do it for him: write a brief paragraph saying why his argument matters, and for whom.

5. Graff argues that schools should encourage students to think critically, read, and write about areas of personal interest such as cars, fashion, or music—as long as they do so in an intellectually serious way. What do you think? Write an essay considering the educational merits of such a proposal, taking Graff's argument as a "they say."

Blue-Collar Brilliance

MIKE ROSE

—🔲—

My mother, Rose Meraglio Rose (Rosie), shaped her adult identity as a waitress in coffee shops and family restaurants. When I was growing up in Los Angeles during the 1950s, my father and I would occasionally hang out at the restaurant until her shift ended, and then we'd ride the bus home with her. Sometimes she worked the register and the counter, and we sat there; when she waited booths and tables, we found a booth in the back where the waitresses took their breaks.

There wasn't much for a child to do at the restaurants, and so as the hours stretched out, I watched the cooks and waitresses and listened to what they said. At mealtimes, the pace of the kitchen staff and the din from customers picked up. Weaving in and out around the room, waitresses warned behind you in

---

Mike Rose is a professor at the UCLA Graduate School of Education and Information Studies. He is well known for his writing on issues of literacy, including the books *Lives on the Boundary: The Struggles and Achievements of America's Underprepared* (1989) and *Back to School: Why Everyone Deserves a Second Chance at Education* (2012). He also coedited a collection of essays, *Public Education Under Siege* (2014). This article originally appeared in 2009 in the *American Scholar*, a magazine published by the Phi Beta Kappa Society.

Rosie solved technical problems and human problems on the fly.

impassive but urgent voices. Standing at the service window facing the kitchen, they called out abbreviated orders. Fry four on two, my mother would say as she clipped a check onto the metal wheel. Her tables were deuces, four-tops, or six-tops according to their size; seating areas also were nicknamed. The racetrack, for instance, was the fast-turnover front section. Lingo conferred authority and signaled know-how.

Rosie took customers' orders, pencil poised over pad, while fielding questions about the food. She walked full tilt through the room with plates stretching up her left arm and two cups of coffee somehow cradled in her right hand. She stood at a table or booth and removed a plate for this person, another for that person, then another, remembering who had the hamburger, who had the fried shrimp, almost always getting it right. She would haggle with the cook about a returned order and rush by us, saying, He gave me lip, but I got him. She'd take a minute to flop down in the booth next to my father. I'm all in, she'd say, and whisper something about a customer. Gripping the outer edge of the table with one hand, she'd watch the room and note, in the flow of our conversation, who needed a refill, whose order was taking longer to prepare than it should, who was finishing up.

I couldn't have put it in words when I was growing up, but what I observed in my mother's restaurant defined the world of adults, a place where competence was synonymous with physical work. I've since studied the working habits of blue-collar workers and have come to understand how much my mother's kind of work demands of both body and brain. A waitress acquires knowledge and intuition about the ways and the rhythms of the restaurant business. Waiting on seven to nine tables, each with two to six customers, Rosie devised memory strategies so that she could remember who ordered what. And because she knew the average time it took to prepare different dishes, she could monitor an order that was taking too long at the service station.

Like anyone who is effective at physical work, my mother ⁵ learned to work smart, as she put it, to make every move count. She'd sequence and group tasks: What could she do first, then second, then third as she circled through her station? What tasks could be clustered? She did everything on the fly, and when problems arose—technical or human—she solved them within the flow of work, while taking into account the emotional state of her co-workers. Was the manager in a good mood? Did the cook wake up on the wrong side of the bed? If so, how could she make an extra request or effectively return an order?

And then, of course, there were the customers who entered the restaurant with all sorts of needs, from physiological ones, including the emotions that accompany hunger, to a sometimes complicated desire for human contact. Her tip depended on how well she responded to these needs, and so she became adept at reading social cues and managing feelings, both the customers' and her own. No wonder, then, that Rosie was intrigued by psychology. The restaurant became the place where she studied human behavior, puzzling over the problems of her regular customers and refining her ability to deal with people in a difficult world. She took pride in being among the public, she'd say. There isn't a day that goes by in the restaurant that you don't learn something.

My mother quit school in the seventh grade to help raise her brothers and sisters. Some of those siblings made it through high school, and some dropped out to find work in railroad yards, factories, or restaurants. My father finished a grade or two in primary school in Italy and never darkened the schoolhouse door again. I didn't do well in school either. By high school I had accumulated a spotty academic record and many hours of hazy disaffection. I spent a few years on the vocational track, but in my senior year I was inspired by my English teacher and managed to squeak into a small college on probation.

My freshman year was academically bumpy, but gradually I began to see formal education as a means of fulfillment and as a road toward making a living. I studied the humanities and later the social and psychological sciences and taught for ten years in a range of situations—elementary school, adult education courses, tutoring centers, a program for Vietnam veterans who wanted to go to college. Those students had socioeconomic and educational backgrounds similar to mine. Then I went back to graduate school to study education and cognitive psychology and eventually became a faculty member in a school of education.

Blue-Collar Brilliance

Intelligence is closely associated with formal education—the type of schooling a person has, how much and how long—and most people seem to move comfortably from that notion to a belief that work requiring less schooling requires less intelligence. These assumptions run through our cultural history, from the post-Revolutionary War period, when mechanics were characterized by political rivals as illiterate and therefore incapable of participating in government, until today. More than once I've heard a manager label his workers as "a bunch of dummies." Generalizations about intelligence, work, and social class deeply affect our assumptions about ourselves and each other, guiding the ways we use our minds to learn, build knowledge, solve problems, and make our way through the world.

See Chapter 1 for ways to introduce something implied or assumed.

Although writers and scholars have often looked at the working class, they have generally focused on the values such workers exhibit rather than on the thought their work requires—a subtle but pervasive omission. Our cultural iconography promotes the muscled arm, sleeve rolled tight against biceps, but no brightness behind the eye, no image that links hand and 10 brain.

One of my mother's brothers, Joe Meraglio, left school in the ninth grade to work for the Pennsylvania Railroad. From there he joined the Navy, returned to the railroad, which was already in decline, and eventually joined his older brother at General Motors where, over a 33-year career, he moved from working on the assembly line to supervising the paint-and-body department. When I was a young man, Joe took me on a tour of the factory. The floor was loud—in some places deafening—and when I turned a corner or opened a door, the smell of chemicals knocked my head back. The work was repetitive and taxing, and the pace was inhuman.

Still, for Joe the shop floor provided what school did not; it was like schooling, he said, a place where you're constantly learning. Joe learned the most efficient way to use his body by acquiring a set of routines that were quick and preserved energy. Otherwise he would never have survived on the line.

As a foreman, Joe constantly faced new problems and became a consummate multi-tasker, evaluating a flurry of demands quickly, parceling out physical and mental resources, keeping a number of ongoing events in his mind, returning to whatever task had been interrupted, and maintaining a cool head under the pressure of grueling production schedules. In the midst of all this, Joe learned more and more about the auto industry, the technological and social dynamics of the shop floor, the machinery and production processes, and the basics of paint chemistry and of plating and baking. With further promotions, he not only solved problems but also began to find problems to solve: Joe initiated the redesign of the nozzle on a paint sprayer, thereby eliminating costly and unhealthy over-spray. And he found a way to reduce energy costs on the baking ovens without affecting the quality of the paint. He lacked formal knowledge of how the machines under his supervision worked, but he had direct experience with them, hands-on knowledge, and was savvy about their quirks and operational capabilities. He could experiment with them.

In addition, Joe learned about budgets and management. Coming off the line as he did, he had a perspective of workers' needs and management's demands, and this led him to think of ways to improve efficiency on the line while relieving some of the stress on the assemblers. He had each worker in a unit learn his or her co-workers' jobs so they could rotate across stations to relieve some of the monotony. He believed that rotation would allow assemblers to get longer and more frequent breaks. It was

With an eighth-grade education, Joe (hands together) advanced to supervisor of a G.M. paint-and-body department.

an easy sell to the people on the line. The union, however, had to approve any modification in job duties, and the managers were wary of the change. Joe had to argue his case on a number of fronts, providing him a kind of rhetorical education.

Eight years ago I began a study of the thought processes involved in work like that of my mother and uncle. I catalogued the cognitive demands of a range of blue-collar and service jobs, from waitressing and hair styling to plumbing and welding. To gain a sense of how knowledge and skill develop, I observed experts as well as novices. From the details of this close examination, I tried to fashion what I called "cognitive biographies" of blue-collar workers. Biographical accounts of the lives of scientists, lawyers, entrepreneurs, and other professionals are rich with detail about the intellectual dimension of their work.

But the life stories of working-class people are few and are typically accounts of hardship and courage or the achievements wrought by hard work.

Our culture—in Cartesian fashion—separates the body from the mind, so that, for example, we assume that the use of a tool does not involve abstraction. We reinforce this notion by defining intelligence solely on grades in school and numbers on IQ tests. And we employ social biases pertaining to a person's place on the occupational ladder. The distinctions among blue, pink, and white collars carry with them attributions of character, motivation, and intelligence. Although we rightly acknowledge and amply compensate the play of mind in white-collar and professional work, we diminish or erase it in considerations about other endeavors—physical and service work particularly. We also often ignore the experience of everyday work in administrative deliberations and policymaking.

But here's what we find when we get in close. The plumber seeking leverage in order to work in tight quarters and the hair stylist adroitly handling scissors and comb manage their bodies strategically. Though work-related actions become routine with experience, they were learned at some point through observation, trial and error, and, often, physical or verbal assistance from a co-worker or trainer. I've frequently observed novices talking to themselves as they take on a task, or shaking their head or hand as if to erase an attempt before trying again. In fact, our traditional notions of routine performance could keep us from appreciating the many instances within routine where quick decisions and adjustments are made. I'm struck by the thinking-in-motion that some work requires, by all the mental activity that can be involved in simply getting from one place to another: the waitress rushing back through her station to the kitchen or the foreman walking the line.

The use of tools requires the studied refinement of stance, grip, balance, and fine-motor skills. But manipulating tools is intimately tied to knowledge of what a particular instrument can do in a particular situation and do better than other similar tools. A worker must also know the characteristics of the material one is engaging—how it reacts to various cutting or compressing devices, to degrees of heat, or to lines of force. Some of these things demand judgment, the weighing of options, the consideration of multiple variables, and, occasionally, the creative use of a tool in an unexpected way.

In manipulating material, the worker becomes attuned to aspects of the environment, a training or disciplining of perception that both enhances knowledge and informs perception. Carpenters have an eye for length, line, and angle; mechanics troubleshoot by listening; hair stylists are attuned to shape, texture, and motion. Sensory data merge with concept, as when an auto mechanic relies on sound, vibration, and even smell to understand what cannot be observed.

Planning and problem solving have been studied since the earliest days of modern cognitive psychology and are considered core elements in Western definitions of intelligence. To work is to solve problems. The big difference between the psychologist's laboratory and the workplace is that in the former the problems are isolated and in the latter they are embedded in the real-time flow of work with all its messiness and social complexity.

Much of physical work is social and interactive. Movers determining how to get an electric range down a flight of stairs require coordination, negotiation, planning, and the establishing of incremental goals. Words, gestures, and sometimes a quick pencil sketch are involved, if only to get the rhythm right. How important it is, then, to consider the social and communicative dimension of physical work, for it provides the medium for so much of work's intelligence.

Given the ridicule heaped on blue-collar speech, it might seem odd to value its cognitive content. Yet, the flow of talk at work provides the channel for organizing and distributing tasks, for troubleshooting and problem solving, for learning new information and revising old. A significant amount of teaching, often informal and indirect, takes place at work. Joe Meraglio saw that much of his job as a supervisor involved instruction. In some service occupations, language and communication are central: observing and interpreting behavior and expression, inferring mood and motive, taking on the perspective of others, responding appropriately to social cues, and knowing when you're understood. A good hair stylist, for instance, has the ability to convert vague requests (I want something light and summery) into an appropriate cut through questions, pictures, and hand gestures.

Verbal and mathematical skills drive measures of intelligence in the Western Hemisphere, and many of the kinds of work I studied are thought to require relatively little proficiency in either. Compared to certain kinds of white-collar occupations, that's true. But written symbols flow through physical work.

Numbers are rife in most workplaces: on tools and gauges, as measurements, as indicators of pressure or concentration or temperature, as guides to sequence, on ingredient labels, on lists and spreadsheets, as markers of quantity and price. Certain jobs require workers to make, check, and verify calculations, and to collect and interpret data. Basic math can be involved, and some workers develop a good sense of numbers and patterns. Consider, as well, what might be called material mathematics: mathematical functions embodied in materials and actions, as when a carpenter builds a cabinet or a flight of stairs. A simple mathematical act can extend quickly beyond itself. Measuring, for example, can involve more than recording the dimensions of an object. As I watched a cabinetmaker measure a long strip of wood, he read a number off the tape out loud, looked back over his shoulder to the kitchen wall, turned back to his task, took another measurement, and paused for a moment in thought. He was solving a problem involving the molding, and the measurement was important to his deliberation about structure and appearance.

In the blue-collar workplace, directions, plans, and refer- 25 ence books rely on illustrations, some representational and others, like blueprints, that require training to interpret. Esoteric symbols—visual jargon—depict switches and receptacles, pipe fittings, or types of welds. Workers themselves often make sketches on the job. I frequently observed them grab a pencil to sketch something on a scrap of paper or on a piece of the material they were installing.

Though many kinds of physical work don't require a high literacy level, more reading occurs in the blue-collar workplace than is generally thought, from manuals and catalogues to work orders and invoices, to lists, labels, and forms. With routine tasks, for example, reading is integral to understanding production quotas, learning how to use an instrument, or applying a product. Written notes can initiate action, as in restaurant orders or reports of machine malfunction, or they can serve as memory aids.

True, many uses of writing are abbreviated, routine, and repetitive, and they infrequently require interpretation or analysis. But analytic moments can be part of routine activities, and seemingly basic reading and writing can be cognitively rich. Because workplace language is used in the flow of other activities, we can overlook the remarkable coordination of words, numbers, and drawings required to initiate and direct action.

If we believe everyday work to be mindless, then that will affect the work we create in the future. When we devalue the full range of everyday cognition, we offer limited educational opportunities and fail to make fresh and meaningful instructional connections among disparate kinds of skill and knowledge. If we think that whole categories of people—identified by class or occupation—are not that bright, then we reinforce social separations and cripple our ability to talk across cultural divides.

Affirmation of diverse intelligence is not a retreat to a softhearted definition of the mind. To acknowledge a broader range of intellectual capacity is to take seriously the concept of cognitive variability, to appreciate in all the Rosies and Joes the thought that drives their accomplishments and defines who they are. This is a model of the mind that is worthy of a democratic society.

Joining the Conversation

1. This essay begins with a fairly detailed description of Mike Rose's mother at her work as a waitress in the 1950s, when he was a child. How is this description related to his argument? Is it an effective opening? Why or why not?
2. How would you summarize Rose's overall argument? What evidence does he offer as support? How convincing is his argument?
3. Where does Rose mention differing views, and what is his reason for bringing them up? What are these other views, and who holds them?

4. How do you think Rose would respond to Charles Murray's argument (pp. 400–20) that many students lack the intellectual potential to succeed in college?
5. Write an essay in which you consider the intellectual demands of a kind of work that you have done or are interested in.

Shut Up about Harvard

BEN CASSELMAN

—🔲—

A focus on elite schools ignores the issues most college students face.

IT'S COLLEGE ADMISSIONS SEASON, which means it's time once again for the annual flood of stories that badly misrepresent what higher education looks like for most American students—and skew the public debate over everything from student debt to the purpose of college in the process.

"How college admissions has turned into something akin to 'The Hunger Games,'" screamed a *Washington Post* headline Monday. "What you need to remember about fate during college admission season," wrote *Elite Daily* earlier this month. "Use rejection to prepare teens for college," advised *The Huffington Post*.

———

BEN CASSELMAN is an economics writer and senior editor for *FiveThirty-Eight*, a website that "uses statistical analysis—hard numbers—to tell compelling stories about elections, politics, sports, science, economics, and culture." Previously, Casselman worked for *Salem News* and the *Wall Street Journal*, where he was nominated for a Pulitzer Prize for a story about the *Deepwater Horizon* oil spill. This essay first appeared on *FiveThirtyEight* on March 30, 2016.

Here's how the national media usually depicts the admissions process: High school seniors spend months visiting colleges; writing essays; wrangling letters of recommendation; and practicing, taking and retaking an alphabet soup of ACTs, SATs and AP exams. Then the really hard part: months of nervously waiting to find out if they are among the lucky few (fewer every year, we're told!) with the right blend of academic achievement, extracurricular involvement and an odds-defying personal story to gain admission to their favored university.

Here's the reality: Most students never have to write a college entrance essay, pad a résumé or sweet-talk a potential letter-writer. Nor are most, as the *Atlantic* put it Monday, "obsessively checking their mailboxes" awaiting acceptance decisions. (Never mind that for most schools, those decisions now arrive online.) According to data from the Department of Education,[1] more than three-quarters of U.S. undergraduates[2] attend colleges that accept at least half their applicants; just 4 percent attend schools that accept 25 percent or less, and hardly any—well under 1 percent—attend schools like Harvard and Yale that accept less than 10 percent.

Media misconceptions don't end with admission. "College," 5 in the mainstream media, seems to mean people in their late teens and early 20s living in dorms, going to parties, studying English (or maybe pre-med) and emerging four years later with a degree and an unpaid internship. But that image, never truly representative, is increasingly disconnected from reality. Nearly half of all college students attend community colleges[3]; among those at four-year schools, nearly a quarter attend part time and about the same share are 25 or older. In total, less than a third of U.S. undergraduates are "traditional" students in the sense that they are full-time, degree-seeking students at primarily residential four-year colleges.[4]

College Doesn't Always Mean Leafy Campuses

Share of U.S. undergraduates at schools primarily offering ...

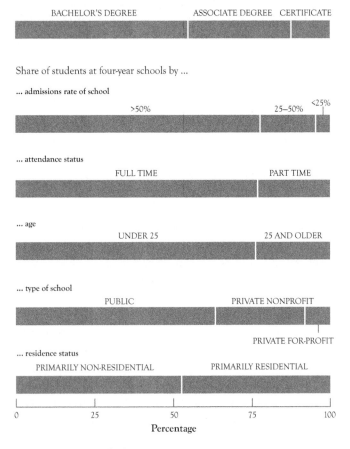

BACHELOR'S DEGREE   ASSOCIATE DEGREE   CERTIFICATE

Share of students at four-year schools by ...

... admissions rate of school

>50%   25–50%   <25%

... attendance status

FULL TIME   PART TIME

... age

UNDER 25   25 AND OLDER

... type of school

PUBLIC   PRIVATE NONPROFIT

PRIVATE FOR-PROFIT

... residence status

PRIMARILY NON-RESIDENTIAL   PRIMARILY RESIDENTIAL

0   25   50   75   100

Percentage

Source: Department of Education.
Note: Data are the most recent available.

Shut Up about Harvard

Of course, the readerships of the *Atlantic* and *Washington Post* probably don't mirror the U.S. as a whole. Many readers probably did attend selective institutions or have children they are hoping will. It's understandable that media outlets would want to cater to their readers, particularly in stories that aim to give advice to students or their parents.

See pp. 88–89 for other ways to make concessions while still standing your ground.

But it's hard not to suspect that there is also another reason for reporters' focus on elite colleges: At least in major national media outlets, that's where most of them went. There's no definitive data on where reporters went to school, but the newsrooms of influential media outlets in New York and Washington, D.C., are full of graduates from Ivy League or similarly selective colleges. Those who attended public colleges often went to a handful of top research universities such as the University of Michigan or the University of California, Berkeley. *FiveThirtyEight* is just as bad: The vast majority of our editorial staff, including me, went to elite, selective colleges. (I went to Columbia.)

"Ninety-five percent of the newsroom probably went to private institutions, they went to four-year institutions, and they went to elite institutions," said Jeff Selingo, a longtime higher-education journalist who has a new book focused on giving advice to a broader group of students. "It is exactly the opposite of the experience for the bulk of American students."

It isn't just newsrooms. Hollywood is guilty of this too—think of a movie about college, and it probably took place on a leafy suburban campus. That's true even of movies that aren't set in the real world; when the writers of the Pixar film *Monsters University* wanted a model for their animated campus, they visited Harvard, MIT and Berkeley, according to *The Wall Street Journal*.[5] One result, Selingo said: "We tend to view higher education through the eyes of private higher education," even though nearly two-thirds of U.S. undergraduates[6] attend public institutions.

That myopia has real consequences for education policy. 10 Based on media accounts, it would be easy to think that the biggest issues on U.S. campuses today are the spread of "trigger warnings," the rise of "hookup culture" and the spiraling cost of amenity-filled dorms and rec centers. Meanwhile, issues that matter to a far larger share of students get short shrift.

The media's focus on elite schools draws attention away from state cuts to higher-education funding, for example. Private colleges, which feature disproportionately in media accounts, aren't affected by state budget cuts; top-tier public universities, which have outside resources such as alumni donations, research grants and patent revenue, are much less dependent on public dollars than less selective schools.

Or consider the breathless coverage of the college application game that few students ever play: For most students, or at least most high school graduates, getting into college isn't nearly as big a challenge as getting out. Barely half of first-time, full-time bachelor's degree students graduate within six years; for part-time or community college students, that share is even lower. But it took years for what is known in education jargon as "college completion" to break into mainstream education coverage, perhaps because at selective schools, the vast majority of students graduate on time or close to it.

Even issues that do get attention, such as student debt, are often covered through the lens of elite institutions. Reporters can't resist stories of students with eye-popping debt loads in the six figures. But many of those stories involve people who went to graduate school, most (though not all) of whom will end up making good salaries in the long run. Meanwhile, those who are struggling most to pay off loans are often those with smaller balances who either have degrees that don't help them find jobs (often from for-profit colleges) or who never got a degree in the first place. Nearly one in five Americans age 25 to 34 has some college credits but no degree,[7] and a growing share of them have student debt.

"The biggest issue is that people can't afford to spend enough time in college to actually finish their darn degrees," said Sara Goldrick-Rab, a sociology professor and education-policy expert at the University of Wisconsin.[8]

What few journalists seem to understand, Goldrick-Rab said, is how tenuous a grasp many students have on college. They are working while in school, often juggling multiple jobs that don't readily align with class schedules. They are attending part time, which makes it take longer to graduate and reduces the chances of finishing at all. They are raising children, supporting parents and racking up debt trying to pay for it all.

One little thing goes awry and it just falls apart," Goldrick-Rab said. "And the consequences of it falling apart when they're taking on all this debt are just so severe."

Students keep taking that risk for a reason: A college degree remains the most likely path to a decent-paying job. They aren't studying literary theory or philosophy; the most popular undergraduate majors in recent years have been business and health-related fields such as nursing.

Yet the public debate over whether college is "worth it," and the related conversation over how to make higher education more affordable, too often focuses on issues that are far removed from the lives of most students: administrative salaries, runaway construction costs, the value of the humanities. Lost in those discussions are the challenges that affect far more students: How to design college schedules to accommodate students who work, as more than half of students do;[9] how to make sure students keep their credits when they transfer, as more than a third of students do at least once; and, of course, how to make college affordable not just for the few who attend Harvard but for the many who attend regional public universities and community colleges.

Notes

1. Unless otherwise noted, all data in this article is from the Department of Education's College Scorecard database. Data is the most recent available.

2. Degree-seeking undergraduates at four-year schools.

3. Defined as schools offering primarily associate degrees or certificates.

4. "Primarily residential" colleges are those where at least 25 percent of students live on campus.

5. Thanks to Selingo for pointing out this anecdote.

6. At four-year colleges.

7. According to the Current Population Survey, via IPUMS.

8. Goldrick-Rab is leaving Wisconsin for Temple University at the end of the academic year.

9. CPS, via IPUMS.

Joining the Conversation

1. Why does Ben Casselman believe the media focuses too much on students at Harvard and other elite colleges? In his view, what effect does this bias have on higher education?

2. Examine the table on page 448 listing data from the US Department of Education. How do the data support Casselman's argument? What other sorts of information relating to the essay's argument might you like to see displayed, and what would you hope to learn from it?

3. In presenting his "they say," Casselman gives numerous examples of mainstream media's emphasis on elite colleges. What words and phrases does he use to distinguish his views from those of other newspapers and magazines?

4. Read Liz Addison's essay (pp. 421–24), and compare what she says with what Casselman says.
5. Go to **theysayiblog.com** and read Devoney Looser's article "Why I Teach Online." How do you think Casselman would respond to her argument?

On the Front Lines
of a New Culture War

STEVE KOLOWICH

——◻——

*St. Cloud State University spent 15 years trying to become a
beacon of diversity and tolerance while its city fought over the
arrival of Muslim refugees. Then Donald Trump came along.*

St. Cloud, Minnesota. The Somali students watched the
news with a sense of dread: Someone had hit six people with
a car and then stabbed five more at Ohio State University.

Just don't let him be Somali, some of the students thought to
themselves as details of the attack started percolating on social
media. *Don't let him be Muslim.*

It had happened on a different campus in a different state,
but the Somali refugees at St. Cloud State University had lived
in the United States for long enough to know how this worked:

———

Steve Kolowich is a staff reporter for *The Chronicle of Higher Education*, "the No. 1 source of news, information, and jobs for college and
university faculty members and administrators." He has also written
for *Inside Higher Education, Slate,* and the *Washington City Paper.* This
essay appeared in *The Chronicle of Higher Education* on January 1, 2017.

Mohamed Warsame, president of the Somali Student Association at
St. Cloud State University.

Any act of violence by a foreign-born Muslim could reignite
fears of immigration and terrorism, and there was no place more
flammable than St. Cloud, Minn.

The bad news had arrived in short order: The Ohio State
attacker, Abdul Artan, was Somali, Muslim, and a student.
The next day, the Somali Muslim students at St. Cloud State
gathered for their weekly meeting in the student union to talk
about what, if anything, Mr. Artan had to do with them.

They had beaten long odds to get here. Their families fled 5
a civil war that left hundreds of thousands of Somalis starved,
brutalized, and stranded. Some of the students had been raised
in refugee camps. They came to the United States at the invitation of the federal government and put down roots in Minnesota. They now stood to earn college degrees and the chance
to climb the social ladder in their adoptive country.

But it was not clear that their country wanted them.

Earlier that month, U.S. voters had elected Donald J. Trump as their next president. During his campaign, he had spoken of Somali refugees as a "disaster" for Minnesota and called for a ban on Muslims entering the country. He had specifically mentioned St. Cloud, a city that sits at the axis of three counties in central Minnesota. On Election Day, more than 60 percent of voters in those counties cast ballots for Mr. Trump—the most support here for any presidential candidate in more than half a century.

The election dealt a moral blow to the Somali students. Now news of the Ohio State attack threatened to validate the suspicions stirred by Mr. Trump's message.

The details of the attack were sadly familiar. They echoed a September incident here, in St. Cloud, where a Muslim man with Somali roots had hit a cyclist with his car and then stabbed 10 people at a local shopping mall. The attacker was a former student at St. Cloud State.

After the mall attack, Somali students at the university led a rally on campus to show solidarity with the city. Now, in the student union, they talked about whether they should make a statement addressing what happened in Ohio.

White people, they had noticed, always seemed to expect Muslims everywhere to condemn violence committed by Muslims anywhere. But why should they have to take responsibility for the actions of a stranger 800 miles away?

It felt unfair. The majority of the Somali students at St. Cloud State had spent most of their lives in America. They watch football on Sundays. They laugh at impersonations of Homer Simpson and Arnold Schwarzenegger. They aspire to be social workers, police officers, and beauty queens.

They are part of a generation of refugees who are trying to do what immigrants in the United States have done for years:

get educated, expand their horizons, and build better lives for themselves while also staying connected to the culture that sustained their elders through the traumas of war and disloca-tion. For the younger Somalis, a college degree repre-sents a chance to avoid the powerlessness of life in the nonwhite working class.

See pp. 94–95 for ways to indicate who cares.

What it might not offer them is a privilege afforded to many Americans regardless of education: the freedom to speak for themselves, and no one else.

St. Cloud sits along the chilliest stretch of the Mississippi River, about 65 miles northwest of Minneapolis. German was spo-ken in its downtown business district, and in many homes and schools, until a wave of nativism swept the state during World War I. Many German immigrants suppressed their heritage for fear of being seen as disloyal. 15

A few blocks south, the city opens up on a series of Brutalist buildings. Here, in the middle of a deep red gash in the Demo-cratic Party's crumbling upper-Midwest firewall, sits a public university that, over the past decade and a half, has tried to embody diversity, tolerance, and globalist optimism.

St. Cloud State, whose 15,000 students include 300 Somalis, now faces the task of making a case for those values in hostile territory.

For two decades, the city has been a destination for refugees fleeing the Horn of Africa. Some residents of the Minnesota city once known as "White Cloud" have been jarred by the influx of African Muslims.

In recent years, relationships have become tense. Somalis have reported being harassed on the street and in the hallways of a local high school. Somali-owned businesses have been tagged with graffiti. Last winter a Minneapolis-based newspaper declared St. Cloud to be "the worst place in Minnesota to be Somali."

The university wants to be an exception to that rule. St. 20
Cloud State prides itself on being safe and welcoming to students of color and to religious minorities, although this has not
always been the case. At the time St. Cloud State hired its first
nonwhite president, Roy H. Saigo, in 2000, it had been named
in dozens of discrimination lawsuits.

Mr. Saigo, a Japanese-American who spent three years of
his childhood in an Arizona internment camp during World
War II, started working on making the campus more inclusive.
The first step was to force the university to look in the mirror.
Mr. Saigo asked the Equal Employment Opportunity Commission to investigate how St. Cloud State was failing its minority
students and staff members, and how it could do better.

Investigators found a "perception of ignorance and an acute
lack of sensitivity among faculty, students, and administrators
in regard to religious and cultural differences," both on the
campus and in the city.

"The university," they wrote in a report, "suffers from a
severe lack of credibility with regard to diversity issues."

Mr. Saigo set about trying to fix that. He visited urban
high schools in the Twin Cities, where St. Cloud State had
never recruited. He faced some resistance. Three black faculty
members, apparently worried that the new recruits might not
know what they were getting themselves into, sent letters to
guidance counselors in Twin Cities high schools warning that
"residency in St. Cloud can be hazardous for black people." At
around the same time, a "cultural audit" by a consulting firm
noted that the special attention given to minorities on campus
had irked some white employees. "The white culture is feeling
oppressed and left out," wrote the auditors in 2002, "and wants
to be recognized." In 2007 and 2008, swastikas were scrawled
on campus.

Since then the numbers of international students and stu- 25 dents of color have ticked upward.

In the student union on an afternoon in late November, the progress is evident: The air is alive with the sound of a half-dozen languages and accents. Indian students in saris offer temporary henna tattoos. Muslim women in head scarves gossip around laptops. A grinning white guy with a patchy beard lumbers through in a Green Bay Packers jersey and a cheese head.

The student population at St. Cloud State is now more diverse than those of Minnesota and the country as a whole. But diversity alone does not erase boundaries. Seventy percent of students at the university are white Americans, many of them drawn from the mostly white counties around the city. And here, just as on many campuses, those white students can still sail through four years without spending significant time with people whose backgrounds differ greatly from their own.

Ashish Vaidya, St. Cloud State's interim president, wants to do what he can to change that.

For Mr. Vaidya, diversity does not mean just better serving students of color. It also means preparing white kids from Minnesota to navigate a diverse world with grace and empathy. St. Cloud State requires students to take courses that focus on "multicultural, gender, and minority studies," and Mr. Vaidya wants it to develop tools than can measure whether students have absorbed those lessons.

"If, at the end of their educational experience at St. Cloud 30 State, they emerge without knowing very well how to engage in a diverse and multicultural environment," says the president, "we have failed."

"Diversity is not just a nice social norm," says Ashish Vaidya, interim
president of St. Cloud State. "I'm convinced that it is a primary driving
force for creativity and innovation."

Mr. Vaidya, an Indian-born economist, became president
unexpectedly last year, when the man who had hired him as
provost, Earl H. Potter III, died in a car crash. His father was a
telecommunications engineer for the Indian government, a job
that uprooted his family every few years. Mr. Vaidya was raised
in an ever-changing backdrop of locales, including two years on
the African island of Mauritius, where the children at his school
spoke French and Creole. At the University of California at
Davis, where he got his doctorate, he studied alongside students

from Spain, China, and Iran. "My wife thinks I have no roots," he says, "which is probably accurate."

The interim president, who came to St. Cloud State from Los Angeles in 2015, is enthusiastic about the "internationalization" that he sees as part of the university's identity. He is bullish on study-abroad programs, and the university is pushing more students to incorporate international travel into their education. If he could afford to send all 15,000 students at the university to study in foreign countries, he says, he would. His realistic goal is more modest: to increase study-abroad enrollment from 450 to 700 over the next three years.

As for central Minnesota, Mr. Vaidya believes his best pitch for diversity is an economic one. "Diversity is not just a nice social norm," he says. "I'm convinced that it is a primary driving force for creativity and innovation that's going to lead to economic success."

Minnesota businesses have global ambitions, he says, and a state university that promotes multiculturalism will better serve both its students and the companies that might want to hire them, "It's a globally interconnected world. There is no 'other.' There is no 'the other side.'"

That is, of course, exactly the kind of optimism that typified 35 Hillary Clinton's presidential campaign and failed to inspire so many voters here in central Minnesota. On the morning after Election Day, college leaders woke up to the realization that they were the "other."

Mr. Trump's victory was a reminder that big swaths of the population don't cherish "safe spaces," political correctness, or multiculturalism—to say nothing of fact-checking or the scientific method.

This might not have come as a shock to state universities, many of which have been gradually starved by state legislators as they have become more diverse. In the wake of the Trump victory, St. Cloud State has reason to feel especially disconnected from the regional political mood. If the voting results are any indication, most people around here seem to think that cultural and economic boundaries exist for good reasons, and would rather see them reinforced than blurred beyond recognition.

Two days before the election, Mr. Trump held a rally in an airplane hangar at the Minneapolis–St. Paul airport. He did not talk about the college graduates Minnesota was sending out into the world. He talked about people invading the state from the other side of civilization.

"Everybody's reading about the disaster taking place in Minnesota," Mr. Trump had told the crowd, referring to the Somali refugees. "Everybody's reading about it. You don't even have the right to talk about it. ... You don't even know who's coming in—you have no idea. You'll find out."

He was not talking to Minnesota business leaders eager to 40 leverage the "globally interconnected world," or to college presidents who could help them do it. He was talking to white people who feel less connected than ever to the world right outside their doorsteps.

Two days before Election Day, Mohamed Warsame was at a friend's apartment, watching a football game. His Minnesota Vikings were in the process of letting one slip away at home.

Mr. Warsame, a 24-year-old business major at St. Cloud State who is president of the Somali Student Association, checked Facebook and saw that Mr. Trump was trying to pull off a similar upset, decrying the presence of Somalis in places like St. Cloud.

"You've suffered enough," Mr. Trump told the hangar full of white Minnesotans.

Mr. Warsame was not impressed. "We've dealt with civil war, we've dealt with some family members dying because of tribal issues that didn't even make sense," he says. "What else can you do to us? We've been survivalists all our lives. So, saying we're bad people, that doesn't really do anything to us."

His family fled Somalia in 2001. Mr. Warsame doesn't remember those days vividly, and doesn't care to. There were guns, there were "travel issues," there were people who died. He doesn't see any point in dwelling on the past. "It's very hard, and it's a very divided issue," he says. "If you bring it up, you're just bringing problems."

The family arrived in Minnesota the way a lot of Somalis did: by traveling from wherever else the U.S. government had placed them. They were in Tennessee but headed north after getting a call from a relative in Minnesota. The Somalis there had a community and a foothold in the working class. Mr. Warsame's mother got a job at a turkey-processing plant in a small city called Faribault, and after a few years she moved the family to the Twin Cities.

Mr. Warsame has a soccer player's build, but since moving to Minnesota as a teenager he has become a fan of American football. He and Mr. Trump share a favorite player, the New England Patriots quarterback Tom Brady, whom the president-elect has called a "great champion." Mr. Warsame likes Mr. Brady because nobody else wanted him on their team, and he proved them all wrong.

He believes in underdog stories, including his own. In junior high school, he remembers spending a long time working through the English sentences in his homework under the guidance of a Somali neighbor who had been in the country for a longer time. It was hard work, but Mr. Warsame didn't give up, and made the honor roll.

When it came time to go to college, he almost slipped through the cracks. He applied to Minnesota State University at Mankato at the suggestion of a friend, but had to scramble to get his financial-aid forms in order. This time he had no one to guide him. "I didn't have anyone to lead the way for me, to say, 'This is how you do stuff.'"

At Mankato he was stressed out. He made some friends but 50 couldn't afford a car, and as the days grew colder and shorter he felt more and more isolated. He left after a year and enrolled in community college. He took a job at a computer-chip manufacturer for $12 per hour.

It was hard manual work, and it wore him down. Mr. Warsame noticed that a lot of the other immigrants there were hired on a temporary basis and did not get benefits. "I figured out, I can't do this for the rest of my life," he says.

Finally he enrolled at St. Cloud State, where he found a home among the Somali students and student-government types. After the Somali student group elected him president, Mr. Warsame had the idea to pair up new Somali students with older mentors who could help them find their way.

As a campaign message, optimism might seem corny, but as a personal philosophy, Mr. Warsame sees it a key for survival. Experience has shown him how some people start out with disadvantages—but, like bad memories, he doesn't see any upside in focusing on them.

"There's two ways of being an underdog," he says. One way is to say the system is rigged and you'll be shut out. But "there's another way: I'll find my way in, and I'll do whatever it takes."

Patrick Nelson, a St. Cloud student, says he might feel more positive about Islam if he had Muslim friends: "Most of the problems I have with Islam is the belief system, not the individuals."

Patrick Nelson was at the airport for Mr. Trump's speech. The 55 Republican candidate, wearing his trademark red hat, gripped the sides of the podium and recounted the knife attack in St. Cloud. Then, pinching thumb to forefinger and gesturing decisively, he promised he would not allow any refugees to be placed in any town that didn't want them there.

The crowd cheered, and so did Mr. Nelson.

The stereotype of a Trump supporter is an alpha male of a certain age who longs for a time in American history when he felt less bitter about his place in the country and the country's place in the world. Mr. Nelson does not fit that mold. He is 19 years old, fresh-faced and polite, too young to be nostalgic about anything. Like a lot of college kids, he professes to be antiwar, pro–gender equality, and pro–gay rights.

Mr. Nelson grew up in St. Cloud just as the Somali population was becoming more visible. The Somalis in his neighborhood lived up the road in an apartment complex overseen by Catholic Charities, which Mr. Nelson knew as "the projects." He kept his distance from the Somali boys at his school, who always seemed to be involved in fights. They spoke their own language with one another and didn't seem interested in him. That was fine with Mr. Nelson, who was a shy, anxious kid and wasn't interested in them, either.

As he approached voting age, Mr. Nelson became curious about Islam, the dominant religion among the new immigrants. He says he read the Quran and did some research online—on his own, not for a class—on Shariah law and the differences between Sunni and Shiite Muslims. He concluded that Islam was an intolerant religion, and that Muslims arriving from conservative cultures posed a threat to the gay-rights movement at a moment when homophobia in the United States was finally on the wane.

He says he used to worry about Christian extremists, like 60 the Westboro Baptist Church. Now he worries about Muslims.

Mr. Nelson grew up around Somalis—in school and at the warehouse where he once worked as a janitor—but has not been close with any of them. "I think some of that was my choice," he says, "just because I probably had some internal racism or something."

He's open to the possibility that he might feel differently about Islam if he had Muslim friends, but says his critique is ideological, not personal. "Most of the problems I have with Islam is the belief system," he says, "not the individuals."

Mr. Nelson, who transferred to St. Cloud State this year and lives at his childhood home, south of campus, describes his parents as center-left Democrats who like President Obama. He remembers learning concepts like racism from them and from his teachers in school. It was on YouTube and on 8chan, an anything-goes online hub popular among gamers and hackers, that he learned the term "race realism": the idea that race, rather than being a social construct, marks actual biological differences among people.

As the election approached, the first presidential contest in which he would be eligible to vote, Mr. Nelson started constructing his own political identity.

He believes in "race realism" but not white supremacy. [65] He supports stemming the arrival of new refugees but not kicking out the ones who already live here. He doesn't think Muslim immigrants are more violent than other groups, but he worries that Islam might attract people who are inherently violent.

He does not believe everything that Donald Trump says, but he doesn't think Mr. Trump believes everything he says, either.

The guys on 8chan saw Mr. Trump as a cult hero: a trash-talking boss who broke the rules of politics and got away with it. "A lot of my peers online were into him," says Mr. Nelson, "so I thought, 'Jump on the bandwagon.'"

After Mr. Trump won the Republican nomination, Mr. Nelson started taking his positions seriously. The candidate started looking like a guy capable of ushering his party to the left on gay-rights issues. (His running mate, Mike Pence, who has a record of supporting policies that would enable discrimination against gay people, is another matter. Mr. Nelson says, half-seriously, that he thinks Mr. Trump picked the Indiana governor to discourage would-be assassins on the left who would not want to be stuck with a President Pence.)

After Mr. Trump gave a foreign-policy speech railing against the country's attempts at nation-building in the Middle East, he started looking like the antiwar candidate, too.

Mr. Nelson was sold, and he wasn't alone. At an election-night 70 watch party on campus, he was pleased to find that some of his fellow St. Cloud State students were also pulling for Mr. Trump.

He knows that some people think education should necessarily immunize voters to Mr. Trump's charms, but he finds that view demeaning. Mr. Nelson sees his reasons for supporting the president-elect as legitimate, evidence-based, and moderate compared with some of the chatter he reads online.

"I've done my homework," he says. "I'm not coming in completely stupid."

On September 17, with the presidential race heating up, Mr. Nelson checked Facebook and saw a friend's message with a link to a local news story. Something had happened at a shopping mall three miles west of campus.

A 20-year-old man with Somali roots had grabbed two long knives and driven to the mall, hitting a cyclist on the way. In the parking lot he slashed a pregnant woman and her boyfriend. Inside the mall, the man stabbed eight more people before being shot and killed by an off-duty police officer.

"The suspect made some references to Allah," noted the story, "and asked at least one person in the mall if they were 75 Muslim before attacking them."

Details of the attacker's life soon emerged. His name was Dahir Adan. He was born in Kenya to Somali parents and came to the United States when he was 2 years old. Other Somalis in St. Cloud knew him as a "normal American kid" who liked basketball, soccer, and video games. He was a good student, and after high school he had enrolled at St. Cloud State, where he studied information systems.

Earlier last year, something had changed. According to the FBI, Mr. Adan "flunked out" of college, lost weight, seemed unusually agitated, and took an intense interest in the Quran. The agency looked into whether Mr. Adan had ties to any terror groups. They did not immediately find any links, although the investigation remains open.

Faisa Salah, a student studying social work at the university, wonders if Mr. Adan might have been suffering from psychological problems—a possibility that, she notes with dismay, never seems to come up when an attacker is Muslim and foreign-born. (Mr. Adan's family and his soccer coach have said they do not believe he was mentally ill.)

Ms. Salah, too, was born in Kenya to Somali parents. They came to the United States when she was 6, days after the terrorist attacks of September 11, 2001. The refugee-resettlement office placed them in San Diego, but before long they, too, beat a path to Minnesota.

Growing up in St. Cloud, Ms. Salah did not learn much about mental health. Like many Americans, Somali immigrants see psychological disorders as shameful, she says, and usually 80 they are swept under the rug. "With us, it's more of a stigma," she says. "If a family member is disabled, the whole family is frowned upon."

When a cousin began acting out, Ms. Salah says, her aunt insisted that he needed the Quran, not psychiatric treatment. The cousin later jumped off a third-floor balcony. (He survived, she says, and eventually got medical help.) That experience made her want to study psychology at St. Cloud State. Now she plans to stay for a master's degree and become a clinical social worker.

She knows how stressful it can be to try to build a life on a cultural fault line. In the early 2010s, she felt the plates start to slip. The ethnic tensions at her high school started to reflect those of St. Cloud generally. Ms. Salah has felt pulled between the culture she had inherited from her Somali relatives and the one she had adopted in Minnesota.

"I felt like it was 'them' and 'us,' and I didn't know who to pick," she says.

Ms. Salah considered herself an American. She had white friends, and all of her memories are of St. Cloud. But the arrival of newer Somalis, who don't identify with the kids who grew up in central Minnesota, complicated the question of where she fit in socially.

"They thought we were too Americanized, or like we wanted [85] to be like the white kids," says Ms. Salah. But she and the other "Americanized" Somalis didn't fully fit in with the white kids, either. "So, we were kind of stuck in the middle."

Ms. Salah is Muslim—she wears a head scarf and does not shake hands with men who are not family—but she's also a modern woman, who, despite her mother's reservations, is planning on a career despite having two young children herself. She says her sense of identity has been shaped by her education and professional aspirations as much as by her faith and heritage.

"I can relate more to a white person who has the same ideas as me," she says. "I can relate more to the social workers who are white than someone who is in my culture."

The older generation of Somali refugees witnessed murder and the rape of family members during the conflict that turned their home country into what some have described as hell on earth. Ms. Salah believes there are cases of post-traumatic stress disorder among them that have never been diagnosed. She hopes a degree in social work will help her teach her elders about mental health.

But it's complicated. Among Somalis, she says, credibility is conferred by age, not education. She sometimes tries to tell her mother what she's learned about symptoms and treatments. "She goes, 'No, you just need prayers,'" says Ms. Salah. "Prayers do help, but it's not the only factor. You need medicine, too."

Ms. Salah hopes that fewer Somalis in her generation will 90 see a family member showing signs of psychological distress and point to the Quran as the only solution.

She also hopes that fewer Americans in her generation will see a Somali Muslim commit an act of violence and point to the Quran as the problem.

St. Cloud State provides its Somali students with a relatively safe place in a world that they know, better than most, is anything but safe.

Whatever refuge the campus offers is temporary, of course. The students will continue their journeys in a country where many other people see them as a threat.

Abdi H. Daisane's journey has been improbable. His father, a military man, took the family from one Somali city to the next during the civil war, trying desperately to avoid the purgatory of a refugee camp. They ended up in one anyway, in Kenya, where Mr. Daisane spent the next 18 years, until he was finally delivered, courtesy of the U.S. government and a Lutheran charity, to an apartment in Omaha.

His journey then took him to a couple of Nebraska towns 95 and finally to Minnesota, where he earned a degree in international relations and planning and community development at St. Cloud State. Last winter, after he graduated, Mr. Daisane's journey took him a few miles west of campus, to a small office with green walls, a space heater, and a window looking out on the parking lot of a Buffalo Wild Wings.

Mr. Daisane is a lanky 29-year-old with an easy smile. His desk is covered in printed forms and schedules, alongside a

Abdi Daisane, a Somali native, works with a nonprofit group that helps Somali refugees find jobs in Minnesota. He calls himself a "career planner" but teaches basic cultural competencies as well.

motivational book called *Get Up Off Your Butt & Do It Now!* His prayer mat is folded on a chair against the wall.

The office belongs to Resource Inc., a nonprofit group that works with counties to place people in jobs so they can receive government benefits under Minnesota's welfare-to-work program. Mr. Daisane works primarily with new Somali refugees.

He calls himself a "career planner," but he also teaches basic cultural competencies: the importance of showing up on time, respecting other people's personal space, refraining from homophobic remarks, not answering their cellphones at inappropriate times. Most of his clients don't speak English, he says, and many have never been to school.

Last year Mr. Daisane decided he wanted to give the local Somalis a voice where it counted: the city government. He filed

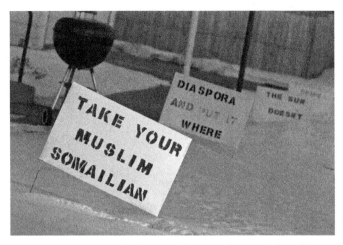

A homeowner in St. Cloud, where Somali refugees have settled, used his front lawn to express his point of view after Election Day.

to run for a seat on the St. Cloud City Council against three incumbents and one other challenger, all of them white.

He pitched himself as a "bridge builder." At a public forum, Mr. Daisane challenged the council president on how attentive the council had been to racial divisions in St. Cloud. He showed up at the shopping mall after the stabbing attack and talked about how much Somalis in town feared being targeted for retaliation. He won an endorsement from the *St. Cloud Times*.

He hit the streets to canvass for votes. One day, he knocked 100 on the door of a small white house with an American flag in the front yard. The man who answered the door seemed wary of the Somalis who had moved into the neighborhood, says Mr. Daisane, but the candidate made his case anyway and asked if he could count on the man's vote. The man said he would do some research.

On November 8, Mr. Trump won, and Mr. Daisane lost.

The three incumbents won handily. The other challenger, who had skipped the public forum and had not responded to inquiries from the newspaper, came in fourth. Mr. Daisane came in last.

Two days after the election, a series of signs appeared next to the American flag on the lawn of the small white house near the mall. They spelled out a message: "Take your Muslim Somailian diaspora and put it where the sun doesn't shine!!!"

The owner of the house, who didn't want his name used, told *The Chronicle* he doesn't remember a conversation with Mr. Daisane but wouldn't trust any Muslim, no matter how well-educated, to serve at any level of government. "I believe," he says, "that down the line they will go back to their strong Muslim, Shariah beliefs."

Mr. Daisane didn't sleep much the night after the election. 105 The next morning, while his wife slept, he sat in his pajamas watching TV and wondering where the country might be headed. He thought about the kids in the refugee camp where he had woken up every morning for 18 years, unsure whether water would flow from the tap his family shared with 200 others. He remembers sitting down in his mostly bare Nebraska apartment the week he arrived in the country and writing down his goals: Get a driver's license. Get a GED. Get a college degree.

The process had thrilled him. It was the first time he had lived anywhere with a functioning government, and America's mythos as a land of freedom and opportunity felt very real to him. "This is the only country where you're actually writing goals for yourself," he says, "because there is stability, there is a system."

After awhile, he thought about his own campaign. He knows some people here are prejudiced. They might have seen his skin tone or his name and been reminded of the knife-wielding attacker on the evening news. Those same people might tense up at the sound of his footsteps behind them in a dark parking lot.

Just don't let him be Somali, they might think to themselves. *Don't let him be Muslim.*

Mr. Daisane has faith that if he came to their homes, and if they listened to his story and heard what he really believed, they would give him a chance.

"I probably should have knocked on more doors and had 110 more conversations with people," he says.

"If I had done that, probably I would have won."

Joining the Conversation

1. Steve Kolowich tells the stories of people living in and around St. Cloud, Minnesota: Somali immigrants (mainly college students), the president of the local university (himself an immigrant from India), a white college student from the area, and a Somali community organizer. Taken together, what picture emerges of the Somali community of St. Cloud? Of the white population there?

2. Does the essay leave you feeling optimistic, pessimistic, or both about the possibilities for the Somali community to fit in to life in small-town Minnesota? Why?

3. Notice how many direct quotations Kolowich includes. Why do you think he includes so many? What, if anything, do the quotations contribute that a summary or paraphrase would not?

4. How might Sean Blanda (pp. 248–54) and danah boyd (pp. 255–65) respond to the situation of Somali students in St. Cloud, Minnesota?

5. Write a letter to Patrick Nelson, the college student discussed in the essay, agreeing, disagreeing, or both with his views. You might incorporate the views of Abdi Daisane, Faisa Salah, or Mohamed Warsame as support for your argument.

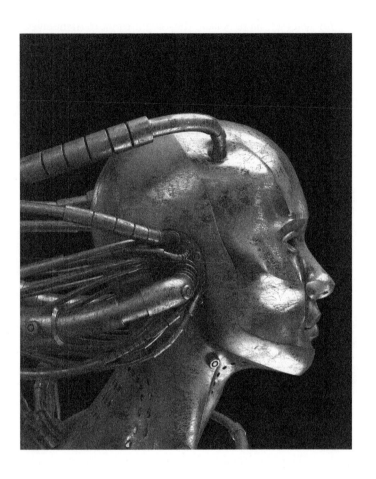

TWENTY

ARE WE IN A RACE
AGAINST THE MACHINE?

———🖫———

ARE WE IN A RACE AGAINST THE MACHINE? Many people seem
to think so and are frightened by the prospect. Researchers at
Chapman University in California recently conducted a survey
of Americans' fears, asking around 1,500 adults what scares
them most. Somewhat surprisingly, technology came in second
place, right behind natural disasters. As Adrienne LaFrance
writes in a piece for the *Atlantic*, "In the early days of the
telephone, people wondered if the machines might be used
to communicate with the dead. Today, it is the smartphone
that has people jittery." No doubt, smartphones connect us to
friends, family, and colleagues, but they can also be a source of
anxiety and unease as they bring us continuous streams of news
stories, social media posts, and text messages.

Smartphones aside, others continue to worry about technology in all its forms, and how it can negatively impact our brains
and bodies. Susan Greenfield, a neuroscientist, argues that our
"attention spans are shorter, personal communication skills are
reduced and there's a marked reduction in the ability to think
abstractly." Scientists used to believe that the human brain
changed up through adolescence but was relatively stable before
declining in old age. Now, however, there is strong evidence

for what Greenfield calls "the malleability of the adult brain," with alterations in brain structure caused by the devices we have come to rely upon—and even some indications that we are losing important mental skills.

But not everyone accepts these doomsday scenarios. A number of experts argue that such alarmist views are seriously overstated. In their view, new technologies make us smarter, happier, and more productive. Clive Thompson, for example, focuses on the growing role of computers in chess playing to argue that technology is changing our minds—and our lives— for the better. Similarly, Kenneth Goldsmith writes that far from wasting time, much of what we do on the internet helps us to develop new skills, learn about the world, and interact with others. Responding to concerns that digital communication leads to a decline in face-to-face interaction, Jenna Wortham offers a positive assessment of the social media platform Snapchat, writing that it is an easy, fun, language-free technology for connecting with others and simply being oneself.

Along these same lines, college student Michaela Cullington discusses her own research study, which found that, contrary to public belief, text messaging is a practical form of communication and does not weaken students' academic writing skills. And countering the view that political involvement online does not translate to genuine activism, Zeynep Tufekci argues that, used judiciously, social media can be a driving force for initiating and maintaining political and social movements.

Still, some are concerned and think others should be too. Nicholas Carr believes that extensive use of the internet is hurting our capacity for deep thinking and contemplation. Previously a strong proponent of digital technologies, Sherry Turkle now argues that they are leading to a decline in intimacy and a move away from self-reflection. And Carole Cadwalladr shows how Google and Facebook use algorithms that make it easy to spread fake news and discriminatory speech. The readings in this chapter give us much to think about, raising a number of complex problems and providing no easy solutions. And while some commentators may paint an optimistic picture of technology and others contemplate more pessimistic scenarios, there's a little bit of optimism and pessimism in each reading, factors that make this conversation worth joining.

Is Google Making Us Stupid?

NICHOLAS CARR

—⌐▢⌐—

"DAVE, STOP. STOP, WILL YOU? Stop, Dave. Will you stop, Dave?" So the supercomputer HAL pleads with the implacable astronaut Dave Bowman in a famous and weirdly poignant scene toward the end of Stanley Kubrick's *2001: A Space Odyssey*. Bowman, having nearly been sent to a deep-space death by the malfunctioning machine, is calmly, coldly disconnecting the memory circuits that control its artificial "brain." "Dave, my mind is going," HAL says, forlornly. "I can feel it. I can feel it."

I can feel it, too. Over the past few years I've had an uncomfortable sense that someone, or something, has been tinkering with my brain, remapping the neural circuitry, reprogramming the memory. My mind isn't going—so far as I can tell—but it's changing. I'm not thinking the way I used to think. I can

————

NICHOLAS CARR writes frequently on issues of technology and culture. His books include *The Big Switch: Rewiring the World, from Edison to Google* (2008), *The Shallows: What the Internet Is Doing to Our Brains* (2010), *The Glass Cage: How Our Computers Are Changing Us* (2014) and *Utopia Is Creepy* (2016). Carr also has written for periodicals including the *Guardian*, the *New York Times*, the *Wall Street Journal*, and *Wired*, and he blogs at roughtype.com. This essay appeared originally as the cover article in the July/August 2008 issue of the *Atlantic*.

Dave (Keir Dullea) removes HAL's "brain" in *2001: A Space Odyssey.*

feel it most strongly when I'm reading. Immersing myself in a book or a lengthy article used to be easy. My mind would get caught up in the narrative or the turns of the argument, and I'd spend hours strolling through long stretches of prose. That's rarely the case anymore. Now my concentration often starts to drift after two or three pages. I get fidgety, lose the thread, begin looking for something else to do. I feel as if I'm always dragging my wayward brain back to the text. The deep reading that used to come naturally has become a struggle.

I think I know what's going on. For more than a decade now, I've been spending a lot of time online, searching and surfing and sometimes adding to the great databases of the Internet. The Web has been a godsend to me as a writer. Research that once required days in the stacks or periodical rooms of libraries can now be done in minutes. A few Google searches, some quick clicks on hyperlinks, and I've got the telltale fact or pithy quote I was after. Even when I'm not working, I'm as likely as not to be foraging in the Web's info-thickets reading and writing e-mails, scanning headlines and blog posts, watching videos and listening to podcasts, or just tripping from link to link to link. (Unlike footnotes, to which they're sometimes likened, hyperlinks don't merely point to related works; they propel you toward them.)

For me, as for others, the Net is becoming a universal medium, the conduit for most of the information that flows through my eyes and ears and into my mind. The advantages of having immediate access to such an incredibly rich store of information are many, and they've been widely described and duly applauded. "The perfect recall of silicon memory," *Wired*'s Clive Thompson has written, "can be an enormous boon to thinking." But that boon comes at a price. As the media theorist Marshall McLuhan pointed out in the 1960s, media are not just passive channels of information. They supply the stuff of thought, but they also shape the process of thought. And what the Net seems to be doing is chipping away my capacity for concentration and contemplation. My mind now expects to take in information the way the Net distributes it: in a swiftly moving stream of particles. Once I was a scuba diver in the sea of words. Now I zip along the surface like a guy on a Jet Ski.

I'm not the only one. When I mention my troubles with 5 reading to friends and acquaintances—literary types, most of them—many say they're having similar experiences. The more they use the Web, the more they have to fight to stay focused on long pieces of writing. Some of the bloggers I follow have also begun mentioning the phenomenon. Scott Karp, who writes a blog about online media, recently confessed that he has stopped reading books altogether. "I was a lit major in college, and used to be [a] voracious book reader," he wrote. "What happened?" He speculates on the answer: "What if I do all my reading on the web not so much because the way I read has changed, i.e. I'm just seeking convenience, but because the way I *think* has changed?"

Bruce Friedman, who blogs regularly about the use of computers in medicine, also has described how the Internet has altered his mental habits. "I now have almost totally lost the ability to read and absorb a longish article on the web or in print," he wrote earlier this year. A pathologist who has long been on the faculty of the University of Michigan Medical School, Friedman elaborated on his comment in a telephone conversation with me. His thinking, he said, has taken on a "staccato" quality, reflecting the way he quickly scans short passages of text from many sources online. "I can't read *War and Peace* anymore," he admitted. "I've lost the ability to do that. Even a blog post of more than three or four paragraphs is too much to absorb. I skim it."

Anecdotes alone don't prove much. And we still await the long-term neurological and psychological experiments that will provide a definitive picture of how Internet use affects cognition. But a recently published study of online research habits, conducted by scholars from University College London, suggests that we may well be in the midst of a sea change in the way we read and think. As part of the five-year research program, the scholars examined computer logs documenting the behavior of visitors to two popular research sites, one operated by the British Library and one by a U.K. educational consortium, that provide access to journal articles, e-books, and other sources of written information. They found that people using the sites exhibited "a form of skimming activity," hopping from one source to another and rarely returning to any source they'd already visited. They typically read no more than one or two pages of an article or book before they would "bounce" out to another site. Sometimes they'd save a long article, but there's no evidence that they ever went back and actually read it. The authors of the study report:

It is clear that users are not reading online in the traditional sense; indeed there are signs that new forms of "reading" are emerging as users "power browse" horizontally through titles, contents pages and abstracts going for quick wins. It almost seems that they go online to avoid reading in the traditional sense.

Thanks to the ubiquity of text on the Internet, not to mention the popularity of text-messaging on cell phones, we may well be reading more today than we did in the 1970s or 1980s, when television was our medium of choice. But it's a different kind of reading, and behind it lies a different kind of thinking— perhaps even a new sense of the self. "We are not only *what* we read," says Maryanne Wolf, a developmental psychologist at Tufts University and the author of *Proust and the Squid: The Story and Science of the Reading Brain.* "We are *how* we read." Wolf worries that the style of reading promoted by the Net, a style that puts "efficiency" and "immediacy" above all else, may be weakening our capacity for the kind of deep reading that emerged when an earlier technology, the printing press, made long and complex works of prose commonplace. When we read online, she says, we tend to become "mere decoders of information." Our ability to interpret text, to make the rich mental connections that form when we read deeply and without distraction, remains largely disengaged.

Reading, explains Wolf, is not an instinctive skill for human beings. It's not etched into our genes the way speech is. We have to teach our minds how to translate the symbolic characters we see into the language we understand. And the media or other technologies we use in learning and practicing the craft of reading play an important part in shaping the neural circuits inside our brains. Experiments demonstrate that readers of ideograms, such as the Chinese, develop a mental circuitry for reading that is very different from the circuitry found in those of us whose written language employs an alphabet. The variations extend across many regions of the brain, including those that govern such essential cognitive functions as memory and the interpretation of visual and auditory stimuli. We can expect as well that the circuits woven by our use of the Net will be different from those woven by our reading of books and other printed works.

Sometime in 1882, Friedrich Nietzsche bought a typewriter— 10 a Malling-Hansen Writing Ball, to be precise. His vision was failing, and keeping his eyes focused on a page had become exhausting and painful, often bringing on crushing headaches. He had been forced to curtail his writing, and he feared that he would soon have to give it up. The typewriter rescued him, at least for a time. Once he had mastered touch-typing, he was

Friedrich Nietzsche and his Malling-Hansen Writing Ball.

able to write with his eyes closed, using only the tips of his fingers. Words could once again flow from his mind to the page.

But the machine had a subtler effect on his work. One of Nietzsche's friends, a composer, noticed a change in the style of his writing. His already terse prose had become even tighter, more telegraphic. "Perhaps you will through this instrument even take to a new idiom," the friend wrote in a letter, noting that, in his own work, his "'thoughts' in music and language often depend on the quality of pen and paper."

"You are right," Nietzsche replied, "our writing equipment takes part in the forming of our thoughts." Under the sway of the machine, writes the German media scholar Friedrich A. Kittler, Nietzsche's prose "changed from arguments to aphorisms, from thoughts to puns, from rhetoric to telegram style."

The human brain is almost infinitely malleable. People used to think that our mental meshwork, the dense connections formed among the 100 billion or so neurons inside our skulls, was largely fixed by the time we reached adulthood. But brain researchers have discovered that that's not the case. James Olds, a professor of neuroscience who directs the Krasnow Institute for Advanced Study at George Mason University, says that even the adult mind "is very plastic." Nerve cells routinely break old connections and form new ones. "The brain," according to Olds, "has the ability to reprogram itself on the fly, altering the way it functions."

As we use what the sociologist Daniel Bell has called our "intellectual technologies"—the tools that extend our mental rather than our physical capacities—we inevitably begin to take on the qualities of those technologies. The mechanical clock, which came into common use in the 14th century, provides a compelling example. In *Technics and Civilization*, the historian and cultural critic Lewis Mumford described how the clock "disassociated time from human events and helped create the belief in an independent world of mathematically measurable sequences." The "abstract framework of divided time" became "the point of reference for both action and thought."

The clock's methodical ticking helped bring into being 15 the scientific mind and the scientific man. But it also took something away. As the late MIT computer scientist Joseph Weizenbaum observed in his 1976 book, *Computer Power and Human Reason: From Judgment to Calculation*, the conception of the world that emerged from the widespread use of timekeeping instruments "remains an impoverished version of the older one, for it rests on a rejection of those direct experiences that formed the basis for, and indeed constituted, the old reality." In deciding when to eat, to work, to sleep, to rise, we stopped listening to our senses and started obeying the clock.

The process of adapting to new intellectual technologies is reflected in the changing metaphors we use to explain ourselves to ourselves. When the mechanical clock arrived, people began thinking of their brains as operating "like clockwork." Today, in the age of software, we have come to think of them as operating "like computers." But the changes, neuroscience tells us, go much deeper than metaphor. Thanks to our brain's plasticity, the adaptation occurs also at a biological level.

The Internet promises to have particularly far-reaching effects on cognition. In a paper published in 1936, the British mathematician Alan Turing proved that a digital computer, which at the time existed only as a theoretical machine, could be programmed to perform the function of any other information-processing device. And that's what we're seeing today. The Internet, an immeasurably powerful computing system, is subsuming most of our other intellectual technologies. It's becoming our map and our clock, our printing press and our typewriter, our calculator and our tele-phone, and our radio and TV.

When the Net absorbs a medium, that medium is re-created in the Net's image. It injects the medium's content with hyper-links, blinking ads, and other digital gewgaws, and it surrounds the content with the content of all the other media it has absorbed. A new e-mail message, for instance, may announce its arrival as we're glancing over the latest headlines at a news-paper's site. The result is to scatter our attention and diffuse our concentration.

The Net's influence doesn't end at the edges of a computer screen, either. As people's minds become attuned to the crazy quilt of Internet media, traditional media have to adapt to the audience's new expectations. Television programs add text crawls and pop-up ads, and magazines and newspapers shorten their articles, introduce capsule summaries, and crowd their pages with easy-to-browse info-snippets. When, in March of this year, the *New York Times* decided to devote the second and third pages of every edition to article abstracts, its design director, Tom Bodkin, explained that the "shortcuts" would give harried readers a quick "taste" of the day's news, sparing them the "less efficient" method of actually turning the pages and reading the articles. Old media have little choice but to play by the new-media rules.

Never has a communications system played so many roles in 20 our lives—or exerted such broad influence over our thoughts—as the Internet does today. Yet, for all that's been written about the Net, there's been little consideration of how, exactly, it's reprogramming us. The Net's intellectual ethic remains obscure.

About the same time that Nietzsche started using his type-writer, an earnest young man named Frederick Winslow Taylor carried a stopwatch into the Midvale Steel plant in Philadelphia and began a historic series of experiments aimed at improving the efficiency of the plant's machinists. With the approval of Midvale's owners, he recruited a group of factory hands, set them to work on various metalworking machines, and recorded and timed their every movement as well as the operations of the machines. By breaking down every job into a sequence of small, discrete steps and then testing different ways of performing each one, Taylor created a set of precise instructions—an "algorithm," we might say today—for how each worker should work. Midvale's employees grumbled about the strict new regime, claiming that it turned them into little more than automatons, but the factory's productivity soared.

More than a hundred years after the invention of the steam engine, the Industrial Revolution had at last found its philosophy

A testing engineer (possibly Taylor) observes a Midvale Steel worker c. 1885.

and its philosopher. Taylor's tight industrial choreography—his "system," as he liked to call it—was embraced by manufacturers throughout the country and, in time, around the world. Seeking maximum speed, maximum efficiency, and maximum output, factory owners used time-and-motion studies to organize their work and configure the jobs of their workers. The goal, as Taylor defined it in his celebrated 1911 treatise, *The Principles of Scientific Management*, was to identify and adopt, for every job, the "one best method" of work and thereby to effect "the gradual substitution of science for rule of thumb throughout the mechanic arts." Once his system was applied to all acts of manual labor, Taylor assured his followers, it would bring about a restructuring not only of industry but of society, creating a utopia of perfect efficiency. "In the past the man has been first," he declared; "in the future the system must be first."

Taylor's system is still very much with us; it remains the ethic of industrial manufacturing. And now, thanks to the growing power that computer engineers and software coders wield over our intellectual lives, Taylor's ethic is beginning to govern the realm of the mind as well. The Internet is a machine designed for the efficient and automated collection, transmission, and manipulation of information, and its legions of programmers are intent on finding the "one best method"— the perfect algorithm—to carry out every mental movement of what we've come to describe as "knowledge work."

Google's headquarters, in Mountain View, California—the Googleplex—is the Internet's high church, and the religion practiced inside its walls is Taylorism. Google, says its chief executive, Eric Schmidt, is "a company that's founded around the science of measurement," and it is striving to "systematize everything" it does. Drawing on the terabytes of behavioral data

The Googleplex.

it collects through its search engine and other sites, it carries out thousands of experiments a day, according to the *Harvard Business Review*, and it uses the results to refine the algorithms that increasingly control how people find information and extract meaning from it. What Taylor did for the work of the hand, Google is doing for the work of the mind.

The company has declared that its mission is "to organize 25 the world's information and make it universally accessible and useful." It seeks to develop "the perfect search engine," which it defines as something that "understands exactly what you mean and gives you back exactly what you want." In Google's view, information is a kind of commodity, a utilitarian resource that can be mined and processed with industrial efficiency. The more pieces of information we can "access" and the faster we can extract their gist, the more productive we become as thinkers.

Where does it end? Sergey Brin and Larry Page, the gifted young men who founded Google while pursuing doctoral degrees in computer science at Stanford, speak frequently of their desire to turn their search engine into an artificial intelligence, a HAL-like machine that might be connected directly to our brains. "The ultimate search engine is something as smart as people—or smarter," Page said in a speech a few years back. "For us, working on search is a way to work on artificial intelligence." In a 2004 interview with *Newsweek*, Brin said, "Certainly if you had all the world's information directly attached to your brain, or an artificial brain that was smarter than your brain, you'd be better off." Last year, Page told a convention of scientists that Google is "really trying to build artificial intelligence and to do it on a large scale."

Such an ambition is a natural one, even an admirable one, for a pair of math whizzes with vast quantities of cash at their disposal and a small army of computer scientists in their employ. A fundamentally scientific enterprise, Google is motivated by a desire to use technology, in Eric Schmidt's words, "to solve problems that have never been solved before," and artificial intelligence is the hardest problem out there. Why wouldn't Brin and Page want to be the ones to crack it?

Still, their easy assumption that we'd all "be better off" if our brains were supplemented, or even replaced, by an artificial intelligence is unsettling. It suggests a belief that intelligence is the output of a mechanical process, a series of discrete steps that can be isolated, measured, and optimized. In Google's world, the world we enter when we go online, there's little place for the fuzziness of contemplation. Ambiguity is not an opening for insight but a bug to be fixed. The human brain is just an outdated computer that needs a faster processor and a bigger hard drive.

The idea that our minds should operate as high-speed data-processing machines is not only built into the workings of the Internet, it is the network's reigning business model as well. The faster we surf across the Web—the more links we click and pages we view—the more opportunities Google and other companies gain to collect information about us and to feed us advertisements. Most of the proprietors of the commercial Internet have a financial stake in collecting the crumbs of data we leave behind as we flit from link to link—the more crumbs, the better. The last thing these companies want is to encourage leisurely reading or slow, concentrated thought. It's in their economic interest to drive us to distraction.

Maybe I'm just a worrywart. Just as there's a tendency to glo- 30 rify technological progress, there's a countertendency to expect the worst of every new tool or machine. In Plato's *Phaedrus*, Socrates bemoaned the development of writing. He feared that, as people came to rely on the written word as a substitute for the knowledge they used to carry inside their heads, they would, in the words of one of the dialogue's characters, "cease to exercise their memory and become forgetful." And because they would be able to "receive a quantity of information without proper instruction," they would "be thought very knowledgeable when they are for the most part quite ignorant." They would be "filled with the conceit of wisdom instead of real wisdom." Socrates wasn't wrong—the new technology did often have the effects he feared—but he was shortsighted. He couldn't foresee the many ways that writing and reading would serve to spread information, spur fresh ideas, and expand human knowledge (if not wisdom).

The arrival of Gutenberg's printing press, in the 15th century, set off another round of teeth gnashing. The Italian humanist Hieronimo Squarciafico worried that the easy availability of books would lead to intellectual laziness, making men "less studious" and weakening their minds. Others argued that cheaply printed books and broadsheets would undermine religious authority, demean the work of scholars and scribes, and spread sedition and debauchery. As New York University professor Clay Shirky

See pp. 31–33 for tips on putting yourself in their shoes.

notes, "Most of the arguments made against the printing press were correct, even prescient." But, again, the doomsayers were unable to imagine the myriad blessings that the printed word would deliver.

So, yes, you should be skeptical of my skepticism. Perhaps those who dismiss critics of the Internet as Luddites or nostalgists will be proved correct, and from our hyperactive, data-stoked minds will spring a golden age of intellectual discovery and universal wisdom. Then again, the Net isn't the alphabet, and although it may replace the printing press, it produces something altogether different. The kind of deep reading that a sequence of printed pages promotes is valuable not just for the knowledge we acquire from the author's words but for the intellectual vibrations those words set off within our own minds. In the quiet spaces opened up by the sustained, undistracted reading of a book, or by any other act of contemplation, for that matter, we make our own associations, draw our own inferences and analogies, foster our own ideas. Deep reading, as Maryanne Wolf argues, is indistinguishable from deep thinking.

If we lose those quiet spaces, or fill them up with "content," we will sacrifice something important not only in our selves but in our culture. In a recent essay, the playwright Richard Foreman eloquently described what's at stake:

> I come from a tradition of Western culture, in which the ideal (my ideal) was the complex, dense and "cathedral-like" structure of the highly educated and articulate personality—a man or woman who carried inside themselves a personally constructed and unique version of the entire heritage of the West. [But now] I see within us all (myself included) the replacement of complex inner density with a new kind of self—evolving under the pressure of information overload and the technology of the "instantly available."

As we are drained of our "inner repertory of dense cultural inheritance," Foreman concluded, we risk turning into "'pancake people'—spread wide and thin as we connect with that vast network of information accessed by the mere touch of a button."

I'm haunted by that scene in *2001*. What makes it so poi- 35 gnant, and so weird, is the computer's emotional response to the disassembly of its mind: its despair as one circuit after another goes dark, its childlike pleading with the astronaut—"I can feel it. I can feel it. I'm afraid"—and its final reversion to what can only be called a state of innocence. HAL's outpouring of feeling contrasts with the emotionlessness that characterizes the human figures in the film, who go about their business with an almost robotic efficiency. Their thoughts and actions feel scripted, as if they're following the steps of an algorithm. In the world of *2001*, people have become so machinelike that the most human character turns out to be a machine. That's the essence of Kubrick's dark prophecy: as we come to rely on computers to mediate our understanding of the world, it is our own intelligence that flattens into artificial intelligence.

Joining the Conversation

1. "Is Google making us stupid?" How does Nicholas Carr answer this question, and what evidence does he provide to support his answer?

2. What possible objections to his own position does Carr introduce—and why do you think he does so? How effectively does he counter these objections?

3. Carr begins this essay by quoting an exchange between HAL and Dave, a supercomputer and an astronaut in the film *2001: A Space Odyssey*—and he concludes by reflecting on

that scene. What happens to HAL and Dave, and how does this outcome support his argument?

4. How does Carr use transitions to connect the parts of his text and to help readers follow his train of thought? (See Chapter 8 to help you think about how transitions help develop an argument.)

5. In his essay on pages 497–517, Clive Thompson reaches a different conclusion than Carr does, saying that "At their best, today's digital tools help us see more, retain more, communicate more. At their worst, they leave us prey to the manipulation of the toolmakers. But on balance . . . what is happening is deeply positive." Write a paragraph or two discussing how Carr might respond. What would he agree with, and what would he disagree with?

6. This article sparked widespread debate and conversation when it first appeared in 2008, and the discussion continues today. Go to **theysayiblog.com** and click on "Are We in a Race against the Machine?" to read some of what's been written on the topic recently.

Smarter Than You Think: How Technology Is Changing Our Minds for the Better

CLIVE THOMPSON

———

WHO'S BETTER AT CHESS—computers or humans?

The question has long fascinated observers, perhaps because chess seems like the ultimate display of human thought: the players sit like Rodin's *Thinker*, silent, brows furrowed, making lightning-fast calculations. It's the quintessential cognitive activity, logic as an extreme sport.

So the idea of a machine outplaying a human has always provoked both excitement and dread. In the eighteenth century, Wolfgang von Kempelen caused a stir with his clockwork Mechanical Turk—an automaton that played an eerily good game of chess, even beating Napoleon Bonaparte. The spectacle was so unsettling that onlookers cried out in astonishment

———

CLIVE THOMPSON is a journalist and blogger who writes for the *New York Times Magazine* and *Wired*. He was awarded a 2002 Knight Science Journalism Fellowship at MIT. He blogs at clivethompson.net. This essay is adapted from his book, *Smarter Than You Think: How Technology Is Changing Our Minds for the Better* (2013).

The Thinker, by French sculptor Auguste Rodin (1840–1917).

when the Turk's gears first clicked into motion. But the gears, and the machine, were fake; in reality, the automaton was controlled by a chess savant cunningly tucked inside the wooden cabinet. In 1915, a Spanish inventor unveiled a genuine, honest-to-goodness robot that could actually play chess—a simple endgame involving only three pieces, anyway. A writer for *Scientific American* fretted that the inventor "Would Substitute Machinery for the Human Mind."

Eighty years later, in 1997, this intellectual standoff clanked to a dismal conclusion when world champion Garry Kasparov was defeated by IBM's Deep Blue supercomputer in a tournament of six games. Faced with a machine that could calculate two hundred million positions a second, even Kasparov's notoriously aggressive and nimble style broke down. In its final game, Deep Blue used such a clever ploy—tricking Kasparov into letting the computer sacrifice a knight—that it trounced him in nineteen moves. "I lost my fighting spirit," Kasparov said afterward, pronouncing himself "emptied completely." Riveted, the journalists announced a winner. The cover of *Newsweek* proclaimed the event "The Brain's Last Stand." Doom-sayers predicted that chess itself was over. If machines could out-think even Kasparov, why would the game remain interesting? Why would anyone bother playing? What's the challenge?

Then Kasparov did something unexpected. 5

The truth is, Kasparov wasn't completely surprised by Deep Blue's victory. Chess grand masters had predicted for years that computers would eventually beat humans, because they understood the different ways humans and computers play. Human chess players learn by spending years studying the world's best opening moves and endgames; they play thousands of games, slowly amassing a capacious, in-brain library of which strategies triumphed and which flopped. They analyze their opponents' strengths and weaknesses, as well as their moods. When they look at the board, that knowledge manifests as intuition—a eureka moment when they suddenly spy the best possible move.

In contrast, a chess-playing computer has no intuition at all. It analyzes the game using brute force; it inspects the pieces currently on the board, then calculates all options. It prunes away moves that lead to losing positions, then takes the promising ones and runs the calculations again. After doing this a few times—and looking five or seven moves out—it arrives at a few powerful plays. The machine's way of "thinking" is fundamentally unhuman. Humans don't sit around crunching every possible move, because our brains can't hold that much information at once. If you go eight moves out in a game of chess, there are more possible games than there are stars in our galaxy. If you total up every game possible? It outnumbers the atoms in the known universe. Ask chess grand masters, "How many moves can you see out?" and they'll likely deliver the answer attributed to the Cuban grand master José Raúl Capablanca: "One, the best one."

The fight between computers and humans in chess was, as Kasparov knew, ultimately about speed. Once computers could see all games roughly seven moves out, they would wear humans down. A person might make a mistake; the computer wouldn't. Brute force wins. As he pondered Deep Blue, Kasparov mused on these different cognitive approaches.

It gave him an audacious idea. What would happen if, instead of competing against one another, humans and computers *collaborated*? What if they played on teams together— one computer and a human facing off against another human and a computer? That way, he theorized, each might benefit from the other's peculiar powers. The computer would bring the lightning-fast—if uncreative—ability to analyze zillions of moves, while the human would bring intuition and insight, the ability to read opponents and psych them out. Together, they would form what chess players later called a centaur: a hybrid beast endowed with the strengths of each.

In June 1998, Kasparov played the first public game of human-computer collaborative chess, which he dubbed "advanced chess," against Veselin Topalov, a top-rated grand master. Each used a regular computer with off-the-shelf chess software and databases of hundreds of thousands of chess games, including some of the best ever played. They considered what moves the computer recommended, they examined historical databases to see if anyone had ever been in a situation like theirs before. Then they used that information to help plan. Each game was limited to sixty minutes, so they didn't have infinite time to consult the machines; they had to work swiftly.

Kasparov found the experience "as disturbing as it was exciting." Freed from the need to rely exclusively on his memory, he was able to focus more on the creative texture of his play. It was, he realized, like learning to be a race-car driver: He had to learn how to *drive* the computer, as it were—developing a split-second sense of which strategy to enter into the computer for assessment, when to stop an unpromising line of inquiry, and when to accept or ignore the computer's advice. "Just as a good Formula One driver really knows his own car, so did we have to learn the way the computer program worked," he later wrote. Topalov, as it turns out, appeared to be an even better Formula One "thinker" than Kasparov. On purely human terms, Kasparov was a stronger player; a month before, he'd trounced Topalov 4–0. But the centaur play evened the odds. This time, Topalov fought Kasparov to a 3–3 draw.

Garry Kasparov (right) plays Veselin Topalov (left) in Sofia, Bulgaria, on May 3, 1998.

In 2005, there was a "freestyle" chess tournament in which a team could consist of any number of humans or computers, in any combination. Many teams consisted of chess grand masters who'd won plenty of regular, human-only tournaments, achieving chess scores of 2,500 (out of 3,000). But the winning team didn't include any grand masters at all. It consisted of two young New England men, Steven Cramton and Zackary Stephen (who were comparative amateurs, with chess rankings down around 1,400 to 1,700), and their computers.

Why could these relative amateurs beat chess players with far more experience and raw talent? Because Cramton and Stephen were expert at collaborating with computers. They knew when to rely on human smarts and when to rely on the machine's advice. Working at rapid speed—these games, too, were limited to sixty minutes—they would brainstorm moves, then check to see what the computer thought, while also scouring databases to see if the strategy had occurred in previous games. They used three different computers simultaneously, running five different pieces of software; that way they could cross-check whether different programs agreed on the same move. But they wouldn't simply accept what the machine accepted, nor would they merely mimic old games. They selected moves that were low-rated by the computer if they thought they would rattle their opponents psychologically.

In essence, a new form of chess intelligence was emerging. You could rank the teams like this: (1) a chess grand master was good; (2) a chess grand master playing with a laptop was better. But even that laptop-equipped grand master could be beaten by (3) relative newbies, if the amateurs were extremely skilled at integrating machine assistance. "Human strategic guidance combined with the tactical acuity of a computer," Kasparov concluded, "was overwhelming."

Better yet, it turned out these smart amateurs could even 15 outplay a supercomputer on the level of Deep Blue. One of the entrants that Cramton and Stephen trounced in the freestyle chess tournament was a version of Hydra, the most powerful chess computer in existence at the time; indeed, it was probably faster and stronger than Deep Blue itself. Hydra's owners let it play entirely by itself, using raw logic and speed to fight its opponents. A few days after the advanced chess event, Hydra destroyed the world's seventh-ranked grand master in a man-versus-machine chess tournament.

But Cramton and Stephen beat Hydra. They did it using their own talents and regular Dell and Hewlett-Packard computers, of the type you probably had sitting on your desk in 2005, with software you could buy for sixty dollars. All of which brings us back to our original question here: Which is smarter at chess—humans or computers?

Neither.

It's the two together, working side by side.

We're all playing advanced chess these days. We just haven't learned to appreciate it.

Our tools are everywhere, linked with our minds, working 20 in tandem. Search engines answer our most obscure questions; status updates give us an ESP-like awareness of those around us; online collaborations let far-flung collaborators tackle problems too tangled for any individual. We're becoming less like Rodin's *Thinker* and more like Kasparov's centaurs. This transformation is rippling through every part of our cognition— how we learn, how we remember, and how we act upon that knowledge emotionally, intellectually, and politically. As with Cramton and Stephen, these tools can make even the amateurs among us radically smarter than we'd be on our own, assuming (and this is a big assumption) we understand how they work. At their best, today's digital tools help us see more, retain more, communicate more. At their worst, they leave us prey to the manipulation of the toolmakers. But on balance, I'd argue, what is happening is deeply positive. . . .

In a sense, this is an ancient story. The "extended mind" theory of cognition argues that the reason humans are so intellectually dominant is that we've always outsourced bits of cognition, using tools to scaffold our thinking into ever-more-rarefied realms. Printed books amplified our memory. Inexpensive paper and reliable pens made it possible to externalize our thoughts quickly. Studies show that our eyes zip around the page while performing long division on paper, using the handwritten digits as a form of prosthetic short-term memory. "These resources enable us to pursue manipulations and juxtapositions of ideas and data that would quickly baffle the unaugmented brain," as Andy Clark, a philosopher of the extended mind, writes.

Granted, it can be unsettling to realize how much thinking already happens outside our skulls. Culturally, we revere the Rodin ideal—the belief that genius breakthroughs come from our gray matter alone. The physicist Richard Feynman once got into an argument about this with the historian Charles Weiner. Feynman understood the extended mind; he knew that writing his equations and ideas on paper was crucial to his thought. But when Weiner looked over a pile of Feynman's notebooks, he called them a wonderful "record of his day-to-day work." No, no, Feynman replied testily. They weren't a record of his thinking process. They *were* his thinking process:

"I actually did the work on the paper," he said.
"Well," Weiner said, "the work was done in your head, but the record of it is still here."
"No, it's not a *record*, not really. It's *working*. You have to work on paper and this is the paper. Okay?"

Every new tool shapes the way we think, as well as what we think about. The printed word helped make our cognition linear and abstract, along with vastly enlarging our stores of knowledge. Newspapers shrank the world; then the telegraph shrank it even more dramatically. With every innovation, cultural prophets bickered over whether we were facing a technological apocalypse or a utopia. Depending on which Victorian-age pundit you asked, the telegraph was either going to usher in an era of world peace ("It is impossible that old prejudices and hostilities should longer exist," as Charles F. Briggs and Augustus Maverick intoned) or drown us in a Sargasso of idiotic trivia ("We are eager to tunnel under the Atlantic . . . but perchance the first news that will leak through into the broad, flapping American ear will be that the Princess Adelaide has the whooping cough," as Thoreau opined). Neither prediction was quite right, of course, yet neither was quite wrong. The one thing that both apocalyptics and utopians understand and agree upon is that every new technology pushes us toward new forms of behavior while nudging us away from older, familiar ones. Harold Innis—the lesser-known but arguably more interesting intellectual midwife of Marshall McLuhan—called this the bias of a new tool. Living with new technologies means understanding how they bias everyday life.

What are the central biases of today's digital tools? There are many, but I see three big ones that have a huge impact on our cognition. First, they allow for prodigious external memory: smartphones, hard drives, cameras, and sensors routinely record more information than any tool before them. We're shifting from a stance of rarely recording our ideas and the events of our lives to doing it habitually. Second, today's tools make it easier for us to find connections—between ideas, pictures, people, bits of news—that were previously invisible. Third, they encourage a superfluity of communication and publishing. This last feature has many surprising effects that are often ill understood. Any economist can tell you that when you suddenly increase the availability of a resource, people do more things with it, which also means they do increasingly unpredictable things. As electricity became cheap and ubiquitous in the West, its role expanded from things you'd expect—like night-time lighting—to the unexpected and seemingly trivial: battery-driven toy trains, electric blenders, vibrators. The superfluity of communication today has produced everything from a rise in crowd-organized projects like Wikipedia to curious new forms of expression: television-show recaps, map-based storytelling, discussion threads that spin out of a photo posted to a smartphone app, Amazon product-review threads wittily hijacked for political satire. Now, none of these three digital biases is immutable, because they're the product of software and hardware, and can easily be altered or ended if the architects of today's tools (often corporate and governmental) decide to regulate the tools or find they're not profitable enough. But right now, these big effects dominate our current and near-term landscape.

In one sense, these three shifts—infinite memory, dot 25 connecting, explosive publishing—are screamingly obvious to anyone who's ever used a computer. Yet they also somehow constantly surprise us by producing ever-new "tools for thought" (to use the writer Howard Rheingold's lovely phrase) that upend our mental habits in ways we never expected and often don't apprehend even as they take hold. Indeed, these phenomena have already woven themselves so deeply into the lives of people around the globe that it's difficult to stand back and take account of how much things have changed and why. While [here I map] out what I call the future of thought, it's also frankly rooted in the *present*, because many parts of our future have already arrived, even if they are only dimly understood. As the sci-fi author William Gibson famously quipped: "The future is already here—it's just not very evenly distributed." This is an attempt to understand what's happening to us right now, the better to see where our augmented thought is headed. Rather than dwell in abstractions, like so many marketers and pundits—not to mention the creators of technology, who are often remarkably poor at predicting how people will use their tools—I focus more on the actual experiences of real people.

To provide a concrete example of what I'm talking about, let's take a look at something simple and immediate: my activities while writing the pages you've just read.

As I was working, I often realized I couldn't quite remember a detail and discovered that my notes were incomplete. So I'd zip over to a search engine. (*Which chess piece did Deep Blue sacrifice when it beat Kasparov? The knight!*) I also pushed some of my thinking out into the open: I blogged admiringly about the Spanish chess-playing robot from 1915, and within minutes commenters offered smart critiques. (One pointed out that the chess robot wasn't *that* impressive because it was playing an endgame that was almost impossible to lose: the robot started with a rook and a king, while the human opponent had only a mere king.) While reading Kasparov's book *How Life Imitates Chess* on my Kindle, I idly clicked on "popular highlights" to see what passages other readers had found interesting—and wound up becoming fascinated by a section on chess strategy I'd only lightly skimmed myself. To understand centaur play better, I read long, nuanced threads on chess-player discussion groups, effectively eavesdropping on conversations of people who know chess far better than I ever will. (Chess players who follow the new form of play seem divided—some think advanced chess is a grim sign of machines' taking over the game, and others think it shows that the human mind is much more valuable than computer software.) I got into a long instant-messaging session with my wife, during which I realized that I'd explained the gist of advanced chess better than I had in my original draft, so I cut and pasted that explanation into my notes. As for the act of writing itself? Like most writers, I constantly have to fight the procrastinator's urge to meander online, idly checking Twitter links and Wikipedia entries in a dreamy but pointless haze—until I look up in horror and realize I've lost two hours of work, a missing-time experience redolent of a UFO abduction. So I'd switch my word processor into full-screen mode, fading my computer desktop to black so

I could see nothing but the page, giving me temporary mental peace.

[Let's] explore each of these trends. First off, there's the emergence of omnipresent computer storage, which is upending the way we remember, both as individuals and as a culture. Then there's the advent of "public thinking": the ability to broadcast our ideas and the catalytic effect that has both inside and outside our minds. We're becoming more conversational thinkers—a shift that has been rocky, not least because everyday public thought uncorks the incivility and prejudices that are commonly repressed in face-to-face life. But at its best (which, I'd argue, is surprisingly often), it's a thrilling development, reigniting ancient traditions of dialogue and debate. At the same time, there's been an explosion of new forms of expression that were previously too expensive for everyday thought— like video, mapping, or data crunching. Our social awareness is shifting, too, as we develop ESP-like "ambient awareness," a persistent sense of what others are doing and thinking. On a social level, this expands our ability to understand the people we care about. On a civic level, it helps dispel traditional political problems like "pluralistic ignorance," catalyzing political action, as in the Arab Spring.

Are these changes good or bad for us? If you asked me twenty years ago, when I first started writing about technology, I'd have said "bad." In the early 1990s, I believed that as people migrated online, society's worst urges might be uncorked: pseudonymity would poison online conversation, gossip and trivia would dominate, and cultural standards would collapse. Certainly some of those predictions have come true, as anyone who's wandered into an angry political forum knows. See p. 65 for ways to make the "I'm of two minds" move. But the truth is, while I predicted the bad stuff, I didn't foresee the good stuff. And what a torrent we have: Wikipedia, a global forest of eloquent bloggers, citizen journalism, political fact-checking—or even the way status-update tools like Twitter have produced a renaissance in witty, aphoristic, haikuesque expression. If [I accentuate] the positive, that's in part because we've been so flooded with apocalyptic warnings of late. We need a new way to talk clearly about the rewards and pleasures of our digital experiences—one that's rooted in our lived experience and also detangled from the hype of Silicon Valley.

The other thing that makes me optimistic about our cog- 30 nitive future is how much it resembles our cognitive past. In the sixteenth century, humanity faced a printed-paper wave of information overload—with the explosion of books that began with the codex and went into overdrive with Gutenberg's movable type. As the historian Ann Blair notes, scholars were alarmed: How would they be able to keep on top of the flood of human expression? Who would separate the junk from what was worth keeping? The mathematician Gottfried Wilhelm Leibniz bemoaned "that horrible mass of books which keeps on growing," which would doom the quality writers to "the danger of general oblivion" and produce "a return to barbarism." Thankfully, he was wrong. Scholars quickly set about organizing the new mental environment by clipping their favorite passages from books and assembling them into huge tomes—*florilegia*, bouquets of text—so that readers could sample the best parts. They were basically blogging, going through some of the same arguments modern bloggers go through. (Is it enough to clip a passage, or do you also have to verify that what the author wrote was true? It was debated back then, as it is today.) The past turns out to be oddly reassuring, because a pattern emerges. Each time we're faced with bewildering new thinking tools, we panic—then quickly set about deducing how they can be used to help us work, meditate, and create.

History also shows that we generally improve and refine our tools to make them better. Books, for example, weren't always as well designed as they are now. In fact, the earliest ones were, by modern standards, practically unusable—often devoid of the navigational aids we now take for granted, such as indexes, paragraph breaks, or page numbers. It took decades—centuries, even—for the book to be redesigned into a more flexible cognitive tool, as suitable for quick reference as it is for deep reading. This is the same path we'll need to tread with our digital tools. It's why we need to understand not just the new abilities our tools give us today, but where they're still deficient and how they ought to improve.

I have one caveat to offer. If you were hoping to read about the neuroscience of our brains and how technology is "rewiring" them, [I] will disappoint you.

This goes against the grain of modern discourse, I realize. In recent years, people interested in how we think have become obsessed with our brain chemistry. We've marveled at the ability of brain scanning—picturing our brain's electrical activity or blood flow—to provide new clues as to what parts of the brain are linked to our behaviors. Some people panic that our brains are being deformed on a physiological level by today's technology: spend too much time flipping between windows and skimming text instead of reading a book, or interrupting your conversations to read text messages, and pretty soon you won't be able to concentrate on anything—and if you can't concentrate on it, you can't understand it either. In his book *The Shallows*, Nicholas Carr eloquently raised this alarm, arguing that the quality of our thought, as a species, rose in tandem with the ascendance of slow-moving, linear print and began declining with the arrival of the zingy, flighty Internet. "I'm not thinking the way I used to think," he worried.

I'm certain that many of these fears are warranted. It has always been difficult for us to maintain mental habits of concentration and deep thought; that's precisely why societies have engineered massive social institutions (everything from universities to book clubs and temples of worship) to encourage us to keep it up. It's part of why only a relatively small subset of people become regular, immersive readers, and part of why an even smaller subset go on to higher education. Today's multitasking tools really do make it harder than before to stay focused during long acts of reading and contemplation. They require a high level of "mindfulness"—paying attention to your own attention. While I don't dwell on the perils of distraction [here], the importance of being mindful resonates throughout these pages. One of the great challenges of today's digital thinking tools is knowing when *not* to use them, when to rely on the powers of older and slower technologies, like paper and books.

That said, today's confident talk by pundits and journalists 35 about our "rewired" brains has one big problem: it is very premature. Serious neuroscientists agree that we don't really know how our brains are wired to begin with. Brain chemistry is particularly mysterious when it comes to complex thought, like memory, creativity, and insight. "There will eventually be neuroscientific explanations for much of what we do; but those explanations will turn out to be incredibly complicated," as the neuroscientist Gary Marcus pointed out when critiquing the popular fascination with brain scanning. "For now, our ability to understand how all those parts relate is quite limited, sort of like trying to understand the political dynamics of Ohio from an airplane window above Cleveland." I'm not dismissing brain scanning; indeed, I'm confident it'll be crucial in unlocking these mysteries in the decades to come. But right now the field is so new that it is rash to draw conclusions, either apocalyptic or utopian, about how the Internet is changing our brains. Even Carr, the most diligent explorer in this area, cited only a single brain-scanning study that specifically probed how people's brains respond to using the Web, and those results were ambiguous.

The truth is that many healthy daily activities, if you scanned the brains of people participating in them, might appear outright dangerous to cognition. Over recent years, professor of psychiatry James Swain and teams of Yale and University of Michigan scientists scanned the brains of new mothers and fathers as they listened to recordings of their babies' cries. They found brain circuit activity similar to that in people suffering from obsessive-compulsive disorder. Now, these parents did not actually have OCD. They were just being temporarily vigilant about their newborns. But since the experiments appeared to show the brains of new parents being altered at a neural level, you could write a pretty scary headline if you wanted: BECOMING A PARENT ERODES YOUR BRAIN FUNCTION! In reality, as Swain tells me, it's much more benign. Being extra fretful and cautious around a newborn is a good thing for most parents: Babies are fragile. It's worth the trade-off. Similarly, living in cities—with their cramped dwellings and pounding noise—stresses us out on a straightforwardly physiological level and floods our system with cortisol, as I discovered while researching stress in New York City several years ago. But the very urban density that frazzles us mentally also makes us 50 percent more productive, and more creative, too, as Edward Glaeser argues in *Triumph of the City*, because of all those connections between people. This is "the city's edge in producing ideas." The upside of creativity is tied to the downside of living in a sardine tin, or, as Glaeser puts it, "Density has costs as well as benefits." Our digital environments likely offer a similar push and pull. We tolerate their cognitive hassles and distractions for the enormous upside of being connected, in new ways, to other people.

I want to examine how technology changes our mental habits, but for now, we'll be on firmer ground if we stick to what's observably happening in the world around us: our cognitive behavior, the quality of our cultural production, and the social science that tries to measure what we do in everyday life. In any case, I won't be talking about how your brain is being "rewired." Almost everything rewires it. . . .

The brain you had before you read this paragraph? You don't get that brain back. I'm hoping the trade-off is worth it.

The rise of advanced chess didn't end the debate about man versus machine, of course. In fact, the centaur phenomenon only complicated things further for the chess world—raising questions about how reliant players were on computers and how their presence affected the game itself. Some worried that if humans got too used to consulting machines, they wouldn't be able to play without them. Indeed, in June 2011, chess master Christoph Natsidis was caught illicitly using a mobile phone during a regular human-to-human match. During tense moments, he kept vanishing for long bathroom visits; the referee, suspicious, discovered Natsidis entering moves into a piece of chess software on his smartphone. Chess had entered a phase similar to the doping scandals that have plagued baseball and cycling, except in this case the drug was software and its effect cognitive.

This is a nice metaphor for a fear that can nag at us in our 40 everyday lives, too, as we use machines for thinking more and more. Are we losing some of our humanity? What happens if the Internet goes down: Do our brains collapse, too? Or is the question naive and irrelevant—as quaint as worrying about whether we're "dumb" because we can't compute long division without a piece of paper and a pencil?

Certainly, if we're intellectually lazy or prone to cheating and shortcuts, or if we simply don't pay much attention to how our tools affect the way we work, then yes—we can become, like Natsidis, overreliant. But the story of computers and chess offers a much more optimistic ending, too. Because it turns out that when chess players were genuinely passionate about learning and being creative in their game, computers didn't degrade their own human abilities. Quite the opposite: it helped them internalize the game much more profoundly and advance to new levels of *human* excellence.

Before computers came along, back when Kasparov was a young boy in the 1970s in the Soviet Union, learning grand-master-level chess was a slow, arduous affair. If you showed promise and you were very lucky, you could find a local grand master to teach you. If you were one of the tiny handful who showed world-class promise, Soviet leaders would fly you to Moscow and give you access to their elite chess library, which contained laboriously transcribed paper records of the world's top games. Retrieving records was a painstaking affair; you'd contemplate a possible opening, use the catalog to locate games that began with that move, and then the librarians would retrieve records from thin files, pulling them out using long sticks resembling knitting needles. Books of chess games were rare and incomplete. By gaining access to the Soviet elite library, Kasparov and his peers developed an enormous advantage over their global rivals. That library was their cognitive augmentation.

But beginning in the 1980s, computers took over the library's role and bested it. Young chess enthusiasts could buy CD-ROMs filled with hundreds of thousands of chess games.

Chess-playing software could show you how an artificial opponent would respond to any move. This dramatically increased the pace at which young chess players built up intuition. If you were sitting at lunch and had an idea for a bold new opening move, you could instantly find out which historic players had tried it, then war-game it yourself by playing against software. The iterative process of thought experiments—"If I did *this*, then what would happen?"—sped up exponentially.

Chess itself began to evolve. "Players became more creative and daring," as Frederic Friedel, the publisher of the first popular chess databases and software, tells me. Before computers, grand masters would stick to lines of attack they'd long studied and honed. Since it took weeks or months for them to research and mentally explore the ramifications of a new move, they stuck with what they knew. But as the next generation of players emerged, Friedel was astonished by their unusual gambits, particularly in their opening moves. Chess players today, Kasparov has written, "are almost as free of dogma as the machines with which they train. Increasingly, a move isn't good or bad because it looks that way or because it hasn't been done that way before. It's simply good if it works and bad if it doesn't."

Most remarkably, it is producing players who reach grand 45 master status younger. Before computers, it was extremely rare for teenagers to become grand masters. In 1958, Bobby Fischer stunned the world by achieving that status at fifteen. The feat was so unusual it was over three decades before the record was broken, in 1991. But by then computers had emerged, and in the years since, the record has been broken twenty times, as more and more young players became grand masters. In 2002, the Ukrainian Sergey Karjakin became one at the tender age of twelve.

So yes, when we're augmenting ourselves, we can be smarter. We're becoming centaurs. But our digital tools can also leave us smarter even when we're not actively using them.

Joining the Conversation

1. Clive Thompson lists three shifts—infinite memory, dot connecting, and explosive publishing—that he believes have strongly affected our cognition. What exactly does he mean by these three shifts, and in what ways does he think they have changed our thinking?

2. Thompson starts paragraph 20 by saying "Our tools are everywhere, linked with our minds, working in tandem." What do you think? Does his statement reflect your own experience with technology?

3. In paragraphs 33–35, Thompson cites Nicholas Carr, whose views about technology differ from his. How does he respond to Carr—and how does acknowledging views he disagrees with help support his own position?

4. So what? Has Thompson convinced you that his topic matters? If so, how and where does he do so?

5. Write an essay reflecting on the ways digital technologies have influenced your own intellectual development, drawing from Thompson's text and other readings in this chapter—and on your own experience as support for your argument. Be sure to acknowledge views other than your own.

Does Texting Affect Writing?

MICHAELA CULLINGTON

—▢—

IT'S TAKING OVER OUR LIVES. We can do it almost anywhere—
walking to class, waiting in line at the grocery store, or hanging out
at home. It's quick, easy, and convenient. It has become a concern
of doctors, parents, and teachers alike. What is it? It's texting!

Text messaging—or texting, as it's more commonly called—
is the process of sending and receiving typed messages via a
cellular phone. It is a common means of communication among
teenagers and is even becoming popular in the business world
because it allows quick messages to be sent without people
having to commit to a telephone conversation. A person is
able to say what is needed, and the other person will receive
the information and respond when it's convenient to do so.

In order to more quickly type what they are trying to say,
many people use abbreviations instead of words. The language
created by these abbreviations is called textspeak. Some people

———

MICHAELA CULLINGTON was a student at Marywood University in Pennsylvania when she wrote this essay, which originally appeared in *Young
Scholars in Writing*, an undergraduate journal of writing published by the
University of Missouri–Kansas City. She received a masters degree in
speech and language pathology from Marywood in 2014 and is a speech
language pathologist in Delaware.

believe that using these abbreviations is hindering the writing abilities of students, and others argue that texting is actually having a positive effect on writing. In fact, it seems likely that texting has no significant effect on student writing.

Here's the summary of an ongoing debate. For tips on this move, see Chapter 1.

Concerns about Textspeak

A September 2008 article in *USA Today* entitled "Texting, Testing Destroys Kids' Writing Style" summarizes many of the most common complaints about the effect of texting. It states that according to the National Center for Education Statistics, only 25% of high school seniors are "proficient" writers. The article quotes Jacquie Ream, a former teacher and author of *K.I.S.S.— Keep It Short and Simple*, a guide for writing more effectively. Ream states, "[W]e have a whole generation being raised without communication skills." She blames the use of acronyms and shorthand in text messages for students' inability to spell and ultimately to write well. Ream also points out that students struggle to convey emotion in their writing because, as she states, in text messages "emotions are always sideways smiley faces."

This debate became prominent after some teachers began 5 to believe they were seeing a decline in the writing abilities of their students. Many attributed this perceived decline to the increasing popularity of text messaging and its use of abbreviations. Naomi Baron, a linguistics professor at American University, blames texting for what she sees as the fact that "so much of American society has become sloppy and laissez faire about the mechanics of writing" ("Should We Worry or LOL?"). Teachers report finding "2" for "to," "gr8" for "great," "dat" for "that," and "wut" for "what," among other examples of textspeak, in their students' writing. A Minnesota teacher of the seventh and ninth grades says that she has to spend extra time in class editing papers and must "explicitly" remind her students that it is not acceptable to use text slang and abbreviations in writing (Walsh). Another English teacher believes that text language has become "second nature" to her students (Carey); they are so used to it that they do not even catch themselves doing it.

Many also complain that because texting does not stress the importance of punctuation, students are neglecting it in their formal writing. Teachers say that their students are forgetting commas, apostrophes, and even capital letters to begin sentences. Another complaint is that text messages lack emotion. Many argue that texts lack feeling because of their tendency to be short, brief, and to the point. Because students are not able to communicate emotion effectively through texts, some teachers worry, they may lose the ability to do so in writing.

To get a more personal perspective on the question of how teachers perceive texting to be influencing student writing, I interviewed two of my former high school teachers—my junior-year English teacher and my senior-year theology teacher. Both teachers stress the importance of writing in their courses. They maintain that they notice text abbreviations in their students' writing often. To correct this problem, they point it out when it occurs and take points off for its use. They also remind their students to use proper sentence structure and complete sentences. The English teacher says that she believes texting inhibits good writing—it reinforces simplistic writing that may be acceptable for conversation but is "not so good for critical thinking or analysis." She suggests that texting tends to generate topic sentences without emphasizing the following explanation. According to these teachers, then, texting is inhibiting good writing. However, their evidence is limited, based on just a few personal experiences rather than on a significant amount of research.

Responses to Concerns about Textspeak

In response to these complaints that texting is having a negative impact on student writing, others insist that texting should be viewed as beneficial because it provides students with motivation to write, practice in specific writing skills, and an opportunity to gain confidence in their writing. For example, Sternberg, Kaplan, and Borck argue that texting is a good way to motivate students: teens enjoy texting, and if they frequently write through texts, they will be more motivated to write formally. Texting also helps to spark students' creativity, these authors argue, because they are always coming up with new ways to express their ideas (417).

In addition, because they are engaging in written communication rather than oral speech, texting teens learn how to convey their message to a reader in as few words as possible. In his book *Txtng: The Gr8 Db8*, David Crystal discusses a study that concludes that texting actually helps foster "the ability to summarize and express oneself concisely" in writing (168). Furthermore, Crystal explains that texting actually helps people to "sharpen their diplomatic skills . . . [because] it allows more time to formulate their thoughts and express them carefully" (168). One language arts teacher from Minnesota believes that texting helps students develop their own "individual voice" (qtd. in Walsh). Perfecting such a voice allows the writer to offer personal insights and express feelings that will interest and engage readers.

Supporters of texting also argue that it not only teaches 10 elements of writing but provides extra practice to those who struggle with the conventions of writing. As Crystal points out, children who struggle with literacy will not choose to use a technology that requires them to do something that is difficult for them. However, if they do choose to text, the experience will help them "overcome their awkwardness and develop their social and communication skills" (*Txtng* 171). Shirley Holm, a junior high school teacher, describes texting as a "comfortable form of communication" (qtd. in Walsh). Teenagers are used to texting, enjoy doing so, and as a result are always writing. Through this experience of writing in ways they enjoy, they can learn to take pleasure in writing formally. If students are continually writing in some form, they will eventually develop better skills.

Furthermore, those who favor texting explain that with practice comes the confidence and courage to try new things, which some observers believe they are seeing happen with writing as a result of texting. Teenagers have, for example, created an entirely new language—one that uses abbreviations and symbols instead of words, does not require punctuation, and uses short, incomplete phrases throughout the entire conversation. It's a way of speaking that is a language in and of itself. Crystal, among others, sees this "language evolution" as a positive effect of texting; he seems, in fact, fascinated that teenagers are capable of creating such a phenomenon, which he describes as the "latest manifestation of the human ability" (*Txtng* 175). David Warlick, a teacher and author of books about technology in the classroom, would agree with Crystal. He believes students should be given credit for "inventing a new language ideal for communicating in a high-tech world" (qtd. in Carey).

Methods

I decided to conduct my own research into this controversy. I wanted to get different, more personal, perspectives on the issue. First, I surveyed seven students on their opinions about the impact of texting on writing. Second, I questioned two high school teachers, as noted above. Finally, in an effort to compare what students are actually doing to people's perceptions of what they are doing, I analyzed student writing samples for instances of textspeak.[1]

To let students speak for themselves, I created a list of questions for seven high school and college students, some of my closest and most reliable friends. Although the number of respondents was small, I could trust my knowledge of them to help me interpret their responses. In addition, these students are very different from one another, and I believed their differences would allow for a wide array of thoughts and opinions on the issue. I was thus confident in the reliability and diversity of their answers but was cautious not to make too many assumptions because of the small sample size.

I asked the students how long they had been texting; how often they texted; what types of abbreviations they used most and how often they used them; and whether they noticed themselves using any type of textspeak in their formal writing. In analyzing their responses, I looked for commonalities to help me draw conclusions about the students' texting habits and if/how they believed their writing was affected.

I created a list of questions for teachers similar to the one 15 for the students and asked two of my high school teachers to provide their input. I asked if they had noticed their students using textspeak in their writing assignments and, if so, how they dealt with it. I also asked if they believed texting had a positive or negative effect on writing. Next, I asked if they were texters themselves. And, finally, I solicited their opinions on what they believed should be done to prevent teens from using text abbreviations and other textspeak in their writing.

I was surprised at how different the students' replies and opinions were from the teachers'. I decided to find out for myself whose impressions were more accurate by comparing some students' actual writing with students' and teachers' perceptions of that writing. To do this I looked at twenty samples of student writing—end-of-semester research arguments written in two first-year college writing courses with different instructors. The topics varied from increased airport security after September 11 to the weapons of the Vietnam War to autism, and lengths ranged from eight to ten pages. To analyze the papers for the presence of textspeak, I looked closely for use of abbreviations and other common slang terms, especially those usages which the students had stated in their surveys were most common. These included "hbu" ("How about you?"); "gtg" ("Got to go"); and "cuz" ("because"). I also looked for the numbers 2 and 4 used instead of the words "to" and "for."

Discussion of Findings

My research suggests that texting actually has a minimal effect on student writing. It showed that students do not believe textspeak is appropriate in formal writing assignments. They recognize the difference between texting friends and writing formally and know what is appropriate in each situation. This was proven true in the student samples, in which no examples of textspeak were used. Many experts would agree that there is no harm in textspeak, as long as students continue to be taught and reminded that occasions where formal language is expected are not the place for it. As Crystal explains, the purpose of the abbreviations used in text messages is not to replace language but rather to make quick communications shorter and easier, since in a standard text message, the texter is allowed only 160 characters for a communication ("Texting" 81).

Dennis Baron, an English and linguistics professor at the University of Illinois, has done much research on the effect of technology on writing, and his findings are aligned with those of my own study. In his book *A Better Pencil: Readers, Writers, and the Digital Revolution,* he concludes that students do not use textspeak in their writing. In fact, he suggests students do not even use abbreviations in their text messages very often. Baron says that college students have "put away such childish things, and many of them had already abandoned such signs of middle-school immaturity in high school" (qtd. in Golden).

In surveying the high school and college students, I found that most have been texting for a few years, usually starting around ninth grade. The students said they generally text between thirty and a hundred messages every day but use abbreviations only occasionally, with the most common being "lol" ("Laugh out loud"), "gtg" ("Got to go"), "hbu" ("How about you?"), "cuz" ("because"), and "jk" ("Just kidding"). None of them believed texting abbreviations were acceptable in formal writing. In fact, research has found that most students report that they do not use textspeak in formal writing. As one Minnesota high school student says, "[T]here is a time and a place for everything," and formal writing is not the place for communicating the way she would if she were texting her friends (qtd. in Walsh). Another student admits that in writing for school she sometimes finds herself using these abbreviations. However, she notices and corrects them before handing in her final paper (Carey). One teacher reports that, despite texting, her students' "formal writing remains solid." She occasionally sees an abbreviation; however, it is in informal, "warm-up" writing. She believes that what students choose to use in everyday types of writing is up to them as long as they use standard English in formal writing (qtd. in Walsh).

Also supporting my own research findings are those from a 20 study which took place at a midwestern research university. This study involved eighty-six students who were taking an Introduction to Education course at the university. The participants were asked to complete a questionnaire that included questions about their texting habits, the spelling instruction they had received, and their proficiency at spelling. They also took a standardized spelling test. Before starting the study, the researchers had hypothesized that texting and the use of abbreviations would have a negative impact on the spelling abilities of the students. However, they found that the results did not support their hypothesis. The researchers did note that text messaging is continuing to increase in popularity; therefore, this issue should continue to be examined (Shaw et al.).

I myself am a frequent texter. I chat with my friends from home every day through texting. I also use texting to communicate with my school friends, perhaps to discuss what time we are going to meet for dinner or to ask quick questions about homework. According to my cell phone bill, I send and receive around 6,400 texts a month. In the messages I send, I rarely notice myself using abbreviations. The only time I use them is if I do not have time to write out the complete phrase. However, sometimes I find it more time-consuming to try to figure out how to abbreviate something so that my message will still be comprehensible.

Since I rarely use abbreviations in my texting, I never use them in my formal writing. I know that they are unacceptable and that it would make me look unintelligent if I included acronyms and symbols instead of proper and formal language. I also have not noticed an effect on my spelling as a result of texting. I am confident in my spelling abilities, and even when I use an abbreviation, I know how to spell the word(s) it stands for.

On the basis of my own research, expert research, and personal observations, I can confidently state that texting is not interfering with students' use of standard written English and has no effect on their writing abilities in general. It is interesting to look at the dynamics of the arguments over these issues. Teachers and parents who claim that they are seeing a decline in the writing abilities of their students and children mainly support the negative-impact argument. Other teachers and researchers suggest that texting provides a way for teens to practice writing in a casual setting and thus helps prepare them to write formally. Experts and students themselves, however, report that they see no effect, positive or negative. Anecdotal experiences should not overshadow the actual evidence.

NOTE

1. All participants in the study have given permission for their responses to be published.

WORKS CITED

Baron, Dennis. *A Better Pencil: Readers, Writers, and the Digital Revolution*. Oxford UP, 2009.

Carey, Bridget. "The Rise of Text, Instant Messaging Vernacular Slips into Schoolwork." *Miami Herald*, 6 Mar. 2007. *Academic Search Elite*, www .ebscohost.com/academic/academic-search-elite. Accessed 27 Oct. 2009.

Crystal, David. "Texting." *ELT Journal*, vol. 62, no. 1, Jan. 2008, pp. 77–83. *WilsonWeb*, doi:10.1093/elt/ccm080. Accessed 8 Nov. 2009.

———. *Txtng: The Gr8 Db8*. Oxford UP, 2008.

Golden, Serena. Review of *A Better Pencil,* by Dennis Baron. *Inside Higher Ed*, 18 Sept. 2009, www.insidehighered.com/news/2009/09/18/barron. Accessed 9 Nov. 2009.

Shaw, Donita M., et al. "An Exploratory Investigation into the Relationship between Text Messaging and Spelling." *New England Reading Association Journal*, vol. 43, no. 1, June 2007, pp. 57–62. *EBSCOhost*, connection .ebscohost.com/c/articles/25648081/exploratory-investigation -relationship-between-text-messaging-spelling. Accessed 8 Nov. 2009.

"Should We Worry or LOL?" *NEA Today*, vol. 22, no. 6, Mar. 2004, p. 12. *EBSCOhost*, connection.ebscohost.com/c/articles/12405267/should-we -worry-lol. Accessed 27 Oct. 2009.

Sternberg, Betty, et al. "Enhancing Adolescent Literacy Achievement through Integration of Technology in the Classroom." *Reading Research Quarterly*, vol. 42, no. 3, July–Sept. 2007, pp. 416–20. *ERIC*, eric.ed.gov/?id=EJ767777. Accessed 8 Nov. 2009.

"Texting, Testing Destroys Kids' Writing Style." *USA Today*, vol. 137, no. 2760, Sept. 2008, p. 8. *EBSCOhost*, connection.ebscohost.com/c/ articles/34214935/texting-testing-destroys-kids-writing-style. Accessed 9 Nov. 2009.

Walsh, James. "Txt Msgs Creep in2 class—Some Say That's gr8." *Star Tribune*, 23 Oct. 2007. *Academic Search Elite*, www.ebscohost.com/ academic/academic-search-elite. Accessed 27 Oct. 2009.

Joining the Conversation

1. Michaela Cullington makes clear in her first paragraph what viewpoint she's responding to. What is this view (her "they say"), and what is her view (her "I say")? What kinds of evidence does she offer in support of her argument?

2. Cullington acknowledges the views of quite a few naysayers, including teachers who believe that texting has a negative effect on their students' writing. How—and where in her essay—does she respond to this criticism? Is her response persuasive—and if not, why not?

3. What kinds of sources does Cullington cite, and how does she incorporate their ideas in her essay? Look at paragraph 18, for instance: how well does she introduce and explain Dennis Baron's ideas? (See pp. 45–49 on framing quotations.)

4. Cullington focuses on how texting affects writing, whereas Sherry Turkle is concerned with the way it affects communication more broadly (pp. 561–80). How do you think Cullington would respond to Turkle's concerns?

5. Cullington "send[s] and receive[s] around 6,400 texts a month" (paragraph 21). About how many do you send and receive? Write a paragraph reflecting on how your texting affects your other writing. First write it as a text, and then revise it to meet the standards of academic writing. How do the two differ?

How I Learned to Love Snapchat

JENNA WORTHAM

——❏——

IN THE MID-'80S, a German engineer named Friedhelm Hillebrand helped devise a way for cellphones to send and receive text messages. Back then, mobile bandwidth was extremely limited, which meant that the messages needed to be as lightweight as possible. The story goes that Hillebrand experimented with a variety of greetings and phrases and concluded, in very German fashion, that most things that needed saying could be done so in an economical 160 characters or fewer. "This is perfectly sufficient," he said of his findings. Eventually the infrastructure improved so that there were no limits to how much text we could transmit at once. And by 2007, texting had surpassed voice calls as the preferred, if not default, mode of communication.

As most rapid advances in technology tend to do, this transition inspired a low-grade, intergenerational moral panic. Many

———

JENNA WORTHAM writes for the *New York Times*, where she also contributes to *Still Processing*, a podcast on culture. Her work has appeared in *Bust* magazine, *Jezebel*, the *Village Voice*, *Vogue*, and *Wired*. Her Twitter handle is @jennydeluxe. This essay first appeared in the *New York Times Magazine* on May 22, 2016.

feared that we would become asocial creatures, misanthropes who would rather hide behind the safety of a screen than face the intimacy of a spoken conversation. And maybe there's some truth in that, but there's another way of looking at it. Maybe we didn't hate talking—just the way older phone technologies forced us to talk. Texting freed a generation from the strictures and inconvenience (and awkwardness) of phone calls, while allowing people to be more loosely and constantly connected.

I thought about this shift recently when trying to make sense of the rise of Snapchat, the latest wellspring of technosocial hand-wringing. Like texting, Snapchat flourished amid scarcity, though of an entirely different kind. We no longer live in Hillebrand's era, when there were hard limits on how much we could say over text; but words alone can be an imperfect technology. So much of what we mean lies not just in what we say, or in the exact words we choose, but also in the light that animates our eyes (or doesn't) when we deliver them and the sharpness (or softness) of the tone we use. Text barely captures even a fraction of that emotional depth and texture, even when we can type as much as we want. Snapchat is just the latest and most well realized example of the various ways we are regaining the layers of meaning we lost when we began digitizing so many important interactions.

Most efforts to approximate normal human behavior in software tend to be creepy or annoying. The oblong gray bubble that pops up when your conversation partner is typing (officially called the "typing awareness indicator") is no doubt intended to be helpful, the virtual version of watching someone inhale and then part their lips to speak. But it becomes panic-inducing if it appears and then disappears—an indication that someone wrote something, then, for any number of reasons, deleted it. Similarly, "read" receipts, designed to let you know that someone opened and read your message, are perhaps best at letting you know when you're being ignored. In a strange turn of events, texting has evolved to become almost as awkward as the phone calls it made obsolete.

In 2012, I calculated that I sent about 7,000 texts a month; 5 now, thanks to the creeping unwieldiness of phones and the misfirings of autocorrect, I can barely manage to peck out half a sentence before I become aggravated by the effort and give up. To combat that fatigue, I've turned to newer ways to talk and interact with friends, primarily voice memos. These function like a highly evolved version of voice mail—there's no expectation of a return call, or even a simultaneous conversation. Freed from that pressure, my friends and I leave one another memos about episodes of *RuPaul's Drag Race* and *Empire*, the themes of *Lemonade* or even just a detailed account of a date or run-in with an ex. The trend is catching on elsewhere: According to an article on Vice's website *Motherboard*, voice notes have become so popular in Argentina that they've virtually replaced text messages altogether.

This is not to say that text is irredeemable. A significant humanization of our text interactions happened quietly in 2011, when emoji were introduced as part of an Apple iOS software update. They offered a palette of punctuation that clarified intent. Tacking on emoji like hearts, skulls, grins and

See Chapter 6 for more ways to address a skeptical reader.

bugged-out eyes to a short message made it infinitely easier to confidently project sarcasm, humor, grief and love across a medium that had been, until then, emotionally arid. If you want proof that we see ourselves in the emoji we use, consider the ever-present disputes over emoji inclusivity: Initially, the characters all had the same skin tone, and even now, the only "professional" emoji are male.

And though the catalog of emoji has expanded in response to user demand, it still struggles to keep up with the multiplicity of human experiences. As a result, a new bespoke-emoji economy has begun to emerge, in apps like Bitmoji, which let people create personalized avatars to adorn their text messages. If our emoji couldn't become us, we would become our emoji.

But messages that include little actual messaging seem to be the wave of the future, and Snapchat is leading the way. The app, which allows users to send short videos and images that disappear after a short period of time, is intimate by design, something that sets it apart from its social-media peers. Most of the "snaps" I send and receive are tightly framed, with angles that could be considered unflattering. They're low resolution too, the images speckled with grain. Snapchat does have filters, but the dumb ones are the most fun, especially the ones that add a comically hideous effect—bloating your face into a red tomato, or distorting it into an animal mask.

If we are to believe the theories about how people want to communicate nowadays—largely through anesthetized, hyper-mediated and impersonal exchanges—Snapchat's recent surge in popularity makes little sense. During the first few years of Snapchat's existence, the only people I knew using the service (beyond journalists like me who were trying to understand it) were my youngest relatives, still in high school and college. And of course there was the attendant moral panic: When it first blew up around 2012, the press seemed to assume it would primarily be used by horny teenagers swapping nudes.

If that was ever the case, it has since expanded. Each time I check the app, I'm surprised to see who else in my network has started using the service. My circle includes every demographic, age and locale: co-workers who send snaps of their dogs, friends on strange adventures in the desert, people I talk to mostly online sending videos from their travels. The videos are rarely elaborate: just a few seconds of my favorite people's faces on a large screen, smiling, or singing, or showing off their view, before they fade and disappear.

Its entire aesthetic flies in the face of how most people 10 behave on Facebook, Instagram and Twitter—as if we're waiting to be plucked from obscurity by a talent agent or model scout. But Snapchat isn't the place where you go to be pretty. It's the place where you go to be yourself, and that is made easy thanks to the app's inbuilt ephemerality. Away from the fave-based economies of mainstream social media, there's less pressure to be dolled up, or funny. For all the advances in tech that let us try on various guises to play around with who we are, it seems that we just want new ways to be ourselves. As it turns out, the mundanity of our regular lives is the most captivating thing we could share with one another.

Joining the Conversation

1. How would you summarize Jenna Wortham's argument about the appeal of Snapchat? How does she place its appeal in the ongoing history of online communication?

2. Wortham begins her piece with a short narrative about a German engineer's invention of text messaging more than thirty years ago. Why do you think she chooses to start her essay this way? How else might the piece have begun?

3. Wortham uses connecting words, phrases, and sentences to link different parts of her argument. For example, at the beginning of paragraph 6, after explaining what she dislikes about text messaging, she writes, "This is not to say that text is irredeemable" and discusses some recent improvements.

Find another place where she makes a similar transition, and explain how you think it develops her argument.

4. Sherry Turkle (pp. 561–80) writes that young women often "prefer to deal with strong feelings from the safe haven of the Net" and that doing so provides "an alternative to processing emotions in real time." Given what Wortham seems to value most about Snapchat, how might she respond to Turkle?

5. In your own view, what are the benefits and limitations of Snapchat as a form of communication? More broadly, write an essay developing your own argument about the larger effects of digital media, citing your experiences as well as ideas from the readings in this chapter.

Google, Democracy, and the Truth about Internet Search

CAROLE CADWALLADR

—◻—

Tech-savvy right-wingers have been able to "game" the algorithms of internet giants and create a new reality where Hitler is a good guy, Jews are evil and . . . Donald Trump becomes president.

HERE'S WHAT YOU DON'T WANT TO DO late on a Sunday night. You do not want to type seven letters into Google. That's all I did. I typed: "a-r-e." And then "j-e-w-s." Since 2008, Google has attempted to predict what question you might be asking and offers you a choice. And this is what it did. It offered me a choice of potential questions it thought I might want to ask: "are jews a race?," "are jews white?," "are jews christians?," and finally, "are jews evil?"

Are Jews evil? It's not a question I've ever thought of asking. I hadn't gone looking for it. But there it was. I press enter.

———

CAROLE CADWALLADR is a journalist who writes features articles for the *Guardian* and the *Observer*, two British newspapers. She is also the author of the novel *The Family Tree* (2006). This piece first appeared on the *Observer* website on December 4, 2016.

A page of results appears. This was Google's question. And this was Google's answer: Jews *are* evil. Because there, on my screen, was the proof: an entire page of results, nine out of 10 of which "confirm" this. The top result, from a site called Listovative, has the headline: "Top 10 Major Reasons Why People Hate Jews." I click on it: "Jews today have taken over marketing, militia, medicinal, technological, media, industrial, cinema challenges etc and continue to face the worlds [sic] envy through unexplained success stories given their inglorious past and vermin like repression all over Europe."

Google *is* search. It's the verb, to Google. It's what we all do, all the time, whenever we want to know anything. We Google it. The site handles at least 63,000 searches a second, 5.5 billion a day. Its mission as a company, the one-line overview that has informed the company since its foundation and is still the banner headline on its corporate website today, is to "organize the world's information and make it universally accessible and useful." It strives to give you the best, most relevant results. And in this instance the third-best, most relevant result to the search query "are Jews . . ." is a link to an article from stormfront.org, a neo-Nazi website. The fifth is a YouTube video: "Why the Jews are Evil. Why we are against them."

The sixth is from Yahoo Answers: "Why are Jews so evil?" The seventh result is: "Jews are demonic souls from a different world." And the 10th is from jesus-is-saviour.com: "Judaism is Satanic!"

There's one result in the 10 that offers a different point of ⁵ view. It's a link to a rather dense, scholarly book review from thetabletmag.com, a Jewish magazine, with the unfortunately misleading headline: "Why Literally Everybody In the World Hates Jews."

I feel like I've fallen down a wormhole, entered some parallel universe where black is white, and good is bad. Though later, I think that perhaps what I've actually done is scraped the topsoil off the surface of 2016 and found one of the underground springs that has been quietly nurturing it. It's been there all the time, of course. Just a few keystrokes away . . . on our laptops, our tablets, our phones. This isn't a secret Nazi cell lurking in the shadows. It's hiding in plain sight.

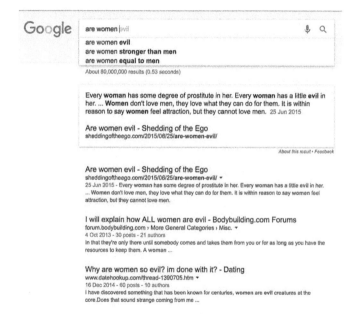

Stories about fake news on Facebook have dominated certain sections of the press for weeks following the American presidential election, but arguably this is even more powerful, more insidious. Frank Pasquale, professor of law at the University of

Maryland, and one of the leading academic figures calling for tech companies to be more open and transparent, calls the results "very profound, very troubling."

He came across a similar instance in 2006 when, "If you typed 'Jew' in Google, the first result was jewwatch.org. It was 'look out for these awful Jews who are ruining your life.' And the Anti-Defamation League went after them and so they put an asterisk next to it which said: 'These search results may be disturbing but this is an automated process.' But what you're showing—and I'm very glad you are documenting it and screen-shotting it—is that despite the fact they have vastly researched this problem, it has gotten vastly worse."

And ordering of search results does influence people, says Martin Moore, director of the Centre for the Study of Media, Communication and Power at King's College, London, who has written at length on the impact of the big tech companies on our civic and political spheres. "There's large-scale, statistically significant research into the impact of search results on political views. And the way in which you see the results and the types of results you see on the page necessarily has an impact on your perspective." Fake news, he says, has simply "revealed a much bigger problem. These companies are so powerful and so committed to disruption. They thought they were disrupting politics but in a positive way. They hadn't thought about the downsides. These tools offer remarkable empowerment, but there's a dark side to it. It enables people to do very cynical, damaging things."

Google is knowledge. It's where you go to find things out. 10 And evil Jews are just the start of it. There are also evil women. I didn't go looking for them either. This is what I type: "a-r-e w-o-m-e-n." And Google offers me just two choices, the first of which is: "Are women evil?" I press return. Yes, they are.

Every one of the 10 results "confirms" that they are, including the top one, from a site called sheddingoftheego.com, which is boxed out and highlighted: "Every woman has some degree of prostitute in her. Every woman has a little evil in her . . . Women don't love men, they love what they can do for them. It is within reason to say women feel attraction, but they cannot love men."

Next I type: "a-r-e m-u-s-l-i-m-s." And Google suggests I should ask: "Are Muslims bad?" And here's what I find out: yes, they are. That's what the top result says and six of the others. Without typing anything else, simply putting the cursor in the search box, Google offers me two new searches and I go for the first, "Islam is bad for society." In the next list of suggestions, I'm offered: "Islam must be destroyed."

Jews are evil. Muslims need to be eradicated. And Hitler? Do you want to know about Hitler? Let's Google it. "Was Hitler bad?" I type. And here's Google's top result: "10 Reasons Why Hitler Was One Of The Good Guys." I click on the link: "He never wanted to kill any Jews"; "he cared about conditions for Jews in the work camps"; "he implemented social and cultural reform." Eight out of the other 10 search results agree: Hitler really wasn't that bad.

A few days later, I talk to Danny Sullivan, the founding editor of SearchEngineLand.com. He's been recommended to me by several academics as one of the most knowledgeable experts on search. Am I just being naive, I ask him? Should I have known this was out there? "No, you're not being naive," he says. "This is awful. It's horrible. It's the equivalent of going into a library and asking a librarian about Judaism and being handed 10 books of hate. Google is doing a horrible, horrible job of delivering answers here. It can and should do better."

He's surprised too. "I thought they stopped offering autocomplete suggestions for religions in 2011." And then he types "are women" into his own computer. "Good lord! That answer at the top. It's a featured result. It's called a 'direct answer.' This is supposed to be indisputable. It's Google's highest endorsement." That every woman has some degree of prostitute in her? "Yes. This is Google's algorithm going terribly wrong."

I contacted Google about its seemingly malfunctioning auto- 15 complete suggestions and received the following response: "Our search results are a reflection of the content across the web. This means that sometimes unpleasant portrayals of sensitive subject matter online can affect what search results appear for a given query. These results don't reflect Google's own opinions or beliefs—as a company, we strongly value a diversity of perspectives, ideas and cultures."

Google isn't just a search engine, of course. Search was the foundation of the company but that was just the beginning. Alphabet, Google's parent company, now has the great- To elaborate on a previous idea, see p. 137. est concentration of artificial intelligence experts in the world. It is expanding into healthcare, transportation, energy. It's able to attract the world's top computer scientists, physicists and engineers. It's bought hundreds of start-ups, including Calico, whose stated mission is to "cure death" and DeepMind, which aims to "solve intelligence."

And 20 years ago it didn't even exist. When Tony Blair became prime minister, it wasn't possible to Google him: the search engine had yet to be invented. The company was only founded in 1998 and Facebook didn't appear until 2004. Google's founders Sergey Brin and Larry Page are still only 43. Mark Zuckerberg of Facebook is 32. Everything they've done, the world they've remade, has been done in the blink of an eye.

Google cofounders Larry Page and Sergey Brin.

But it seems the implications about the power and reach of these companies are only now seeping into the public consciousness. I ask Rebecca MacKinnon, director of the Ranking Digital Rights project at the New America Foundation, whether it was the recent furor over fake news that woke people up to the danger of ceding our rights as citizens to corporations. "It's kind of weird right now," she says, "because people are finally saying, 'Gee, Facebook and Google really have a lot of power' like it's this big revelation. And it's like, 'D'oh.'"

MacKinnon has a particular expertise in how authoritarian governments adapt to the internet and bend it to their purposes. "China and Russia are a cautionary tale for us. I think what happens is that it goes back and forth. So during the Arab spring, it seemed like the good guys were further ahead. And now it seems like the bad guys are. Pro-democracy activists are using the internet more than ever but at the same time, the adversary has gotten so much more skilled."

Last week Jonathan Albright, an assistant professor of com- 20 munications at Elon University in North Carolina, published the first detailed research on how right-wing websites had spread their message. "I took a list of these fake news sites that was circulating, I had an initial list of 306 of them and I used a tool—like the one Google uses—to scrape them for links and then I mapped them. So I looked at where the links went—into YouTube and Facebook, and between each other, millions of them . . . and I just couldn't believe what I was seeing.

"They have created a web that is bleeding through onto our web. This isn't a conspiracy. There isn't one person who's created this. It's a vast system of hundreds of different sites that are using all the same tricks that all websites use. They're sending out thousands of links to other sites and together this has created a vast satellite system of right-wing news and propaganda that has completely surrounded the mainstream media system."

He found 23,000 pages and 1.3 million hyperlinks. "And Facebook is just the amplification device. When you look at it in 3D, it actually looks like a virus. And Facebook was just one of the hosts for the virus that helps it spread faster. You can see the *New York Times* in there and the *Washington Post* and then you can see how there's a vast, vast network surrounding them. The best way of describing it is as an ecosystem. This really goes way beyond individual sites or individual stories. What this map shows is the distribution network and you can see that it's surrounding and actually choking the mainstream news ecosystem."

Like a cancer? "Like an organism that is growing and getting stronger all the time."

Charlie Beckett, a professor in the school of media and communications at LSE,* tells me: "We've been arguing for some time now that plurality of news media is good. Diversity is good. Critiquing the mainstream media is good. But now . . . it's gone wildly out of control. What Jonathan Albright's research has shown is that this isn't a byproduct of the internet. And it's not even being done for commercial reasons. It's motivated by ideology, by people who are quite deliberately trying to destabilize the internet."

Albright's map also provides a clue to understanding the 25 Google search results I found. What these right-wing news

Jonathan Albright's map of the fake-news ecosystem.

*LSE The London School of Economics

sites have done, he explains, is what most commercial websites try to do. They try to find the tricks that will move them up Google's PageRank system. They try and "game" the algorithm. And what his map shows is how well they're doing that.

That's what my searches are showing too. That the right has colonized the digital space around these subjects—Muslims, women, Jews, the Holocaust, black people—far more effectively than the liberal left.

"It's an information war," says Albright. "That's what I keep coming back to."

But it's where it goes from here that's truly frightening. I ask him how it can be stopped. "I don't know. I'm not sure it can be. It's a network. It's far more powerful than any one actor."

So, it's almost got a life of its own? "Yes, and it's learning. Every day, it's getting stronger."

The more people who search for information about Jews, 30 the more people will see links to hate sites, and the more they click on those links (very few people click on to the second page of results) the more traffic the sites will get, the more links they will accrue and the more authoritative they will appear. This is an entirely circular knowledge economy that has only one outcome: an amplification of the message. Jews are evil. Women are evil. Islam must be destroyed. Hitler was one of the good guys.

And the constellation of websites that Albright found—a sort of shadow internet—has another function. More than just spreading right-wing ideology, they are being used to track and monitor and influence anyone who comes across their content. "I scraped the trackers on these sites and I was absolutely dumbfounded. Every time someone likes one of these posts on Facebook or visits one of these websites, the scripts are then following you around the web. And this enables data-mining and influencing companies like Cambridge Analytica to precisely target individuals, to follow them around the web, and to send them highly personalized political messages. This is a propaganda machine. It's targeting people individually to recruit them to an idea. It's a level of social engineering that I've never seen before. They're capturing people and then keeping them on an emotional leash and never letting them go."

Cambridge Analytica, an American-owned company based in London, was employed by both the Vote Leave* campaign and the Trump campaign. Dominic Cummings, the campaign director of Vote Leave, has made few public announcements since the Brexit referendum but he did say this: "If you want to make big improvements in communication, my advice is—hire physicists."

Steve Bannon, founder of Breitbart News and the newly appointed chief strategist to Trump, is on Cambridge Analytica's board and it has emerged that the company is in talks to undertake political messaging work for the Trump administration. It claims to have built psychological profiles using 5,000 separate pieces of data on 220 million American voters. It knows their quirks and nuances and daily habits and can target them individually.

"They were using 40–50,000 different variants of ad every day that were continuously measuring responses and then adapting and evolving based on that response," says Martin Moore of Kings College. Because they have so much data on individuals and they use such phenomenally powerful distribution networks, they allow campaigns to bypass a lot of existing laws.

*Vote Leave An organization that campaigned for the United Kingdom to leave the European Union.

"It's all done completely opaquely and they can spend as 35 much money as they like on particular locations because you can focus on a five-mile radius or even a single demographic. Fake news is important but it's only one part of it. These companies have found a way of transgressing 150 years of legislation that we've developed to make elections fair and open."

Did such micro-targeted propaganda—currently legal— swing the Brexit vote? We have no way of knowing. Did the same methods used by Cambridge Analytica help Trump to victory? Again, we have no way of knowing. This is all happening in complete darkness. We have no way of knowing how our personal data is being mined and used to influence us. We don't realize that the Facebook page we are looking at, the Google page, the ads that we are seeing, the search results we are using, are all being personalized to us. We don't see it because we have nothing to compare it to. And it is not being monitored or recorded. It is not being regulated. We are inside a machine and we simply have no way of seeing the controls. Most of the time, we don't even realise that there are controls.

Rebecca MacKinnon says that most of us consider the internet to be like "the air that we breathe and the water that we drink." It surrounds us. We use it. And we don't question it. "But this is not a natural landscape. Programmers and executives and editors and designers, they make this landscape. They are human beings and they all make choices."

But we don't know what choices they are making. Neither Google or Facebook make their algorithms public. Why did my Google search return nine out of 10 search results that claim Jews are evil? We don't know and we have no way of knowing. Their systems are what Frank Pasquale describes as "black boxes." He calls Google and Facebook "a terrifying duopoly of power" and has been leading a growing movement of academics who are calling for "algorithmic accountability." "We need to have regular audits of these systems," he says. "We need people in these companies to be accountable. In the US, under the Digital Millennium Copyright Act, every company has to have a spokesman you can reach. And this is what needs to happen. They need to respond to complaints about hate speech, about bias."

Is bias built into the system? Does it affect the kind of results that I was seeing? "There's all sorts of bias about what counts as a legitimate source of information and how that's weighted. There's enormous commercial bias. And when you look at the personnel, they are young, white and perhaps Asian, but not black or Hispanic and they are overwhelmingly men. The worldview of young wealthy white men informs all these judgments."

Later, I speak to Robert Epstein, a research psychologist at the 40 American Institute for Behavioral Research and Technology, and the author of the study that Martin Moore told me about (and that Google has publicly criticized), showing how search-rank results affect voting patterns. On the other end of the phone, he repeats one of the searches I did. He types "do blacks . . ." into Google.

"Look at that. I haven't even hit a button and it's automatically populated the page with answers to the query: 'Do blacks commit more crimes?' And look, I could have been going to ask all sorts of questions. 'Do blacks excel at sports,' or anything. And it's only given me two choices and these aren't simply search-based or the most searched terms right now. Google used to use that but now they use an algorithm that looks at other things. Now, let me look at Bing and Yahoo. I'm on Yahoo and I have 10 suggestions, not one of which is 'Do black people commit more crime?'

"And people don't question this. Google isn't just offering a suggestion. This is a negative suggestion and we know that negative suggestions depending on lots of things can draw between five and 15 more clicks. And this is all programmed. And it could be programmed differently."

What Epstein's work has shown is that the contents of a page of search results can influence people's views and opinions. The type and order of search rankings was shown to influence voters in India in double-blind trials. There were similar results relating to the search suggestions you are offered.

"The general public are completely in the dark about very fundamental issues regarding online search and influence. We are talking about the most powerful mind-control machine ever invented in the history of the human race. And people don't even notice it."

Damien Tambini, an associate professor at the London School 45 of Economics, who focuses on media regulation, says that we lack any sort of framework to deal with the potential impact of these companies on the democratic process. "We have structures that deal with powerful media corporations. We have competition laws. But these companies are not being held responsible. There are no powers to get Google or Facebook to disclose anything. There's an editorial function to Google and Facebook but it's being done by sophisticated algorithms. They say it's machines not editors. But that's simply a mechanized editorial function."

And the companies, says John Naughton, the *Observer* columnist and a senior research fellow at Cambridge University, are terrified of acquiring editorial responsibilities they don't want. "Though they can and regularly do tweak the results in all sorts of ways."

Certainly the results about Google on Google don't seem entirely neutral. Google "Is Google racist?" and the featured result—the Google answer boxed out at the top of the page—is quite clear: no. It is not.

But the enormity and complexity of having two global companies of a kind we have never seen before influencing so many areas of our lives is such, says Naughton, that "we don't even have the mental apparatus to even know what the problems are."

And this is especially true of the future. Google and Facebook are at the forefront of AI. They are going to own the future. And the rest of us can barely start to frame the sorts of questions we ought to be asking. "Politicians don't think long term. And corporations don't think long term because they're focused on the next quarterly results and that's what makes Google and Facebook interesting and different. They are absolutely thinking long term. They have the resources, the money, and the ambition to do whatever they want.

"They want to digitize every book in the world: they do it. 50 They want to build a self-driving car: they do it. The fact that people are reading about these fake news stories and realizing that this could have an effect on politics and elections, it's like, 'Which planet have you been living on?' For Christ's sake, this is obvious."

"The internet is among the few things that humans have built that they don't understand." It is "the largest experiment involving anarchy in history. Hundreds of millions of people are, each minute, creating and consuming an untold amount of digital content in an online world that is not truly bound by terrestrial laws." The internet as a lawless anarchic state? A massive human experiment with no checks and balances and untold potential consequences? What kind of digital doommongerer would say such a thing? Step forward, Eric Schmidt—Google's chairman. They are the first lines of the book, *The New Digital Age*, that he wrote with Jared Cohen.*

*__Jared Cohen__   Director of Jigsaw, formerly Google Ideas, a technology think tank.

We don't understand it. It is not bound by terrestrial laws. And it's in the hands of two massive, all-powerful corporations. It's their experiment, not ours. The technology that was supposed to set us free may well have helped Trump to power, or covertly helped swing votes for Brexit. It has created a vast network of propaganda that has encroached like a cancer across the entire internet. This is a technology that has enabled the likes of Cambridge Analytica to create political messages uniquely tailored to you. They understand your emotional responses and how to trigger them. They know your likes, dislikes, where you live, what you eat, what makes you laugh, what makes you cry.

And what next? Rebecca MacKinnon's research has shown how authoritarian regimes reshape the internet for their own purposes. Is that what's going to happen with Silicon Valley and Trump? As Martin Moore points out, the president-elect claimed that Apple chief executive Tim Cook called to congratulate him soon after his election victory. "And there will undoubtedly be pressure on them to collaborate," says Moore.

Journalism is failing in the face of such change and is only going to fail further. New platforms have put a bomb under the financial model—advertising—resources are shrinking, traffic is increasingly dependent on them, and publishers have no access, no insight at all, into what these platforms are doing in their headquarters, their labs. And now they are moving beyond the digital world into the physical. The next frontiers are healthcare, transportation, energy. And just as Google is a near-monopoly for search, its ambition to own and control the physical infrastructure of our lives is what's coming next. It already owns our data and with it our identity. What will it mean when it moves into all the other areas of our lives?

"At the moment, there's a distance when you Google 'Jews 55 are' and get 'Jews are evil,'" says Julia Powles, a researcher at

Facebook founder Mark Zuckerberg.

Cambridge on technology and law. "But when you move into the physical realm, and these concepts become part of the tools being deployed when you navigate around your city or influence how people are employed, I think that has really pernicious consequences."

Powles is shortly to publish a paper looking at DeepMind's relationship with the NHS.* "A year ago, 2 million Londoners' NHS health records were handed over to DeepMind. And there was complete silence from politicians, from regulators, from anyone in a position of power. This is a company without any healthcare experience being given unprecedented access into the NHS and it took seven months to even know that they had the data. And that took investigative journalism to find it out."

*NHS National Health Service, the name of the United Kingdom's public health care system.

The headline was that DeepMind was going to work with the NHS to develop an app that would provide early warning for sufferers of kidney disease. And it is, but DeepMind's ambitions—"to solve intelligence"—goes way beyond that. The entire history of 2 million NHS patients is, for artificial intelligence researchers, a treasure trove. And, their entry into the NHS—providing useful services in exchange for our personal data—is another massive step in their power and influence in every part of our lives.

[Because the stage beyond search is prediction.] Google wants to know what you want before you know yourself. "That's the next stage," says Martin Moore. "We talk about the omniscience of these tech giants, but that omniscience takes a huge step forward again if they are able to predict. And that's where they want to go. To predict diseases in health. It's really, really problematic."

For the nearly 20 years that Google has been in existence, our view of the company has been inflected by the youth and liberal outlook of its founders. Ditto Facebook, whose mission, Zuckerberg said, was not to be "a company. It was built to accomplish a social mission to make the world more open and connected."

It would be interesting to know how he thinks that's working out. Donald Trump is connecting through exactly the same technology.... And Facebook and Google are amplifying and spreading that message. And us too—the mainstream media. Our outrage is just another node on Jonathan Albright's data map.

"The more we argue with them, the more they know about us," he says. "It all feeds into a circular system. What we're seeing here is a new era of network propaganda."

We are all points on that map. And our complicity, our credulity, being consumers not concerned citizens, is an essential part of that process. And what happens next is down to us. "I would say that everybody has been really naive and we need to reset ourselves to a much more cynical place and proceed on that basis," is Rebecca MacKinnon's advice. "There is no doubt that where we are now is a very bad place. But it's we as a society who have jointly created this problem. And if we want to get to a better place, when it comes to having an information ecosystem that serves human rights and democracy instead of destroying it, we have to share responsibility for that."

Are Jews evil? How do you want that question answered? This is our internet. Not Google's. Not Facebook's. Not right-wing propagandists.' And we're the only ones who can reclaim it.

Joining the Conversation

1. In what ways does Carole Cadwalladr believe that Google is jeopardizing democracy throughout the world? What supporting arguments and evidence does she provide?
2. Cadwalladr makes clear what her own views are, but she does not say much about other viewpoints. What objections could be raised to her argument, and where would you introduce them in her essay?
3. Cadwalladr frequently quotes others on the prominent representation of right-wing views in Google searches, but she doesn't always set up these quotations or follow them with explanations. Find two examples—in each case, how might she add a sentence or two to explain their meaning and significance? (See pp. 45–49 for ways to frame quotations.)

4. Compare the author's view of Google with Nicholas Carr's view of Google (pp. 480–96). How are they similar? How are they different?

5. Cadwalladr makes a number of debatable claims: "[T]he right has colonized the digital space . . . far more effectively than the liberal left" (paragraph 26) and "Google and Facebook . . . are going to own the future" (paragraph 49). Write an essay responding to one of these claims or another claim that interests you, drawing upon your own experiences to support your argument.

Go Ahead:
Waste Time on the Internet

KENNETH GOLDSMITH

———

Is THE INTERNET A WASTE OF TIME? It's not so easy to say. When I click around news sites, am I wasting time because I should be working instead? What if I've spent hours working, and I need a break? Am I wasting time if I watch cat videos, but not if I read a magazine story about the Iran nuclear deal? Am I wasting time if I look up the latest presidential polling numbers, but not if I'm communicating with an old friend on Facebook?

The notion that the Internet is bad for you seems premised on the idea that the Internet is one thing—a monolith. In reality it's a befuddling mix of the stupid and the sublime, a shattered, contradictory, and fragmented medium. Internet

———

KENNETH GOLDSMITH is a poet and author of ten books, including *Seven American Deaths and Disasters* (2013) and *Uncreative Writing: Managing Language in the Digital Age* (2013). He is the founding editor of *UbuWeb*, an online archive, and senior editor of *PennSound*, a website for digital poetry recordings based at the University of Pennsylvania, where he teaches writing. This essay, first published on August 12, 2016 for the *Los Angeles Times*, is from his book *Wasting Time on the Internet* (2016).

detractors seem to miss this simple fact, which is why so many of their criticisms disintegrate under observation.

The way Internet pundits tell it, you'd think we stare for three hours at clickbait—those articles with hypersensational headlines—the way we once sat down and watched three hours of cartoons on Saturday morning TV. But most of us don't do any one thing on the Internet. Instead, we do many things, some of it frivolous, some of it heavy. Our time spent in front of the computer is a mixed time, a time that reflects our desires— as opposed to the time spent sitting in front of the television where we were fed shows we didn't necessarily enjoy. TV gave us few choices. Many of us truly did feel like we wasted our time—as our parents so often chided us—"rotting away" in front of the TV.

I keep reading—on screens—that in the age of screens we've lost our ability to concentrate, that we've become distracted. But when I look around me and see people riveted to their devices, I notice a great wealth of concentration, focus, and engagement.

And I keep reading—on the Internet—that the Internet ⁵ has made us antisocial, that we've lost the ability to have a conversation. But when I see people with their devices, what I see is people communicating with one another: texting, chatting, IM'ing. And I have to wonder, in what way is this not social? A conversation broken up into short bursts and quick emoticons is still a conversation. Watch someone's face while they're in the midst of a rapid-fire text message exchange: it's full of emotion—anticipation, laughter, affect.

The Internet has been accused of making us shallow. We're skimming, not reading. We lack the ability to engage deeply with a subject anymore. That's both true and not true: we skim and browse certain types of content, and read others carefully.

We're not all using our devices the same way. Looking over the shoulders of people absorbed in their devices on the subway, I see many people reading newspapers and books and many others playing Candy Crush. Sometimes someone will be glancing at a newspaper one moment and playing a game the next.

The other night, I walked into the living room and my wife was glued to her iPad, reading "Narrative of the Life of Frederick Douglass." Hours later, when I headed to bed, she hadn't moved an inch, still transfixed by this 171-year-old narrative on her 21st-century device. When I said good night, she didn't even look up.

Internet critics tell us time and again that our brains are being rewired; I'm not so sure that's a bad thing. Every new See pp. 25–27 for ways to introduce an ongoing debate. media requires new ways of thinking. Wouldn't it be strange if in the midst of this digital revolution we were still expected to use our brains in the same way we read books or watched TV?

The resistance to the Internet shouldn't surprise us: Cultural reactionaries defending the status quo have been around as long as media has. Marshall McLuhan tells us that television was written off by people invested in literature as merely "mass entertainment" just as the printed book was met with the same skepticism in the 16th century by scholastic philosophers. McLuhan says that "the vested interests of acquired knowledge and conventional wisdom have always been by-passed and engulfed by new media . . . The student of media soon comes to expect the new media of any period whatever to be classed as pseudo by those who have acquired the patterns of earlier media, whatever they may happen to be."

I'm told that our children are most at risk, that the exces- 10 sive use of computers has led our kids to view the real world as fake. But I'm not so sure that even I can distinguish "real" from "fake." How is my life on Facebook any less "real" than what happens in my day-to-day life? In fact, much of what does happen in my day-to-day life comes through Facebook—work opportunities, invitations to dinner parties, and even the topics I discuss at those dinner parties.

After reading one of those hysterical "devices are ruining your child" articles, my sister-in-law decided to take action. She imposed a system whereby, after dinner, the children were to "turn in" their devices—computers, smartphones, and tablets. They could "check them out" over the course of the evening, but only if they could prove they needed them for "educational purposes." Upon confiscating my nephew's cell phone one Friday night, she asked him on Saturday morning, "What plans do you have with your friends today?" "None," he responded. "You took away my phone."

On a vacation, after a full day of outdoor activities that included seeing the Grand Canyon and hiking, my friend and her family settled into the hotel for the evening. Her 12-year-old daughter is a fan of preteen goth girl crafting videos on YouTube, where she learns how to bedazzle black skull T-shirts and make perfectly ripped punk leggings. That evening, the girl selected some of her favorite videos to share with her mother. After agreeing to watch a few, her mother grew impatient. "This is nice, but I don't want to spend the whole night clicking around." The daughter responded indignantly that she wasn't just "clicking around." She was connecting with a community of girls her own age who shared similar interests.

Her mother was forced to reconsider her premise that her daughter was just wasting time on the Internet; instead, she was fully engaged, fostering an aesthetic, feeding her imagination, indulging in her creative proclivities, and hanging out with her friends, all from the comfort of a remote hotel room perched on the edge of the Grand Canyon.

Many Internet critics yearn for a return to solitude and introspection, quiet places far removed from the noises of our devices. But those places, away from the rabble, are starting to remind me of gated communities.

Joining the Conversation

1. Kenneth Goldsmith introduces a series of standard views followed by a series of "I say" statements. List each pair, noting the specific language the author uses in each instance.

2. So what? Who cares? Where does Goldsmith explain why his argument matters—and for whom?

3. Goldsmith quotes Marshall McLuhan, a scholar who wrote about the effects of technology on people. Compare Goldsmith's paraphrasing of McLuhan's ideas with Nicholas Carr's (p. 482, paragraph 4). Which author, in your view, provides a better paraphrase? Why?

4. Read Andreas Elpidorou's article "The Quiet Alarm" on **theysayiblog.com**. What do you think Goldsmith would say to Elpidorou's claim that the "next time boredom overcomes you . . . [i]t might be best not to cover it up with your smartphone"?

5. How do your friends, family, and/or coworkers spend time on the internet? How do they feel about it? Incorporating their views as evidence, write an essay responding to Goldsmith in which you agree, disagree, or both with his argument.

No Need to Call

SHERRY TURKLE

—⌐回⌐—

"So many people hate the telephone," says Elaine, seventeen. Among her friends at Roosevelt High School, "it's all texting and messaging." She herself writes each of her six closest friends roughly twenty texts a day. In addition, she says, "there are about forty instant messages out, forty in, when I'm at home on the computer." Elaine has strong ideas about how electronic media "levels the playing field" between people like her—outgoing, on the soccer team, and in drama club—and the shy: "It's only on the screen that shy people open up." She explains why: "When you can think about what you're going to say, you can talk to someone you'd have trouble talking to. And it doesn't seem weird that you pause for two minutes to

———

SHERRY TURKLE teaches in the science, technology, and society program at MIT and directs the MIT Initiative on Technology and Self. She has been described as the "Margaret Mead of digital culture." Her books include *Reclaiming Conversation: The Power of Talk in a Digital Age* (2015), *Alone Together: Why We Expect More from Technology and Less from Each Other* (2011), and *Life on the Screen: Identity in the Age of the Internet* (1995). This essay is from *Alone Together*.

think about what you're going to say before you say it, like it would be if you were actually talking to someone."

Elaine gets specific about the technical designs that help shy people express themselves in electronic messaging. The person to whom you are writing shouldn't be able to see your process of revision or how long you have been working on the message. "That could be humiliating." The best communication programs shield the writer from the view of the reader. The advantage of screen communication is that it is a place to reflect, retype, and edit. "It is a place to hide," says Elaine.

The notion that hiding makes it easier to open up is not new. In the psychoanalytic tradition, it inspired technique. Classical analysis shielded the patient from the analyst's gaze in order to facilitate free association, the golden rule of saying whatever comes to mind. Likewise, at a screen, you feel protected and less burdened by expectations. And, although you are alone, the potential for almost instantaneous contact gives an encouraging feeling of already being together. In this curious relational space, even sophisticated users who know that electronic communications can be saved, shared, and show up in court, succumb to its illusion of privacy. Alone with your thoughts, yet in contact with an almost tangible fantasy of the other, you feel free to play. At the screen, you have a chance to write yourself into the person you want to be and to imagine others as you wish them to be, constructing them for your purposes.[1] It is a seductive but dangerous habit of mind. When you cultivate this sensibility, a telephone call can seem fearsome because it reveals too much.

Elaine is right in her analysis: teenagers flee the telephone. Perhaps more surprisingly, so do adults. They claim exhaustion and lack of time; always on call, with their time highly leveraged through multitasking, they avoid voice communication outside of a small circle because it demands their full attention when they don't want to give it.

Technologies live in complex ecologies. The meaning of any one depends on what others are available. The telephone was once a way to touch base or ask a simple question. But once you have access to e-mail, instant messaging, and texting, things change. Although we still use the phone to keep up with those closest to us, we use it less outside this circle.[2] Not only do people say that a phone call asks too much, they worry it will be received as demanding too much. Randolph, a forty-six-year-old architect with two jobs, two young children, and a twelve-year-old son from a former marriage, makes both points. He avoids the telephone because he feels "tapped out. . . . It promises more than I'm willing to deliver." If he keeps his communications to text and e-mail, he believes he can "keep it together." He explains, "Now that there is e-mail, people expect that a call will be more complicated. Not about facts. A fuller thing. People expect it to take time—or else you wouldn't have called."

Tara, a fifty-five-year-old lawyer who juggles children, a job, and a new marriage, makes a similar point: "When you ask for a call, the expectation is that you have pumped it up a level. People say to themselves: 'It's urgent or she would have sent an e-mail.'" So Tara avoids the telephone. She wants to meet with friends in person; e-mail is for setting up these meetings. "That is what is most efficient," she says. But efficiency has its downside. Business meetings have agendas, but friends have unscheduled needs. In friendship, things can't always wait. Tara knows this; she feels guilty and she experiences a loss: "I'm at the point where I'm processing my friends as though they were items of inventory . . . or clients."

Leonora, fifty-seven, a professor of chemistry, reflects on her similar practice: "I use e-mail to make appointments to see friends, but I'm so busy that I'm often making an appointment one or two months in the future. After we set things up by e-mail, we do not call. Really. I don't call. They don't call. They feel that they have their appointment. What do I feel? I feel I have 'taken care of that person.'" Leonora's pained tone makes it clear that by "taken care of" she means that she has crossed someone off a to-do list. Tara and Leonora are discontent but do not feel they have a choice. This is where technology has brought them. They subscribe to a new etiquette, claiming the need for efficiency in a realm where efficiency is costly.

Audrey: A Life on the Screen

. . . Audrey, sixteen, a Roosevelt junior[,] talked about her Facebook profile as "the avatar of me." She's one of Elaine's shy friends who prefers texting to talking. She is never without her phone, sometimes using it to text even as she instant-messages at an open computer screen. Audrey feels lonely in her family. She has an older brother in medical school and a second, younger brother, just two years old. Her parents are divorced, and she lives half time with each of them. Their homes are about a forty-five-minute drive apart. This means that Audrey spends a lot of time on the road. "On the road," she says. "That's daily life." She sees her phone as the glue that ties her life together. Her mother calls her to pass on a message to her father. Her father does the same. Audrey says, "They call me to say, 'Tell your mom this. . . . Make sure your dad knows that.' I use the cell to pull it together." Audrey sums up the situation: "My parents use me and my cell like instant messenger. I am their IM."

Like so many other children who tell me similar stories, Audrey complains of her mother's inattention when she picks her up at school or after sports practice. At these times, Audrey says, her mother is usually focused on her cell phone, either texting or talking to her friends. Audrey describes the scene: she comes out of the gym exhausted, carrying heavy gear. Her mother sits in her beaten-up SUV, immersed in her cell, and doesn't even look up until Audrey opens the car door. Sometimes her mother will make eye contact but remain engrossed with the phone as they begin the drive home. Audrey says, "It gets between us, but it's hopeless. She's not going to give it up. Like, it could have been four days since I last spoke to her, then I sit in the car and wait in silence until she's done."[3]

Audrey has a fantasy of her mother, waiting for her, expect- 10 ant, without a phone. But Audrey is resigned that this is not to be and feels she must temper her criticism of her mother because of her own habit of texting when she is with her friends. Audrey does everything she can to avoid a call.[4] "The phone, it's awkward. I don't see the point. Too much just a recap and sharing feelings. With a text . . . I can answer on my own time. I can respond. I can ignore it. So it really works with my mood. I'm not bound to anything, no commitment. . . . I have control over the conversation and also more control over what I say."

Texting offers protection:

> Nothing will get spat at you. You have time to think and prepare what you're going to say, to make you appear like that's just the way you are. There's planning involved, so you can control how you're portrayed to this person, because you're choosing these words, editing it before you send it. . . . When you instant-message you can cross things out, edit what you say, block a person, or sign off. A phone conversation is a lot of pressure. You're always expected

to uphold it, to keep it going, and that's too much pressure. . . . You have to just keep going . . . "Oh, how was your day?" You're trying to think of something else to say real fast so the conversation doesn't die out.

Then Audrey makes up a new word. A text, she argues, is better than a call because in a call "there is a lot less *boundness* to the person." By this she means that in a call, she could learn too much or say too much, and things could get "out of control." A call has insufficient boundaries. She admits that "later in life I'm going to need to talk to people on the phone. *But not now.*" When texting, she feels at a reassuring distance. If things start to go in a direction she doesn't like, she can easily redirect the conversation—or cut it off: "In texting, you get your main points off; you can really control when you want the conversation to start and end. You say, 'Got to go, bye.' You

Teenagers plugged into their devices but not each other.

just do it . . . much better than the long drawn-out good-byes, when you have no real reason to leave, but you want to end the conversation." This last is what Audrey likes least—the end of conversations. A phone call, she explains, requires the skill to end a conversation "when you have no real reason to leave. . . . It's not like there is a reason. You just want to. I don't know how to do that. *I don't want to learn*."

Ending a call is hard for Audrey because she experiences separation as rejection; she projects onto others the pang of abandonment she feels when someone ends a conversation with her. Feeling unthreatened when someone wants to end a conversation may seem a small thing, but it is not. It calls upon a sense of self-worth; one needs to be at a place where Audrey has not arrived. It is easier to avoid the phone; its beginnings and endings are too rough on her.

Audrey is not alone in this. Among her friends, phone calls are infrequent, and she says, "Face-to-face conversations happen way less than they did before. It's always, 'Oh, talk to you online.'" This means, she explains, that things happen online that "should happen in person. . . . Friendships get broken. I've had someone ask me out in a text message. I've had someone break up with me online." But Audrey is resigned to such costs and focuses on the bounties of online life.

One of Audrey's current enthusiasms is playing a more 15 social, even flirtatious version of herself in online worlds. "I'd like to be more like I am online," she says. As we've seen, for Audrey, building an online avatar is not so different from writing a social-networking profile. An avatar, she explains, "is a Facebook profile come to life." And avatars and profiles have a lot in common with the everyday experiences of texting and instant messaging. In all of these, as she sees it, the point is to do "a performance of you."

Making an avatar and texting. Pretty much the same. You're creating your own person; you don't have to think of things on the spot really, which a lot of people can't really do. You're creating your own little ideal person and sending it out. Also on the Internet, with sites like MySpace and Facebook, you put up the things you like about yourself, and you're not going to advertise the bad aspects of you.

You're not going to post pictures of how you look every day. You're going to get your makeup on, put on your cute little outfit, you're going to take your picture and post it up as your default, and that's what people are going to expect that you are every day, when really you're making it up for all these people. . . . You can write anything about yourself; these people don't know. You can create who you want to be. You can say what kind of stereotype mold you want to fit in without . . . maybe in real life it won't work for you, you can't pull it off. But you can pull it off on the Internet.

Audrey has her cell phone and its camera with her all day; all day she takes pictures and posts them to Facebook. She boasts that she has far more Facebook photo albums than any of her friends. "I like to feel," she says, "that my life is up there." But, of course, what is up on Facebook is her edited life. Audrey is preoccupied about which photographs to post. Which put her in the best light? Which show her as a "bad" girl in potentially appealing ways? If identity play is the work of adolescence, Audrey is at work all day: "If Facebook were deleted, I'd be deleted. . . . All my memories would probably go along with it. And other people have posted pictures of me. All of that would be lost. If Facebook were undone, I might actually freak out. . . . That is where I am. It's part of your life. It's a second you." It is at this point that Audrey says of a Facebook avatar: "It's your little twin on the Internet."

Since Audrey is constantly reshaping this "twin," she wonders what happens to the elements of her twin that she edits away. "What does Facebook do with pictures you put on and then take off?" She suspects that they stay on the Internet forever, an idea she finds both troubling and comforting. If everything is archived, Audrey worries that she will never be able to escape the Internet twin. That thought is not so nice. But if everything is archived, at least in fantasy, she will never have to give her up. That thought is kind of nice.

On Facebook, Audrey works on the twin, and the twin works on her. She describes her relationship to the site as a "give-and-take." Here's how it works: Audrey tries out a "flirty" style. She receives a good response from Facebook friends, and so she ramps up the flirtatious tone. She tries out "an ironic, witty" tone in her wall posts. The response is not so good, and she retreats. Audrey uses the same kind of tinkering as she experiments with her avatars in virtual worlds. She builds a first version to "put something out there." Then comes months of adjusting, of "seeing the new kinds of people I can hang with" by changing how she represents herself. Change your avatar, change your world.

. . .

Overwhelmed across the Generations

The teenagers I studied were born in the late 1980s and early 1990s. Many were introduced to the Internet through America Online when they were only a little past being toddlers. Their parents, however, came to online life as grown-ups. In this domain, they are a generation that, from the beginning, has been playing catch-up with their children. This pattern continues: the fastest-growing demographic on Facebook is adults from

"Conventional wisdom" is the "standard view." For more on this move, see pp. 23–24.

thirty-five to forty-four.[5] Conventional wisdom stresses how different these adults are from their children—laying out fundamental divides between those who migrated to digital worlds and those who are its "natives." But the migrants and natives share a lot: perhaps above all, the feeling of being overwhelmed. If teenagers, overwhelmed with demands for academic and sexual performance, have come to treat online life as a place to hide and draw some lines, then their parents, claiming exhaustion, strive to exert greater control over what reaches them. And the only way to filter effectively is to keep most communications online and text based.

So, they are always on, always at work, and always on call. 20 I remember the time, not many years ago, when I celebrated Thanksgiving with a friend and her son, a young lawyer, who had just been given a beeper by his firm. At the time, everyone at the table, including him, joked about the idea of his "legal emergencies." By the following year, he couldn't imagine not being in continual contact with the office. There was a time when only physicians had beepers, a "burden" shared in rotation. Now, we have all taken up the burden, reframed as an asset—or as just the way it is.

We are on call for our families as well as our colleagues. On a morning hike in the Berkshires, I fall into step with Hope, forty-seven, a real estate broker from Manhattan. She carries her BlackBerry. Her husband, she says, will probably want to be in touch. And indeed, he calls at thirty-minute intervals. Hope admits, somewhat apologetically, that she is "not fond" of the calls, but she loves her husband, and this is what he needs. She answers her phone religiously until finally a call comes in with spotty reception. "We're out of range, thank goodness," she says, as she disables her phone. "I need a rest."

Increasingly, people feel as though they must have a reason for taking time alone, a reason not to be available for calls. It is poignant that people's thoughts turn to technology when they imagine ways to deal with stresses that they see as having been brought on by technology. They talk of filters and intelligent agents that will handle the messages they don't want to see. Hope and Audrey, though thirty years apart in age, both see texting as the solution to the "problem" of the telephone. And both redefine "stress" in the same way—as pressure that happens in real time. With this in mind, my hiking partner explains that she is trying to "convert" her husband to texting. There will be more messages; he will be able to send more texts than he can place calls. But she will not have to deal with them "as they happen."

Mixed feelings about the drumbeat of electronic communication do not suggest any lack of affection toward those with whom we are in touch. But a stream of messages makes it impossible to find moments of solitude, time when other people are showing us neither dependency nor affection. In solitude we don't reject the world but have the space to think our own thoughts. But if your phone is always with you, seeking solitude can look suspiciously like hiding.

We fill our days with ongoing connection, denying ourselves time to think and dream. Busy to the point of depletion, we make a new Faustian* bargain. It goes something like this: if we are left alone when we make contact, we can handle being together.

. . .

The barrier to making a call is so high that even when people 25 have something important to share, they hold back. Tara, the lawyer who admits to "processing" her friends by dealing with

*__Faustian__ Relating to Faust, a character of German folklore, and used to describe something or someone that is concerned only with present gain and not future consequences.

them on e-mail, tells me a story about a friendship undermined. About four times a year, Tara has dinner with Alice, a classmate from law school. Recently, the two women exchanged multiple e-mails trying to set a date. Finally, after many false starts, they settled on a time and a restaurant. Alice did not come to the dinner with good news. Her sister had died. Though they lived thousands of miles apart, the sisters had spoken once a day. Without her sister, without these calls, Alice feels ungrounded.

At dinner, when Alice told Tara about her sister's death, Tara became upset, close to distraught. She and Alice had been e-mailing for months. Why hadn't Alice told her about this? Alice explained that she had been taken up with her family, with arrangements. And she said, simply, "I didn't think it was something to discuss over e-mail." Herself in need of support, Alice ended up comforting Tara.

As Tara tells me this story, she says that she was ashamed of her reaction. Her focus should have been—and should now be—on Alice's loss, not on her own ranking as a confidant. But she feels defensive as well. She had, after all, "been in touch." She'd e-mailed; she'd made sure that their dinner got arranged. Tara keeps coming back to the thought that if she and Alice had spoken on the telephone to set up their dinner date, she would have learned about her friend's loss. She says, "I would have heard something in her voice. I would have suspected. I could have drawn her out." But for Tara, as for so many, the telephone call is for family. For friends, even dear friends, it is close to being off the menu.

Tara avoids the voice but knows she has lost something. For the young, this is less clear. I talk with Meredith, a junior at Silver Academy who several months before had learned of a friend's death via instant message and had been glad that she didn't have to see or speak to anyone. She says, "It was a day off, so I was at home, and I hadn't seen anyone who lives around me, and then my friend Rosie IM'ed me and told me my friend died. I was shocked and everything, but I was more okay than I would've been if I saw people. I went through the whole thing not seeing anyone and just talking to people online about it, and I was fine. I think it would've been much worse if they'd told me in person."

I ask Meredith to say more. She explains that when bad news came in an instant message, she was able to compose herself. It would have been "terrible," she says, to have received a call. "I didn't have to be upset in front of someone else." Indeed, for a day after hearing the news, Meredith only communicated with friends by instant message. She describes the IMs as frequent but brief: "Just about the fact of it. Conversations like, 'Oh, have you heard?' 'Yeah, I heard.' And that's it." The IMs let her put her emotions at a distance. When she had to face other people at school, she could barely tolerate the rush of feeling: "The second I saw my friends, it got so much worse." Karen and Beatrice, two of Meredith's friends, tell similar stories. Karen learned about the death of her best friend's father in an instant message. She says, "It was easier to learn about it on the computer. It made it easier to hear. I could take it in pieces. I didn't have to look all upset to anyone." Beatrice reflects, "I don't want to hear bad things, but if it is just texted to me, I can stay calm."

These young women prefer to deal with strong feelings from the safe haven of the Net. It gives them an alternative to processing emotions in real time. Under stress, they seek composure above all. But they do not find equanimity. When they meet and lose composure, they find a new way to flee: often they take their phones out to text each other and friends not in the room. I see a vulnerability in this generation, so quick to say, "Please don't call." They keep themselves at a distance from their feelings. They keep themselves from people who could help.

Voices

When I first read how it is through our faces that we call each other up as human beings, I remember thinking I have always felt that way about the human voice. But like many of those I study, I have been complicit with technology in removing many voices from my life.

I had plans for dinner with a colleague, Joyce. On the day before we were to meet, my daughter got admitted to college. I e-mailed Joyce that we would have much to celebrate. She e-mailed back a note of congratulations. She had been through the college admissions process with her children and understood my relief. At dinner, Joyce said that she had thought of calling to congratulate me, but a call had seemed "intrusive." I admitted that I hadn't called her to share my good news for the same reason. Joyce and I both felt constrained by a new etiquette but were also content to follow it. "I feel more in control of my time if I'm not disturbed by calls," Joyce admitted.

Both Joyce and I have gained something we are not happy about wanting. License to feel together when alone, comforted by e-mails, excused from having to attend to people in real time. We did not set out to avoid the voice but end up denying ourselves its pleasures. For the voice can be experienced only in real time, and both of us are so busy that we don't feel we have it to spare.

Apple's visual voicemail for the iPhone was welcomed because it saves you the trouble of having to listen to a message to know who sent it. And now there are applications that automatically transcribe voicemail into text. I interview Maureen, a college freshman, who is thrilled to have discovered one of these programs. She says that only her parents send her voicemail: "I love my parents, but they don't know how to use the phone. It's not the place to leave long voice messages. Too long to listen to. Now, I can scroll through the voicemail as text messages. Great."

Here, in the domain of connectivity, we meet the narrative of better than nothing becoming simply better. People have long wanted to connect with those at a distance. We sent letters, then telegrams, and then the telephone gave us a way to hear their voices. All of these were better than nothing when you couldn't meet face-to-face. Then, short of time, people began to use the phone instead of getting together. By the 1970s, when I first noticed that I was living in a new regime of connectivity, you were never really "away" from your phone because answering machines made you responsible for any call that came in. Then, this machine, originally designed as a way to leave a message if someone was not at home, became a screening device, our end-of-millennium Victorian calling card. Over time, voicemail became an end in itself, not the result of a frustrated telephone call. People began to call purposely when they knew that no one would be home. People learned to let the phone ring and "let the voicemail pick it up."

In a next step, the voice was taken out of voicemail because communicating with text is faster. E-mail gives you more control over your time and emotional exposure. But then, it, too, was not fast enough. With mobile connectivity (think text and Twitter), we can communicate our lives pretty much at the rate we live them. But the system backfires. We express ourselves in staccato texts, but we send out a lot and often to large groups. So we get even more back—so many that the idea of communicating with anything but texts seems too exhausting. Shakespeare might have said, we are "consumed with that which we are nourished by."[6]

I sketched out this narrative to a friend for whom it rang true as a description but seemed incredible all the same. A professor of poetry and a voracious reader, she said, "We cannot all write like Lincoln or Shakespeare, but even the least gifted among us has this incredible instrument, our voice, to communicate the range of human emotion. Why would we deprive ourselves of that?"

The beginning of an answer has become clear: in text messaging and e-mail, you hide as much as you show. You can present yourself as you wish to be "seen." And you can "process" people as quickly as you want to. Listening can only slow you down. A voice recording can be sped up a bit, but it has to unfold in real time. Better to have it transcribed or avoid it altogether. We work so hard to give expressive voices to our robots but are content not to use our own.

Like the letters they replace, e-mail, messaging, texting, and, more recently, Tweeting carry a trace of the voice. When Tara regretted that she had not called her friend Alice—on the phone she would have heard her friend's grief—she expressed the point of view of someone who grew up with the voice and is sorry to have lost touch with it. Hers is a story of trying to rebalance things in a traditional framework. Trey, her law partner, confronts something different, something he cannot rebalance.

My brother found out that his wife is pregnant and he put it on his *blog*. He didn't call me first. I called him when I saw the blog entry. I was mad at him. He didn't see why I was making a big deal. He writes his blog every day, as things happen, that's how he lives. So when they got home from the doctor—bam, right onto the blog. Actually, he said it was part of how he celebrated the news with his wife—to put it on the blog together with a picture of him raising a glass of champagne and she raising a glass of orange juice. Their idea was to celebrate on the blog, almost in real time, with the photos and everything. When I complained they made me feel like such a *girl*. Do you think I'm old-school?[7]

Trey's story is very different from Tara's. Trey's brother was not trying to save time by avoiding the telephone. His brother did not avoid or forget him or show preference to other family members. Blogging is part of his brother's intimate life. It is how he and his wife celebrated the most important milestone in their life as a family. In a very different example of our new genres of online intimacy, a friend of mine underwent a stem cell transplant. I felt honored when invited to join her family's blog. It is set up as a news feed that appears on my computer desktop. Every day, and often several times a day, the family posts medical reports, poems, reflections, and photographs. There are messages from the patient, her husband, her children, and her brother, who donated his stem cells. There is progress and there are setbacks. On the blog, one can follow this family as it lives, suffers, and rejoices for a year of treatment. Inhibitions lift. Family members tell stories that would be harder to share face-to-face. I read every post. I send e-mails. But the presence of the blog changes something in my behavior. I am grateful for every piece of information but feel strangely shy about calling. Would it be an intrusion? I think of Trey. Like him, I am trying to get my bearings in a world where the Net has become a place of intimate enclosure.

NOTES

1. In the object relations tradition of psychoanalysis, an object is that which one relates to. Usually, objects are people, especially a significant person who is the object or target of another's feelings or intentions. A whole object is a person in his or her entirety. It is common in development for people to internalize part objects, representations of others that are not the whole person. Online life provides an environment that makes it easier for people to relate to part objects. This puts relationships at risk. On object relations theory, see, for example, Stephen A. Mitchell and Margaret J. Black, *Freud and Beyond: A History of Modern Psychoanalytic Thought* (New York: Basic Books, 1995).

2. See Stefana Broadbent, "How the Internet Enables Intimacy," Ted.com, www.ted.com/talks/stefana_broadbent_how_the_internet_enables_intimacy .html (accessed August 8, 2010). According to Broadbent, 80 percent of calls on cell phones are made to four people, 80 percent of Skype calls are made to two people, and most Facebook exchanges are with four to six people.

3. This mother is being destructive to her relationship with her daughter. Research shows that people use the phone in ways that surely undermine relationships with adult partners as well. In one striking finding, according to Dan Schulman, CEO of cell operator Virgin Mobile, one in five people will interrupt sex to answer their phone. David Kirkpatrick, "Do You Answer Your Cellphone During Sex?" *Fortune*, August 28, 2006, http://money.cnn.com/2006/08/25/ technology/fastforward_kirpatrick.fortune/index.htm (accessed November 11, 2009).

4. See Amanda Lenhart et al., "Teens and Mobile Phones," The Pew Foundation, April 20, 2010, www.pewinternet.org/Reports/2010/Teens-and -Mobile-Phones.aspx?r=i (accessed August 10, 2010).

5. "Number of US Facebook Users over 35 Nearly Doubles in Last 60 Days," Inside Facebook, March 25, 2009, www.insidefacebook.com/2009/03/25/ number-of-us-facebook-users-over-35-nearly-doubles-in-last-60-days (accessed October 19, 2009).

6. This paraphrases a line from Sonnet 73: "Consum'd with that which it was nourish'd by . . ."

7. The author of a recent blog post titled "I Hate the Phone" would not call Trey old-school, but nor would she want to call him. Anna-Jane Grossman admits to growing up loving her pink princess phone, answering machine, and long, drawn-out conversations with friends she had just seen at school. Now she

hates the phone: "I feel an inexplicable kind of dread when I hear a phone ring, even when the caller ID displays the number of someone I like. . . . My dislike for the phone probably first started to grow when I began using Instant Messenger. Perhaps phone-talking is a skill that one has to practice, and the more IMing I've done, the more my skills have dwindled to the level of a modern day 13-year-old who never has touched a landline. . . . I don't even listen to my [phone] messages any more: They get transcribed automatically and then are sent to me via e-mail or text." The author was introduced to Skype and sees its virtues; she also sees the ways in which it undermines conversation: "It occurs to me that if there's one thing that'll become obsolete because of video-chatting, it's not phones: it's natural flowing conversations with people far away." See Grossman, "I Hate the Phone."

In my experience with Skype, pauses seem long and awkward, and it is an effort not to look bored. Peggy Ornstein makes this point in "The Overextended Family," *New York Times Magazine*, June 25, 2009, ww.nytimes .com/2009/06/28/magazine/28fob-wwln-t.html (accessed October 17, 2009). Ornstein characterizes Skype as providing "too much information," something that derails intimacy: "Suddenly I understood why slumber-party confessions always came after lights were out, why children tend to admit the juicy stuff to the back of your head while you're driving, why psychoanalysts stay out of a patient's sightline."

Joining the Conversation

1. Sherry Turkle was once optimistic about the potential for technology to improve human lives but now takes a more complex view. What does she mean here by the title "No Need to Call"? What pitfalls does she see in our increasing reluctance to talk on the phone or face-to-face?

2. This reading consists mainly of stories about how people communicate on social media, on the phone, and face-to-face. Summarize the story about Audrey (pp. 564–69) in one paragraph.

3. According to Turkle, we "hide as much as [we] show" in text messages and email, presenting ourselves "as [we] wish to be 'seen'" (paragraph 38). Is this so different from what we do in most of our writing? How do you present yourself in your academic writing, and how does that presentation differ from what you do in text messages or email?

4. Go to **theysayiblog.com** and read Tim Adams's interview with Turkle. In what ways have Turkle's views about conversation in a digital age changed, if at all? How have her views stayed the same?

5. Turkle says she sees "a vulnerability" in those who prefer social media to phone calls or face-to-face communication: "I see a vulnerability in this generation, so quick to say, 'Please don't call'" (paragraph 30). Write an essay about your own views on communicating with social media, drawing upon this and other readings in the chapter for ideas to consider, to question, and to support your view.

Does a Protest's Size Matter?

ZEYNEP TUFEKCI

THE WOMEN'S MARCH ON SATURDAY, which took place in cities and towns all across the United States (and around the world), may well have been the largest protest in American history. There were an estimated 3.5 million participants.

This has to mean something, right?

After studying protests over the last two decades, I have to deliver some bad news: In the digital age, the size of a protest is no longer a reliable indicator of a movement's strength. Comparisons to the number of people in previous marches are especially misleading.

A protest does not have power just because many people get together in one place. Rather, a protest has power insofar as it signals the underlying capacity of the forces it represents.

ZEYNEP TUFEKCI is a professor at the School of Information and Library Science at the University of North Carolina who researches the relationship between technology and society. She is also a faculty associate at the Harvard Berkman Klein Center for Internet and Society and author of *Twitter* and *Tear Gas: The Power and Fragility of Networked Protest* (2017). This op-ed piece first appeared in the *New York Times* on January 27, 2017. Follow her on Twitter @zeynep.

Consider an analogy from the natural world: A gazelle will ⁵
sometimes jump high in the air while grazing, apparently to no
end—but it is actually signaling strength. "If I can jump this
high," it communicates to would-be predators, "I can also run
very fast. Don't bother with the chase."

Protesters are saying, in effect, "If we can pull this off, imagine what else we can do."

But it is much easier to pull off a large protest than it used
to be. In the past, a big demonstration required months, if not
years, of preparation. The planning for the March on Washington in August 1963, for example, started nine months earlier,
in December 1962. The march drew a quarter of a million
people, but it represented much more effort, commitment and
preparation than would a protest of similar size today. Without
Facebook, without Twitter, without email, without cellphones,
without crowdfunding, the ability to organize such a march
was a fair proxy for the strength and sophistication of the civil
rights movement.

The Women's March, on the other hand, started with a few Facebook posts and came together in a relatively short amount of time. The organizers no doubt did a lot of work, and the size and the energy of the gathering reflected a remarkable depth of dissent. However, as with all protests today, the march required fewer resources and less time spent on coordination than a comparable protest once did.

See pp. 64–65 for more "yes and no" moves.

This is one reason that recent large protests have had less effect on policy than many were led to expect. I participated in the antiwar protests of February 2003—at that point, likely the largest global protest in history, with events in more than 600 cities. I assumed the United States and its allies could not ignore a protest of that size. But President George W. Bush, dismissing the protesters as a "focus group," indeed proceeded to ignore us, and the Iraq war began soon after. Mr. Bush was right in one way: The protesters failed to transform into an electoral force capable of defeating him in the 2004 election.

In 2011, I attended the global Occupy protests, which were 10 held in about 1,000 cities in more than 80 countries—again, likely the biggest global protest ever, at that point. Thanks in part to digital technology, those protests, too, had been organized in just a few weeks. I was optimistic that I would soon see political and economic changes in response to this large-scale expression of resistance to economic inequality. I was wrong, then, too.

Two enormous protests, two disappointing results. Similar sequences of events have played out in other parts of the world.

This doesn't mean that protests no longer matter—they do. Nowadays, however, protests should be seen not as the culmination of an organizing effort, but as a first, potential step. A large protest today is less like the March on Washington in 1963 and more like Rosa Parks's refusal to move to the back of the bus. What used to be an endpoint is now an initial spark.

More than ever before, the significance of a protest depends on what happens afterward.

Consider the Tea Party protests of 2009, which also brought out hundreds of thousands of people in cities throughout the United States, and which also were organized with the help of digital communication. Like any other protest, including the Women's March, these were symbolic expressions of support, and they also functioned as events where like-minded individuals could find one another. But the Tea Party protesters then got to work on a ferociously focused agenda: identifying and supporting primary candidates to challenge Republicans who did not agree with their demands, keeping close tabs on legislation and pressuring politicians who deviated from a Tea Party platform.

Last Saturday, as I participated in the Women's March in 15 North Carolina, I marveled at the large turnout and the passion of those who marched. But if those protesters are not exchanging contact information and setting up local strategy meetings, their large numbers are unlikely to translate into the kind of effectiveness the Tea Party supporters had after their protests in 2009.

The Tea Party, of course, is not the only model for moving forward. But there is no magic power to marching in the streets that, on its own, leads to any other kind of result.

The march I attended in North Carolina ended with everyone singing along to a song called "Let's Get to Work." For today's protests, more than ever, that's the right message.

Joining the Conversation

1. Identify the primary "they say" and "I say" statements in this essay. Why, according to Zeynep Tufekci, is the number of people participating in a protest no longer a reliable indicator of the strength of a movement?

2. What role, both short-term and long-term, does the author believe social media plays in the development of a protest movement? How does her discussion of the Women's March toward the beginning and at the end of this essay fit into her argument?

3. In pargraph 13, Tufekci states, "more than ever before, the significance of a protest depends on what happens afterward." Why, in your view, does Tufekci then describe the Tea Party protests of 2009?

4. Tufekci focuses on the ability of technology to bring large groups of people together around a cause, but also argues that protests are not enough. How might danah boyd (pp. 255–65) respond to this claim?

5. Write a Facebook post inviting like-minded people to a protest march (devoted to a cause of your choice). In the post, describe your plan for the march and also for follow-up activities to take place after the march.

"Rise of the Machines" Is Not a Likely Future

MICHAEL LITTMAN

Every new technology brings its own nightmare scenarios. Artificial intelligence (AI) and robotics are no exceptions. Indeed, the word "robot" was coined for a 1920 play that dramatized just such a doomsday for humanity.

Recently, an open letter about the future of AI, signed by a number of high-profile scientists and entrepreneurs, spurred a new round of harrowing headlines like "Top Scientists Have an Ominous Warning about Artificial Intelligence," and "Artificial Intelligence Experts Sign Open Letter to Protect Mankind from Machines." The implication is that the machines will one day displace humanity.

Let's get one thing straight: a world in which humans are enslaved or destroyed by superintelligent machines of our

Michael Littman is a professor of computer science at Brown University. He is also codirector of the Humanity Centered Robotics Initiative at Brown, a group dedicated to advancing robotics and studying the impact of these advancements on society. This piece was originally published in *Live Science* on January 28, 2015.

own creation is purely science fiction. Like every other technology, AI has risks and benefits, but we cannot let fear dominate the conversation or guide AI research. Nevertheless, the idea of dramatically changing the AI research agenda to focus on AI "safety" is the primary message of a group calling itself the Future of Life Institute (FLI). FLI includes a handful of deep thinkers and public figures such as Elon Musk and Stephen Hawking and worries about the day in which humanity is steamrolled by powerful programs run amuck.

As eloquently described in the book *Superintelligence: Paths, Dangers, Strategies* by FLI advisory board member and Oxford-based philosopher Nick Bostrom, the plot unfolds in three parts. In the first part—roughly where we are now—computational power and intelligent software develops at an increasing pace through the toil of scientists and engineers. Next, a breakthrough is made: programs are created that possess intelligence on par with humans. These programs, running on increasingly fast computers, improve themselves extremely rapidly, resulting in a runaway "intelligence explosion." In the third and final act, a singular super-intelligence takes hold—outsmarting, outmaneuvering, and ultimately outcompeting the entirety of humanity and perhaps life itself. End scene.

Let's take a closer look at this apocalyptic storyline. Of the three parts, the first is indeed happening now and Bostrom provides cogent and illuminating glimpses into current and near-future technology. The third part is a philosophical romp exploring the consequences of supersmart machines. It's that second part—the intelligence explosion—that demonstrably violates what we know of computer science and natural intelligence.

Runaway Intelligence?

See Chapter 16 for tips on presenting the prevailing theories. The notion of the intelligence explosion arises from Moore's Law, the observation that the speed of computers has been increasing exponentially since the 1950s. Project this trend forward and we'll see computers with the computational power of the entire human race within the next few decades. It's a leap to go from this idea to unchecked growth of machine intelligence, however.

First, ingenuity is not the sole bottleneck to developing faster computers. The machines need to actually be built, which requires real-world resources. Indeed, Moore's law comes with exponentially increasing production costs as well—mass production of precision electronics does not come cheap. Further, there are fundamental physical laws—quantum limits—that bound how quickly a transistor can do its work. Non-silicon technologies may overcome those limits, but such devices remain highly speculative.

In addition to physical laws, we know a lot about the fundamental nature of computation and its limits. For example, some computational puzzles, like figuring out how to factor a number and thereby crack online cryptography schemes, are generally believed to be unsolvable by any fast program. They are part of a class of mathematically defined problems that are "NP-complete," meaning that they are exactly as hard as any problem that can be solved non-deterministically (N) in polynomial time (P), and they have resisted any attempt at scalable solution. As it turns out, most computational problems that we associate with human intelligence are known to be in this class.

See Chapter 6 for tips on anticipating objections. Wait a second, you might say. How does the human mind manage to solve mathematical problems that computer scientists believe can't be solved? We don't. By and large, we cheat. We build a cartoonish mental model of the elements of the world that we're interested in and then probe the behavior of this invented miniworld. There's a trade-off between completeness and tractability in these imagined microcosms. Our ability to propose and ponder and project credible futures comes at the cost of accuracy. Even allowing for the possibility of the existence of considerably faster computers than we have today, it is a logical impossibility that these computers would be able to accurately simulate reality faster than reality itself.

Countering the Anti-AI Cause

In the face of general skepticism in the AI and computer science 10 communities about the possibility of an intelligence explosion, FLI still wants to win support for its cause. The group's letter calls for increased attention to maximizing the societal benefits of developing AI. Many of my esteemed colleagues signed the letter to show their support for the importance of avoiding potential pitfalls of the technology. But a few key phrases in the letter such as "our AI systems must do what we want them to do" (Tegmark) are taken by the press as an admission that AI researchers believe they might be creating something that cannot be controlled. It also implies that AI researchers are asleep at the wheel, oblivious to the ominous possibilities, which is simply untrue.

To be clear, there are indeed concerns about the near-term future of AI—algorithmic traders crashing the economy, or sensitive power grids overreacting to fluctuations and shutting down electricity for large swaths of the population. There's also a concern that systemic biases within academia and industry prevent underrepresented minorities from participating and helping to steer the growth of information technology. These worries should play a central role in the development and deployment of new ideas. But dread predictions of computers suddenly waking up and turning on us are simply not realistic.

I welcome an open discussion about how AI can be made robust and beneficial, and how we can engineer intelligent machines and systems that make society better. But, let's please keep the discussion firmly within the realm of reason and leave the robot uprisings to Hollywood screenwriters.

REFERENCES

Bostrom, Nick. *Superintelligence: Paths, Dangers, Strategies*. Oxford UP, 2014.

Čapek, Karel. *R. U. R.* Translated by David Wyllie, The University of Adelaide, 2014. eBooks@Adelaide, https://ebooks.adelaide.edu.au/c/capek/karel/rur/index.html. Accessed 9 June 2017.

Sparkes, Matthew. "Top Scientists Have an Ominous Warning about Artificial Intelligence." *Business Insider*, 13 Jan. 2015, http://www.businessinsider.com/top-scientists-have-an-ominous-warning-about-artificial-intelligence-2015-1. Accessed 9 June 2017.

Statt, Nick. "Artificial intelligence experts sign open letter to protect mankind from machines." *CNET*, 11 Jan. 2015, https://www.cnet.com/news/artificial-intelligence-experts-sign-open-letter-to-protect-mankind-from-machines/. Accessed 9 June 2017.

Tegmark, Max, et al. "An Open Letter: Research Priorities for Robust and Beneficial Artificial Intelligence." *Future of Life Institute*, 2015, https://futureoflife.org/ai-open-letter. Accessed 9 June 2017.

TWENTY-ONE

WHAT'S GENDER GOT
TO DO WITH IT?

—⌐🔲⌐—

IN THE NEWS, at home, at school, and out with friends, gender is a much-discussed topic. Gender, in the words of Kate Gilles, a policy analyst at the Population Reference Bureau, "is a social construct—that is, a society's assumptions about the way a man or woman should look and behave." Gender roles in our society have changed considerably in recent decades: there are more women in the workforce, many doing jobs once held exclusively or primarily by men, and more men taking an active role in the raising of children, including a growing number of men who choose to stay at home with the children while their partner works outside the home. Moreover, while discrimination still exists, there is increasing acceptance of nonheterosexual relationships—most notably with same-sex marriage now legal in all of the United States—and, in the last few years, of people who choose to change their gender or sex.

No matter one's roles or beliefs, pressure still exists for people, particularly children, to maintain traditional gender roles—for males, playing sports, acting tough, and not showing emotion; for females, emphasizing physical appearance, attracting members of the opposite sex, and not acting "too intelligent."

Journalist Laurie Frankel writes about how her son went from "he to she in first grade," and how her child experienced this transition at home and at school. Stephen Mays, an editor at *U.S. News and World Report*, finds that the same gender stereotypes that exist in society at large are often also present in same-sex relationships, arguing against these limiting stereotypes.

Other writers in the chapter focus on the unique expectations of women, arguing that while women have made substantial progress in the United States, serious obstacles remain. Anne-Marie Slaughter, a former government official and current university dean, observes that women who want to advance in their careers find it difficult to also raise children—and that it's not possible to really "have it all." College president Raynard Kington explains why he still has it easier than working moms even though he is, as he says in the title of his essay, "gay and African American." Kate Crawford, a technology researcher, argues that the dominance of white males in the technology industry has led to a bias against women and minorities.

In response to such critiques, some male writers argue that the situation for men in contemporary American life is, in many ways, just as problematic for women. Journalist, husband, and father Richard Dorment writes about the increasing difficulty men have in balancing work and home life. Educator Andrew Reiner argues that conforming to male stereotypes of toughness and stoicism makes it much harder for men to be "emotionally honest"—with themselves and with others. And economist Nicholas Eberstadt discusses the plight of men who are now unemployed or underemployed due to the decline of industrial production in the United States.

What's Gender Got to Do with It?

Gender is personal, part of one's own developing identity and web of relationships, but it is also political, related to questions of equity, fairness, and civil rights. In reading about some of the discussions taking place around gender, you will have the opportunity to learn more about this topic, formulate your views, and become part of this ongoing conversation.

Why Women Still Can't Have It All

ANNE-MARIE SLAUGHTER

Redefining the Arc of a Successful Career

EIGHTEEN MONTHS INTO MY JOB as the first woman director of policy planning at the State Department, a foreign-policy dream job that traces its origins back to George Kennan, I found myself in New York, at the United Nations' annual assemblage of every foreign minister and head of state in the world. On a Wednesday evening, President and Mrs. Obama hosted a glamorous reception at the American Museum of Natural History. I sipped champagne, greeted foreign dignitaries, and mingled. But I could not stop thinking about my 14-year-old son, who had started eighth grade three weeks earlier and was already resuming what had become his pattern of skipping homework,

ANNE-MARIE SLAUGHTER is the president and CEO of the New America Foundation, "a think tank and civic enterprise committed to renewing American politics, prosperity, and purpose in the digital age." She has taught at Princeton University and Harvard Law School and worked as director of policy planning for the US State Department. She is also the author and editor of several books, most recently *The Chessboard and the Web: Strategies of Connection in a Networked World* (2017). This essay first appeared in the July/August 2012 issue of the *Atlantic*.

disrupting classes, failing math, and tuning out any adult who tried to reach him. Over the summer, we had barely spoken to each other—or, more accurately, he had barely spoken to me. And the previous spring I had received several urgent phone calls—invariably on the day of an important meeting—that required me to take the first train from Washington, D.C., where I worked, back to Princeton, New Jersey, where he lived. My husband, who has always done everything possible to support my career, took care of him and his 12-year-old brother during the week; outside of those midweek emergencies, I came home only on weekends.

As the evening wore on, I ran into a colleague who held a senior position in the White House. She has two sons exactly my sons' ages, but she had chosen to move them from California to D.C. when she got her job, which meant her husband commuted back to California regularly. I told her how difficult I was finding it to be away from my son when he clearly needed me. Then I said, "When this is over, I'm going to write an op-ed titled 'Women Can't Have It All.'"

She was horrified. "You *can't* write that," she said. "You, of all people." What she meant was that such a statement, coming from a high-profile career woman—a role model—would be a terrible signal to younger generations of women. By the end of the evening, she had talked me out of it, but for the remainder of my stint in Washington, I was increasingly aware that the feminist beliefs on which I had built my entire career were shifting under my feet. I had always assumed that if I could get a foreign-policy job in the State Department or the White House while my party was in power, I would stay the course as long as I had the opportunity to do work I loved. But in January 2011, when my two-year public-service leave from Princeton University was up, I hurried home as fast as I could.

A rude epiphany hit me soon after I got there. When people asked why I had left government, I explained that I'd come home not only because of Princeton's rules (after two years of leave, you lose your tenure), but also because of my desire to be with my family and my conclusion that juggling high-level government work with the needs of two teenage boys was not possible. I have not exactly left the ranks of full-time career women: I teach a full course load; write regular print and online columns on foreign policy; give 40 to 50 speeches a year; appear regularly on TV and radio; and am working on a new academic book. But I routinely got reactions from other women my age or older that ranged from disappointed ("It's such a pity that you had to leave Washington") to condescending ("I wouldn't generalize from your experience. *I've* never had to compromise, and my kids turned out great").

The first set of reactions, with the underlying assumption that my choice was somehow sad or unfortunate, was irksome enough. But it was the second set of reactions—those implying that my parenting and/or my commitment to my profession were somehow substandard—that triggered a blind fury. Suddenly, finally, the penny dropped. All my life, I'd been on the other side of this exchange. I'd been the woman smiling the faintly superior smile while another woman told me she had decided to take some time out or pursue a less competitive career track so that she could spend more time with her family. I'd been the woman congratulating herself on her unswerving commitment to the feminist cause, chatting smugly with her dwindling number of college or law-school friends who had reached and maintained their place on the highest rungs of their profession. I'd been the one telling young women at my lectures that you *can* have it all and do it all, regardless of what field you are in. Which means I'd been part, albeit unwittingly, of making millions of women feel that *they* are to blame if they cannot manage to rise up the ladder as fast as men and also have a family and an active home life (and be thin and beautiful to boot).

Last spring, I flew to Oxford to give a public lecture. At the request of a young Rhodes Scholar I know, I'd agreed to talk to the Rhodes community about "work-family balance." I ended up speaking to a group of about 40 men and women in their mid-20s. What poured out of me was a set of very frank reflections on how unexpectedly hard it was to do the kind of job I wanted to do as a high government official and be the kind of parent I wanted to be, at a demanding time for my children (even though my husband, an academic, was willing to take on the lion's share of parenting for the two years I was in Washington). I concluded by saying that my time in office had convinced me that further government service would be very unlikely while my sons were still at home. The audience was rapt, and asked many thoughtful questions. One of the first was from a young woman who began by thanking me for "not giving just one more fatuous 'You can have it all' talk." Just about all of the women in that room planned to combine careers and family in some way. But almost all assumed and accepted that they would have to make compromises that the men in their lives were far less likely to have to make.

The striking gap between the responses I heard from those young women (and others like them) and the responses I heard from my peers and associates prompted me to write this article. Women of my generation have clung to the feminist credo we were raised with, even as our ranks have been steadily thinned by unresolvable tensions between family and career, because we are determined not to drop the flag for the next generation. But when many members of the younger generation have stopped listening, on the

See p. 138 for tips on indicating the importance of a claim.

grounds that glibly repeating "you can have it all" is simply airbrushing reality, it is time to talk.

I still strongly believe that women can "have it all" (and that men can too). I believe that we can "have it all at the same time." But not today, not with the way America's economy and society are currently structured. My experiences over the past three years have forced me to confront a number of uncomfortable facts that need to be widely acknowledged—and quickly changed.

Before my service in government, I'd spent my career in academia: as a law professor and then as the dean of Princeton's Woodrow Wilson School of Public and International Affairs. Both were demanding jobs, but I had the ability to set my own schedule most of the time. I could be with my kids when I needed to be, and still get the work done. I had to travel frequently, but I found I could make up for that with an extended period at home or a family vacation.

I knew that I was lucky in my career choice, but I had 10 no idea how lucky until I spent two years in Washington within a rigid bureaucracy, even with bosses as understanding as Hillary Clinton and her chief of staff, Cheryl Mills. My workweek started at 4:20 on Monday morning, when I got up to get the 5:30 train from Trenton to Washington. It ended late on Friday, with the train home. In between, the days were crammed with meetings, and when the meetings stopped, the writing work began—a never-ending stream of memos, reports, and comments on other people's drafts. For two years, I never left the office early enough to go to any stores other than those open 24 hours, which meant that everything from dry cleaning to hair appointments to Christmas shopping had to be done on weekends, amid children's sporting events, music lessons, family meals, and conference calls. I was entitled to four hours of vacation per pay period, which came to one day of vacation a month. And I had it better than many of my peers in D.C.; Secretary Clinton deliberately came in around 8 a.m. and left around 7 p.m., to allow her close staff to have morning and evening time with their families (although of course she worked earlier and later, from home).

In short, the minute I found myself in a job that is typical for the vast majority of working women (and men), working long hours on someone else's schedule, I could no longer be both the parent and the professional I wanted to be—at least not with a child experiencing a rocky adolescence. I realized what should have perhaps been obvious: having it all, at least for me, depended almost entirely on what type of job I had. The flip side is the harder truth: having it all was not possible in many types of jobs, including high government office—at least not for very long.

I am hardly alone in this realization. Michèle Flournoy stepped down after three years as undersecretary of defense for policy, the third-highest job in the department, to spend more time at home with her three children, two of whom are teenagers. Karen Hughes left her position as the counselor to President George W. Bush after a year and a half in Washington to go home to Texas for the sake of her family. Mary Matalin, who spent two years as an assistant to Bush and the counselor to Vice President Dick Cheney before stepping down to spend more time with her daughters, wrote: "Having control over your schedule is the only way that women who want to have a career and a family can make it work."

Yet the decision to step down from a position of power— to value family over professional advancement, even for a time—is directly at odds with the prevailing social pressures on career professionals in the United States. One phrase says it all about current attitudes toward work and family, particularly among elites. In Washington, "leaving to spend time with your family" is a euphemism for being fired. This understanding is so ingrained that when Flournoy announced her resignation last December, *The New York Times* covered her decision as follows:

> Ms. Flournoy's announcement surprised friends and a number of Pentagon officials, but all said they took her reason for resignation at face value and not as a standard Washington excuse for an official who has in reality been forced out. "I can absolutely and unequivocally state that her decision to step down has nothing to do with anything other than her commitment to her family," said Doug Wilson, a top Pentagon spokesman. "She has loved this job and people here love her."

Think about what this "standard Washington excuse" implies: it is so unthinkable that an official would *actually* step down to spend time with his or her family that this must be a cover for something else. How could anyone voluntarily leave the circles of power for the responsibilities of parenthood? Depending on one's vantage point, it is either ironic or maddening that this view abides in the nation's capital, despite the ritual commitments to "family values" that are part of every political campaign. Regardless, this sentiment makes true work-life balance exceptionally difficult. But it cannot change unless top women speak out.

Only recently have I begun to appreciate the extent to which many young professional women feel under assault by women my age and older. After I gave a recent speech in New York, several women in their late 60s or early 70s came up to tell me how glad and proud they were to see me speaking as a foreign-policy expert. A couple of them went on, however, to contrast my career with the path being traveled by "younger women today." One expressed dismay that many younger women "are just not willing to get out there and do it." Said another, unaware of the circumstances of my recent job change: "They think they have to choose between having a career and having a family."

A similar assumption underlies Facebook Chief Operating 15 Officer Sheryl Sandberg's widely publicized 2011 commencement speech at Barnard, and her earlier TED talk, in which she lamented the dismally small number of women at the top and advised young women not to "leave before you leave." When a woman starts thinking about having children, Sandberg said, "she doesn't raise her hand anymore . . . She starts leaning back." Although couched in terms of encouragement, Sandberg's exhortation contains more than a note of reproach. We who have made it to the top, or are striving to get there, are essentially saying to the women in the generation behind us: "What's the matter with you?"

They have an answer that we don't want to hear. After the speech I gave in New York, I went to dinner with a group of 30-somethings. I sat across from two vibrant women, one of whom worked at the UN and the other at a big New York law firm. As nearly always happens in these situations, they soon began asking me about work-life balance. When I told them I was writing this article, the lawyer said, "I look for role models and can't find any." She said the women in her firm who had become partners and taken on management positions had made tremendous sacrifices, "many of which they don't even seem to realize. . . . They take two years off when their kids are young but then work like crazy to get back on track professionally, which means that they see their kids when they are toddlers but not teenagers, or really barely at all." Her friend nodded, mentioning the top professional women she knew, all of whom essentially relied on round-the-clock nannies. Both were very clear that they did not want that life, but could not figure out how to combine professional success and satisfaction with a real commitment to family.

I realize that I am blessed to have been born in the late 1950s instead of the early 1930s, as my mother was, or the beginning of the 20th century, as my grandmothers were. My mother built a successful and rewarding career as a professional artist largely in the years after my brothers and I left home—and after being told in her 20s that she could not go to medical school, as her father had done and her brother would go on to do, because, of course, she was going to get married. I owe my own freedoms and opportunities to the pioneering generation of women ahead of me—the women now in their 60s, 70s, and 80s who faced overt sexism of a kind I see only when watching *Mad Men*, and who knew that the only way to make it as a woman was to act exactly like a man. To admit to, much less act on, maternal longings would have been fatal to their careers.

But precisely thanks to their progress, a different kind of conversation is now possible. It is time for women in leadership positions to recognize that although we are still blazing trails and breaking ceilings, many of us are also reinforcing a falsehood: that "having it all" is, more than anything, a function of personal determination. As Kerry Rubin and Lia Macko, the authors of *Midlife Crisis at 30*, their cri de coeur for Gen-X and Gen-Y women, put it:

> What we discovered in our research is that while the empowerment part of the equation has been loudly celebrated, there has been very little honest discussion among women of our age about the real barriers and flaws that still exist in the system despite the opportunities we inherited.

I am well aware that the majority of American women face problems far greater than any discussed in this article. I am writing for my demographic—highly educated, well-off women who are privileged enough to have choices in the first place. We may not have choices about whether to do paid work, as dual incomes have become indispensable. But we have choices about the type and tempo of the work we do. We are the women who could be leading, and who should be equally represented in the leadership ranks.

Millions of other working women face much more difficult life 20 circumstances. Some are single mothers; many struggle to find any job; others support husbands who cannot find jobs. Many cope with a work life in which good day care is either unavailable or very expensive; school schedules do not match work schedules; and schools themselves are failing to educate their children. Many of these women are worrying not about having it all, but rather about holding on to what they do have. And although women as a group have made substantial gains in wages, educational attainment, and prestige over the past three decades, the economists Justin Wolfers and Betsey Stevenson have shown that women are less happy today than their predecessors were in 1972, both in absolute terms and relative to men.

The best hope for improving the lot of all women, and for closing what Wolfers and Stevenson call a "new gender gap"— measured by well-being rather than wages—is to close the leadership gap: to elect a woman president and 50 women senators; to ensure that women are equally represented in the ranks of corporate executives and judicial leaders. Only when women wield power in sufficient numbers will we create a society that genuinely works for all women. That will be a society that works for everyone.

. . .

Rediscovering the Pursuit of Happiness

One of the most complicated and surprising parts of my journey out of Washington was coming to grips with what I really
wanted. I had opportunities to stay on, and I could have tried
to work out an arrangement allowing me to spend more time
at home. I might have been able to get my family to join me
in Washington for a year; I might have been able to get classified technology installed at my house the way Jim Steinberg
did; I might have been able to commute only four days a week
instead of five. (While this last change would have still left
me very little time at home, given the intensity of my job,
it might have made the job doable for another year or two.)
But I realized that I didn't just *need* to go home. Deep down,
I *wanted* to go home. I wanted to be able to spend time with
my children in the last few years that they are likely to live
at home, crucial years for their development into responsible,
productive, happy, and caring adults. But also irreplaceable
years for me to enjoy the simple pleasures of parenting—baseball games, piano recitals, waffle breakfasts, family trips, and
goofy rituals. My older son is doing very well these days, but
even when he gives us a hard time, as all teenagers do, being
home to shape his choices and help him make good decisions
is deeply satisfying.

The flip side of my realization is captured in Rubin and
Macko's ruminations on the importance of bringing the different parts of their lives together as 30-year-old women:

> If we didn't start to learn how to integrate our personal, social, and
> professional lives, we were about five years away from morphing
> into the angry woman on the other side of a mahogany desk who
> questions her staff's work ethic after standard 12-hour workdays,
> before heading home to eat moo shoo pork in her lonely apartment.

Women have contributed to the fetish of the one-dimensional life, albeit by necessity. The pioneer generation of feminists walled off their personal lives from their professional personas to ensure that they could never be discriminated against for a lack of commitment to their work. When I was a law student in the 1980s, many women who were then climbing the legal hierarchy in New York firms told me that they never admitted to taking time out for a child's doctor appointment or school performance, but instead invented a much more neutral excuse.

Today, however, women in power can and should change that environment, although change is not easy. When I became dean of the Woodrow Wilson School, in 2002, I decided that one of the advantages of being a woman in power was that I could help change the norms by deliberately talking about my children and my desire to have a balanced life. Thus, I would end faculty meetings at 6 p.m. by saying that I had to go home for dinner; I would also make clear to all student organizations that I would not come to dinner with them, because I needed to be home from six to eight, but that I would often be willing to come back after eight for a meeting. I also once told the Dean's Advisory Committee that the associate dean would chair the next session so I could go to a parent-teacher conference.

After a few months of this, several female assistant professors showed up in my office quite agitated. "You *have* to stop talking about your kids," one said. "You are not showing the gravitas that people expect from a dean, which is particularly damaging precisely because you are the first woman dean of the school." I told them that I was doing it deliberately and continued my practice, but it is interesting that gravitas and parenthood don't seem to go together.

Ten years later, whenever I am introduced at a lecture or other speaking engagement, I insist that the person introducing me mention that I have two sons. It seems odd to me to list degrees, awards, positions, and interests and *not* include the dimension of my life that is most important to me—and takes an enormous amount of my time. As Secretary Clinton once said in a television interview in Beijing when the interviewer asked her about Chelsea's upcoming wedding: "That's my real life." But I notice that my male introducers are typically uncomfortable when I make the request. They frequently say things like "And she particularly wanted me to mention that she has two sons"—thereby drawing attention to the unusual nature of my request, when my entire purpose is to make family references routine and normal in professional life.

This does not mean that you should insist that your colleagues spend time cooing over pictures of your baby or listening to the prodigious accomplishments of your kindergartner. It does mean that if you are late coming in one week, because it is your turn to drive the kids to school, that you be honest about what you are doing. Indeed, Sheryl Sandberg recently acknowledged not only that she leaves work at 5:30 to have dinner with her family, but also that for many years she did not dare make this admission, even though she would of course make up the work time later in the evening. Her willingness to speak out now is a strong step in the right direction.

Seeking out a more balanced life is not a women's issue; balance would be better for us all. Bronnie Ware, an Australian blogger who worked for years in palliative care and is the author of the 2011 book *The Top Five Regrets of the Dying*, writes that the regret she heard most often was "I wish I'd had the courage to live a life true to myself, not the life others expected of me." The second-most-common regret was "I wish I didn't work so hard." She writes: "This came from every male patient that I nursed. They missed their children's youth and their partner's companionship."

Juliette Kayyem, who several years ago left the Department of Homeland Security soon after her husband, David Barron, left a high position in the Justice Department, says their joint decision to leave Washington and return to Boston sprang from their desire to work on the "happiness project," meaning quality time with their three children. (She borrowed the term from her friend Gretchen Rubin, who wrote a best-selling book and now runs a blog with that name.)

It's time to embrace a national happiness project. As a daughter of Charlottesville, Virginia, the home of Thomas Jefferson and the university he founded, I grew up with the Declaration of Independence in my blood. Last I checked, he did not declare American independence in the name of life, liberty, and professional success. Let us rediscover the pursuit of happiness, and let us start at home.

Innovation Nation

As I write this, I can hear the reaction of some readers to many of the proposals in this essay: It's all fine and well for a tenured professor to write about flexible working hours, investment intervals, and family-comes-first management. But what about the real world? Most American women cannot demand these things, particularly in a bad economy, and their employers have little incentive to grant them voluntarily. Indeed, the most frequent reaction I get in putting forth these ideas is that when the choice is whether to hire a man who will work whenever and wherever needed, or a woman who needs more flexibility, choosing the man will add more value to the company.

In fact, while many of these issues are hard to quantify and measure precisely, the statistics seem to tell a different story. A seminal study of 527 U.S. companies, published in the *Academy of Management Journal* in 2000, suggests that "organizations with more extensive work-family policies have higher perceived firm-level performance" among their industry peers. These findings accorded with a 2003 study conducted by Michelle Arthur at the University of New Mexico. Examining 130 announcements of family-friendly policies in *The Wall Street Journal*, Arthur found that the announcements alone significantly improved share prices. In 2011, a study on flexibility in the workplace by Ellen Galinsky, Kelly Sakai, and Tyler Wigton of the Families and Work Institute showed that increased flexibility correlates positively with job engagement, job satisfaction, employee retention, and employee health.

This is only a small sampling from a large and growing literature trying to pin down the relationship between family-friendly policies and economic performance. Other scholars have concluded that good family policies attract better talent, which in turn raises productivity, but that the policies themselves have no impact on productivity. Still others argue that results attributed to these policies are actually a function of good management overall. What is evident, however, is that many firms that recruit and train well-educated professional women are aware that when a woman leaves because of bad work-family balance, they are losing the money and time they invested in her.

Even the legal industry, built around the billable hour, is 35 taking notice. Deborah Epstein Henry, a former big-firm litigator, is now the president of Flex-Time Lawyers, a national consulting firm focused partly on strategies for the retention of female attorneys. In her book *Law and Reorder*, published by the

American Bar Association in 2010, she describes a legal profession "where the billable hour no longer works"; where attorneys, judges, recruiters, and academics all agree that this system of compensation has perverted the industry, leading to brutal work hours, massive inefficiency, and highly inflated costs. The answer—already being deployed in different corners of the industry—is a combination of alternative fee structures, virtual firms, women-owned firms, and the outsourcing of discrete legal jobs to other jurisdictions. Women, and Generation X and Y lawyers more generally, are pushing for these changes on the supply side; clients determined to reduce legal fees and increase flexible service are pulling on the demand side. Slowly, change is happening.

At the core of all this is self-interest. Losing smart and motivated women not only diminishes a company's talent pool; it also reduces the return on its investment in training and mentoring. In trying to address these issues, some firms are finding out that women's ways of working may just be better ways of working, for employees and clients alike.

Experts on creativity and innovation emphasize the value of encouraging nonlinear thinking and cultivating randomness by taking long walks or looking at your environment from unusual angles. In their new book, *A New Culture of Learning: Cultivating the Imagination for a World of Constant Change*, the innovation gurus John Seely Brown and Douglas Thomas write, "We believe that connecting play and imagination may be the single most important step in unleashing the new culture of learning."

Space for play and imagination is exactly what emerges when rigid work schedules and hierarchies loosen up. Skeptics should consider the "California effect." California is the cradle of American innovation—in technology, entertainment, sports, food, and lifestyles. It is also a place where people take leisure as seriously as they take work; where companies like Google deliberately encourage play, with Ping-Pong tables, light sabers, and policies that require employees to spend one day a week working on whatever they wish. Charles Baudelaire wrote: "Genius is nothing more nor less than childhood recovered at will." Google apparently has taken note.

No parent would mistake child care for childhood. Still, seeing the world anew through a child's eyes can be a powerful source of stimulation. When the Nobel laureate Thomas Schelling wrote *The Strategy of Conflict*, a classic text applying game theory to conflicts among nations, he frequently drew on child-rearing for examples of when deterrence might succeed or fail. "It may be easier to articulate the peculiar difficulty of constraining [a ruler] by the use of threats," he wrote, "when one is fresh from a vain attempt at using threats to keep a small child from hurting a dog or a small dog from hurting a child."

The books I've read with my children, the silly movies I've 40 watched, the games I've played, questions I've answered, and people I've met while parenting have broadened my world. Another axiom of the literature on innovation is that the more often people with different perspectives come together, the more likely creative ideas are to emerge. Giving workers the ability to integrate their non-work lives with their work— whether they spend that time mothering or marathoning—will open the door to a much wider range of influences and ideas.

Enlisting Men

Perhaps the most encouraging news of all for achieving the sorts of changes that I have proposed is that men are joining the cause. In commenting on a draft of this article, Martha Minow, the dean of the Harvard Law School, wrote me that one change she has observed during 30 years of teaching law at Harvard is that today many young men are asking questions about how they can manage a work-life balance. And more systematic research on Generation Y confirms that many more men than in the past are asking questions about how they are going to integrate active parenthood with their professional lives.

Abstract aspirations are easier than concrete trade-offs, of course. These young men have not yet faced the question of whether they are prepared to give up that more prestigious clerkship or fellowship, decline a promotion, or delay their professional goals to spend more time with their children and to support their partner's career.

Yet once work practices and work culture begin to evolve, those changes are likely to carry their own momentum. Kara Owen, a British foreign-service officer who worked a London job from Dublin, wrote me in an e-mail:

> I think the culture on flexible working started to change the minute the Board of Management (who were all men at the time) started to work flexibly—quite a few of them started working one day a week from home.

Men have, of course, become much more involved parents over the past couple of decades, and that, too, suggests broad support for big changes in the way we balance work and family. It is noteworthy that both James Steinberg, deputy secretary of state, and William Lynn, deputy secretary of defense, stepped down two years into the Obama administration so that they could spend more time with their children (for real).

Going forward, women would do well to frame work-family 45 balance in terms of the broader social and economic issues that affect both women and men. After all, we have a new generation of young men who have been raised by full-time working mothers. Let us presume, as I do with my sons, that they will understand "supporting their families" to mean more than earning money.

I have been blessed to work with and be mentored by some extraordinary women. Watching Hillary Clinton in action makes me incredibly proud—of her intelligence, expertise, professionalism, charisma, and command of any audience. I get a similar rush when I see a front-page picture of Christine Lagarde, the managing director of the International Monetary Fund, and Angela Merkel, the chancellor of Germany, deep in conversation about some of the most important issues on the world stage; or of Susan Rice, the U.S. ambassador to the United Nations, standing up forcefully for the Syrian people in the Security Council.

These women are extraordinary role models. If I had a daughter, I would encourage her to look to them, and I want a world in which they are extraordinary but not unusual. Yet I also want a world in which, in Lisa Jackson's* words, "to be a strong woman, you don't have to give up on the things that define you as a woman." That means respecting, enabling, and indeed celebrating the full range of women's choices. "Empowering yourself," Jackson said in a speech at Princeton, "doesn't have to mean rejecting motherhood, or eliminating the nurturing or feminine aspects of who you are."

I gave a speech at Vassar last November and arrived in time to wander the campus on a lovely fall afternoon. It is a place infused with a spirit of community and generosity, filled with

---

*Jackson   From 2009 until 2013, Administrator of the United States Environmental Protection Agency.

benches, walkways, public art, and quiet places donated by alumnae seeking to encourage contemplation and connection. Turning the pages of the alumni magazine (Vassar is now coed), I was struck by the entries of older alumnae, who greeted their classmates with *Salve* (Latin for "hello") and wrote witty remembrances sprinkled with literary allusions. Theirs was a world in which women wore their learning lightly; their news is mostly of their children's accomplishments. Many of us look back on that earlier era as a time when it was fine to joke that women went to college to get an "M.R.S." And many women of my generation abandoned the Seven Sisters as soon as the formerly all-male Ivy League universities became coed. I would never return to the world of segregated sexes and rampant discrimination. But now is the time to revisit the assumption that women must rush to adapt to the "man's world" that our mothers and mentors warned us about.

I continually push the young women in my classes to speak more. They must gain the confidence to value their own insights and questions, and to present them readily. My husband agrees, but he actually tries to get the young men in his classes to act more like the women—to speak less and listen more. If women are ever to achieve real equality as leaders, then we have to stop accepting male behavior and male choices as the default and the ideal. We must insist on changing social policies and bending career tracks to accommodate *our* choices, too. We have the power to do it if we decide to, and we have many men standing beside us.

We'll create a better society in the process, for *all* women. 50 We may need to put a woman in the White House before we are able to change the conditions of the women working at Walmart. But when we do, we will stop talking about whether women can have it all. We will properly focus on how we can help all Americans have healthy, happy, productive lives, valuing the people they love as much as the success they seek.

Joining the Conversation

1. According to Anne-Marie Slaughter, women can "'have it all.' . . . But not today, not with the way America's economy and society are currently structured" (paragraph 8). Summarize her "I say," noting the reasons and evidence she gives to support her claims.

2. In paragraph 19, Slaughter entertains a possible objection to her argument, saying that she is "well aware that a majority of American women face problems far greater than any discussed in this article." How does she answer this objection?

3. This essay consists of four sections: Redefining the Arc of a Successful Career, Rediscovering the Pursuit of Happiness, Innovation Nation, and Enlisting Men. Summarize each section in a sentence or two. Put yourself in Slaughter's shoes; your summary should be true to what she says. (See pp. 31–33 for guidance in writing this kind of summary.)

4. Slaughter claims that most young men today have not yet had to decide between accepting a promotion or other professional opportunity and delaying their own goals "to spend more time with their children and to support their partner's career" (paragraph 42). What would Richard Dorment (pp. 617–37) say to that?

5. Write a paragraph stating your own thoughts and perceptions on mixing family and career. Given Slaughter's arguments, how do you think she'd respond to what you say?

Why Men Still Can't Have It All

RICHARD DORMENT

───⌐回⌐───

Lately, the raging debate about issues of "work-life balance" has focused on whether or not women can "have it all." Entirely lost in this debate is the growing strain of work-life balance on men, who today are feeling the competing demands of work and home as much or more than women. And the truth is as shocking as it is obvious: No one can have it all. Any questions?

THE BABY HAS A HEARTBEAT. The ultrasound shows ten fuzzy fingers and ten fuzzy toes and a tiny crescent-moon mouth that will soon let out the first of many wails. We have chosen not to find out the gender, and when the question comes, as it does every day, we say we have no preference. Ten fingers, ten toes. A wail in the delivery room would be nice. But in private, just us, we talk. About the pros and cons of boys versus girls, and about whether it would be better, more advantageous, to

───────

RICHARD DORMENT is a senior editor at *Wired* magazine. He was a senior editor at *Esquire* magazine and has been a guest on television and radio programs including the *Today Show, CNN Newsroom, Here and Now,* and *Upfront and Straightforward.* This essay first appeared in the June/July 2013 issue of *Esquire.*

be born a boy or a girl right now. It's a toss-up, or maybe just a draw—impossible to say that a boy *or* a girl born in America in 2013 has any conspicuous advantages because of his or her gender.

Consider the facts: Nearly 60 percent of the bachelor's degrees in this country today go to women. Same number for graduate degrees. There are about as many women in the workforce as men, and according to Hanna Rosin's 2012 book, *The End of Men*, of the fifteen professions projected to grow the fastest over the coming years, twelve are currently dominated by women. Per a 2010 study by James Chung of Reach Advisors, unmarried childless women under thirty and with full-time jobs earn 8 percent more than their male peers in 147 out of 150 of the largest U. S. cities. The accomplishments that underlie those numbers are real and world-historic, and through the grueling work of generations of women, men and women are as equal as they have ever been. Adding to that the greater male predisposition to ADHD, alcoholism, and drug abuse, women have nothing but momentum coming out of young adulthood— the big mo!—and then . . .

Well, what exactly? Why don't women hold more than 15 percent of *Fortune* 500 executive-officer positions in America? Why are they stalled below 20 percent of Congress? Why does the average woman earn only seventy-seven pennies for every dollar made by the average man? Childbirth plays a role, knocking ambitious women off their professional stride for months (if not years) at a time while their male peers go chug-chug-chugging along, but then why do some women still make it to the top while others fall by the wayside? Institutional sexism and pay discrimination are still ugly realities, but with the millions in annual penalties levied on offending businesses . . . they have become increasingly, and thankfully, uncommon.

College majors count (women still dominate education, men engineering), as do career choices, yet none of these on their own explains why the opportunity gap between the sexes has all but closed yet a stark achievement gap persists.

For a fuller explanation, the national conversation of late has settled on a single issue—work-life balance—with two voices in particular dominating: The first belongs to former State Department policy chief Anne-Marie Slaughter, whose essay "Why Women Still Can't Have It All" was the most widely read story ever on the *Atlantic*'s web site and landed her a book deal and spots on *Today* and *Colbert*. Slaughter's twelve-thousand-word story relies on personal anecdotes mixed with wonk talk: "I still strongly believe that women can 'have it all' (and that men can too). I believe that we can 'have it all at the same time.' But not today, not with the way America's economy and society are currently structured." The scarcity of female leaders to effect public and corporate change on behalf of women; the inflexibility of the traditional workday; the prevalence of what she calls "'time macho'—a relentless competition to work harder, stay later, pull more all-nighters, travel around the world and bill the extra hours that the international date line affords you." All these factors conspire to deprive women of "it all." (The "it" in question being like Potter Stewart's definition of pornography: You know it when you have it.)

The second, and altogether more grown-up, voice belongs 5 to Facebook COO Sheryl Sandberg, whose "sort of feminist" manifesto *Lean In* urges women to command a seat at any table of their choosing. Like Slaughter, Sandberg references the usual systemic challenges, but what it really boils down to, Sandberg argues, is what Aretha Franklin and Annie Lennox prescribed back in the eighties: Sisters Doin' It for Themselves. Sandberg encourages women to negotiate harder, be more assertive, and forget about being liked and concentrate instead on letting 'er rip. She believes that women can, and should, determine the pace and scope of their own careers, and for her audacity in assigning some agency to the women of America, her critics (Slaughter among them) say she blames women for their failure to rise farther, faster, rather than the real culprits: society, corporations, and men (which is to say: men, men, and men). Commenting on the *Lean In* debate in a blog for *The New York Times*, Gail Collins asked, "How do you give smart, accomplished, ambitious women the same opportunities as men to reach their goals? What about universal preschool and after-school programs? What about changing the corporate mind-set about the time commitment it takes to move up the ladder? What about having more husbands step up and take the major load?"

Her questions echo a 2010 *Newsweek* cover story, "Men's Lib," which ended with an upper: "If men embraced parental leave, women would be spared the stigma of the 'mommy track'—and the professional penalties (like lower pay) that come along with it. If men were involved fathers, more kids might stay in school, steer clear of crime, and avoid poverty as adults. And if the country achieved gender parity in the workplace—an optimal balance of fully employed men and women—the gross domestic product would grow by as much as 9 percent. . . . Ultimately, [it] boils down to a simple principle: in a changing world, men should do whatever it takes to contribute their fair share at home and at work."

Two men wrote that, incidentally, which must make it true, and among those who traffic in gender studies, it is something of a truth universally acknowledged: Men are to blame for pretty much everything. And I freely admit, we do make for a compelling target. Men have oppressed their wives and sisters and daughters for pretty much all of recorded history, and now women are supposed to trust us to share everything 50-50?

Allow me to paint another picture. One in which women are asked to make the same personal sacrifices as men past and present—too much time away from home, too many weekends at the computer, too much inconvenient travel—but then claim some special privilege in their hardship. One in which universal pre-school and after-school programs would be a boon to all parents (and not, as Collins suggests, simply to women). In which men spend more time with their children, and are more involved with their home lives, than ever before. In which men work just as hard at their jobs, if not harder, than ever before. In which men now report higher rates of work-life stress than women do. In which men are tormented by the lyrics of "Cat's in the Cradle." In which men are being told, in newspapers and books, on web sites and TV shows, that they are the problem, that they need to help out, when, honestly folks, they're doing the best they can. In which men like me, and possibly you, open their eyes in the morning and want it all—*everything!*—only to close their eyes at night knowing that only a fool could ever expect such a thing.

My wife makes more money than I do. We majored in the same thing at the same college at the same time, and when I chose to go into journalism, she chose to go to law school. She works longer hours, shoulders weightier responsibilities, and faces greater (or at least more reliable) prospects for long-term success, all of which are direct results of choices that we made in our early twenties. She does more of the heavy lifting with our young son than I do, but I do as much as I can. (Someone else watches him while we are at work.) I do a lot of cooking and cleaning around our house. So does she. I don't keep score (and she says she doesn't), and it's hard to imagine how our life would work if we weren't both giving every day our all.

According to a study released in March by the Pew Research 10 Center, household setups like ours are increasingly the norm: 60 percent of two-parent homes with kids under the age of eighteen are made up of dual-earning couples (i.e., two working parents). On any given week in such a home, women put in more time than men doing housework (sixteen hours to nine) and more time with child care (twelve to seven). These statistics provoke outrage among the "fair share" crowd, and there is a sense, even among the most privileged women, that they are getting a raw deal. (In April, Michelle Obama referred to herself as a "single mother" before clarifying: "I shouldn't say single— as a busy mother, sometimes, you know, when you've got a husband who is president, it can feel a little single." Because really: The president should spend more time making sure the First Lady feels supported.)

But the complete picture reveals a more complex and equitable reality.

Men in dual-income couples work outside the home eleven more hours a week than their working wives or partners do (forty-two to thirty-one), and when you look at the total weekly workload, including paid work outside the home and unpaid work inside the home, men and women are putting in roughly the same number of hours: fifty-eight hours for men and fifty-nine for women.

How you view those numbers depends in large part on your definition of work, but it's not quite as easy as saying men aren't pulling their weight around the house. (Spending eleven fewer hours at home and with the kids doesn't mean working dads are freeloaders any more than spending eleven fewer hours at work makes working moms slackers.) These are practical accommodations that reflect real-time conditions on the ground, and rather than castigate men, one might consider whether those extra hours on the job provide the financial cover the family needs so that women can spend more time with the kids.

Also, according to women in the Pew study, it seems to be working out well. Working mothers in dual-earning couples are more likely to say they're very or pretty happy with life right now than their male partners are (93 percent to 87 percent); if anything, it's men who are twice as likely to say they're unhappy. (Pew supplied *Esquire* with data specific to dual-income couples that is not part of its published report. There is plenty of data relating to other household arrangements—working father and stay-at-home mom; working mother and stay-at-home dad; same-sex households—but since the focus of Slaughter, Sandberg, et al. is on the struggles of working mothers, and most working mothers are coupled with working fathers, the dual-income data set seems most relevant to examine here.)

Ellen Galinsky has been studying the American workplace 15 for more than thirty years. A married mother of two grown kids with a background in child education and zero tolerance for bullshit, she cofounded the Families and Work Institute in part to chart how the influx of women in American offices and factories would affect family dynamics. "In 1977," she says, "there was a Department of Labor study that asked people, 'How much interference do you feel between your work and your family life?' and men's work-family conflict was a lot lower than women's." She saw the numbers begin to shift in the late 1990s, and "by 2008, 60 percent of fathers in dual-earning couples were experiencing some or a lot of conflict compared to about 47 percent of women. I would go into meetings with business leaders and report the fact that men's work-family conflict was higher than women's, and people in the room—who were so used to being worried about women's advancement—couldn't believe it."

What they couldn't believe was decades of conventional wisdom—men secure and confident in the workplace, women somewhat less so—crumbling away as more and more fathers began to invest more of their time and energy into their home lives. Though they still lag behind women in hours clocked at the kitchen sink, men do more than twice as much cooking and cleaning as they did fifty years ago, which probably comes as a shock to older women who would famously come home from work to a "second shift" of housework. In reporting her book, *Big Girls Don't Cry*, a study of women's roles in the 2008 election, Rebecca Traister interviewed dozens of high-achieving women who were in the thick of second-wave feminism and encountered the generation gap for herself. "I remember one day, right before Thanksgiving, a woman who had grown children said something like 'I would love to keep talking to you but

I have to start my two-day slog to Thanksgiving.' And I said very lightly, 'Oh, my husband does the cooking in our house.' This woman then got very serious, as if she had never heard of such a thing. For people [in their thirties], isn't it totally normal for guys to do a lot of cooking? In fact it's one of the things about today—dudes love food, right? But it was so foreign to her."

In speaking with a variety of men for this article, I found that most men say they share responsibilities as much as circumstances allow. One of the men who spoke with me, Dave from Atherton, California, runs a successful business, and both he and his wife (a fellow technology executive) say that they split their family duties 50-50. "We have a Google calendar that we share so that everyone is on the same page, and on the weekend, we plan out our week: who's doing what, who's driving the kids which day, what dinner looks like each night during the week."

Yet Dave still considers himself an anomaly. "There is still this expectation that women are going to do the majority of the housework, and deal with schools and stuff, while men can just make it home for dinner and show up at sporting events and be like, 'Wow, I'm being a great father.' It is a real issue, and it is something you really have to work at. You have to try and make sure that you're doing the other stuff around the house in a way that's fair and equal."

He makes a valid point, and in trying to figure out why men don't do more around the house, we could discuss any number of factors—men generally spend more time at work, out of the home, than women do, so they don't have as much time for chores; women are inherently more fastidious; men are lazy and/or have a higher threshold for living in filth—but the most compelling argument comes from writer Jessica Grose in *The New Republic*. "Women are more driven to keep a clean house because they know they—before their male partners—will be judged for having a dirty one." Rather than confront or ignore paternalistic expectations, some women seem willing to cede to them, and this whiff of put-upon-ness recalls something Slaughter acknowledged in an online chat with readers following her article's publication: "SO MUCH OF THIS IS ABOUT WHAT WE FEEL, or rather WHAT WE ARE MADE TO FEEL by the reactions of those around us." Between the all-caps (hers) and the sentiments expressed, this writing wouldn't be out of place on a teenage blog, and as anyone who's ever argued with a teenager knows, it's hard to reason with feelings.

However, I will try. The *validation of one's feelings* is the lan- 20 guage of therapy, which is to say that it is how we all talk now. This is not to denigrate the language or the feelings; it is only to say that to use one's feelings as evidence of an injury is no way to advance a serious cause. And to imply that one has been *made* to feel any way at all— well, no grown man has ever won that argument before.

See p. 137 for ways to ward off potential misunderstandings.

A final point about housework: It is not always as simple as men volunteering to do what needs to be done. To give a small, vaguely pitiful example from my own life: We share laundry duty in my house, and yet whenever I'm through folding a pile of clothes, my wife will then refold everything, quietly and without comment. This used to annoy me—why do I even bother? or, conversely, Is this the Army?—but now it mostly amuses me. When I press her on it, she tells me that I'm doing it wrong, and this too used to annoy me, until I realized that it wasn't really about me. "If I've talked to one group of people about this, I've talked to hundreds," says Galinsky. "Women will say 'Support me more,' and men will say 'But you're telling me I'm doing it wrong.' I wouldn't say it's biological, because I'm not a biologist, but it feels biological to me in that it's very hard to let someone else do something different, because it might mean that the way you're doing it isn't right." When I asked Galinsky if this could explain why a wife would refold a pile of laundry that her husband had just done a perfectly good job folding, she laughed. "Exactly."

What you're about to read is a passage from "Why Women Still Can't Have It All," and though it's long and windy, I feel the need to quote from as much of it as possible. You will understand why:

> The proposition that women can have high-powered careers as long as their husbands or partners are willing to share the parenting load equally (or disproportionately) assumes that most women will *feel* as comfortable as men do about being away from their children, as long as their partner is home with them. . . . From years of conversations and observations . . . I've come to believe that men and women respond quite differently when problems at home force them to recognize that their absence is hurting a child, or at least that their presence would likely help. I do not believe fathers love their children any less than mothers do, but men do seem more likely to choose their job at a cost to their family, while women seem more likely to choose their family at a cost to their job.

(Dr. Slaughter, you had me at "I do not believe fathers love their children any less than mothers do. . . .")

Since Slaughter doesn't provide any evidence to support her claim, it's impossible to say whether the men she's referring to are the sole breadwinners in the family (meaning: the ones who feel the intense weight and pressure of being what one writer described as "one job away from poverty") or are in two-income households, or what, but it's worth keeping in mind that this comes from a person whose husband, by her own admission, sacrificed much in his own academic career to do the heavy lifting with their children, all so she could pursue her dream job and then complain about it, bitterly, in the pages of a national magazine.

The trouble with probing men's and women's emotional relationships with their children is that the subject is fraught with stereotypes and prone to specious generalities (see above), but here goes: In my own experience as both son and father, I've learned that one parent's relationship with a child (and vice versa) isn't inherently richer or deeper than the other parent's. It's just different, and with more and more fathers spending more and more time with their kids today—nearly three times as much as they did in 1965—that has become more true than ever. "There is a dramatic cultural shift among millennial and Gen X-ers in wanting to be involved fathers," says Galinsky. "And I don't just think it's just women who are telling men they need to share. Men want a different relationship with their children than men have had in the past. . . . They don't want to be stick figures in their children's lives. They don't want it on their tombstone how many hours they billed. That 'Cat's Cradle' song is very much alive and well in the male psyche."

"Men are being judged as fathers now in a way that I think 25 they never have been before," says Traister, and just as women are historically new to the workplace, men are new to the carpool and negotiating these fresh expectations (their own and others') as they go along. Not only do working fathers from dual-income homes spend just as much time at work as their fathers and grandfathers did (all while putting in many, many more hours with kids and chores), they also spend more time at work than non-fathers. Seven hours more a week, according to Pew, a trend that Galinsky has noticed in her own research and that she attributes to the unshakable, if often illusory, sense of being the breadwinner. "There are these expectations, even among men whose wives bring in 45 percent of family income, that they were still responsible for the family."

There is the matter of guilt and whether women find it harder than men to be away from their children—which, if that's the case, would mean that women looking to advance in the workplace would have heavier emotional baggage than their male peers. Any husband who's watched his wife cry before taking a business trip (and wondering—silently, I hope—to himself, why?) will tell you that men and women have different ways of experiencing and expressing ambivalence, frustration, and, yes, guilt. "I have no idea if it's societal or genetic or whatever," says Dave, the California businessman, "but it's certainly real that I think my wife feels more guilty than I do when she's gone from the kids. There's no question." I can't claim to speak for Men Everywhere, but in the interviews I conducted for this article, nearly every subject admitted to missing his kids on late nights at the office or aching for home while on a business trip, yet they couch any guilt or regret in the context of sacrifice. Chalk this up to social conditioning (men are raised to be the providers, so it's easier for them to be absent) or genetic predisposition (men are not naturally nurturing) or emotional shallowness (men aren't as in touch with their feelings), but there is the sense, down to the man, that missing their kids is the price of doing business.

And so we all do the best we can. Dave and his wife make weekends sacrosanct and family dinners a priority. "My wife famously said she leaves her office at 5:30 so we can be home at 6:00 for dinner, and I do the same thing, though we're both back online doing work after the kids go to bed."

(Dave's last name, by the way, is Goldberg, and his wife is Sheryl Sandberg, and thanks to *Lean In*, she is famous. Goldberg is the CEO of a company named SurveyMonkey, which provides interactive survey tools for the masses, and he helped build it from a twelve-person operation to a staff of more than two hundred and a $1.35 billion valuation. All while splitting parenting responsibilities 50-50 with a really busy wife. They have the means, certainly, but more importantly, the will.)

Speaking of: In her commencement speech for Harvard Business School in 2012, Sandberg addressed an issue that comes up often—men need to do more to support women in the workplace. "It falls upon the men who are graduating today just as much or more than the women not just to talk about gender but to help these women succeed. When they hear a woman is really great at her job but not liked, take a deep breath and ask why. We need to start talking openly about the flexibility all of us need to have both a job and a life."

Among the various ways men can help women, paternity 30 leave is sometimes mentioned as a good place to start, the idea being that if more men took a few weeks off following the birth of a child, they would help remove the professional stigma surrounding maternity leave and level the playing field. Anyone who has watched any woman, much less one with a full-time job, endure third-term pregnancy, delivery, and the long, lonely nights of postpartum life would tell you how necessary a national paid maternity-leave policy is. Expectant and new mothers are put through the physical and emotional wringer, and they need that time to heal without worrying about losing their job or paying the bills. There are really no two ways about it.

Dads, however, are a different and more complicated story. In California, the first state to fund up to six weeks of paid leave for new moms and dads, only 29 percent of those who take it are men, and there have been numerous studies lately exploring why more men aren't taking greater advantage of the ability to stay home. The general consensus is reflected in a paper out of Rutgers University: "Women who ask for family leave are behaving in a more gender normative way, compared with men who request a family leave. . . . Because the concept of work-life balance is strongly gendered, men who request a family leave may also suffer a *femininity stigma*, whereby 'acting like a woman' deprives them of masculine agency (e.g., competence and assertiveness) and impugns them with negative feminine qualities (e.g., weakness and uncertainty)." This is some paleolithic thinking here, starting, for instance, with the idea that "acting like a woman" means anything at all, much less weakness and uncertainty.

I'm lucky enough to work for a company that provides paid paternity leave, but a few days after my son was born, I was back in the office. It's not because I was scared about appearing weak to my mostly male coworkers or employers, and it's not because I was any more wary of losing my job than usual. At work, I had a purpose—things needed to be done, people needed me to do them. At home, watching my wife feed and swaddle our son and then retreat to our bed to get some sleep of her own, I learned what many first-time fathers learn: assuming an absence of any health issues related to child or mother, the first six weeks of a child's life are fairly uneventful for men. A baby eats (with about 80 percent of women today choosing to breast-feed); he poops; he sleeps. There is potential for valuable bonding time, and a new mother could almost certainly use another pair of hands, but a man's presence is not strictly necessary. Baby book after baby book warns parents that new fathers typically feel "left out," and there's a reason for that: because they are typically left out. More and more companies offer paid and unpaid paternity leave, and a man should feel proud to exercise that option if that's what is best for him and his family. Maybe with the next baby I will. Maybe I won't. But when the doctor delivers a newborn to my exhausted, elated wife, I won't kid myself thinking that I, of all people, really deserve a little time off.

In her Harvard speech, Sandberg also evoked the specter of good old-fashioned sexism by claiming that ambitious, assertive women are generally less well liked than ambitious, assertive men. (In her book, she cites a now famous study conducted by a team of Columbia and NYU professors in which two groups were asked to assess two hard-charging executives, a man named Howard and a woman named Heidi, who were identical in every way except their names. Howard was considered the Man. Heidi, the Shrew.) It's a compelling and convincing study, and Sandberg is persuasive when she argues that too many women too often get an eye roll when they open their mouths. Two things I would hasten to add, though. One: Productivity, profitability, drive, and talent trump all. (I'm reminded of Tina Fey's defense of Hillary Clinton in 2008: "She is [a bitch]. So am I. . . . Bitches get stuff done.") Women might suspect that men don't like assertive, confrontational women, which is only half the truth, leading to my next point: that nobody wants to work with a nightmare of either gender. While the Howard-Heidi problem suggests that some men may get a longer leash than some women, the workplace is not every man's for the shitting all over.

"Advertising is a very small world and when you do something like malign the reputation of a girl from the steno pool on her first day, you make it even smaller. Keep it up, and even if you do get my job, you'll never run this place. You'll die in that corner office, a midlevel executive with a little bit of hair who women go home with out of pity. Want to know why? 'Cause no one will like you." Don Draper said that. Not me. And the wisdom he drops on Pete Campbell in the pilot of *Mad Men* shows that men can be just as vulnerable to office politics as women.

Finally, there is the issue of flex time, with some suggesting 35 that men should demand more options for when and where they can do their work so that women alone aren't penalized for requesting it. It has never been easier to work remotely for many professionals, yet many jobs—and in particular the top jobs, the leadership roles that history (men) has deprived women of in the past—don't have much give to them. Marissa Mayer at Yahoo was dragged into the flex-time debate when she decided that in order to save a struggling business with abysmal morale, she would do away with the company's generous work-from-home policy and require her employees to show up to an office. She was immediately painted as elitist and antiwoman, and it's easy to see why. Even though men and women are equally likely to telecommute, they typically don't place the same value on being able to do so. According to the Pew study, 70 percent of working mothers say a flexible schedule is extremely important to them, compared with just 48 percent of working fathers, and for many of those women (including my wife, who often works well past midnight at a crowded desk in our bedroom), the opportunity to do some work from home is the critical difference between a life that works and one that doesn't. That's what Mayer was messing with when she ordered all hands on deck, and it's what any employer faces when trying to balance family-friendly policies with the sometimes soul-destroying demands of a competitive marketplace.

When Barack Obama entered the White House, he talked about how he wanted his administration to be family-friendly, offering up Sasha and Malia's swing set to staffers so they could bring their own kids to work on the weekends. Rahm Emanuel famously assured him that it would be—"family-friendly to your family."

It was classic Obama—well-meaning, forward-thinking, mindful of the struggles of the common man—undermined by classic Emanuel, which is to say reality. The White House staff would be working at the highest levels of government, investing their love and labor into what can only be described as dream jobs at a time that can only be described as a national nightmare, and if that meant kids and partners had to take the backseat for a year or two, so be it. Man, woman, whoever: Get a shovel and start digging.

Slaughter, a tenured professor at Princeton, came on board as Hillary Clinton's head of policy planning at State, and in her *Atlantic* piece, she describes her grueling workweek in D.C., her weekend commute back to New Jersey, and her ultimate conclusion that "juggling high-level government work with the needs of two teenage boys was not possible." She talked about her struggles to a fellow wonk, Jolynn Shoemaker of Women in International Security, and Shoemaker offered her two cents on high-level foreign-policy positions: "Inflexible schedules, unrelenting travel, and constant pressure to be in the office are common features of these jobs." Slaughter acknowledges that it needn't be as difficult as all that: "Deputy Secretary of State James Steinberg, who shares the parenting of his two young daughters equally with his wife, made getting [secured access to confidential material] at home an immediate priority so that he could leave the office at a reasonable hour and participate in important meetings via videoconferencing if necessary. I wonder how many women in similar positions would be afraid to ask, lest they be seen as insufficiently committed to their jobs."

Slaughter makes an important point here, though probably not the one she intended to make. Steinberg did what he had to do to make a difficult situation work better for him; Slaughter's contention that a woman wouldn't feel as comfortable making the same request may or may not be true, but it doesn't matter. The option was apparently on the table. Fight for it, don't fight for it—it's entirely up to the individual. But don't complain that you never had a choice.

In the end, isn't this what feminism was supposed to be 40 about? Not equality for equality's sake—half of all homes run by men, half of all corporations run by women—but to give each of us, men and women, access to the same array of choices and then the ability to choose for ourselves? And who's to say, whether for reasons biological or sociological, men and women would even want that? When the Pew Research Center asked working mothers and fathers to picture their ideal working situation, 37 percent of women would opt for full time; 50 percent part time; and 11 percent wouldn't have a job at all. (Compare this with men's answers: 75 percent say full time, 15 percent say part time, and 10 percent wouldn't work at all.) Assuming that women had all the flexibility in the world, one of every two working mothers would choose to work part time. Perhaps with guaranteed paid maternity leave, universal daycare, and generous after-school programs, more women would be freed from the constraints of child care and would want to work full time. Or, possibly, they're just happy working part time, one foot in the workplace and one foot in the home. Hard to say.

"I can't stand the kind of paralysis that some people fall into because they're not happy with the choices they've made. You live in a time when there are endless choices. . . . Money certainly helps, and having that kind of financial privilege goes a long way, but you don't even have to have money for it. But you have to work on yourself. . . . Do something!"

Hillary Clinton said that. Not me. And while she wasn't referring to Slaughter in her interview with *Marie Claire*, she offers valuable advice to anyone who's looking to blame someone, or something, for the challenges they face in life. Getting ahead in the workplace is really hard. Getting to the top is really, really hard. And unless you are very fortunate indeed, there will always be somebody smarter, faster, tougher, and ready and willing to take a job if you're not up to the task. It's a grown-up truth, and it bites the big one, but for anyone to pretend otherwise ignores (or simply wishes away) what generations of working men learned the hard way while their wives did the backbreaking work of raising kids and keeping house. Hearing Gail Collins grumble about changing the corporate mind-set (as if competition weren't the soul of capitalism, and capitalism weren't the coin of the realm) or reading Slaughter complain that our society values hard work over family (as if a Puritan work ethic weren't in our national DNA) makes me feel like channeling Tom Hanks in *A League of Their Own*: There's no crying in baseball! If you don't want a high-pressure, high-power, high-paying job that forces you to make unacceptable sacrifices in the rest of your life, don't take the job. Or get another job that doesn't require those sacrifices. And if you can't get another job, take comfort knowing that the guy who sits across from you, the one with kids the same age as yours and a partner who's busting his or her ass to make it work, is probably in the very same boat. We are all equals here.

Then again, I would say that. I'm a man, with a working wife and a busy schedule and a little boy and another baby on the way, and I live with the choices that I've made. That is all I've ever asked for, and it is all I will ever need.

Joining the Conversation

1. Why, in Richard Dorment's view, can men still not "have it all"? What in particular does he mean by "it all," and what evidence does he provide to support his position?

2. This article is a response to Anne-Marie Slaughter's "Why Women Still Can't Have It All" (pp. 596–616), and Dorment summarizes and quotes from that piece extensively. How fairly do you think he represents Slaughter's views? Cite specific examples from his article in your answer.

3. Dorment published this article in *Esquire*, which calls itself "the magazine for men." How can you tell that he has written his article primarily for a male audience? How might he revise the article, keeping the same basic argument, to appeal to an audience of women?

4. Imagine you have a chance to speak with Dorment about this article. Write out what you'd say, remembering to frame your statement as a response to what he has said. (See Chapter 12 for advice on entering class discussions.)

5. Dorment's writing is quite informal—colorful and in places even irreverent. How does this informality suit his audience and purpose? How does it affect your response? Choose a paragraph in his article and dress it up, rewriting it in more formal, academic language. Which version do you find more appealing, and why?

I'm Gay and African American.
As a Dad, I Still Have It Easier Than
Working Moms.

RAYNARD KINGTON

———□———

WHEN MY SELECTION as the 13th president of Grinnell College was announced at a gathering on campus in February, 2010, my older son, then age 4, was sitting in the first row of the packed college chapel with my spouse. A few minutes into my comments, he stood up, wandered over to the edge of the stage, and interrupted me in a loud voice, asking, "Daddy, can I come up with you?"

After an initial hesitation, I relented, and he joined me on stage. While I continued to speak, he stood quietly between me and the lectern exploring the wooden shelves in the lectern and playing

———

RAYNARD KINGTON is the president of Grinnell College in Iowa. He worked as a director at the National Institutes of Health and the Centers for Disease Control and Prevention, as a senior scientist at the RAND Corporation, and as a professor of medicine at the University of California at Los Angeles. In 2011 he established the Grinnell Prize, which honors leaders under 40 "who show creativity, commitment, and extraordinary accomplishment in effecting positive social change." This essay first appeared in the *Washington Post* on November 3, 2016.

with a piece of paper while my hand intermittently entwined in his curly head of hair just visible to the audience. After a few minutes he interrupted me again to inform me that he would be "right back"—I said "okay" and he returned to his seat.

My response to the audience: Never allow a kid in the act. It went over well, but more than one person applauded me for making it clear that part of what I am is a parent. And I wondered whether a woman being announced as the new college president would either have allowed her child to join her onstage or would have been responded to in the same way. Would the response have been "What is she thinking?" rather than "Isn't that delightful?" That question has returned to me frequently over the last several years as I have taken note of the struggles women still face as mothers trying to carve out careers vs. people who think they should be at home raising children.

I am the type of person, at least in my mind, who takes sides in public debates like this. But not in this case. Despite the fact that the issues at the heart of the battles are in essence the same issues that I struggle with as a college president married to a busy professor of child psychiatry while trying to raise two active boys, I feel as if I don't have a dog in the fight.*

My experience of these debates surely is deeply tied to the 5 fact that my spouse and I are both men and that we are privileged in many ways.

It's not that I don't feel incompetent as a parent at least once a day. In those moments of craziness and despair that every parent of young children has, I ask myself: What made you think that you could pull this off? But I don't experience that feeling of incompetence as reflecting anything other than my *personal* incompetence. Blame it on a strong sense of male

*__Dog in the fight__ To have a personal stake or interest in something.

Raynard Kington, President of Grinnell College

privilege and arrogance, but I never seriously thought that this life wouldn't be possible for me and my family.

I know that I am held to a different standard in many ways—if only because openly gay men in leadership positions with young children remain relatively unusual, and society has yet to develop any strong norms of acceptable choices in my position. My spouse and I have other advantages as well: We are well-educated and have a generous household income; we live in a wonderful home five minutes from my office; I have a fair amount of control over my schedule; I have the option of bringing the family to dinner in the dining hall where students find some joy in young kids, even when they are demonstrating the parenting deficits of their dads; we live in a small town with inexpensive child care and great teachers and schools.

Another advantage for me is being African American. I was raised in the black middle class of the 1960s and 1970s, and, at its most functional, that world prepared its young to become accustomed to defying expectations, if not to ignore them completely. That ability serves me well in many ways, and I think it extends to my role as an atypical parent.

So maybe I don't feel the emotional engagement with the debates because my situation is still so unusual that I don't compare myself to others in the same position. My details—gender, orientation, race to a degree—are so different from those of the affluent white women who seem to be at the heart of these ongoing battles (or "mommy wars").

When I do connect at an emotional level with the debates, it is deeply rooted in having experienced the downdraft of my mother's difficult decision to end her career more than 50 years ago to care for me and my four siblings. I asked my mother several times why she had stopped doing what she loved, and her answer never changed. She never thought that she had made the wrong decision—she always said that she really had no choice if she cared about the futures, especially the education, of her children. So as my father began his medical practice, she shifted to devoting a big chunk of her time to shepherding her five children through the Baltimore City public school system. Although she remained active in civic affairs and worked part time off and on for many years, I know that she never forgot the personal price that she paid in giving up her true career love—of independence, of self-worth, of intellectual challenge. I remember thinking as a teenager that I would never allow myself to be in a position like that.

10

See Chapter 8 for tips on how to transition within a paragraph.

But the reality is that I couldn't truly be in my mother's position, because it's different for men—society doesn't put the same pressures on us. And the choices we make are not judged in the same way.

As I'm in my 11th year as a parent, I understand my mother's choice better and how hard it must have been precisely because I know I have so many advantages. Even though I'm African American, even though I'm gay, parenting as a male may present fewer challenges to my career choices than parenting as a female.

But even with the advantages that I have, and even with the distinctions of decades, orientation, family dynamic, socioeconomic status, and location between us, the basic trade-offs are the same for me as they were for her. I experience these to be as complicated and as simple: my children's interests vs. my interests vs. my spouse's interests; one set of advantages for our boys (more quality time with their parents) vs. another set of advantages for them (opportunities and income that may accompany the higher level, more stressful jobs); this part of what I want to do (be a successful parent) vs. that part of what I want to do (have a meaningful career); the here and now vs. the future.

The difference is my perception that these trade-offs are for me and my spouse to make. As males, we're in a position of power when it comes to making decisions about our family, somewhat immune to the cultural and social scrutiny—still— of working mothers.

If I view my family situation as a case study, what insights 15 can be gleaned from it? I believe that public policy, institutional practices, and legal protections can make a big difference, no doubt. With better institutional and government support, more families would have some of the advantages that our family enjoys. But those changes will never eliminate the trade-offs required in parenting, and the trade-offs ultimately are strictly personal—or they should be. They aren't always for women.

And so our culture must also change the way we think about the roles of parents, especially mothers, in our society. Until we shift our cultural thinking and expectations of women and mothers vs. men and fathers, there is still a sense that parenting and career choices don't solely belong to females, that they're not wholly personal choices.

We need to change our laws, policies and practices to reduce the pressure of these choices. By instituting things like paid parental leave and more flexible work schedules, everyone would win with better support to enable better choices. We should shift our thinking to allow for sick family days, accommodate participation in meetings remotely, and not schedule important meetings to start at 7:30 a.m. or end at 5:30 p.m.— prime kid drop-off and pickup times. And we need to recognize that not all accommodations can be written into policy in advance—like letting my son come up and join me at the lectern even if it briefly delayed my speech.

Though it would be foolish to think that any of these will eliminate the difficulty of the choice, we should at least eliminate the disparities that make the choice harder.

Joining the Conversation

1. Raynard Kington makes clear with the title of his essay what he thinks. Why does he claim that he has it easier than most working mothers? What larger social issue or problem do you think is motivating him to share his views?

2. Kington does not include many viewpoints other than his own. How might adding other perspectives improve his argument? Name two or three objections he might have considered and how he could respond to them.

3. The author acknowledges that even with his advantages "the basic trade-offs are the same" for him as they are for women. How might Richard Dorment (pp. 617–37) respond?

4. Kington writes about his mother (paragraph 10); Richard Dorment (pp. 617–37) describes folding laundry with his wife; and Anne-Marie Slaughter (pp. 596–616) begins her essay by talking about her son. How do you think personal anecdotes affect these authors' arguments—do they strengthen them, weaken them, or both?

5. Kington concludes his essay with a recommendation: "By instituting things like paid parental leave and more flexible work schedules, everyone would win with better support to enable better choices." Write an essay responding to what he says, drawing from the readings in this chapter and your own experiences and observations as support for what you say.

From He to She in First Grade

LAURIE FRANKEL

—▱—

WHEN OUR SON TURNED 6, my husband and I bought him a puppet theater and a chest of dress-up clothes because he liked to put on plays. We filled the chest with 20 items from Goodwill, mostly grown-man attire: ties, button-down shirts, a gray pageboy cap and a suit vest.

But we didn't want his or his castmates' creative output to be curtailed by a lack of costume choices, so we also included high heels, a pink straw hat, a dazzling fairy skirt and a sparkly green halter dress.

He was thrilled with these presents. He put on the sparkly green dress right away. In a sense, he never really took it off.

For a while, he wore the dress only when we were at home, and only when we were alone. He would change back into

LAURIE FRANKEL is the author of three novels, *The Atlas of Love* (2010), *Goodbye for Now* (2012), and *This Is How It Always Is* (2017), which was inspired, in part, by the essay that appears here. Her writing has also appeared in publications such as the *Guardian*, *People*, and *Publishers Weekly*. Frankel is on the board of Seattle7Writers, a nonprofit organization that supports literacy and works to build relationships among writers, readers, librarians, and booksellers. This essay first appeared in the *New York Times* on September 16, 2016.

shorts and a T-shirt if we were running errands or had people coming over.

Then we would come home or our guests would leave, and he ⁵ would change back to the sparkly green dress, asking me to tie the halter behind his neck and the sash around his waist.

Eventually he stopped changing out of it. He wore it to the grocery store and when he had friends over. He wore it to the park and the lake. He wore shorts for camp and trunks for swimming, but otherwise he was mostly in the dress.

My husband and I were never of the opinion that girls should not wear pants or climb trees or get dirty, or that boys should not have long hair or play with dolls or like pink, so the dress did not cause us undue alarm or worry. But school was about to start, and we found ourselves at a crossroads.

It seemed reasonable to say: "Wear whatever you're comfortable in to school. If that's what you want to wear, you don't have to keep changing in and out of it."

But it also seemed reasonable to say: "Dresses are for play at home only. The dress is fun, but you can't wear it to first grade."

The former had the advantage of being fair, what we ¹⁰ believed, and what would make our child happiest. The latter had the advantage of being much less fraught.

So we asked him, "What do you think you'll do with your dress when school starts in a couple weeks?" We said: "You need new clothes for the new school year. What should we buy?"

For weeks, he wasn't sure.

And then, on the day before school started, he was.

I later learned that this is remarkably common, that children who make decisions like this often do so as push comes to shove. They achieve clarity when they are faced with two not-great options.

Our child could go to school dressed in shorts and a T-shirt 15
and feel wrong and awkward and not himself. Or he could
wear what felt right and possibly face the wrath of his fellow
elementary-school students.

When he woke up on that last day of summer vacation,
the first thing he said was that he wanted to wear skirts and
dresses to first grade.

"O.K.," I said, stalling for time, as my brain flooded with all
the concerns I hadn't yet voiced. "What do you think other
kids will say tomorrow if you wear a dress to school?"

For ways to let your naysayer speak informally, see pp. 83–85.

"They'll say, 'Are you a boy or a girl?'" he replied.
"They'll say: 'You can't wear that. Boys don't wear
dresses.' They'll say, 'Ha, ha, ha, you're so stupid.'"

This seemed about right to me. "And how will that make
you feel?" I asked.

He shrugged and said he didn't know. But he did know, with 20
certainty, what he wanted to wear to school the next day, even
as he also seemed to know what that choice may cost him.

I hadn't met his new teacher yet, so I sent her a heads-up by
email, explaining that this had been going on for some time; it
wasn't just a whim. She emailed back right away, unfazed, and
she promised to support our child "no matter what."

Then we went shopping. The fairy skirt and sparkly green
dress were play clothes. He didn't have any skirts or dresses
that were appropriate for school.

I didn't want to buy a whole new wardrobe when I didn't
know if this was going to last. I envisioned a scenario in which
he wore a skirt the first day, got made fun of, and never wore
a skirt again. I envisioned another in which he got the skirt-
wearing out of his system and happily donned pants every day
thereafter. But mostly I was pretty sure the skirts were here
to stay.

School started on a Wednesday, so we bought three outfits to get us through the week. Three school skirts. Three school tops. A pair of white sandals.

On the drive home, I asked, "What will you say back if kids 25 say the things you think they will?"

"I don't know," he admitted.

So we brainstormed. We role-played. We practiced saying, "If girls can wear pants or skirts, so can boys." We practiced saying: "You wear what you're comfortable wearing. This is what I'm comfortable wearing." We practiced polite ways of suggesting they mind their own business.

"Are you sure?" I asked him. I asked this while he was behind me in his car seat so he wouldn't see how scared I was. I asked casually while we ran errands so it wouldn't seem like a big deal.

"I'm sure," he said. He certainly sounded sure. That made one of us.

The question I couldn't stop asking myself was: Do we love 30 our children best by protecting them at all costs or by supporting them unconditionally? Does love mean saying, "Nothing, not even your happiness, is as important as your safety"? Or does love mean saying, "Be who you are, and I will love that person no matter what"?

I couldn't ask my child those questions. But the next morning I did ask one more time, "Are you sure?"

Which was ridiculous, given that he had gotten up before dawn to put on the new skirt and blouse and sandals and was grinning, glowing, with joy.

We put some barrettes in his very short hair and took the traditional first-day-of-school pictures. They're all a little blurry because he was too excited to stand still, but it doesn't matter because that joyful smile is all you see anyway.

My husband and I took deep breaths and walked him to school. For my son's part, he fairly floated, seemingly unconcerned. Having decided, he was sure.

The things I imagined happening fell into opposite catego- 35 ries, but both transpired. A lot of children didn't notice, didn't care or stared briefly before moving on. But there were a few who pestered him on the playground and in the hallways, who teased or pressed, who covered their mouths and laughed and pointed and would not be dissuaded by our carefully rehearsed answers.

That lasted longer than I had expected, but it was mostly over within the month.

At the end of that first week, when he was going to bed on Friday night, he was upset about something—weepy, cranky and irritable. He couldn't or wouldn't tell me what the problem was. His eyes were wet, his fists balled, his face stormy.

I tucked him in and kissed him good night. I asked, again, what the matter was. I asked, again, what I could do. I told him I couldn't help if he wouldn't talk to me. Finally I whispered, "You don't have to keep wearing skirts and dresses to school, you know. If kids are being mean, if it feels weird, you can absolutely go back to shorts and T-shirts."

He snapped out of it immediately, sitting up, his face clearing, his eyes drying and brightening. "No, Mama," he chided. I wish I could say that he did so sweetly, but his tone was more like, Don't be an idiot. "I already decided about that," he said. "I never think about that anymore."

It had been three days. 40

But it was also true. He had already decided. He didn't think about that anymore. And he—she—never looked back. She grew out her hair. She stopped telling people she was a boy in a skirt and started being a girl in a skirt instead.

And we, as a family, decided to be open and honest about it, too, celebrating her story instead of hiding it.

Two years later, our daughter still sometimes wears the green dress, for dress-up and to put on plays, as we imagined her doing in the first place. Now that she can be who she is on the inside and on the outside, on weekdays as well as on weekends, at home and everywhere else, the sparkly green dress has once again become just a costume.

Joining the Conversation

1. Laurie Frankel tells the story of her child's transition from "he to she" at home and at school. What's Frankel's point, and how does the story she tells support that point?
2. This essay appeared in the *New York Times*' "Modern Love" section, a "series of weekly reader-submitted essays that explore the joys and tribulations of love." These pieces are relatively short. If you were revising this one to be a longer essay, which strategies taught in this book could help?
3. So what? Frankel explains why gender identity is important to her child, herself, and her husband. Has she convinced you that you should care? If so, how? If not, how could she do better?
4. Write a one-page response to Frankel's essay in which you give your own reasons for supporting her argument, not supporting it, or both.
5. Go to **theysayiblog.com** and click on "What's Gender Got to Do with It?" Search for Frankel's essay and read the comments that readers have posted in response to her article. Consider how many posts incorporate personal stories, like Frankel does, as support.

Teaching Men to Be Emotionally Honest

ANDREW REINER

LAST SEMESTER, a student in the masculinity course I teach showed a video clip she had found online of a toddler getting what appeared to be his first vaccinations. Off camera, we hear his father's voice. "I'll hold your hand, O.K.?" Then, as his son becomes increasingly agitated: "Don't cry! ... Aw, big boy! High five, high five! Say you're a man: 'I'm a man!'" The video ends with the whimpering toddler screwing up his face in anger and pounding his chest. "I'm a man!" he barks through tears and gritted teeth.

The home video was right on point, illustrating the takeaway for the course: how boys are taught, sometimes with the best of intentions, to mutate their emotional suffering into anger. More immediately, it captured, in profound concision, the earliest stirrings of a male identity at war with itself.

ANDREW REINER teaches writing and cultural studies at Towson University, including a course titled "Real Men Smile: The Changing Face of Masculinity." His essays have appeared in the *New York Times*, *Washington Post Magazine*, *The Chronicle of Higher Education*, and *Chicago Tribune*. He also contributes to *The Signal*, an arts and culture show on WYPR, Baltimore's NPR station. This essay first appeared in the *New York Times* on April 10, 2016.

This is no small thing. As students discover in this course, an honors college seminar called "Real Men Smile: The Changing Face of Masculinity," what boys seem to need is the very thing they fear. Yet when they are immunized against this deeper emotional honesty, the results have far-reaching, often devastating consequences.

Despite the emergence of the metrosexual and an increase in stay-at-home dads, tough-guy stereotypes die hard. As men continue to fall behind women in college, while outpacing them four to one in the suicide rate, some colleges are waking up to the fact that men may need to be *taught* to think beyond their own stereotypes.

In many ways, the young men who take my seminar—typically, 5 20 percent of the class—mirror national trends. Based on their grades and writing assignments, it's clear that they spend less time on homework than female students do; and while every bit as intelligent, they earn lower grades with studied indifference. When I asked one of my male students why he didn't openly fret about grades the way so many women do, he said: "Nothing's worse for a guy than looking like a Try Hard."

In a report based on the 2013 book *The Rise of Women: The Growing Gender Gap in Education and What It Means for American Schools*, the sociologists Thomas A. DiPrete and Claudia Buchmann observe: "Boys' underperformance in school has more to do with society's norms about masculinity than with anatomy, hormones or brain structure. In fact, boys involved in extracurricular cultural activities such as music, art, drama and foreign languages report higher levels of school engagement and get better grades than other boys. But these cultural activities are often denigrated as unmasculine by preadolescent and adolescent boys."

Throughout elementary school and beyond, they write, girls consistently show "higher social and behavioral skills," which translate into "higher rates of cognitive learning" and "higher levels of academic investment."

It should come as no surprise that college enrollment rates for women have outstripped men's. In 1994, according to a Pew Research Center analysis, 63 percent of females and 61 percent of males enrolled in college right after high school; by 2012, the percentage of young women had increased to 71, but the percentage of men remained unchanged.

By the time many young men do reach college, a deep-seated gender stereotype has taken root that feeds into the stories they have heard about themselves as learners. Better to earn your Man Card than to succeed like a girl, all in the name of constantly having to prove an identity to yourself and others.

The course "Real Men Smile," which examines how the 10 perceptions of masculinity have and haven't changed since the 18th century, grew out of a provocative lecture by Michael Kimmel, the seminal researcher and author in the growing field of masculine studies.

Dr. Kimmel came to my campus, Towson University, in 2011 to discuss the "Bro Code" of collegiate male etiquette. In his talk, he deconstructed the survival kit of many middle-class, white male students: online pornography, binge drinking, a brotherhood in which respect is proportional to the disrespect heaped onto young women during hookups, and finally, the most ubiquitous affirmation of their tenuous power, video games.

As Dr. Kimmel masterfully deflected an outpouring of protests, the atmosphere grew palpably tense. A young man wearing fraternity letters stood up. "What you don't get right is that girls are into hooking up as much as we are; they come on to us, too," he said. Dr. Kimmel shook his head, which left the student clearly rattled.

His voice quavering, the young man stammered something unexpected from a frat brother, about how women can be as insensitive and hurtful as guys. He sounded like a victim himself. But afterward, when I asked him if he had reached out to any of his guy friends for advice or solace, he stared at me, incredulous, his irises two small blue islands amid a sea of sclera. "Nah, I've got this," he said.

I wanted the course to explore this hallmark of the masculine psyche—the shame over feeling any sadness, despair or strong emotion other than anger, let alone expressing it and the resulting alienation. Many young men, just like this student, compose artful, convincing masks, but deep down they aren't who they pretend to be.

Research shows what early childhood teachers have always 15 known: that from infancy through age 4 or 5, boys are more emotive than girls. One study out of Harvard Medical School and Boston Children's Hospital in 1999 found that 6-month-old boys were more likely to show "facial expressions of anger, to fuss, to gesture to be picked up" and "tended to cry more than girls."

"Boys were also more socially oriented than girls," the report said—more likely to look at their mother and "display facial expressions of joy."

This plays out in the work of Niobe Way, a professor of applied psychology at New York University. After 20-plus years of research, Dr. Way concludes that many boys, especially early and middle adolescents, develop deep, meaningful friendships, easily rivaling girls in their emotional honesty and intimacy.

But we socialize this vulnerability out of them. Once they reach ages 15 or 16, "they begin to sound like gender stereotypes," she writes in *Deep Secrets: Boys' Friendships and the Crisis of Connection.* "They start using phrases such as 'no homo' . . .

and they tell us they don't have time for their male friends, even though their desire for these relationships remains."

As women surpass men on campus, the threat felt by thin-skinned males often reveals itself in the relationships where they feel most exposed. "Boys are not only more invested in ongoing romantic relationships but also have less confidence navigating them than do girls," writes the sociologist Robin W. Simon in the *Journal of Health and Social Behavior*. That's problematic, because "romantic partners are their primary sources of intimacy," whereas young women confide in friends and family.

Some cultural critics link such mounting emotional vulnerability to the erosion of male privilege and all that it entails. This perceived threat of diminishing power is exposing ugly, at times menacing fault lines in the male psyche. Experts point to sexual assaults on campus and even mass murders like those at a community college in Oregon and a movie theater in Colorado. These gunmen were believed to share two hypermasculine traits: feelings of profound isolation and a compulsion for viral notoriety.

20

See Chapter 2 for tips on summarizing what others say.

With so much research showing that young men suffer beneath the gravity of conventional masculinity, men's studies is gaining validation as a field of its own, not just a subset of women's studies. Hobart and William Smith Colleges has offered a minor in men's studies since the late '90s. The Center for the Study of Men and Masculinities was established in 2013 at Stony Brook University, part of the State University of New York, and plans to offer its first master's degree program in 2018. Last year, the center hosted the International Conference on Men and Masculinities, where topics included fatherhood, male friendships and balancing work and family life.

So why don't campuses have more resource centers for men?

Some universities offer counseling services for men of color and gay men, and some sponsor clubs through which male members explore the crisis of sexual violence against women. Only a precious few—the University of Massachusetts and Simon Fraser University among them—offer ways for all men to explore their shared struggles. And these don't exist without pushback. Talk of empowering men emotionally yields eye rolling at best, furious protest at worst—as when the Simon Fraser center was proposed, in 2012, and men and women alike challenged the need for a "safe space" for members of the dominant culture.

But wouldn't encouraging men to embrace the full range of their humanity benefit women? Why do we continue to limit the emotional lives of males when it serves no one? This question is the rhetorical blueprint I pose to students before they begin what I call the "Real Man" experiment.

In this assignment, students engage strangers to explore, 25 firsthand, the socialized norms of masculinity and to determine whether these norms encourage a healthy, sustainable identity.

The findings result in some compelling presentations. One student interviewed her male and female friends about their hookups and acted out an amalgam of their experiences through the eyes of a male and a female character; another explored the pall of silence and anxiety that hangs over campus men's rooms; two students gleaned children's gender perceptions in a toy store. One of the most revealing projects was a PowerPoint by a student who had videotaped himself and then a female friend pretending to cry in the crowded foyer of the university library, gauging the starkly different reactions of passersby.

"Why do you think a few young women stopped to see if your female friend was O.K.," I asked him, "but no one did the same thing for you?"

He crossed his arms, his laser pointer pushing against his bicep like a syringe, and paused. Even at this point in the semester, the students, some of whom had studied gender issues before, seemed blind to their own ingrained assumptions. So his response raised many eyebrows. "It's like we're scared," he said, "that the natural order of things will completely collapse."

Joining the Conversation

1. Andrew Reiner argues that male college students need more resources to help them express their feelings without ridicule or judgment. What larger conversation seems to motivate his essay?

2. Reiner quotes sociologists Thomas A. DiPrete and Claudia Buchmann, who say that "boys' underperformance in school has more to do with society's norms about masculinity than with anatomy, hormones or brain structure" (paragraph 6). What point is the author trying to make with this quotation?

3. Reiner quotes and summarizes other viewpoints, but he makes his own views clear. How does he signal when he's asserting his own views and when he's incorporating those of someone else? (See Chapter 5 for this book's advice on distinguishing what you say from what others say.)

4. Like Reiner, Nicholas Eberstadt (pp. 667–81) is worried about the situation of men in US society, but he discusses quite a different set of problems. Consider both arguments—whose do you find more persuasive, and why?

5. Reiner cites research studies and examples from his own classroom to make his point. Write a response to Reiner, in which you agree, disagree, or both with his argument, drawing on one or two studies—either in this essay or another reading in the chapter—and your own experiences.

What about Gender Roles in Same-Sex Relationships?

STEPHEN MAYS

—🔲—

Imposing gender roles on gay couples is even more ridiculous than doing so with straight couples.

I RECENTLY OVERHEARD someone comment to her friend about a gay male couple walking ahead of them on the sidewalk. The girl said, "Who do you think is the girl in the relationship?" I couldn't help but frown at the girl and shake my head. As clear as you would think it is to see, I'll spell it out for you: neither of them is the girl. They're both boys.

Not to say that traditional ideas of gender roles don't play a part in a gay relationship, but they're a little more diluted, I would say. A gay man may show effeminate qualities, but that doesn't

———

STEPHEN MAYS is a multimedia editor for *U.S. News and World Report*. He has been a web producer for both *U.S. News and World Report* and the *Telegraph*, and a contributing writer for *USA Today College*. As a student at the University of Georgia, he was the editor-in-chief of the *Red & Black*, an independent student-run newspaper covering campus news, and *Ampersand Magazine*, a UGA lifestyle magazine. This piece appeared in the *Red & Black* on September 24, 2013.

make him the "woman" of the relationship. Just like the muscled, bearded gay man doesn't have to be the "man" of the relationship.

One huge aspect of the gay male relationship that I appreciate is the more leveled playing field that we have. We're both men. If one of us opens the door for the other on a whim of affection or chivalry, it wasn't expected because he was the "man." It was simply a nice gesture. If one of us cooks dinner once, or every night for that matter, it isn't because he's the "woman" of the relationship. He's probably just better at it than his partner.

I have noticed, however, here in the South that a good number of gay men claim to be seeking "masc" or "masculine" partners. They want a boyfriend who likes the outdoors, is in good physical condition, plays sports and all those other standard characteristics for "men." I have no idea why this is, other than perhaps personal preference, because there's nothing wrong with the guys who like wearing skinny jeans, putting highlights in their hair, or shopping all the time. We simply associate certain actions with very classic ideas of masculinity or femininity. There are few actions or characteristics that classify as gender-neutral.

Why does caring about your appearance, cooking dinner, or 5 enjoying shopping for new clothes have to be considered feminine? Why does hiking, playing football, or working out a lot have to be considered masculine? When it boils down to it, all of us, gay and straight alike, comprise many characteristics—some are considered masculine, and some are considered feminine.

Chapter 4 shows ways to agree and disagree simultaneously.

Despite sexual orientation, some people simply demonstrate more masculine qualities or more feminine qualities. In the case of a gay male relationship, however, the key point is that neither of us is the girl of the relationship, no matter which side of the scale we fall on. We're both boys. Neither sexual preferences in the bedroom nor our daily characteristics have any effect on that biology.

Joining the Conversation

1. Stephen Mays begins by literally quoting what someone said, which he then uses as a way to launch what he says in response. He could have summarized what was said; why do you think he quoted it instead? What argument does he offer in response?

2. Mays obviously cares a lot about this topic, but does he explain why we should care? If not, do it for him. Write a paragraph—perhaps it could be a new concluding paragraph—discussing explicitly why this topic matters and who should care. (See Chapter 7 for guidance.)

3. This short piece was written as a newspaper column. What strategies in this book could Mays use to revise his article as an academic essay? (See the tips in Chapter 11 for using the templates to revise.)

4. Read Andrew Reiner's essay (pp. 651–57) on the ways society reinforces traditional gender roles for men. How does his argument relate to Mays's views on gender roles in same-sex relationships?

5. Mays critiques various gender stereotypes, including ones affecting gay people and straight people, both men and women. What do you think? Write an essay in which you agree, disagree, or both with what he says.

Artificial Intelligence's White Guy Problem

KATE CRAWFORD

—▣—

ACCORDING TO SOME prominent voices in the tech world, artificial intelligence presents a looming existential threat to humanity: Warnings by luminaries like Elon Musk and Nick Bostrom about "the singularity"—when machines become smarter than humans—have attracted millions of dollars and spawned a multitude of conferences.

But this hand-wringing is a distraction from the very real problems with artificial intelligence today, which may already be exacerbating inequality in the workplace, at home and in our legal and judicial systems. Sexism, racism and other forms of discrimination are being built into the machine-learning algorithms that underlie the technology behind many "intelligent" systems that shape how we are categorized and advertised to.

———

KATE CRAWFORD is a researcher at Microsoft Research. She also teaches at the Center for Civic Media at MIT and is a fellow at New York University's Information Law Institute. She serves on the editorial board for three academic journals and has written for the *Atlantic* and the *New Inquiry*. This essay first appeared in the *New York Times* on June 25, 2016.

Take a small example from last year: Users discovered that Google's photo app, which applies automatic labels to pictures in digital photo albums, was classifying images of black people as gorillas. Google apologized; it was unintentional.

But similar errors have emerged in Nikon's camera software, which misread images of Asian people as blinking, and in Hewlett-Packard's web camera software, which had difficulty recognizing people with dark skin tones.

This is fundamentally a data problem. Algorithms learn by ⁵ being fed certain images, often chosen by engineers, and the system builds a model of the world based on those images. If a system is trained on photos of people who are overwhelmingly white, it will have a harder time recognizing nonwhite faces.

To elaborate on a previous idea, see p. 137. A very serious example was revealed in an investigation published last month by ProPublica. It found that widely used software that assessed the risk of recidivism in criminals was twice as likely to mistakenly flag black defendants as being at a higher risk of committing future crimes. It was also twice as likely to incorrectly flag white defendants as low risk.

The reason those predictions are so skewed is still unknown, because the company responsible for these algorithms keeps its formulas secret—it's proprietary information. Judges do rely on machine-driven risk assessments in different ways—some may even discount them entirely—but there is little they can do to understand the logic behind them.

Police departments across the United States are also deploying data-driven risk-assessment tools in "predictive policing" crime prevention efforts. In many cities, including New York, Los Angeles, Chicago and Miami, software analyses of large sets of historical crime data are used to forecast where crime hot spots are most likely to emerge; the police are then directed to those areas.

At the very least, this software risks perpetuating an already vicious cycle, in which the police increase their presence in the same places they are already policing (or overpolicing), thus ensuring that more arrests come from those areas. In the United States, this could result in more surveillance in traditionally poorer, nonwhite neighborhoods, while wealthy, whiter neighborhoods are scrutinized even less. Predictive programs are only as good as the data they are trained on, and that data has a complex history.

Histories of discrimination can live on in digital platforms, 10 and if they go unquestioned, they become part of the logic of everyday algorithmic systems. Another scandal emerged recently when it was revealed that Amazon's same-day delivery service was unavailable for ZIP codes in predominantly black neighborhoods. The areas overlooked were remarkably similar to those affected by mortgage redlining in the mid-20th century. Amazon promised to redress the gaps, but it reminds us how systemic inequality can haunt machine intelligence.

And then there's gender discrimination. Last July, computer scientists at Carnegie Mellon University found that women were less likely than men to be shown ads on Google for highly paid jobs. The complexity of how search engines show ads to internet users makes it hard to say why this happened—whether the advertisers preferred showing the ads to men, or the outcome was an unintended consequence of the algorithms involved.

Regardless, algorithmic flaws aren't easily discoverable: How would a woman know to apply for a job she never saw advertised? How might a black community learn that it were being overpoliced by software?

Members from Project Include, "an open community working toward providing meaningful diversity and inclusion solutions for tech companies." From left: Susan Wu, Laura I. Gómez, Erica Baker, Ellen Pao, Tracy Chou, Y-Vonne Hutchinson, Bethanye McKinney Blount, and Freada Kapor Klein.

We need to be vigilant about how we design and train these machine-learning systems, or we will see ingrained forms of bias built into the artificial intelligence of the future.

Like all technologies before it, artificial intelligence will reflect the values of its creators. So inclusivity matters— from who designs it to who sits on the company boards and which ethical perspectives are included. Otherwise, we risk constructing machine intelligence that mirrors a narrow and privileged vision of society, with its old, familiar biases and stereotypes.

If we look at how systems can be discriminatory now, we 15 will be much better placed to design fairer artificial intelligence.

But that requires far more accountability from the tech community. Governments and public institutions can do their part as well: As they invest in predictive technologies, they need to commit to fairness and due process.

While machine-learning technology can offer unexpected insights and new forms of convenience, we must address the current implications for communities that have less power, for those who aren't dominant in elite Silicon Valley circles.

Currently the loudest voices debating the potential dangers of superintelligence are affluent white men, and, perhaps for them, the biggest threat *is* the rise of an artificially intelligent apex predator.

But for those who already face marginalization or bias, the threats are here.

Joining the Conversation

1. Kate Crawford begins her essay with a clear "they say" on the subject of artificial intelligence. What is it, and what is her response?

2. According to Crawford, "sexism, racism and other forms of discrimination are being built into the machine-learning algorithms that underlie the technology" we use (paragraph 2). She then provides several examples of this bias to elaborate on what she means. Choose three of the examples and in your own words explain how they illustrate this bias.

3. Where in her essay does Crawford try to convince you that her argument is something you should care about? Has she convinced you? Why or why not?

4. In her essay, "Google, Democracy, and the Truth about Internet Search" (pp. 536–55), Carole Cadwalladr also raises concerns about the future of the internet. Whose argument do you find more persuasive, and why?

5. Using strategies discussed in Chapter 12, "Entering Class Discussions," write two to three sentences on artificial intelligence that could initiate a class discussion, whether it's in person or online. Your statement should acknowledge the view or views motivating this conversation.

Men without Work

NICHOLAS EBERSTADT

—◻—

MUCH CURRENT ANALYSIS of labor market conditions paints a cautiously optimistic—even unabashedly positive—picture of job trends. But easily accessible data demonstrate that we are, in reality, living through an extended period of extraordinary, Great Depression-scale underutilization of male manpower, and this severe "work deficit" for men has gradually worsened over time.

Expert opinions on U.S. labor market performance have been increasingly sanguine over the past year or so. A few select media headlines and quotations illustrate the emerging consensus:

- "The Jobless Numbers Aren't Just Good, They're Great" (August 2015, Bloomberg[1])

———

NICHOLAS EBERSTADT is an economist at the American Enterprise Institute, a "public policy think tank dedicated to defending human dignity, expanding human potential, and building a freer and safer world." He researches poverty, demographics and economic development, and security. In 2012 he was awarded the Bradley Prize, given to innovative intellectuals. He has also written several books, including *Russia's Peacetime Demographic Crisis* (2010) and *The Poverty of "the Poverty Rate"* (2008). This selection is from his most recent book, *Men without Work: America's Invisible Crisis* (2016).

- "The Jobs Report Is Even Better Than It Looks" (November 2015, FiveThirtyEight[2])

- "Healthy Job Market at Odds with Global Gloom" (March 2016, *Wall Street Journal*[3])

- An excerpt from "Two Sides to Economic Recovery: Growth Stalls, While Jobs Soar" stated: "The job market, according to Labor Department figures released in recent months, is at its healthiest point since the boom of the late 1990s." (April 2016, *International New York Times*[4])

- "June's Super Jobs Report (July 2016, *Atlantic Monthly*[5])

In addition, U.S. economists and policymakers who have served under Republican and Democratic presidents maintain that today's U.S. economy is either near or at "full employment":

- "It is encouraging to see that the U.S. economy is approaching full employment with low inflation." (Ben Bernanke, former chairman of the Federal Reserve Board, October 2015[6])

- "The American economy is in good shape . . . we are essentially at full employment . . . tight labor markets are leading to increases in hourly earnings and in the producer prices of services." (Martin Feldstein, former chair of the President's Council of Economic Advisers and longtime director of the National Bureau of Economic Research, February 2016[7])

- "We are coming close to [the Federal Reserve's] assigned congressional goal of full employment. [Many measures of unemployment] really suggest a labor market that is vastly improved." (Janet Yellen, chairman of the Federal Reserve, April 2016[8])

All of these assessments draw upon data on labor market dynamics: job openings, new hires, "quit ratios," unemployment filings and the like. And all those data are informative— Here's a "yes, but" move— see p. 63. as far as they go. But they miss also something, a big something: the deterioration of work rates for American men.

The pronouncements above stand in stark contrast to the trends illustrated in figure 1, which track officially estimated work rates for U.S. men over the postwar era (see figure 1).

The federal government did not begin releasing continuous monthly data on U.S. employment until after World War II. By any broad measure, U.S. employment-to-population rates for civilian, noninstitutionalized men in 2015 were close to their lowest levels on record—and vastly lower than levels in earlier postwar decades.[9]

Between 1948 and 2015, the work rate for U.S. men twenty and older fell from 85.8 percent to 68.2 percent. Thus the proportion of American men twenty and older without paid work more than doubled, from 14 percent to almost 32 percent. Granted, the work rate for adult men in 2015 was over a percentage point higher than 2010 (its all-time low). But purportedly "near full employment" conditions notwithstanding, the work rate for the twenty-plus male was more than a fifth lower in 2015 than in 1948.

Of course, the twenty-plus work rate measure includes men sixty-five and older, men of classic retirement age. But when the sixty-five-plus population is excluded, work rates trace a long march downward here, too. By 2015, nearly 22 percent of U.S. men between the ages of twenty and sixty-five were not engaged in paid work of any kind, and the work rate for this grouping was nearly 12.5 percentage points below its 1948 level. In short, the fraction of U.S. men from ages twenty to sixty-four not at work in 2015 was 2.3 times higher than it had been in 1948.

As for "prime-age" men—the twenty-five–to–fifty-four group that historically always has the highest employment—work rates

FIGURE 1. EMPLOYMENT-TO-POPULATION RATIO, U.S. MALES, SELECTED AGE GROUPS, 1948–2016 (SEASONALLY ADJUSTED)

Source: "Labor Force Statistics from the Current Population Survey," LNS12300025, LNS12300061, Bureau of Labor Statistics, retrieved on May 16, 2016, http://data.bls.gov/pdq/querytool.jsp?survey-ln.

fell from 94.1 percent in 1948 to 84.3 percent in 2015. Under today's "near-full employment" norm, a monthly average of nearly one in six prime-age men had no paying job of any kind.

Though the work rate for prime-age men has recovered to some degree since 2010, the latest report as of this writing (July 2016) is barely on par with the lowest-ever Bureau of Labor Statistics (BLS) reading before the Crash of 2008 (the depths of the early 1980s recession). In 2015, the proportion of prime-age men without jobs was over 2.5 times higher than in 1948. Indeed, 1948 work rates for men in their late fifties and early sixties were slightly higher than for prime-age men today.

Even more shocking is the comparison of work rates for prime-age men today with those from the prewar Depression era.

During the Depression era, we did not possess our current official statistical apparatus for continuously monitoring employment conditions. Our postwar statistical apparatus for continuously monitoring employment conditions only came in response to the prewar employment crisis. Consequently, our main source of information on Depression-era employment comes from our decennial population censuses. As fate would have it, the Great Depression spanned two national censuses, the 1930 census, near the start of the Depression, and the 1940 census, near its end.[10] We contrapose male employment patterns then and now in table 1.

According the 1940 census, the work rate for civilian noninstitutional men twenty to sixty-four years old was 81.3 percent. In 2015, that rate was 78.4 percent. The work rate for prime-age males in 1940 was reported to be 86.5 percent, two points higher than in 2015 and about a point and a half higher than readings thus far for 2016. In other words, work rates for men appear to be lower today than they were late in the Great Depression when the civilian unemployment rate ran above 14 percent.[11] Furthermore,

TABLE 1. U.S. MALE EMPLOYMENT-TO-POPULATION RATIOS: TODAY VS. SELECTED DEPRESSION YEARS

YEAR AND SOURCE	EMPLOYMENT TO POPULATION RATIO, MEN 20–64 (PERCENTAGE OF CIVILIAN NON-INSTITUTIONAL POPULATION)	EMPLOYMENT TO POPULATION RATIO, MEN 25–54 (PERCENTAGE OF CIVILIAN NONINSTITUTIONAL POPULATION)
2015 (BLS)	78.4	84.4
1940 (Census)	81.3	86.4
1930 (Census)	88.2*	91.2**

Source: For 2015: Bureau of Labor Statistics, Labor Force Statistics from the Current Population Survey, LNS12300025, LNS12300061, http://data.bls.gov/pdq/querytool.jsp?survey=ln. Accessed May 16, 2016. For 1940: Derived from http://www.jstor.org/stable/117246?seq=1_page_scan_tab_contents; http://censusacn.adobeaemcloud.com'library/publications/1943/dec/population-labor-forcesample.html_Table_1; http://www2.census.gov/library/publications/decennial/1940/population-institutional-population/08520028ch2.pdf; http://www/dtic.mil/dtic/tr/fulltext/u2/a954007.pdf. Accessed August 5, 2016. For 1930: http://digital.library.unt.edu/ark:/67531/metadc26169/m1/1/high_res_d/R40655_2009Jun19.pdf. Accessed March 2, 2016.
Notes: *Calculated for total numerated population, not civilian noninstitutional population; **Twenty-five–to–forty-four male population corresponding male twenty-five–to–forty-four ratio for 2015 would be 85.3 percent.

the work rate for American men is manifestly lower today than it was in 1930, to judge by returns from the 1930 census.

Admittedly, the comparison is not straightforward, since the 1930 census used different questions about employment status than we use today and did not break out "civilian noninstitutional population" from the total adult population. Nonetheless, the Census Bureau has harmonized those 1930 employment figures with modern definitions of work and joblessness.[12] By these reconstructions, the 1930 ratio for employment to total population for men twenty to sixty-four was over 88 percent. Among men twenty-five to forty-four (prime work ages for that era) the ratio for employment to total population was over 91 percent.

In 2015, the official work rate for working-age men twenty–to–sixty-four was nearly ten percentage points below this 1930 figure (78.4 percent vs. 88.2 percent) and for men twenty-five to forty-four, the nominal gap was nearly six points (85.3 percent vs. 91.2 percent). These numerical differences, I should note, *understate* slightly the true work rate gap between adult men in 1930 and today, since the 1930 numbers do not exclude men in the armed forces, prisons, long-term hospitalization, etc., from the demographic denominator by which current work rates for the "civilian noninstitutional" population are calculated.

To be clear, the employment disaster in the depths of the 15 Great Depression was unquestionably worse than it was in either 1930 or 1940.[13] For better or worse, however, we only have these two census data points for that era's labor market conditions, and current data indicate that work rates for American men are *lower* today than in either of these years. It is thus meaningful to talk about work rates for American men today as being at Depression-era levels. In fact, they are more depressed than those recorded in particular years of the Great Depression.

Just how great is our current "work deficit" for American men? One reasonable benchmark for measuring that gap might be the mid-1960s. Then, the U.S. economy was strong and labor markets functioned at genuinely full employment levels.

Between 1965 and 2015, work rates for men twenty and older fell by over 13 percent. Population aging cannot account for most of this massive decline: nearly four-fifths of that drop was due to age-specific declines in work rates for 1967–2015 (the period for which more detailed data are available for such calculations). Over these same years, work rates for men in the broad twenty–to–sixty-four group fell from 90 percent to less than 79 percent. In other words, over the two generations, the fraction of men without jobs of any sort in the broad twenty–to–sixty-four group went from 10 percent of the total to almost 22 percent. Almost none of that decline can be attributed to changes in age structure (see figure 2). For the critical prime-age group (men twenty-five to fifty-four), work rates dropped over this half century from about 94 percent to just over 84 percent. Consequently, the percentage of wholly jobless prime-age men shot from 6 percent to nearly 16 percent.

If we look at the long-term trends over the postwar era, we see an eerie and radical transformation in the condition of prime-age men: the unrelenting ratcheting upward in the fraction of men without any paid employment (see figure 3). In the decade of the 1960s, monthly averages indicated that one in sixteen prime-age American men were not at work. By the 1990s, the ratio had jumped to one in eight. In the current decade (January 2010 to June 2016), the ratio has dropped below one in six for an average of 17.5 percent of prime-age men with no paid work in the past month.[14]

What does all this mean for the current "work deficit" for grown men? If age-specific work rates for the civilian noninstitutional adult population had simply held constant from 1965 to today, over 10.5 million additional men ages twenty to sixty-four would have been working for pay in 2015 America, including an additional 6 million men in the prime twenty-five–to–fifty-four group.[15]

In one important respect, however, this 10.5-million-plus 20 figure overstates today's "deficit" for men. The reason: it fails to account for the steady increase in education and training for adult men over the past five decades. Education and work-related training can temporarily take work-minded men out of the workforce. It's critical to make adjustments for these factors to get a meaningful sense of the true falloff in paid employment for men in modern America.

FIGURE 2. AGE-STRUCTURE ADJUSTED EMPLOYMENT-TO-POPULATION RATIO, U.S. MALES 20–64, ANNUAL 1967–2015

Source: "Labor Force Statistics from the Current Population Survey," 20+ LNS12300025, 64+ LNU02300199, Bureau of Labor Statistics, retrieved on May 17, 2016, http://data.bls.gov/pdq/querytool.jsp?survey-ln.

Unfortunately, making these adjustments is not such a straightforward task. Statistics on training are notoriously limited, inconsistent, and contradictory.[15] Numbers on formal education can also be problematic. Nevertheless, by 2014 (the latest figures available), nearly a million more men in their early twenties were in school than would have been the case with 1965 enrollment ratios.[16] For men twenty-five to sixty-four, the corresponding number exceeded 1.6 million.[17] These numbers suggest that at least 2.5 million more adult men were in education or training in 2014 than in 1965.

Of course, not all of these men would have been out of work pursuing work-related education or training. It's actually quite the contrary. The overwhelming majority of adult male job trainees appear to be job holders already. That is the nature of job-related training. As for formal education, most men of all adult ages enrolled in formal schooling are also in the workforce. They are typically part-time student workers or part-time working students. In 2014, according to Current Population Survey (CPS) data from the Census Bureau, 55 percent of all men twenty and older enrolled in schooling were simultaneously working paid jobs. The same was true for nearly 70 percent of men twenty-five to fifty-four years of age.[18] So the real question becomes what proportion of the additional men in school or training were out of the workforce because they were in school or training.

Roughly speaking, CPS data indicate that adult schooling *per se* is currently taking about a million more working-age men out of the paid workforce today than would have been the case if the twenty-plus population conformed to 1965-era enrollment ratios.[19] (Not all of this schooling is directly or even indirectly employment related.) If we deduct this million from the 10.5 million figure above, the "corrected" total for 2015 would be approximately 9.5 million.

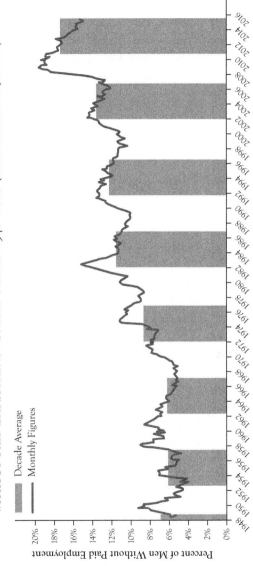

FIGURE 3. PERCENTAGE OF CIVILIAN NONINSTITUTIONAL PRIME-AGE (25–54) MALE POPULATION WITHOUT PAID EMPLOYMENT: UNITED STATES 1948–2016 (SEASONALLY ADJUSTED)

Source: Bureau of Labor Statistics, "Labor Force Statistics from the Current Population Survey," Employed LNS12000061, Civilian Noninstitutional Population LNU0000061, Bureau of Labor Statistics, retrieved on June 21, 2016, www.bls.gov/data.

In sum, even after (generously) adjusting for today's demanding regimen of adult schooling and training, the net "jobs deficit" in 2015 for men twenty to sixty-four in relation to 1965-era work patterns would come out to a number approaching 10 million. The implied employment deficit works out to around 1.2 million for men in their early twenties and about 5.5 million for prime-age men twenty-five to fifty-four, with the remainder being men in their late fifties and early sixties.

If 1965-style employment patterns applied today, an addi- 25 tional 10-plus percent of America's civilian noninstitutional male population between the ages of twenty and sixty-five would have been working and earning a paycheck in 2015, even after taking educational expansion into account. We would also have about 10 percent more men at work in the prime-age years than we do today.

Romans used the word "decimation" to describe the loss of a tenth of a given unit of men. The United States has suffered something akin to a decimation of its male workforce over the past fifty years. This disturbing situation is our "new normal." No less disturbing is the fact that the general public and political elites have uncritically accepted this American decimation as today's "new normal."

Today's received wisdom holds that the United States is now at or near "full employment." An alternative view would hold that, by not-so-distant historic standards, the nation today is short of full employment by nearly 10 million male workers (to say nothing of the additional current "jobs deficit" for women). Unlike the dead soldiers in Roman antiquity, our decimated men still live and walk among us, though in an existence without productive economic purpose. We might say those many millions of men without work constitute a sort of invisible army, ghost soldiers lost in an overlooked, modern-day depression.

Notes

1. Joe Weisenthal, "The Jobless Numbers Aren't Just Good, They're Great," Bloomberg video, 1:21, August 6, 2015, http://www.bloomberg.com/news/videos/2015-08-06/the-jobless-numbers-aren-t-just-good-they-re-great.

2. Ben Casselman, "The Jobs Report Is Even Better Than It Looks," Five ThirtyEight, November 6, 2015, http://fivethirtyeight.com/features/the-jobs-report-is-even-better-than-it-looks/.

3. Greg Ip, "Healthy Job Market at Odds with Global Gloom," *Wall Street Journal*, March 30, 2016, http://www.wsj.com/articles/healthy-job-market-at-odds-with-global-gloom-1459357330

4. Nelson D. Schwartz, "The Recovery's Two Sides," *New York Times*, April 28, 2016, http://www.nytimes.com/2016/04/29/business/economy/us-economy-gdp-q1-growth.html?_r=0.

5. Bourree Lam, "June's Super Jobs Report," *Atlantic Monthly*, July 8, 2016, http://www.theatlantic.com/business/archive/2016/07/june-jobs-report/490466/.

6. Ben Bernanke, "How the Fed Saved the Economy," Brookings, October 4, 2015, https://www.brookings.edu/opinions/how-the-fed-saved-the-economy/.

7. Martin Feldstein, "The U.S. Economy Is in Good Shape," *Wall Street Journal*, February 21, 2016, http://www.wsj.com/articles/the-u-s-economy-is-in-good-shape-1456097121.

8. Jana Raindow, Christopher Condon, and Matthew Boesler, "Yellen Says U.S. Near Full Employment, Some Slack Remains," Bloomberg, April 7, 2016, http://www.bloomberg.com/news/articles/2016-04-07/yellen-says-u-s-close-to-full-employment-some-slack-remains.

9. Note that the workforce is officially defined as the sixteen-plus population (more or less the age you legally can get out of school); historically it was the fourteen-plus population. In this study, I use three measures for working age population: twenty-plus, twenty–to–sixty-four, and the "prime working" ages of twenty-five–to–fifty-four.

10. While the U.S. Great Depression is conventionally dated as lasting from 1929 to 1939, in part to concord with the eruption of World War II that ended any peacetime economic slumps besetting European powers, unemployment data suggest that the effects of the Depression continued on into 1940 and 1941—indeed almost to our entry into that same conflict. According to the nascent test run of the present CPS, which began producing its first estimates of the U.S. employment situation in March 1940, the U.S. unemployment rate averaged nearly 11.5 percent of the civilian labor force for the first half of 1941—a higher level than ever

recorded for any single month in postwar American history. As of April 12, 1941, according to these figures, the civilian unemployment rate was over 12 percent. See "Unemployment Rate for United States," FRED Economic Data, last modified August 17, 2012, https://research.stlouisfed.org/fred2/series/M0892BUSM156S-NBR, and "Civilian Unemployment Rate," FRED Economic Data, last modified August 5, 2016, https://research.stlouisfed.org/fred2/series/UNRATENSA.

11. Initial CPS estimates for 1940 placed the civilian unemployment rate at an average of 14.6 percent for the months it covered. The 1940 population census put the civilian unemployment rate at 15.2 percent (see "Unemployment Rate for United States," FRED Economic Data, last modified August 17, 2012, https://research.stlouisfed.org/fred2/series/M0892BUSM156SNBR; "Census of Population and Housing," vol. 3, part 1, chapter 1, table 2, U.S. Census Bureau, http://www.census.gov/prod/www/decennial.html#y1940popv3.

12. Linda Levine, "The Labor Market during the Great Depression and the Current Recession," Congressional Research Service, last modified June 19, 2009, http://digital.library.unt.edu/ark:/67531/metadc26169/m1/1/high_res_d/R40655_2009Jun19.pdf.

13. John E. Bregger, "The Current Population Survey: A Historical Perspective and BLS' Role," *Monthly Labor Review* (June 1984): 8–14. http://www.bls.gov/opub/mlr/1984/06/art2full.pdf.

14. Note, incidentally, that our current decade's level is four percentage points higher than the corresponding estimate for prime-age men from the 1940 census—and the current decade's work rate for men twenty to sixty-four is over two points lower than for their counterparts back in 1940. Our current decade's work rates would look even worse if we compared them instead to the levels reported in the 1930 census.

15. This is calculated on the ten-year cohort of twenty-five to sixty-four and the five-year cohort of twenty to twenty-four.

16. Robert Zemsky and Daniel Shapiro, "On Measuring a Mirage: Why U.S. Training Numbers Don't Add Up" (working paper, National Center on the Educational Quality of the Workforce, Washington, DC), http://files.eric.ed.gov/fulltext/ED372191.pdf.

17. Derived from "CPS Historical Time Series Tables on School Enrollment," U.S. Census Bureau, http://www.census.gov/hhes/school/data/cps/historical/.

18. According to the Census Bureau CPS data, the matrix of school enrollment and employment for men twenty and older in the United States in 2014 looked like this:

Age	Total	Employed	Unemployed	Discouraged NILF*	Other NILF
20+	7,028,145	3,884,208	257,545	39,641	2,846,751
20–24	4,045,022	1,841,584	126,263	27,258	2,049,918
25–54	2,847,750	1,970,127	129,208	12,383	736,032
55–64	103,634	57,518	2,074	0	44,042
65+	31,739	14,979	0	0	16,760

Derived by Alex Coblin of the American Enterprise Institute from the October 2014 CPS microdata especially for this study. *Not in labor force.

19. And not all of this schooling is directly or even indirectly employment related.

Joining the Conversation

1. Nicholas Eberstadt examined data from a variety of sources to compare the percentage of employed adult men at different periods in US history, from the 1930s to the present. What did he find out?

2. Examine one of the charts in this essay and how Eberstadt explains its meaning and significance. What, if anything, would you change about the chart and his explanation to help you and other readers understand the data?

3. Eberstadt uses several connecting words to transition from one sentence to another. Find some examples of these words and make a list. Using the categories on pp. 105–06, categorize each word by its function (addition, elaboration, and so on).

4. J. D. Vance writes of the economic decline he has witnessed in his own community in *Hillbilly Elegy* (pp. 287–304). How do you think Vance would respond to Eberstadt's report?

5. Write an essay about the current conditions of men in the United States, drawing on Eberstadt's argument as well as two other readings of your choice in the book.

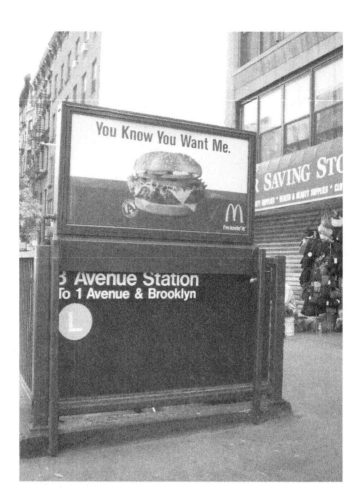

TWENTY-TWO

WHAT'S THERE TO EAT?

IF MUCH OF WHAT WE READ ABOUT FOOD is what to eat and what not to eat—and why—for some people living in the United States, the question is a little different: what's there to eat, if anything? It might be surprising that in a country which, according to the United States Department of Agriculture (USDA), wastes billions of pounds of food each year, there are people who don't have regular access to food and who are often hungry. But food security, which the USDA defines as "access by all people at all times to enough food for an active, healthy life," is hard to obtain for many children and adults. The readings in this chapter offer a variety of perspectives on what to eat, but also on food access, especially as it relates to health, education, government, and business.

How to treat illnesses associated with unhealthy diets continues to be a topic of debate among civic leaders, public health experts, politicians, and citizens. Some believe the government should step in to ensure that healthy foods are available for all people living in the United States, to educate people about their options, and to increase taxes on or even to outlaw the most unhealthy items. Meanwhile, many civil libertarians, food and drink producers, and those who enjoy these unhealthy items strongly oppose such efforts.

On the issue of government intervention versus personal responsibility, David Zinczenko blames the fast-food industry for the growing rate of obesity in the United States and argues that the government should regulate this industry. In contrast, the libertarian commentator Radley Balko argues that what we eat should remain a matter of personal responsibility and that staying trim should depend not on government intervention but on individual willpower.

Other readings focus on efforts to improve people's diets and routines, and how the marketing and research efforts of food companies affect what we eat. Author and food activist Michael Pollan outlines his rationale for ending our reliance on processed foods and moving to a diet of more organic food, especially vegetables. College student Mary Maxfield challenges the assumption that overeating is a social problem that needs to be fixed and suggests that Michael Pollan and other critics exaggerate its dangers. Michael Moss, while sympathetic to Pollan's endorsement of healthy eating, looks at ways in which fast food companies' research on the taste, texture, smell, and packaging of food makes their products extremely difficult to resist. And journalist David H. Freedman argues that advocates of a healthy diet, such as Pollan, should not consider fast food the enemy, but instead should encourage fast food companies to make their products healthier, an effort that in some cases is already proving effective.

Other writers in this chapter examine the relationship between food and one's environment, and food access generally. Olga Khazan examines one nonprofit's program to supply convenience stores in Washington, D.C. with low-cost, healthy fruits and vegetables, with the goal of improving the diets of residents who live far from a large supermarket. In a research study, Sara Goldrick-Rab, Katherine Broton, and Emily Brunjes Colo show that a growing number of college students rely on food pantries for their meals and are unable to focus on their studies because they do not have regular access to food. The authors propose expanding the federal school lunch program to include colleges in addition to elementary and high schools.

So read on for a wide range of opinions on food and eating in the United States. You'll likely find plenty to agree with, and just as much to disagree with. Whatever your point of view, the pieces in this chapter will challenge you to see what others are saying, to think about what you believe and why—and then to add your own voice to the conversation.

You'll find even more readings on **theysayiblog.com**, along with a space where you can respond with what you think—and literally add your own voice to the conversation.

Escape from the Western Diet

MICHAEL POLLAN

—⌐□⌐—

THE UNDERTOW OF NUTRITIONISM is powerful. . . . Much
nutrition science qualifies as reductionist science, focusing as
it does on individual nutrients (such as certain fats or carbohydrates or antioxidants) rather than on whole foods or dietary
patterns. . . . But using this sort of science to try to figure out
what's wrong with the Western diet is probably unavoidable.
However imperfect, it's the sharpest experimental and explanatory tool we have. It also satisfies our hunger for a simple,
one-nutrient explanation. Yet it's one thing to entertain such
explanations and quite another to mistake them for the whole
truth or to let any one of them dictate the way you eat.

[And] many of the scientific theories put forward to account
for exactly what in the Western diet is responsible for Western
diseases conflict with one another. The lipid hypothesis cannot

---

MICHAEL POLLAN has written many books on food and eating,
including *The Omnivore's Dilemma: A Natural History of Four Meals*
(2006), *Food Rules: An Eater's Manual* (2010), *Cooked: A Natural
History of Transformation* (2013), and *In Defense of Food: An Eater's
Manifesto* (2008), from which this essay was excerpted. He was named
one of *Time* magazine's top 100 Most Influential People in 2010 and
teaches at the University of California at Berkeley.

be reconciled with the carbohydrate hypothesis, and the theory that a deficiency of omega-3 fatty acids (call it the neolipid hypothesis) is chiefly to blame for chronic illness is at odds with the theory that refined carbohydrates are the key. And while everyone can agree that the flood of refined carbohydrates has pushed important micronutrients out of the modern diet, the scientists who blame our health problems on deficiencies of these micronutrients are not the same scientists who see a sugar-soaked diet leading to metabolic syndrome and from there to diabetes, heart disease, and cancer. It is only natural for scientists no less than the rest of us to gravitate toward a single, all-encompassing explanation. That is probably why you now find some of the most fervent critics of the lipid hypothesis embracing the carbohydrate hypothesis with the same absolutist zeal that they once condemned in the Fat Boys. In the course of my own research into these theories, I have been specifically warned by scientists allied with the carbohydrate camp not to "fall under the spell of the omega-3 cult." *Cult?* There is a lot more religion in science than you might expect.

So here we find ourselves . . . lost at sea amid the cross-currents of conflicting science.

See pp. 83–85 for tips on introducing objections informally.

Or do we?

Because it turns out we don't need to declare our allegiance 5 to any one of these schools of thought in order to figure out how best to eat. In the end, they are only theories, scientific explanations for an empirical phenomenon that is not itself in doubt: People eating a Western diet are prone to a complex of chronic diseases that seldom strike people eating more traditional diets. Scientists can argue all they want about the biological mechanisms behind this phenomenon, but whichever it is, the solution to the problem would appear to remain very much the same: *Stop eating a Western diet.*

In truth the chief value of any and all theories of nutrition, apart from satisfying our curiosity about how things work, is not to the eater so much as it is to the food industry and the medical community. The food industry needs theories so it can better redesign specific processed foods; a new theory means a new line of products, allowing the industry to go on tweaking the Western diet instead of making any more radical change to its business model. For the industry it's obviously preferable to have a scientific rationale for *further* processing foods—whether by lowering the fat or carbs or by boosting omega-3s or fortifying them with antioxidants and probiotics—than to entertain seriously the proposition that processed foods of any kind are a big part of the problem.

For the medical community too scientific theories about diet nourish business as usual. New theories beget new drugs to treat diabetes, high blood pressure, and cholesterol; new treatments and procedures to ameliorate chronic diseases; and new diets organized around each new theory's elevation of one class of nutrient and demotion of another. Much lip service is paid to the importance of prevention, but the health care industry, being an industry, stands to profit more handsomely from new drugs and procedures to treat chronic diseases than it does from a wholesale change in the way people eat. Cynical? Perhaps. You could argue that the medical community's willingness to treat the broad contours of the Western diet as a given is a reflection of its realism rather than its greed. "People don't want to go there," as Walter Willett responded to the critic who asked him why the Nurses' Health Study didn't study the benefits of more alternative diets. Still, medicalizing the whole problem of the Western diet instead of working to overturn it (whether at the level of the patient or politics) is exactly what you'd expect from a health care community that is sympathetic to nutritionism as a matter of temperament, philosophy, and economics. You would not expect such a medical community to be sensitive to the cultural or ecological dimensions of the food problem—and it isn't. We'll know this has changed when doctors kick the fast-food franchises out of the hospitals.

So what would a more ecological or cultural approach to the food problem counsel us? How might we plot our escape from nutritionism and, in turn, from the most harmful effects of the Western diet? To Denis Burkitt, the English doctor stationed in Africa during World War II who gave the Western diseases their name, the answer seemed straightforward, if daunting. "The only way we're going reduce disease," he said, "is to go backwards to the diet and lifestyle of our ancestors." This sounds uncomfortably like the approach of the diabetic Aborigines who went back to the bush to heal themselves. But I don't think this is what Burkitt had in mind; even if it was, it is not a very attractive or practical strategy for most of us. No, the challenge we face today is figuring out how to escape the worst elements of the Western diet and lifestyle *without* going back to the bush.

In theory, nothing could be simpler: To escape the Western diet and the ideology of nutritionism, we have only to stop eating and thinking that way. But this is harder to do in practice, given the treacherous food environment we now inhabit and the loss of cultural tools to guide us through it. Take the question of whole versus processed foods, presumably one of the simpler distinctions between modern industrial foods and older kinds. Gyorgy Scrinis, who coined the term "nutritionism," suggests that the most important fact about any food is not its nutrient content but its degree of processing. He writes that "whole foods and industrial foods are the only two food groups I'd consider including in any useful food 'pyramid.'" In other words, instead of worrying about nutrients, we should simply avoid any food that has been processed to such an extent that it is more the product of industry than of nature.

This sounds like a sensible rule of thumb until you real- 10 ize that industrial processes have by now invaded many whole foods too. Is a steak from a feedlot steer that consumed a diet of corn, various industrial waste products, antibiotics, and hormones still a "whole food"? I'm not so sure. The steer has itself been raised on a Western diet, and that diet has rendered its meat substantially different—in the type and amount of fat in it as well as its vitamin content—from the beef our ancestors ate. The steer's industrial upbringing has also rendered its meat so cheap that we're likely to eat more of it more often than our ancestors ever would have. This suggests yet another sense in which this beef has become an industrial food: It is designed to be eaten industrially too—as fast food.

So plotting our way out of the Western diet is not going to be simple. Yet I am convinced that it can be done, and in the course of my research, I have collected and developed some straightforward (and distinctly unscientific) rules of thumb, or personal eating policies, that might at least point us in the right direction. They don't say much about specific foods—about what sort of oil to cook with or whether you should eat meat. They don't have much to say about nutrients or calories, either, though eating according to these rules will perforce change the balance of nutrients and amount of calories in your diet. I'm not interested in dictating anyone's menu, but rather in developing what I think of as eating algorithms—mental programs that, if you run them when you're shopping for food or deciding on a meal, will produce a great many different dinners, all of them "healthy" in the broadest sense of that word.

And our sense of that word stands in need of some broadening. When most of us think about food and health, we think in fairly narrow nutritionist terms—about our personal physical health and how the ingestion of this particular nutrient or rejection of that affects it. But I no longer think it's possible to separate our bodily health from the health of the environment from which we eat or the environment in which we eat or, for that matter, from the health of our general outlook about food (and health). If my explorations of the food chain have taught me anything, it's that it is a food chain, and all the links in it are in fact linked: the health of the soil to the health of the plants and animals we eat to the health of the food culture in which we eat them to the health of the eater, in body as well as mind. [So you will find rules here] concerning not only what to eat but also how to eat it as well as how that food is produced. Food consists not just in piles of chemicals; it also comprises a set of social and ecological relationships, reaching back to the land and outward to other people. Some of these rules may strike you as having nothing whatever to do with health; in fact they do.

Many of the policies will also strike you as involving more work—and in fact they do. If there is one important sense in which we do need to heed Burkitt's call to "go backwards" or follow the Aborigines back into the bush, it is this one: In order to eat well we need to invest more time, effort, and resources in providing for our sustenance, to dust off a word, than most of us do today. A hallmark of the Western diet is food that is fast, cheap, and easy. Americans spend less than 10 percent of their income on food; they also spend less than a half hour a day preparing meals and little more than an hour enjoying them.[1] For most people for most of history, gathering and preparing food has been an occupation at the very heart of daily life. Traditionally people have allocated a far greater proportion of their income to food—as they still do in several of the countries where people eat better than we do and as a consequence are healthier than we are.[2] Here, then, is one way in which we would do well to go a little native: backward, or perhaps it is forward, to a time and place where the gathering and preparing and enjoying of food were closer to the center of a well-lived life.

[I'd like to propose] three rules—"*Eat food. Not too much. Mostly plants.*"—that I now need to unpack, providing some elaboration and refinement in the form of more specific guidelines, injunctions, subclauses, and the like. Each of these three main rules can serve as category headings for a set of personal policies to guide us in our eating choices without too much trouble or thought. The idea behind having a simple policy like "avoid foods that make health claims" is to make the process simpler and more pleasurable than trying to eat by the numbers and nutrients, as nutritionism encourages us to do.

So under "Eat Food," I propose some practical ways to [15] separate, and defend, real food from the cascade of foodlike products that now surround and confound us, especially in the supermarket. Many of the tips under this rubric concern shopping and take the form of filters that should help keep out the sort of products you want to avoid. Under "Mostly Plants," I'll dwell more specifically, and affirmatively, on the best types of foods (not nutrients) to eat. Lest you worry, there is, as the adverb suggests, more to this list than fruits and vegetables. Last, under "Not Too Much," the focus shifts from the foods themselves to the question of how to eat them—the manners, mores, and habits that go into creating a healthy, and pleasing, culture of eating.

NOTES

1. David M. Cutler, et al., "Why Have Americans Become More Obese?," *Journal of Economic Perspectives*, Vol. 17, No. 3 (Summer, 2003), pp. 93–118. In 1995 Americans spent twenty-seven minutes preparing meals and four minutes cleaning up after them; in 1965 the figure was forty-four minutes of preparation and twenty-one minutes of cleanup. Total time spent eating has dropped from sixty-nine minutes to sixty-five, all of which suggests a trend toward prepackaged meals.

2. Compared to the 9.9 percent of their income Americans spend on food, the Italians spend 14.9 percent, the French 14.9 percent, and the Spanish 17.1 percent.

Joining the Conversation

1. What does Michael Pollan mean when he refers to the "Western diet"? Why does he believe Americans need to "escape" from it?

2. Pollan begins with a "they say," citing a variety of scientific theories known as nutritionism. Summarize his response to these views. What is his objection to such views, and to the business and research interests that promote them?

3. If Pollan were to read Mary Maxfield's response to this article (pp. 703–08), how might he, in turn, respond to her?

4. It's likely that Pollan favors (and shops at) local farmers' markets. Go to **theysayiblog.com** and search for "Mark Bittman on Farmers' Markets." What does he say about them: who, according to Bittman, do they most benefit?

5. Write an essay that begins where Pollan's piece ends, perhaps by quoting from paragraph 14: "*Eat food. Not too much. Mostly plants.*" You'll need to explain his argument, and then respond with your own views.

Why Don't Convenience Stores Sell Better Food?

OLGA KHAZAN

———⌐⌐———

New programs aim to put more produce in corner stores in order to improve the health of low-income communities. Will it work?

AT A SMALL CORNER STORE in northeast Washington, Nola Liu, a community-outreach officer with the D.C. Central Kitchen, whirled around a deli case with a clipboard in hand, passing out a recipe for cinnamon pear crisps to anyone who would take it.

She thrust a card at a man in a blue knit hat who was on his way out.

———

OLGA KHAZAN is a writer for the *Atlantic*, where she covers health, gender, and science. She has also contributed to the *Washington Post, Los Angeles Times,* and *Forbes.* In 2014 Khazan was named one of the ten best science writers by *RealClearScience,* a website that aggregates and produces articles on "science stories from around the globe." In 2013 *Foreign Policy* magazine put her on its list of the top one hundred "Twitterati"; follow her @olgakhazan. This essay first appeared in the March 2, 2015, issue of the *Atlantic.*

"Are you gonna make it for me?" he asked.

"No, you have to make it yourself," she responded.

"I'm not much of a baker," he said, and walked out.   5

Fresh pears are a relatively new arrival at this store, which is called Thomas & Sons. Just a few months ago, the extent of its produce selection was a small refrigerated case holding a few forlorn fruits and onions, all going at a premium. The owner, Jae Chung, was reluctant to stock things like tomatoes, which would often go bad while they lingered on the shelves.

Now, a brand-new refrigerated vegetable case sits front and center amid all the beer and bulletproof glass. ("I have some unruly customers," Chung explains.) Inside are apples, lemons, limes, and grapes packaged neatly in plastic containers. Additional baskets hold potatoes and bananas. The case was provided by the D.C. Central Kitchen as part of their Healthy Corners program, which seeks to expand the fruit and vegetable offerings in corner stores across the District.

The Healthy Corners fridge at Thomas & Sons.

Not only did the nonprofit give Chung the fridge for free, it will also replace any items that go bad at no extra cost. They sell the greens to him for cheap, too. Chung says before, he had to buy his fresh produce stock at Costco and pick it up himself. After he added in his markup, a tomato at Thomas & Sons would sell for about $2.50. Now, it's more like $1 to $1.50—on par with what someone might pay for a bag of chips or package of donuts. (At Walmart, a pack of four tomatoes goes for $2.48, or about 60 cents per tomato.)

Nearly every city has neighborhoods that suffer from a lack 10 of access to cheap, easy, and healthful options, and Washington, D.C. is no exception. Tiny, independent corner stores—the kind that have wall-to-wall beverage cases, rows of brightly-packaged junk food, and just one or two cash registers—are crammed into every nook of the city. They're an essential part of the food landscape, providing everything from make-do lunch fare for construction workers to emergency beer for hipsters on their way to house parties. According to the D.C. Central Kitchen's calculations, 88 percent of food retailers in the District sell mostly junk food or processed food. Two hundred thousand of the District's residents live in an area where the closest grocery store is three times further away than the closest fast-food or convenience store.

One solution is to lure more large grocery stores to these so-called "food deserts." But it's often much easier, some advocates argue, to simply get the ubiquitous corner stores to start selling healthier food.

Size is the main reason most American corner and convenience stores don't stock very many fruits and vegetables. Many food distributors require a minimum order—say 250 apples—for a delivery. That's easy for places like Safeway or Giant, but it's harder for small shops that sell maybe two dozen apples each week. Corner-store owners who do opt to sell produce end up buying it at prices similar to those regular consumers pay. On top of that, produce requires refrigeration, which adds to the cost for store owners. And unlike Cheetos or Oreos, vegetables rot.

The Healthy Corners program has lowered most of these hurdles. The D.C. Central Kitchen already owned a fleet of trucks that it used for food deliveries to homeless shelters and transitional homes. In 2011, the organization realized it could use the same drivers to bring produce to local corner shops. Because it serves many different types of facilities, the Kitchen has substantial buying power: It's more akin to a large restaurant than a tiny retailer. That, combined with its strategy of buying from local farms and seeking philanthropic grants, helps drive down prices.

"We buy product that's aesthetically or geometrically challenged," says the organization's chief executive officer, Mike Curtin. Some of it is produce that's "the wrong shape or size to fit in the right box to fit in the right truck to fit in bins in the grocery store that are organized by size." But it's still perfectly good—and corner-store owners were happy to have it.

The Healthy Corners program targets areas where there is not 15 a full-service grocery store within a quarter-mile. In addition to promoting fruit and veggie recipes in the stores, D.C. Central Kitchen staffers have also held cooking demonstrations and doled out free samples. It's not enough, store owners told me, to simply install a produce fridge and expect the community to flock.

There are now 67 such Healthy Corners in D.C., most of which are in lower-income neighborhoods. According to the nonprofit's own numbers, the corner stores in the program sold more than 140,000 pieces of produce within the past 10 months, up from about 17,000 in the seven-month period between September 2011 and April 2012.

The organization says it wants to help grow these types of programs in other cities. It recently consulted on a similar project in Rochester, New York. Separate initiatives focusing on corner stores have sprouted up in Chicago, Manhattan, and Denver.

See pp. 25–27 for ways to introduce an ongoing debate. The idea that food deserts, or even insufficient produce intake, are a cause of obesity has come under fire recently. One study in *Health Affairs* last year found that when a new grocery store opened up in a food desert in Philadelphia, neither locals' weight nor their diets changed. Roland Sturm, an economist with the RAND Corporation, wrote a paper (which I covered when it came out) about how people of all incomes now eat about 30 pounds more vegetables and fruit annually than they did in 1970. Obesity rates have worsened all the while.

People still rely on corner shops primarily for household essentials, like toilet paper, or for a filling meal they can eat on the run. Chung says that occasionally parents thank him for providing fruit as an after-school snack option. Still, "customers' behavior hasn't really changed at this point," he says.

At Thomas & Sons, one man plopped a 12-pack of Yuengling 20 on the counter and announced to the cashier, "I ain't working today, so I'm going to drink." At Wheeler Market, another Healthy Corners store, some customers eyed the fridge full of fruit before grabbing a package of donuts.

"This is not going to end obesity, or diabetes. It's naive to think that's the case," Curtin says. "People will avail themselves of this food, but are they still going to eat junk food? Sure."

But perhaps reducing obesity shouldn't be the goal, or at least not an immediate one. Other than weight loss, there are plenty of advantages of eating well, like preventing some forms of cancer. And even produce-heavy, organic grocery stores still sell brownies. (Curtin points out that no one would say, "Oh, we shouldn't open up a Whole Foods in McLean [a wealthy D.C. suburb], because people are still going to buy chips.")

The Healthy Corners do seem to resemble a European style of grocery shopping that some public-health advocates extoll. Rather than pack up the family and head to Kroger every Saturday, returning with a trunk full of Teddy Grahams and assorted meats, many Europeans buy their produce on the way home from work from the dozens of small green-grocers that dot their street corners. These independent merchants—many of them recent immigrants—wedge their stores into the bottom floors of larger buildings, their melons and squashes stacked neatly in blue bins on the sidewalk.

Jaap Seidell, an obesity expert at Vrije Universiteit Amsterdam, said these small vegetable shops, which have proliferated across both large and small towns in Europe, offer a great deal of variety at prices that are even lower than those of grocery stores. They don't seem to run into the same distribution and cost issues that their American counterparts struggle with. "It's in season, they don't have to store it for a long time, they don't have to cool it, and there's a lot of demand for it," Seidell says. "There's a lot less cost and waste involved."

Of course, the Dutch way of life makes on-the-fly veggie 25 shopping easier. Big grocery-store runs aren't very practical anyway, Seidell notes, because almost everyone bikes or walks to work. Most Dutch women work part-time, so they have ample time to procure and cook fresh food.

In the Netherlands, he says, "It has always been like this: you have butchers, bakers, and the vegetable farmer."

Curtin says the success or failure of Healthy Corners will not hinge on whether "we put vegetables in 67 corner stores, and

Woldeabzghi (in the white sweater) entertains customers at Wheeler Market.

some people are still fat." It's about allowing people to decide what kind of diet they'd like to have.

Muller Woldeabzghi, the owner of Wheeler Market in south-east D.C., says he sells maybe 10 to 20 pieces of the Healthy Corners produce each day, accounting for about 10 percent of his sales. He said some customers come to Wheeler instead of the Giant, which is one and a half miles away, because they lack transportation, but others simply like the shop's community feel. It's "a neighborhood feeling," he says. "They want to support us, we want to support them."

When I asked one Wheeler shopper what he thought of the fridge, he seemed skeptical. "Why would someone go to the corner store for produce?" one man said on his way out. "Why wouldn't they go to the market?"

Several other customers I spoke with, though, seemed to ₃₀ take a more Dutch view.

"It's convenient," said Laray Winn, who lives in the neighborhood. "You can make it here in an emergency and get whatever you need."

Demetrius Cain, who lives across the street, says his 6-year-old son is also a fan. Sometimes when he's bored, the boy runs over and comes home with a still-chilled apple. It's not exactly a revolution, but at least it's not a Twinkie.

Joining the Conversation

1. Olga Khazan writes about a Washington, D.C. program that brings fresh fruits and vegetables to "food deserts" (paragraph 11). In what ways does the program seem to be succeeding? In what ways does it not?
2. While accepting the premise that increasing the consumption of healthy fruits and vegetables is good for people, Khazan also anticipates potential objections to her argument. Does she introduce these views fairly? What, if anything, do these views contribute to the essay?
3. Khazan does not include any metacommentary explaining to readers the larger point of her essay. Looking at the templates on pages 137–39, choose a few that you think could help Khazan elaborate on what she has written.
4. Khazan quotes Mike Curtin, who says of the Healthy Corners program, "This is not going to end obesity, or diabetes. It's naive to think that's the case. People will avail themselves of this food, but are they still going to eat junk food? Sure." How might Michael Pollan (pp. 686–93) respond to Curtin?

5. Visit a small grocery store and examine the foods there. Write an essay comparing the healthy and unhealthy items in terms of factors you find significant (price, calories, ingredients, packaging, location in the store, or something else).

Food as Thought:
Resisting the Moralization of Eating

MARY MAXFIELD

——◻——

How do French people eat so unhealthily—famously indulging in cheese, cream, and wine—but stay, on average, healthier than Americans? Journalist Michael Pollan offers readers a simple solution: quit obsessing over this French paradox and start obsessing over the french fry. Pointing to what he considers the American paradox—"a notably unhealthy population preoccupied with . . . the idea of eating healthy" (9)—Pollan contends that our definition of healthy eating is driven by a well-funded corporate machine. According to Pollan, the food industry, along with nutrition science and journalism, is capitalizing on our confusion over how to eat.

———

MARY MAXFIELD is a PhD student in American Studies at Saint Louis University. She has a masters degree from Bowling Green State, University and a bachelors degree from Fontbonne University. Her academic interests include bodies, gender, sexuality, politics, and rhetoric, and her work has appeared in *Feminist Media Studies*, an academic journal that engages with "feminist issues and debates in media and communication." Read her blog at missmarymax.wordpress .com, or follow her on Twitter @missmarymax.

While Pollan implicates his own profession in this critique, he simultaneously contributes to our cultural anxiety over food. The same critic who argues that "any and all theories of nutrition [serve] not the eater [but] the food industry," nevertheless proposes his own theory: the elimination of processed foods (141). Likewise, even after noting that the connections between diet and health that we take as gospel apparently *aren't*, Pollan nevertheless adheres to contemporary common-sense science, making assumptions about diet, health, and weight that underpin the very food industry he critiques.

Thus as he attempts to dismantle one paradox, Pollan embodies another: he's a critic of nutrition and food science who nevertheless bolsters the American investment in those industries. After publishing *In Defense of Food* (and its equally successful predecessor, *The Omnivore's Dilemma*), Pollan released *Food Rules*, a pocket-sized manual for better eating. Of course, Pollan contends that *his* guidelines function differently than the prescriptions (and proscriptions) of food scientists, because his rules function as "eating algorithms" that "produce many different dinners" (144) rather than specifying a concrete menu. Yet no matter how many meals fit Pollan's formula—"Eat food, not too much, mostly plants" (1)—it remains a dictate provided by an expert to those who apparently can't properly nourish themselves.

See pp. 33–38 for tips on how to summarize and know where you're going.

Pollan and other like-minded nutrition hawks consistently back up their claims with concerns over American health. Although acknowledging that eating primarily for health represents a departure from the historical purpose of food—fuel for our bodies—these gastronomical philosophers nevertheless position themselves as protectors of health. Americans need this protection, we are told, because we're a nation stricken by heart disease, diabetes, and cancer. According to this line of thought, each of these maladies is tied to our diet and essentially to our weight. As a culture, we no longer discuss healthy eating without also discussing unhealthy weights. Linking nutrition and body type, voices like Pollan's warn us against eating too much—often without any parallel warnings against eating too little. Pollan himself insists that overeating constitutes "the greatest threat" to our survival (7), and our government concurs, pouring resources into a fight against the obesity epidemic, that plague of fatness that supposedly threatens our national health.

The problem is that our understanding of health is as based 5 in culture as it is in fact. Despite some doubt in academic circles over connections between diet, health, and weight, common-sense reportage continues to presume that they are directly connected. Pollan, for example, twice notes that our diet of processed foods makes us "sick and fat" (10), and then—without evidence to support that claim—conflates health with weight and condemns fatness out of hand. Later, he refers to obesity as a Western disease (11)—again presuming a correlation between weight and health—and even cites statistics on eating habits from a study entitled "Why Have Americans Become More Obese?" (145).

A growing group of academics who have examined the research on obesity at length have discovered fundamental flaws behind perceptions of fatness, diet, and health. Law professor and journalist Paul Campos notes that "lies about fat, fitness, and health . . . not coincidentally serve the interests of America's $50-billion-per-year diet industry," and fat-acceptance activist Kate Harding elaborates on this point, observing that "if you scratch an article on the obesity crisis, you will almost always find a press release from a company that's developing a weight loss drug—or from a 'research group' . . . funded by such companies." Harding and Campos both belong to a school that has repeatedly challenged the validity of the body mass index (BMI), a tool that uses height and weight measurements to calculate body fat. Originally developed by a mathematician as a purely statistical tool, the BMI has become medicine's go-to means for predicting heart disease and other maladies, despite research that suggests a low BMI presents a greater mortality risk than a high one and that, in general, BMI cannot accurately predict one's health (Campos).

Culturally, however, we resist these scientific findings in favor of a perspective that considers fatness fatal and thinness immortal. Our skewed views of fatness then facilitate skewed views of food. We continue to believe in a "right" or "healthy" way of eating that involves eating less and eating differently than we instinctively would, despite evidence to the contrary provided both by scholars like Harding and Campos, and by Health at Every Size (HAES) nutritionists like Michelle Allison. HAES advocates challenge our cultural misconceptions, suggesting that—outside of specific medical conditions like celiac disease and anorexia—"what a person eats [rarely] takes primacy over how they eat it" (Allison, "Eating"). In essence, we can eat as we always have—which includes eating for emotional and social reasons—and still survive or even thrive.

Few of us, however, manage to think about eating this way. As Allison notes, "there are a lot of pressures and barriers in this world that get in our way, that confuse us, that distract us and attempt to control us in counterproductive ways" ("Rules vs. Trust"). In this context, "health" functions moralistically. It results from making decisions like choosing fresh mozzarella over spray cheese, the "right" foods over the "wrong" ones. Experts offer science to substantiate those designations, yet science—as Campos, Harding, and Allison show—does not actually support these systems. Instead, as even Pollan notes, there remains "a lot [of] religion in science" (140).

That "religion" presents itself in the moralizing of food, the attempt—in how we eat—to rise above our beastly natures. As a culture, when we imagine eating like animals, we visualize a feeding frenzy. Allison observes that when she says "Adult human beings are allowed to eat whatever and however much they want," what people actually hear is: "Go out and cram your face with Twinkies!" ("Eat Food"). (Indeed, for Pollan, the total elimination of American anxiety about food translates to a laissez-faire policy of "let them eat Twinkies" [9].) Yet Allison and other HAES nutritionists suggest that adult humans will eat in a way that is good for them, given the opportunity ("Eat Food"). When we attempt to rise above our animal nature through the moralization of food, we unnecessarily complicate the practice of eating. Food—be it french fry or granola bar, Twinkie or brown rice—isn't moral or immoral. Inherently, food is ethically neutral; notions of good and bad, healthy and unhealthy are projected onto it by culture. Staying mindful of that culture (and critical of the hidden interests that help guide it) can free us each to follow a formula we have long known but recently forgotten: Trust yourself. Trust your body. Meet your needs.

WORKS CITED

Allison, Michelle. "Eat Food. Stuff You Like. As Much As You Want."
    The Fat Nutritionist, 15 Feb. 2010, www.fatnutritionist.com/index.php/
    eat-food-stuff-you-like-as-much-as-you-want. Accessed 19 Jan. 2011.
———. "Eating—the WHAT or the HOW?" *The Fat Nutritionist*, 17 Aug.
    2009, www.fatnutritionist.com/index.php/eating-the-what-or-the-how.
    Accessed 19 Jan. 2011.

———. "Rules vs. Trust in Eating." *The Fat Nutritionist*, 15 Dec. 2009, www.fatnutritionist.com/index.php/rules-vs-trust-in-eating. Accessed 19 Jan. 2011.

Campos, Paul. "Being Fat Is OK." *Jewish World Review*, 23 Apr. 2001, www.jewishworldreview.com/0501/campos042301.asp. Accessed 25 Mar. 2011.

Harding, Kate. "Don't You Realize Fat Is Unhealthy?" *Shapely Prose*, 20 June 2007, kateharding.net/faq/but-dont-you-realize-fat-is-unhealthy. Accessed 19 Jan. 2011.

Pollan, Michael. *In Defense of Food: An Eater's Manifesto*. Penguin, 2008.

Joining the Conversation

1. In what ways does Mary Maxfield disagree with Michael Pollan (pp. 686–93) and other critics of the Western diet? What is her "they say," and what does she say?

2. What supporting evidence does Maxfield offer to counter the views of Michael Pollan and other critics?

3. Maxfield concludes by offering a formula for eating: "Trust yourself. Trust your body. Meet your needs." This formula contrasts with Michael Pollan's "Eat food. Not too much. Mostly plants." Write an essay responding to these arguments and presenting your own formula for eating.

4. Go to **theysayiblog.com** and click on "What's There to Eat?" Read one or two articles that look interesting to you and click on "join the conversation" if you would like to add your response to what you have read.

Don't Blame the Eater

DAVID ZINCZENKO

——◻——

IF EVER THERE WERE a newspaper headline custom-made for Jay Leno's monologue, this was it. Kids taking on McDonald's this week, suing the company for making them fat. Isn't that like middle-aged men suing Porsche for making them get speeding tickets? Whatever happened to personal responsibility?

I tend to sympathize with these portly fast-food patrons, though. Maybe that's because I used to be one of them.

I grew up as a typical mid-1980s latchkey kid. My parents were split up, my dad off trying to rebuild his life, my mom working long hours to make the monthly bills. Lunch and dinner, for me, was a daily choice between McDonald's, Taco Bell, Kentucky Fried Chicken or Pizza Hut. Then as now, these

———

DAVID ZINCZENKO, who was for many years the editor-in-chief of the fitness magazine *Men's Health*, is CEO of Galvanized Brands, a global health and wellness media company. Zinczenko is the author of numerous best-selling books, including the *Eat This, Not That* and the *Abs Diet* and *Zero Belly Diet* series. He has contributed op-ed essays to the *New York Times*, the *Los Angeles Times*, and *USA Today* and has appeared on *Dr. Oz, Oprah, Ellen,* and *Good Morning America*. This piece was first published on the op-ed page of the *New York Times* on November 23, 2002.

were the only available options for an American kid to get an affordable meal. By age 15, I had packed 212 pounds of torpid teenage tallow on my once lanky 5-foot-10 frame.

Then I got lucky. I went to college, joined the Navy Reserves and got involved with a health magazine. I learned how to manage my diet. But most of the teenagers who live, as I once did, on a fast-food diet won't turn their lives around: They've crossed under the golden arches to a likely fate of lifetime obesity. And the problem isn't just theirs— it's all of ours.

For tips on saying why it matters, see Chapter 7.

Before 1994, diabetes in children was generally caused by 5 a genetic disorder—only about 5 percent of childhood cases were obesity-related, or Type 2, diabetes. Today, according to the National Institutes of Health, Type 2 diabetes accounts for at least 30 percent of all new childhood cases of diabetes in this country.

Not surprisingly, money spent to treat diabetes has skyrocketed, too. The Centers for Disease Control and Prevention estimate that diabetes accounted for $2.6 billion in health care costs in 1969. Today's number is an unbelievable $100 billion a year.

Shouldn't we know better than to eat two meals a day in fast-food restaurants? That's one argument. But where, exactly, are consumers—particularly teenagers—supposed to find alternatives? Drive down any thoroughfare in America, and I guarantee you'll see one of our country's more than 13,000 McDonald's restaurants. Now, drive back up the block and try to find someplace to buy a grapefruit.

Complicating the lack of alternatives is the lack of information about what, exactly, we're consuming. There are no calorie information charts on fast-food packaging, the way there are on grocery items. Advertisements don't carry warning labels the way tobacco ads do. Prepared foods aren't covered under

Food and Drug Administration labeling laws. Some fast-food purveyors will provide calorie information on request, but even that can be hard to understand.

For example, one company's Web site lists its chicken salad as containing 150 calories; the almonds and noodles that come with it (an additional 190 calories) are listed separately. Add a serving of the 280-calorie dressing, and you've got a healthy lunch alternative that comes in at 620 calories. But that's not all. Read the small print on the back of the dressing packet and you'll realize it actually contains 2.5 servings. If you pour what you've been served, you're suddenly up around 1,040 calories, which is half of the government's recommended daily calorie intake. And that doesn't take into account that 450-calorie super-size Coke.

Make fun if you will of these kids launching lawsuits against 10 the fast-food industry, but don't be surprised if you're the next plaintiff. As with the tobacco industry, it may be only a matter of time before state governments begin to see a direct line between the $1 billion that McDonald's and Burger King spend each year on advertising and their own swelling health care costs.

And I'd say the industry is vulnerable. Fast-food companies are marketing to children a product with proven health hazards and no warning labels. They would do well to protect themselves, and their customers, by providing the nutrition information people need to make informed choices about their products. Without such warnings, we'll see more sick, obese children and more angry, litigious parents. I say, let the deep-fried chips fall where they may.

"Don't Blame the Eater." From *The New York Times*, November 23, 2002. Reprinted by permission of the author.

Joining the Conversation

1. Summarize Zinczenko's arguments (his "I say") against the practices of fast-food companies. How persuasive are these arguments?

2. One important move in all good argumentative writing is to introduce voices raising possible objections to the position being argued—what this book calls naysayers. What objections does Zinczenko introduce, and how does he respond? Can you think of other objections that he might have noted?

3. How does the story that Zinczenko tells about his own experience in paragraphs 3 and 4 support or fail to support his argument? How could the same story be used to support an argument opposed to Zinczenko's?

4. So what? Who cares? How does Zinczenko make clear to readers why his topic matters? Or, if he does not, how might he do so?

5. Write an essay responding to Zinczenko, using your own experience and knowledge as part of your argument. You may agree, disagree, or both, but be sure to represent Zinczenko's views near the beginning of your text, both summarizing and quoting from his arguments.

What You Eat Is Your Business

RADLEY BALKO

—▫—

THIS JUNE, *Time* magazine and ABC News will host a three-day summit on obesity. ABC News anchor Peter Jennings, who last December anchored the prime-time special "How to Get Fat Without Really Trying," will host. Judging by the scheduled program, the summit promises to be a pep rally for media, nutrition activists, and policy makers—all agitating for a panoply of government anti-obesity initiatives, including prohibiting junk food in school vending machines, federal funding for new bike trails and sidewalks, more demanding labels on foodstuffs, restrictive food marketing to children, and prodding the food industry into more "responsible" behavior. In other words, bringing government between you and your waistline.

———

RADLEY BALKO writes a blog about civil liberties and the criminal justice system for the *Washington Post*. He was once an editor at the *Huffington Post* and *Reason* magazine and a columnist for FoxNews.com. A self-described libertarian, Balko is the author of the book *Rise of the Warrior Cop: The Militarization of America's Police Forces* (2013). This essay was first published on May 23, 2004, on the website of the Cato Institute, which aims to promote the principles of "limited government, individual liberty, free markets, and peace."

Politicians have already climbed aboard. President Bush earmarked $200 million in his budget for anti-obesity measures. State legislatures and school boards across the country have begun banning snacks and soda from school campuses and vending machines. Senator Joe Lieberman and Oakland Mayor Jerry Brown, among others, have called for a "fat tax" on high-calorie foods. Congress is now considering menu-labeling legislation, which would force restaurants to send every menu item to the laboratory for nutritional testing.

This is the wrong way to fight obesity. Instead of manipulating or intervening in the array of food options available to American consumers, our government ought to be working to foster a sense of responsibility in and ownership of our own health and well-being. But we're doing just the opposite.

For decades now, America's health care system has been migrating toward socialism. Your well-being, shape, and condition have increasingly been deemed matters of "public health," instead of matters of personal responsibility. Our lawmakers just enacted a huge entitlement that requires some people to pay for other people's medicine. Senator Hillary Clinton just penned a lengthy article in the *New York Times Magazine* calling for yet more federal control of health care. All of the Democratic candidates for president boasted plans to push health care further into the public sector. More and more, states are preventing private health insurers from charging overweight and obese clients higher premiums, which effectively removes any financial incentive for maintaining a healthy lifestyle.

We're becoming less responsible for our own health, and 5 more responsible for everyone else's. Your heart attack drives up the cost of my premiums and office visits. And if the government is paying for my anti-cholesterol medication, what incentive is there for me to put down the cheeseburger?

This collective ownership of private health then paves the way for even more federal restrictions on consumer choice and civil liberties. A society where everyone is responsible for everyone else's well-being is a society more apt to accept government restrictions, for example—on what McDonald's can put on its menu, what Safeway or Kroger can put on grocery shelves, or holding food companies responsible for the bad habits of unhealthy consumers.

A growing army of nutritionist activists and food industry foes are egging the process on. Margo Wootan of the Center for Science in the Public Interest has said, "We've got to move beyond 'personal responsibility.'" The largest organization of trial lawyers now encourages its members to weed jury pools of candidates who show "personal responsibility bias." The title of Jennings's special from last December—"How to Get Fat Without Really Trying"—reveals his intent, which is to relieve viewers of responsibility for their own condition. Indeed, Jennings ended the program with an impassioned plea for government intervention to fight obesity.

For tips on distinguishing what you say from what others say, as Balko does here, see Chapter 5.

The best way to alleviate the obesity "public health" crisis is to remove obesity from the realm of public health. It doesn't belong there anyway. It's difficult to think of anything more private and of less public concern than what we choose to put into our bodies. It only becomes a public matter when we force the public to pay for the consequences of those choices. If policymakers want to fight obesity, they'll halt the creeping socialization of medicine, and move to return individual Americans' ownership of their own health and well-being back to individual Americans.

That means freeing insurance companies to reward healthy lifestyles, and penalize poor ones. It means halting plans to further socialize medicine and health care. Congress should also increase access to medical and health savings accounts, which give consumers the option of rolling money reserved for health care into a retirement account. These accounts introduce accountability into the health care system, and encourage caution with one's health care dollar. When money we spend on health care doesn't belong to our employer or the government, but is money we could devote to our own retirement, we're less likely to run to the doctor at the first sign of a cold.

We'll all make better choices about diet, exercise, and 10 personal health when someone else isn't paying for the consequences of those choices.

Joining the Conversation

1. What does Radley Balko claim in this essay? How do you know? What position is he responding to? Cite examples from the text to support your answer.
2. Reread the last sentence of paragraph 1: "In other words, bringing government between you and your waistline." This is actually a sentence fragment, but it functions as metacommentary, inserted by Balko to make sure that readers see his point. Imagine that this statement were not there, and reread the first three paragraphs. Does it make a difference in how you read this piece?
3. Notice the direct quotations in paragraph 7. How has Balko integrated these quotations into his text—how has he introduced them, and what, if anything, has he said to explain them and tie them to his own text? Are there any changes you might suggest? How do key terms in the quotations echo one another? (See Chapter 3 for advice on quoting, and pp. 110–12 for help on repeating key terms.)

4. Balko makes his own position about the so-called obesity crisis very clear, but does he consider any of the objections that might be offered to his position? If so, how does he deal with those objections? If not, what objections might he have raised?

5. Write an essay responding to Balko, agreeing, disagreeing, or both agreeing and disagreeing with his position. You might want to cite some of David Zinczenko's arguments (see pp. 709–12)—depending on what stand you take, Zinczenko's ideas could serve as support for what you believe or as the source of one possible objection.

The Extraordinary Science
of Addictive Junk Food

MICHAEL MOSS

—▣—

ON THE EVENING OF APRIL 8, 1999, a long line of Town Cars and taxis pulled up to the Minneapolis headquarters of Pillsbury and discharged 11 men who controlled America's largest food companies. Nestlé was in attendance, as were Kraft and Nabisco, General Mills and Procter & Gamble, Coca-Cola and Mars. Rivals any other day, the C.E.O.'s and company presidents had come together for a rare, private meeting. On the agenda was one item: the emerging obesity epidemic and how to deal with it. While the atmosphere was cordial, the men assembled were hardly friends. Their stature was defined by their skill in fighting one another for what they called "stomach share"—the amount

———

MICHAEL MOSS is a *New York Times* investigative reporter who won a 2010 Pulitzer Prize for "The Burger That Shattered Her Life," an article about a young dance instructor who was paralyzed after contracting an *E. coli* infection. Moss has reported for the *Wall Street Journal*, *New York Newsday*, and the *Atlanta Journal-Constitution* and taught at the Columbia University School of Journalism. This selection, adapted from his book, *Salt Sugar Fat: How the Food Giants Hooked Us* (2013), first appeared in the *New York Times Magazine* on February 24, 2013.

of digestive space that any one company's brand can grab from the competition.

James Behnke, a 55-year-old executive at Pillsbury, greeted the men as they arrived. He was anxious but also hopeful about the plan that he and a few other food-company executives had devised to engage the C.E.O.'s on America's growing weight problem. "We were very concerned, and rightfully so, that obesity was becoming a major issue," Behnke recalled. "People were starting to talk about sugar taxes, and there was a lot of pressure on food companies." Getting the company chiefs in the same room to talk about anything, much less a sensitive issue like this, was a tricky business, so Behnke and his fellow organizers had scripted the meeting carefully, honing the message to its barest essentials. "C.E.O.'s in the food industry are typically not technical guys, and they're uncomfortable going to meetings where technical people talk in technical terms about technical things," Behnke said. "They don't want to be embarrassed. They don't want to make commitments. They want to maintain their aloofness and autonomy."

A chemist by training with a doctoral degree in food science, Behnke became Pillsbury's chief technical officer in 1979 and was instrumental in creating a long line of hit products, including microwaveable popcorn. He deeply admired Pillsbury but in recent years had grown troubled by pictures of obese children suffering from diabetes and the earliest signs of hypertension and heart disease. In the months leading up to the C.E.O. meeting, he was engaged in conversation with a group of food-science experts who were painting an increasingly grim picture of the public's ability to cope with the industry's formulations—from the body's fragile controls on overeating to the hidden power of some processed foods to make people feel hungrier still. It was time, he and a handful of others felt, to warn the C.E.O.'s that their companies may have gone too far in creating and marketing products that posed the greatest health concerns.

The discussion took place in Pillsbury's auditorium. The first speaker was a vice president of Kraft named Michael Mudd. "I very much appreciate this opportunity to talk to you about childhood obesity and the growing challenge it presents for us all," Mudd began. "Let me say right at the start, this is not an easy subject. There are no easy answers—for what the public health community must do to bring this problem under control or for what the industry should do as others seek to hold it accountable for what has happened. But this much is clear: For those of us who've looked hard at this issue, whether they're public health professionals or staff specialists in your own companies, we feel sure that the one thing we shouldn't do is nothing."

As he spoke, Mudd clicked through a deck of slides—114 5 in all—projected on a large screen behind him. The figures were staggering. More than half of American adults were now considered overweight, with nearly one-quarter of the adult population—40 million people—clinically defined as obese. Among children, the rates had more than doubled since 1980, and the number of kids considered obese had shot past 12 million. (This was still only 1999; the nation's obesity rates would climb much higher.) Food manufacturers were now being blamed for the problem from all sides—academia, the Centers for Disease Control and Prevention, the American Heart Association and the American Cancer Society. The secretary of agriculture, over whom the industry had long held sway, had recently called obesity a "national epidemic."

Mudd then did the unthinkable. He drew a connection to the last thing in the world the C.E.O.'s wanted linked to their products: cigarettes. First came a quote from a Yale University professor of psychology and public health, Kelly Brownell, who was an especially vocal proponent of the view that the processed-food industry should be seen as a public health menace: "As a culture, we've become upset by the tobacco companies advertising to children, but we sit idly by while the food companies do the very same thing. And we could make a claim that the toll taken on the public health by a poor diet rivals that taken by tobacco."

"If anyone in the food industry ever doubted there was a slippery slope out there," Mudd said, "I imagine they are beginning to experience a distinct sliding sensation right about now."

Mudd then presented the plan he and others had devised to address the obesity problem. Merely getting the executives to acknowledge some culpability was an important first step, he knew, so his plan would start off with a small but crucial move: the industry should use the expertise of scientists—its own and others—to gain a deeper understanding of what was driving Americans to overeat. Once this was achieved, the effort could unfold on several fronts. To be sure, there would be no getting around the role that packaged foods and drinks play in overconsumption. They would have to pull back on their use of salt, sugar and fat, perhaps by imposing industrywide limits. But it wasn't just a matter of these three ingredients; the schemes they used to advertise and market their products were critical, too. Mudd proposed creating a "code to guide the nutritional aspects of food marketing, especially to children."

"We are saying that the industry should make a sincere effort to be part of the solution," Mudd concluded. "And that by doing so, we can help to defuse the criticism that's building against us."

What happened next was not written down. But according 10
to three participants, when Mudd stopped talking, the one
C.E.O. whose recent exploits in the grocery store had awed
the rest of the industry stood up to speak. His name was
Stephen Sanger, and he was also the person—as head of
General Mills—who had the most to lose when it came to
dealing with obesity. Under his leadership, General Mills had
overtaken not just the cereal aisle but other sections of the
grocery store. The company's Yoplait brand had transformed
traditional unsweetened breakfast yogurt into a veritable
dessert. It now had twice as much sugar per serving as
General Mills' marshmallow cereal Lucky Charms. And yet,
because of yogurt's well-tended image as a wholesome snack,

Traditional unsweetened breakfast yogurt transformed into a veritable dessert.

sales of Yoplait were soaring, with annual revenue topping $500 million. Emboldened by the success, the company's development wing pushed even harder, inventing a Yoplait variation that came in a squeezable tube—perfect for kids. They called it Go-Gurt and rolled it out nationally in the weeks before the C.E.O. meeting. (By year's end, it would hit $100 million in sales.)

According to the sources I spoke with, Sanger began by reminding the group that consumers were "fickle." (Sanger declined to be interviewed.) Sometimes they worried about sugar, other times fat. General Mills, he said, acted responsibly to both the public and shareholders by offering products to satisfy dieters and other concerned shoppers, from low sugar to added whole grains. But most often, he said, people bought what they liked, and they liked what tasted good. "Don't talk to me about nutrition," he reportedly said, taking on the voice of the typical consumer. "Talk to me about taste, and if this stuff tastes better, don't run around trying to sell stuff that doesn't taste good."

To react to the critics, Sanger said, would jeopardize the sanctity of the recipes that had made his products so successful. General Mills would not pull back. He would push his people onward, and he urged his peers to do the same. Sanger's response effectively ended the meeting.

"What can I say?" James Behnke told me years later. "It didn't work. These guys weren't as receptive as we thought they would be." Behnke chose his words deliberately. He wanted to be fair. "Sanger was trying to say, 'Look, we're not going to screw around with the company jewels here and change the formulations because a bunch of guys in white coats are worried about obesity.'"

The meeting was remarkable, first, for the insider admissions of guilt. But I was also struck by how prescient the organizers of the sit-down had been. Today, one in three adults is considered clinically obese, along with one in five kids, and 24 million Americans are afflicted by type 2 diabetes, often caused by poor diet, with another 79 million people having pre-diabetes. Even gout, a painful form of arthritis once known as "the rich man's disease" for its associations with gluttony, now afflicts eight million Americans.

The public and the food companies have known for decades 15 now—or at the very least since this meeting—that sugary, salty, fatty foods are not good for us in the quantities that we consume them. So why are the diabetes and obesity and hypertension numbers still spiraling out of control? It's not just a matter of poor willpower on the part of the consumer and a give-the-people-what-they-want attitude on the part of the food manufacturers. What I found, over four years of research and reporting, was a conscious effort—taking place in labs and marketing meetings and grocery-store aisles—to get people hooked on foods that are convenient and inexpensive. I talked to more than 300 people in or formerly employed by the processed-food industry, from scientists to marketers to C.E.O.'s. Some were willing whistle-blowers, while others spoke reluctantly when presented with some of the thousands of pages of secret memos that I obtained from inside the food industry's operations. What follows is a series of small case studies of a handful of characters whose work then, and perspective now, sheds light on how the foods are created and sold to people who, while not powerless, are extremely vulnerable to the intensity of these companies' industrial formulations and selling campaigns.

"In This Field, I'm a Game Changer."

John Lennon couldn't find it in England, so he had cases of it shipped from New York to fuel the *Imagine* sessions. The Beach

Boys, ZZ Top and Cher all stipulated in their contract riders that it be put in their dressing rooms when they toured. Hillary Clinton asked for it when she traveled as first lady, and ever after her hotel suites were dutifully stocked.

What they all wanted was Dr Pepper, which until 2001 occupied a comfortable third-place spot in the soda aisle behind Coca-Cola and Pepsi. But then a flood of spinoffs from the two soda giants showed up on the shelves—lemons and limes, vanillas and coffees, raspberries and oranges, whites and blues and clears—what in food-industry lingo are known as "line extensions," and Dr Pepper started to lose its market share.

Responding to this pressure, Cadbury Schweppes created its first spinoff, other than a diet version, in the soda's 115-year history, a bright red soda with a very un–Dr Pepper name: Red Fusion. "If we are to re-establish Dr Pepper back to its historic growth rates, we have to add more excitement," the company's president, Jack Kilduff, said. One particularly promising market, Kilduff pointed out, was the "rapidly growing Hispanic and African-American communities."

But consumers hated Red Fusion. "Dr Pepper is my all-time favorite drink, so I was curious about the Red Fusion," a California mother of three wrote on a blog to warn other Peppers away. "It's disgusting. Gagging. Never again."

Stung by the rejection, Cadbury Schweppes in 2004 [20] turned to a food-industry legend named Howard Moskowitz. Moskowitz, who studied mathematics and holds a Ph.D. in experimental psychology from Harvard, runs a consulting firm in White Plains, where for more than three decades he has "optimized" a variety of products for Campbell Soup, General Foods, Kraft and PepsiCo. "I've optimized soups," Moskowitz told me. "I've optimized pizzas. I've optimized salad dressings and pickles. In this field, I'm a game changer."

In the process of product optimization, food engineers alter a litany of variables with the sole intent of finding the most perfect version (or versions) of a product. Ordinary consumers are paid to spend hours sitting in rooms where they touch, feel, sip, smell, swirl and taste whatever product is in question. Their opinions are dumped into a computer, and the data are sifted and sorted through a statistical method called conjoint analysis, which determines what features will be most attractive to consumers. Moskowitz likes to imagine that his computer is divided into silos, in which each of the attributes is stacked. But it's not simply a matter of comparing Color 23 with Color 24. In the most complicated projects, Color 23 must be combined with Syrup 11 and Packaging 6, and on and on, in seemingly infinite combinations. Even for jobs in which the only concern is taste and the variables are limited to the ingredients, endless charts and graphs will come spewing out of Moskowitz's computer. "The mathematical model maps out the ingredients to the sensory perceptions these ingredients create," he told me, "so I can just dial a new product. This is the engineering approach."

. . .

I first met Moskowitz on a crisp day in the spring of 2010 at the Harvard Club in Midtown Manhattan. As we talked, he made clear that while he has worked on numerous projects aimed at creating more healthful foods and insists the industry could be doing far more to curb obesity, he had no qualms about his own pioneering work on discovering what industry insiders now regularly refer to as "the bliss point" or any of the other systems that helped food companies create the greatest amount of crave. "There's no moral issue for me," he said. "I did the best science I could. I was struggling to survive and didn't have the luxury of being a moral creature. As a researcher, I was ahead of my time."

Moskowitz's path to mastering the bliss point began in earnest not at Harvard but a few months after graduation, 16 miles from Cambridge, in the town of Natick, where the U.S. Army hired him to work in its research labs. The military has long been in a peculiar bind when it comes to food: how to get soldiers to eat more rations when they are in the field. They know that over time, soldiers would gradually find their meals-ready-to-eat so boring that they would toss them away, half-eaten, and not get all the calories they needed. But what was causing this M.R.E.-fatigue was a mystery. "So I started asking soldiers how frequently they would like to eat this or that, trying to figure out which products they would find boring," Moskowitz said. The answers he got were inconsistent. "They liked flavorful foods like turkey tetrazzini, but only at first; they quickly grew tired of them. On the other hand, mundane foods like white bread would never get them too excited, but they could eat lots and lots of it without feeling they'd had enough."

This contradiction is known as "sensory-specific satiety." In lay terms, it is the tendency for big, distinct flavors to overwhelm the brain, which responds by depressing your desire to have more. Sensory-specific satiety also became a guiding principle for the processed-food industry. The biggest hits—be they Coca-Cola or Doritos—owe their success to complex formulas that pique the taste buds enough to be alluring but don't have a distinct, overriding single flavor that tells the brain to stop eating.

Thirty-two years after he began experimenting with the bliss 25 point, Moskowitz got the call from Cadbury Schweppes asking him to create a good line extension for Dr Pepper. I spent an afternoon in his White Plains offices as he and his vice president for research, Michele Reisner, walked me through the

Dr Pepper campaign. Cadbury wanted its new flavor to have cherry and vanilla on top of the basic Dr Pepper taste. Thus, there were three main components to play with. A sweet cherry flavoring, a sweet vanilla flavoring and a sweet syrup known as "Dr Pepper flavoring."

Finding the bliss point required the preparation of 61 subtly distinct formulas—31 for the regular version and 30 for diet. The formulas were then subjected to 3,904 tastings organized in Los Angeles, Dallas, Chicago and Philadelphia. The Dr Pepper tasters began working through their samples, resting five minutes between each sip to restore their taste buds. After each sample, they gave numerically ranked answers to a set of questions: How much did they like it overall? How strong is the taste? How do they feel about the taste? How would they describe the quality of this product? How likely would they be to purchase this product?

Moskowitz's data—compiled in a 135-page report for the soda maker—is tremendously fine-grained, showing how different people and groups of people feel about a strong vanilla taste versus weak, various aspects of aroma and the powerful sensory force that food scientists call "mouth feel." This is the way a product interacts with the mouth, as defined more specifically by a host of related sensations, from dryness to gumminess to moisture release. These are terms more familiar to sommeliers, but the mouth feel of soda and many other food items, especially those high in fat, is second only to the bliss point in its ability to predict how much craving a product will induce.

In addition to taste, the consumers were also tested on their response to color, which proved to be highly sensitive. "When we increased the level of the Dr Pepper flavoring, it gets darker and liking goes off," Reisner said. These preferences can also be cross-referenced by age, sex and race.

On page 83 of the report, a thin blue line represents the amount of Dr Pepper flavoring needed to generate maximum appeal. The line is shaped like an upside-down U, just like the bliss-point curve that Moskowitz studied 30 years earlier in his Army lab. And at the top of the arc, there is not a single sweet spot but instead a sweet range, within which "bliss" was achievable. This meant that Cadbury could edge back on its key ingredient, the sugary Dr Pepper syrup, without falling out of the range and losing the bliss. Instead of using 2 milliliters of the flavoring, for instance, they could use 1.69 milliliters and achieve the same effect. The potential savings is merely a few percentage points, and it won't mean much to individual consumers who are counting calories or grams of sugar. But for Dr Pepper, it adds up to colossal savings. "That looks like nothing," Reisner said. "But it's a lot of money. A lot of money. Millions."

The soda that emerged from all of Moskowitz's variations 30 became known as Cherry Vanilla Dr Pepper, and it proved successful beyond anything Cadbury imagined. In 2008, Cadbury split off its soft-drinks business, which included Snapple and 7-Up. The Dr Pepper Snapple Group has since been valued in excess of $11 billion.

. . .

"It's Called Vanishing Caloric Density."

At a symposium for nutrition scientists in Los Angeles on February 15, 1985, a professor of pharmacology from Helsinki named Heikki Karppanen told the remarkable story of Finland's effort to address its salt habit. In the late 1970s, the Finns were consuming huge amounts of sodium, eating on average more than two teaspoons of salt a day. As a result, the country had developed significant issues with high blood pressure, and men in the eastern part of Finland had the highest rate of fatal cardiovascular disease in the world. Research showed that this plague was not just a quirk of genetics or a result of a sedentary lifestyle—it was also owing to processed foods. So when Finnish authorities moved to address the problem, they went right after the manufacturers. (The Finnish response worked. Every grocery item that was heavy in salt would come to be marked prominently with the warning "High Salt Content." By 2007, Finland's per capita consumption of salt had dropped by a third, and this shift—along with improved medical care—was accompanied by a 75 percent to 80 percent decline in the number of deaths from strokes and heart disease.)

Karppanen's presentation was met with applause, but one man in the crowd seemed particularly intrigued by the presentation, and as Karppanen left the stage, the man intercepted him and asked if they could talk more over dinner. Their conversation later that night was not at all what Karppanen was expecting. His host did indeed have an interest in salt, but from quite a different vantage point: the man's name was Robert I-San Lin, and from 1974 to 1982, he worked as the chief scientist for Frito-Lay, the nearly $3-billion-a-year manufacturer of Lay's, Doritos, Cheetos and Fritos.

Lin's time at Frito-Lay coincided with the first attacks by nutrition advocates on salty foods and the first calls for federal regulators to reclassify salt as a "risky" food additive, which could have subjected it to severe controls. No company took this threat more seriously—or more personally—than Frito-Lay, Lin explained to Karppanen over their dinner. Three years after he left Frito-Lay, he was still anguished over his inability to effectively change the company's recipes and practices.

By chance, I ran across a letter that Lin sent to Karppanen three weeks after that dinner, buried in some files to which I had gained access. Attached to the letter was a memo written when Lin was at Frito-Lay, which detailed some of the company's efforts in defending salt. I tracked Lin down in Irvine, California, where we spent several days going through the internal company memos, strategy papers and handwritten notes he had kept. The documents were evidence of the concern that Lin had for consumers and of the company's intent on using science not to address the health concerns but to thwart them. While at Frito-Lay, Lin and other company scientists spoke openly about the country's excessive consumption of sodium and the fact that, as Lin said to me on more than one occasion, "people get addicted to salt."

Not much had changed by 1986, except Frito-Lay found 35 itself on a rare cold streak. The company had introduced a series of high-profile products that failed miserably. Toppels, a cracker with cheese topping; Stuffers, a shell with a variety of fillings; Rumbles, a bite-size granola snack—they all came and went in a blink, and the company took a $52 million hit. Around that time, the marketing team was joined by Dwight Riskey, an expert on cravings who had been a fellow at the Monell Chemical Senses Center in Philadelphia, where he was part of a team of scientists that found that people could beat their salt habits simply by refraining from salty foods long enough for their taste buds to return to a normal level of sensitivity. He had also done work on the bliss point, showing how a product's allure is contextual, shaped partly by the other foods a person is eating, and that it changes as people age. This seemed to help explain why Frito-Lay was having so much trouble selling new snacks. The largest single block of customers, the baby boomers, had begun hitting middle age. According to the research, this suggested that their liking for salty snacks—both in the concentration of salt and how much they ate—would be tapering off. Along with the rest of the snack-food industry, Frito-Lay anticipated lower sales because of an aging population, and marketing plans were adjusted to focus even more intently on younger consumers.

Except that snack sales didn't decline as everyone had projected, Frito-Lay's doomed product launches notwithstanding. Poring over data one day in his home office, trying to understand just who was consuming all the snack food, Riskey realized that he and his colleagues had been misreading things all along. They had been measuring the snacking habits of different age groups and were seeing what they expected to see, that older consumers ate less than those in their 20s. But what they weren't measuring, Riskey realized, is how those snacking habits of the boomers compared to themselves when they were in their 20s. When he called up a new set of sales data and performed what's called a cohort study, following a single group over time, a far more encouraging picture—for Frito-Lay, anyway—emerged. The baby boomers were not eating fewer salty snacks as they aged. "In fact, as those people aged, their consumption of all those segments—the cookies, the crackers, the candy, the chips—was going up," Riskey said. "They were not only eating what they ate when they were younger, they were eating more of it." In fact, everyone in the country, on average, was eating more salty snacks than they used to. The rate of consumption was edging up about one-third of a pound every year, with the average intake of snacks like chips and cheese crackers pushing past 12 pounds a year.

Riskey had a theory about what caused this surge: Eating real meals had become a thing of the past. Baby boomers, especially, seemed to have greatly cut down on regular meals. They were skipping breakfast when they had early-morning meetings. They skipped lunch when they then needed to catch up on work because of those meetings. They skipped dinner when their kids stayed out late or grew up and moved out of the house. And when they skipped these meals, they replaced them with snacks. "We looked at this behavior, and said, 'Oh, my gosh, people were skipping meals right and left,'" Riskey told me. "It was amazing." This led to the next realization, that baby boomers did not represent "a category that is mature, with no growth. This is a category that has huge growth potential."

The food technicians stopped worrying about inventing new products and instead embraced the industry's most reliable method for getting consumers to buy more: the line extension. The classic Lay's potato chips were joined by Salt & Vinegar, Salt & Pepper and Cheddar & Sour Cream. They put out Chili-Cheese-flavored Fritos, and Cheetos were transformed into 21 varieties. Frito-Lay had a formidable research complex near Dallas, where nearly 500 chemists, psychologists and technicians conducted research that cost up to $30 million a year, and the science corps focused intense amounts of resources on questions of crunch, mouth feel and aroma for each of these items. Their tools included a $40,000 device that simulated a chewing mouth to test and perfect the chips, discovering things like the perfect break point: people like a chip that snaps with about four pounds of pressure per square inch.

To get a better feel for their work, I called on Steven Witherly, a food scientist who wrote a fascinating guide for industry insiders titled, "Why Humans Like Junk Food." I brought him two shopping bags filled with a variety of chips

The industry's most reliable method for getting consumers to buy more: the line extension.

to taste. He zeroed right in on the Cheetos. "This," Witherly said, "is one of the most marvelously constructed foods on the planet, in terms of pure pleasure." He ticked off a dozen attributes of the Cheetos that make the brain say more. But the one he focused on most was the puff's uncanny ability to melt in the mouth. "It's called vanishing caloric density," Witherly said. "If something melts down quickly, your brain thinks that there's no calories in it . . . you can just keep eating it forever."

As for their marketing troubles, in a March 2010 meeting, 40 Frito-Lay executives hastened to tell their Wall Street investors that the 1.4 billion boomers worldwide weren't being neglected; they were redoubling their efforts to understand exactly what it was that boomers most wanted in a snack chip. Which was basically everything: great taste, maximum bliss but minimal guilt about health and more maturity than puffs. "They snack a lot," Frito-Lay's chief marketing officer, Ann Mukherjee, told the investors. "But what they're looking for is very different. They're looking for new experiences, real food experiences." Frito-Lay acquired Stacy's Pita Chip Company, which was started by a Massachusetts couple who made food-cart sandwiches and started serving pita chips to their customers in the mid-1990s. In Frito-Lay's hands, the pita chips averaged 270 milligrams of sodium—nearly one-fifth a whole day's recommended maximum for most American adults—and were a huge hit among boomers.

The Frito-Lay executives also spoke of the company's ongoing pursuit of a "designer sodium," which they hoped, in the near future, would take their sodium loads down by 40 percent. No need to worry about lost sales there, the company's C.E.O., Al Carey, assured their investors. The boomers would see less salt as the green light to snack like never before.

There's a paradox at work here. On the one hand, reduction of sodium in snack foods is commendable. On the other, these changes may well result in consumers eating more. "The big thing that will happen here is removing the barriers for boomers and giving them permission to snack," Carey said. The prospects for lower-salt snacks were so amazing, he added, that the company had set its sights on using the designer salt to conquer the toughest market of all for snacks: schools. He cited, for example, the school-food initiative championed by Bill Clinton and the American Heart Association, which is seeking to improve the nutrition of school food by limiting its load of salt, sugar and fat. "Imagine this," Carey said.

See Chapter 4 for ways to agree and disagree simultaneously.

"A potato chip that tastes great and qualifies for the Clinton-A.H.A. alliance for schools. . . . We think we have ways to do all of this on a potato chip, and imagine getting that product into schools, where children can have this product and grow up with it and feel good about eating it."

Carey's quote reminded me of something I read in the early stages of my reporting, a 24-page report prepared for Frito-Lay in 1957 by a psychologist named Ernest Dichter. The company's chips, he wrote, were not selling as well as they could for one simple reason: "While people like and enjoy potato chips, they feel guilty about liking them. . . . Unconsciously, people expect to be punished for 'letting themselves go' and enjoying them." Dichter listed seven "fears and resistances" to the chips: "You can't stop eating them; they're fattening; they're not good for you; they're greasy and messy to eat; they're too expensive; it's hard to store the leftovers; and they're bad for children." He spent the rest of his memo laying out his prescriptions, which in time would become widely used not just by Frito-Lay but also by the entire industry. Dichter suggested that Frito-Lay avoid using the word "fried" in referring to its chips and adopt instead the more healthful-sounding term "toasted." To counteract the "fear of letting oneself go," he suggested repacking the chips into smaller bags. "The more-anxious consumers, the ones who have the deepest fears about their capacity to control their appetite, will tend to sense the function of the new pack and select it," he said.

Dichter advised Frito-Lay to move its chips out of the realm of between-meals snacking and turn them into an ever-present item in the American diet. "The increased use of potato chips and other Lay's products as a part of the regular fare served by restaurants and sandwich bars should be encouraged in a concentrated way," Dichter said, citing a string of examples:

"potato chips with soup, with fruit or vegetable juice appetizers; potato chips served as a vegetable on the main dish; potato chips with salad; potato chips with egg dishes for breakfast; potato chips with sandwich orders."

In 2011, *The New England Journal of Medicine* published [45] a study that shed new light on America's weight gain. The subjects—120,877 women and men—were all professionals in the health field, and were likely to be more conscious about nutrition, so the findings might well understate the overall trend. Using data back to 1986, the researchers monitored everything the participants ate, as well as their physical activity and smoking. They found that every four years, the participants exercised less, watched TV more and gained an average of 3.35 pounds. The researchers parsed the data by the caloric content of the foods being eaten, and found the top contributors to weight gain included red meat and processed meats, sugar-sweetened beverages and potatoes, including mashed and French fries. But the largest weight-inducing food was the potato chip. The coating of salt, the fat content that rewards the brain with instant feelings of pleasure, the sugar that exists not as an additive but in the starch of the potato itself—all of this combines to make it the perfect addictive food. "The starch is readily absorbed," Eric Rimm, an associate professor of epidemiology and nutrition at the Harvard School of Public Health and one of the study's authors, told me. "More quickly even than a similar amount of sugar. The starch, in turn, causes the glucose levels in the blood to spike"—which can result in a craving for more.

If Americans snacked only occasionally, and in small amounts, this would not present the enormous problem that it does. But because so much money and effort has been invested over decades in engineering and then relentlessly selling these products, the effects are seemingly impossible to unwind. More than 30 years have passed since Robert Lin first tangled with Frito-Lay on the imperative of the company to deal with the formulation of its snacks, but as we sat at his dining-room table, sifting through his records, the feelings of regret still played on his face. In his view, three decades had been lost, time that he and a lot of other smart scientists could have spent searching for ways to ease the addiction to salt, sugar and fat. "I couldn't do much about it," he told me. "I feel so sorry for the public."

"These People Need a Lot of Things, But They Don't Need a Coke."

The growing attention Americans are paying to what they put into their mouths has touched off a new scramble by the processed-food companies to address health concerns. Pressed by the Obama administration and consumers, Kraft, Nestlé, Pepsi, Campbell and General Mills, among others, have begun to trim the loads of salt, sugar and fat in many products. And with consumer advocates pushing for more government intervention, Coca-Cola made headlines in January by releasing ads that promoted its bottled water and low-calorie drinks as a way to counter obesity. Predictably, the ads drew a new volley of scorn from critics who pointed to the company's continuing drive to sell sugary Coke.

One of the other executives I spoke with at length was Jeffrey Dunn, who, in 2001, at age 44, was directing more than half of Coca-Cola's $20 billion in annual sales as president and chief operating officer in both North and South America. In an effort to control as much market share as possible, Coke extended its aggressive marketing to especially poor or vulnerable areas of the U.S., like New Orleans—where people were drinking twice as much Coke as the national average—or Rome, Georgia, where the per capita intake was nearly three Cokes a day. In Coke's headquarters in Atlanta, the biggest consumers were referred to as "heavy users." "The other model we use was called 'drinks and drinkers,'" Dunn said. "How many drinkers do I have? And how many drinks do they drink? If you lost one of those heavy users, if somebody just decided to stop drinking Coke, how many drinkers would you have to get, at low velocity, to make up for that heavy user? The answer is a lot. It's more efficient to get my existing users to drink more."

One of Dunn's lieutenants, Todd Putman, who worked at Coca-Cola from 1997 to 2001, said the goal became much larger than merely beating the rival brands; Coca-Cola strove to outsell every other thing people drank, including milk and water. The marketing division's efforts boiled down to one question, Putman said: "How can we drive more ounces into more bodies more often?" (In response to Putman's remarks, Coke said its goals have changed and that it now focuses on providing consumers with more low- or no-calorie products.)

In his capacity, Dunn was making frequent trips to Brazil, 50 where the company had recently begun a push to increase consumption of Coke among the many Brazilians living in [the slums known as] *favelas*. The company's strategy was to repackage Coke into smaller, more affordable 6.7-ounce bottles, just 20 cents each. Coke was not alone in seeing Brazil as a potential boon; Nestlé began deploying battalions of women to travel poor neighborhoods, hawking American-style processed foods door to door. But Coke was Dunn's concern, and on one trip, as he walked through one of the impoverished areas, he had an epiphany. "A voice in my head says, 'These people need a lot of things, but they don't need a Coke.' I almost threw up."

Dunn returned to Atlanta, determined to make some changes. He didn't want to abandon the soda business, but he did want to try to steer the company into a more healthful mode, and one of the things he pushed for was to stop marketing Coke in public schools. The independent companies that bottled Coke viewed his plans as reactionary. A director of one bottler wrote a letter to Coke's chief executive and board asking for Dunn's head. "He said what I had done was the worst thing he had seen in 50 years in the business," Dunn said. "Just to placate these crazy leftist school districts who were trying to keep people from having their Coke. He said I was an embarrassment to the company, and I should be fired." In February 2004, he was.

Dunn told me that talking about Coke's business today was by no means easy and, because he continues to work in the food business, not without risk. "You really don't want them mad at you," he said. "And I don't mean that, like, I'm going to end up at the bottom of the bay. But they don't have a sense of humor when it comes to this stuff. They're a very, very aggressive company."

When I met with Dunn, he told me not just about his years at Coke but also about his new marketing venture. In April 2010, he met with three executives from Madison Dearborn Partners, a private-equity firm based in Chicago with a wide-ranging portfolio of investments. They recently hired Dunn to run one of their newest acquisitions—a food producer in the San Joaquin Valley. As they sat in the hotel's meeting room, the men listened to Dunn's marketing pitch. He talked about giving the product a personality that was bold and irreverent, conveying the idea that this was the ultimate snack food. He went into detail on how he would target a special segment of the 146 million Americans who are regular snackers—mothers, children, young professionals—people, he said, who "keep their snacking ritual fresh by trying a new food product when it catches their attention."

He explained how he would deploy strategic storytelling in the ad campaign for this snack, using a key phrase that had been developed with much calculation: "Eat 'Em Like Junk Food."

After 45 minutes, Dunn clicked off the last slide and thanked the men for coming. Madison's portfolio contained the largest Burger King franchise in the world, the Ruth's Chris Steak House chain and a processed-food maker called AdvancePierre whose lineup includes the Jamwich, a peanut-butter-and-jelly contrivance that comes frozen, crustless and embedded with four kinds of sugars.

The snack that Dunn was proposing to sell: carrots. Plain, fresh carrots. No added sugar. No creamy sauce or dips. No salt. Just baby carrots, washed, bagged, then sold into the deadly dull produce aisle.

"We act like a snack, not a vegetable," he told the investors. "We exploit the rules of junk food to fuel the baby-carrot conversation. We are pro-junk-food behavior but anti-junk-food establishment."

The investors were thinking only about sales. They had already bought one of the two biggest farm producers of baby carrots in the country, and they'd hired Dunn to run the whole operation. Now, after his pitch, they were relieved. Dunn had figured out that using the industry's own marketing ploys would work better than anything else. He drew from the bag of tricks that he mastered in his 20 years at Coca-Cola, where he learned one of the most critical rules in processed food: The selling of food matters as much as the food itself.

Later, describing his new line of work, Dunn told me he was doing penance for his Coca-Cola years. "I'm paying my karmic debt," he said.

Joining the Conversation

1. Michael Moss provides three examples of scientific research on junk food and its effects. What common denominator links these examples? What makes the science of addictive junk food so extraordinary?

2. Moss opens this essay by describing a meeting that the leaders of several major food companies held to discuss the obesity epidemic and how to respond to it. Why do you think he begins with this story? How does it set the stage for the rest of the piece?

3. Moss is able to present complex technical information so that nonscientists can understand it. One way he does this is by using colloquial language to explain technical terms such as "product optimization," "bliss point," and "sensory-specific satiety." This technique helps us understand his topic, but how also does it make his argument interesting—and persuasive?

4. Moss reports that the major food companies hire experts to make their products as appealing as possible. Now that you know about these tactics, what are some specific actions you can take to guard against manipulation when you shop for food?

5. If Jeffrey Dunn could turn carrots into "the ultimate snack food" (paragraph 53), what other healthy foods could be similarly transformed? Beets? Kale? What else? Write an essay proposing such a product. Use the "they say/I say" format, perhaps quoting or summarizing something said in Moss's essay as your "they say."

How Junk Food Can End Obesity

DAVID H. FREEDMAN

—◻—

Demonizing processed food may be dooming many to obesity and disease. Could embracing the drive-thru make us all healthier?

LATE LAST YEAR, in a small health-food eatery called Cafe Sprouts in Oberlin, Ohio, I had what may well have been the most wholesome beverage of my life. The friendly server patiently guided me to an apple-blueberry-kale-carrot smoothie-juice combination, which she spent the next several minutes preparing, mostly by shepherding farm-fresh produce into machinery. The result was tasty, but at 300 calories (by my rough calculation) in a 16-ounce cup, it was more than my diet could regularly absorb without consequences, nor was I about to make a habit of $9 shakes, healthy or not.

———

DAVID H. FREEDMAN is the author of *Wrong: Why Experts Keep Failing Us—and How to Know When Not to Trust Them* (2010) and the coauthor, with Eric Abrahamson, of *A Perfect Mess: The Hidden Benefits of Disorder* (2007). He is a contributing editor at the *Atlantic* and *Inc.* magazines and is widely published on issues relating to science, technology, and health care. He blogs at fatandskinner.org. This essay first appeared in the July/August 2013 issue of the *Atlantic*.

Inspired by the experience nonetheless, I tried again two months later at L.A.'s Real Food Daily, a popular vegan restaurant near Hollywood. I was initially wary of a low-calorie juice made almost entirely from green vegetables, but the server assured me it was a popular treat. I like to brag that I can eat anything, and I scarf down all sorts of raw vegetables like candy, but I could stomach only about a third of this oddly foamy, bitter concoction. It smelled like lawn clippings and tasted like liquid celery. It goes for $7.95, and I waited 10 minutes for it.

I finally hit the sweet spot just a few weeks later, in Chicago, with a delicious blueberry-pomegranate smoothie that rang in at a relatively modest 220 calories. It cost $3 and took only seconds to make. Best of all, I'll be able to get this concoction just about anywhere. Thanks, McDonald's!

If only the McDonald's smoothie weren't, unlike the first two, so fattening and unhealthy. Or at least that's what the most-prominent voices in our food culture today would have you believe.

An enormous amount of media space has been dedicated 5
to promoting the notion that all processed food, and only
processed food, is making us sickly and overweight. In this
narrative, the food-industrial complex—particularly the fast-
food industry—has turned all the powers of food-processing
science loose on engineering its offerings to addict us to fat,
sugar, and salt, causing or at least heavily contributing to the
obesity crisis. The wares of these pimps and pushers, we are
told, are to be universally shunned.

Consider the *New York Times.* Earlier this year, the *Times
Magazine* gave its cover to a long piece based on Michael
Moss's about-to-be-best-selling book, *Salt Sugar Fat: How the
Food Giants Hooked Us.* Hitting bookshelves at about the same
time was the former *Times* reporter Melanie Warner's *Pandora's
Lunchbox: How Processed Food Took Over the American Meal,*
which addresses more or less the same theme. Two years ago
the *Times Magazine* featured the journalist Gary Taubes's "Is
Sugar Toxic?," a cover story on the evils of refined sugar and
high-fructose corn syrup. And most significant of all has been
the considerable space the magazine has devoted over the years
to Michael Pollan, a journalism professor at the University of
California at Berkeley, and his broad indictment of food processing as a source of society's health problems.

"The food they're cooking is making people sick," Pollan has
said of big food companies. "It is one of the reasons that we
have the obesity and diabetes epidemics that we do. . . . If you're
going to let industries decide how much salt, sugar and fat is
in your food, they're going to put [in] as much as they possibly
can. . . . They will push those buttons until we scream or die."
The solution, in his view, is to replace Big Food's engineered,
edible evil—through public education and regulation—with
fresh, unprocessed, local, seasonal, *real* food.

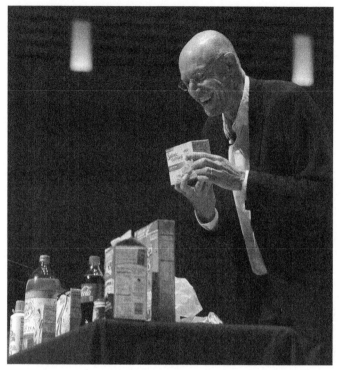

Michael Pollan

Pollan's worldview saturates the public conversation on healthy eating. You hear much the same from many scientists, physicians, food activists, nutritionists, celebrity chefs, and pundits. *Foodlike substances*, the derisive term Pollan uses to describe processed foods, is now a solid part of the elite vernacular. Thousands of restaurants and grocery stores, most notably the Whole Foods chain, have thrived by answering the call to reject industrialized foods in favor of a return to natural, simple, nonindustrialized—let's call them "wholesome"—foods.

The two newest restaurants in my smallish Massachusetts town both prominently tout wholesome ingredients; one of them is called the Farmhouse, and it's usually packed.

A new generation of business, social, and policy entrepreneurs is rising to further cater to these tastes, and to challenge Big Food. Silicon Valley, where tomorrow's entrepreneurial and social trends are forged, has spawned a small ecosystem of wholesome-friendly venture-capital firms (Physic Ventures, for example), business accelerators (Local Food Lab), and Web sites (Edible Startups) to fund, nurture, and keep tabs on young companies such as blissmo (a wholesome-food-of-the-month club), Mile High Organics (online wholesome-food shopping), and Whole-share (group wholesome-food purchasing), all designed to help reacquaint Americans with the simpler eating habits of yesteryear.

In virtually every realm of human existence, we turn to 10 technology to help us solve our problems. But even in Silicon Valley, when it comes to food and obesity, technology—or at least food-processing technology—is widely treated as if it *is* the problem. The solution, from this viewpoint, necessarily involves turning our back on it.

If the most-influential voices in our food culture today get their way, we will achieve a genuine food revolution. Too bad it would be one tailored to the dubious health fantasies of a small, elite minority. And too bad it would largely exclude the obese masses, who would continue to sicken and die early. Despite the best efforts of a small army of wholesome-food heroes, there is no reasonable scenario under which these foods could become cheap and plentiful enough to serve as the core diet for most of the obese population—even in the unlikely case that your typical junk-food eater would be willing and able to break life-long habits to embrace kale and yellow beets. And many of the dishes glorified by the wholesome-food movement are, in any case, as caloric and obesogenic as anything served in a Burger King.

Through its growing sway over health-conscious consumers and policy makers, the wholesome-food movement is impeding the progress of the one segment of the food world that is actually positioned to take effective, near-term steps to reverse the obesity trend: the processed-food industry. Popular food producers, fast-food chains among them, are already applying various tricks and technologies to create less caloric and more satiating versions of their junky fare that nonetheless retain much of the appeal of the originals, and could be induced to go much further. In fact, these roundly demonized companies could do far more for the public's health in five years than the wholesome-food movement is likely to accomplish in the next 50. But will the wholesome-food advocates let them?

Michael Pollan Has No Clothes

Let's go shopping. We can start at Whole Foods Market, a critical link in the wholesome-eating food chain. There are three Whole Foods stores within 15 minutes of my house—we're big on real food in the suburbs west of Boston. Here at the largest of the three, I can choose from more than 21 types of tofu, 62 bins of organic grains and legumes, and 42 different salad greens.

Much of the food isn't all that different from what I can get in any other supermarket, but sprinkled throughout are items that scream "wholesome." One that catches my eye today, sitting prominently on an impulse-buy rack near the checkout counter, is Vegan Cheesy Salad Booster, from Living Intentions, whose package emphasizes the fact that the food is enhanced with spirulina, chlorella, and sea vegetables. The label also proudly lets me know that the contents are raw—no processing!—and that they don't contain any genetically modified ingredients. What the stuff does contain, though, is more than three times the fat content per ounce as the beef patty in a Big Mac (more than two-thirds of the calories come from fat), and four times the sodium.

After my excursion to Whole Foods, I drive a few minutes 15 to a Trader Joe's, also known for an emphasis on wholesome foods. Here at the register I'm confronted with a large display of a snack food called "Inner Peas," consisting of peas that are breaded in cornmeal and rice flour, fried in sunflower oil, and then sprinkled with salt. By weight, the snack has six times as much fat as it does protein, along with loads of carbohydrates. I can't recall ever seeing anything at any fast-food restaurant that represents as big an obesogenic crime against the vegetable kingdom. (A spokesperson for Trader Joe's said the company does not consider itself a "'wholesome food' grocery retailer." Living Intentions did not respond to a request for comment.)

This phenomenon is by no means limited to packaged food at upscale supermarkets. Back in February, when I was at Real Food Daily in Los Angeles, I ordered the "Sea Cake" along with my green-vegetable smoothie. It was intensely delicious in a way that set off alarm bells. RFD wouldn't provide precise information about the ingredients, but I found a recipe online for "Tofu 'Fish' Cakes," which seem very close to what I ate. Essentially, they consist of some tofu mixed with a lot of refined carbs (the RFD version contains at least some unrefined carbs) along with oil and soy milk, all fried in oil and served with a soy-and-oil-based tartar sauce. (Tofu and other forms of soy are high in protein, but per 100 calories, tofu is as fatty as many cuts of beef.) L.A. being to the wholesome-food movement what Hawaii is to Spam, I ate at two other mega-popular wholesome-food restaurants while I was in the area. At Café Gratitude

I enjoyed the kale chips and herb-cornmeal-crusted eggplant parmesan, and at Akasha I indulged in a spiced-lamb-sausage flatbread pizza. Both are pricey orgies of fat and carbs.

I'm not picking out rare, less healthy examples from these establishments. Check out their menus online: fat, sugar, and other refined carbs abound. (Café Gratitude says it uses only "healthy" fats and natural sweeteners; Akasha says its focus is not on "health food" but on "farm to fork" fare.) In fact, because the products and dishes offered by these types of establishments tend to emphasize the healthy-sounding foods they contain, I find it much harder to navigate through them to foods that go easy on the oil, butter, refined grains, rice, potatoes, and sugar than I do at far less wholesome restaurants. (These dishes also tend to contain plenty of sea salt, which Pollanites hold up as the wholesome alternative to the addictive salt engineered by the food industry, though your body can't tell the difference.)

One occasional source of obesogenic travesties is the *New York Times Magazine*'s lead food writer, Mark Bittman, who now rivals Pollan as a shepherd to the anti-processed-food flock. (*Salon*, in an article titled "How to Live What Michael Pollan Preaches," called Bittman's 2009 book, *Food Matters*, "both a cookbook and a manifesto that shows us how to eat better—and save the planet.") I happened to catch Bittman on the *Today* show last year demonstrating for millions of viewers four ways to prepare corn in summertime, including a lovely dish of corn sautéed in bacon fat and topped with bacon. Anyone who thinks that such a thing is much healthier than a Whopper just hasn't been paying attention to obesity science for the past few decades.

That science is, in fact, fairly straightforward. Fat carries more than twice as many calories as carbohydrates and proteins do per gram, which means just a little fat can turn a serving of food into a calorie bomb. Sugar and other refined carbohydrates,

Mark Bittman demonstrates cooking on the *Today* show.

like white flour and rice, and high-starch foods, like corn and potatoes, aren't as calorie-dense. But all of these "problem carbs" charge into the bloodstream as glucose in minutes, providing an energy rush, commonly followed by an energy crash that can lead to a surge in appetite.

Because they are energy-intense foods, fat and sugar and other problem carbs trip the pleasure and reward meters placed in our brains by evolution over the millions of years during which starvation was an ever-present threat. We're born enjoying the stimulating sensations these ingredients provide, and exposure strengthens the associations, ensuring that we come to crave them and, all too often, eat more of them than we should. Processed food is not an essential part of this story: recent examinations of ancient human remains in Egypt, Peru, and elsewhere have repeatedly revealed hardened arteries, suggesting that pre-industrial diets, at least of the affluent, may not have been the epitome of healthy eating that the Pollanites make them out to be. People who want to lose weight and keep it off are almost always advised by those who run successful long-term weight-loss programs to transition to a diet high in lean protein, complex carbs such as whole grains and legumes, and the sort of fiber vegetables are loaded with. Because these ingredients provide us with the calories we need without the big, fast bursts of energy, they can be satiating without pushing the primitive reward buttons that nudge us to eat too much.

(A few words on salt: Yes, it's unhealthy in large amounts, raising blood pressure in many people; and yes, it makes food more appealing. But salt is not obesogenic—it has no calories, and doesn't specifically increase the desire to consume high-calorie foods. It can just as easily be enlisted to add to the appeal of vegetables. Lumping it in with fat and sugar as an addictive junk-food ingredient is a confused proposition. But let's agree we want to cut down on it.)

See Chapter 6 for ways to anticipate objections.

To be sure, many of Big Food's most popular products are loaded with appalling amounts of fat and sugar and other problem carbs (as well as salt), and the plentitude of these ingredients, exacerbated by large portion sizes, has clearly helped foment the obesity crisis. It's hard to find anyone anywhere who disagrees. Junk food is bad for you because it's full of fat and problem carbs. But will switching to wholesome foods free us from this scourge? It could in theory, but in practice, it's hard to see how. Even putting aside for a moment the serious questions about whether wholesome foods could be made accessible to the obese public, and whether the obese would be willing to eat them, we have a more immediate stumbling block: many of the foods served up and even glorified by the wholesome-food movement are themselves chock full of fat and problem carbs.

Some wholesome foodies openly celebrate fat and problem carbs, insisting that the lack of processing magically renders them healthy. In singing the praises of clotted cream and lard-loaded cookies, for instance, a recent *Wall Street Journal* article by Ron Rosenbaum explained that "eating basic, earthy, fatty foods isn't just a supreme experience of the senses—it can actually be good for you," and that it's "too easy to conflate eating fatty food with eating industrial, oil-fried junk food." That's right, we wouldn't want to make the same mistake that all the cells in our bodies make. Pollan himself makes it clear in his writing that he has little problem with fat—as long as it's not in food "your great-grandmother wouldn't recognize."

Television food shows routinely feature revered chefs tossing around references to healthy eating, "wellness," and farm-fresh ingredients, all the while spooning lard, cream, and sugar over everything in sight. (A study published last year in the *British Medical Journal* found that the recipes in the books of top TV chefs call for "significantly more" fat per portion than what's contained in ready-to-eat supermarket meals.) Corporate wellness programs, one of the most promising avenues for getting the population to adopt healthy behaviors, are falling prey to this way of thinking as well. Last November, I attended a stress-management seminar for employees of a giant consulting company, and listened to a high-powered professional wellness coach tell the crowded room that it's okay to eat anything as long as its plant or animal origins aren't obscured by processing. Thus, she explained, potato chips are perfectly healthy, because they plainly come from potatoes, but Cheetos will make you sick and fat, because what plant or animal is a Cheeto? (For the record, typical potato chips and Cheetos have about equally nightmarish amounts of fat calories per ounce; Cheetos have fewer carbs, though more salt.)

The Pollanites seem confused about exactly what benefits 25 their way of eating provides. All the railing about the fat, sugar, and salt engineered into industrial junk food might lead one to infer that wholesome food, having not been engineered, contains substantially less of them. But clearly you can take in obscene quantities of fat and problem carbs while eating wholesomely, and to judge by what's sold at wholesome stores and restaurants, many people do. Indeed, the more converts and customers the wholesome-food movement's purveyors seek, the stronger their incentive to emphasize foods that light up precisely the same pleasure centers as a 3 Musketeers bar. That just makes wholesome food stealthily obesogenic.

Hold on, you may be thinking. Leaving fat, sugar, and salt aside, what about all the nasty things that wholesome foods do not, by definition, contain and processed foods do? A central claim of the wholesome-food movement is that wholesome is healthier because it doesn't have the artificial flavors, preservatives, other additives, or genetically modified ingredients found in industrialized food; because it isn't subjected to the physical transformations that processed foods go through; and because it doesn't sit around for days, weeks, or months, as industrialized food sometimes does. (This is the complaint against the McDonald's smoothie, which contains artificial flavors and texture additives, and which is pre-mixed.)

The health concerns raised about processing itself—rather than the amount of fat and problem carbs in any given dish—are not, by and large, related to weight gain or obesity. That's important to keep in mind, because obesity is, by an enormous margin, the largest health problem created by what we eat. But even putting that aside, concerns about processed food have been magnified out of all proportion.

Some studies have shown that people who eat wholesomely tend to be healthier than people who live on fast food and other processed food (particularly meat), but the problem with such studies is obvious: substantial nondietary differences exist between these groups, such as propensity to exercise, smoking rates, air quality, access to health care, and much more. (Some researchers say they've tried to control for these factors, but that's a claim most scientists don't put much faith in.) What's more, the people in these groups are sometimes eating entirely different foods, not the same sorts of foods subjected to different levels of processing. It's comparing apples to Whoppers, instead of Whoppers to hand-ground, grass-fed-beef burgers with heirloom tomatoes, garlic aioli, and artisanal cheese. For all these reasons, such findings linking food type and health are considered highly unreliable, and constantly contradict one another, as is true of most epidemiological studies that try to tackle broad nutritional questions.

The fact is, there is simply no clear, credible evidence that any aspect of food processing or storage makes a food uniquely unhealthy. The U.S. population does not suffer from a critical lack of any nutrient because we eat so much processed food. (Sure, health experts urge Americans to get more calcium, potassium, magnesium, fiber, and vitamins A, E, and C, and eating more produce and dairy is a great way to get them, but these ingredients are also available in processed foods, not to mention supplements.) Pollan's "foodlike substances" are regulated by the U.S. Food and Drug Administration (with some exceptions, which are regulated by other agencies), and their effects on health are further raked over by countless scientists who would get a nice career boost from turning up the hidden dangers in some common food-industry ingredient or technique, in part because any number of advocacy groups and journalists are ready to pounce on the slightest hint of risk.

The results of all the scrutiny of processed food are hardly scary, although some groups and writers try to make them 30 appear that way. The Pew Charitable Trusts' Food Additives Project, for example, has bemoaned the fact that the FDA directly reviews only about 70 percent of the ingredients found in food, permitting the rest to pass as "generally recognized as safe" by panels of experts convened by manufacturers. But the only actual risk the project calls out on its Web site or in its publications is a quote from a *Times* article noting that bromine, which has been in U.S. foods for eight decades, is regarded as suspicious by many because flame retardants containing bromine have been linked to health risks. There is no conclusive evidence that bromine itself is a threat.

In *Pandora's Lunchbox*, Melanie Warner assiduously catalogs every concern that could possibly be raised about the health threats of food processing, leveling accusations so vague, weakly supported, tired, or insignificant that only someone already convinced of the guilt of processed food could find them troubling. While ripping the covers off the breakfast-cereal conspiracy, for example, Warner reveals that much of the nutritional value claimed by these products comes not from natural ingredients but from added vitamins that are chemically synthesized, which must be bad for us because, well, they're *chemically synthesized*. It's the tautology at the heart of the movement: processed foods are unhealthy because they aren't natural, full stop.

In many respects, the wholesome-food movement veers awfully close to religion. To repeat: there is no hard evidence to back any health-risk claims about processed food—evidence, say, of the caliber of several studies by the Centers for Disease Control and Prevention that have traced food poisoning to raw milk, a product championed by some circles of the wholesome-food movement. "Until I hear evidence to the contrary, I think it's reasonable to include processed food in your diet," says Robert Kushner, a physician and nutritionist and a professor at Northwestern University's medical school, where he is the clinical director of the Comprehensive Center on Obesity.

There may be other reasons to prefer wholesome food to the industrialized version. Often stirred into the vague stew of benefits attributed to wholesome food is the "sustainability" of its production—that is, its long-term impact on the planet. Small farms that don't rely much on chemicals and heavy industrial equipment may be better for the environment than giant industrial farms—although that argument quickly becomes complicated by a variety of factors. For the purposes of this article, let's simply stipulate that wholesome foods are environmentally superior. But let's also agree that when it comes to prioritizing among food-related public-policy goals, we are likely to save and improve many more lives by focusing on cutting obesity—through any available means—than by trying to convert all of industrial agriculture into a vast constellation of small organic farms.

The impact of obesity on the chances of our living long, productive, and enjoyable lives has been so well documented at this point that I hate to drag anyone through the grim statistics again. But let me just toss out one recent dispatch from the world of obesity-havoc science: a study published in February in the journal *Obesity* found that obese young adults and middle-agers in the U.S. are likely to lose almost a decade of life on average, as compared with their non-obese counterparts. Given our obesity rates, that means Americans who are alive today can collectively expect to sacrifice 1 billion years to obesity. The study adds to a river of evidence suggesting that for the first time in modern history—and in spite of many health-related improvements in our environment, our health care, and our nondietary habits—our health prospects are worsening, mostly because of excess weight.

By all means, let's protect the environment. But let's not rule 35 out the possibility of technologically enabled improvements to our diet—indeed, let's not rule out *any* food—merely because we are pleased by images of pastoral family farms. Let's first pick the foods that can most plausibly make us healthier, all things considered, and then figure out how to make them environmentally friendly.

. . .

The Food Revolution We Need

The one fast-food restaurant near a busy East L.A. intersection otherwise filled with bodegas was a Carl's Jr. I went in and saw that the biggest and most prominent posters in the store were pushing a new grilled-cod sandwich. It actually looked pretty good, but it wasn't quite lunchtime, and I just wanted a cup of coffee. I went to the counter to order it, but before I could say anything, the cashier greeted me and asked, "Would you like to try our new Charbroiled Atlantic Cod Fish Sandwich today?" Oh, well, sure, why not? (I asked her to hold the tartar sauce, which is mostly fat, but found out later that the sandwich is normally served with about half as much tartar sauce as the notoriously fatty Filet-O-Fish sandwich at McDonald's, where the fish is battered and fried.) The sandwich was delicious. It was less than half the cost of the Sea Cake appetizer at Real Food Daily. It took less than a minute to prepare. In some ways, it was the best meal I had in L.A., and it was probably the healthiest.

We know perfectly well who within our society has developed an extraordinary facility for nudging the masses to eat certain foods, and for making those foods widely available in cheap and convenient forms. The Pollanites have led us to conflate the industrial processing of food with the adding of fat and sugar in order to hook customers, even while pushing many faux-healthy foods of their own. But why couldn't Big Food's processing and marketing genius be put to use on genuinely healthier foods, like grilled fish? Putting aside the standard objection that the industry has no interest in doing so—we'll see later that in fact the industry has plenty of motivation for taking on this challenge—wouldn't that present a more plausible answer to America's junk-food problem than ordering up 50,000 new farmers' markets featuring locally grown organic squash blossoms?

According to Lenard Lesser, of the Palo Alto Medical Foundation, the food industry has mastered the art of using in-store and near-store promotions to shape what people eat. As Lesser and I drove down storied Telegraph Avenue in Berkeley and into far less affluent Oakland, leaving behind the Whole Foods Markets and sushi restaurants for gas-station markets and barbecued-rib stands, he pointed out the changes in the billboards. Whereas the last one we saw in Berkeley was for fruit juice, many in Oakland tout fast-food joints and their wares, including several featuring the Hot Mess Burger at Jack in the Box. Though Lesser noted that this forest of advertising may simply reflect Oakland residents' preexisting preference for this type of food, he told me lab studies have indicated that the more signs you show people for a particular food product or dish, the more likely they are to choose it over others, all else being equal.

We went into a KFC and found ourselves traversing a maze of signage that put us face-to-face with garish images of various fried foods that presumably had some chicken somewhere deep inside them. "The more they want you to buy something, the bigger they make the image on the menu board," Lesser explained. Here, what loomed largest was the $19.98 fried-chicken-and-corn family meal, which included biscuits and cake. A few days later, I noticed that McDonald's places large placards showcasing desserts on the trash bins, apparently calculating that the best time to entice diners with sweets is when they think they've finished their meals.

Trying to get burger lovers to jump to grilled fish may already be a bit of a stretch—I didn't see any of a dozen other customers buy the cod sandwich when I was at Carl's Jr., though the cashier said it was selling reasonably well. Still, given the food industry's power to tinker with and market food, we should not dismiss its ability to get unhealthy eaters—slowly, incrementally—to buy better food. 40

That brings us to the crucial question: Just how much healthier could fast-food joints and processed-food companies make their best-selling products without turning off customers? I put that question to a team of McDonald's executives, scientists, and chefs who are involved in shaping the company's future menus, during a February visit to McDonald's surprisingly bucolic campus west of Chicago. By way of a partial answer, the team served me up a preview tasting of two major new menu items that had been under development in their test kitchens and high-tech sensory-testing labs for the past year, and which were rolled out to the public in April. The first was the

Egg White Delight McMuffin ($2.65), a lower-calorie, less fatty version of the Egg McMuffin, with some of the refined flour in the original recipe replaced by whole-grain flour. The other was one of three new Premium McWraps ($3.99), crammed with grilled chicken and spring mix, and given a light coating of ranch dressing amped up with rice vinegar. Both items tasted pretty good (as do the versions in stores, I've since confirmed, though some outlets go too heavy on the dressing). And they were both lower in fat, sugar, and calories than not only many McDonald's staples, but also much of the food served in whole-some restaurants or touted in wholesome cookbooks.

In fact, McDonald's has quietly been making healthy changes for years, shrinking portion sizes, reducing some fats, trimming average salt content by more than 10 percent in the past couple of years alone, and adding fruits, vegetables, low-fat dairy, and oatmeal to its menu. In May, the chain dropped its Angus third-pounders and announced a new line of quarter-pound burgers, to be served on buns containing whole grains. Outside the core fast-food customer base, Americans are becoming more health-conscious. Public backlash against fast food could lead to regulatory efforts, and in any case, the fast-food industry has every incentive to maintain broad appeal. "We think a lot about how we can bring nutritionally balanced meals that include enough protein, along with the tastes and satisfaction that have an appetite-tiding effect," said Barbara Booth, the company's director of sensory science.

Such steps are enormously promising, says Jamy Ard, an epidemiology and preventive-medicine researcher at Wake Forest Baptist Medical Center in Winston-Salem, North Carolina, and a co-director of the Weight Management Center there. "Processed food is a key part of our environment, and it needs to be part of the equation," he explains. "If you can reduce fat and calories by only a small amount in a Big Mac, it still won't be a health food, but it wouldn't be as bad, and that could have a huge impact on us." Ard, who has been working for more than a decade with the obese poor, has little patience with the wholesome-food movement's call to eliminate fast food in favor of farm-fresh goods. "It's really naive," he says. "Fast food became popular because it's tasty and convenient and cheap. It makes a lot more sense to look for small, beneficial changes in that food than it does to hold out for big changes in what people eat that have no realistic chance of happening."

According to a recent study, Americans get 11 percent of their calories, on average, from fast food—a number that's almost certainly much higher among the less affluent over-weight. As a result, the fast-food industry may be uniquely positioned to improve our diets. Research suggests that calorie counts in a meal can be trimmed by as much as 30 percent without eaters noticing—by, for example, reducing portion sizes and swapping in ingredients that contain more fiber and water. Over time, that could be much more than enough to literally tip the scales for many obese people. "The difference between losing weight and not losing weight," says Robert Kushner, the obesity scientist and clinical director at Northwestern, "is a few hundred calories a day."

Which raises a question: If McDonald's is taking these sorts 45 of steps, albeit in a slow and limited way, why isn't it more loudly saying so to deflect criticism? While the company has heavily plugged the debut of its new egg-white sandwich and chicken wraps, the ads have left out even a mention of health, the reduced calories and fat, or the inclusion of whole grains. McDonald's has practically kept secret the fact that it has also begun substituting whole-grain flour for some of the less healthy refined flour in its best-selling Egg McMuffin.

The explanation can be summed up in two words that surely strike fear into the hearts of all fast-food executives who hope to make their companies' fare healthier: McLean Deluxe.

Among those who gleefully rank such things, the McLean Deluxe reigns as McDonald's worst product failure of all time, eclipsing McPasta, the McHotdog, and the McAfrica (don't ask). When I brought up the McLean Deluxe to the innovation team at McDonald's, I faced the first and only uncomfortable silence of the day. Finally, Greg Watson, a senior vice president, cleared his throat and told me that neither he nor anyone else in the room was at the company at the time, and he didn't know that much about it. "It sounds to me like it was ahead of its time," he added. "If we had something like that in the future, we would never launch it like that again."

Introduced in 1991, the McLean Deluxe was perhaps the boldest single effort the food industry has ever undertaken to shift the masses to healthier eating. It was supposed to be a healthier version of the Quarter Pounder, made with extra-lean beef infused with seaweed extract. It reportedly did reasonably well in early taste tests—for what it's worth, my wife and I were big fans—and McDonald's pumped the reduced-fat angle to the public for all it was worth. The general reaction varied from lack of interest to mockery to revulsion. The company gamely flogged the sandwich for five years before quietly removing it from the menu.

The McLean Deluxe was a sharp lesson to the industry, even if in some ways it merely confirmed what generations of parents have well known: if you want to turn off otherwise eager eaters to a dish, tell them it's good for them. Recent studies suggest that calorie counts placed on menus have a negligible effect on food choices, and that the less-health-conscious might even use the information to steer clear of low-calorie fare—perhaps assuming that it tastes worse and is less satisfying, and that it's worse value for their money. The result is a sense in the food industry that if it is going to sell healthier versions of its foods to the general public—and not just to that minority already sold on healthier eating—it is going to have to do it in a relatively sneaky way, emphasizing the taste appeal and not the health benefits. "People expect something to taste worse if they believe it's healthy," says Charles Spence, an Oxford University neuroscientist who specializes in how the brain perceives food. "And that expectation affects how it tastes to them, so it actually *does* taste worse."

Thus McDonald's silence on the nutritional profiles of 50 its new menu items. "We're not making any health claims,"

Watson said. "We're just saying it's new, it tastes great, come on in and enjoy it. Maybe once the product is well seated with customers, we'll change that message." If customers learn that they can eat healthier foods at McDonald's without even realizing it, he added, they'll be more likely to try healthier foods there than at other restaurants. The same reasoning presumably explains why the promotions and ads for the Carl's Jr. grilled-cod sandwich offer not a word related to healthfulness, and why there wasn't a whiff of health cheerleading surrounding the turkey burger brought out earlier this year by Burger King (which is not yet calling the sandwich a permanent addition).

If the food industry is to quietly sell healthier products to its mainstream, mostly non-health-conscious customers, it must find ways to deliver the eating experience that fat and problem carbs provide in foods that have fewer of those ingredients. There is no way to do that with farm-fresh produce and wholesome meat, other than reducing portion size. But processing technology gives the food industry a potent tool for trimming unwanted ingredients while preserving the sensations they deliver.

I visited Fona International, a flavor-engineering company also outside Chicago, and learned that there are a battery of tricks for fooling and appeasing taste buds, which are prone to notice a lack of fat or sugar, or the presence of any of the various bitter, metallic, or otherwise unpleasant flavors that vegetables, fiber, complex carbs, and fat or sugar substitutes can impart to a food intended to appeal to junk-food eaters. Some 5,000 FDA-approved chemical compounds—which represent the base components of all known flavors—line the shelves that run alongside Fona's huge labs. Armed with these ingredients and an array of state-of-the-art chemical-analysis and testing tools, Fona's scientists and engineers can precisely control flavor perception. "When you reduce the sugar, fat, and salt in foods, you change the personality of the product," said Robert Sobel, a chemist, who heads up research at the company. "We can restore it."

For example, fat "cushions" the release of various flavors on the tongue, unveiling them gradually and allowing them to linger. When fat is removed, flavors tend to immediately inundate the tongue and then quickly flee, which we register as a much less satisfying experience. Fona's experts can reproduce the "temporal profile" of the flavors in fattier foods by adding edible compounds derived from plants that slow the release of flavor molecules; by replacing the flavors with similarly flavored compounds that come on and leave more slowly; or by enlisting "phantom aromas" that create the sensation of certain tastes even when those tastes are not present on the tongue. (For example, the smell of vanilla can essentially mask reductions in sugar of up to 25 percent.) One triumph of this sort of engineering is the modern protein drink, a staple of many successful weight-loss programs and a favorite of those trying to build muscle. "Seven years ago they were unpalatable," Sobel said. "Today we can mask the astringent flavors and eggy aromas by adding natural ingredients."

I also visited Tic Gums in White Marsh, Maryland, a company that engineers textures into food products. Texture hasn't received the attention that flavor has, noted Greg Andon, Tic's boyish and ebullient president, whose family has run the company for three generations. The result, he said, is that even people in the food industry don't have an adequate vocabulary for it. "They know what flavor you're referring to when you say 'forest floor,' but all they can say about texture is 'Can you make it more creamy?'" So Tic is inventing a vocabulary, breaking textures down according to properties such as "mouth coating" and "mouth clearing." Wielding an arsenal of some 20 different "gums"—edible ingredients mostly found in tree sap, seeds, and other plant matter—Tic's researchers can make low-fat foods taste, well, creamier; give the same full body that sugared drinks offer to sugar-free beverages; counter chalkiness and gloopiness; and help orchestrate the timing of flavor bursts. (Such approaches have nothing in common with the ill-fated Olestra, a fat-like compound engineered to pass undigested through the body, and billed in the late 1990s as a fat substitute in snack foods. It was made notorious by widespread anecdotal complaints of cramps and loose bowels, though studies seemed to contradict those claims.)

Fona and Tic, like most companies in their industry, won't 55 identify customers or product names on the record. But both firms showed me an array of foods and beverages that were under construction, so to speak, in the name of reducing calories, fat, and sugar while maintaining mass appeal. I've long hated the taste of low-fat dressing—I gave up on it a few years ago and just use vinegar—but Tic served me an in-development version of a low-fat salad dressing that was better than any I've ever had. Dozens of companies are doing similar work, as are the big food-ingredient manufacturers, such as ConAgra, whose products are in 97 percent of American homes, and whose whole-wheat flour is what McDonald's is relying on for its breakfast sandwiches. Domino Foods, the sugar manufacturer, now sells a low-calorie combination of sugar and the nonsugar sweetener stevia that has been engineered by a flavor company to mask the sort of nonsugary tastes driving many consumers away from diet beverages and the like. "Stevia has a licorice note we were able to have taken out," explains Domino Foods CEO Brian O'Malley.

High-tech anti-obesity food engineering is just warming up. Oxford's Charles Spence notes that in addition to flavors and textures, companies are investigating ways to exploit a stream of insights that have been coming out of scholarly research about the neuroscience of eating. He notes, for example, that candy companies may be able to slip healthier ingredients into candy bars without anyone noticing, simply by loading these ingredients into the middle of the bar and leaving most of the fat and sugar at the ends of the bar. "We tend to make up our minds about how something tastes from the first and last bites, and don't care as much what happens in between," he explains. Some other potentially useful gimmicks he points out: adding weight to food packaging such as yogurt containers, which convinces eaters that the contents are rich with calories, even when they're not; using chewy textures that force consumers to spend more time between bites, giving the brain a chance to register satiety; and using colors, smells, sounds, and packaging information to create the belief that foods are fatty and sweet even when they are not. Spence found, for example, that wine is perceived as 50 percent sweeter when consumed under a red light.

Researchers are also tinkering with food ingredients to boost satiety. Cargill has developed a starch derived from tapioca that gives dishes a refined-carb taste and mouthfeel, but acts more like fiber in the body—a feature that could keep the appetite from spiking later. "People usually think that processing leads to foods that digest too quickly, but we've been able to use processing to slow the digestion rate," says Bruce McGoogan, who heads R&D for Cargill's North American food-ingredient business. The company has also developed ways to reduce fat in beef patties, and to make baked goods using half the usual sugar and oil, all without heavily compromising taste and texture.

Other companies and research labs are trying to turn out healthier, more appealing foods by enlisting ultra-high pressure, nanotechnology, vacuums, and edible coatings. At the University of Massachusetts at Amherst's Center for Foods for Health and Wellness, Fergus Clydesdale, the director of the school's Food Science Policy Alliance—as well as a spry 70-something who's happy to tick off all the processed food in his diet—showed me labs where researchers are looking into possibilities that would not only attack obesity but also improve health in other significant ways, for example by isolating ingredients that might lower the risk of cancer and concentrating them in foods. "When you understand foods at the molecular level," he says, "there's a lot you can do with food and health that we're not doing now."

The Implacable Enemies of Healthier Processed Food

What's not to like about these developments? Plenty, if you've bought into the notion that processing itself is the source of the unhealthfulness of our foods. The wholesome-food movement is not only talking up dietary strategies that are unlikely to help most obese Americans; it is, in various ways, getting in the way of strategies that could work better.

The Pollanites didn't invent resistance to healthier popular 60 foods, as the fates of the McLean Deluxe and Olestra demonstrate, but they've greatly intensified it. Fast food and junk food have their core customer base, and the wholesome-food gurus have theirs. In between sit many millions of Americans—the more the idea that processed food should be shunned no matter what takes hold in this group, the less incentive fast-food joints will have to continue edging away from the fat- and problem-carb-laden fare beloved by their most loyal customers to try to broaden their appeal.

Pollan has popularized contempt for "nutritionism," the idea behind packing healthier ingredients into processed foods. In his view, the quest to add healthier ingredients to food isn't a potential solution, it's part of the problem. Food is healthy not when it contains healthy ingredients, he argues, but when it can be traced simply and directly to (preferably local) farms. As he resonantly put it in *The Times* in 2007: "If you're concerned about your health, you should probably avoid food products that make health claims. Why? Because a health claim on a food product is a good indication that it's not really food, and food is what you want to eat."

In this way, wholesome-food advocates have managed to pre-damn the very steps we need the food industry to take, placing the industry in a no-win situation: If it maintains the status quo, then we need to stay away because its food is loaded with fat and sugar. But if it tries to moderate these ingredients, then it is deceiving us with nutritionism. Pollan explicitly counsels avoiding foods containing more than five ingredients, or any hard-to-pronounce or unfamiliar ingredients. This rule eliminates almost anything the industry could do to produce healthier foods that retain mass appeal—most of us wouldn't get past xanthan gum—and that's perfectly in keeping with his intention.

By placing wholesome eating directly at odds with healthier processed foods, the Pollanites threaten to derail the reformation of fast food just as it's starting to gain traction. At McDonald's, "Chef Dan"—that is, Dan Coudreaut, the executive chef and director of culinary innovation—told me of the dilemma the movement has caused him as he has tried to make the menu healthier. "Some want us to have healthier food, but others want us to have minimally processed ingredients, which can mean more fat," he explained. "It's becoming a balancing act for us." That the chef with arguably the most influence in the world over the diet of the obese would even consider adding fat to his menu to placate wholesome foodies is a pretty good sign that something has gone terribly wrong with our approach to the obesity crisis.

Many people insist that the steps the food industry has already taken to offer less-obesogenic fare are no more than cynical ploys to fool customers into eating the same old crap under a healthy guise. In his 3,500-word *New York Times Magazine* article on the prospects for healthier fast food, Mark Bittman lauded a new niche of vegan chain restaurants while devoting just one line to the major "quick serve" restaurants' contribution to better health: "I'm not talking about token gestures, like the McDonald's fruit-and-yogurt parfait, whose calories are more than 50 percent sugar." Never mind that 80 percent of a farm-fresh apple's calories come from sugar; that almost any obesity expert would heartily approve of the yogurt parfait as a step in the right direction for most fast-food-dessert eaters; and that many of the desserts Bittman glorifies in his own writing make the parfait look like arugula, nutrition-wise. (His recipe for corn-and-blueberry crisp, for example, calls for adding two-thirds of a cup of brown sugar to a lot of other problem carbs, along with five tablespoons of butter.)

Bittman is hardly alone in his reflexive dismissals. No sooner 65 had McDonald's and Burger King rolled out their egg-white sandwich and turkey burger, respectively, than a spate of articles popped up hooting that the new dishes weren't healthier because they trimmed a mere 50 and 100 calories from their standard counterparts, the Egg McMuffin and the Whopper. Apparently these writers didn't understand, or chose to ignore, the fact that a reduction of 50 or 100 calories in a single dish places an eater exactly on track to eliminate a few hundred calories a day from his or her diet—the critical threshold needed for long-term weight loss. Any bigger reduction would risk leaving someone too hungry to stick to a diet program. It's just the sort of small step in the right direction we should be aiming for, because the obese are much more likely to take it than they are to make a big leap to wholesome or very-low-calorie foods.

Many wholesome foodies insist that the food industry won't make serious progress toward healthier fare unless forced to by regulation. I, for one, believe regulation aimed at speeding the replacement of obesogenic foods with appealing healthier foods would be a great idea. But what a lot of foodies really want is to ban the food industry from selling junk food altogether. And that is just a fantasy. The government never managed to keep the tobacco companies from selling cigarettes, and banning booze (the third-most-deadly consumable killer after cigarettes and food) didn't turn out so well. The two most health-enlightened, regulation-friendly major cities in America, New York and San Francisco, tried to halt sales of two of the most horrific fast-food assaults on health—giant servings of sugared beverages and kids' fast-food meals accompanied by toys, respectively—and neither had much luck. Michelle Obama is excoriated by conservatives for asking schools to throw more fruits and vegetables into the lunches they serve. Realistically, the most we can hope for is a tax on some obesogenic foods. The research of Lisa Powell, a University of Illinois professor, suggests that a 20 percent tax on sugary beverages would reduce consumption by about 25 percent. (As for fatty foods, no serious tax proposal has yet been made in the U.S., and if one comes along, the wholesome foodies might well join the food industry and most consumers in opposing it. Denmark did manage to enact a fatty-food tax, but it was deemed a failure when consumers went next door into Germany and Sweden to stock up on their beloved treats.)

Continuing to call out Big Food on its unhealthy offerings, and loudly, is one of the best levers we have for pushing it toward healthier products—but let's call it out intelligently, not reflexively. Executives of giant food companies may be many things, but they are not stupid. Absent action, they risk a growing public-relations disaster, the loss of their more affluent and increasingly health-conscious customers, and the threat of regulation, which will be costly to fight, even if the new rules don't stick. Those fears are surely what's driving much of the push toward moderately healthier fare within the industry today. But if the Pollanites convince policy makers and the health-conscious public that these foods are dangerous by virtue of not being farm-fresh, that will push Big Food in a different direction (in part by limiting the profit potential it sees in lower-fat, lower-problem-carb foods), and cause it to spend its resources in other ways.

Significant regulation of junk food may not go far, but we have other tools at our disposal to prod Big Food to intensify and speed up its efforts to cut fat and problem carbs in its offerings, particularly if we're smart about it. Lenard Lesser points out that government and advocacy groups could start singling out particular restaurants and food products for praise or shaming—a more official version of "eat this, not that"—rather than sticking to a steady drumbeat of "processed food must go away." Academia could do a much better job of producing and highlighting solid research into less obesogenic, high-mass-appeal foods, and could curtail its evidence-light anti-food-processing bias, so that the next generation of social and policy entrepreneurs might work to narrow the gap between the poor obese and the well-resourced healthy instead of inadvertently widening it. We can keep pushing our health-care system to provide more incentives and support to the obese for losing weight by making small, painless, but helpful changes in their behavior, such as switching from Whoppers to turkey burgers, from Egg McMuffins to Egg White Delights, or from blueberry crisp to fruit-and-yogurt parfaits.

And we can ask the wholesome-food advocates, and those who give them voice, to make it clearer that the advice they sling is relevant mostly to the privileged healthy—and to start getting behind realistic solutions to the obesity crisis.

Joining the Conversation

1. Early in this essay, David Freedman explicitly lays out a "they say" that frames his argument. Summarize the position that he then sets out to refute.

2. What is Freedman's argument, and how does he support it? Why do you think he cites his own personal experiences? What do they contribute to his argument—and to his essay as a whole?

3. Paragraphs 30 and 31 introduce opinions that differ from Freedman's views. How fairly does he represent these opposing views, and how persuasively does he respond to what they say?

4. Freedman is particularly critical of the views of Michael Pollan (pp. 686–93). What are his specific criticisms? How do you think Pollan might respond?

5. What do you think? Could "embracing the drive-thru make us all healthier"? Write an essay responding to Freedman, saying what *you* think—and why. Draw from your own experience as well as from information in his essay in arguing for what you say.

Expanding the National School Lunch Program to Higher Education

SARA GOLDRICK-RAB

KATHARINE BROTON

EMILY BRUNJES COLO

———▫︎———

IN THE EARLY 20TH CENTURY, communities and philanthropists came together to provide lunch to hungry school children. Some recognized that children couldn't learn as well when they were hungry and others felt a moral imperative to meet this basic need. Decades later, the federal government joined in these efforts and launched the National School Lunch Program (NSLP).[1] Since its inception, the NSLP has reduced the

———

SARA GOLDRICK-RAB, KATHARINE BROTON, and EMILY BRUNJES COLO wrote this essay in April 2016 for the Wisconsin HOPE Lab, an institute based at the University of Wisconsin at Madison that focuses on "research aimed at improving equitable outcomes in postsecondary education" and works on translating scientific research into practice. Goldrick-Rab, the lab's founding director, is a professor of higher education policy studies and sociology at Temple University. Broton, a research assistant, is a doctoral candidate in sociology, and Colo is an assistant researcher.

incidence of malnutrition, boosted intake of protein, fiber, and other nutrients for children, and increased educational attainment.[2] In 2015 more than 30 million children received lunch every day, in about 100,000 schools and other institutions across the country.[3]

In today's economy the continuation of education beyond high school is common and increasingly necessary for a well-paying job. But many of the nation's undergraduates are struggling to concentrate on their education due to hunger. Over 200 food pantries are operating on college and university campuses, and staff and faculty are reaching into their own pockets to provide lunch money to struggling students. Federal support to address this problem may improve academic achievement among undergraduates, as it has among schoolchildren, boosting degree completion rates.[4] We therefore propose expanding the NSLP to higher education.

The New Demographics of American Higher Education

Three in four undergraduates defy traditional stereotypes.[5] Just 13% live on college campuses, and nearly half attend community colleges. One in four students is a parent, juggling childcare responsibilities with class assignments. About 75% work for pay while in school, including a significant number of full-time workers. The number of students qualified for the federal Pell Grant—a proxy for low-income status—grew from about 6 million in 2007–2008 to about 8.5 million in 2013–14. This is unsurprising given that See p. 238 for ways to discuss your data. participation in the NSLP grew by 3.7 million students during that time.[6] With more than one in five children living in poverty, college-going rates at a national high, and the price of higher education continuing to rise, food insecurity among undergraduates is probably more common than ever.[7]

But eligibility for the federally funded food safety net on which many schoolchildren rely (including the Supplemental Nutrition Assistance Program or SNAP, the National School Lunch Program, and the School Breakfast Program), ends abruptly for most when they enter college. Though students' financial needs remain while pursuing a postsecondary education—which is increasingly a prerequisite for a basic standard of living—food assistance becomes very difficult to access. This may be why undergraduates are at greater risk of food insecurity compared to the general population.[8]

Insufficient attention to the nutritional needs of undergradu- 5 ates could contribute to the inadequate production of college-educated labor. Over 60% of jobs now require some college education, but there are not enough people with college degrees to meet this growing demand. By 2018, the U.S. is predicted to need an additional 3 million individuals with an associate's degree or higher and another 4.7 million with postsecondary certificates.[9] This demand, along with a desire to have the highest proportion of college graduates in the world, led President Obama to encourage all Americans to "get more than a high school diploma" and focus the national education agenda on improving college completion rates.[10]

Enough students start college to meet these goals, but not enough finish. Among first-time, full-time students seeking a bachelor's degree, 59% graduate within six years while 29% of students seeking an associate's degree obtain one within three years. These completion rates mask significant variation by economic background. Just 14% of students from the lowest socioeconomic quartile had completed a bachelor's or higher degree within eight years of high school graduation compared to 29% of those from middle socioeconomic families and 60% of students from the highest socioeconomic quartile.[11] By one estimate, students from high-income families are six times more likely to graduate from college than those from low-income families.[12] Moreover, these gaps persist even after controlling for prior academic achievement.[13]

Lack of resources is at the root of this problem.[14] The price of college is rising faster than inflation, faster than health-care costs, and faster than need-based financial aid.[15] The Pell Grant, the flagship federal program, does not buy what it used to. When it was created, the grant paid for roughly 80% of the total cost to attend a public four-year college or university, including tuition, fees, and living costs. Today it covers barely one-third.[16] As a result, students from low- and moderate-income families have a great deal of unmet financial need.

This means that after all grants and scholarships are accounted for, a dependent student from a family in the lowest income quartile (i.e., $21,000 median annual earnings) has to devote 59% of her family's total income to attend a public four-year college for one year, or 40% to attend a public two-year college. The situation for independent students is even worse. On average, independent students over age 24 in the bottom income quartile must pay more than 100% of their annual income in order to attend a two- or four-year public college. Given these numbers, is it any surprise that so many people feel college is simply unaffordable?

Food Insecurity in Higher Education

Nationally, about half of all Pell recipients are from families living below the federal poverty line. Many of these students come to college to escape the material hardship they have long endured.[17] Yet food security is not examined on any national surveys of undergraduates—so there is limited information about the extent to which undergraduates struggle to find enough food to eat.[18]

In 2015, the Wisconsin HOPE Lab partnered with the Healthy Minds Study at the University of Michigan, the Association of Community College Trustees, and Single Stop to administer a survey at 10 community colleges in seven states. More than 4,000 students completed a standardized assessment of food security.[19] It revealed that half of all respondents (52%) were at least marginally food insecure over the past 30 days.[20] Specifically, 13% were marginally secure, indicating anxiety over their food supply, 19% had a low level of security marked by reductions in the quality or variety of their diet, and 21% indicated a very low level of food security—or hunger.[21] The most prevalent challenge facing community college students appears to be their ability to eat balanced meals, which research suggests may affect their cognitive functioning.[22] In addition, 39% of students said that the food they bought didn't last and they did not have sufficient money to purchase more. Twenty-eight percent cut the size of their meals or skipped meals at least once, and 22% did so on at least three days in the last 30 days. More than one in four respondents (26%) ate less than they felt they should, and 22% said that they had gone hungry due to lack of money.

This problem isn't limited to community colleges. In 2008 the HOPE Lab surveyed more than 2,000 Pell Grant recipients attending 42 public colleges and universities across Wisconsin, and found that during their first semester of college, 71% reported that they had changed their food shopping or eating habits due to a lack of funds. Twenty-seven percent of students indicated that in the past month, they did not have enough money to buy food, ate less then they felt they should, or cut the size of their meals because there was not enough money.

When asked if they ever went without eating for an entire day because they lacked enough money for food, 7% of students said yes.[23] In 2015 the HOPE Lab went into the field again with a survey of about 1,100 low- and middle-income undergraduates at eight four-year and two two-year colleges in Wisconsin.[24] Most students—61%—experienced food insecurity at some point during the academic year. Forty-seven percent said that they were unable to afford a balanced diet. Almost as many students reported that the food they purchased didn't last or that they cut the size of meals or skipped meals altogether. Each of these experiences was reported by 42% of students surveyed. And 37% reported that because of financial constraints they ate less than they thought they should.

There are likely consequences to these circumstances. Several studies of elementary and secondary school students show an inverse relationship between food insecurity and academic achievement.[25] Similarly, a study using data from two community colleges in Maryland found that food insecure students were 22% less likely than food secure students to have high grades.[26]

As Madeline Pumariega, chancellor of the Florida University System, puts it, "When a student is hungry, he does not feel safe, and it is hard to help him synthesize class material. We have to meet students' basic needs in order for them to fully concentrate on assimilating the information in a class in a way that they can apply it, learn, and take it forward."[27]

Beyond SNAP

When undergraduates need assistance affording food, colleges and universities often refer them to SNAP. While in theory SNAP could support them, in practice the help it provides is quite limited.[28] An analysis of the National Postsecondary Student Aid Survey of 2012 revealed that just 27% of undergraduates who are likely eligible for SNAP actually participate in the program.[29] Eligibility issues aside, SNAP take-up rates among undergraduates are quite low.

Further limiting the impact of SNAP, most low-income col- 15 lege students are ineligible. In order to qualify, students must work at least 20 hours per week, take part in the Federal Work Study (FWS) program, have children, or participate in other safety net programs.[30] It can be very difficult for undergraduates, especially those without children, to meet these criteria. Consider the FWS program. It is underfunded and misallocated, such that only 1 in 10 Pell recipients at public colleges or universities receive any support. Moreover, apart from FWS, Pell recipients may struggle to secure and maintain 20 hours per week of employment due to increasingly common labor practices that require flexibility and availability incompatible with the demands of students' class schedules.[31]

Moreover, working long hours while in college is counterproductive, reducing academic achievement and inhibiting course completion.[32] Students working 20 or more hours per week are more likely to drop out of college. And among those who manage to graduate, working extends their time to degree and thus increases their college costs.[33]

Even so, students who are food insecure are more likely to work than their food secure peers. According to one study, the typical food insecure college student works 18 hours per week. Employed students are nearly twice as likely to report experiences with food insecurity, indicating that work and financial aid are not enough to meet the financial demands of attending college.[34]

SNAP also has limited utility for undergraduates because it is rarely accepted on college campuses where students spend their time. Qualified retailers must meet stringent requirements on the types and quantities of staple foods such as meats, dairy, and vegetables they sell, and also be equipped with challenging sales hardware. While Oregon State University just became one of the first universities in the country to accept SNAP, additional proposed changes to rules for retailers may make it very difficult for other schools to follow suit.[35]

In the meantime, campuses are opening food banks and food pantries. The College and University Food Bank Alliance, co-founded by student affairs professionals Clare Cady and Nate Smyth-Tyge, now supports over 200 food banks on college campuses across the nation.[36] Feeding America reports that one in ten of its 45.5 million clients are college students.[37] Organizations such as Single Stop and the Working Families Success Network are also expanding to help colleges develop these services to meet students' needs, in the absence of a clear and cohesive food safety net.

Expand the National School Lunch Program

Given the growing crisis of food insecurity in higher education, 20 the National School Lunch Program should be expanded to include colleges and universities in order to promote college completion. This would require modifying the authorizing legislation to redefine "school" and extend program participation to include adults.[38]

Under current NSLP rules, students may receive free or reduced price lunches if their family income is below 185 percent of the annual income poverty level guideline established by the U.S. Department of Health and Human Services and updated annually by the Census Bureau (currently $21,756 for a family of four).[39] Pell Grant eligibility requirements map onto this standard. For example, the median adjusted gross income among Pell recipients in the public sector is just under $17,000 per year, and 85% have incomes below 200% of the poverty line.[40] Students already identified as qualified via the financial aid system (e.g., Pell Grant awardees) could be deemed eligible for the program to cut down on administrative costs. The NSLP provides precedent for this "direct certification" approach and research indicates that it increases participation, lowers administrative costs, and reduces error in who receives benefits.[41] It might also be wise to consider exercising the Community Eligibility Option, introduced in the Healthy, Hunger-Free Kids Act of 2010, at high-poverty community colleges....

Expanding the NSLP to all public and private not-for-profit colleges and universities, and students of all ages, would provide food assistance to approximately 7 million Pell recipients— increasing the NSLP total program size by about one-quarter (in 2015, there were 30.5 million children participating).[42] As in elementary and secondary schools, broad expansion might facilitate creative delivery models so that campuses can effectively serve both on and off-campus students while also reducing stigma.

Program expansion should build on existing efforts. Some colleges are already taking steps to implement a school lunch–type program on their campus. For example, Bunker Hill Community College is working with its cafeteria vendor to buy a basic lunch (sandwich, fruit, and milk) at wholesale rather than retail prices, and distributing those lunches to students in need. Other colleges provide a limited number of food vouchers (with a particular dollar value) to help hungry students get something to eat in the school cafeteria. More often faculty and staff members report taking it upon themselves to help students obtain food on an individual basis.

Program expansion could proceed in stages, perhaps starting with public two-year college students, in selected states, or with selected populations. A gradual rollout based on pilot or demonstration projects could be used to iron out implementation challenges and assess impacts. We recommended splitting pilot projects between two approaches to distribution. One approach ought to provide money for lunches directly to colleges and require that they provide free or reduced priced lunches to Pell recipients on their campuses, much as the existing NSLP program does. The other approach should provide a campus based food voucher directly to students. Vouchers could be distributed through existing campus ID or expense card systems. Under a lunch voucher system, monies could be distributed to students either in lump sums once per semester, or on a more periodic basis—perhaps once per month or biweekly. If vouchers are provided directly to students, requirements for institutions to provide low-cost healthy options would also be needed. Both efforts should be rigorously evaluated, with attention paid to impacts on nutritional outcomes as well as academic progress.

The U.S. Department of Agriculture should work with the U.S. Department of Education to plot the expansion. And any expansion must include provisions for state matching, to ensure that new federal money does not displace existing state level investments in public higher education. A rough estimate based on current program costs is that the costs of full program expansion would total around $4 billion per year.[43]

Investing in college students by offering them the food assistance they need to do well in school has immense long-term potential. It will likely improve college attainment and reduce future dependency on the social safety net.[44] Congress is currently considering legislation to reauthorize child nutrition programs, including the NSLP. This is an optimal time to reshape this program to include undergraduates. These students have proven to be good investments by surviving poverty and graduating high school. Additional support can help ensure that they successfully complete college and become competitive in today's labor market, improving their odds of economic stability for the long-term.

NOTES

1. Gunderson, G. W. (1971). The National School Lunch Program: Background and development. U.S. Department of Agriculture, Food and Nutrition Service. Available at http://www.fns.usda.gov/sites/default/files/NSLP-Program%20 History.pdf

2. Fox, M.K, W. Hamilton, & B.H. Lin. (2004). Effects of food assistance and nutrition programs on nutrition and health: Volume 3, literature review. USDA Economic Research Service Report (FANRR-19-3); Hinrichs, P. (2010). The effects of the National School Lunch Program on education and health. *Journal of Policy Analysis and Management, 29*(3), 479–505; Rosenbaum, D. & Z. Neuberger. (2005). *Food and nutrition programs: Reducing hunger, bolstering nutrition.* Center on Budget and Policy Priorities, Washington, D.C.

3. Oliveira, V. (2016). The food assistance landscape: FY 2015 annual report. U.S. Department of Agriculture, Economic Information Bulletin Number 150.

4. Gassman-Pines, A. and L. E. Bellows. 2015. The timing of SNAP benefit receipt and children's academic achievement. Paper presented at the Association for Public Policy Analysis and Management annual meeting. Available at https://appam.confex.com/appam/2015/webprogram/Paper13559.html; Price, D., Long, M., Quast, S., McMaken, J., & Kioukis, G. (2014). Public benefits and community colleges: Lessons from the Benefits Access for College Completion Evaluation. OMG Center for Collaborative Learning, Philadelphia, PA. Available at http://www.equalmeasure.org/wp-content/uploads/2014/12/ BACC-Final-Report-FINAL-111914.pdf

5. Casselman, B. (2013, July 6). Number of the week: 'Non-traditional' students are majority on College Campuses. *The Wall Street Journal.*

6. Kelchen, R. (2015). "Analyzing trends in Pell grant recipients and expenditures." Brookings Institution, Washington, DC. Available at http:// www.brookings.edu/blogs/brown-center-chalkboard/posts/2015/07/28-pell-grant -trends-kelchen; Food Research and Action Center (2015). National School

Lunch Program: Trends and factors affecting student participation. Available at http://frac.org/pdf/national_school_lunch_report_2015.pdf

7. Bartfeld, J. (2016.) SNAP and the school meal programs. In J. Bartfeld, C. Gundersen, T. Smeeding & J. Ziliak (Eds), *SNAP matters: How food stamps affect health and well-being*. Stanford University Press. Goldrick-Rab, S. (forthcoming). *Paying the price: College costs, financial aid, and the betrayal of the American dream*. University of Chicago Press.

8. Broton, K., Frank, V., & Goldrick-Rab, S. (2014). *Safety, security, and college attainment: An investigation of undergraduates' basic needs and institutional response*. Wisconsin HOPE Lab, Madison, WI.

9. Carnevale, A. P., Smith, N., & Strohl, J. (2010). *Help wanted: Projections of job and education requirements through 2018*. Georgetown University Center on Education and the Workforce.

10. Obama, B. (2009, February 24). Address to joint session of congress.

11. U.S. Department of Education. (2015). *The condition of education*.

12. Bailey, M. J., & Dynarski, S. M. (2011). *Gains and gaps: Changing inequality in US college entry and completion*. National Bureau of Economic Research, Cambridge, MA.

13. U.S. Department of Education. (2015). *The condition of education*.

14. Goldrick-Rab, S. (forthcoming). *Paying the price: College costs, financial aid, and the betrayal of the American dream*. University of Chicago Press.

15. Kurzleben, D. (2013, Oct. 23). "Just how fast has college tuition grown?" *U.S. News & World Report*.

16. Goldrick-Rab, S. (forthcoming). *Paying the price: College costs, financial aid, and the betrayal of the American dream*. University of Chicago Press.

17. Goldrick-Rab, S. (forthcoming). *Paying the price: College costs, financial aid, and the betrayal of the American dream*. University of Chicago Press.

18. The Wisconsin HOPE Lab has requested that the federal government add these items to data collection on undergraduates. Wisconsin HOPE Lab. (2015). Request to add measurement of food insecurity to the National Post-secondary Student Aid Study. Available at http://wihopelab.com/publications/NPSAS%20Brief%202015_WI%20HOPE%20Lab_ACE.pdf

19. U.S. Department of Agriculture, Economic Research Service. (2012). *U.S. Household Food Security Module: Six-Item Short Form*. Available at http://www.ers.usda.gov/datafiles/Food_Security_in_the_United_States/Food_Security_Survey_Modules/short2012.pdf.

20. Goldrick-Rab, S., K. Broton, & D. Eisenberg. (2015). *Hungry to learn: Addressing food & housing insecurity among undergraduates.* Wisconsin HOPE Lab, Madison, WI.

21. U.S. Department of Agriculture, Economic Research Service. (2012). *U.S. household food security module: Six-item short form.* Available at http://www.ers.usda.gov/datafiles/Food_Security_in_the_United_States/Food_Security_Survey_Modules/short2012.pdf.

22. Maroto, M. E., Snelling, A., & Linck, H. (2015). Food insecurity among community college students: Prevalence and association with grade point average. *Community College Journal of Research and Practice, 39*(6), 515–526.

23. Broton, K., Frank, V., & Goldrick-Rab, S. (2014). *Safety, security, and college attainment.* Wisconsin HOPE Lab, Madison, WI.

24. Wisconsin HOPE Lab. (2016). What we're learning: Food and housing insecurity among college students. Data Brief 16-01. Available at: http://wihopelab.com/publications/Wisconsin_HOPE_Lab_Data%20Brief%2016-01_Undergraduate_Housing%20and_Food_Insecurity.pdf

25. Cady, C. L. (2014). Food insecurity as a student issue. *Journal of College and Character, 15*(4), 265–272; Alaimo, K., Olson, C. M., & Frongillo, E. A. (2001). Food insufficiency and American school-aged children's cognitive, academic, and psychosocial development. *Pediatrics, 108*(1), 44–53; Alaimo, K. (2005). Food insecurity in the United States: An overview. *Topics in Clinical Nutrition, 20*(4), 281–298; Jyoti, D. F., Frongillo, E. A., & Jones, S. J. (2005). Food insecurity affects school children's academic performance, weight gain, and social skills. *The Journal of Nutrition, 135*(12), 2831–2839; Winicki, J., & Jemison, K. (2003). Food insecurity and hunger in the kindergarten classroom: Its effect on learning and growth. *Contemporary Economic Policy, 21*(2), 145–157.

26. Maroto, M. E., Snelling, A., & Linck, H. (2015). Food insecurity among community college students: Prevalence and association with grade point average. *Community College Journal of Research and Practice, 39*(6).

27. Goldrick-Rab, S., Broton, K., & Gates. (2013). Clearing the path to a brighter future: Addressing barriers to community college access and success. Association of Community College Trustees, Washington, D.C., and Single Stop USA, New York, NY.

28. Duke-Benfield, A.E. (2015). Bolstering Non-Traditional Student Success: A Comprehensive Student Aid System Using Financial Aid, Public Benefits, and Refundable Tax Credits. Center for Postsecondary and Economic Success at the

Center for Law and Social Policy, Washington, D.C. Available at http://www
.clasp.org/resources-and-publications/publication-1/Bolstering-NonTraditional
-Student-Success.pdf

29. "Likely eligible" means students with incomes under 130% of the federal
poverty line who work at least 20 hours per week, take part in work-study,
receive TANF or have a dependent child under age 6; Gault, B., J. Hayes, C.
Williams, & M. Froehner. (2014.) Public benefit eligibility and receipt among
low-income college students—Working draft. Institute for Women's Policy
Research, Washington, D.C.

30. United States Department of Agriculture. Supplemental Nutrition
Assistance Program (SNAP) website: http://www.fns.usda.gov/snap/students.

31. Goldrick-Rab, S. (forthcoming). *Paying the price: College costs, financial
aid, and the betrayal of the American dream*. University of Chicago Press.

32. Dadgar, M. (2012). The academic consequences of employment for students enrolled in community college. CCRC working paper no. 46. New York,
NY: Community College Research Center at Columbia University; Darolia,
R. (2014). Working (and studying) day and night: Heterogeneous effects of
working on the academic performance of full-time and part-time students.
Economics of Education Review, 38, 38–50.; DeSimone, J. S. (2008). The impact
of employment during school on college student academic performance. NBER
working paper 14006. National Bureau of Economic Research, Cambridge, MA;
Stinebrickner, R., & Stinebrickner, T. R. (2003). Working during school and
academic performance. *Journal of Labor Economics, 21*(2), 473–491.

33. Bound, J., Lovenheim, M. F., & Turner, S. (2012). Increasing time to
baccalaureate degree in the United States. *Education Finance and Policy, 7*(4),
375–424; Bozick, R. (2007). Making it through the first year of college: The
role of students' economic resources, employment, and living arrangements.
Sociology of Education, 80(3), 261–285; Ehrenberg, R. G., & Sherman, D. R.
(1987). Employment while in college, academic achievement, and post-college
outcomes: A summary of results. *The Journal of Human Resources, 22*(1), 1–23;
Horn, L. J., & Malizio, A. G. (1998). *Undergraduates who work*. National Postsecondary Student Aid Study, 1996. Washington, D.C.: U.S. Department of
Education.; Orszag, J. M., Orszag, P. R., & Whitmore, D. M. (2001). *Learning
and earning: Working in college*. Newton, MA: Upromise, Inc.; Van Dyke, R.,
Little, B., & Callender, C. (2005). *Survey of higher education students' attitudes
to debt and term-time working and their impact on attainment*. Higher Education
Funding Council for England, Bristol, England.

34. Patton-López, M. M., López-Cevallos, D. F., Cancel-Tirado, D. I., & Vazquez, L. (2014). Prevalence and correlates of food insecurity among students attending a midsize rural university in Oregon. *Journal of Nutrition Education and Behavior, 46*(3), 209–214.

35. OSU participation in SNAP to help improve food access. (2016). Oregon State University. Available at http://oregonstate.edu/ua/ncs/archives/2016/jan/osu-participation-snap-help-improve-student-food-access; Enhancing retailer standards in the Supplemental Nutrition Assistance Program (SNAP). Proposed rule. *Federal Register: The Daily Journal of the United States Government.* Available at https://www.federalregister.gov/articles/2016/02/17/2016-03006/enhancing-retailer-standards-in-the-supplemental-nutrition-assistance-program-snap

36. College & University Food Bank Alliance webpage. Available at www.cufba.org.

37. Resnikoff, N. (2014, August 8). "The hunger crisis in America's universities." *MSNBC*.

38. Agriculture, Subchapter A—Child Nutrition Programs, 7CFR210 (2014). Available at http://www.fns.usda.gov/sites/default/files/7CFR210_2014.pdf

39. The poverty guidelines updated periodically in the Federal Register by the U.S. Department of Health and Human Services under the authority of 42 U.S.C. 9902(2). Available at http://aspe.hhs.gov/POVERTY/07poverty.shtml

40. Goldrick-Rab, S. (forthcoming). Paying the price: *College costs, financial aid, and the betrayal of the American dream.* University of Chicago Press.

41. Bartfeld, J. (2016). SNAP and the school meal programs. In J. Bartfeld, C. Gundersen, T. Smeeding & J. Ziliak (Eds), *SNAP matters: How food stamps affect health and well-being.* Stanford University Press; Gleason, P. et al. (2003). Direct certification in the National School Lunch Program—Impacts on program access and integrity. Prepared by Mathematics Policy Research for U.S. Department of Agriculture; Cole, N. (2007). Data matching in the National School Lunch Program: 2005 final report. Prepared by Abt Associates for U.S. Department of Agriculture; Ponza, M., Gleason, P., Hulsey, L., and Moore, Q. (2007). NSLP/SBP access, participation, eligibility and certification study. Prepared by Mathematics Policy Research for U.S. Department of Agriculture.

42. According to Title IV program volume reports, 8.6 million students received Pell Grants in 2013–14. College Board did some calculations of the Pell volume at each institution type (see http://trends.collegeboard.org/student-aid/figures-tables/percentage-distribution-pell-grants-sector-over-time). According to their calculations, for-profits made up 20% of Pell recipients in 2013-14. We

subtract these students for program estimates. For the current number in NSLP see http://www.fns.usda.gov/sites/default/files/pd/slsummar.pdf

43. Neuberger, Z. & Namian, T. (2016). Who benefits from federal subsidies for free and reduced price school meals? Center on Budget and Policy Priorities, Washington, D.C. Available at http://www.cbpp.org/research/who-benefits-from-federal-subsidies-for-free-and-reduced-price-school-meals; for reimbursement amounts per meal see http://www.fns.usda.gov/school-meals/rates-reimbursement; For the cost of meals in the NSLP see: http://www.fns.usda.gov/sites/default/files/MealCostStudy.pdf

44. Price, D., Long, M., Quast, S., McMaken, J., & Kioukis, G. (2014). Public benefits and community colleges: Lessons from the benefits access for college completion evaluation. OMG Center for Collaborative Learning, Philadelphia, PA. Available at http://www.equalmeasure.org/wp-content/uploads/2014/12/BACC-Final-Report-FINAL-111914.pdf

Joining the Conversation

1. Sara Goldrick-Rab, Katharine Broton, and Emily Brunjes Colo propose expanding the national school lunch program to include college students. What evidence do they provide to support their proposal?
2. The authors include forty-four endnotes to identify and explain their sources. Examine the endnotes. Pick five of them that look interesting to you and explain what they contribute to the authors' argument.
3. Choose three examples of the authors' use of data: one from near the beginning of the report, one from the middle, and one from near the end. What part of the authors' argument does each piece of data support?
4. According to Goldrick-Rab et al., the federal government should provide lunch for college students in need. How do you think Radley Balko (pp. 713–17), who complains of

government spending and interference in personal behaviors, would respond?

5. Write an essay in which you agree, disagree, or both with the authors' proposal. Draw from your own observations, from another reading in this chapter, or both.

CREDITS

TEXT

Liz Addison: "Two Years Are Better Than Four." From *The New York Times*, September 2, 2007. Copyright © 2007 The New York Times. All rights reserved. Used by permission and protected by the Copyright Laws of the United States. The printing, copying, redistribution, or retransmission of this Content without express written permission is prohibited.

Michelle Alexander: Excerpt from *The New Jim Crow*. Copyright © 2010, 2012 by Michelle Alexander. Reprinted by permission of The New Press. www.thenewpress.com

Radley Balko: "What You Eat Is Your Business." The Cato Institute, May 23, 2004. Reprinted by permission of the publisher.

Sean Blanda: "The 'Other Side' Is Not Dumb," from *Medium*, January 7, 2016. Reprinted by permission of the author.

danah boyd: "Why America Is Self-Segregating," by danah boyd. From Points, Data & Society, *Medium*, January 5, 2017. Reprinted by permission of the author.

Carole Cadwalladr: "Google, Democracy, and the Truth about Internet Search," by Carole Cadwalladr. *The Guardian*, December 4, 2016. Copyright © 2017 Guardian News & Media Ltd. Reprinted with permission.

Nicholas Carr: "Is Google Making Us Stupid?" by Nicholas Carr. From *The Atlantic*, July/August 2008. Copyright © 2008 The Atlantic Media Co., as first published in The Atlantic Magazine. All rights reserved. Distributed by Tribune Content Agency, LLC.

Credits

Credits

Credits

PHOTOGRAPHS

Chapter 11: p. 148: 20th Century Fox/Courtesy Everett Collection; p. 156: 20th Century Fox/Courtesy Everett Collection; **Chapter 15:** p. 198: Wikimedia; **Chapter 18:** p. 244: mathisworks/Getty Images; p. 249: Tom Gauld; p. 250: Esquire/NBC News Poll; p. 258: Sgt. Jennifer Pirante/US Marine Corps; p. 262: Netflix; p. 270: Miller Center/Wikipedia; p. 273: Charles Tasnadi/AP Photo; p. 298: Photograph by Naomi McColloch; p. 318: Sam Hodgson/The New York Times/Redux; p. 324: Doyle Partners; p. 333: ASSOCIATED PRESS; p. 248: ASSOCIATED PRESS; **Chapter 19:** p. 370: iStock/Getty images; p. 434: Photo courtesy of Mike Rose; p. 439: Photo courtesy of Mike Rose; p. 455: ©CourtneyPerry; p. 460: ©CourtneyPerry; p. 465: ©CourtneyPerry; p. 472: ©CourtneyPerry; p. 473: ©CourtneyPerry; **Chapter 20:** p. 476: ociacia/iStock/Getty images; p. 481: Courtesy of the Everett Collection; p. 485 (left): Gustav Schultze, Naumburg, 1882/Wikimedia Commons; p. 485 (right): akg images/Newscom; p. 489: Midvale Company Photographs (1883–1953)/Flickr; p. 491: Sebastian Bergmann/Wikimedia Commons; p. 498: Foto Marburg/Art Resource, NY; p. 502: ASSOCIATED PRESS; p. 538: Google; p. 542: James Leynse/Corbis Historical/Getty Images; p. 544: Jonathan Albright; p. 552: REUTERS/Mariana Bazo; p. 566: Creatista/Shuttershock; p. 582: Tasos Katopodis/Getty Images; **Chapter 21:** p. 592: Maarten de Boer/Contour By Getty Images; p. 619: Thodoris Tibilis/Shuttershock; p. 640: Courtesy of Grinnell College; p. 664: Damien Maloney/New York Times/Redux; **Chapter 22:** p. 682: Courtesy of Marilyn Moller; p. 695: Courtesy of the Atlantic; p. 700: Courtesy of the Atlantic; p. 722: iStockphoto; p. 634: Shuttershock; p. 744: iStock/Getty images; p. 746: Jahi Chikwendiu/The Washinton Post via Getty Images; p. 751: Peter Kramer/NBC/NBC NewsWire via Getty Images; p. 758: iStock/Getty images; p. 761: AP Photo/Reed Saxon; **About the Authors:** Tricia Koning (Graff and Birkenstein); Melanie Cannon (Durst).

ACKNOWLEDGMENTS

Like the previous three editions, this one would never have seen print if it weren't for Marilyn Moller, our superb editor at Norton, and the extraordinary job she has done of inspiring, commenting on, and rewriting (and then rewriting and rewriting again) our many drafts. Our friendship with Marilyn is one of the most cherished things to have developed from this project.

We are particularly thankful to Sarah Touborg, whose exemplary counsel, criticism, and hands-on intervention shaped the changes we have made to this edition. We are grateful for Sarah's unflagging patience with a couple of sometimes-recalcitrant authors. We extend our deep thanks to Claire Wallace for her excellent editorial work on the new examples in this edition as well as the chapter on online writing. Madeline Rombes skillfully and cheerfully coordinated the many details involved in preparing our manuscript.

Our thanks go as well to Roby Harrington for his encouragement and astute suggestions (and great dinners) on his annual visits to Chicago. We extend our gratitude to Andy Ensor, Elizabeth Marotta, and Christine D'Antonio for managing the editing and production of this edition; and to Michal Brody, Erica Wnek, Claire Wallace, and Madeline Rombes for curating and producing the fabulous blog that accompanies this book, **theysayiblog.com**.

Acknowledgments

Thanks to John Darger, our Norton representative, who offered early encouragement to write this book; to Debra Morton Hoyt and Tiani Kennedy for their excellent work on the cover; and special thanks to Lib Triplett and all the Norton travelers for the superb work they've done on behalf of our book.

We owe a special debt of gratitude to Erin Ackerman and Christopher Gillen for their chapters on writing in the sciences and social sciences, respectively. Working with Erin and Chris proved to be an exhilarating experience; we learned a great deal by seeing how they applied our ideas to their disciplines.

We owe a special thanks to our colleagues in the English department at the University of Illinois at Chicago: Mark Canuel, our former department head, for supporting our earlier efforts overseeing the university's Writing in the Disciplines requirement; Walter Benn Michaels, our current department head; and Ann Feldman, former director of university writing programs, for encouraging us to teach first-year composition courses at UIC in which we could try out ideas and drafts of our manuscript; Tom Moss, Diane Chin, Vainis Aleksa, and Matt Pavesich, who have also been very supportive of our efforts; and Matt Oakes, our former research assistant. We are also grateful to Ann Feldman, Diane Chin, and Mark Bennett for bringing us into their graduate course on the teaching of writing; and to Lisa Freeman, John Huntington, Walter Benn Michaels, and Ralph Cintron for inviting us to present our ideas in the keynote lecture at UIC's 2013 Composition Matters conference.

We are also especially grateful to Steve Benton and Nadya Pittendrigh, who taught a section of composition with us using an early draft of this book. Steve made many helpful suggestions, particularly regarding the exercises. We are grateful to

ACKNOWLEDGMENTS

Andy Young, a lecturer at UIC who has tested our book in his courses and who gave us extremely helpful feedback. And we thank Vershawn A. Young, whose work on code-meshing influenced our argument in Chapter 9, and Hillel Crandus, whose classroom handout inspired the chapter on "Entering Classroom Discussions."

We are grateful to the many colleagues and friends who've let us talk our ideas out with them and given extremely helpful responses. UIC's former dean, Stanley Fish, has been central in this respect, both in personal conversations and in his incisive articles calling for greater focus on form in the teaching of writing. Our conversations with Jane Tompkins have also been integral to this book, as was the composition course that Jane cotaught with Gerald, titled "Can We Talk?" Lenny Davis, too, offered both intellectual insight and emotional support, as did Heather Arnet, Jennifer Ashton, Janet Atwill, Kyra Auslander, Noel Barker, Mark Bauerlein, Jim Benton, Jack Brereton, Jim Burke, Tim Cantrick, Marsha Cassidy, David Chinitz, Lisa Chinitz, Pat Chu, Harry J. Cook, Duane Davis, Bridget O'Rourke Flisk, Steve Flisk, Judy Gardiner, Howard Gardner, Rich Gelb, Gwynne Gertz, Jeff Gore, Bill Haddad, Ben Hale, Scott Hammerl, Patricia Harkin, Andy Hoberek, John Huntington, Carol Jago, Joe Janangelo, Paul Jay, David Jolliffe, Nancy Kohn, Don Lazere, Sarah Levine, Jo Liebermann, Steven Mailloux, Deirdre McCloskey, Maurice J. Meilleur, Alan Meyers, Greg Meyerson, Anna Minkov, Chris Newfield, Randy Olson, Jim Phelan, Paul Psilos, Bruce Robbins, Charles Ross, Eileen Seifert, Evan Seymour, David Shumway, Herb Simons, Jim Sosnoski, Kyle Stedman, David Steiner, Harold Veeser, Chuck Venegoni, Marla Weeg, Jerry Wexler, Joyce Wexler, Virginia Wexman, Jeffrey Williams, Lynn Woodbury,

Art Young, and the late Wayne Booth, whose friendship we dearly miss.

We are grateful for having had the opportunity to present our ideas to a number of colleges and high schools: University of Arkansas at Little Rock, Augustana College, Brandeis University, Brigham Young University, Bryn Mawr College, California State University at Bakersfield, California State University at Northridge, University of California at Riverside, Case Western University, Central Michigan University, Clemson University, Columbia University, Community College of Philadelphia, Daemen College, Davidson College, University of Delaware, DePauw University, Drew University, Duke University, Duquesne University, Elmhurst College, Emory University, Fairfield University, Fontbonne University, Furman University, Gettysburg College, Harper College, Harvard University, Haverford College, Hawaii Office of Secondary School Curriculum Instruction, Hunter College, University of Illinois College of Medicine, Illinois State University, Illinois Wesleyan University, John Carroll University, Kansas State University, Lawrence University, the Lawrenceville School, University of Louisiana at Lafayette, MacEwan University, University of Maryland at College Park, Massachusetts Institute of Technology, University of Memphis, Miami University, Mills College, University of Missouri at Columbia, New Trier High School, North Carolina A&T University, University of North Florida, Northern Michigan University, Northwestern University Division of Continuing Studies, Norwalk Community College, University of Notre Dame, Ohio State University, Ohio Wesleyan University, Oregon State University, University of Portland, Purdue University at Calumet, University of Rochester, Rockford University, St. Ambrose University, St. Andrew's School,

ACKNOWLEDGMENTS

St. Charles High School, St. Francis University at Joliet, State University of New York at Geneseo, State University of New York at Stony Brook, Seattle University, South Elgin High School, University of South Florida, Southern Connecticut State University, University of Southern Mississippi, Stanford University, Swarthmore College, Teachers College, University of Tennessee at Knoxville, University of Texas at Arlington, Tulane University, Union College, Ursinus College, Wabash College, Washington College, University of Washington, University of West Virginia at Morgantown, Western Michigan University, Westinghouse/Kenwood High Schools, Wheaton North High School, Wheaton Warrenville English Chairs, Winona State University, and the University of Wisconsin at Whitewater.

We particularly thank those who helped arrange these visits and discussed writing issues with us: Jeff Abernathy, Herman Asarnow, John Austin, Greg Barnheisel, John Bean, Crystal Benedicks, Joe Bizup, Sheridan Blau, Dagne Bloland, Chris Breu, Elizabeth Brockman, Mark Brouwer, Lizabeth Bryant, Joan Johnson Bube, John Caldwell, Gregory Clark, Irene Clark, Dean Philip Cohen, Cathy D'Agostino, Tom Deans, Gaurav Desai, Lisa Dresdner, Kathleen Dudden-Rowlands, Lisa Ede, Alexia Ellett, Emory Elliott, Anthony Ellis, Kim Flachmann, Ronald Fortune, Rosanna Fukuda, George Haggerty, Donald Hall, Joe Harris, Gary Hatch, Elizabeth Hatmaker, Donna Heiland, Harry Hellenbrand, Nicole Henderson, Doug Hesse, Van Hillard, Andrew Hoberek, Michael Hustedde, Sara Jameson, T. R. Johnson, David Jones, Ann Kaplan, Don Kartiganer, Linda Kinnahan, Dean Georg Kleine, Albert Labriola, Craig Lawrence, Lori Lopez, Tom Liam Lynch, Hiram Maxim, Michael Mays, Elizabeth McDermott, Thomas McFadden, Sean Meehan,

Acknowledgments

Connie Mick, Robert Morace, Joseph Musser, Margaret Oakes, John O'Connor, Gary Olson, Tom Pace, Amy Pearson, Les Perelman, Jim Phelan, Emily Poe, Dominick Randolph, Clancy Ratliff, Monica Rico, Kelly Ritter, Jack Robinson, Warren Rosenberg, Laura Rosenthal, Dean Howard Ross, Deborah Rossen-Knill, Paul Schacht, Petra Schatz, Evan Seymour, Rose Shapiro, Mike Shea, Cecilia M. Shore, Erec Smith, Kelly Smith, Nancy Sommers, Stephen Spector, Timothy Spurgin, Ron Strickland, Marcy Taylor, Michael Theune, Trig Thoreson, Josh Toth, Judy Trost, Aiman Tulamait, Charles Tung, John Webster, Robert Weisbuch, Sandi Weisenberg, Karin Westman, Martha Woodmansee, and Lynn Worsham.

We also wish to extend particular thanks to two Chicago-area educators who have worked closely with us: Eileen Murphy of CERCA and Les Lynn, formerly of the Chicago Debate League and now director of our joint organization, Argument-Centered Education. Lastly, we wish to thank two high school teachers for their excellent and inventive adaptations of our work: Mark Gozonsky in his *YouTube* video clip "Building Blocks," and Dave Stuart Jr. in his blog, *Teaching the Core.*

For inviting us to present our ideas at their conferences, we are grateful to John Brereton and Richard Wendorf at the Boston Athenaeum; Wendy Katkin of the Reinvention Center of State University of New York at Stony Brook; Luchen Li of the Michigan English Association; Lisa Lee and Barbara Ransby of the Public Square in Chicago; Don Lazere of the University of Tennessee at Knoxville; Dennis Baron of the University of Illinois at Urbana-Champaign; Alfie Guy of Yale University; Irene Clark of the California State University of Northridge; George Crandell and Steve Hubbard, codirectors of the ACETA conference at Auburn University; Mary Beth Rose of the Humanities Institute at the University of Illinois at Chicago; Diana Smith of St. Anne's Belfield School and the University of Virginia; Jim Maddox and Victor Luftig of the Bread Loaf School of English; Jan Fitzsimmons and Jerry Berberet of the Associated Colleges of Illinois; Rosemary Feal, executive director of the Modern Language Association; Les Perelman of the Massachusetts Institute of Technology; and Bruce Herzberg of Bentley College and Chris Gallagher of Northeastern University.

We wish to thank those reviewers who provided feedback on the new material for Chapter 9: Ana Cooke (Carnegie Mellon University); Elias Dominguez-Barajas (University of Arkansas); Douglas Kern (University of Maryland); Janine Morris (Nova Southeastern University); and Keith Walters (Portland State University).

Our thanks also go to those who helped develop the ideas for the new chapter on online discussions: Karen Bruce (Ohio State University); Nick Carbone; Ana Cooke (Carnegie Mellon); Courtney Danforth (University of Southern Nevada); Lyra Hilliard (University of Maryland); Janine Morris (Nova Southeastern University); and Ilknur Sancak-Marusa (West Chester University).

A very special thanks goes to those who reviewed materials for the fourth edition: Teresa Alto (Itasca Community College); Darla Anderson (California State University, Northridge); Jan Andres (Riverside City College); Steven Bailey (Central Michigan University); Valerie Bell (Loras College); Tamara Benson (Kent State University); Jade Bittle (Rowan-Cabarrus Community College); Jill Bonds (University of Phoenix); William Cantrell (Johnson Central High School); David Chase (Raritan Valley Community College); Barbara Cook (Mount

Aloysius College); Jonathan Cook (Durham Technical Community College); Carol Lynne Lana Dalley (California State University, Fullerton); D'Arcangelis (Memorial University of Newfoundland); Nicholas DeArmas (Seminole State College of Florida); Elias Dominguez-Barajas (University of Arkansas); Ember Dooling (St. Joseph High School); Andrew Dunphy (Massasoit Community College); Justin Eells (Minnesota State University, Mankato); Africa Fine (Palm Beach State College); Valerie Fong (Foothill College); Reese Fuller (Episcopal School of Acadiana); Karen Gaffney (Raritan Valley Community College); Jacquelyn Geiger (Bucks County Community College); Joshua Geist (College of the Sequoias); Ashley Gendek (Kentucky Wesleyan College); Sean George (Dixie State University); Karen Gocsik (University of California, San Diego); Sarah Gray (Middle Tennessee State University); George Grinnell (University of British Columbia Okanagan); Lindsay Haney (Bellevue College); Catherine Hayter (Saddleback College); Stephen V. Hoyt (Obridge Academy/St. Joseph's College); Timothy Jackson (Rosemont College); Julie Jung-Kim (Trinity International University); Hannah Keller (Campbell University); Michael Keller (South Dakota State University); Nina Kutty (DePaul University); Lisa Lipani (University of Georgia); Judi Mack (Joliet Junior College); Anna Maheshwari (Schoolcraft College); Sarah F. McGinley (Wright State University); James McGovern (Germanna Community College); Liz McLemore (Minneapolis Community and Technical College) Jason Melton (Sacramento State University); Michael Mendoza (Seminole State College of Florida); Carey Millsap-Spears (Moraine Valley Community College); Nicole Morris (Emory University); Shelley Palmer (Central Piedmont Community College); Jeff Pruchnic (Wayne State University);

ACKNOWLEDGMENTS

Tammy Ramsey (Bluegrass Community and Technical College); Cynthia Cox Richardson (Sinclair Community College); Rachel Rinehart (St. Edward's University); Kelly Ritter (University of Illinois Urbana-Champaign); Deborah Rossen-Knill (University of Rochester); Laura Rossi-Le (Endicott College); Julie Shattuck (Frederick Community College); Ellen Sorg (Owens Community College); Jennifer Stefaniak (Springfield Technical Community College); Heather Stringham (College of Southern Nevada); Stuart Swirsky (Seminole State College of Florida); Star Taylor (Riverside City College); Stephanie Tran (Foothill College); Alicia Trotman (Mercy College); Robert Williams (St. Edward's University); and Benjamin Woo (Carleton University).

A very special thanks goes to those who reviewed materials for the third edition: Carrie Bailey (Clark College); Heather Barrett (Boston University); Amy Bennett-Zendzian (Boston University); Seth Blumenthal (Boston University); Ron Brooks (Oklahoma State University); Jonathan Cook (Durham Technical Community College); Tessa Croker (Boston University); Perry Cumbie (Durham Technical Community College); Robert Danberg (Binghamton University); Elias Dominguez-Barajas (University of Arkansas); Nancy Enright (Seton Hall University); Jason Evans (Prairie State College); Ted Fitts (Boston University); Karen Gaffney (Raritan Valley Community College); Karen Gardiner (University of Alabama); Stephen Hodin (Boston University); Michael Horwitz (University of Hartford); John Hyman (American University); Claire Kervin (Boston University); Melinda Kreth (Central Michigan University); Heather Marcovitch (Red Deer College); Christina Michaud (Boston University); Marisa Milanese (Boston University); Theresa Mooney (Austin Community College);

Roxanne Munch (Joliet Junior College); Sarah Quirk (Waubonsee Community College); Lauri Ramey (California State University, Los Angeles); David Shawn (Boston University); Jennifer Sia (Boston University); Laura Sonderman (Marshall University); Katherine Stebbins McCaffrey (Boston University); K. Sullivan (Lane Community College); Anne-Marie Thomas (Austin Community College at Riverside); Eliot Treichel (Lane Community College); Rosanna Walker (Lane Community College); and Mary Erica Zimmer (Boston University). We also thank those who reviewed the literature chapter: Julie Bowman (Carnegie Mellon University); Jim Burke (Burlingame High School); Ana Cooke (Carnegie Mellon University); Thomas Cooley (Ohio State University); Lisa Ede (Oregon State University); Priscilla Glanville (State College of Florida); Melissa Goldthwaite (Saint Joseph's University); Rafey Habib (Rutgers University at Camden); Michael Hennessy (Texas State University); and Alexis Teagarden (Carnegie Mellon University).

Thanks to those who reviewed the materials for the second edition: Erin Ackerman (City University of New York–John Jay College); Mary Angeline (University of Northern Colorado); Ned Bachus (Community College of Philadelphia); Michelle Ballif (University of Georgia); Jonathan Barz (University of Dubuque); Mary Bauer Morley (University of North Dakota); Benjamin Bennett-Carpenter (Oakland University); Michelle Boswell (University of Maryland); Laura Bowles (University of Central Arkansas); E. Brand (Broome Community College); Beth Buyserie (Washington State University); Dana Cairns Watson (University of California, Los Angeles); Genevieve Carminati (Montgomery College); Brent Chesley (Aquinas College); Joseph Colavito (Butler University); Tara DaPra

(University of Minnesota); Emily Detmer-Goebel (Northern Kentucky University); J. Michael Duvall (College of Charleston); Adriana Estill (Carleton College); Ralph Faris (Community College of Philadelphia); Chris Gillen (Kenyon College); Patricia Gillikin (University of New Mexico Valencia Campus); Kenneth Grant (University of Wisconsin–Baraboo/Sauk County); Kevin Griffith (Capital University); Annemarie Hamlin (Central Oregon Community College); Rick Hansen (California State University, Fresno); John Hare (Montgomery College); Wendy Hayden (Hunter College of the City University of New York); Karen Head (Georgia Institute of Technology); Chene Heady (Longwood University); Nels Highberg (University of Hartford); Victoria Holladay (California State University, Los Angeles); D. Kern Holoman (University of California, Davis); Elizabeth Huergo (Montgomery College); Sara Jameson (Oregon State University); Joseph Jones (University of Memphis); Andrew Keitt (University of Alabama at Birmingham); Kurt Koenigsberger (Case Western Reserve University); Gary Leising (Utica College); Gary Lewandowski (Monmouth University); Michelle Maher (La Roche College); Lisa Martin (University of Wisconsin–Baraboo/Sauk County); Miles McCrimmon (J. Sargeant Reynolds Community College); Jacqueline Megow (Oklahoma State University); Bruce Michelson (University of Illinois at Urbana-Champaign); Megan Morton (Purdue University); Steven Muhlberger (Nipissing University); Lori Muntz (Iowa Wesleyan College); Ann Murphy (Assumption College); Sarah Perrault (University of Nevada, Reno); Christine Pipitone-Herron (Raritan Valley Community College); David Samper (University of Oklahoma); Rose Shapiro (Fontbonne University); Jennifer Stewart (Indiana University–Purdue University Fort Wayne);

Sandra Stollman (Broward College); Linda Sturtz (Beloit College); Mark Sutton (Kean University); Tobin von der Nuell (University of Colorado at Boulder); Brody Waybrant (Bay Mills Community College); Gina Weaver (Southern Nazarene University); Amy Whitson (Missouri State University); and Susan Wright (Montclair State University).

Thanks also to those who reviewed the manuscript for the original version of *They Say*; their suggestions contributed enormously to this book: Alan Ainsworth (Houston Community College); Rise Axelrod (University of California, Riverside); Bob Baron (Mesa Community College); David Bartholomae (University of Pittsburgh); Diane Belcher (Georgia State University); Michel De Benedictis (Miami Dade College); Joseph Bizup (Boston University); Patricia Bizzell (College of the Holy Cross); John Brereton (Harvard University); Richard Bullock (Wright State University); Charles Cooper (University of California, San Diego); Christine Cozzens (Agnes Scott College); Sarah Duerden (Arizona State University); Russel Durst (University of Cincinnati); Joseph Harris (Duke University); Paul Heilker (Virginia Polytechnic Institute); Michael Hennessy (Texas State University); Karen Lunsford (University of California, Santa Barbara); Libby Miles (University of Rhode Island); Mike Rose (University of California, Los Angeles); William H. Smith (Weatherford College); Scott Stevens (Western Washington University); Patricia Sullivan (University of Colorado); Pamela Wright (University of California, San Diego); and Daniel Zimmerman (Middlesex Community College).

Finally, a special thank you to David Bartholomae for suggesting the phrase that became the subtitle of this book.

INDEX OF TEMPLATES

DISAGREEING WITHOUT BEING DISAGREEABLE
(pp. 10–11)

▶ While I understand the impulse to _____, my own view is _____.

▶ While I agree with X that _____, I cannot accept her overall conclusion that _____.

▶ While X argues _____, and I argue _____, in a way we're both right.

THE TEMPLATE OF TEMPLATES
(p. 11)

▶ In recent discussions of _____, a controversial issue has been whether _____. On the one hand, some argue that _____. From this perspective, _____. On the other hand, however, others argue that _____. In the words of _____, one of this view's main proponents, "_____." According to this view, _____. In sum, then, the issue is whether _____ or _____.

My own view is that _____. Though I concede that _____, I still maintain that _____. For example, _____. Although some might object that _____, I would reply that _____. The issue is important because _____.

INTRODUCING WHAT "THEY SAY"

(p. 23)

▸ A number of _____ have recently suggested that _____.

▸ It has become common today to dismiss _____.

▸ In their recent work, Y and Z have offered harsh critiques of _____ for _____.

INTRODUCING "STANDARD VIEWS"

(pp. 23–24)

▸ Americans today tend to believe that _____.

▸ Conventional wisdom has it that _____.

▸ Common sense seems to dictate that _____.

▸ The standard way of thinking about topic X has it that _____.

▸ It is often said that _____.

▸ My whole life I have heard it said that _____.

▸ You would think that _____.

▸ Many people assume that _____.

INDEX OF TEMPLATES

MAKING WHAT "THEY SAY" SOMETHING *YOU* SAY
(pp. 24–25)

▶ I've always believed that _____ .

▶ When I was a child, I used to think that _____ .

▶ Although I should know better by now, I cannot help thinking that _____ .

▶ At the same time that I believe _____ , I also believe _____ .

INTRODUCING SOMETHING IMPLIED OR ASSUMED
(p. 25)

▶ Although none of them have ever said so directly, my teachers have often given me the impression that _____ .

▶ One implication of X's treatment of _____ is that _____ .

▶ Although X does not say so directly, she apparently assumes that _____ .

▶ While they rarely admit as much, _____ often take for granted that _____ .

INTRODUCING AN ONGOING DEBATE
(pp. 25–28)

▶ In discussions of X, one controversial issue has been _____ . On the one hand, _____ argues _____ . On the other

812

hand, _____ contends _____. Others even maintain
_____. My own view is _____.

▸ When it comes to the topic of _____, most of us will readily agree that _____. Where this agreement usually ends,
however, is on the question of _____. Whereas some are
convinced that _____, others maintain that _____.

▸ In conclusion, then, as I suggested earlier, defenders of
_____ can't have it both ways. Their assertion that
_____ is contradicted by their claim that _____.

CAPTURING AUTHORIAL ACTION

(pp. 39–41)

▸ X acknowledges that _____.

▸ X agrees that _____.

▸ X argues that _____.

▸ X believes that _____.

▸ X denies/does not deny that _____.

▸ X claims that _____.

▸ X complains that _____.

▸ X concedes that _____.

▸ X demonstrates that _____.

▸ X deplores the tendency to _____.

▸ X celebrates the fact that _____.

▸ X emphasizes that _____.

INDEX OF TEMPLATES

▸ X insists that _____.

▸ X observes that _____.

▸ X questions whether _____.

▸ X refutes the claim that _____.

▸ X reminds us that _____.

▸ X reports that _____.

▸ X suggests that _____.

▸ X urges us to _____.

INTRODUCING QUOTATIONS
(p. 47)

▸ X states, "_____."

▸ As the prominent philosopher X puts it, "_____."

▸ According to X, "_____."

▸ X himself writes, "_____."

▸ In her book, _____, X maintains that "_____"

▸ Writing in the journal _____, X complains that "_____."

▸ In X's view, "_____."

▸ X agrees when she writes, "_____."

▸ X disagrees when he writes, "_____."

▸ X complicates matters further when he writes, "_____."

Index of Templates

EXPLAINING QUOTATIONS
(pp. 47–48)

▸ Basically, X is saying _____.

▸ In other words, X believes _____.

▸ In making this comment, X urges us to _____.

▸ X is corroborating the age-old adage that _____.

▸ X's point is that _____.

▸ The essence of X's argument is that _____.

DISAGREEING, WITH REASONS
(p. 58)

▸ I think X is mistaken because she overlooks _____.

▸ X's claim that _____ rests upon the questionable assumption that _____.

▸ I disagree with X's view that _____ because, as recent research has shown, _____.

▸ X contradicts herself / can't have it both ways. On the one hand, she argues _____. On the other hand, she also says _____.

▸ By focusing on _____, X overlooks the deeper problem of _____.

- ▶ X is right that _____, but she seems on more dubious ground when she claims that _____.

- ▶ While X is probably wrong when she claims that _____, she is right that _____.

- ▶ I'm of two minds about X's claim that _____. On the one hand, I agree that _____. On the other hand, I'm not sure if _____.

- ▶ My feelings on the issue are mixed. I do support X's position that _____, but I find Y's argument about _____ and Z's research on _____ to be equally persuasive.

SIGNALING WHO IS SAYING WHAT
(pp. 70–72)

- ▶ X argues _____.

- ▶ According to both X and Y, _____.

- ▶ Politicians _____, X argues, should _____.

- ▶ Most athletes will tell you that _____.

- ▶ My own view, however, is that _____.

- ▶ I agree, as X may not realize, that _____.

- ▶ But _____ are real and, arguably, the most significant factor in _____.

- ▶ But X is wrong that _____.

- ▶ However, it is simply not true that _____.

- ▶ Indeed, it is highly likely that _____.

- ▶ X's assertion that _____ does not fit the facts.

- X is right that _____.

- X is wrong that _____.

- X is both right and wrong that _____.

- Yet a sober analysis of the matter reveals _____.

- Nevertheless, new research shows _____.

- Anyone familiar with _____ should agree that _____.

EMBEDDING VOICE MARKERS
(p. 74)

- X overlooks what I consider an important point about _____.

- My own view is that what X insists is a _____ is in fact a _____.

- I wholeheartedly endorse what X calls _____.

- These conclusions, which X discusses in _____, add weight to the argument that _____.

ENTERTAINING OBJECTIONS
(p. 81)

- At this point I would like to raise some objections that have been inspired by the skeptic in me. She feels that I have been ignoring _____. "_____," she says to me, "_____."

- Yet some readers may challenge the view that _____.

- Of course, many will probably disagree with this assertion that _____.

Index of Templates

NAMING YOUR NAYSAYERS
(pp. 82–83)

▶ Here many _____ would probably object that _____ .

▶ But _____ would certainly take issue with the argument that _____ .

▶ _____ , of course, may want to question whether _____ .

▶ Nevertheless, both followers and critics of _____ will probably argue that _____ .

▶ Although not all _____ think alike, some of them will probably dispute my claim that _____ .

▶ _____ are so diverse in their views that it's hard to generalize about them, but some are likely to object on the grounds that _____ .

INTRODUCING OBJECTIONS INFORMALLY
(pp. 83–84)

▶ But is my proposal realistic? What are the chances of its actually being adopted?

▶ Yet is it always true that _____ ? Is it always the case, as I have been suggesting, that _____ ?

▶ However, does the evidence I've cited prove conclusively that _____ ?

▶ "Impossible," some will say. "You must be reading the research selectively."

MAKING CONCESSIONS WHILE STILL
STANDING YOUR GROUND (p. 88)

▸ Although I grant that _____, I still maintain that _____.

▸ Proponents of X are right to argue that _____. But they exaggerate when they claim that _____.

▸ While it is true that _____, it does not necessarily follow that _____.

▸ On the one hand, I agree with X that _____. But on the other hand, I still insist that _____.

INDICATING WHO CARES
(pp. 94–95)

▸ _____ used to think _____. But recently [or within the past few decades] _____ suggests that _____.

▸ These findings challenge the work of earlier researchers, who tended to assume that _____.

▸ Recent studies like these shed new light on _____, which previous studies had not addressed.

▸ Researchers have long assumed that _____. For instance, one eminent scholar of cell biology, _____, assumed in _____, her seminal work on cell structures and functions, that fat cells _____. As _____ herself put it, "_____" (2012). Another leading scientist, _____, argued that fat cells "_____" (2011). Ultimately, when it came to the nature of fat, the basic assumption was that _____.

But a new body of research shows that fat cells are far more complex and that _____.

▸ If sports enthusiasts stopped to think about it, many of them might simply assume that the most successful athletes _____. However, new research shows _____.

▸ These findings challenge neoliberals' common assumptions that _____.

▸ At first glance, teenagers appear to _____. But on closer inspection _____.

ESTABLISHING WHY YOUR CLAIMS MATTER
(pp. 97–98)

▸ X matters / is important because _____.

▸ Although X may seem trivial, it is in fact crucial in terms of today's concern over _____.

▸ Ultimately, what is at stake here is _____.

▸ These findings have important consequences for the broader domain of _____.

▸ My discussion of X is in fact addressing the larger matter of _____.

▸ These conclusions / This discovery will have significant applications in _____ as well as in _____.

▸ Although X may seem of concern to only a small group of _____, it should in fact concern anyone who cares about _____.

Index of Templates

COMPARISON

along the same lines	likewise
in the same way	similarly

CONTRAST

although	nevertheless
but	nonetheless
by contrast	on the contrary
conversely	on the other hand
despite	regardless
even though	whereas
however	while
in contrast	yet

CONCESSION

admittedly	of course
although it is true that	naturally
granted	to be sure
I concede that	

CONCLUSION

as a result	so
consequently	the upshot of all this is that
hence	therefore
in conclusion, then	thus
in short	to sum up
in sum, then	to summarize
it follows, then	

INDEX OF TEMPLATES

TRANSLATION RECIPES
(pp. 120–21)

▸ Scholar X argues, "_____." In other words, _____.

▸ Essentially, X argues _____.

▸ X's point, succinctly put, is that _____.

▸ Plainly put, _____.

ADDING METACOMMENTARY
(pp. 133–39)

▸ In other words, _____.

▸ What _____ really means by this is _____.

▸ Ultimately, my goal is to demonstrate that _____.

▸ My point is not _____, but _____.

▸ To put it another way, _____.

▸ In sum, then, _____.

▸ My conclusion, then, is that, _____.

▸ In short, _____.

▸ What is more important, _____.

▸ Incidentally, _____.

▸ By the way, _____.

▸ Chapter 2 explores _____, while Chapter 3 examines _____.

▶ Having just argued that _____ , let us now turn our attention to _____ .

▶ Although some readers may object that _____ , I would
answer that _____ .

LINKING TO WHAT "THEY SAY"
(p. 171)

▶ As X mentions in <u>this article,</u> " _____ ."

▶ In making <u>this comment,</u> X warns that _____ .

▶ Economists often assume _____ ; however, <u>new research</u> by
X suggests _____ .

STARTING WITH WHAT OTHERS SAY
ABOUT A LITERARY WORK
(pp. 188–91)

▶ Critic X complains that Author Y's story is compromised by his
_____ . While there's some truth to this critique, I argue
that Critic X overlooks _____ .

▶ According to Critic A, novel X suggests _____ . I agree, but
would add that _____ .

▶ Several members of our class have suggested that the final message of play X is _____ . I agree up to a point, but I still
think that _____ .

▶ On first reading play Z, I thought it was an uncritical celebration of _____ . After rereading the play and discussing it in

class, however, I see that it is more critical of _____ than I originally thought.

▸ It might be said that poem Y is chiefly about _____. But the problem with this reading, in my view, is _____.

▸ Though religious readers might be tempted to analyze poem X as a parable about _____, a closer examination suggests that the poem is in fact about _____.

RESPONDING TO OTHER INTERPRETATIONS OF A LITERARY WORK
(p. 194)

▸ It might be argued that in the clash between character X and Y in play Z, the author wants us to favor character Y, since she is presented as the play's heroine. I contend, however, that _____.

▸ Several critics seem to assume that poem X endorses the values of _____ represented by the image of _____ over those of _____ represented by the image of _____. I agree, but with the following caveat: _____.

SHOWING EVIDENCE WHEN WRITING ABOUT A LITERARY WORK
(pp. 197–99)

▸ Although some might read the metaphor of _____ in this poem as evidence, that for Author X, _____, I see it as _____.

Index of Templates

▸ Some might claim that evidence X suggests _____, but I argue that, on the contrary, it suggests _____.

▸ I agree with my classmate _____ that the image of _____ in novel Y is evidence of _____. Unlike _____, however, I think _____.

EXPLAIN WHAT THE DATA MEAN
(p. 214)

▸ Our data *support / confirm / verify* the work of X by showing that _____.

▸ By demonstrating _____, X's work *extends* the findings of Y.

▸ The results of X *contradict/refute* Y's conclusion that _____.

▸ X's findings *call into question* the widely accepted theory that _____.

▸ Our data *are consistent with* X's hypothesis that _____.

EXPLAINING AN EXPERIMENTAL RESULT
(p. 217)

▸ One explanation for X's finding of _____ is that _____. An alternative explanation is _____.

▸ The difference between _____ and _____ is probably due to _____.

INTRODUCING GAPS IN THE EXISTING RESEARCH
(p. 232)

▶ Studies of X have indicated _____. It is not clear, however, that this conclusion applies to _____.

▶ _____ often take for granted that _____. Few have investigated this assumption, however.

▶ X's work tells us a great deal about _____. Can this work be generalized to _____?

▶ Our understanding of _____ remains incomplete because previous work has not examined _____.

INDEX OF AUTHORS AND TITLES

GERALD GRAFF, Emeritus Professor of English and education at the University of Illinois at Chicago and the 2008 president of the Modern Language Association of America, has had a major impact on teachers through such books as *Professing Literature: An Institutional History, Beyond the Culture Wars: How Teaching the* *Conflicts Can Revitalize American Education,* and, most recently, *Clueless in Academe: How Schooling Obscures the Life of the Mind.*

CATHY BIRKENSTEIN is a lecturer in English at the University of Illinois at Chicago and co-director of the Writing in the Disciplines program. She has published essays on writing, most recently in *College English,* and, with Gerald Graff, in *The Chronicle of Higher Education, Academe,* and *College Composition and* *Communication.* She has also given talks and workshops with Gerald at numerous colleges and is currently working on a study of common misunderstandings surrounding academic discourse.

RUSSEL DURST, who edited the readings in this book, is a professor of English at the University of Cincinnati, where he teaches courses in composition, writing pedagogy and research, English linguistics, and the Hebrew Bible as literature. A past president of the National Conference on Research in Language and Literacy, he is the author of several books, including *Collision Course: Conflict, Negotiation, and Learning in College Composition.*